THE NEW MODEL ARMY

THE NEW MODEL ARMY

Agent of Revolution

Ian Gentles

YALE UNIVERSITY PRESS
NEW HAVEN AND LONDON

For information about this and other Yale University Press publications, please contact:
U.S. Office: sales.press@yale.edu   yalebooks.com
Europe Office: sales@yaleup.co.uk   yalebooks.co.uk

Set in Minion Pro by IDSUK (DataConnection) Ltd
Printed in Great Britain by TJ Books, Padstow, Cornwall

Library of Congress Control Number: 2021950214

ISBN 978-0-300-22683-6

A catalogue record for this book is available from the British Library.

10 9 8 7 6 5 4 3 2 1

To Frances Henderson

CONTENTS

MAPS AND ILLUSTRATIONS

Maps

Plates

PREFACE AND ACKNOWLEDGEMENTS

More years ago than I care to remember, Heather McCallum asked me if I would be interested in preparing a second edition of my *The New Model Army in England, Ireland and Scotland, 1645–1653* (Oxford: Blackwell, 1992). I said yes, and in response to a reader's suggestion, undertook to bring the army's history up to its ushering in of the king in 1660, shepherded by its own General George Monck. In undertaking a second edition I almost bit off more than I could chew. Not only did I have to assimilate the great volume of work that has been published in the more than quarter-century since the first edition, I had to write three important new chapters and add a great deal more to two existing chapters. To make the book more manageable and appealing to readers, I also had to condense what I had previously written. The result is a very different book from the one I first published. As such I think it also merits a new title: *The New Model Army: Agent of Revolution.*

Several people besides my editor have helped to turn this new edition into a reality. Anica Bakalic-Radic, the reference librarian at York University, Toronto, was a great help in locating for me during the COVID-19 pandemic a number of primary and secondary sources that I was unable to locate for myself. Polly Ha and David Como sent me copies of articles on Henry Ireton and the climactic events of 1647 in advance of publication. Ismini Pells allowed me to read her biography of Philip Skippon in advance of publication. Frances Henderson, despite a number of obstacles, provided me with a copy of her decipherment of William Clarke's shorthand notes on General George Monck's campaign against Glencairn's rising of 1654 (Worcester College MS xxvi). This hitherto inaccessible source added immediacy to my account of an important episode in the New Model Army's history. The book is dedicated to Frances in gratitude for her great generosity. I also benefited from discussions about the army with David Scott, John Morrill,

Henry Reece, Micheál Ó Siochrú, David Farr, Stephen Roberts, Barbara Donagan, Jason Peacey, Paul Griffiths and William Gairdner. To them all I owe an immense debt of gratitude. In addition I am most grateful to Sarah Mortimer and David Scott for their gracious hospitality to me on several visits to Oxford, to Jane Ohlmeyer on visits to Dublin, and to Kay Senior on visits to London. Above all I am thankful to my wife Caroline for her many acts of kindness, which helped to preserve my sanity during the years it took to complete this book.

PROLOGUE

The first of Europe's great revolutions was unleashed in England in the autumn of 1642 when King Charles I declared war on his own Parliament. The resulting Civil War spread to his other two kingdoms, and was rapidly transformed into a revolution that shook monarchy, aristocracy and church to their foundations. By the time its energy was spent, it had cost well over half a million lives throughout the Stuart kingdoms. How are we to understand this cataclysm, its passionate fury, its colossal violence? What were its mainsprings?[1]

Many people living at the time thought they knew. Clothworkers in Essex maintained that the root cause of England's troubles was Parliament's failure to stand up to the expansionary forces of international Roman Catholicism ('popery'), rampant both at home and in Ireland, where a popish rebellion had led to the massacre of countless thousands of innocent Protestants. Set beside the need for action on this existential religious threat, the social and economic problems of the day were inconsequential. A similar petition from Norfolk made the same point: only when 'religion [is] established in the purity both of doctrine and discipline' will the kingdom 'be established in peace and the land shall be at rest'.[2]

Such was the message of these citizens. Did they have a point? The founders of the New Model Army certainly thought so, as we shall see. One of the aims of this book is to listen to the voices of those who lived through the Revolution, to attend to what they said and wrote, and to refrain from subjecting them to 'the enormous condescension of posterity'.[3]

It was the king who fired the opening shot in England when he declared war on Parliament in August 1642. The rebels, as he regarded them, had been systematically challenging his attempts to govern as an absolute king on the European model. They had rejected his arguments for collecting taxes without the approval of Parliament and were appalled at his muzzling of those who disagreed with him. More alarming in their eyes was his perceived drift towards popery, and his clearly expressed desire to suppress the Puritan movement in the church in favour of the Arminian or High Church faction. Now that Charles had declared his implacable hostility towards his parliamentary critics, the MPs, hastily, and in fear for their lives, appointed military leaders and set about organising armed resistance and raising money. Their initial success was striking – not only on the battlefield but in the Treasury. For at least a year the parliamentary war effort against the king was awash in money, while the king struggled to find cash to pay his troops.[4]

The first battle of the English Civil War pitted two armies of nearly 15,000 each against each other at Edgehill (23 October 1642). The result was a virtual draw. For the next twenty months, Parliament and king each struggled to gain the upper hand, until the parliamentary leader, John Pym, just before his death, achieved his masterstroke by forging a religious and military alliance with Scotland. Known as the Solemn League and Covenant, the treaty released formidable spiritual and political energy on both sides of the border.

> We profess and declare before God and the world our unfeigned desire
> to be humbled for our own sins and for the sins of these kingdoms,
> and . . . receive Christ into our hearts, that the Lord may turn away his
> wrath, and heavy indignation, and establish these churches and king-
> doms in truth and peace.[5]

What other revolutionary movement has ever confessed a desire to 'be humbled for our sins' or 'receive Christ in our hearts'? This alliance bore fruit at the battle of Marston Moor in Yorkshire, nearly the greatest battle ever fought on English soil (2 July 1644). The outcome, thanks to the presence of the Scots, was a crushing defeat for the king. Oliver Cromwell was there with his double regiment of Ironsides. He exulted that God had used them to make the royalists 'stubble to our swords'.[6] It looked as though the war was all but over, except that Charles, obstinate to the end, refused to throw in the towel. Instead, he regrouped his forces in the south and chased the army of Robert Devereux, third earl of Essex, almost to the end of the Cornish peninsula. There at Lostwithiel he achieved his own masterstroke, inflicting a humiliating defeat on the main parliamentary army.

Now it was voices on the parliamentary side who wanted to throw in the towel. Sir William Waller, one of Parliament's generals, had already called it 'this war without an enemy'.[7] Edward Montagu, second earl of Manchester, had been heard to ponder that 'if we beat the king ninety-nine times he would be king still and his posterity; and we subjects still. But if he beat us once we should be hanged and our posterity undone.'[8] The earl of Essex for his part had been known to be seeking a compromise peace since the summer of 1643. This was all too much for the militant win-the-war party led by William Fiennes, first Viscount Saye and Sele, Sir Henry Vane, Oliver St John, Sir Arthur Hesilrige and Oliver Cromwell. Nothing less would satisfy them than wiping the slate clean of Parliament's effete upper-class military leadership and radically revamping its armies.

CHAPTER ONE

THE FOUNDING OF THE NEW MODEL ARMY

After waging war upon their anointed monarch for two years, the armies of Parliament found themselves at a low ebb. For all their success at raising money and troops, and forging a coalition with the Scots, their military effort to defeat the king's forces had run out of steam. Their aristocratic leaders, the earls of Essex and Manchester, seemed plagued with doubts about the justice of their cause, and were looking for a compromise peace that would bring an end to the appalling bloodshed they had witnessed at Edgehill (October 1642), Marston Moor (July 1644) and a dozen other battlefields and sieges. Their numbers had swelled and deflated like a balloon: the earl of Essex's army between 5,000 and 19,000; the earl of Manchester's usually well under 11,000; and Sir William Waller's never more than 6,000, and usually many fewer.[1]

This crisis had materialised very suddenly. In the summer of 1644 Parliament's armed forces, with a big boost from the Scots, had won a stunning victory against the royalist armies at Marston Moor. Almost before the smoke had cleared from the battlefield, however, things began to go wrong, as the generals proved unable to follow up their victory. By the autumn the war effort against the king seemed to have unravelled completely. Wide cracks began to disfigure the fragile façade of parliamentary unity. The victory at Marston Moor, which might have been expected to soften the discord, only sharpened it. The English win-the-war party, known as the Independents, many of whom were also Congregationalist in religion, cried up Oliver Cromwell as the hero of the battle, causing fierce resentment among the Scots against the neglect of their leader Lord Leven's contribution. From then on the split in Manchester's army widened to a gaping chasm. Its chief cause was Manchester's sudden loss of appetite for fighting the king. Paradoxically, his altered attitude may have been due to the allies' sweeping success, which for the first time opened up the prospect of total victory. The moderate earl, who had hoped all along for a negotiated peace that would preserve Parliament, and head off a social revolution, was appalled. He was also acutely conscious of the unpredictable dangers of the battlefield, as well as the poor condition of his troops.[2]

Manchester's growing caution manifested itself in a deliberate policy of inactivity.[3] To vent their frustration against their idle commander-in-chief, Cromwell and his allies in the army launched a purge of their foes. Officers who would not support religious toleration were cashiered, though the attempt to drive out Major-General Lawrence Crawford foundered on Manchester's resistance.[4]

After the combined armies of Manchester, Essex and Waller failed to defeat the numerically far inferior royalist army at the second battle of Newbury or to engage the king at Donnington Castle, the Committee of Both Kingdoms, Parliament's executive committee directing the war, expressed bitter disappointment, while public opinion in London blamed Manchester, Crawford and Sir William Balfour, one of Essex's cavalry commanders.[5]

With the end of the fighting season the parliamentary commanders were now free to carry on their quarrel by other means. In the Commons, Cromwell and Waller launched an attack on Manchester, aiming at his removal as commander-in-chief of the Eastern Association. Cromwell's allegations were referred to the Committee for the Army chaired by the MP Zouch Tate, a Presbyterian member of the war party, for further examination and a speedy report back to the House.[6] In the Lords, Manchester delivered a blistering indictment of Cromwell's military record, while raising the alarm against his religious and political radicalism:

> For his expressions were sometimes against the nobility, that he hoped to live to see never a noble man in England . . . His animosity against the Scottish nation . . . was such as he told me, that . . . he could as soon draw his sword against them as against any in the king's army. And he . . . told me that he . . . desired to have none in my army but such as were of the Independent judgement . . .[7]

In London everyone understood that the quarrel was about more than military competence and obedience. It was about the antagonism between the win-the-war and peace groups, which had been embittered by religious difference. In the weeks following, a fierce conflict raged behind the scenes.

What was not widely known was that Cromwell had an even more dangerous enemy in the earl of Essex.[8]

One night around the beginning of December Essex summoned to his house in the Strand the Scottish commissioners, and five leading MPs. The purpose of the meeting was to bring down Oliver Cromwell by having him condemned as an incendiary. Denzil Holles and Philip Stapilton, the leaders of the parliamentary Peace Party, were keen to launch the indictment at once. Bulstrode Whitelocke, a lawyer and admirer of Essex, urged tactical caution. When it came to political manoeuvre no one was more adroit than Oliver Cromwell, 'a gentleman of quick and subtle parts'. His extensive network of friends in both houses, made him someone not to be trifled with. The Scottish commissioners, impressed by this judicious assessment, drew back.[9]

In the Committee for the Army Cromwell and his friends pulled out all the stops in their campaign to convict Manchester of military incompetence, unwillingness to fight the king, and contempt of Parliament. To their enemies their intentions were crystal clear: a 'high and mighty plot of the Independent party to have gotten an army for themself [sic] under Cromwell'.[10]

The Self-Denying Ordinance

The combination of the armies' indifferent record since the summer of 1644, and their officers' incorrigible tendency to fracture along political and religious lines, provided compelling reasons to turn the page. On 9 December members crowded into the House of Commons to hear Zouch Tate report from the Committee for the Army that the chief causes of division were 'pride and covetousness'. After many had spoken Oliver Cromwell rose to his feet. With a show of magnanimity he admitted that he had been guilty of oversights, along with the other commanders on the battlefield. However, the time had come to put aside private interests for the public good: 'If the army be not put into another method, and the war more vigorously prosecuted, the people can bear the war no longer, and will enforce you to a dishonourable peace.' Another speaker echoed his argument, adding that more damaging than financial exhaustion and the wasted state of the country was the divided leadership of Parliament's armies.[11] The stage had been set for Tate to introduce his resolution, seconded by the war party spokesman, Sir Henry Vane the younger, 'That during the time of this war, no member of either House shall have or execute any office or command, military or civil . . . and that an ordinance be brought in accordingly.' The resolution appealed to both peace and win-the-war advocates. It defused the criticism that too many people in Parliament were profiting from the war.[12]

Several London newspaper editors congratulated the MPs on their statesmanship and impartiality in giving up their commands for the sake of reconciliation. There was also a clear awareness of the political implications of the proposed Self-Denying Ordinance. One editor tried to quash the popular view that the resolution was a radical manoeuvre, by pointing out that Cromwell was to be dismissed along with the others, and that he had already announced his willingness to resign.[13]

The question of which faction would gain or lose by the passage of the ordinance did not escape the attention of MPs. There was a close division over whether to make an exception for Essex, but no one spoke up for Manchester. Whitelocke, always alert to other people's hidden agendas, believed that the ordinance 'was set on by that party who contrived the outing of the lord-general'.[14]

On 19 December the Commons debated and rejected an amendment to require all officers and officials to take the Solemn League and Covenant and submit to the government and discipline of the church laid down by Parliament. The amendment, which would be revived by the Lords, illustrates the continuing split over religion. The whole bill was then debated till late at night, when, in the words of an embittered eyewitness, 'envy and self ends prevailing', it passed.[15]

The bill was not, however, expected to clear the upper house. In fact the Lords shunted the 'Great Ordinance' aside until 3 January, by which time they had come to a firm decision not to pass it. They professed alarm at the great changes being suggested. Even though the war-party lords led by Viscount Saye and Sele supported the bill, the majority interpreted it as an insult to their honour. It treated them 'worse . . . than any free subject' since it excluded them all without exception, whereas only those commoners who were MPs were excluded. The ordinance also flew in the face of centuries of practice, the peers always having taken the lead in defending the liberties of England.[16]

Instantly the Commons appointed a committee dominated by war-party members to answer the peers' objections. Ten days later the whole house, led by the Speaker, Sir William Lenthall, trooped up to the Lords to present their arguments in person. Unimpressed by this show of determination, the

Lords drily responded that they saw no need to return the ordinance for amendment since they objected to its entirety.[17]

Seeing that the bill's prospects now appeared hopeless, the war party in the lower house began implementing their alternative plan, a protracted outflanking manoeuvre against the Lords' refusal to sanction a purge of the existing armies' leadership. The manoeuvre consisted simply of setting up a new army with new commanders. The three existing southern armies would be bled of their officers and men in order to fill up the new one. At the same time they would be denied funding; all new revenues would be devoted to the new force. Finally demoralised and in a state of imminent disintegration, the remnants of the existing armies would be absorbed into the new one. If the Lords refused to step aside gracefully they would have the rug ruthlessly pulled from under their feet.

The plan originated in the Committee of Both Kingdoms, where the war party was dominant. The idea of unifying the three armies of Essex, Manchester and Waller had been sketched out as early as the previous October. Having failed initially to reconstruct their armies from the top down the Commons resolved on 11 January to work from the bottom up. A new army would be mobilised, numbering 6,000 horse (later increased to 6,600), 1,000 dragoons and 14,400 foot, as well as officers. Two days later the financing of the new army was mapped out. A monthly assessment was levied on the seventeen counties of East Anglia, the Midlands, and the south-east.[18]

To impress upon the upper house the seriousness of this project, the Commons leaders let it be known that they would not let the peace negotiations with the king at Uxbridge go forward until the armies had been remodelled. At the same time they retaliated against the peers' obstructionism by reviving the allegations against the earl of Manchester.[19]

Having decided the size of the new army, and taken steps to finance it, the Commons war party now set about the sensitive task of choosing its commanders. In doing this they circumvented the Lords' rejection of the Self-Denying Ordinance. By naming new officers, none of whom was a member of either House, the Commons achieved their end 'as well as if the said ordinance were passed'. Who would replace Essex as commander-in-chief? In January the war-party MP James Chaloner wrote to Ferdinando, Lord Fairfax of Cameron to tell him that his son Sir Thomas was the most likely candidate for the generalship of the cavalry in the new army. On 21 January the nomination of Sir Thomas Fairfax as commander-in-chief came before the House. The vote was a clear trial of strength between war and peace parties. This time the peace party could only muster sixty-nine votes, but the number who voted for Fairfax was almost identical (at 101) to the number who had voted against keeping Essex a month earlier. While Fairfax would later become a moderate Presbyterian, in early 1645 he was known as a good friend of Oliver Cromwell and therefore aligned with the war party.[20]

The Commons then proceeded to name the major-general of the new army's infantry, Philip Skippon, and also the colonels of the twelve foot and eleven horse regiments as well as the regiment of dragoons. The names, which included men of widely differing political and religious complexions, as well as a handful of Scots, were adopted without division, though later there would be a fierce debate over whether the religious radical Nathaniel Rich ought to be a colonel.[21]

After several long sessions the Commons passed the ordinance for a new army under the command of Sir Thomas Fairfax on 28 January. They sent it up to the Lords, urging their speedy concurrence. After stalling for a week the Lords finally addressed it. After lengthy debate they adopted two sweeping changes to make the ordinance more palatable to the peace group. First, all officers should be nominated by the joint houses of Parliament rather than the commander-in-chief. Secondly, all officers should take the Solemn League and Covenant and submit to the form of church government to be laid down by Parliament.[22]

Meanwhile, political opinion was making itself felt on the issue of a new army.[23] The Commons fell to debating the Lords' amendments as soon as they came down. On the question of Fairfax's right to appoint his own officers, the war party wanted to reject the Lords' amendment out of hand. However, after a five-hour debate, a compromise was reached. Fairfax would appoint his officers in the first instance, but would submit them to both houses for approval. The next day the Commons continued to debate the Lords' amendments for another twelve hours, in the end passing all of them except the requirement that the common soldiers submit to the form of church laid down by Parliament – this, for the common-sense reason that, if it passed, anyone wanting to evade military service would only have to refuse the oath. On 11 February the Lords and Commons held an all-day conference to thrash out their differences, then the Lords put off further debate for another two days.[24]

Against a background of mounting anxiety over the imminent collapse of the parliamentary forces, the Commons exploited the sense of panic welling up among Parliament's most dedicated supporters to force the Lords' compliance. At the end of January 'robberies, ravishings and innumerable wicked actions' were alleged by parliamentary soldiers in the south-east. To all appearances the Commons majority was deliberately allowing the existing forces to disintegrate in order to coerce the Lords into sanctioning the creation of the New Model Army for lack of any alternative. When war party MP Sir John Evelyn went to the peers to desire their urgent attention to the amended ordinance, he hinted broadly that the Commons might invoke its power of the purse to impose its will. Action was necessary 'because there are no monies to be raised for the supply of the forces without the passing of that ordinance'. In other words, the Commons would starve the three existing armies out of existence by denying them funds. Only one army would be allowed to operate in the south – the New Model – and the Lords would have to choose between that or no army at all.[25]

While putting on a show of political muscle for the peers' benefit, the Commons in fact were bitterly divided. On the question of displacing officers who declined to swear the Solemn League and Covenant as the Lords demanded, the lower house split along party lines. After a long debate it agreed to administer the Covenant to all the officers but not to fire those who refused. As the news filtered back to London of the imminent breakdown of negotiations with the king at Uxbridge, the war party pressed its case all the more strongly. In the end the Lords swallowed their objections and allowed the ordinance for remodelling the army to pass into law.[26]

In its final form the ordinance called for the creation of an army led by Sir Thomas Fairfax of twenty-four regiments – eleven of horse, one of dragoons, twelve of foot – for a total of 22,000 men besides officers. The commander of the cavalry was left unnamed. A monthly assessment of £53,436 was levied on the counties under parliamentary control. County committees were nominated to bring in the money. Then came the 'provisos' or amendments adopted to appease the Lords. The most important required Fairfax to nominate his officers out of Parliament's existing forces, with the approval of both houses. This proviso was aimed at minimising the number of officers who would lose their jobs, since there were almost twice as many officers as posts available. Next, all officers and private soldiers were required to take the Covenant. The Commons war party had resorted to ruthless tactics to bring the Lords to heel. They had cut off funding from the existing armies, and exploited the resulting disorder in these forces to drive home the argument for the reorganisation of the southern forces. They had unceremoniously robbed the commanders of the existing armies of men to command.[27]

Once the ordinance was passed the Commons sped ahead with their plans to raise men and money. Sir Thomas Fairfax was brought to the Commons, where he was ushered in with elaborate ceremony. As he stood, bareheaded, before the assembled MPs, Speaker Lenthall praised him warmly for his valour and experience. After his glowing reception Fairfax paid a courtesy call on the man he had just supplanted – the earl of Essex.[28]

Initially the troops in the earl of Essex's cavalry regiments would not march under new commanders. 'This new model causeth a great alteration', wrote one MP; 'there are great distractions in our army'.[29]

The Choosing of Officers

With effort being exerted on all fronts to get the new army into the field by the spring, the Commons now turned their attention to Sir Thomas Fairfax's list of officers. Contrary to what they would later say, the Commons scrutinised Fairfax's nominations closely and subjected at least eight (4 per cent of the total) to heated debate. The war party suffered a sharp reverse when the majority voted to replace Nathaniel Rich, an ally of Oliver Cromwell, with the younger Sir Robert Pye, son of a prominent peace-party MP.[30]

As soon as the three-day debate was over, the officer list was sent to the upper house. At the same time, a large committee was appointed to bargain with the London Common Council for a loan of £80,000 to launch the army. The loan was made possible by large contributions from the leadership of the Irish Adventurers, prominent London financiers and parliamentarians who had invested in the reconquest of Ireland. Their quick support would make possible the New Model's victory at Naseby three months later. Meanwhile, the Lords yielded to Commons' pressure to the extent of approving six 'safe regiments' – the two belonging to Fairfax, those of the future Presbyterian Richard Graves, the Dutch colonel Bartholomew Vermuyden and Philip Skippon, plus Ralph Weldon's Kentish foot regiment. In sum, fifty officers, just over a quarter of the total, were approved almost immediately. But then the Lords dug in their heels and refused to be rushed, subjecting the remaining names to microscopic scrutiny. The fruit of their deliberations was a demand for fifty-seven changes among the 143 officers in the eighteen remaining regiments.[31]

The large number of alterations demanded in Manchester's regiments reflects both the size of his army's contribution to the New Model, and the advanced state of politicisation already prevailing among his officers.

The Lords attempted to alter close to one-third of Fairfax's nominations, interfering more with the foot than with the horse and dragoons. Evidence about the political and religious leanings of those whom the Lords wished to demote or expel has been easier to turn up for the period after their appointment than before it. Evidence of later political behaviour by itself would be of little value. However, in this instance the later evidence points in the same direction as the evidence for 1644–45. Overwhelmingly, the officers of whom the Lords disapproved were radicals or Independents, or would later show themselves to be such, while those whom the Lords wished to promote or to introduce into the army, were moderates, Presbyterians, or protégés or kinsmen of the earl of Essex.

In short, many if not most of the proposed fifty-seven changes were politically or religiously motivated. Some of them were doubtless prompted by considerations of seniority or a desire to preserve the integrity of regiments. Moreover, the peers were not the only ones politically motivated. In his nominations, Fairfax favoured Cromwellians and conducted a thorough purge of officers who had stood against Cromwell in his quarrel with Manchester the previous autumn. What the success of Fairfax and his parliamentary allies meant was 'not that moderates were purged from the New Model, but that *radicals were not purged*'. Considerations of patronage and kinship were at work on both sides, but the partisans of the new army interpreted the peers' changes as springing from nothing less than simple negativity. As one MP commented, Fairfax's list had been 'much obstructed in the Lords' house'. Thomas Juxon, the radical London common councillor, believed that the peers, alienated by their exclusion from all commands in the new army, formed an alliance with the Scots and the peace party in the Commons to alter the list, putting out 'not only Independents but such as were good . . . by which it appears . . . how little they regard the real good of the nation, their peerage being their great idol'.[32]

After exerting unremitting pressure on the Lords for several days, the war party devised a 'subtle ruse' to break their will. They went to the London Common Council and persuaded the City magistrates to make their £80,000 loan conditional upon there being no tampering with Fairfax's list. Still the resistance of the upper house continued. The Commons then sent a powerful nine-man delegation headed by Sir Henry Vane and Oliver St John to meet with the lords in a joint conference. The Commons bluntly told them that if they would not approve of what was 'for the apparent good of the kingdom' they would go ahead without them. Allowing each house to alter the list 'must make the difference endless', and the consequent delay would give the king the advantage of recruiting his forces earlier. Taking their cue from the Commons' message, the war party in the Lords moved to pass the list 'as presented by Sir Thomas Fairfax to the House of Commons'.[33]

In the end the Lords passed the motion by the narrowest of margins. The old military leadership remained alienated and unreconciled. Excluded from the command of the new army, which had already been labelled 'the chief visible strength upon which we are to rely for the safety of the parliament and kingdom', Essex, Manchester and two others bitterly registered their dissent.[34]

With the passage of Fairfax's officer list the Commons moved to reintroduce the Self-Denying Ordinance. A day later the ordinance to secure the £80,000 loan for the New Model was also read twice and committed. Without waiting for the Lords' agreement, the Commons pressed on, voting £7,000 out of the loan for a fortnight's pay to those who enlisted voluntarily. The following day they sent Independent, war party MP Sir Henry Mildmay, to acquaint the peers with the necessity of speedily passing the ordinance, 'otherwise no money can be had for the immediate and present service'. By now the heart had gone out of the Lords' opposition; they gave in to the Commons' badgering, and passed the bill without a division the same day.[35]

It took some time for the full political significance of the creation of the new army to sink in. Only gradually was it realised that the exclusion or resignation of over 300 Scottish officers from the new army considerably diminished that nation's role in English affairs.[36] Even then, the Lords had not completely given up the political struggle.

Fairfax's Commission

At the end of March 1645 a fierce and prolonged argument flared up over the wording of Sir Thomas Fairfax's commission. At issue was whether he should be required, as every previous commander had been, to preserve the safety of the king's person. On 24 March, leading Independent MP Robert Scawen reported from the Committee for the Army an ordinance hedging in this requirement. Entitled 'an ordinance for giving more power to Sir Thomas Fairfax', it was passed the same day and sent to the Lords. The Commons gave two reasons for no longer respecting the king's life. The first denied that the king was in fact defending 'the true Protestant religion'. The second claimed that it would give the king too much of a military advantage.

They further warned that the Lords' fear of granting Fairfax too much power could end by destroying the army.[37]

Two days later, stepping up the pressure once more, the Commons informed the Lords 'that the army is in mutiny and disorder and they know not who to obey: and until this ordinance be passed Sir Thomas Fairfax has no power to do anything'. Any misfortune that arose from this delay would not be their fault.[38]

The Lords began to wilt under the pressure. Essex announced that he was resigning his commission. He was shortly followed by Manchester and Basil Feilding, second earl of Denbigh, the three of them 'having opposed the others [i.e. the war party] to the last'. Wearied by the hectoring of militant MPs, they finally caved in and allowed the ordinance to pass.[39]

The next day Essex delivered up his commission, sardonically expressing the hope that his resignation 'may prove as good an expedient to the present distempers as some will have it believed'. He and the earls of Manchester and Denbigh quit in order to spare themselves the humiliation of dismissal. For almost four months these noblemen had fought tenaciously against a purge of the army command, but events had swept them along. Parliament's desperate military situation, and the tidal wave of discontent generated by those who would be satisfied with nothing less than outright victory over the king, finally swamped them. They had been obliged to yield on one point after another. While they staved off the Self-Denying Ordinance, the war-party majority in the Commons and the Committee of Both Kingdoms went ahead and built a new army out of the wreckage of the old ones. A monthly assessment was approved, to commence on 1 February. An immediate transfusion of funds was supplied in the form of an £80,000 loan from the City of London and the Irish Adventurers. To this the Lords had been compelled to assent. We don't know who advised Fairfax on his selections of officers, but the Lords found almost 30 per cent of them unsatisfactory. Once again the militants forced them to back down. Finally, the Lords were deeply disturbed by the draft terms of Fairfax's commission. Essex's party fought even harder over this question than they had over Fairfax's nominations. The ordinance that was whisked through three readings in a single morning was blocked for days in the upper house. The principle at stake was of the highest importance: was Parliament waging war on papists, Irishmen and wicked counsellors who had misled the king, or was it waging war on Charles himself? The elimination of the clause obliging Fairfax to protect the person of the king meant the abandonment of the fiction that they were fighting only the king's evil counsellors. It was the first step in the conversion of the Civil War into a revolution.[40]

The Self-Denying Ordinance (Revised Version)

Having retreated while managing to preserve a modicum of self-respect, Essex's party now lifted their veto of the Self-Denying Ordinance, passing it on 3 April 1645. Its content was significantly different from the resolution passed by the Commons four months earlier. Instead of making parliamentarians incapable of holding any office or command for the duration of the war it simply dismissed them without ruling out the possibility of reappointment. Ironically the Lords recovered their civilian appointments, when what had offended them most about the draft ordinance was its robbing the nobility of their historic military function. Having lost the main bone of contention, they had to be content with a few crumbs.

The totality of the collapse of lordly opposition is seen in how they participated in a joint committee named to recommend what to do with MPs displaced by the Self-Denying Ordinance. At first the peers appointed a balanced membership of twelve on which the supporters of the New Model had a slight edge over the members of Essex's party. Later in the day, however, all of Essex's supporters withdrew from the committee, which was reduced to only five members from the upper house, every one of whom had been a consistent supporter of the New Model Army. The problem of what to do with the many unemployed officers occupied much parliamentary time.[41]

The Return of Oliver Cromwell

The Lords' resentment against the New Model Army flared up yet again over the question of continuing Oliver Cromwell's commission as a cavalry commander. The grace period allowed under the Self-Denying Ordinance ended on 13 May 1645. At the end of April, the Committee of Both Kingdoms decided that Cromwell and Major-General Richard Browne would continue in their commands until further notice. A few days later the Commons extended Cromwell's commission another forty days. The Lords went along, but not before members of Essex's party had spoken sharply against it as a breach of the ordinance.[42]

When did Cromwell form his intention to carry on in active military service? Had he planned it all along? Was there a precise moment between

December 1644 and June 1645 when he decided that he would strive to remain in the army? Or did he simply surrender to the popular demand that he be made lieutenant-general of the cavalry, for the good reason that he was supremely qualified for the position? Why had the post of lieutenant-general been left conspicuously vacant, ever since 21 January? The evidence does not permit definitive answers. Cromwell may have decided to seek the command of the New Model cavalry at the point when the ordinance was converted from one that barred members of both houses from wartime service, to one that merely discharged them without ruling out their re-appointment. This change was part of the second version of the ordinance passed on 3 April.

Two months before that Cromwell had been active in the Committee of Both Kingdoms, devising plans for the new army establishment. At the end of February he left to join Waller fighting the royalists in the west. Unlike Waller, who responded to the passage of the Self-Denying Ordinance by resigning immediately, Cromwell stayed on, mustering all the forces he could collect. He managed to take the strongly fortified post of Bletchingdon House without firing a shot. Encouraged by this success he proceeded to beat up the country around Oxford, further disrupting the king's communications with Worcester. Parliament gave him an additional 4,000 men (bringing his total force to about 5,500) to block up Oxford. As he performed this service he continued helping to organise the new army. By early May he was coordinating a march on Oxford with Major-General Browne. He now commanded five horse and six foot regiments, totalling 7,000 men. Bowing to Fairfax's request, the houses extended his commission by another forty days.[43]

At the end of May, fearing an attack on the eastern counties, the Committee of Both Kingdoms ordered Cromwell to fortify the Isle of Ely. He quickly assembled 3,000 horse for that purpose. Then came the royalist storm and sack of Leicester, which unexpectedly enhanced his prospects. This shocking reversal produced dismay bordering on panic in the capital, prompting the City authorities to frame a petition extremely critical of the conduct of the war. Pointing to various signs of feeble resolution on the part of Parliament's strategists, they called for an end to remote-control warfare, firm orders to the Scottish army to move southward, a vigorous campaign to meet the New Model's recruitment targets, speedy engagement with the enemy, and the appointment of Cromwell as commander of the Eastern Association. The Lords did not thank the City for this petition, yet they gave it their close attention, and implemented most of its demands over the next two weeks.[44]

In a separate, uncoordinated petition, Fairfax, his Council of War and the parliamentary commissioners residing with the army wrote to both houses in early June requesting Cromwell's appointment as lieutenant-general of cavalry in the New Model. The Lords did not answer this petition either. The Commons on the other hand wrote Fairfax giving him the green light. The general at once sent a message to Cromwell at Ely telling him of his appointment and ordering him to report to the main army without delay. In the face of the Lords' unalterable opposition to Cromwell's nomination, the Commons simply ignored the requirement that military appointments be approved by both houses. However, the stunning victory at Naseby a few days later, where Cromwell's contribution was undeniable, transformed the political situation. The war party pressed home the advantage that Naseby created, to make Cromwell's appointment permanent. The Lords would still do no more than sanction it for another three months.[45]

The insistence by the upper house that the appointment be only temporary reflects the enduring antagonism of Essex's supporters towards Cromwell, as well as their recapture of a majority in the House of Lords. Cromwell was perfectly aware that any reappointment would depend on the approval of the upper chamber, where his enemies were again dominant. We may infer therefore that he had been sincere when he spoke for the principle of self-denial in December 1644. His own resignation was not too high a price to pay to be rid of a bagful of aristocratic and other enemies. Yet with the advent of the spring fighting season his desire to be militarily active was re-ignited, and he did everything in his power to stave off the inevitable day of his dismissal. Only the unforeseen victory at Naseby on 14 June was overwhelming enough to override the Lords' opposition and obtain for him the commission that by now he fiercely coveted.

CHAPTER TWO

RECRUITMENT, PROVISIONING AND PAY

A new army had been formed. The old aristocratic leaders had been fired; three armies had been merged into one; a new roster of officers had been approved. Money, arms, ammunition, clothing and provisions now had to be amassed to put this army into the field. Men had to be rounded up to fill the vacancies in the infantry and dragoon regiments. Parliament's success in meeting the challenges of money, supply and recruitment would contribute tremendously to Fairfax's unbroken chain of victories in the coming year.

Revenue

The New Model was extremely fortunate in having as its advocate in the House of Commons Robert Scawen, the member for Berwick-on-Tweed, client of Algernon Percy, tenth earl of Northumberland, and chairman of the Committee for the Army. It was Scawen who saw to it that the New Model received priority in funding, supply and recruitment in preference to all the remaining forces under parliamentary authority. Unabashedly partisan, the committee was dominated by political Independents, Presbyterian followers of the earl of Essex having been effectively frozen out. Because of his constant attention to the New Model's material needs between 1645 and 1648, Scawen can claim a major role in its victories.[1]

One of his chief tasks was ensuring the timely collection of the army's chief revenue source, the monthly assessment. For a time the sales tax known as the excise, first introduced in 1643, was intended to be the main form of war taxation, but from 1645 the assessment replaced it as the foundation of army finance until the end of the Interregnum. The Treasurers at War accounts show that from February 1645 until the end of 1651, of their total revenue of £7,621,149, fully £5,228,873 came from the assessment. The remainder came from delinquents' fines, the sale of crown fee farm rents and last, the excise.[2]

Totalling £53,436 a month, 87 per cent of the amount due for the first twenty months was collected, a strikingly high rate of return for the seventeenth century. The only problem was that the revenue was slow to reach the Treasurers at War in Guildhall.[3]

At no time during its twenty-month history was the first assessment actually sufficient to finance the New Model. A common hindrance to the smooth flow of assessment money was the practice of free quarter. Colonel Edward King complained that Lincolnshire, after paying its assessment of £2,800 a month for a year, was still prey to the exactions of Colonel Edward Rossiter's regiment, which was based there. The New Model as a whole first resorted to free quarter in September 1645. By that month the assessment had to be supplemented by borrowing against the future receipts of the excise. Borrowing against the excise was repeated in October, December and March 1646. During the first fifteen months of the army's existence over £200,000, or 25 per cent, of the £801,540 budgeted revenue from the monthly assessment actually came from other sources.[4]

After the assessment expired on 1 October 1646 there was a six-month hiatus until its renewal on 25 March 1647. The rate was then increased to £60,000 a month and spread over all the counties of England and Wales. But tax resistance had by now taken root. For nine months – until December 1647 – not a penny of the new assessment was received. Nor was there anything from the excise after November 1646. Despite the evaporation of current revenue from the autumn of 1646, arrears from the first twenty months' assessment continued to trickle in. Moreover, Robert Scawen's Army Committee ordered extraordinary payments in November and December 1646, so that the army was able to avoid financial crisis until the spring of 1647.[5]

Recruitment

With the ordinance for a monthly assessment in place, the Commons next set about raising men for the new army. Again, it was Robert Scawen's Army Committee that organised the recruiting effort. By the end of February 1645 an impressment (or conscription) bill had become law. From the long list of people exempt from impressment it was clear that the poor were the ones being targeted. In principle all men between the ages of eighteen and sixty-five were liable to impressment, but any man, or the son of any man rated at £5 in goods or £3 in land, was exempt. So were all clergymen, scholars, students at law or university, esquires' sons, MPs, peers, mariners, watermen, fishermen and tax officials – in other words, the middle classes and those in three essential trades.[6]

By mid-March, with his officer list only partially approved, Fairfax was authorised to take all the soldiers and officers of the rank of lieutenant and lower from the armies of Essex, Manchester and Waller. Those three armies had still not been formally abolished, the Self-Denying Ordinance had still not been passed, and the three commanders still held their commissions. Yet their armies were being cannibalised to furnish regiments for Fairfax. The recruitment of regiments already approved by both houses went ahead without delay. In addition, Essex's remaining infantry regiments were condensed into another three regiments. This delicate task was entrusted to Major-General Philip Skippon. Given their previous rebelliousness, there was more than a little anxiety that the prospect of reorganisation would only further inflame these regiments. In the event, the promise of two weeks' pay for reduced officers, and new clothes and weapons for the rank and file, as well as Skippon's diplomatic finesse, allowed the assimilation to be effected without incident. Skippon's success with these regiments, potentially the most volatile in the old armies, set an example to the others, so that in a short time the balance of Essex's army was merged into the New Model. Regiments from the other two armies were also absorbed smoothly, so that the quota of 6,600 horse troopers was easily met. In fact, service in Fairfax's cavalry was so coveted that numbers of redundant officers from the old armies signed on as private troopers in the New Model. With 3,048 men from Essex's infantry, 3,578 from Manchester's and 600 from Waller's, the strength of the new army's foot stood at 7,226, exclusive of officers.[7]

Service was far less attractive in the infantry than in the cavalry. Impressment was therefore a costly and arduous business. Not only did the conscripts have to be clothed and fed; they had to be closely guarded until their escorts delivered them to the assembly point at Reading. There were the expenses of county officials, high collectors and local militia to be reimbursed.[8]

London, Westminster and the suburbs, with their great reserves of population, were expected to be the most fertile soil from which to harvest conscripts. In the event the authorities would be disappointed. Conscripts came in slowly, and from nowhere more slowly than the City. Some conscripts mutinied; others perpetrated robberies and other felonies on their march towards Reading.[9]

Fairfax was always short of foot soldiers during the first year and a quarter of active fighting. The army's strength was constantly bled by desertions; almost two men had to be conscripted for every one that was retained. Recruiting infantry was like ladling water into a leaky bucket. During the weeks leading up to Naseby, for example, conscripts, having received their shilling of 'pressed money' did 'daily run away'. Alarmed at this haemorrhaging of strength, Parliament took the drastic step of authorising the death penalty for deserters.[10]

Immediately after Naseby there was a massive drain in the army's numbers. Following the capture of Bristol in September 1645, the army's numbers again contracted. Demoralised by harsh weather, shortages of pay, food and clothing, and the absence of many of their officers, who had retreated to the comfort of London, the numbers of foot fell to 8,000. By April 1646 the winter recruiting campaign had restored the army's total strength to about 17,000.[11]

Why did the foot desert in such large numbers? Apart from their low pay (eightpence a day), the soldiers struggled under a 60-pound load and often slept beneath the open sky. Few foot soldiers understood or cared about the reasons for fighting against the king. Drawn from the lowest ranks of society, often without a fixed address, some of them found it easy to desert because they were next to impossible to trace once they had fled. Colonel John Venn reflected the frustration caused by the low quality of conscripted men when he wrote to Parliament in April 1646: 'most countries press the scum of all their inhabitants, the king's soldiers, men taken out of prison, tinkers, pedlars and vagrants that have no dwelling, and such of whom no account can be given. It is no marvel if such run away.' If the next batch of recruits was of the same abysmal quality, Venn declared, he would rather face the enemy without them.[12]

There were frequent, exaggerated accusations that the New Model was riddled with royalism. It is worth noting that by mid-1646 there were already in the army a significant number of men who had previously fought on the king's side. Besides royalists, there were also West Country Clubmen. They were a regionally organised movement of resistance to the ravages of war. What united them was outrage at plundering by undisciplined troops and a passionate yearning for peace. Initially more hostile to Parliament than to the king, these professed neutralists were won over by the New Model's superior conduct. A few days after the storming of Bristol their numbers were reported by Fairfax as 3,500 from Somerset and Gloucestershire.[13]

An unforeseen source of recruits was deserters from Colonel Edward Massie's Western Brigade. As early as April 1645 Massie complained that troops were leaving him because he was unable to horse, clothe and arm them properly. Massie's losses to the New Model showed no sign of letting up several months later, leading the House of Lords to move that Fairfax be forbidden to receive deserters from the Western Brigade. But the Commons refused to agree, so the practice continued unchecked.[14]

Royalists, Clubmen and deserters from other parliamentary forces never comprised more than a fraction of the New Model foot. The great bulk were pressed men from the south-east in 1645 and from the south-east and south-west in 1646. Raw force was necessary to get them to serve, which made it expensive to round them up, usually £2 to £2 10s per man.[15]

The second and third recruitment campaigns were a great disappointment, partly because of the growing lack of cooperation from London. Fairfax was therefore authorised to recruit men where he was, in the west, as well as in the counties newly brought under parliamentary control.[16]

To summarise the recruitment campaigns and their impact upon the fluctuating strength of the New Model Army during the first year, from April 1645 to April 1646: 7,226 infantry, and most of the 6,600 cavalry were voluntarily recruited from the defunct armies of Essex, Manchester and Waller. This left 7,174 foot and 1,000 dragoons still to be raised. A target of 8,460 was set for London and the ten south-eastern counties. Every pressed man was to be supplied with a suit of clothes, including a red coat faced with blue.[17]

The Army Committee, the general staff and county officials worked together rapidly to meet this target. By the end of April 1645 the army's strength had reached between 20,000 and 21,000. Included in this total were the 7,000 men of Oliver Cromwell's brigade.[18]

After Fairfax had left to relieve Taunton at the beginning of May, 2,000 more troops arrived at Reading, and at least another 2,000 flowed in at the end of May. These figures yield a total of 24,000–25,000, two weeks before the battle of Naseby. Only half that number were under Fairfax's immediate command.[19] Although combat and sickness had as yet claimed few casualties, men were already running away in large numbers. Around the beginning of June, Cromwell's brigade was divided between the Isle of Ely, where Cromwell himself led a force of 3,000–4,000, to protect the eastern counties, and Oxford, where the remainder under Major-General Richard Browne kept watch on the king's headquarters. With the arrival of Cromwell's troops on 6 June and Vermuyden's on the 8th, the New Model reached a strength of over 20,000, made up as follows:

At Taunton	4,000
Under Cromwell	3,000+
Under Vermuyden	2,500
At Boarstall	500
Under Fairfax	10,000
Total	**20,000+**

In theory, then, there were over 15,500 troops available at Naseby. The arrival of Rossiter's Lincolnshire regiment at the very last moment added another 500, making the total about 16,000. However, under-strength regiments may have reduced the actual numbers to perhaps 15,000, or 17,000 if officers are included in the count. The army, it seems, had already lost well over 4,000 of the men it had recruited over the previous two months.[20]

It was to lose a similar number after Naseby. At the end of June the Committee of Both Kingdoms ordered a second major recruitment campaign in London and eleven south-eastern counties. Owing to the New Model's weakness in numbers, an immediate assault on Oxford had to be put off. At the beginning of July Fairfax was again in command of only 10,000 troops apart from the 4,000 still at Taunton.[21] How are we to explain this drastic drop in numbers?

The dead and wounded at Naseby came to about 500, but when they are subtracted there are still nearly 5,000 missing men to be accounted for. Observers at the time agreed that a large number of them – both horse and foot – had quit the army to find safe storage for the booty they had taken on the battlefield. Fairfax, never a man to exaggerate, declared to the House of Lords that both his horse and foot had been depleted, the latter by at least 50 per cent. The situation had hardly changed by the end of July when similar figures were again broadcast: a shortfall of 6,000 foot and 1,400 horse. It was confidently expected that the second recruitment campaign would make good this lack, but the army commanders were to be bitterly disappointed. It is not known how many horse were raised, but the foot came to scarcely over 2,000, including 100 Cavaliers.[22]

In the autumn of 1645 a third recruitment campaign was launched with a target of 500 horse, 500 dragoons and 5,489 foot. Again it seems that the New Model had declined to barely two-thirds of its intended strength. Responsibility for finding the 1,000 horse and dragoons was laid on the London Militia Committee, which was told to collect either a horse and rider or £12 from every qualified householder. This is the one time we hear of coercion being applied to raise mounted troops for the New Model Army. The mounted troops were quickly mobilised, but only 2,080, or 38 per cent, of the infantry quota were recruited. London's record was the worst: fifty-seven out of a quota of 1,469. Desperate for more infantry, Fairfax accepted Clubmen from Somerset and Gloucestershire, but they do not seem to have stayed long in the army.[23]

By October 1645 the third press produced 3,000 men. Yet the idleness of the autumn months, the wet weather and disease, food scarcities throughout the south-west, and delays in sending money and clothing to the front meant that this gain was completely wiped out by December. Again the principal reason was desertion.[24]

The army's fourth recruitment campaign was launched in January 1646. The county quotas added up to 8,800, implying that the New Model was at its lowest ebb since its launching almost a year before. The campaign was a relative success, but half the pressed men ran away, which meant that the New Model only attained a strength of 17,000 by April 1646.[25]

The strength of the army does not always reflect the results of these official recruitment campaigns. Other counties also contributed; royalist soldiers switched sides on at least three occasions; and the army had some success in recruiting locally, notably when the Somerset and Gloucestershire Clubmen threw their weight behind the New Model for the assault on Bristol in September 1645. The figures for the army's strength on a particular date,

Recruitment campaign	Numbers raised	Army strength	Date
April to May 1645	11,000	24,800	31 May 1645
		20,000+	10 June 1645
		16,000	1 July 1645
		13,800	31 July 1645
July 1645	1,300	15,100	15 August 1645
		18,600	15 September 1645
September to October 1645	2,080	?	31 October 1645
		14,000	December 1645
		13,400	January 1646
January to April 1646	3,400	16,800	30 April 1646

while based on a sifting of official records, newsbook reports and other contemporary sources, are inevitably approximate.

Among the rank and file the turnover was mainly due to desertion and, to a much lesser extent, death from disease or wounds. Among the officers on the other hand, for the first two years, there was virtually no desertion; most of those lost were killed in action, or died from disease. At least 38 – 19 per cent of the total – disappeared from the army for such reasons. In the late spring and summer of 1647, however, a much higher number left or were driven out for political reasons. By August 1647 at least 132 had gone, or about 70 per cent of the total for the two and a quarter years since the army's founding.[26]

The picture that emerges from this examination of army recruitment and retention is different from the traditional one in several respects. First, the gulf separating the horse and the foot was even wider than used to be thought. The men of the cavalry were clearly the sons of yeomen and craftsmen – 'middling sort of people' in the terminology of the seventeenth century. While most of them could not afford to equip themselves with a horse, weapons and armour, they thought for themselves to the extent of wishing to serve voluntarily under the parliamentary standard. The foot by contrast were drawn from the lowest ranks of society. They were 'scum', as one officer called them in a moment of exasperation, men who, once clothed and given their shilling of 'pressed money', wanted nothing more than to run away. Only a minority engaged in the luxury of political opinions.

While the number of horse remained fairly stable, between 5,000 and 6,600, the foot and dragoons underwent violent fluctuations in numbers, from 18,000 to 7,000, owing to massive desertions. The men who stamped the New Model with its distinctive character were a tight group of about 5,000 horse and 7,000 foot. For the rest the army was no more than a revolving door through which they exited almost as quickly as they entered. By the summer of 1646 the number of men who had served in Sir Thomas Fairfax's army must have been well over 30,000. If we add to this total those who were conscripted but ran away before seeing active service we arrive at 40,000 as the total number of men who were recruited in a period of twelve months. Ironically, great victories such as Naseby and Bristol brought no influx of new recruits, but only accelerated the already worrying attrition rate. Parliament's experience in raising troops was not much different from the king's. Both sides ran into the same resistance, and both suffered constant haemorrhaging of their numbers, resulting in chronic shortages of infantry.

All we can say about the difference between the two armies is that the royalist army, plagued by inferior financing, bitterly divided leadership and a mounting tally of defeats, suffered recruitment problems even more acutely than the army of Fairfax.[27]

Arms, Clothing and Food

The gigantic task of outfitting the new army began as soon as the officer list was complete, the monthly assessment scheme in place, and the loan from London arranged. A committee of six MPs was named to contract for arms, ammunition, clothing and other equipment needed for the summer campaign. Contracts were let almost immediately, and by early April supplies were pouring into army stores at Reading. The system of provisioning was administered efficiently and, by delivering matériel to the army on time, was instrumental in achieving the victories of 1645. Based on prompt payment in cash, this new centralised system soon supplanted other schemes for equipping the army.[28]

About 200 suppliers, virtually all of them based in or near London, were given contracts. The revenues from the London loan, the monthly assessment, and – when these fell short – 'delinquents' compositions' (royalist fines) and the excise, were always adequate to ensure prompt payment. The contracts vividly illustrate the economic power of the metropolis to feed the army's voracious appetite. The records also document the privileged position enjoyed by the New Model vis-à-vis Parliament's other armies.[29]

With the membership of the Army Committee reflecting the ascendancy of the Independent war party, it is not surprising to find that a number of suppliers were men of the same political stripe.[30]

All the suppliers, whatever their political colours, were paid promptly, and prospered from the war. But there were no scandals connected with provisioning the army, not even allegations of profiteering. The Army Committee drove hard bargains for everything it bought.[31]

A great volume of supplies left London for the army during the first twelve months of its existence. In value they amounted to £116,823. Fairfax and his London friends, who included several newspaper editors, lost no opportunity to publicise the army's needs. In December 1645 Robert Scawen brought down a lengthy report on the condition of the army. Adopted by the Commons, the report set targets for various kinds of clothing, arms and ammunition. Several of the targets, including those for swords and suits of clothing, were impressively met over the next three months.[32]

These financial records tell us much about the operation of a seventeenth-century army. They show, for example, how much better the cavalry were treated than the dragoons, and how much better the dragoons were treated than the infantry. Dragoon horses were lighter, weaker and cheaper than those of the cavalry. The wide range in seventeenth-century horse prices is analogous to the range in car prices today. At one end of the scale a dragoon horse could be had for £2. At the other end, Major Thomas Harrison, who always loved to outfit himself stylishly, spent £50 on two horses.[33]

Everyone in the rank and file, whether horse trooper or foot soldier, had the same quality of sword, but dragoon muskets, even though shorter barrelled, cost 20–30 per cent more than the matchlock muskets supplied to the foot. Some dragoons carried carbines, which were also more expensive than infantry muskets. Cavalry troopers sat in saddles that were more substantial, fancier and twice as costly as the saddles provided for their comrades in the dragoons. Pistols, which were highly prized, and upon which a great deal of money was lavished, were supplied only to the cavalry. They doubtless contributed to a trooper's sense of well-being, but posed little threat to the enemy.

A great deal of money was spent on firearms in general. Pistols, muskets and carbines cost more than pikes and halberds, and many more of them were bought. Everyone carried a sword, which was still the most lethal hand weapon, but musketeers outnumbered pikemen by two to one or more.

Powder, match, shot and shells ate up considerable sums of money, but the New Model purchased only three new pieces of artillery during its first year. The explanation is simple: a good deal of ordnance was inherited from the three armies that went out of existence in 1645. We know the size of the artillery train from the description of the army's marching formation in the spring of 1645. The carriages and main body of the train marched in the middle of the army, flanked by troops of horse on all sides. In addition, four pieces of ordnance were drawn between each of the twenty-four regiments.[34] Ordnance was not used to much effect on the battlefield, but it came into its own during the many sieges that began in July 1645. Fairfax's preference for lightning assaults against royalist castles and fortified towns was made feasible by the gigantic haul of royalist ordnance at Naseby (much of it previously captured from Essex at Lostwithiel). Over the previous century on the Continent the new cannon had sounded the death knell for the high stone walls of mediaeval cities. The same sentence was now executed in England as one castle and city-wall after another crumpled before the shock of the New Model artillery. Yet the heavy guns were still not fully exploited in the sieges of 1645–46. Poor road conditions and sometimes lack of transport meant that they could not always be brought into play.

What did it cost to outfit a foot soldier? The Commons directive was that a coat, breeches, shirt, pair of shoes and stockings, and knapsack were to cost not more than 24 shillings, and the army normally did not exceed that maximum. In addition, most new dragoons and cavalry troopers had to be provided with a horse. Those who came from the previous armies usually brought their horses with them, so that only 280 had to be bought before the battle of Naseby. During the next ten months, thousands of horses were taken from the enemy – most notably at Naseby where 2,000 were taken, and at the surrender of Sir Ralph Hopton's army in Cornwall, when another 2,500 were acquired. Nevertheless, the demand for troop horses was insatiable, as the account book of horses showed.[35]

The creation of the New Model was also marked by the introduction of the British Army's distinctive uniform for two centuries: the redcoat. It was faced with blue, Sir Thomas Fairfax's colour, while the breeches were grey.[36]

In addition to being clothed and transported to the army's assembly point at Reading, the new troops were fed until the time they received their first wages. The basic staples – cheese and hard biscuit – were purchased centrally. Until Naseby and beyond, the army was supplied by a commissariat that purchased food through London merchants and transported it by road to wherever the army was stationed. This was economically practical within a short distance from London – as far as Leicester and Oxford. Farther than that, the soldiers were on their own. The New Model, as with other contemporary European armies, procured a good 90 per cent of its provisions locally. Not only were soldiers expected to buy food out of their wages, the cavalry were also responsible for feeding their own horses. Sympathetic journalists made much of the soldiers' relatively good record of paying for what they consumed. Once it was known that the soldiers could be trusted to pay in cash, farmers were only too happy to sell. Local economies were quickened by the infusion of money from soldiers' pockets.[37]

But if the army stayed too long in one place a local economy could be devastated. The region near Crediton, Devon, in February 1646, where a large part of the army was stationed for several weeks, became 'miserably exhausted and ruined' with hardly any food or fodder to be had, despite the fact that the soldiers had cash to pay for them.[38] Given the relative immobility of food supplies and the very high cost of inland transport in the seventeenth century, an army that did not keep moving became an insupportable burden to the region where it was stationed.

Shortage of pay merely exacerbated a problem that was continually on the verge of spiralling out of control. At the time of Naseby for example, the army descended like clouds of locusts on the defenceless countryside of Northamptonshire and Warwickshire. For four months, from April to July, it was relatively well paid.[39] Yet if the householders of both counties are to be believed, Fairfax's men devoured mammoth quantities of butter, cheese, beer, wheat, barley, peas, oats, malt, mutton, lamb, pork, veal and bacon. Bored with their spartan diet of cheese and hard biscuit, the soldiers were ravenous for meat on the eve of battle. Their horses, between 7,000 and 8,000 of them, were no less hungry. They consumed whole meadows and pastures, some freshly seeded. The loss of grass was a leading complaint heard time and again. Horses needed to be shod as well as fed, and horseshoes were a further item for which compensation was often demanded. Another expense borne locally was the wagons commandeered by the New Model to transport goods and equipment for short distances.

No article in the agrarian inventory was safe from the soldiers' grasping fingers. In addition to foodstuffs, claims were submitted for clothing – shoes, shirts, gloves and stockings; for bedding and linen; for fuel – coal, turf and firewood; and for a whole miscellany of items – straw, a brass pot, a bottle, money and a Bible. Besides burning some families' entire stores of firewood in the space of a few nights, soldiers cut down trees, or quartered on unwilling householders without paying their way. The taking of free quarter – so potent a source of animosity between soldier and civilian – was more the rule than the exception in the spring of 1645. A year later the inhabitants of Stretton under Fosse reported wearily, 'we have been charged so often with so many for free quarter that we cannot make any certainty thereof'.[40]

Accounts in the army's own records give the lie to contemporary publicists' boast that it behaved honourably at all times towards its civilian hosts. Military conduct towards civilians does seem to have improved after Naseby, however. The two and a half months leading up to that great milestone in the war were a time of administrative chaos, as officers tried to discipline an infantry, a good half of whom were raw, disorderly recruits. Over the succeeding months Fairfax and his staff knocked the army into shape by punishing harshly those who took from civilians without paying. When money ran short, as it often did, soldiers were more inclined to tighten their belts than risk punishment for seizing food they could not pay for. It was said that one of the causes of the widespread sickness in the army in the late autumn of 1645, apart from poor accommodation and lack of warm clothing, was the inability to pay for bread. This reduced the soldiers to living off 'fruit and roots', a demoralising experience to men not inspired with the modern enthusiasm for vegetables.[41]

As soon as it became evident that the war was won, taxpayers and Parliament both slackened their efforts to keep the army well provisioned and paid. From the late spring to the autumn of 1646, the army's financial position steadily deteriorated. Ironically, at the very moment when a pro-army newspaper was boasting that the soldiers besieging Oxford paid in ready money for everything they consumed, Fairfax published a severe proclamation against taking free quarter:

> Forasmuch as the army under my command have for some time past for want of pay practised free quarter ... I do hereby strictly ... order all officers and soldiers ... to discharge their quarters according to the several rates ... (*viz.*), 4d a night hay, 2d a night grass, 4d a peck oats, 6d a peck peas and beans, and also 8d a day for the diet of every trooper or horseman, 7d a day for every dragooner, and 6d a day for every foot soldier, pioneer, waggoner or carter ...[42]

In the next breath the order was undercut by a proviso that unpaid soldiers were to give receipts, signed by their commanding officers, for what they received in board and lodging. It may be that soldiers paid for what they obtained in the marketplace, but fell down when it came to honouring their obligations to those who gave them shelter.

The improvement in the army's conduct during the ten months after Naseby does not alter the reality that the New Model fundamentally lived off the countryside where it was stationed. However much was paid centrally for food, many times that value was taken locally. Some was paid for at the time; some was commandeered in return for receipts promising future payment, and some was unceremoniously seized. The localities did not just yield food and lodging; they also gave up carts and wagons, spades and shovels, horses, and occasionally clothing. The only thing that can be said for New Model soldiers is that they were less oppressive and undisciplined in their exploitation of the countryside than their royalist counterparts.

Pay

Once men had been recruited, clothed and equipped, the chief continuing expense was their daily wage, ranging from eightpence for a foot soldier, 1 shilling and sixpence for a dragoon and 2 shillings for a cavalry trooper, to 30 shillings for a colonel and £10 for the commander-in-chief. Officers whose pay was between 5 and 10 shillings a day had one third of it withheld or 'respited', while those whose pay was above 10 shillings a day saw half of it withheld. Even the cavalry trooper saw a quarter of his pay deducted in forced savings.[43] Private foot soldiers were expected to feed and clothe themselves out of their wages, while cavalry troopers also had to feed their horses.

In theory the system of paying the troops was both rational and centralised. Regiments were mustered every four to six weeks. A warrant would then be drawn up for one, two or four weeks' pay for the company of foot or dragoons or regiment of horse in question, signed by Fairfax and dispatched to the Treasurers at War. Roughly once a month a shipment of silver coin would leave London for the army in its several locations. The money was weighty; delivering it involved wagons, teams of horses and guards. In October 1645 the pay sent to Cheshire was conveyed by no fewer than 500 cavalry and 1,000 dragoons.[44]

Once it reached the army, the money was paid out to the officers, who then distributed it among their men. The virtual absence of any complaints against New Model officers for withholding money from their troops suggests that this final stage was carried out honestly. Over the twenty-seven months from April 1645 to June 1647, the foot received pay for approximately eighty-nine weeks, or 76 per cent of the whole period. The horse, whose standard of living was slightly higher than subsistence, were deliberately paid less regularly, their total pay coming to sixty-eight weeks, or 58 per cent of the whole period. The army was surprisingly well paid in late 1646 and early 1647. The fighting had been over for many months, yet during the half-year ending in April 1647 both horse and foot received virtually full pay.[45]

Paradoxically, it was after the army's political triumph in the summer of 1647 that its pay fell seriously into arrears. It had tried and failed to persuade Parliament to double the monthly assessment to £120,000. Instead Parliament agreed to earmark the excise to fund the army's reorganisation and reduction in numbers. There was then a rapid and drastic disbandment of nearly 4,000 men from the original New Model regiments in early 1648, accompanied by a much greater disbandment of provincial forces. The shrunken numbers were paid in full for the first half of 1648.[46]

Not until after the king's execution and the establishment of the Commonwealth in early 1649 were the army's needs addressed by raising the assessment from £60,000 to £90,000 a month and assigning each regiment to a different county. For this reason most counties paid their assessment locally. The assessment actually reached £120,000 for a time, and during the period that the army was in control of the government, between 1653 and 1659, the collection rate averaged 88 per cent. Yet the army constantly felt hard done by. Why was this? There was at all times stubborn resistance to taxes that were several times greater than Charles I had ever levied, and the money was slow to be collected, which threw the soldiers back onto free quarter. This only generated a vicious circle of increasing reluctance to pay taxes, which in turn forced the army to rely more on free quarter, which in turn provoked greater tax resistance. Before long the army was sending soldiers around to collect the assessment, and this became an endless source of friction with the civilian population. The army's control of the assessment was formalised by appointing officers as assessment commissioners, from which position they were able to chivvy local collectors into action. That, plus the physical presence of soldiers, largely cured London's recalcitrance after the army's invasions of 1647 and 1648. The cost in popular resentment was high.[47]

After the occupation of Ireland and Scotland in the 1650s the New Model soldiers in both countries were paid from the local assessment, and excise topped up by supplementary payments from English revenues. In spite of these subsidies the army in England continued to be better paid than the armies of occupation.

There were a number of expedients apart from free quarter to stave off hunger when pay was slow in arriving: loans from innkeepers, loans from borough corporations, and loans from commanding officers. The battle of Worcester (3 September 1651), led to a three-year period during which the army in England received regular pay. Then under the Protectorate the government twice reduced the assessment. On the eve of the first Protectoral Parliament in 1654 it came down to £90,000, and down again to £60,000 by 1655. But there were no cuts in the number of troops. General Monck, ever the realist, wrote to Cromwell: 'it passes my understanding how your Highness will be able to carry on your business with this £60,000 a month'. He was right. Soon there was a growing chorus complaining of lack of pay and the return of free quarter. At length the government responded in the summer of 1655 by cutting soldiers' wages, and then by significantly reducing the size of the payroll. In place of the disbanded troops the government set up a much cheaper militia that was to muster only four times a year.[48]

Thanks to the various sources of credit, as well as free quarter, arrears were never in fact a pressing grievance for the soldiers; they only became so at the time of disbanding. Nevertheless, short-term delays in the delivery of money to the army could produce acute suffering. In their desperation to head off desertion, officers dug into their pockets to feed their men. The army also enlisted publicists like Lord Fairfax of Cameron, Sir Thomas's father, who had taken up residence in the capital, and the preacher Hugh Peters, to highlight the soldiers' plight. They teamed up with journalists to stir up guilty feelings among well-fed Londoners living safe, warm, comfortable lives while shivering soldiers fell sick for lack of warm clothing or decent food.[49]

In the face of this heart-rending publicity, it should not be forgotten that the New Model was better paid than the three armies it replaced, and other contemporary armies. That is why men fled from Massie's brigade to the New Model (see above, pp. 21–2). It is why hundreds of royalist soldiers signed on for the New Model. And it illuminates the soldiers' statement in June 1647 that their pre-New Model arrears were much greater than what they had accumulated since 1645. The total arrears owing to all the forces of Parliament by early 1647 was nearly £3 million, but over half that sum was due to non-New Model forces. Of the roughly £1.5 million due to the New Model, three-fifths were for pre-New Model service. Close to half the arrears from 1645 on were owed to officers. Of the remainder, almost all belonged to the cavalry troopers who were on three-quarters pay. The back pay of the infantry was negligible. Most noteworthy, both infantry and cavalry had been paid punctually and nearly in full for four months before the New Model became politically active in March 1647, and for two months after that time. As we shall see, pay and arrears were negligible factors in its revolt of 1647.

CHAPTER THREE

THE YEAR OF VICTORIES, 1645–46

The New Model Army got off to an unpromising start. Essex's former foot regiments seemed reluctant to accept Fairfax's authority. Colonel John Dalbier with his eight troops of horse, stood aloof, apparently ready to join the king at Oxford. Sir Michael Livesey led his regiment in a mutiny against the new dispensation and was at once replaced by Henry Ireton. A number of other officers wasted their time in 'idleness and profaneness' in London, scandalising citizens with their drunken brawling. Fairfax, whose health was fragile at the best of times, succumbed to a fever, just before he was to conduct the new army from Windsor to Reading. The key post of lieutenant-general of the cavalry remained unfilled.[1]

More seriously, Fairfax and his commanders found their freedom of manoeuvre hobbled by the Committee of Both Kingdoms, which continued to direct military strategy from London. It took a major disaster to bring the armchair strategists in London to their senses. By their restless shifting of pieces over the chessboard of southern England, the committee had inadvertently created a vacuum at the centre. In late May the New Model forces were distributed between Taunton (5,000), Oxford (10,000), the north (2,500) – where Vermuyden had been dispatched to assist the Scots – and East Anglia (5,000), where Cromwell had been stationed. The whole strategy began to unravel when the Scots, worried about the royalist menace from the marquess of Montrose, withdrew towards Scotland. The king chose this moment to storm and brutally sack Leicester, without a finger being raised to stop him. A week later the Committee of Both Kingdoms acknowledged the futility of trying to direct field operations from London, and gave Fairfax the free hand he sought.[2]

By the beginning of June, thanks to political infighting, poor strategy and administrative delay, Parliament's fortunes were at their lowest ebb since 1643. Objectively, however, the king's were even lower. If Fairfax was straitjacketed by the Committee of Both Kingdoms, Charles was distracted by irreconcilable divisions within his council. Isolated from his supporters in the west and the north, he commanded fewer than 9,000 troops, while Fairfax's ranks swelled by the day.

Fairfax's Council of War chose this juncture to urge that Oliver Cromwell be nominated to the vacant lieutenant-generalship of the cavalry. The Commons – though not the Lords – quickly agreed to the request, a mere four days before battle was joined at Naseby. By the time Cromwell rode into the New Model's lines with 600 horse and dragoons from the Eastern Association, that climactic event was only a day away.[3]

Naseby

That the battle occurred at all was thanks to Charles's indecision about whether to link up with George, Lord Goring in the south-west, meet Sir Marmaduke Langdale in the north, or launch an attack on the Eastern Association. When he found himself close to Fairfax's army he listened to Prince Rupert, whose contempt for the New Model was boundless. Yet Charles might still have postponed the battle had he received Goring's intercepted letter promising to overrun Taunton and then hasten to his aid within three weeks.[4]

On 14 June 1645, Fairfax disposed of eleven horse regiments more or less at full strength, a regiment of dragoons, eight regiments of foot and 200 lifeguards, as well as a similar number of firelocks. As we have seen in Chapter 2 (p. 23), his total strength cannot have been less than 15,000. Charles could boast barely three-fifths that number. The parliamentary generals chose their ground well. In the early morning of 14 June, the armies faced each other on two low hills just north of Naseby. Finding that the king's army had the advantage of the westerly wind, Fairfax shifted to the left so that the two armies now faced each other on a north–south axis.

He then backed his troops 100 paces behind the brow of the hill in order to conceal them from the king. In addition to facing an uphill charge, Charles's cavalry would have to wade through low, wet ground. Fairfax's cavalry was augmented by Colonel John Fiennes's regiment and the regiment delivered by Cromwell from the Eastern Association. The cavalry on the left wing were under the command of Henry Ireton, who had been made commissary-general that morning. Thanks to the last-minute arrival of Rossiter's regiment

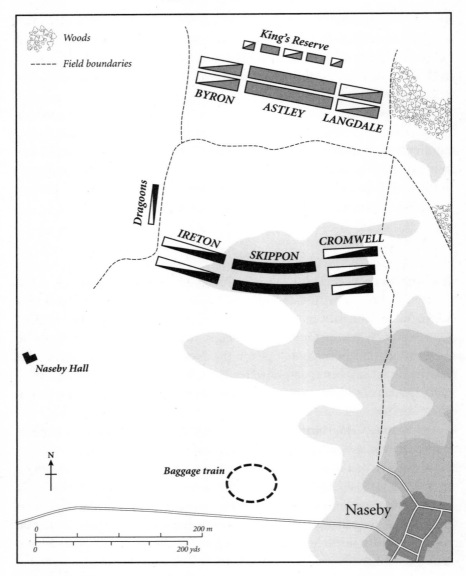

Woods

Field boundaries

King's Reserve

BYRON   ASTLEY   LANGDALE

Dragoons

IRETON   SKIPPON   CROMWELL

Naseby Hall

N

Baggage train

Naseby

0   200 m

0   200 yds

1. The battle of Naseby, 14 June 1645

from Lincolnshire, the right wing under Cromwell was a trifle heavier, and was drawn up three lines deep instead of the usual two. The left wing's slight inferiority in numbers was more than offset by the stationing of Colonel John Okey's crack regiment of dragoons behind the hedges on the far left at right angles to the line of battle. From that position they would be able to pour galling musket fire across the flank of the king's advancing horse. At a later stage in the battle the dragoons' intervention would be decisive. Between the two wings of cavalry were eight infantry regiments drawn up in two lines, with a 'forlorn hope' (a small advance force) of 300 musketeers ahead of the front line. The battle line was over 1.5 miles in breadth. About 900 yards back, just west of Naseby, was the baggage and artillery train, guarded by 200 firelocks. It was a simple order of battle, apart from 'one touch of tactical subtlety' – the placement of the dragoons. For ease of communication, the eight infantry regiments were divided into three brigades.[5] Around ten o'clock the cannon on both sides began to play, but the exchange lasted less than an hour, since the parliamentary commanders wanted all the daylight hours for fighting. (The conventional wisdom of the day was that artillery scarcely affected the outcome of a battle.)

In a scant two hours the battle was over. Between ten and eleven o'clock Prince Rupert advanced with his cavalry against the left wing under Ireton, who tried to gain the upper hand by charging down the hill to meet him. The charge was ragged, and some of the horse stumbled into shallow water-holes and ditches. Ireton in his inexperience allowed himself to become distracted by the distress of the infantry. He ordered the detachment nearest to him to ride to their rescue. While he was preoccupied with this diversion, his own horse was shot under him; he was wounded and taken prisoner. He remained out of action until the tide turned. One regiment was saved from the general disaster on Ireton's left wing by musket fire from the dragoons in the hedges. Despite being routed, Ireton's regiments did not turn tail and flee. As many as 1,500 troopers remained on the field.[6] Having overrun nearly half the New Model cavalry and left it headless, Prince Rupert now tried to capture the artillery train on the other side of the field. He met with unexpectedly fierce resistance from Thomas Hammond's seasoned men.

At the same time as Ireton was being captured, Cromwell led a successful charge on the right wing against Langdale's horse. His two regiments of Ironsides were 'like a torrent driving all before them'. After putting up a stiff resistance, the whole of Langdale's wing was pushed back, leaving the flank of the royalist infantry exposed to cavalry attack. But the parliamentary foot under Skippon was in an even worse jam. The enemy had rolled back the front line, except for Fairfax's own foot regiment. Skippon now brought up the reserves, under Colonels Thomas Rainborowe, Thomas Pride and Robert Hammond. As he did so he was wounded by a musket ball, said to have been fired accidentally by one of his own men, which pierced right through his armour and his body. Though severely wounded,

Skippon insisted on remaining at his post. By bringing up the infantry reserves he halted the royalist advance before all was lost. It was now about noon and the New Model had lost two of its field generals, only Fairfax, Cromwell and Thomas Hammond remaining. By a monumental, co-ordinated effort, they managed to save the day.[7]

Seeing the distress on the left wing and the middle, Fairfax and Cromwell wheeled about. With a detachment of horse, Cromwell crossed the field to rally Ireton's fragmented regiments. He and Fairfax then charged from opposite sides into the main body of the king's infantry with the intent of relieving their own boxed-in regiments. The manoeuvre worked. Having restored order to the parliamentary line, Fairfax now prepared to lead a second charge against the king's left wing of horse, which had regrouped and been reinforced by Prince Rupert's divisions, now back on the field. Fairfax had to wait until the parliamentary foot recovered the quarter-mile they had lost at the beginning of the battle. As soon as the horse and foot were abreast and the horse arranged again in two wings, the whole army advanced under Fairfax's direction. This time the general was careful to ensure that the horse did not leave the flanks of the infantry exposed by too impetuous a charge. Sighting the monolithic approach of the New Model and overawed by its crushing superiority of numbers, the remnant of the king's army now turned tail and fled. Cromwell directed the pursuit of these demoralised forces for 13 or 14 miles to Leicester.

All contemporary narratives of the battle of Naseby are clear about the central role of Sir Thomas Fairfax. True, Cromwell's arrival on the day before gave a fillip to the soldiers' morale. It was he who suggested moving the army west to the higher ground of Mill Hill; he who arranged the cavalry, making his right wing three lines deep; he who led the first charge. But when his friend Ireton, to whom he had handed the leadership of the left wing, faltered and fell, Cromwell raced to rescue him and re-inspire his shattered regiments. Skippon, though severely wounded, brought up the infantry reserves, while Fairfax helped to save the infantry by his own courage and leadership. At most times a quiet and even sickly man – he suffered the agonies of kidney stones among other complaints – Fairfax's personality was transformed on the battlefield. In the words of one eyewitness, he 'did so animate the soldiers as is hardly to be expressed. Sir, had you seen him and how his spirit was raised, it would have made an impression on you never to be obliterated.' Fairfax did not hesitate to expose himself to personal danger by wading into the thick of the battle at critical moments. More important, he kept his head amidst the terrible confusion, flux and panic of an actual battle. Cromwell chose the ground, set the troops in order and decisively broke Langdale's horse. Fairfax, thirteen years his junior, but with the benefit of several years of battlefield experience on the Continent and in the north, directed troop movements, and responded to the unpredictable fluidity, the overwhelming rush of events that were compressed into the two hours when the outcome of the English Civil War was decided. In the opinion of the army's secretary John Rushworth, always a shrewd observer, 'what made our horse so terrible to them was the thickness of our reserves and their orderly and timely coming on, not one failing to come on in time'.[8]

The human cost of victory was cheap. Fairfax lost 150 men, the king about 1,000. Charles also lost most of his infantry, 4,000 of whom were taken prisoner, 2,000 horses, his entire artillery and baggage train, and his chest of secret letters. Parliament's published excerpts from these letters would soon do terrible damage to the king's reputation as a man of honour. The ugliest episode of the day was the massacre of over 100 women as whores, Irishwomen 'of cruel countenance', and possibly witches. Rushworth admitted the truth: many of them were royalist soldiers' wives.[9]

The South-Western Campaign

The next day Fairfax advanced his army to Leicester, where the king's remaining forces had fled. Two days later he retook the town. Turning his mind to Taunton, he bent his steps westward. When at the beginning of July he crossed into Dorset, he came up against a group of Clubmen. There was no uncertainty about his intention towards the Clubmen who stood in his way: it was to crush them. For the time being, however, he dealt with them courteously, watching and waiting. Early in July he met with a leader of the Dorset–Wiltshire Clubmen, Robert Hollis. The Clubmen wanted to travel through his lines and deliver petitions to king and Parliament. Fairfax said no. After his sweeping victory over Goring at Langport on 10 July, Fairfax encountered a much friendlier reception from the mid-Somerset Clubmen under Humphrey Willis. They confiscated the royalists' horses and arms, and took some of the fleeing soldiers prisoner. Over the next ten days Clubmen blocked the road to Bristol, preventing Goring from fleeing to join

Prince Rupert's garrison. They also joined the conquest of Bridgwater, where they helped Colonel Massie's forces on the opposite side of the River Parrett. When the royalist infantry came fleeing down the hedge-lined roads, they stopped them, disarmed them, and sent them home. After Bridgwater, Clubmen from Somerset, Wiltshire and Devon slid more and more rapidly into Fairfax's camp. The parliamentary commissioners who accompanied the army were convinced that the army's prompt payment for food and lodgings was instrumental in winning the hearts and minds of the Clubmen: 'Thousands have laid down their arms merely upon the attention of the soldiers' carriage, which worketh upon them more than laws will.' The power of the New Model Army, combined with its excellent conduct, enabled the 'submerged parliamentarianism' of many West Country Clubmen to rise to the surface.[10]

The Dorset Clubmen, however, as well as some from Wiltshire and the Somerset border, continued to hold out against Fairfax, even after Bridgwater. Fairfax dispatched two of his best cavalry regiments – Colonel Charles Fleetwood's and Colonel Edward Whalley's – to deal with them. They surprised the leaders in the midst of their deliberations, and brought them back to the general, who shipped them to London with other royalist prisoners. A few days later at least 2,000 armed men of Dorset gathered at Hambledon Hill to demand the release of their leaders. Fairfax sent Cromwell with 1,000 horse against them. Cromwell in turn sent Captain-Lieutenant John Gladman with a squadron of Fairfax's horse to scatter them. But the Clubmen presented a wall of pikes and halberds that the horse could not penetrate. Cromwell then ordered his own troop of horse under Captain James Berry to charge them, but Berry too was beaten back. Finally Major John Disbrowe led another troop of horse around a ledge of the hill and surprised them from the rear. Only after this third charge by Ironside cavalry were the Dorset Clubmen routed.[11]

The capture of Bridgwater and Sherborne removed centres of active encouragement for royalist-leaning Clubmen in the Dorset and Somerset border region, while repeated outrages by Goring farther west would cause that region to rise up against him. Confident that he now had the upper hand, Fairfax ordered the sheriff of Somerset to 'raise the power of the country'. By the end of August, volunteers were flocking to be listed. A large force of Clubmen assisted operations against the fort at Portishead on the Bristol Channel, which surrendered on 28 August. A few days later Sheriff Sir John Horner mobilised a great meeting of 4,000–5,000 horse and foot on the hills near Chewton Mendip. Fairfax's chaplain, Hugh Peters, preached to them twice on horseback. Next day 2,000 men turned up to assist with the siege. Another 1,500 arrived from Gloucestershire. They fell on Bedminster, one of the outposts, striking terror into the defenders, who soon surrendered.[12]

From beginning to end, Fairfax's handling of the Clubmen was a diplomatic and military triumph. Thanks to his tact, as well as the Clubmen's disenchantment with the king, he was able to draw the West Country Clubmen more and more into the orbit of the New Model. Only the Dorset Clubmen remained faithful to the royalists, but a calculated show of force was enough to eliminate them as a military threat. From that point (August 1645) until the end of the First Civil War the majority of the West Country Clubmen kept loyal to Fairfax, not only because they detested marauding Cavaliers, but also because they were convinced that total victory held out the best hope of lifting the curse of civil war from their counties. A year later they would come to the bitter realisation that their new masters were hardly better than the old.

The Summer Campaign

In the wake of Naseby, the Committee of Both Kingdoms voted that the enemy should be vigorously prosecuted in the field. Fairfax hardly needed this advice. After recapturing Leicester for Parliament he wheeled around to take on the second most important royalist army led by George, Lord Goring at Taunton. From the opposite direction Massie approached with a brigade of 2,200 horse and dragoons. Goring's army was said to number 10,000. The New Model, despite its great haul of treasure, artillery and secret papers at Naseby, was in some distress as it moved west. It was suffering from reduced numbers, scarcity of arms and lack of horses.[13]

On 4 July 1645, Goring abandoned his siege of Taunton and fell back to Langport, where the rivers Yeo and Parrett protected him against surprise attack. He was playing for time, but Fairfax's mission was to engage with him as speedily as possible. On Tuesday the 8th Fairfax dispatched Massie's brigade, reinforced with New Model horse and dragoons, in pursuit of Goring's force. On the 9th they came upon the royalists relaxing by a stream, their horses at grass in the meadow, the men bathing, drinking or strolling along the riverbank. Catching them unawares, Massie pounced, took 500 prisoners, and chased the rest back to Langport. On the morning of the 10th Goring drew up his army on a hill outside Langport, hoping to block the enemy's advance. He chose his ground well. At the bottom of the hill was a stream that Fairfax's men had to ford. Though the day was hot and dry, recent rains had swollen the stream so that when the soldiers crossed it they were belly-high in water. From the ford a narrow hedged lane ascended the hill towards Goring's position. He stationed a strong force of musketeers behind the hedges that both traversed the fields and lined the lane leading up to his position. At this point Goring had no intention of fighting; he believed his position impregnable.

For his part Fairfax disposed of barely 2,000 cavalry troopers that morning (the rest were with Massie). However, because the lane was too narrow for more than two horses to ride abreast, he could only employ a fraction of them. Against Goring's tactical cleverness Fairfax had three telling advantages: intelligence, firepower and morale. From scouts and local inhabitants he learned that Goring lacked baggage and artillery; in other words he had already opted for a retreat. Fairfax and his Council of War were now emboldened to strike. They drew up their 10,000 men in battle forma-tion on the other side of the valley.

Their second advantage was that they had with them all the New Model's heavy guns. With these they soon silenced the royalists' two remaining small cannon, and 'made the other side of the hill so hot' that Goring pulled his cavalry back, leaving the musketeers in the hedges devoid of support. After fifty or sixty cannonades, Fairfax sent Colonel Rainborowe and 1,500 muske-teers splashing across the stream. 'With admirable resolution', they advanced up the lane from hedge to hedge until the entire passage was theirs. It was now midday under a blazing July sun. Sensing that the moment was ripe, Fairfax sent two troops of horse (200 men) galloping up the lane under Major Christopher Bethell. It was an audacious stroke, which tested the mettle of his cavalry. When they reached the top of the hill they charged straight at Goring's brigade, which outnumbered them perhaps six or eight to one. For a few moments there was a hectic struggle at sword-point, but then Major Disbrowe appeared on the scene with another detachment of horse. Colonel Rainborowe's musketeers had by now also arrived, and the dispirited royalists began to scatter. The chaplain Richard Baxter watched fascinated from the opposite bank. As the Cavalier army crumbled he heard Major Thomas Harrison, who was standing nearby, 'with a loud voice break forth into the praises of God with fluent expressions as if he had been in a rapture'. Bethell and Disbrowe wanted to pursue the terrified Cavaliers, but Fairfax ordered them to wait until reinforcements came up. The discipline of the soldiers was such that they instantly halted their pursuit. The full body of Fairfax's horse now advanced to within 2 miles of Bridgwater, taking along the way 1,400 prisoners, 2,000 horses, 4,000 arms, two cannon and three wagonloads of ammunition. As at Naseby, the human cost of this stunning victory was not high: about 300 royalists and thirty parliamentarians were killed. 'To see this,' exclaimed Cromwell, 'is it not to see the face of God!' Fairfax had triumphantly attained his objective of engaging Goring before he could be strengthened by Welsh reinforcements. The events of June and July had been decisive. At Naseby, Fairfax had struck the king a mortal blow. 'Then swinging round to face the only other army in the field he lunged at Goring.' The war had been effectively won in less than four weeks.[14]

Mopping up the West

Ahead lay eleven more months of sieges, pitched battles, cold, hunger, sickness and anxiety. The New Model carried all before it, and royalist resistance became ever more feeble. The major conquests were Bridgwater, Bath, Sherborne, Bristol, Basing, Tiverton, Dartmouth and Torrington.[15]

At Bristol Prince Rupert was forced to yield up the second city of the kingdom, and the king's main distribution centre for weaponry, ammunition and supplies. Bristol was a euphoric highpoint for the New Model. Welded together by the thrilling experience of shared danger and total victory, the army momentarily breathed the spirit of complete unity. In this mood of unalloyed exaltation Cromwell wrote to the Speaker of the Commons with an appeal for liberty of conscience: 'Presbyterians, Independents, all have here the same spirit of faith and prayer, the same presence and answer; they agree here, pity it should be otherwise anywhere . . . We look for no compulsion, but that of light and reason.' When the letter was printed by Parliament the above passage was deleted. Cromwell's friends in the House retaliated by anonymously printing the suppressed portion, and scattering it up and down the streets of London. Informed opinion on both sides in the capital was highly sensitised to the political implication of the army's lengthening string of victories.[16]

Oxford

The victory at Torrington in February scattered the last remaining body of royalist infantry under Sir Ralph Hopton. There was now only one major fortress in royalist hands: Oxford. With the army's military duties winding down, Cromwell returned to his seat in the Commons. As he passed through Westminster Hall, his colleagues stared at him in awe. Charles meanwhile slipped out of Oxford in disguise, leaving its governor, Sir Thomas Glemham, the humiliating job of yielding the garrison. A few days later the king gave himself up to the Scottish army near Newark.[17]

All the New Model's top commanders – Cromwell, Ireton, Fleetwood, Skippon (the latter greeted with 'much joy and acclamations' by the foot after his long convalescence) – now gravitated to Oxford to be on hand for the dénouement. There was a momentary rush of excitement when artillery fire was briefly exchanged, but on 15 June word came from the king that all his strongholds were to surrender.[18]

Glemham handed over the city to Fairfax on 24 June. Aiming to spare Oxford's intellectual and aesthetic treasures, the general consented to terms so generous as to earn him harsh criticism in London. The defenders were permitted to exit with dignity to wherever they liked: 'colours flying, trumpets sounding, drums beating, matches lighted at both ends, bullet in their mouths, and every soldier to have twelve charges of powder'.[19]

The army's opening and closing actions of the war had been at Oxford. Fairfax, his work accomplished, now took a long break to nurse his kidney stone and repair his ruined health. In November he rode to London and a hero's welcome. The City militia and many citizens turned out to greet him; Parliament formally welcomed him; two days later several peers arrived in their coaches at his house in Queen Street. The earl of Manchester delivered a speech of thanks, following which the Speaker of the Commons, William Lenthall, gave a longer, more effusive address, comparing Fairfax to Julius Caesar. Three days later the mayor and aldermen of the City arrived in another train of coaches with their own expressions of homage. These expressions of delight and gratitude were short-lived, soon to be overtaken by resentment at the cost of the army, and impatience with its religious diversity.[20]

The year of wonders was over. What lay ahead was a more treacherous and complicated war that would be fought with petitions, pamphlets and plots.

CHAPTER FOUR

RELIGION AND MORALE

[The officers] were better Christians than soldiers and wiser in faith than in fighting . . . Many of them with their soldiery, were much in prayer and reading scripture, an exercise that soldiers till of late have used but little, and thus [they] went on and prospered.

Ioshua Sprigge, *Anglia Rediviva*[1]

In a famous dictum Napoleon pronounced that in war 'the moral is to the physical as three is to one'. About 2,000 years before him, Xenophon declared that 'not numbers or strength bring victory in war, but whichever army goes into battle stronger in their soul'. An army's spirit or morale is of crucial importance, but what exactly does it consist of? According to the military historian S.L.A. Marshall, morale is the 'whole complex body of an army's thought'.[2]

Normal preconditions for high morale are that the troops should be in good health, with adequate medical care, sufficient food and water, regular pay, and adequate rest and sleep. These depend not only on resources being available, but on a commanding officer's ability to organise and administer them. They were matters upon which Oliver Cromwell bestowed infinite care. For example, on the way to the battle of Preston (1648), he stopped for several days until his men had been shod with the boots and stockings shipped from Northampton. James Hamilton, first duke of Hamilton, was already in the north with 10,000 marauding Scots at his back, but Cromwell refused to be rushed. Similarly, the following year he refused to take the army to Ireland until Parliament had furnished him with a war chest of £100,000.[3]

A military leader makes a crucial contribution to the morale of his troops if he can bring them to feel that they are safe in his hands, that he will not be careless of their lives and welfare. This Cromwell was able to do almost better than anyone else. By contrast, his opponent at the battle of Dunbar, David Leslie, lacked the power to persuade his troops that they were safe with him, even though they were fighting on home ground and outnumbered their adversary two to one.[4]

Another indispensable ingredient of morale is strong primary-group loyalty. The primary group can be as small as a file of two or three men, or perhaps a company of sixty to 100 men, but never larger than a regiment of 1,000 men. In the turmoil of an actual battle the overriding concern of most soldiers is to protect the lives of those few close comrades who can make a difference to their own chances of survival. Fundamental too is the desire not to be thought a coward by the members of one's group. Primary-group loyalty was reinforced in the seventeenth century by the remarkable discovery by Prince Maurice of Nassau that long hours of drill make men more obedient and more efficient in battle. Accidentally it transpired that when a group of men move their arm and leg muscles in unison for prolonged periods, a primitive and powerful social bond wells up among them. Drill is after all a form of dance, and dance is one of humanity's earliest, most primary vehicles of sociability.[5]

The New Model Army enjoyed markedly higher morale than most armies of the seventeenth century. High morale contributed to, and was enhanced by, the army's battlefield victories. A variety of other factors contributed to its morale, but most distinctive was its collective religious consciousness. Cromwell was in no doubt about the contribution this made to the army's spirit: 'I had rather have a plain, russet-coated captain that knows what he fights for and loves what he knows, than that which you call a gentleman and is nothing else.'[6]

To what extent was the army permeated with religion? We know that most of the time there were several chaplains who preached often, that there was frequent prayer and fasting, and that scripture study was promoted. Were these religious observances meaningful to those who took part in them? Did they make a difference to the soldiers' conduct?

We have seen (above, pp. 20–1) that a large proportion of the soldiers were conscripts. Once in the army they were all too ready to desert. Their demoralising example encouraged others to do the same. It is questionable if any of these runaways were consumed with religious zeal. Another fact that must give us pause is the existence of extremist ideas bordering on scepticism and unbelief. In 1645 and 1646 evidence of unbelief was eagerly collected and purveyed to shocked readers by the London Presbyterian minister Thomas Edwards. One alleged incident involved a blasphemous parody of baptism in which soldiers took a horse into a parish church, filled the baptismal font with urine, and then poured it over the hapless animal while reciting the service from the Book of Common Prayer. In 1646 Captain Paul Hobson was said to have preached that Christians were liberated from the moral law and that the Puritan saints were equal in perfection to Christ. Another officer was reported to have repudiated morality, the Sabbath, the sacraments, the authority of the Bible and the need for forgiveness. Some officers and soldiers rejected the divinity of Christ and scoffed at prayer. Still others reasoned that every spirit was God, that hell did not exist, or that God was as much in hell as in heaven.[7]

If a soldier asserted such views publicly he violated the first article of the army's Laws and Ordinances, which expressly declared 'the holy and blessed Trinity' as an article of belief. By September 1649 the officers were so worried by irreligion that they kept a 'day of humiliation' to combat the 'atheism and profaneness' that had crept into the army.[8]

With the passage of time the army experienced a greater and greater fracturing of the spiritual unity it had briefly known on the battlefield. Such a devout observer as Colonel John Jones was depressed by the endless arid debates over inessentials such as infant baptism, and by the growth of religious subjectivism which rejected prayer, a transcendent God and the reality of sin. The end of it all, thought Jones, could only be 'a fearful spiritual Babel'. Certainly by the early 1650s the forces of religious heterodoxy seemed to be making alarming inroads into the army. Besides radical sceptics there were substantial numbers of Fifth Monarchists, who believed in the imminent return of Christ to rule the earth with his saints, and Quakers, who held that all religious truth was subjective, emanating from the holy spirit dwelling within each individual. During the last years of the Protectorate, Quakerism grew to alarming proportions and was a major source of antagonism between the army and civilian society.[9]

In the beginning, however, when the army was preoccupied on the battle-field, little was heard of debate or heresy and much of sweet unity and a passionate fervour that sometimes reached intoxicating heights. In fact the evidence for devoutness and piety in the New Model Army is overwhelming from beginning to end. This piety extended from the highest to the lowest ranks. The commander-in-chief, Sir Thomas Fairfax, exemplified it well. He always liked to consult religious men before embarking on any course of action, 'as if the best place he could find for counsel and action was there where God was; and he prospered accordingly'. That was why Fairfax appointed Hugh Peters, 'the strenuous Puritan', as chief chaplain to the army, and gave him great latitude and responsibility in preaching, recruiting, negotiating with the enemy, and corresponding with Parliament and the public. On several occasions Fairfax exhibited an acute sense of God's special favour towards him and the army.[10]

The major-general of the infantry, Philip Skippon, was, like Fairfax, a man of few words. By the same token, he had an unquestioning confidence in God's favour, which he was able to communicate to the rank and file. In 1642 at Turnham Green he exhorted them with the words, 'come my honest brave boys, pray heartily and fight heartily and God will bless us'. Skippon published three books of devotion addressed to his fellow soldiers, and at his death, left a lengthy will that breathed an elaborate Puritan piety.[11]

The lieutenant-general of the cavalry, Oliver Cromwell, is renowned for his colossal, exuberant religious zeal. His habit of wearing his spiritual heart on his sleeve has caused many to doubt his sincerity, and in his own day he was regularly accused of hypocrisy. But his private letters are of a piece with his public statements and testify to his sincerity. Writing to his daughter Bridget shortly after her marriage to Henry Ireton, he urged on her the joy of being a religious seeker: 'Who ever tasted that graciousness of His, and could go less in desire, and less than pressing after full enjoyment? Dear Heart, press on; let not husband, let not anything cool thy affections after Christ.'[12] His letters to his daughter give us a glimpse of the personal, private side of Cromwell's religion. As for the public, political face of his religion, its chief ingredients were the sovereignty of conscience, the continual looking to providence as a warrant for action, and the belief in an imminent millennium which made moral reformation urgent. In his observances and his dispatches, Cromwell revealed his Calvinist belief in a ceaselessly active God, a God of battles who in his overarching cosmic strategy, as well as his attention to the smallest details, helped those who were on his side. Thus on the eve of the assault on Basing House, a 'nest of idolatrous papists', we see Cromwell on his knees most of the night, praying and reading scripture. He was strengthened by the scriptural text 'They that make idols are like unto them' (Psalm 115:8). During this period there was never any doubt in Cromwell's mind that he understood the mind and the plans of God. Trumpeting the crushing victory at Naseby, he told the Speaker, 'Sir, this is none other but the hand of God; and to Him alone belongs the glory.' The victory at Bristol three months later was 'none other than the work of God. He must be a very atheist that doth not acknowledge it.' He went on to expound one of his favourite themes: the efficacy of aggressive, combative prayer: 'faith and prayer obtained this city for you. . . . The people of God with you and all England over . . . have wrestled with God for a blessing in this very thing.'[13]

Cromwell was honest enough with himself to accept that God could chastise his followers as well as reward them. His loss of three children, frequent illness and economic misfortune were setbacks he regarded as part of the spiritual discipline by which his character was strengthened. But when, in July 1655, he received the news that his navy's expedition to capture Hispaniola, the jewel of the Spanish empire in the West Indies, had met with ignominious failure (see below, pp. 261–7), he at first could not comprehend the news, and was plunged into a depression from which he never seems to have recovered. Hispaniola taught Cromwell to think less boldly and less simply about the ways of God. In the days of his triumphs providence had been 'clear and unclouded', but towards the end of his life he came to refer to 'the dark paths through the providence and dispensations of God'.[14]

Not just the field commanders, but the officers as a whole were a religious vanguard who set their stamp on the army. The rank and file were a more mixed bag, but there were plenty of godly men among them; the chaplain William Dell recalled 'the spirit of prayer' that he had often witnessed among the rank and file. On occasion he had accidentally overheard troopers praying 'with that faith and familiarity with God that I have stood wondering at the grace'. This habit of praying aloud extemporaneously won for the New Model a reputation among London sectaries as 'the praying army'. Soldiers customarily carried pocket Bibles in their breast pockets; according to the puritan writer Ambrose Barnes, many had their faith confirmed when these Bibles shielded them from enemy bullets.[15]

Sermons often drew large crowds, with the soldiers straining to hear the preachers. On a Sunday in May 1646 William Dell and William Sedgwick preached in the morning and afternoon, while John Saltmarsh preached a day later. Each of their sermons was two hours long, yet they were well attended, many soldiers climbing trees in order to hear better. The regimental chaplains played a key part in stirring up the fervour of the rank and file. They encouraged the conviction that the events the soldiers were witnessing were holy history, part of God's own plan for their country. Appointed by the army commanders, chaplains such as Peters, Saltmarsh, Dell and Sedgwick were powerful personalities in their own right. By their eloquence they reinforced the conviction that the army was an almost passive instrument in the hands of the Almighty. Peters loved to describe to anyone who would listen 'the pieces of God's providence' he had witnessed in the army, such as the celebrated catch of fish near Dartmouth. For seven weeks before the New Model's approach no fish had been caught along the coast. 'But now there were so many mullets taken as comfortably supplied our army.' As for the royalists, 'the Lord hath scattered them like chaff before the wind; they fly when none pursues them; they are broken and divided in their counsels'. Both Peters and Dell were proud of the superior standard of conduct that characterised not only the officer corps but the lowest ranks. It was Peters's claim that whereas in most armies men emerged coarser and more brutal from the experience of war, 'here men grow more religious and spiritual thriving, than in any place of the kingdom'. Dell agreed. It was the army's faith, together with its special sense of the presence of God, that explained why small numbers of soldiers were able to put much larger numbers of royalists to flight.[16]

The chaplains were not merely expressing their own views. They were also articulating the army's interpretation of what it had done. Chaplains were appointed personally by the colonels, and while they were not simple mouthpieces for their officers, they tended to reflect their views. Well-educated men, they were always in short supply, though forty-three are known to have served between 1645 and 1651. Four of them were Presbyterian in 1645; that number shrank to zero before 1649. Their main function was to persuade the soldiers of the righteousness of fighting against their fellow Englishmen. At Naseby, for example, Peters rode from rank to rank with a Bible in one hand and a pistol in the other, exhorting the men to do their duty.[17]

When the army was not fighting, the chaplains and officers devised an elaborate programme of religious exercises to occupy it. Sunday was normally observed as a day of rest and prayer. On that day, as well as after major battles, the soldiers would 'exercise their minds' in Bible study. The sharing of religious experience could bind soldiers more tightly together. In 1647, for example, a soldier from Colonel Hewson's regiment, writing of 'the manifest presence of God' among them, exclaimed 'the sweet union we had with God doth endear us together in love'.[18]

Pictures and written slogans were also deployed to remind soldiers of the godly character of their mission. Major-General Skippon's flag read 'Pray

and fight. May Jehovah help us, and help us he will'; Colonel Ludlow's 'The
Word of God', and Colonel Sheffield's, 'With God as our guide there is no
need to despair.' Another standard depicted Ireland as a house on fire with
the flames of popish rebellion; Skippon's depicted a sword of heaven and
a Bible; Captain John Blackwell's pictured a walled city above a clutch of
flaming hearts and the motto 'Aflame with love for Sion'. In all, 72 per cent
of the surviving parliamentary standards expressed religious themes.[19]

Fasting and 'humiliation' were among the more intense techniques used
to raise consciousness for the trials ahead. The officers frequently resorted
to fasting. At Bristol it was combined with sermons and a resolution by the
Council of War 'to punish the vices in the army'. A day of humiliation was
held a few months later to discover if the Lord wanted the army to advance
on the enemy in Devon. Days of humiliation and fasting continued to be a
favoured activity of the high command long after the emotional high points
of the First Civil War were behind them. In 1649 and 1650 all the garrisons
in England were urged to join with headquarters in such exercises to prepare
for the invasions of Ireland and Scotland. When, in August 1650, the army
was racked by plague in Munster, Ireton imposed an eight-day fast spread
over three weeks to beg the Lord 'to remove the heavy judgement of pestilence in our quarters'. In late 1652, when there was growing anxiety about
the troubles with the Netherlands and the failure of the Rump Parliament
to enact the army's political programme, fasts, prayers and days of humiliation were laid on again. Indeed, the jaundiced editor of *Mercurius Militaris*
noted that all the officers' political 'mischief' was 'ever done after fasting
and prayer'.[20]

For many in the army, God was political. Thus, at the beginning of 1648,
the army secretary William Clarke, uneasy that political pressure was forcing
the army to reduce its strength drastically, was fortified by his personal faith,
as expressed in a letter to his friend Lieutenant-Colonel John Rede, governor
of Poole: 'I fear we go on to support a rotten structure which God will have
fall. He's happy that can escape crushing if once the pillars break. Lay then a
foundation of peace and comfort in the bosom of Christ, which will keep
us safe and secure in storms and calms.' Officers such as Colonels Hewson
and Whalley displayed a crude arrogance in their self-assurance that God
backed the conquest of Ireland and Scotland. The regicide Colonel John
Jones expressed a similar faith in divine providence with greater delicacy:
'This comfort remains firm, that although we are weak, dark, deformed and
peevish, we steadfastly believe, that we are completely strong, wise, beautiful

and meek in the Lord Jesus'. Most remarkable of all is the message addressed to their fellow soldiers in Wallingford Garrison by about thirty London officers and separatist clergy on the eve of the invasion of Ireland. An incandescent fervour suffuses the whole letter. Lamenting that their neglect of duty had caused 'the glory of Christ to be eclipsed', they had attempted to rectify matters by coming together 'to seek the face of God'. Acknowledging their failure in 'provoking one another to love and to good works, of pouring out our souls together before the Lord and of that care and watchfulness over each other's souls as became those who had received God', they prayed that their joint religious exercises would all make them 'burning and shining lights in our generation, to the stopping of the mouths of our enemies, the cheering of the upright in heart, and above all, the glorifying of our father which is in heaven'.[21]

Intense piety was frequently accompanied by exaggerated humility and self-abasement. Paradoxically, the more powerful the army became, the more it insisted on its weakness and humility. At Naseby, declared Cromwell, God had given the victory to 'a company of poor, ignorant men'. The storming of Bridgwater was led by Lieutenant-Colonel Hewson, a shoemaker: 'Thus God gets glory by things despised, and not by humane great ones'. Cromwell was certain 'he that prays and preaches best will fight best'. When Fairfax crossed intellectual swords with Lord Hopton in 1646, he acknowledged that divine favour did not spring from any merit on the part of the army, 'but from his own free grace and goodness towards his people'. In December 1648, when the army was poised for its most daring stroke – the king's execution – Colonel Humphrey Mackworth mused that 'God who comforteth the abject and loves to turn the wisdom of carnal men into folly hath in part freed us from our former fears'. It did not cross Mackworth's mind that at that moment the abject ones were the king and the recently expelled and imprisoned MPs, not the all-powerful army. Still, the unconscious irony of Mackworth's words gives a clue to the psychology of self-abasement. In a flattering sermon preached to the army on the eve of its departure for Ireland in 1649, John Maudit counselled the officers that 'God is doing his greatest work when he takes to him the weakest means'. He chooses 'the contemptible ones of the world that are rich in faith . . . to bring his great designs about'.[22]

Whether the army had ever been poor and contemptible, for the decade after 1649 it was the master of England. Yet it was flattering to be counselled not to trust 'the arm of flesh', not to be daunted by persecution, and to visualise oneself as the underdog. Never mind that the army commanded overwhelming superiority of resources. It gave the soldiers greater confidence to think of themselves as God's humble servants. Their morale was enhanced by the conviction that the victory was His alone, not theirs. Success in the 'arm of flesh' only reinforced the myth, as when the officers referred to their subjugation of the three kingdoms, sealed at Worcester, as 'the poor endeavours of his servants', or when, after taking Ross in October 1649, Cromwell called his comrades and himself 'a company of poor worthless creatures'.[23]

Evangelism and Lay Preaching

Besides the dimension of personal piety, Puritan zeal also possessed an outward, dynamic, proselytising thrust. This outwardness is seen most strikingly in the phenomenon of lay preaching practised by officers and common soldiers alike. Before the New Model took the field, Colonel John Pickering had already caused division in his regiment by exercising his gifts of religious oratory. Parliament reacted with an ordinance banning lay preaching and issuing strict orders to Fairfax to enforce it in the army.[24]

But the practice was irrepressible. In June 1645 Pickering's was one of the seven 'chiefest praying and preaching regiments in the army'. In the end, lay preaching unavoidably implies the principle of liberty of conscience. Thomas Edwards's *Gangraena* is replete with horrified accounts of officers and common soldiers interrupting sermons, usurping pulpits, and boldly claiming equality with the clergy. The army was unrepentant. Colonel William Goffe and Lieutenant Edmund Chillenden penned eloquent apologies for the right of the humblest soldier to act as a channel of divine revelation.[25]

The volume and range of religious activities engaged in by the New Model Army – prayer, both private and collective, fasting, reading and expounding of scripture, alternately listening to and delivering sermons – show that there was in the army a great store of spiritual and intellectual energy. It found expression in the vocabularies of both Calvinistic Puritanism and libertarianism. How did this spiritual energy impinge on the army's military and political activities?

Egalitarianism

Clearly a godly army was an army with high morale. This condition was first noted in the summer of 1645 and it continued through the bad months of early 1646, when disease, dismal weather, and shortages of money and supplies might have been expected to promote discontent and unhappiness. Soon after the army's founding, journalists remarked on the sense of unity, fellowship and love that they observed among all ranks. This harmony existed even though the army was populated with Presbyterians, Independents and sectaries, and it manifested itself in a high standard of conduct. 'Instead of drinking, gaming, plundering,' exclaimed the *Moderate Intelligencer,* 'they pray and discourse.' Reporting on the storming of Bristol, Oliver Cromwell cited the fraternal feeling among the soldiers to make a point about religious toleration. The feeling of fellowship and unity was reinforced by the spiritual egalitarianism preached by Dell, Saltmarsh and Peters. God was no respecter of persons; works were useless to salvation; grace was available to all; Christ judged by the heart rather than outward show. If all this was true, then everyone was of equal importance. During the Putney debates of October to November 1647 (see below, pp. 94–101), Henry Ireton asserted that the Holy Spirit 'is the only searcher of hearts' who can reveal to a man 'the error of his own ways and . . . the workings of his own heart'. The creation of the General Council of the Army in 1647 and the Reading and Putney debates of that year are emblematic of the conviction that even the lowliest individual has immeasurable value in the eyes of God. For several months the rank and file through their elected agitators were, formally at least, on an equal footing with the higher officers in making policy for the army.[26]

The commanders were well aware of the benefits of spiritual egalitarianism in welding men into an effective fighting unit. During the first month after the army took the field, Fairfax stipulated that every foot regiment should take turns marching at the head. This small gesture made a deep impression on the soldiers. Morale was also fortified by the willingness of officers to share the risks of battle equally with their men. Thus, Major Disbrowe led Fairfax's horse regiment up Hambleton Hill in an assault on the Clubmen. At the dangerous storm of Bridgwater, the forlorn hope of foot was led by Lieutenant-Colonel Hewson. Once they had got over the outworks and let down the drawbridge the forlorn hope of horse streamed into the town, with Captain John Reynolds at their head. Major Bethell was shot through the hand while taking his troops through the narrow pass below Langport. Similar bravery at Bristol cost him his life. Captain Thomas Ireton led the horse in attacking the line at Bristol. In the same battle Captain Waldive Lagoe of the infantry scrambled up a ladder at Prior's Hill Fort, and was the first man to lay hold on the enemy's colours. Colonel Herbert led his men in a daring assault on the heavily fortified stronghold of Berkeley Castle, narrowly escaping death when he was shot through the hat.[27] With the possible exception of Herbert, all these officers were men of piety.

Extraordinary displays of courage are an unfailing means of cementing solidarity between officers and men. Another means is shared financial hardship. Many higher officers emptied their own pockets to promote Parliament's war effort. Cromwell, for example, was reported to have made great personal sacrifices, while Fairfax renounced his pay as colonel. Other officers dug deep into their pockets to help their men when pay fell behind. This practical concern for material welfare was encouraged by the spiritual egalitarianism that the chaplains preached.[28]

'The sweetness, union and love that is amongst the saints' was most intensely experienced at the regimental and garrison level. Some units formed themselves into 'gathered churches' or voluntary associations for religious worship, like Cromwell's regiment of Ironsides early in the war. In a broad sense William Dell regarded the whole New Model in 1646 as a gathered church after its bonding experience of battle over the previous twelve months. Smaller units within the army viewed themselves through the same prism. Each troop in Colonel Whalley's regiment acted as a gathered church when they were stationed in Nottinghamshire and Derbyshire in the 1650s. By 1649 the officers at headquarters in Whitehall had also come together as a church and sought to transmit their practices to the garrisons. Their model was widely imitated. As Colonel John Jones said to a friend, 'the communion and fellowship of saints . . . is one of the most principal parts of the saints' privileges and enjoyment'.[29]

The other side of the coin of fellowship and unity was a sense of separateness from the rest of society. At Putney, Lieutenant-Colonel William Goffe admonished his fellow officers and agitators that their ways should not be 'such as the world hath walked in'. In July 1651 the English Council of Officers in Ireland wrote to their counterparts in Scotland to behave in such a way 'that our conversation may tell the world we are not of it, but are strangers and pilgrims here, travelling through it towards our own country and city, whose maker and builder is God'. The soldiers were under no illusion that their vision was shared by the majority of the English people. Internal spiritual solidarity combined with alienation from the bulk of the population also explains the army's aggressive behaviour in suppressing traditional religious observances, enforcing the reformation of manners, and protecting like-minded sectarian congregations.[30]

Courage, Discipline and Personal Conduct

The conviction that their army was bathed in the rays of providential favour, that they were fighting the 'warfare of heaven', 'overcoming evil by doing good', had a liberating effect throughout the army that led to many acts of exceptional courage and improvisation, as at Bath, Sherborne Castle, Bristol and Tiverton.[31]

The accumulation of successes bred steadily increasing self-confidence. Because they were saturated with religious thinking, victory confirmed their providentialist outlook, while providentialism contributed to victory. Providentialism was not just the smug attribution of success to divine favour. Risk-taking was also required. When in the spring of 1649 there were bitter differences over which regiments should be sent to Ireland, the conflict was resolved by drawing lots (see below, p. 176). This signified that the officers were turning the decision over to God, and each one was accepting the chance that he would be selected for a dangerous and unpalatable mission.

That the army's high morale was not due merely to its military success is suggested by the strict code of personal conduct that was imposed during at least the first year and a half of its existence. For the first three months Fairfax employed harsh measures to knock it into shape. Deserters, mutineers and plunderers were shot. Then, with the most serious threats to the army's survival regulated, Fairfax took aim at lesser sins: swearing, drunkenness and whoring. In most armies these behaviours have been – are – regarded with indulgence, but in the New Model, blasphemy (swearing) was a crime often punished. A man unfortunate enough to be convicted had his tongue pulled out of his mouth with surgeon's pincers and bored through with a hot iron. The speech impediment this left him with was a permanent reminder to him and his comrades of the gravity of taking the Lord's name in vain. Officers were occasionally cashiered for quarrelling and falsifying their musters, while drunkards were made to ride the wooden horse with papers pinned to their hats describing their crime. This punishment, and running the gauntlet, were also inflicted for other misdemeanours. Besides being painful they were meant to humiliate. They depended on the approval and support of the rank and file. Flogging, which would become the most common punishment in the eighteenth-century army and navy, seems initially to have been reserved for sexual offences. Whores were whipped and sent on their way, while soldiers found guilty of fornication and adultery received the same treatment. Rape was extremely rare: none being alleged against the New Model in England or Ireland, and only one case of attempted rape being heard in the Dundee court-martial of 1651.[32]

Because the army was well paid, fed and clothed by the standards of the day, the harsh code of discipline was accepted and even internalised. For at least two years, pro-army journalists were able to boast, without fear of contradiction, of the troops' admirable conduct. 'A general reformation is passed through the soldiery,' enthused Henry Walker, 'no oaths, no cursing, no drunkenness, no quarrelling, but love, unanimity is amongst them.' To the intellectually simple it was self-evident that God delighted in the army's good behaviour. His delight meant His blessing and His blessing meant victory in battle.[33]

Ruthlessness and Iconoclasm

Success added to a providentialist world view banished self-doubt. As victory piled upon victory, the army became imbued with a holy ruthlessness. This phenomenon is seen most vividly in the army's iconoclasm – its destruction of stained glass, religious statuary, stone altars, altar rails, rood screens, brasses, crosses, vestments, prayerbooks, organs and printed music. To many this orgy of destruction was an incomprehensible outrage, but to the soldiers it was a necessary purging of the relics of popish superstition, justified by the biblical commandment against the making of graven images. In fact they were carrying on the revolutionary iconoclasm that had already been begun by local officials before the creation of the New Model.[34]

Desecration seems to have horrified royalist commentators more than iconoclasm: soldiers stabling horses in the nave of St Paul's Cathedral and other sacred places, setting hounds to hunt cats in the aisles of Lichfield, using churches to 'ease nature', turning stone altars into chopping blocks for meat, dressing up in priests' or bishops' vestments, and brazenly smoking, drinking and swearing inside the sacred space of churches.[35]

Most soldierly attention was focused on cathedrals. The army was responsible for extensive destruction in Canterbury, Rochester, Winchester, Peterborough, Lincoln, Worcester, Chichester, Lichfield, Exeter, Salisbury and Gloucester, as well as Westminster Abbey. York Minster, on the other hand, managed to preserve the biggest collection of mediaeval stained glass in Europe thanks to Sir Thomas Fairfax's intervention.[36]

The building that suffered perhaps most from the violent hands of soldiers was St Paul's Cathedral. In December 1648 soldiers were lodged there; to keep warm they tore the carved wainscotting from the walls and lit bonfires on the floor. Throughout the Interregnum the nave was used to stable horses belonging to the cavalry. Besides these cathedrals a few parish churches also suffered military iconoclasm.[37]

The Reformation of Manners

Soldiers were also in the forefront of the campaign to correct social practices that offended Puritan sensibilities. From the establishment of the republic in 1649 they went about aggressively suppressing stage plays, Morris dancing, maypoles, alehouses and horse-racing. Some of their campaigns would qualify as enlightened by modern standards – their attacks on cock-fighting, bear- and bull-baiting, and prize fencing, for example. There are also the examples of Lieutenant-Colonel Paul Hobson, who blocked the efforts of the Scottish witch-finder in Newcastle in 1650, and the New Model soldiers who freed several accused witches in Stirling in 1652 (see below, p. 224).[38]

The army took seriously the Rump Parliament's abolition of Christmas and other 'popish' festivals such as Ascension Day. In London soldiers attempted to tear down the holly with which festive citizens had decorated the streets, and to compel shopkeepers to open on Christmas Day. On 3 May 1649 Colonel Philip Twisleton's troopers rode into Worcester, where Ascension Day was being observed. When they quarrelled with some of the citizens, the mayor intervened, 'until at last it grew hot, one of the horses were killed, and the inhabitants beat the soldiers out of town'. One holy day, however, had to be honoured – the Sabbath. Both work and play on Sunday were forbidden. Notably zealous in Sabbath enforcement was Colonel Thomas Pride, who made his will felt in Chester, Manchester, Liverpool and London. Major-General Robert Lilburne meanwhile had market day in Durham and Yorkshire switched from Monday to Tuesday so that preparation for it would not profane the Lord's Day.[39]

The Protection of the Godly

Even more important to the soldiers was the eradication of what they regarded as popish or Laudian (high church or Anglo-Catholic) practices, and their replacement by acceptably Puritan worship. The campaign to refashion the religion of England gathered momentum after the war had been won. First, disaffected clergy were silenced and the use of the Book of Common Prayer suppressed. Conservative clergymen were often the focus of military anger, for the good reason that they were the ones who rallied popular resistance to the Revolution. Another bone of contention was the days of thanksgiving decreed by Parliament after the army's victories at Dunbar and Worcester. In Exeter, thanks to 'froward [contrary] ministers', only a few people observed the day of thanksgiving in 1650. Elsewhere strong-willed officers like Major Hobson in Newcastle and Colonel Christopher Whichcote in Windsor took matters into their own hands and fired unsatisfactory ministers. Eventually the harassment of conservative clergy and congregations provoked so much resentment that in April 1653 Cromwell's committee of officers in Whitehall ordered soldiers to refrain from disturbing 'any ministers or people peaceably met together in any public places to worship God'.[40]

In all these struggles with civilians the army exhibited an acute conscious-ness of its religious calling. Godly officers were morally certain that the army 'hath been a shelter to honest people that had otherwise been hammered to dust'. Many Independent and sectarian congregations were only too aware that the army was a prop to their survival.[41]

Throughout England the army actively promoted the welfare of sectarian congregations. In Hull, Colonel Robert Overton erected a brick wall between the chancel and the nave of Trinity Church, so that the garrison and its Brownist (radical sectarian) chaplain John Canne could have half of it for their services. In Bristol Colonels John Harrison and Adrian Scrope played an influential role in the city's religious life, protecting and fostering its Quaker minority in the 1650s. In Newcastle, the governor Colonel Robert Lilburne and his deputy Captain Paul Hobson helped found the first Baptist congregations in Tyneside. In London, a radical preacher whose sermon was disturbed by Presbyterian and royalist hecklers found relief when troops of cavalry came and drove them out. In Chester, the 'honest party' (of radical sectarians) testified to the encouragement that the arrival of Colonel John Barkstead's forces had given them in their struggle with the city's clergy, all but one of whom were 'Scottified Presbyterians'. In Manchester, Major-General Harrison fought the conservative clergy by importing a radical preacher, the celebrated Morgan Llwyd, who invaded the pulpit of the leading disaffected minister and 'preached . . . the things of Christ most sweetly'.[42]

In summary, the religious energy that imbued the army affected both its fortunes on the battlefield and its relations with civilians. Religion fostered high morale, even when the army was buffeted by disease, bad weather and hardship. Spiritual equality was demonstrated in the officers' willingness to share risks with their men and in the solidarity that was frequently manifested among them. Solidarity based on a shared conviction of righteousness produced many feats of extraordinary courage, which in turn accelerated the collapse of enemy morale. Thanks to religion large numbers of ordinary soldiers internalised an exacting code of personal discipline. During its early years at least, the New Model was characterised by less drunkenness, swearing and exploitation of civilians than other armies of early modern Europe. Equally, its religiously grounded self-confidence imparted to it an additional edge of ruthlessness. From 1648, if not before, most opponents, whether king, royalists or Irish, were regarded as agents of Antichrist, against whom almost any measure was justified. The army's confidence in its own righteousness led it to interfere with civilian society – demolishing the visible evidence of 'popish superstition', enforcing the Puritan reformation of manners, and nurturing separatist congregations throughout the three nations. These were not the activities of a normal army; they are directly traceable to the New Model's peculiar religious stamp.

The Experience of Defeat

... the Lord is pleased for the present to make them the tail, who before were the head, and that they should bow down that their enemies may go over them.

Edmund Ludlow, *A Voyce from the Watch Tower: Part Five, 1660–1662*[43]

The providentialist view of history is good for morale when things are going well. When success turns to failure, however, it is a harsh doctrine. If God willed the countless illustrious victories of the army, as well as the political revolution that the army imposed on the three nations, did He also will the reversal of that revolution in 1660? Justification by success logically implies condemnation by defeat, but few members of the New Model Army could bring themselves to accept that God had condemned their life's work when Charles II came back to the throne.

Many of them were reduced to silence by the Restoration. Many found solace in a personal, quietistic faith which from that time forward ignored politics. But a few remained defiant to the end and went down with colours flying. A few, such as Edmund Ludlow, were able to persuade themselves that what had happened was only a temporary setback, a sojourn in the wilderness, after which the saints would surely arrive at the promised land.

Belief in providence is perfectly able to accommodate personal setbacks and reverses. Colonel John Jones lost seven of his eight children, as well as his wife. Thomas Harrison buried his first child just after the king's execution, and the other two over the next four years. Cromwell also lost children, and like Fairfax was a frequent prey to sickness. Disappointment and suffering of this kind were familiar to everyone in the seventeenth century, and were regarded by Puritan soldiers as part of a chastening process by which they were spiritually tempered. Fairfax was confident that he would not be burdened with more sickness than he could bear. Cromwell thought that illness taught him not to rely on the 'arm of flesh'.[44]

It was also possible for men functioning within this mental framework to deal with temporary setbacks of a military or political nature. In 1646, when the New Model was beginning to feel the heat of civilian impatience at its continued existence, there was no thought that God too might be impatient with the army. 'But this is our comfort,' confided Cromwell to his commander-in-chief, 'God . . . doth what pleaseth Him . . . whatever the designs of men, and the fury of the people be.'[45]

In 1651 Henry Ireton, now deputy of Ireland, concluded that their humiliation at Clonmel and the 'heavy stroke of the pestilence upon all our garrisons' (see below, pp. 190–1, 288, 312) was God's way of bringing the army back to dependence on Himself. News of the crushing defeat of the expedition to Hispaniola in 1655 prompted Cromwell for several days to seek the Lord's explanation. But in the crisis of 1659–60 the imminent prospect of total political defeat paralysed any constructive response by the officers, with the notable exception of General Monck. Despairingly Major-General Fleetwood concluded that 'the Lord had blasted them and spit in their faces'.[46]

A few senior officers responded heroically. Fortified by their providentialist faith, several of the regicides went unshaken to their deaths, convinced that the triumph of royalism had only temporarily postponed their millenarian expectations. At his trial Thomas Harrison articulated a complete confidence in the rightness of his cause: 'The finger of God hath been amongst us of late years . . . Be not discouraged by reason of the cloud that is now upon you; for the Son will shine and God will give a testimony unto what He hath been a-doing in a short time.' When he was on his way to his execution, a bystander jeered at Harrison, 'Where is your good old cause?'

Smiling he answered, 'Here it is', clapping his hand over his heart, 'and I am going to seal it with my blood'.[47]

At least two other officers in the army – Colonel John Jones and Lieutenant-General Edmund Ludlow – kept the faith. Ludlow did not shrink from acknowledging the full measure of the defeat of the 'Good Old Cause' (see below, pp. 258, 288, 312), but the dignity and optimism of his response bear comparison with Milton's in *Samson Agonistes*.[48]

How do we account for the stunning success of the New Model Army, coming in the wake of so many disasters endured by the parliamentary armies between 1642 and 1645? There is no denying that the army's success was in part due to its being well financed, clothed, provisioned and armed. It also enjoyed excellent leadership, while the blunders and military weakness of its adversary were also major factors. But to complete the picture we must also acknowledge the role of religion and morale. The religious ideas that powered the army may be grouped under the heading of Calvinistic Puritanism and, to a lesser extent, libertarian antinomianism. Together they enabled the soldiers to overcome their anxiety about their social origins, and their fear about challenging their anointed king. They also liberated them psychologically, transformed them into men of iron, endowed them with holy ruthlessness, and furnished them with the conviction that in turning their society upside down, and then exporting their revolution to Ireland and Scotland, they were carrying out the will of God. When in 1660 their revolution came crashing down about their ears, the less religious ones switched sides to become agents of counter-revolution. Others simply crumpled and retreated into silence. Others responded heroically and went with undiminished faith to their deaths. Still others interpreted the catastrophe as merely a temporary detour into the wilderness until God led His saints into the promised land. Such was the force of religious belief in the New Model Army.

CHAPTER FIVE

THE POLITICAL WARS, 1646–48
PART I: FROM THE KING'S SURRENDER
TO THE ASSAULT ON PARLIAMENT

The Growth of Hostility to the Army

Once the fighting was over, people began to worry more about the New Model Army's religious and political character. The strife surrounding its creation, added to its early reputation for religious radicalism, had not been forgotten even during its palmiest days. Right from the start, the New Model had been called 'the Independent Army'. This label did not endear it to Presbyterians and religious conservatives.[1]

In March 1646 an anonymous *Late Letter from Sir Thomas Fairfax's Army Now in Truro* was published with an engraving of the victorious general, below which was the figure of an axe cleaving through a crown. Any political or religious conservative into whose hands this tract fell would have had reason to be worried. Much of the blame for the army's radicalism was heaped on the head of Hugh Peters, chief chaplain to the army.[2]

In July 1646 the House of Lords, dominated by the earl of Essex's faction, responded to the City's demand and to pressure from the Scots by ordering the imposition of the Covenant throughout the army, and the enforcement of a ban on lay preaching. The Commons stonewalled.[3]

The Disbandment of Massie's Brigade

The chief political question at Westminster in the autumn of 1646 was how Parliament should set about disbanding its various armies. Nightmarish accounts from the north about the behaviour of the Scottish soldiers persuaded the majority that they must be sent packing as soon as possible.[4]

But first it was the turn of Colonel Edward Massie's Western Brigade. There had long been friction between the brigade and the New Model. The superior discipline of the New Model proved to be a telling factor in the

Commons' decision to preserve it at the expense of Massie's brigade. Ultimately, however, the survival of the New Model was due to the superior strength of the parliamentary Independents, managed by Viscount Saye and Sele and Sir Arthur Hesilrige, against the Presbyterians led by Essex and Holles. Presbyterian weakness throughout the summer and autumn of 1646 meant that provincial forces were steadily dismantled while the New Model remained intact.[5]

As with most political victories, the triumph of the Independents over the party of Essex and Holles was not a clean one. Before long London was swarming with reformadoes – disbanded troops – from Massie's brigade. With their wives they besieged Parliament, shouting insults at MPs and peers alike, and demanding their back pay. The following summer their willingness to throw their weight behind the projected Presbyterian counter-revolution of June to July 1647 would help to make that scheme a frightening reality.[6]

The Departure of the Scots

Getting the Scottish army out of England would reduce the drain on the Treasury, spare the northern counties further barbarities at the hands of their unwelcome visitors, and lessen the pressure for England to adopt the Scottish brand of church government. Before they would leave, the Scots insisted on being paid a hefty proportion of the money owing them. The only way to meet this demand was to sell off the bishops' lands, and so an ordinance to that effect was passed on 9 October 1646. By February 1647 the money had been paid to the Scots who then handed the king over to Colonel Graves and quit English soil. Soon Charles would be lodged in the royal palace at Holdenby, Northamptonshire.[7]

The Attempt to Disband the New Model

Against all expectations, the parliamentary Presbyterians, who had profound misgivings about the departure of the Scots, were to profit from it. With the Scots gone there was no longer any justification for keeping the New Model in existence. Faced with the prospect of a miserable winter brought on by the recent poor harvest, Londoners looked for any measure that would lighten their financial burden. While praising the New Model for its stellar military successes, the magistrates wrote, 'There are some officers and many common soldiers of that army who either have never taken the Covenant or are disaffected to the church government held forth by Parliament . . . The pulpits of divers godly ministers are often usurped by preaching soldiers . . . What security or settlement can be expected while they are masters of such a power?' Disbanding the army would not only curb sectarianism and save money, it would also enable Parliament to attend to 'gasping, dying Ireland'. The Lords voted the City petition their 'hearty thanks' and ordered it printed. The Commons ignored it. But within days there was a political turnabout that shifted the balance of power in the Commons. The growing number of religious outrages blamed on New Model soldiers contributed to popular disenchantment with the army, as did the high taxes necessary for its upkeep. The day after the London petition was presented to Parliament the City elections were held. They produced an almost exclusively Presbyterian, crypto-royalist Common Council.[8]

The imminent departure of the Scots, combined with the Presbyterian triumph in London, and the beginning of parliamentary lobbying by the City from late December 1646, revived the spirits of the Presbyterians in the Commons. By a large margin they persuaded the House to debate the City petition. The publication of Volume 3 of Thomas Edwards' *Gangraena* at the end of December, with its long catalogue of sacrilegious acts and heretical preaching by New Model soldiers, confirmed the worst suspicions of many. In contrast, Ioshua Sprigge's *Anglia Rediviva*, which came out the following month, full of praise for the exploits and the piety of the New Model, had little impact: hardly anyone read it.[9]

The army commanders met the growing threat to their survival head on. Immediately after the Common Council elections they moved two cavalry regiments to Surrey. The marshal-general of the horse, Richard Lawrence, published a blistering attack on the Presbyterians as representatives of Antichrist.[10]

At Westminster the army's supporters were in disarray. With the Scottish army gone, political moderates gravitated towards Holles and Stapilton and their programme of disbandment and lower taxes. Exacerbating the Independents' political demoralisation was Oliver Cromwell's dangerous illness at the beginning of February. However, there was still a major roadblock standing in the way of the Presbyterian effort to emasculate the New Model. This was the huge debt owed by Parliament to all its soldiers. It would be folly to attempt disbandment of the New Model without reimbursing it at least a major chunk of its back pay. Many Presbyterians were conscious of the problem, but reckoned they could get away with the same shabby treatment that had been meted out to Massie's brigade.[11]

Failing to recognise the New Model's indestructibility, the Commons voted on 18 February to disband all but 5,400 horse and 1,000 dragoons. The infantry would either go to Ireland or be demobbed. Nothing was said about the money owing to the soldiers. The Presbyterians counted on the support of popular opinion to face down the army, and were reassured by the knowledge that the king was being guarded by troops under the Presbyterian Colonel Richard Graves. The Presbyterian majority now threw caution to the winds. They carried a motion that no members of the Commons should hold a military commission. Cromwell, Ireton, Rainborowe, Harrison and Fleetwood would have to choose between quitting their seats or resigning their commissions.[12]

The imminent extinction of the New Model widened political fissures within the City. The Common Council and the opposition radical Independents – soon to be known as Levellers – framed rival petitions. The magistrates urged Parliament to disband the army and turn over to themselves the control of the London militia. They also complained that the soldiers were circulating 'a most dangerous and seditious petition', while the army as a body was drawing nearer the City. The radical *Humble Petition of Many Thousands,* despite its title, represented minority opinion in the City. Its thirteen points mapped out the Leveller programme for the next two years and, in a clear reference to the New Model, exhorted Parliament not to 'lay by that strength, which (under God) hath hitherto made you powerful to all good works'.[13]

Political consciousness was well advanced in the army, although its priorities were different from those of the London radicals. For the soldiers religion came first: the eradication of ungodliness and the preservation of the gospel. The liberty of the subject came second, and the privileges of Parliament third. Reluctantly (so they said) they mentioned 'this our lawful service . . . which we do tender in respect of our liberties ten thousand times more than all our arrears'. Before the end of March, several rank-and-file petitions were circulating in the army. Because some of them were overtly political, the officers gathered them all together, deleted the offending passages and boiled them down to a single document of five points: 1. a parliamentary new ordinance, 'to which the royal assent may be desired', indemnifying them from prosecution for all acts of war; 2. the auditing and payment of arrears before disbandment; 3. no conscription for service outside the kingdom of those who had joined the army voluntarily, and no cavalry to be conscripted into the infantry; 4. fair compensation for maimed soldiers and the families of the slain; 5. regular pay until disbandment. These demands would be the ground bass of all army statements for the remainder of the year. The officers were also confronted with a crisis of conscience. Parliament's decision of 8 March to require them to swear the Solemn League and Covenant split the officer corps and effectively precipitated the army's revolt.[14]

On the day the petition was published, a deputation from the Presbyterian-dominated Derby House Committee for Irish Affairs went to meet the officers at their Saffron Walden headquarters. They were startled to be told that there would be no enlistment for Ireland until they answered four questions: 1. What regiments were to be kept up in England? 2. Who was to command the army in Ireland? 3. How would the soldiers who went to Ireland be paid, fed and clothed? 4. How would the soldiers be satisfied regarding arrears of pay and indemnity? The lack of satisfactory answers deepened the crisis.[15]

The Declaration of Dislike, and Irish Recruitment

By the end of March 1647, the army was pervaded by a deep sense of paranoia, fed by the belief that only the army and a remnant of the civilian population continued to follow God's ways. Had the Presbyterians under Holles and Stapilton handled the army tactfully and attended seriously to its grievances over pay and indemnity, they could have pacified it. As it happened, they were incapable of tact, and unwilling to offer the soldiers a fair deal.

When the Derby House Committee members reported the soldiers' concerns to the Commons, the immediate response of the Presbyterian leaders was to order Fairfax to suppress the petition circulating in the army. Two days later, on 29 March, they were alarmed to hear that soldiers were still being pressured into signing it. Fairfax wrote to the Speaker of the Commons, reluctantly complying with the order to suppress the petition, and sent its organisers to Westminster to explain themselves. The Presbyterian leaders exploded with rage at the army's disobedience. Holles hurriedly scribbled the text of a motion threatening those who persisted in promoting the petition that if they continued their illegal activity they would be 'looked upon and proceeded against as enemies to the state and disturbers of the public peace'. This provocative motion passed late in the evening in a thin house.[16]

Holles's 'Declaration of Dislike', as it came to be known, was his crossing of the Rubicon. It opened a chasm of distrust between the Presbyterian party and the New Model Army that no subsequent concessions could close. A royalist commentator characterised the Presbyterian leaders as 'cocksure' and questioned their wisdom in inflaming an undefeated body of 20,000 armed men. Holles thought he could minimise the danger by segregating those willing to enlist for the Irish service from those who declined it. A campaign was now launched to divide the army by offering back pay to those who quit, and a month's pay in advance to those who volunteered for Ireland. The blunder was compounded by the announcement of the expedition's commanders: Sir William Waller as general of the foot and Edward Massie as general of the horse. When it was also announced that the horse regiments to be retained in England would be commanded by men of the same Presbyterian stripe as Waller and Massie, it dawned on the soldiers that they were soon to be deprived of their trusted commanders in both kingdoms.[17]

The systematic hostility of the Holles–Stapilton party from the end of March onwards converted the army's already sharp political consciousness into revolutionary militancy. The Declaration of Dislike instantly shot to the top of the army's grievance list. To call them enemies of the state was to attack the soldiers' honour. Indignantly they rejected the order to stop petitioning, at once protesting against the imprisonment of Major Alexander Tulidah for promoting the March *Petition of Many Thousands*. The army radicals were now in open sympathy with their counterparts in the City.[18]

So great was the resentment of the eight horse regiments stationed in East Anglia that they pressed their superior officers to draw them all to a rendezvous where they could draft a document vindicating their conduct. There was little Fairfax could do to check the accelerating radicalisation of all ranks. By the middle of April, men in Ireton's regiment in Suffolk were not stickling to call their foes tyrants, and some of them were heard quoting John Lilburne's writings as 'statute law'. At the same time, the soldiers began forging links with their civilian sympathisers. Through Gilbert Mabbott, a radical attached to the army's clerical staff at Fairfax's house in Queen Street, Westminster, they kept themselves informed of developments in the capital.[19]

Unworried by this radical ferment, the party of Holles and Stapilton pressed ahead with the Irish expedition. Disbandment of the forces remaining in England was necessary, they alleged, because these forces were riddled with royalism. In spite of the soldiers' angry denials, there was plenty of evidence of sympathy for the king within the army. Certainly the soldiers were less hostile towards the king than towards the parliamentary Presbyterians.[20] This also makes it more understandable why the higher officers were so marked in their friendliness towards Charles during the summer of 1647. The widespread public perception that they were about to restore him to power did a lot to take the wind out of the sails of the Presbyterian counter-revolution during these same months.

Whatever their feelings about the king, both soldiers and officers became progressively more disenchanted with the prospect of going to Ireland. By the end of March a mere twenty-nine officers of the rank of captain and higher had agreed to lead men across the Irish Sea. Among the rank and file there were many who would have enrolled if they could have been accompanied by their familiar commanders. Give us 'Fairfax and Cromwell and we all go', the men shouted to the parliamentary commissioners in mid-April.[21] Instead they were now offered Massie and Skippon.

On 15 April the parliamentary commissioners came to dine at Fairfax's quarters. After dinner they said how worried they were at the resistance to Irish recruitment, and pulled out a declaration for him to sign. It threatened punishment to anyone who obstructed the service. Fairfax answered evasively. Most officers sat on their hands, and recruitment only limped ahead. For example, the continuing efforts of Lieutenant-Colonel Nicholas Kempson to win over Robert Lilburne's regiment were sabotaged by one of the ensigns, Francis Nicholls. For his pains Nicholls was arrested, his pockets searched, and he was sent to London without Fairfax's knowledge. On 23 April the parliamentary commissioners reported that only 115 officers were ready to serve in Ireland and perhaps 1,000 rank and file soldiers.[22]

What held the New Model together in the face of Presbyterian efforts to dismember it was the solidarity of the rank and file. Forbidden to petition at the end of March, they turned to their commander-in-chief for protection. It did not take long for the majority of the officers to reciprocate this movement for unity, with the consequence that between April and November 1647 there was close collaboration between the leaders and the led. Growing evidence of Presbyterian preparations to intimidate them only knitted soldiers and officers more tightly together.[23]

The Purging of the London Militia and the Rise of the Agitators

For many months the City had been demanding from Parliament the return of the power to nominate the members of its militia committee. In April 1647 the party of Holles and Stapilton, now firmly in control of the House of Commons, granted the City's request. The City magistrates then drew up a slate purged of radical Independents. The new committee at once set about dismissing Independent militia officers and replacing them with men trusted by the Presbyterian regime.[24]

These signs that the groundwork was being laid for a Presbyterian counter-revolution raised the soldiers' anxiety to a new pitch. The eight cavalry regiments quartered in East Anglia drew together, elected two representatives or 'commissioners' each, and addressed an impassioned *Apologie of the Common Souldiers* to Fairfax. They now found themselves, they said, face to face with enemies more dangerous than any they had fought on the battlefield: 'Like foxes they lurk in their dens, and cannot be dealt withall, though discovered, being protected by those who are entrusted with the government of the kingdom.' The Irish expedition was nothing other than 'a design to ruin and break this army in pieces'. Though conscious of 'the bleeding condition of Ireland, crying aloud for a brotherly assistance', they refused to go there until their own grievances had been redressed, and 'the just rights and liberties of the subjects . . . maintained'.[25]

Hard on the heels of this appeal to Fairfax came a *Second Apologie*, much grimmer and more menacing. The officers were exhorted to 'stand fast in your integrity'; any who did not would be 'marked with a brand of infamy forever, as a traitor to his country and an enemy to his army'. In addition to the standard material grievances, the petitioners demanded that the army's honour be vindicated, 'and justice done upon the fomenters' of the Declaration of Dislike. They also pointed out that their reason for taking up arms had been so that 'the meanest subject should fully enjoy his right, liberty and proprieties in all things'.[26]

At this point the officers' and soldiers' thinking was nearly identical. In their own petition published around the same time the officers also declared that they had fought for 'the removal of every yoke from the people's necks'. They then took the bolder step of addressing their petition not to Fairfax, but to Parliament. Defying the recent prohibition against petitions from the army, a high-level delegation led by Colonel John Okey laid it before the Commons on 27 April. Instead of hearing their petition, the Commons chose to summon three other officers to appear before them: Colonel Robert Lilburne for turning his men against the Irish service; and Captain William Style and Major Robert Saunders for handing out copies of the inflammatory pamphlet *A New Found Stratagem*. They also threw Ensign Nicholls in prison. Pressing their current advantage against the parliamentary Independents, the Holles-led majority voted that disbanded troops should receive only six weeks' pay – a tiny fraction of the sum due to them.[27]

The Commons never discussed the officers' petition, but they were forced to address the soldiers' *Apologie* of 3 May when Skippon handed the Speaker a copy given to him by three troopers the previous day. These men were now at the Commons door. As noted above, along with the other thirteen signatories they called themselves 'commissioners' for their regiments. Before long they would be known as 'agitators' or 'adjutators' or, less frequently, 'agents'. (At the time the word 'agitator' meant simply one who had been empowered to act on behalf of others.) The sixteen 'commissioners' had evidently been chosen by their regiments when their officers summoned them to a rendezvous to hear the terms for the Irish Service. The presence of the officers hints at their approval, if not supervision, of this novel form of rank-and-file representation. The action of the eight cavalry regiments was quickly emulated throughout the army. Most regiments selected two agitators from each troop or company. According to a radical source the representatives, or agitators, were elected 'in a parliamentary way . . . by free election'.[28] In other words, they were not chosen by the officers.

In June, when the officers put themselves at the head of the army revolt, the system was formalised by balancing the soldier-agitators with an equal number of officer-agitators from each regiment. Together with the general officers at army headquarters, they formed the General Council of the Army which met between July 1647 and January 1648, when it was dissolved. Little is known about most of the soldier-agitators beyond their names. Their civilian occupations were probably no more exalted than that of William Allen, a felt maker from Southwark. Yet several of them would impress their superiors enough to win rapid promotion. Edward Sexby, perhaps the most active, and certainly one of the most radical, was rewarded with the rank of captain. Thomas Sheppard became cornet to William Cecil's troop, while William Allen rose to be adjutant-general of horse in Ireland. Consolation Fox became a lieutenant, and then captain-lieutenant to Colonel Richard Ingoldsby. Many of the officer-agitators were also promoted. Captains John Reynolds and James Berry, for example, both became colonels. If the higher officers did not actually engineer the election of agitators from the rank and file, they certainly kept a firm grip on them once they had been chosen. Cromwell's great 'favourite' Captain Reynolds became the chairman of the agitators' council. Another officer, Lieutenant Edmund Chillenden, was stationed in London where he issued a series of letters that were central to the agitators' activities in late May and early June. It was he too who directed the agitators to promote the idea of a general rendezvous, which was implemented on 5 June when the army assembled at Kentford Heath to adopt *The Solemne Engagement of the Army.*[29]

Meanwhile, the Commons, after hearing Skippon's information, called in the three troopers to question them directly. They testified that their officers had drawn the eight regiments to separate rendezvous, where they heard the letter read. Although it had been approved unanimously, the three troopers could not – or would not – say who had drafted it, but offered their opinion that few officers were involved. When the MPs tried to elicit the meaning of phrases like 'some that had tasted of sovereignty had degenerated into tyrants', they insisted that all questions be submitted in writing to the regiments, who would answer them collectively. Denzil Holles and his followers were enraged by what they called the impudence of these three men, and demanded that they be punished. But Parliament was divided. When the Presbyterians moved to have the three agitators committed, the MP for Newcastle stood up and said that 'he would have them committed indeed, but it should be to the best inn of the town, and good sack and sugar provided'. The Commons' majority refrained from punishing the agitators, and contented themselves with directing Skippon, Cromwell, Ireton and Fleetwood to repair to their regiments and quieten the distemper.[30]

The officers returned to find their regiments in a state of near-hysteria. On 26 April the four horse regiments stationed in Norfolk had met together to promote their March petition. The meeting almost turned into an insurrection, but a group of officers led by Major Huntington was able to persuade the soldiers instead to appoint one officer and one man from each troop to meet and continue discussing the matter. The soldiers were painfully aware of how they were resented by the people. Small wonder that some of the fiery spirits began to propose extreme measures. Among the papers collected by the army secretary, William Clarke, is a draft 'Heads of demands made to the parliament' which clearly reflects the influence of Leveller thinking on parliamentary and electoral matters. Calling for a reform of election abuses, it advocates annual elections, and closes with ringing assertion of the sovereignty of the people, 'princes being but the kingdom's great servants, entrusted for their weal, not for their woe'. To have gone public with these demands would have been to embrace a revolutionary strategy by claiming the right to speak for the English people and to sit in judgement over Parliament. John

Lilburne threw his weight behind such a strategy, and sometime in May began pressing the soldiers to adopt his personal struggle as their own.[31]

But, whatever the impression of some people, Lilburne's word was far from being statute law throughout the army. The agitator leadership judged that the time was not ripe to take an openly revolutionary line. Publicly they followed Secretary Rushworth's advice to 'demand nothing but what is relating to them as soldiers'. At the same time they quietly prepared to throw down the gauntlet before Parliament. They moved for the creation of a representative body to administer the army's business. From London, Lieutenant Edmund Chillenden wrote instructing his fellow agitators to approach the officers for money to buy a printing press for the army. The press was quickly purchased, and over the next several months produced a stream of army-inspired and Leveller documents. They sent envoys to forge links with non-New Model forces and 'well-affected friends' throughout the kingdom. They took steps to prevent the seizure of the king by men hostile to the army. Anticipating an attempt to remove Charles from the army's control, they put him under more vigilant surveillance.[32]

Regimental committees were set up with representation from every troop and company. The meetings were convened at Bury St Edmunds, well away from army headquarters, the foot soldiers reportedly contributing fourpence each to defray the costs. These regimental meetings were not placid affairs. Colonel John Lambert's men cried out for vengeance against Presbyterian ministers who tried to render the army 'odious to the kingdom'. Sir Hardress Waller's regiment used 'scurrilous language' against Parliament to voice its demand for liberty of conscience. The men of Fairfax's horse regiment complained 'that some who have declared themselves enemies to this present Parliament are in part become our judges'. Calling for the repeal of the Declaration of Dislike, they also demanded the punishment of its framers. Many soldiers harboured a deep sense of wrong at the public's failure to honour the risks they had undergone. The men of Colonel Nathaniel Rich's regiment alluded to 'the scarlet dye of our valiant fellow soldiers' blood'. They went on in this vein to contrast their sacrifice to 'the inveterate malice' of their present enemies, 'who gladly would have sheathed their swords in our bowels'.[33]

While publicly the soldiers declared that their honour was 'more dear to us than anything in the world besides', privately they feared for their safety. What obsessed them about the Declaration of Dislike was the thought that, if they disbanded with it still on the books, they would be vulnerable to

criminal prosecution as 'enemies to the state'. On Saturday 15 May the officers met at Saffron Walden Church to hear the regimental reports. Colonel
Lambert denounced the Presbyterian commanders who refused to let their
regiments voice any grievances. Men, he said, who had failed to endorse the
army's March petition had now cut themselves off from their fellow soldiers.
After all the reports had been aired, a committee was struck to summarise
them for presentation to Skippon and the other parliamentary commissioners. The committee had a summary ready by the next day. It sidestepped
the inflammatory expressions and esoteric demands of some regiments,
confining itself to 'what pertains to them as soldiers'.[34]

The eleven grievances that it selected for presentation to the parliamentary commissioners were limited to army matters. These included the
longstanding bread-and-butter concerns: arrears, free quarter, indemnity,
compensation for the wounded and the families of the slain, and conscription. The less tangible question of the army's reputation or honour also
loomed large. The Declaration of Dislike still stood as 'a memorandum of
infamy upon us to posterity'. But honour obsessed the soldiers less than
simple raw fear of their fate if they were disbanded while the Declaration of
Dislike was still in force, and the calumnies of their enemies unrefuted.[35]

At the meeting with the parliamentary commissioners on 16 May, fierce
conflict erupted between the majority who backed the committee's report
and those who favoured obedience to Parliament. At one point Colonels
Whalley and Sheffield nearly came to blows. The antagonism had now
become so rooted that the two sides could no longer live together within the
same army. In vain Skippon tried to mediate the heated clashes. Cromwell,
always pragmatic, admonished his fellow officers that disobedience to
Parliament could only end in confusion and disaster for the army. When he
returned to the Commons, he warned the Presbyterians that officers could
no longer control their men.[36]

Word of the army's discontent aroused alarm in London. Rumours were
rife of a Presbyterian plan to organise a loyal army in the capital to overawe
the New Model if it refused to disband. The soldiers for their part took the
precaution of strengthening the guard on the magazine at Oxford.[37]

It was still not too late to quench the flames of rebellion in the army. The
revocation of the Declaration of Dislike, an act indemnifying the soldiers
for acts committed while in arms, and a more generous settlement of arrears
would have pacified the bulk of the soldiery. At that juncture, however, the
loss of face entailed in repealing the Declaration of Dislike was too great for

the Presbyterian leadership to accept. An indemnity ordinance had already been introduced in the House, and would be passed in early June. To the soldiers it was unsatisfactory on two counts: first, there was no provision for the king to sign it and thereby guarantee the soldiers that there would be no reprisals should he be re-enthroned; second, the ordinance only indemnified soldiers for illegal acts committed during the war, whereas many offences, including indebtedness, had occurred after its end. Of all the grievances, arrears would have been the easiest to satisfy. For the purpose of disbanding the New Model, a fraction of the total they were owed would have won them over. The French ambassador commented that if the army unrest went unchecked and led to the overthrow of the English monarchy, it would be largely because 'the Presbyterians failed to act generously in the present circumstance'.[38] He had a point.

At this moment, however, the Presbyterians were in no mood to deal generously with the army. After making minor concessions to the soldiers, they left all the major grievances unaddressed. At about the same time the soldiers received a fresh jolt in the form of an intercepted letter to the king from his chief negotiator, John Ashburnham. Counselling Charles not to come to terms with the army, Ashburnham observed that, with peace on the Continent almost concluded, the king could expect the assistance of 40,000 or 50,000 men 'from beyond the seas'. If royalists were plotting to renew the war, reasoned the agitators, why was Parliament so eager to disarm? Why too was it so implacably hostile to those who sought social reform? The rejection of the third Independent petition and its burning by the common hangman drove agitators and London radicals into each other's arms. So deep was their distrust of the parliamentary Presbyterians that, when on 18 May they learned of the House's intention to vote full arrears for the rank and file, the agitators interpreted it as a move to drive a wedge between soldiers and officers.[39]

The agitators had good grounds for their suspicion, since the Presbyterians had now embarked on active counter-revolutionary measures. Orders were issued for the magazine at Oxford to be removed to the Tower of London. Massie was sent to secure the garrison at Gloucester, and Sir Robert Pye to take charge of his regiment at Holdenby. Richard Graves, the king's keeper, was summoned to London for consultation on 22 May. From his testimony the parliamentary leadership concluded that the king was in danger and should be removed from Holdenby.[40]

The fateful day for the Presbyterians was 25 May, when they forced through the Commons a motion for the immediate disbandment of the

New Model foot. At the same time, £12,000 was allotted to the London militia, now under firm Presbyterian control. The Presbyterians were confident that they had so riven the New Model with dissension that it was no longer capable of offering united resistance to disbandment. They had divided volunteers for Ireland from those who declined; officers from men, and foot from horse. Major-General Sedenham Poynts was dispatched from London to York with instructions to draw up the Northern Army in readiness to crush Fairfax's. The second earl of Dunfermline was sent to France, allegedly to persuade Charles's wife Henrietta Maria to send the prince of Wales into Scotland to unite the Presbyterian and loyalist forces there. Men who left the New Model to volunteer for the Irish expedition were quartered in strategic locations. Most of the foot soldiers were sent to Worcestershire, where they were joined with other forces to make up four regiments under Presbyterian commanders. On 6 June they were ordered to advance to Reading. The cavalry and dragoons who split off from the New Model numbered about 400 men. To make the best use of them an ordinance was passed authorising the City to raise its own cavalry. The 400 troopers were thereby incorporated into the London militia and quartered close to the City. All the troops that left the New Model and were being marshalled for the expected showdown with their former comrades-in-arms were rewarded with immediate generous payments. In early June a Committee of Safety was set up to recruit and organise forces from the counties. Colonel John Birch's regiment in Windsor Castle was brought up to strength, moved to Herefordshire and told to await further instructions. Colonel Thornton was sent to rally the forces in the Isle of Ely. In London Colonel Dalbier was put in charge of the large number of reformadoes who had signed on.[41]

On paper this strategy for vanquishing the New Model was impressive; yet by August it was in ruins, and those who framed it had fled. Why did the Presbyterian counter-revolution collapse? In the first place, the New Model presented a united front against disbandment. The number of officers who left the army or volunteered for Ireland in the spring of 1647 was 167, or 7 per cent of the total. The 800 or so rank-and-file soldiers who left the army represented little more than 4 per cent of the whole. Secondly, faced with this unity many elements in the Presbyterian coalition wavered and then caved in before superior force.

Though numerically insignificant, the departure of fifty-seven of the most senior officers had significant political consequences. Had they stayed, they could have been counted on to act as a brake against the more radical demands of the agitators – for a march on London, for example. Equally significant, the individuals who stepped into their shoes – men such as Thomas Harrison, Thomas Pride, Matthew Tomlinson, William Goffe and John Cobbett – were in general less socially distinguished and more politically militant than those they replaced.

When the parliamentary order for disbandment reached the army the Council of War defied it. The regiments were ordered to contract their quarters for a general rendezvous. Fairfax shifted headquarters from Saffron Walden to the agitators' meeting place at Bury St Edmunds. In the meantime, Rainborowe's regiment marched from Hampshire to Oxford to secure the magazine against Parliament's attempts to remove it to London, and the money sent for disbanding Ingoldsby's and Fairfax's regiments was confiscated. Because Fairfax had again fallen ill, a committee of officers was appointed to draft a document for his approval.[42]

The Seizure of the King

The most decisive of the army's moves to avoid extinction was taking Charles I into custody. By the end of May 1647 officers and agitators were sure there was a Presbyterian plot to transfer the king to Scotland. The motive they ascribed to their foes was to make Charles the leader of the coalition force being constructed for military action against the New Model. Already the agitators had been pondering counter-action to remove him from the hands of the parliamentary commissioners and the Presbyterian Colonel Richard Graves. Fairfax was politically too moderate – and too ill – to sanction so brazen a step. But Cromwell had recovered from his illness and knew the full dimensions of the menace facing the army. To his house there now trailed an assortment of army radicals and Levellers. Frugally entertained by Mrs Cromwell with small beer, bread and butter, they laid bare to the lieutenant-general their scheme for the army's salvation. On the night of 31 May, in his garden at Drury Lane, Cromwell approved the plan of Cornet George Joyce of Fairfax's horse regiment to march to Holdenby and replace the guards under Graves with troops loyal to the army.[43]

Cornet Joyce and the agitators had already recruited a detachment of 1,000 horse. Alerted to Presbyterian plans to transfer the magazine from Oxford to the Tower of London, they had ridden on the 29th to Oxford, where they secured the train of artillery with its store of powder and ammunition. On

1 June, armed with Cromwell's blessing, they proceeded to the royal manor of Holdenby to block the anticipated removal of the king by Graves and the parliamentary commissioners. Night had fallen before they reached the manor house, but the reluctance of Graves's men to resist their comrades-in-arms gave the colonel and the handful of officers who were loyal to him no choice but to quit the grounds. The parliamentary commissioners also bowed to superior force, though unlike Graves they did not flee.[44]

Joyce's mission had gone off without a hitch. But he was still very worried that Graves would soon come back with reinforcements to wrest the king from his hands. So, at 8 a.m. on 3 June, he wrote an urgent letter to London asking for further instructions. He directed 'that it should be delivered to Lieutenant-General Cromwell, or in his absence to Sir Arthur Hesilrige or Colonel Fleetwood'.[45] Who answered the letter is a mystery, but there can have been little time for Cromwell to deal with it. By the afternoon of the 3rd he was in imminent personal danger, since all London now knew what Joyce had done. That night Holles's party resolved to arrest Cromwell when he came to the House of Commons the next day. Anticipating their intention, the 'subtle fox' opted to take refuge in the New Model. Before sunrise on the 4th he had set out with Hugh Peters for army headquarters, now at Newmarket. Meanwhile, Joyce had decided that he could not wait for Cromwell's instructions. Late in the evening of the 3rd he had resolved to transport the king and his servants to a safer location. It was after ten o'clock, and Charles was in bed, but Joyce broke into his chamber to tell him that he must leave Holdenby early the next morning.

At daybreak Charles acquiesced but demanded to know by what authority Joyce acted. By 'the soldiery of the army' replied the cornet. The king demanded to know if he had anything in writing from Sir Thomas Fairfax. Joyce evaded the question but Charles would not be put off. 'I pray Mr Joyce, deal ingeniously with me, and tell me what commission you have.' 'Here is my commission,' the cornet answered. 'Where?' asked the king. 'Behind me,' pointing to the mounted soldiers. At which, Charles smiled: 'it is a fair commission and as well written as he had seen a commission in his life; and a company of handsome proper gentlemen as he had seen in a great while'.[46]

Joyce had not decided where they were going, but at length deferred to the king's suggestion that they head for Newmarket 'because the air did very well agree with him'. Was it the superior air, or that it was Fairfax's headquarters, and the army rendezvous was to be held there that prompted Charles?

Whatever the reason, Fairfax would take pains to keep the king well out of sight on that critical occasion.[47]

When they arrived at Newmarket, Fairfax put the more reliable Colonel Whalley with his regiment of horse in charge of the king. He and all the general officers then swore before the king that what Joyce had done was without their consent. Joyce and Cromwell would later exchange heated words, with Cromwell calling Joyce a rascal for insinuating that he was only carrying out Cromwell's instructions.[48]

Was Cromwell lying? Are we to believe that the agitators acted alone, without the sanction of their superior officers? No one could credit such a notion. The general officers stayed just on the right side of the truth. They gave orders to secure the king at Holdenby and prevent his seizure by hostile forces. But they did not agree to his forcible *removal* to army headquarters. That arrangement was negotiated by Joyce and the king alone.[49]

What of the larger question: who at this critical moment was in charge of the army? Fairfax in his memoirs would later claim that he was the helpless puppet of political activists between 1647 and 1649, and at the time he did write to the Commons Speaker, 'I am forced to yield to something out of order, to keep the army from worse disorder, or worse inconveniences.' But he chose not to join the other officers who quit the army. By staying on as commander-in-chief he became complicit in what the agitators had done.[50]

The Army in Revolt

There was to be plenty of conflict between agitators and grandees during the summer and autumn of 1647. Yet the arguments over whether or when to invade London, how to treat with the king, and whether to impose a constitutional settlement on England masked a basic harmony of purpose to which the conflicts were only a secondary theme. All agreed that the army must stay united, that its grievances must be redressed, and that there ought to be an honourable peace with the king.

In contrast to the unity of the army was the disunity of the Presbyterian coalition. It pursued contradictory policies of confrontation and conciliation. The inability of Holles and Stapilton to inspire confidence in their followers led men on the fringe like Philip Skippon to waiver and Whitelocke to withdraw his support. Two of the parliamentary commissioners decided to work for a reconciliation between the two sides of the conflict, warning that to levy troops in London and encourage desertion from the New Model would likely 'beget some disorder'.[51]

The City magistrates too began to waiver, for the good reason that the City militia refused to obey their Presbyterian officers. Even the mayor and sheriffs' command to turn out 'upon pain of death' could not make them budge, and boys jeered at the drummers in the streets. The timorousness of the militia is not surprising. They knew they were no match for Fairfax's battle-scarred veterans.[52]

Responding to popular rejection of the Presbyterian strategy of confrontation, the London Common Council named a committee to work for reconciliation. Once at Fairfax's headquarters these men gained insight into the army's grievances and reported back sympathetically to Common Council. This further undermined Presbyterian militancy.[53]

The hope of aid from the Northern Army under Poynts was dashed by the timely action of the agitators. They sent emissaries to persuade the northern soldiers to throw in their lot with their southern comrades. Early in July militants from his own army arrested Poynts and conveyed him to Fairfax's headquarters. Fairfax released him, but later sent Colonel John Lambert to replace him as commander in the north.[54]

Two other elements in the Presbyterian coalition – the king and the Scots – also turned into broken reeds. Charles, moved by his liberal treatment at the hands of the New Model, ordered London Cavaliers to cease cooperating with the Presbyterians. This royal about-face was instrumental in convincing the City to stop supplying money for a counter-revolutionary force. For their part, the Scots turned a deaf ear to invitations to send troops to overthrow the New Model. Next, the parliamentary majority abandoned the Presbyterian leadership by switching to a policy of appeasement. On the night of 3–4 June, sitting till 2 a.m., the Commons voted to expunge the Declaration of Dislike from their journal. The Lords followed suit a few days later. On 7 June an unqualified ordinance of indemnity for all offences committed by soldiers while in military service became law.[55]

The Solemne Engagement at Newmarket

It was too late, however, for appeasement to work. Concessions that would have quieted the army in April were now derided. The soldiers were crying for vengeance on those who had plotted their destruction, and for fundamental changes in England's constitution. Their aggressiveness was only increased by the intoxicating experience of unity during the rendezvous near Newmarket on 4–5 June. Once the dissenting officers had been 'hooted off the field', the men listened attentively to *The Humble Representation of the Dissatisfactions of the Armie*, which had been inspired – if not written – by the agitators. In addition to rehearsing all the grievances that had accumulated over the previous four months, it excoriated Parliament for failing to punish the authors of the Declaration of Dislike.[56] Relieved that the higher officers had thrown in their lot with them, the soldiers greeted Sir Thomas Fairfax with rapturous joy. He paid them the compliment of visiting each of the thirteen regiments in turn.

Cromwell arrived in Newmarket that evening and was present for the next day's meeting, which was to have momentous consequences. By the terms of the *Solemne Engagement*, officers and men entered into a covenant not to disband until their grievances were redressed. The soldiers' safety and that of the freeborn people of England would have to be guaranteed by a watertight provision of indemnity, and also by the removal from power of those who had abused the army and endangered the kingdom. A general council consisting of the general officers plus two officer- and two soldier-agitators from each regiment would judge whether these conditions had been met. This was the first experiment in military representative government; it was shrewdly arranged that the officers in the council should have a permanent majority over the rank and file.

The *Solemne Engagement* ended with a disavowal of any wish to overthrow the Presbyterian form of church government or establish 'licentiousness in religion under pretence of liberty of conscience'. But the authors did not disguise their desire to 'promote such an establishment of common and equal right and freedom to the whole, as all might equally partake of'.[57]

Who drafted the document? Almost certainly Ireton, but he must have cleared it with the agitators before presenting it to the army as a whole. By instituting a general council the officers assimilated the agitators into the army's command structure.[58] As well, the general's power to convene the council, or not convene it, as he saw fit, meant that it would remain firmly under Fairfax's control. This did not seem to bother the soldier-agitators, nor the fact that they were in a permanent minority, for they doubtless viewed the achievement of unity between officers and men as of greater importance. Later the Levellers would argue that the *Solemne Engagement* had dissolved the existing power structure of the army and vested supreme authority in the General Council. In the heady days of 1647, however, the spirit of trust within the army discouraged anyone from raising such a contentious point.

Between June and November there was close co-operation and unity of purpose between grandees and agitators. The agitators' activities were approved of and even directed by the general staff. The agitators made trips all over the country to explain and garner support for the army's defiance of Parliament – to London, Kent, Wales, Hereford, Bristol and the north. Because of the strategic value of the Northern Army as a buffer against Scottish invasion, the agitators invested much time into winning it over. They downplayed their material grievances, proclaiming instead their goal as 'The glory of God, the just preservation of the king's person, the just privileges of Parliament, the redeeming of the lives and liberties of the free people of England from tyranny, oppression and injustice, the maintenance of just laws ... together with the free and impartial distribution of justice to all'.[59] Key agitators such as Edward Sexby, William Allen, Richard Kingdome, George Joyce, Lieutenant Edmund Chillenden and Captain Edmund Rolphe received substantial sums of money. The grandees' temporary harmony of purpose with both Levellers and military radicals is further suggested by the £2 paid to Ensign Nicholls for his imprisonment, the £19 12s paid to Major Tulidah for his arrears, and the £10 paid to John Lilburne, in the vain hope of persuading him to stop making wounding comments about the grandees.[60]

The Impeachment of the Eleven Members

By July, Lilburne and Overton were complaining that the new arrangements had sapped the agitators' authority, but the documents the agitators published around that time conveyed no sense that they were being abused or cold-shouldered. They were the ones who demanded the impeachment of the eleven leading Presbyterian MPs, and they collaborated closely in drafting and presenting it to the House of Commons. The MPs were charged with having endeavoured to overthrow the rights and liberties of the subject, foment hostility against the army, divide the army against itself, raise another army to embroil the kingdom in a new war, and encourage reformadoes to intimidate the members of the House of Commons. The eleven members fled on 27 June, and both sides heaved a sigh of relief. On 6 July, six senior officers led by Colonel Scrope, and six agitators, led by Edward Sexby, submitted the charge to the House of Commons. It was a formidable thirty-page document. At its core was an indictment of the Presbyterian leadership for having plotted a counter-revolution against the army and its Independent friends. It also accused them of harassing the Leveller petitioners in London, and imprisoning two Leveller leaders – Nicholas Tew and Major Alexander Tulidah. After ducking the issue for several days the Commons commanded the accused to answer the charge. In their absence, however, and in the rush of events that summer, the impeachment was soon forgotten.[61]

The Presbyterian Counter-Revolution and the Army's Invasion of London

Meanwhile, Fairfax summoned another general rendezvous of the army on 10 June at Triploe Heath near Cambridge. The purpose of the meeting was to hear the latest parliamentary response to their demands. So impatient were the soldiers with what they heard that they jeered the parliamentary commissioners off the field. Taking their cue from the militancy of the troops, the army leaders advanced their headquarters to St Albans, just 20 miles from London. Parliament and City now both had second thoughts about their previous belligerence, yet there was a strong pull towards intransigence by the Derby House Committee and the turbulent reformadoes who daily besieged the Commons. On 6 June, Colonel Massie rode through the streets in his coach inciting the citizens to defend themselves against the madmen of the army. That night double guards were posted and the portcullises of all seven gates were slammed down. War preparations were coordinated by Parliament's Committee of Safety and the London Militia Committee. Yet the closer the army drew, the less the inhabitants had any stomach for violence.[62]

In theory, the soldiers' demands from May had already been satisfied, but the contradictory signs from the capital prompted them to continue raising the stakes. No longer concerned about their honour, they still feared for their safety and for the liberty of all Englishmen so long as Holles's party was in power.

On 14 June, without involving the agitators, Fairfax and the Council of War announced an about-face in army policy. Four days earlier they had assured the City that they intended 'no alteration of the civil government'. They now unveiled a full-dress political programme, proclaiming that they 'were not a mere mercenary army, hired to serve any arbitrary power of a state, but called forth and conjured by the several declarations of Parliament to the defence of our own and the people's just rights and liberties'.[63] In the

name of the people they called for a purge of all delinquent and corrupt
members of Parliament, a fixed term for future parliaments, an end to the
king's arbitrary power of dissolution, the right of petition and a public
accounting for the vast sums levied during the war. Tacked on at the end was
a request for 'provision for tender consciences'. The most likely author of
this Declaration or Representation was, again, Commissary-General Henry
Ireton. It was the minimal programme that would satisfy the agitators, who
had now begun to clamour for a march on London to chase away the eleven
members and return the City militia to Independent hands. Fairfax drew
the army steadily closer to London, while its public voice grew harsher. *The
Remonstrance of the Representations of the Army*, published on or before
21 June, demanded unqualified liberty of conscience, reform of the judiciary and that 'the glory of God may be exalted'. Two days later the army
rejected Parliament's order to turn over the king, retorting that this would
put him within reach of those who were plotting against the kingdom.[64]

These words and acts brought home to the moderates in Parliament and
City that the army meant business. The next five weeks were a period of
adroit conflict management on both sides. The Commons unanimously
resolved 'that they do own this army as their army; and will make provision
for their maintenance', and made several concessions. Favourably impressed,
Fairfax removed his headquarters from Uxbridge to Reading, 36 miles west
of London.[65]

On 16 July Fairfax wrote to the Commons Speaker asking that all
the land forces in England be unified under one command. The Commons
responded with alacrity, appointing Fairfax as supreme commander in
England and Ireland. This laid to rest the army's nightmare of a counter-
revolutionary force being organised against it. Fairfax was now at the height
of his authority. At this juncture, in the army's view, only London still lay in
enemy hands. What to do about the capital was the immediate reason for
the assembling of the General Council of the Army for its first meeting
on 16 July.[66]

The Reading Debates and the Heads of the Proposals

For the radicals the chief item on the agenda was their demand to march on
London. They had noticed that the farther they were away from the capital,
the slacker Parliament became in attending to their demands. At the same
time, the militant Presbyterians continued to enlist men to oppose the army.

To a man the grandees opposed an immediate march on London. It seemed like picking a quarrel just when Parliament had satisfied most of their demands. Cromwell exhorted the agitators not to 'quarrel with every dog in the street that barks at us'.[67]

But among the agitators patience was in short supply. Oliver's eloquence failed to convince them of the futility of coercion. 'That which you have by force, I look upon it as nothing,' he declared with unconscious irony. They were particularly incensed by the continued imprisonment of Lilburne, Overton, Tew and others. Cromwell shot back that they should be more concerned with the good of the kingdom than with pleasing the London Levellers. 'That's the question, what's for their good, not what pleases them,' he pontificated.[68]

The next day the higher officers introduced their draft settlement, the Heads of the Proposals. This document was 'very much a product of Ireton's own political vision, industry and management'. As he worked on it he was in daily contact with Philip Wharton, fourth Baron Wharton, one of the commissioners at headquarters. Another peer, Viscount Saye and Sele, was also closely consulted. Radical friends in London visited army headquarters, where they had considerable input into the discussions. After being discussed for a whole day in the Council of War, the Heads of the Proposals went to the Council of the Army on 17 July. Speaking for his comrades, the agitator William Allen asked for more time to assess the document, since 'we are most of us but young statesmen'. Ireton agreed that a committee of twelve officers and twelve agitators should scrutinise the Proposals and report back.[69]

The Heads of the Proposals were simultaneously the most generous and the most radical settlement that Charles was ever offered. Parliament was to control the armed forces for ten years, not twenty. Instead of appointing the chief officers of state in perpetuity, it was to do so for only ten years. In religion there was to be broad liberty of conscience. Use of the Book of Common Prayer was to be allowed. Bishops would not be abolished; they would merely lose their coercive power. The tolerant character of the church envisioned by Ireton and his colleagues was underlined by the abolition of compulsory tithes. The punishment of royalists would be much less harsh; only five would be exempted from the general Act of Oblivion for all acts done in performance of the war.[70]

Their radicalism lay in their refashioning of the English polity. Parliaments would become biennial, and the existing one was to be dissolved within a year. Seats would be redistributed according to taxation. There was a further string of social reforms, probably added by the committee of officers and agitators appointed on 17 July. The burdens of the common people were to be lightened by the abolition of the hated excise, the forest laws, trade monopolies and imprisonment for debt. The people were to enjoy the right of petition and the right not to incriminate themselves in criminal trials. All public debts, including army arrears, were to be paid off. These social reforms reflected Leveller influence – especially that of the London civilian leaders Maximilian Petty, John Wildman and William Walwyn, all of whom were at army headquarters in mid-July.[71]

Before publication the Heads of the Proposals were shown to Charles. The officers' awareness of the pervasive popular longing for the return of the king to his capital made it imperative to show him that the army could bring him back on terms more attractive than Parliament's. If it could then have escorted him back to Westminster in triumph, the popular rejoicing would have stopped the projected Presbyterian coup d'état in its tracks.

Near the end of July, a delegation led by Ireton and Rainborowe rode to the king's residence at Woburn, where they spent three hours in talks with him. Unfortunately Charles entertained them with 'sharp and bitter language'. 'You cannot be without me,' he lectured them, 'you will fall to ruin if I do not sustain you.' Rainborowe walked out of the conference. Returning to headquarters, he retailed the news of Charles's arrogant behaviour.[72]

Charles's arrogance and the upheavals in London delayed publication of the Heads of the Proposals. On 31 July the members of both houses who had fled the disorders in the capital (see next section) met senior officers at Syon House, the earl of Northumberland's Middlesex residence. There the Heads of the Proposals received a final going-over. The following day, the Council of War adopted them, and on 2 August they were printed as the army's own programme for the settlement of the kingdom.[73]

The Assault on Parliament, 26 July 1647

Meanwhile, disillusioned by the king's high-handedness, the senior officers digested the unpalatable truth that they would have to march on the capital unfortified by the most highly prized piece in the political chess game now being played out. London had already erupted in counter-revolutionary violence. This had been brought about by the convergence of several factors: first, popular frustration at the failure of Parliament to reach a settlement with the king that preserved his honour and rights; second, high Presbyterian despair over the army's apparently imminent success at coming to terms with him; third, civic indignation at the loss of control over the London militia.

Although Fairfax had been made commander-in-chief of all Parliament's land forces, for the moment he was not able to bring the City forces under his control. For nearly three months they had been in the hands of men loyal to Holles. In their overweening pride, the new London Militia Committee had also purged the Southwark and Tower Hamlets militias, and continued to prepare for a confrontation with the New Model.[74]

Yet on 22 July, the need for a march on the capital seemingly evaporated when the Commons voted to return the London militia to the Independents who had previously controlled it. That evening between 2,000 and 3,000 reformadoes met in St James's Field, resolving to throw their weight behind the campaign for the restoration of the king. The news that the Commons had voted to restore the old Militia Committee threw these men into a frenzy, as the truth sank in that their vision of a settlement with the king and the disbandment of the New Model had been shattered. In rage and frustration they invaded the meeting of the new Militia Committee in Guildhall and dispersed them, threatening to 'hang their guts about their ears' if they caught them meeting again.[75]

As soon as Parliament resumed sitting on Monday the 26th, both houses were besieged by an angry crowd of apprentices demanding the return of the militia to Presbyterian hands. First they invaded the Lords' chamber, crying for Manchester's blood. He had already fled, so they forced the remaining peers to recall their former resolution on the militia. The peers then hurriedly adjourned, being hailed with a loud cry of 'A king, a king, no government without a king!' as they fled their chamber. Next the crowd turned their attention to the lower house. The Commons held out for five hours, until finally being overrun. Keeping their hats on as a mark of contempt, the apprentices ordered the MPs to pass the same motion as the Lords, with shouts of 'Vote, vote'. No one was allowed to leave until all had resolved that the king should immediately be brought to London.[76]

Was this 'rape of Parliament' on 26 July a spontaneous eruption by the 'rude multitude', a 'sudden tumultury thing of idle people without design' as Holles later claimed? Hardly; there is plenty of evidence that the City magistrates and Presbyterian clergy were heavily involved. It is also known that when the crowd was swirling around Parliament five of the eleven impeached members were sitting only a stone's throw away in the Bell Tavern in King Street. There was no doubt in Bustrode Whitelocke's mind that Holles and his cronies were in the saddle once more, directing resistance to the New Model.[77]

Yet in reality the counter-revolution had already collapsed, and the impeached MPs should have known it. The Scots failed to make good on their promises; the Northern Army rallied behind the agitators and kicked out Colonel-General Poynts; the London militia proved a broken reed; and moderates in Parliament and the City quailed at the prospect of a head-on collision with their undefeated army. That is why Holles and the other ten would shortly flee the country. The reactionary violence of 26 July was a last desperate throw of the dice by men who should have known better.

CHAPTER SIX

THE POLITICAL WARS, 1646–48
PART II: FROM THE OCCUPATION OF
LONDON TO THE SECOND CIVIL WAR

The crowd's assault on Parliament vindicated the agitators' repeated call for a march on London. Overnight, revolutionary theory was converted into practice. The army's hand was strengthened by the co-operation of its parliamentary allies. Sir Arthur Hesilrige and Oliver St John rounded up sympathetic MPs and convinced them to take refuge with the New Model. In the end the Speakers of both houses, as well as fifty-seven MPs and eight peers, made the pilgrimage to Fairfax's headquarters. Meanwhile the remaining MPs reassembled on 30 July and at once tried to re-launch the Presbyterian counter-revolution.[1]

Presbyterian bravado soon wilted, however, in the face of the army's firmness. Fairfax announced that the army would shortly march on the capital in order to restore Parliament's freedom.[2] In the final analysis the army did not need to worry about its failure to win over the king. It still had the bigger battalions, and its confidence swelled as messages of support streamed in from across southern England. Southwark and the Tower Hamlets made it clear that they wished to have no part in the counter-revolution.[3]

Within a few days, Presbyterian euphoria at having bent Parliament to its will had evaporated, and the City was gripped with a terrible fear. By the end of the evening of 2 August a nervous crowd at Guildhall prevailed upon the Common Council to write a letter of submission to Fairfax.[4]

The next morning, the army staged a show of strength on Hounslow Heath, 10 miles west of the City. Besides some 15,000 New Model troops, about 100 MPs and fourteen peers were present. Accompanied by Fairfax the parliamentarians reviewed the assembled ranks. As they rode past each regiment, the soldiers flung their hats into the air, shouting 'Lords and Commons and a free parliament'. Recognising that the game was up, Massie, Poynts and other leading Presbyterians quit the City.[5]

The occupation of London was bloodless, helped by the cooperation of the Southwark trained bands (militia). As soon as the metropolis was secure, Fairfax escorted the two Speakers and the members of both houses back to Westminster. The soldiers decked their hats with laurel leaves, while church bells pealed and the triumphal procession wound its way through the streets.[6]

The final scene in the drama was played out on Saturday 7 August, when the army gathered for a walk through the City. Accompanied by flying colours with trumpets and drums, they tramped through every street from eleven in the morning until eight at night. All observers agreed on their exemplary conduct; they stole not 'so much as an apple' during their whole occupation. What was less widely commented on was the enthusiasm with which many citizens greeted the troops.[7]

The army had won its war with both City and Parliament. For a time there were a few agreeable perks of power. Parliament voted Fairfax constable of the Tower of London, and he in turn appointed the politically reliable Colonel Robert Tichborne and Lieutenant-Colonel William Shambrooke as lieutenant and lieutenant-colonel of the Tower.[8]

Meanwhile the fiery spirits in the army were crying for vengeance against its political enemies. What incensed them was the eleven impeached members, most still sitting in the House, and manipulating Commons business against the agenda of the army. This went on for a full two weeks after the occupation of London. The peers by contrast lost no time passing an ordinance voiding all of Parliament's legislation since the assault of 26 July. They also returned control of the London Militia Committee to the Independents, and voted a month's pay to all non-commissioned officers and private soldiers. Astonishingly, the Commons five times defeated the Lords' ordinance.[9]

By now the agitators were boiling with indignation and insisting that the army expel all MPs who had continued to sit after 26 July. The grandees trembled at the thought of laying violent hands on Parliament, instead asking the Commons itself to punish those who had continued to sit. After the motion nullifying the votes of 26 July to 6 August was defeated for the fifth time, Major John Disbrowe drew up 1,000 cavalry in Hyde Park, scarcely a mile from Parliament. The New Model guards were doubled around both houses and the soldiers openly threatened to pull out by their heads all members who had sat and voted in the Speaker's absence. Several of the New Model officer-MPs also made 'high and menacing speeches' in the House. This calculated show of force had the desired effect. The Commons finally voided the votes between 26 July and 6 August. The last of the eleven impeached MPs took the hint and left. The grandees next tried to procure the release of Lilburne and Overton, but ran into a brick wall – the members of the Saye–Wharton group had little sympathy for the men who had insulted them so often in print. So they remained in custody, though Lilburne was allowed to leave his prison cell pretty much when he pleased.[10]

Having brought the Commons to heel, the army now turned its attention to the City of London. The royalist mayor John Gayre and three high-ranking aldermen were charged with high treason and thrown in the Tower. An assortment of lesser officers, citizens, ministers and apprentices were put on trial for the same offence. The army also imposed its own nominee for lord mayor, John Warner. The Tower guards meanwhile were replaced by Colonel Pride's infantry regiment, and the purged Independents returned to their places on the London Militia Committee. Most dramatic of all was the destruction of the lines of communication. This 11-mile ring of forts and earthworks, erected by the citizens in 1643 as a tremendous work of collective self-defence, was a visual metaphor of civic self-sufficiency. Londoners were understandably loath to undo their own labour, but with the army's help the demolition was carried out before the end of September. The only issue over which the City's truculence could not be conquered was taxation. It owed more on the monthly assessment than any county, and continued paying nothing until the end of 1648. This refusal to cough up for the army was short-sighted, since it only strengthened the hand of radicals within the ranks.[11]

The New Agitators

Once they had achieved most of their objectives, the grandees withdrew from the metropolis and established their headquarters 5 miles upstream on the Thames at Putney. The agitators planted theirs at nearby Hammersmith. The radical Independents, later known as Levellers, had shown a lively interest in the army as early as March 1647. In early July the agitators reciprocated that interest by protesting against the burning of the Leveller petitions by the common hangman. From August to November the army was the object of an intense lobbying effort mounted by the Leveller leaders, facilitated by the swelling of the army's numbers in August by radicals from the metropolis, who enlisted for the purpose of advancing the army's political agenda. The radicals also waged a campaign in the Committee of General Officers for the promotion of like-minded soldiers to officer rank.[12]

Fairfax was impervious to radical lobbying and ignored the pressure. There was more political conflict around Thomas Rainborowe's quest to become vice-admiral of the navy. Cromwell and the grandees tried to prevent the appointment, but Rainborowe triumphed after a violent quarrel.[13]

The chronic irregularity of pay made the army fertile ground for radical ideas. John Lilburne advised the rank and file to trust the grandees 'no further than you can throw an ox'. He also castigated William Allen, one of the agitators of Cromwell's regiment, calling him Oliver's lackey. Cromwell himself braved Lilburne's choleric temper to pay him a personal visit in the Tower. He offered him release from the Tower and a commission in the army if he would cease his attacks on the grandees, but Lilburne turned him down, thereby condemning himself to indefinite imprisonment.[14]

By the end of September, mounting dissatisfaction in five horse regiments led to the emergence of new agitators, or 'agents'. Lilburne's exhortations had borne fruit, and he continued to exercise influence over these men as they met frequently with the London Levellers during the autumn. By the beginning of November the new agents claimed the support of nine horse and seven foot regiments. Their over-arching political objectives were the defeat of Cromwell and his faction, and the dissolution of Parliament. Rather than staying with their regiments, the new agents assembled in London, so that they could keep in constant touch with the civilian Levellers. In their headier moments they dreamt of organising a national convention or parliament of agitators, both military and civilian.[15]

What mandate did the new agents have from the regiments they claimed to represent? They were never recognised by the General Council of the Army, nor did they displace the existing agitators. However, in some regiments at least the agents had a mandate from the rank and file.[16]

The grandees treated the political demands of the new agents with the utmost seriousness. Since early September they had been acutely aware of the army's haemorrhaging popularity among the civilian population, the soldiers' anger over the lack of pay, and their own vulnerability after their dream of a settlement with the king had been dashed. Believing that their main hope of preserving the army's peace lay in keeping a steady stream of money flowing into the soldiers' pockets, they busied themselves with the pay question.[17] All the while, however, the army's malaise worsened.

The new agents announced that the only way for the army to cure this malaise was to embrace a thoroughgoing programme of social justice. Proclaiming that 'the great mansion house of this commonwealth . . . [is] on fire', they told Fairfax that in publishing their *Case of the Armie Truly Stated* they were obeying the dictates of divinity, nature and reason.[18]

Though politely addressed to Sir Thomas Fairfax, this tract was a thoroughgoing indictment of the grandees for their failure to honour and implement the sacred obligations undertaken in the *Solemne Engagement* and *Representation* of 5 and 14 June respectively. Owing to their idleness, the army had been rendered odious to the people, while the wants of the rank and file, maimed soldiers and widows of the slain had been neglected. This failure was traceable to the grandees' reluctance to discipline a defiant and corrupt Parliament. Worse, by accepting schemes for disbanding the artillery, dispersing regiments throughout England, and sending regiments to Ireland before grievances had been redressed, they had broken the June engagements. After the electrifying June and July days they had systematically shut the agitators out of any real consultation about army affairs. They had also betrayed the people's interest by failing to insist on the abolition of monopolies, tithes and excise. The agents did not, however, advocate the abolition of the heaviest tax of all, the monthly assessment, prime source of the army's pay.[19]

The principled and uncompromising tone of *The Case of the Armie Truly Stated* masked the two principal difficulties faced by the agents and their Leveller friends. First they had laid themselves open to the charge of sowing further dissension within the army. Anticipating this charge, they protested that they were only performing their duty to God, and that their goal was nothing less than the wellbeing of country, Parliament and army. The second difficulty was that the interests of the two groups for whom they claimed to speak – the common people and the army – were fundamentally incompatible. The people craved relief from taxation and free quarter, but relief could only come if the army were disbanded. The army could not live without the proceeds of the monthly assessment, and was understandably alarmed at the prospect of disbandment. The authors of the *Case of the Armie* pretended that army pay could be financed out of the large sums previously paid to court parasites and out of the 'millions of money' frozen in the 'dead stocks' of some of the City guilds. The notion of paying the army £45,000 a month out of sinecurists' salaries and the hidden capital of City companies was akin to the belief that the modern welfare state can be financed simply by soaking the rich. The irreconcilability of the people's interests and those of the army was a dilemma that would plague the Levellers for the next two years, and ultimately spell their doom.[20]

The new agents presented the *Case of the Armie* to Fairfax on 18 October, and three days later it was considered by the General Council at its regular weekly meeting. It seems that Cromwell himself was behind the decision to invite the agents to attend. Indeed, the agent Robert Everard testified that he 'was marvellously taken up with the plainness of the carriage' and 'the lieutenant-general's desire for an understanding with us'. The senior officers showed further respect for the new agents by appointing a broadly representative committee of field officers and agitators – both commissioned officers and men – to meet at Ireton's quarters and consider the document. At the same time an order was issued expelling all cavalry troopers who had enlisted since the army's march through London on 6–7 August. The stated reason was infiltration by subversive elements.[21]

The Putney Debates

At the General Council meeting held at Putney on 28 October, the new agents and their civilian supporters were invited guests, but several days were given over to debating a new, more radical document, the *Agreement of the People*. Embodying the truly novel and revolutionary concepts of the sovereignty of the people over Parliament, and a written constitution enacted by the signatures of all the freeborn men of England, it also delineated a set of key powers that were to be reserved to the people alone and that no government could exercise. Without monarch or House of Lords, it envisioned a single-chamber representative model of a free state – in short a republic. Although its authorship was anonymous, the *Agreement* was at one level simply the New Model's 'fulfilling of our Declaration of June the 14', as its authors affirmed in their postscript. Printed on the army's own press, it was essentially an army, not a Leveller document. There was obvious Leveller input – from William Walwyn, John Wildman, Maximilian Petty and Henry Marten. But in the end it came from a 'thoroughly politicised army that was capable of thinking for itself'. In a later speech to the House of Commons, Cromwell would regret that he had permitted the Levellers to 'infect' the army with their ideas, but at the time he did not blame them for the content of the *Agreement*.[22]

When the General Council assembled there was a sense of dismay among the officers over the evaporation of army unity since September, over the loss of Independent dominance in the House of Commons, and over the king's palpable loss of interest in coming to an agreement with either Parliament or army.[23]

The session opened with Cromwell in the chair, since Fairfax was nursing another of his many illnesses. Edward Sexby, speaking for himself and for his fellow agitator/agent Nicholas Lockyer, presented the delegates from the radical caucus. They comprised two soldier-agitators, one from Cromwell's, the other from Whalley's regiment, plus two civilian Levellers, John Wildman and Maximilian Petty. The soldier from Cromwell's regiment, referred to in William Clarke's notes as 'buffcoat', was Robert Everard. The one from Whalley's, whom Clarke called 'Bedfordshire man', was one of the four new agents from that regiment.[24]

Sexby came straight to the point. The army was unhappy because 'we have laboured to please a king . . . and we have gone on to support an house which will prove rotten studs, I mean the parliament which consists of a company of rotten members'. After skirmishing with Cromwell and Ireton, Sexby yielded the floor to Captain Robert Everard who laid the *Agreement of the People* before the council, where it was read out for the first time. Besides the revolutionary concepts noted above, the *Agreement* called for the present Parliament to be dissolved before September 1648, with subsequent parliaments to be elected biennially. The new House of Commons would exercise unfettered sovereignty except that it would have no authority in religion and no power to conscript for the army. Nor would it be permitted to violate the principle of equality before the law.

Despite enjoying general support within the army, the *Agreement* ran into two major obstacles in the persons of Cromwell and Ireton. The reading finished, Cromwell at once jumped in and raised the spectre of anarchy. What was to prevent another group of individuals from concocting an equally radical scheme with a different thrust? 'Would it not be utter confusion? Would it not make England like the Switzerland country, one canton of the Swiss against another, and one county against another?'[25] Cromwell then made his most telling criticism of the *Agreement*. Its root principle was the sovereignty of the people, but what if the people of England refused to accept it? For Cromwell unity was of paramount importance, but in the *Agreement* he saw only a recipe for division and conflict. There was another difficulty: to what extent was this *Agreement* consistent with the engagements that the army had already undertaken? Wildman shot back that no engagement could be binding if it was found to be unjust.

Ireton angrily retorted that if men can break their engagements whenever they consider them unjust, then 'this is a principle that will take away all commonwealth'. Unlike some civilians, he added pointedly, soldiers were required to take their engagements seriously.

At this point Colonel Thomas Rainborowe joined the fray on the side of Wildman and Everard. A truculent character, Rainborowe was untroubled by the radicalism of the *Agreement of the People*. So what if it was 'a huge alteration' to the existing constitution? 'If writings be true there hath been many scufflings between the honest men of England and those that have tyrannised over them.' All of England's good laws had originated as innovations and infringements on the power of kings and lords.[26]

Striving for conciliation, Cromwell conceded that there was a moral duty to break unrighteous engagements, and then moved for a committee to review the army's engagements. The council approved the appointment of an eighteen-member committee to do just that. Lieutenant-Colonel William Goffe, perhaps the most pious of all the officers, proposed collectively seeking God, echoing Hugh Peters's words that 'God hath not been with us as formerly'.[27] Ireton, almost equally pious, seconded Goffe's motion, and it was agreed to set aside the following morning for prayer. Cromwell then assured Everard that he and the other grandees were not 'wedded and glued to forms of government'. In fact he accepted 'that the foundation and supremacy is in the people, radically in them, and to be set down by them in their representations'.[28]

Many officers and agitators got up early the next morning for the prayer meeting. Rainborowe was notably absent, visiting Lilburne in the Tower of London. Meanwhile, Goffe led the meeting, presenting several scriptural texts which had convinced him that the army was to be God's instrument in overthrowing the 'mystery of iniquity' represented by the 'kings of the earth' who had surrendered their power to the 'Beast' (the pope). Though masked in biblical language, Goffe's rejection of Cromwell's and Ireton's efforts to come to an accommodation with the king was evident. Yet he would have pleased Cromwell by his insistence on the paramount need to avoid disunity. He also distanced himself from the Levellers by advocacy of waiting upon God before embarking upon revolutionary action.[29]

The prayer meeting produced a sense of elated harmony and fellow feeling. The arrival of Rainborowe and the agents who had not shared the experience rudely shattered that mood. Despite the fact that the Committee of Eighteen had had no chance to examine the *Agreement* in the context of

the army's engagements, Rainborowe and his supporters pressed for immediate consideration of the document. Ireton yielded to the radicals' demand
but urged his hearers to be guided by wisdom from above.[30]

After the *Agreement* was read out, Ireton pounced on the first article:
electoral redistribution 'according to the number of inhabitants'. Did this
not imply universal manhood suffrage? Rainborowe, confident of his audience, took up Ireton's challenge in words that still ring in our ears after
nearly four centuries: 'Really, I think that the poorest he that is in England
hath a life to live as the greatest he; and therefore truly, Sir, I think it's clear
that every man that is to live under a government ought first by his own
consent to put himself under that government'.

Ireton countered with a doctrine of political rights for the propertied
alone, meaning landowners and merchants: 'No person hath a right . . . in
choosing those that shall determine what laws we shall be ruled by here . . .
that hath not a permanent fixed interest in this kingdom'. This was a narrow
definition of the franchise which did not correspond with electoral reality in
England at the time. All adult males often voted in county elections, while
many boroughs practised a householder franchise.[31]

Seemingly unaware that almost the whole room was against him, Ireton
stubbornly stuck to his position. Raising the spectre of communism, he
warned that votes for the unpropertied would inevitably lead to the abolition of private property. Rainborowe scornfully rejected Ireton's reasoning.
Cromwell, seeing the cherished unity of the army quickly draining away,
pleaded with the two men not to be 'so hot one with another'. The debate
dragged on until finally John Wildman exploded with anger. Contemptuous
of Ireton's reverence for history, precedent and law, he demanded to know
what principle they had fought for if not that 'all government is in the free
consent of the people'. Colonel Rainborowe's brother William pithily
observed that human rights were more important than property rights: 'my
person . . . is more dear than my estate'. Sexby, the only accredited agitator to
speak that day, passionately defended the interests of the private soldiers
who had borne the heat and burden of the day: 'it seems now except a man
hath a fixed estate in this kingdom, he hath no right in this kingdom. I
wonder we were so much deceived.'[32]

Ireton brought Sexby and the others back down to earth by pointing out
that they had not fought the Civil War for manhood suffrage, but to put an
end to royal absolutism. Cromwell, while chiding Sexby for a speech 'that
did savour so much of will', searched for middle ground by proposing that

copyholders of inheritance – the bulk of small landholders in England – ought
to have the vote. This failed to satisfy the radicals, so Cromwell moved for
another committee to try to get round the impasse. Ireton now back-pedalled,
offering to yield on the franchise, provided that a committee should first
weigh his argument in favour of limiting the vote to men 'not given up to the
wills of others'. Colonel Rainborowe apologised for his heated words, but
did not back down on his demand for an immediate vote on the *Agreement*'s
first article. Maximilian Petty, the civilian Leveller, endorsed officer-agitator
Captain Edmund Rolphe's suggestion, that apprentices, servants and those
taking alms should be excluded 'because they depend on the will of other
men'. This was the position of the new agents and those on the conservative
wing of the Leveller movement, such as Petty and Walwyn. The movement's
more prominent spokesmen – Wildman, Sexby, Rainborowe and Lilburne –
did not, at least initially, favour confining the franchise to property-owners,
professional men, merchants and independent tradesmen.[33]

The debate now turned to the issue of monarchy's place in the new constitution. Wildman declared that the only way to make the soldiers safe from
the king's vengeance once he got back into power was to enshrine their protection (indemnity) in an Agreement of the People that no king could repudiate
and no parliament repeal. Ireton answered that to imagine the soldiers would
be more secure if they threw their weight behind the Agreement was a pipe-
dream. Unless the whole kingdom 'to a man' subscribed to it they would still
be vulnerable. If the army tried to impose the Agreement upon the kingdom
by force there would be no peace but only 'the perpetuating of combustions'.

Secretary Clarke's record of the debate breaks off at this point, but two
other sources tell us that, before adjourning, the meeting agreed to extend
the vote to 'all soldiers and others if they be not servants or beggars'. There
were only three votes against this motion.[34]

The committee of eighteen officers and agitators appointed to review the
Agreement of the People got to work the next day. Its recommendations illus-
trated the substantial common ground between the authors of the Heads of
the Proposals and the *Agreement*. It recommended that future parliaments
should be elected biennially. The survival of monarchy and House of Lords
was tacitly assumed, though with drastically reduced powers. Constituencies
were to be redistributed, though whether according to taxation or population was left to Parliament to decide. The qualifications for voting were also
left up to Parliament, provided that all who had fought for Parliament before
the battle of Naseby, or contributed voluntarily to the war effort, should be

included, while all who had opposed Parliament should be excluded. The report was conspicuously silent about the revolutionary concept of an unalterable constitution authorised by the signatures of the people. None the less, the almost equally revolutionary concept of powers reserved from Parliament – religion, conscription, and indemnity for things said or done in the late war – was embraced. The power of the Commons in relation to the other two branches of Parliament was enormously enhanced. Tithes were to be replaced by a land tax or a permanent endowment for the clergy.[35]

There was another meeting of the full General Council on Monday 1 November. Fairfax was still unwell, and so Cromwell presided again. He led off with an invitation to those present to testify what answers God had given them in their prayers the day before. Several officers reported that they and other godly people had been told that they should take away the king's and lords' legislative veto. Cromwell was sceptical. He could not understand their obsession with the royal veto; besides, should the army not confine itself to military matters? In addition, he could discern 'no visible presence of the people, either by subscriptions or number' in favour of the *Agreement*. As far as he was concerned, forms of government were 'dross and dung in comparison of Christ'.[36]

In spite of Cromwell's misgivings, it was becoming increasingly evident that articulate opinion in the army was now implacably hostile to the king. Sexby, echoing the Old Testament prophet Jeremiah, thundered, 'we have gone about to wash a blackamoor, to wash him white, which he will not'. The grandees' attempts to please the king had relegated the army commanders to 'a wilderness condition'. Captain George Bishop, a future Quaker, was about a year ahead of his time when he asserted that if the kingdom were now in a dying condition it was because of their efforts to preserve 'that man of blood' whom God had 'manifestly declared against'.[37]

At the end of that meeting, the General Council agreed to a number of items that were to be framed into a 'Declaration to be Presented to Parliament'. The present Parliament was to be dissolved by 30 September 1648. Future parliaments would meet for six months every two years. Elections would be 'free to freemen', meaning those who were not dependent on the will of others. Of the three branches of Parliament, the Commons were to be supreme. There was to be electoral redistribution. The people were to enjoy liberty of conscience, conscription was to be abolished, and indemnity for acts committed during the Civil War was to be absolute, 'save only what shall be adjudged by the present House of Commons'.[38] Except for the crucial provision that the whole package be submitted to Parliament, the Levellers had virtually won the General Council to their way of thinking. Cromwell and Ireton must have been deeply unhappy at the way the debate had gone.

Meanwhile, the Levellers and the new agents campaigned remorselessly against the grandees. In a demagogic indictment, one Leveller demanded their punishment for 'private tampering' with the king, and Charles's impeachment 'as a man of blood'. He urged the agitators to be militant, and not to shrink from overthrowing their present commanders, for 'ye have men amongst you as fit to govern, as others to be removed, and *with a word, ye can create new officers*'. A few days later John Lilburne told his royalist fellow-prisoner in the Tower, Lewis Dyve, that the new agents were planning to purge Parliament and arrest Cromwell and his faction of officers in the army. The fact that Lilburne, though a prisoner in the Tower, was often seen walking the streets of London cannot have been reassuring to the grandees.[39]

By 3 November the printed version of the *Agreement of the People* was on the bookstalls in London, carrying the boast of 'the general approbation of the army'. The grandees now decided enough was enough. Faced with the reality that the Levellers had captured the General Council and were summoning the soldiers to revolution, Cromwell and Ireton, doubtless with Fairfax's support, resolved to meet the menace head on. They moved to cut off further debate in the council and send the agitators back to their regiments. Their hand was strengthened by the unease in many regiments at the visible collapse of unity in the army. Hewson's regiment bluntly condemned the forces of division, which everyone understood to mean the new agents and their Leveller backers. In the same week an unspecified number of regiments apparently petitioned Fairfax to discharge the agitators. At the 8 November meeting of the General Council, Cromwell went on the offensive and moved to send the representative officers and agitators back to their regiments. We may be sure that Fairfax, who was in the chair that day, threw his full weight behind Cromwell's motion, which passed without a recorded vote.

It is remarkable that Cromwell was apparently unopposed. The prestige of Fairfax's support, together with his promise of a rendezvous of the army, probably won the day for him. The council members must also have been favourably inclined by the knowledge that Fairfax was vigorously prosecuting their material demands with Parliament. Before adjourning, the General Council nominated a committee to draft the text of a *Remonstrance* to be offered to the regiments for their approval. The committee included only two agitators, Allen and Lockyer, as well as two radical officers, Major William Rainborowe and Commissary Cowling. The others were all hard-nosed conservatives such as Cromwell, Ireton, Hewson and Commissary-General Dr William Stane, or moderates such as Tichborne, Captain Richard Deane and Lieutenant-Colonel William Cowell.[40]

Leveller Subversion and the Mutiny at Ware

The General Council met for the last time before the army's rendezvous on 9 November. There it was announced that the rendezvous would be held on different days in three different places. This displeased the Levellers, who had hoped to orchestrate a mass demonstration in favour of the *Agreement of the People*. But the regiments were widely dispersed, and it would have been impractical to summon them all to the same place.

The council's final piece of business before it adjourned was the appointment of another committee, to make a summary of what the army stood committed to in the *Solemne Engagement* and its other declarations concerning the good of the kingdom, the people's liberties and the interests of the army. This done, they were then to consider how these commitments could be harmonised with the *Case of the Armie* and the *Agreement of the People*. They were then to assist Fairfax in drafting an engagement to present to the regiments at the three rendezvous. Though also lacking soldier-agitators, this committee included such radicals as the two Rainborowe brothers – Thomas and William – and John Wildman, the first and only time that a non-soldier was appointed to an army council committee. Colonel Thomas Harrison, who had missed the Putney debates, used the present opportunity to testify that it lay upon his spirit 'that the king was a man of blood' who ought to be prosecuted for his crimes. This statement by a high-ranking officer pointed to a budding conviction in some sectors of the army that Charles had forfeited his right to live. Twenty-one radical officers had just written to Parliament denouncing 'accommodation with perfidious enemies' and identifying the king as 'your capital enemy'.

Charles could be forgiven for fearing that his life was in peril. On the evening of 11 November he fled Hampton Court, arriving on the 14th at Carisbrooke Castle on the Isle of Wight, where he threw himself on the mercy of Colonel Robert Hammond.[41]

Meanwhile, in the army and in London the political temperature climbed higher. The Levellers convened large meetings with the new agents and friends such as Henry Marten at two taverns – the Mouth at Aldersgate and the Windmill near Coleman Street – and also at an unnamed meeting place in Mile End to the east of the City. There they hurled insults at the king and coordinated efforts to organise a civilian presence at the first projected rendezvous at Ware in Hertfordshire.[42]

Within the army, too, Leveller organising went on apace. On 11 November the new agents scattered about the streets of London a printed address to all the soldiers, warning the rank and file not to trust their officers, and demanding a general rendezvous of the whole army.[43]

Most disturbing to the grandees was the disobedience of Harrison's and Lilburne's regiments. Fairfax had ordered Robert Lilburne's foot regiment to Newcastle, but on 13 November agents arrived at the regiment and implored the soldiers to halt their march, since according to the *Solemne Engagement* the army had pledged not to let itself be divided until its demands were met. The soldiers rose up and drove off their officers – except for Captain-Lieutenant William Bray – and seized their horses. The entire regiment, minus officers, then headed south to join the rendezvous at Ware.[44]

Before the generals made their appearance at Corkbush Field outside Ware, Colonel William Eyre and Major Thomas Scot had already arrived and were preaching up the *Agreement of the People* to the seven regiments that had been authorised to attend. Other men busily distributed copies of the document and collected signatures. When Fairfax arrived, a delegation headed by Colonel Rainborowe presented him with a petition urging the army to embrace the *Agreement.* Rainborowe was no longer a member of the army; his presence therefore was highly irregular. (He was punished a few weeks later when the Commons voted to bar him from taking up his command at sea). Major Scot, the recruiter MP for Aldborough, was escorted back to Westminster by Lieutenant Chillenden, while William Eyre, who was also unconnected with the New Model, was arrested, along with Captain-Lieutenant Bray. Major John Cobbett, an officer-agitator from Skippon's regiment, which had not been summoned to the rendezvous, was also disciplined. John Lilburne and Richard Overton avoided arrest by staying at Ware and not approaching Corkbush Field.[45]

The most dangerous moment of the day came when Colonel Thomas Harrison's regiment appeared on the field uninvited and without their officers. Led by Joseph Aleyn, the regiment's new agent, they sported copies of the *Agreement* pinned to their hats with the slogan 'England's Freedoms, Soldiers' Rights'. But the men's defiance collapsed when Fairfax upbraided them, and Cromwell charged into their ranks and ripped the papers from their hats. Fairfax then began the review, pausing before each regiment to have his *Remonstrance* read aloud and subscribed. In it he blamed the indiscipline in the army on the new agents, who had taken it upon themselves to be 'guided by divers private persons that are not of the army'. If discipline was not restored, Fairfax threatened to resign his commission. He then outlined the grandees' platform for the army: 1. constant pay; 2. security for arrears; 3. an improved indemnity ordinance, with commissioners residing in every county, not just London; 4. provision for maimed soldiers, widows and orphans; 5. no conscription; 6. cancellation of apprenticeships for soldiers on active service. And for the kingdom: 1. a time limit for the present Parliament; 2. future parliaments to meet and dissolve at prearranged times and sit for fixed periods; 3. freedom and equality of elections.

While the Levellers had been roundly denounced in the preamble to the *Remonstrance*, they had influenced its content regarding conscription and elections. For most soldiers that was enough. As Wildman ruefully noted, many regiments signified their approval by crying, 'For the king and Sir Thomas, for the king and Sir Thomas.'[46]

In the midst of Fairfax's review, Robert Lilburne's regiment suddenly appeared on the field. The men too defiantly wore the *Agreement* in their hats. Major George Gregson of Pride's regiment pleaded with the mutinous soldiers to submit to discipline. Some of them stoned him, fracturing his skull. Fairfax then rode up to the regiment and ordered them to remove the *Agreement* from their hats. At first they refused, and Cromwell and some officers waded into their ranks, swords drawn. This display of ruthless courage was enough to cow most of the soldiers, and the papers disappeared.[47]

With order restored, Fairfax determined to punish the men who had led the mutiny. Eight or nine ringleaders were court-martialled on the spot and condemned to death. After reducing them to abject fear, Fairfax then pardoned all but three and ordered those to cast lots for their lives. The unlucky one, Richard Arnold, was shot to death by the other two at the head of his regiment.[48] The second and third army rendezvous were held in Essex and Surrey without incident, all the regiments pledging obedience to Fairfax.

In light of the rapid restoration of order in the army, would it be right to conclude that the Levellers commanded less of a following than they and others had thought? This is certainly what some of the grandees and journalists wanted the public to believe. On the other hand, it is significant that among the eight regiments excluded from all three rendezvous were some that were or would become the most turbulent in the army. Besides Harrison's and Lilburne's, who came uninvited to Ware, there was Ingoldsby's in Oxford and Scrope's in Somerset, both of which would mutiny at the Levellers' instigation in 1649 (see below, pp. 166–7, 172). Then there was Twisleton's regiment at Cambridge, which had given a warm reception to the *Case of the Armie*, and had elected two new agents from each troop. Finally, Ireton's and Whalley's regiments, though quiet in 1647, would be turbulent and mutinous in 1649 (see below, pp. 164–5, 168). Nor should we forget that the officer class as a whole had shown itself disturbingly susceptible to Leveller arguments. The conservative grandees had found themselves a beleaguered minority during the Putney debates, while Ireton's long-winded eloquence had only served to trim that minority over the course of ten days.

In the aftermath of the mutiny, Cromwell rose in the Commons to explain why he had suppressed the Levellers. In the beginning he had permitted them to propagandise the army, confident that 'their follies would soon vanish'. But when he saw the inroads they made among the soldiery he changed his mind. He had supported a more equal representative simply because 'many honest officers' wanted it. Much more worrying was their acceptance of the radical Leveller demand to give the unpropertied the vote. It was this 'drive at a levelling and parity' that made him set his face against them.[49] Implicit in Cromwell's speech was a recognition of the gravity of the Leveller threat to take political control of the army, contradicting the earlier glib assumption that only a few soldiers supported the *Agreement*.

Reconciliation and Restructuring

After the three rendezvous, the grandees tried to consolidate their position, first by vigorously pushing the army's material grievances, and second by striving to conciliate the alienated radicals within their ranks. They pressured the City of London to stop dragging its feet on assessment payments by quartering Colonel Hewson's regiment on City householders. The Commons decided that the best way to resolve the army's chronic financial crisis was to shed excess strength. Fairfax then issued orders to discharge all soldiers who had enlisted since the army's occupation of Westminster on 6 August. But when the men arrived at Westminster for dismissal there was no cash on hand to cover their expenses home, so they were sent back to their regiments until Parliament should provide the money.[50]

Fairfax and his advisers then sat down to compose a full-scale Representation of the army's demands, which they delivered to Parliament on 7 December. It substantially replicated the *Remonstrance* that he had read to the regiments at the Ware rendezvous in November, but did not conceal the rage of the grandees at Parliament's dilatory approach to its financial needs. Parliament actually listened to the officers, and as a result during the first six months of 1648 most regiments were paid in full.[51]

It was now the job of army headquarters to uphold its part of the bargain by shaving 20,000 men off the military establishment. This difficult exercise was postponed until January 1648 because the rest of December was devoted to tidying up the discipline issues left over from the Ware mutiny, and re-habilitating army morale.

The catalyst of the army's internal reconciliation was Fairfax's personal chaplain, John Saltmarsh. An austere, radical antinomian, he had quit the army on 26 November, apparently out of disgust with the policies of the grandees. At the beginning of December he had risen from his sickbed in Ilford, Essex, mounted his horse, and set off on a 30-mile journey to Windsor. His purpose, as he told his wife, was to impart to the army a message he had received from heaven. He finally arrived at headquarters to find the General Council in session. Saltmarsh told them that 'he had formerly come to them as a lamb, but now in the spirit of a lion, to tell them [that] . . . the Lord had now forsaken them . . . because they had forsaken him, their first principles, and imprisoned saints'. Later that day he met Fairfax, Cromwell and Ireton, gave them each the same message, keeping his hat on the whole time. Cromwell was visibly moved by the pronouncements of this sepulchral figure, prompting the chaplain to declare that he was 'glad . . . that there is some tenderness of heart in you'. On the 7th he left the army to return home, where he died four days later. At the end of December the army tacitly acknowledged the impact of his visit when it authorised the radical printer Robert Ibbotson to publish a full account of his visit to headquarters.[52]

After Saltmarsh's intervention, most of the punishments connected with the Ware mutiny were dropped or reduced. Major Francis White was re-admitted to the General Council by unanimous vote after apologising for his September statement that there was no power in the kingdom but the sword. Rainborowe also made a full submission for his offence at the Ware rendez-vous. The courts-martial of Bray, Crossman and Joseph Aleyn, who had come uninvited to the rendezvous at Ware, were dropped after they admitted 'their rash and irregular proceedings' and promised to submit to army discipline in the future.[53]

Cromwell was not alone in appreciating the importance of unity to the army's military and political strength. The king's flight from Hampton Court and the daily evidence of his conspiring with the Scots had convinced the grandees that there was no longer any hope of a negotiated settlement with him. From London came ever more disturbing reports of royalist preparations for an insurrection. Yet for all their certainty that armed conflict was again just around the corner, Fairfax and his generals knew that popular opinion required them to make drastic cuts to their payroll.

The Great Disbandment

The disbandment of January and February 1648 was conducted in such a way as to safeguard the military effectiveness and restore the political unity of the New Model. It was done in three stages. First came the reduction of those field regiments that had not taken part in the reconciliation exercise at the end of December and were thought to be infected with Presbyterianism. Second were the garrison and provincial troops unconnected with the New Model. Last came the selective dismissals from New Model itself, mostly targeting known radicals.

The politically untrustworthy troops were based mostly in Wales and the west, and most had been tainted by association with the abortive Presbyterian counter-revolution of the previous summer. They all acquiesced in their demobilisation except for Major-General Rowland Laugharne's regiment.[54]

Another detachment who no longer shared the grandees' political orientation were the gentlemen of Fairfax's lifeguard. Most of them cared chiefly about their back pay and were openly contemptuous of the religious and political radicalism that pervaded the army. They received two months' pay on 21 February and were told to assemble in St James's Fields for disbandment. Instead they mutinied, eight or ten of them carrying off the lifeguard's colours. Fairfax immediately ordered the leaders arrested. His quick action caused the mutiny to collapse. From that time on Fairfax's personal guard was furnished by regular troopers.[55]

The second category of troops to be disbanded included the Northern Army, and most of the garrisons and castles of England and Wales. These disbandments were non-political, as Fairfax emptied dozens of fortresses from Northumberland to Cornwall, and dismissed all except five regiments of the Northern Army.[56]

Finally it was the turn of the New Model regiments. With the approval of the Commons, Fairfax set the establishment at 24,000, but increased the number of regiments to fourteen of horse and seventeen of foot to accommodate more officers. Each cavalry troop and infantry company was reduced from 100 to eighty men. Given the much higher pay scales of officers, the elimination of 20 per cent of the common soldiers produced little net saving.[57]

The reasons for restructuring the army in this way were both administrative and political. None of the New Model regiments would have to be dissolved. All the officers who had proven their political fidelity would be retained. The few essential non-New Model regiments and companies could also be absorbed.[58] About the middle of March, army headquarters commenced the disbandment of nearly 4,000 men from the original New Model regiments. A similar number who had been enlisted since 6 August had already been sent home. The disbandment of March 1648 enabled the officers to weed out the remaining soldiers whom they suspected of radicalism or disaffection.

Harrison's regiment experienced the most sweeping purge. The grandees did not forget its disobedience at the Ware rendezvous, and now cut it by half. Predictably, the drastic expulsions provoked a mutiny. Several men were brought to trial on 26 February, and three found guilty. The penalty was death, but Fairfax postponed the executions and they never seem to have been carried out. The reductions in the other New Model regiments appear to have been carried off without incident.[59]

The great disbandment of 1648 was effected mainly at the expense of provincial forces. Except for a few politically unreliable elements, the bulk of the original New Model regiments remained intact. It was an impressive administrative achievement, demonstrating to the people that Parliament and army had heard their groans against heavy taxation and free quarter, and were determined to lighten their burdens.

By the spring of 1648 the military high command had reshaped Parliament's army into a leaner, more politically unified and less costly body of men. There was to be no pause for this restructured force to catch its breath. Even as the last few thousand men were being demobilised, royalist insurrection was being stirred up in the capital, and rebellion plotted against the regime in the western border counties, Wales, the north, East Anglia, Kent and Essex.

CHAPTER SEVEN

THE SECOND CIVIL WAR

The Second Civil War can be dated from 11 November 1647, when Charles fled from Hampton Court to Carisbrooke Castle, where he found himself under the nervous wardenship of Colonel Robert Hammond. His flight prompted Cromwell and Ireton to jettison any further attempts at reconciliation, and to redirect their energies to unifying the army and turning it once more into an effective fighting instrument. Vexed by Leveller unrest on the one hand, and angered by the Scottish–royalist conspiracy on the other, the grandees were in an ugly mood. It was reported from headquarters that the officers were talking of bringing the monarch to trial. Cromwell was now freely admitting that his previous negotiations with Charles were a blunder, which he blamed on 'the glory of the world [which] had so dazzled his eyes, [that] he could not discern clearly the great works that the Lord was doing'.[1]

Meanwhile, the New Model Army's intelligence activities were stepped up to uncover the schemes that the king and his new allies were concocting. To consolidate their military control, the grandees got their friends in the Commons to move that Colonel Rainborowe should immediately be named vice-admiral in the Downs. Overriding the Lords' opposition, the Commons simply ordered Rainborowe to take command of the ships guarding the Solent.[2]

Responding to growing sympathy for the king in London and in Parliament, the army shifted several regiments closer to the capital. The grandees were also worried that Charles might escape from Carisbrooke Castle and become the rallying point of popular antagonism towards the army. The king's gaoler, Colonel Hammond, was less than wholly reliable, so Cromwell made a special trip to the Isle of Wight to impress upon him the gravity of his responsibility. Troop reinforcements soon followed. Upon his return to London, Cromwell sent Colonel William Constable and Lieutenant-Colonels William Goffe and Edward Salmon to stiffen Hammond's backbone.[3]

Meanwhile, on the floor of the House of Commons, Ireton and Cromwell spoke forcefully in favour of the Vote of No Addresses, cutting off further communication with the king. Ireton declared that since the king had ceased to protect his people they could settle the kingdom without him. Cromwell denounced Charles as a dissembler, citing scripture: 'thou shalt not suffer an hypocrite to reign'. On the same day a new committee of safety was created, soon to be known as the Derby House Committee. It promptly set about putting the country on a war footing. From their listening posts in the Mews (present-day Trafalgar Square) and Whitehall, two of the most trusted regiments – Colonel Rich's horse and Colonel Barkstead's foot – maintained a close watch on parliamentary proceedings. In conjunction with Tichborne's reliable Tower regiment, they were also well placed to keep the lid on seething urban unrest. The grandees also moved Hewson's and Fairfax's foot regiments in Kent closer to London.[4]

By the end of the winter the political temperature in the metropolis had reached fever point. On the anniversary of Charles's coronation – 27 March – scores of bonfires were lit, coaches were stopped, their occupants obliged to drink the king's health, and an effigy of Colonel Hammond was dragged through the streets, drawn, quartered and burnt.[5]

A week later there occurred a much graver incident that culminated in a violent attack on the army-nominated City magistrates. On Easter Sunday, 2 April, the lord mayor John Warner ordered the trained bands to disperse a crowd of apprentices who were violating the Sabbath by playing their customary game of tipcat in Finsbury Fields. The following Sunday an even larger crowd gathered with the same intent. This time the lord mayor sent a company of the Tower Hamlets militia under the radical Captain Peter Gale, 'a tub preacher'. The apprentices soon overpowered these hapless soldiers, and then fanned through the City and its suburbs calling on the people to join their insurrection. The main body, 3,000 or 4,000 strong, surged down Fleet Street in the direction of Rich's and Barkstead's regimental barracks, shouting, 'Now for King Charles!' A detachment of Rich's horse rode out to meet the apprentices and drove them back inside the City gates. Fairfax and his officers then passed an anxious night debating whether to throw the two regiments into the fray at once, or wait for reinforcements. At length they resolved, 'though they [might] perish', to engage the rioters with their limited forces. In quelling the uprising the next day the army killed several apprentices and watermen.[6]

Revolt in the Provinces

It proved easier to keep order in the metropolis than to extinguish the smouldering anger of the countryside. Many risings appealed to features of traditional culture: Christmas celebrations, the drinking of healths, Sunday games, bonfires, maypoles and horse races. They also made real demands: the restoration of the king to his former power and dignity, and the re-establishment of the Church of England, its prayerbook and bishops. On the parliamentary side, 'honest radicals' possessing a national consciousness continued to hold sway in Warwickshire, Somerset, Suffolk, Lancashire and other counties throughout 1648.[7]

After London the next open hostility erupted in Canterbury, where a riot broke out against the law suppressing Christmas and requiring shops to stay open on that day. After Charles's attempt to escape from Carisbrooke Castle on the 29th, the Cavaliers in the city declared their readiness to ally with the Scots and restore the king 'to his just rights'. Not till Sir Anthony Weldon arrived before the walls of Canterbury in early January with 3,000 of the county trained bands did the rebels give up. Another uprising against the anti-Christmas ordinance occurred in Ipswich, and there were pro-Christmas stirrings in London.[8]

Over the next six months, the tempo of provincial protest quickened until the Derby House Committee, the Committee for the Army and the army commanders were hard pressed to maintain control of the country. Although military demobilisation was being carried out rapidly, it never seemed to be going rapidly enough for popular opinion. Free quarter continued to be a huge grievance, yet the field regiments were paid almost in full during the first half of 1648. The explanation for this paradox may be that the regiments and local forces awaiting demobilisation in the early months of 1648 extracted free quarter during the weeks before they received their two months' pay and were sent home. In any case, there was a widespread popular conviction that householders would never be rid of freequartering soldiers until they were rid of the army itself.[9]

A serious disturbance broke out in Norwich on 23 April when soldiers came to fetch the city's mayor to Westminster to explain why he had permitted royalist festivities on the anniversary of Charles's coronation (27 March), and why he had allowed the election of 'malignant' aldermen. A detachment from Fleetwood's regiment attempted to disperse the turbulent crowd. In retaliation the crowd seized the city magazine: accidentally they set it on fire, igniting an explosion that killed forty of their number, and three times as many bystanders.[10]

A month later, neighbouring Suffolk flared into revolt. A crowd gathered around a maypole in Bury St Edmunds when a troop of Fairfax's own cavalry regiment rode into town. To shouts of 'For God and King Charles' the crowd laid into the soldiers and chased them out of town. They then shut the town gates, barricaded the streets, seized the magazine and attacked parliamentarians. Their numbers swelled to 600 armed men on foot, and another 100 on horseback. Major Disbrowe threw five troops around the town to contain the revolt and drove the rioters back when they sallied out. Luckily for Disbrowe there was a solid stratum of parliamentary support in Suffolk, and many of the county militia rallied to him. With their help he was able to put down the rising. Royalists again went underground. Some left for Newmarket, where they congregated 'under pretence of horseracing'.[11]

Much more worrying news arrived from the west. Plymouth mutinied against the imposition of Sir Hardress Waller as its governor. Exeter refused to provide quarters for the soldiers or pay its assessment. Stunned by the depth of neutralist and Cavalier sentiment he encountered, Waller marvelled that the western counties were not 'all in one flame'. The Commons were so taken with the gravity of the situation as to instruct him to withdraw his soldiers from Exeter. Colonel Alexander Popham was sent to neighbouring Somerset to keep the royalist infection from spreading there.[12]

By the end of May the minutes of the Derby House Committee convey a palpable sense of panic. In addition to major conflagrations in Wales, Kent and the northern border, there were brushfires in the counties of Nottingham, Lincoln, Huntingdon, Rutland, Leicester, Hertford, Cambridge, Sussex, Dorset, Hampshire, Surrey, Worcester and Warwick.[13]

Another source of anxiety for Parliament was that as the crisis worsened its military strength was steadily contracting. Most of the demobbed took their two months' pay and went home without a grumble. Wales was the exception. Major-General Rowland Laugharne and Colonel John Poyer were unhappy with the terms they were offered.[14]

Poyer turned increasingly to the bottle to stiffen his courage, blurting out his royalist sympathies while defying Parliament's order to disband and hand over Pembroke Castle. On 24 March Fairfax ordered Colonels Thomas Horton and Christopher Fleming, plus Major-General Laugharne, to bring Poyer to heel. Laugharne chose that moment to reveal his true colours, taking one-third of his regiment to join Poyer. Together they chased Fleming out of Pembroke. Then they swept through the county, proclaiming their royalism, which ignited a passionate response across Wales, where Poyer continued to gather strength. Horton, commanding a brigade of only four under-strength regiments, approached Pembroke with caution. Fairfax, his army shrinking and threatened in Kent and East Anglia, was hard put to come to Horton's aid. Yet on 1 May he sent Cromwell with two horse and three foot regiments to reinforce Horton's effectives.[15]

The Welsh royalists knew that they must engage Horton at all costs before Cromwell arrived on the scene. They fell on him, 7,000 strong, at St Fagans, just outside Cardiff. While they outnumbered Horton by about three to one, they boasted only 500 cavalry, which they had to station in the rear to keep the infantry from turning tail. Although they fought stoutly they were no match for the New Model cavalry and dragoons. The political fallout from Horton's victory was instantaneous: royalist spirits sank while Presbyterians in the capital swung away from the king and towards the army.[16]

The victory in Wales gave a needed boost to army morale, which had been fragile for two months or more. While the great disbandment was proceeding, Cromwell had been wrapped up in politics, labouring to forge a coalition with like-minded men in the City, the army and the two houses of Parliament. In late February he convened a meeting at his house in King Street, Westminster between army and parliamentary grandees on the one hand and republicans on the other. The republican 'commonwealthsmen' forthrightly declared against monarchy, but Cromwell and the grandees 'kept themselves in the clouds and would not declare their judgements'. When he grew tired of the meeting Cromwell seized a cushion, flung it at Colonel Ludlow's head, and ran downstairs, but, as Ludlow related with satisfaction, 'I overtook him with another, which made him hasten down faster than he desired.'[17]

As the omens of war darkened, the coalition that Cromwell had been so arduously knitting together began to fall apart. Not only was England boiling with discontent, but more and more royalists were flocking to Scotland to assist the king's military build-up there. In Ireland Lord Inchiquin had turned his coat and declared for the king. Some members of the parliamentary war party now changed tack, and in a bid to detach the king from his Scottish engagement pressed to cancel the Vote of No Addresses and reopen negotiations. Army thinking was shifting in a diametrically opposite direction. Among the rank and file radical ideology was on the rise again. It may have had its seeds in the disgruntlement felt by many soldiers at the demo-

bilisation of so many of their comrades. On 24 April there was an unauthorised meeting of agitators from several horse regiments at St Albans, a
known centre of political radicalism. Their main order of business was a
petition to Parliament for the *Agreement of the People*. A leading figure in
this renewed agitation was Captain John Reynolds of Cromwell's regiment,
who had also played a dominant political role the previous summer. The
meeting had scarcely got underway when a detachment from Fairfax's horse
regiment arrived on the scene and broke it up. Some of the representatives
were arrested, while Reynolds was sentenced to three months' imprisonment and cashiered. The embittered radicals retaliated by publishing their
petition along with a slashing attack on Cromwell. The men of Rich's regiment also petitioned Fairfax for the release of their imprisoned comrades.[18]

Everything seemed to be going wrong for the army. Threatened by
disunity within and facing mortal peril without, the officers resorted to
the only remedy they knew, a prayer meeting. Amidst a mounting sense
of crisis, they began a three-day fast at Windsor on 27 April. There they
pondered the causes of the 'sad dispensation' they witnessed on every side.
On the second day Cromwell 'did press very earnestly . . . to a thorough
consideration of our actions . . . to see if any iniquity could be found in them
. . . that if possible we might . . . remove the cause of such sad rebukes as
were upon us'. The breakthrough came on the third day, when the highly-
respected Lieutenant-Colonel William Goffe rose to speak. Taking Proverbs
1:23 ff. for his text ('Turn you at my reproof . . .'), he announced that all their
misfortunes were the fruit of not following the ways of the Lord. He spoke
with such intensity that everyone in the room was pierced to the heart:
'None was able to speak a word to each other for bitter weeping, partly in the
sense and shame of our iniquities or unbelief, base fear of men, and carnal
consultations . . . with our own wisdom, and not with the word of the Lord.'
Hard on the heels of this emotional catharsis came consensus. Without a
murmur of dissent they agreed that they must go out and fight all the
enemies arrayed against them, 'with an humble confidence in the name of
the Lord'. They further agreed that it was their duty 'to call Charles Stuart,
that man of blood, to an account for that blood he had shed'.[19]

The Renewal of Fighting

During the prayer meeting the Derby House Committee sent Fairfax an
urgent call to deliver more effectives to south Wales. On the last day of the

meeting the news came through that Adjutant-General Fleming had been killed by Welsh royalists. As soon as they broke up, the officers dispersed to fight royalist insurgencies in Wales, Cornwall, the north, Kent, Surrey and Essex. They would not meet again under the same roof for four months.[20]

With the army's men and matériel sorely stretched in all parts of the country, royalists now redoubled their efforts to assault the capital. On 16 May a contingent of 3,000 well-armed men from Surrey arrived at Westminster to petition for a personal treaty with the king. A group of them invaded Westminster Hall, picked a quarrel with the guards, and killed one of them. Reinforcements were rushed in from Rich's and Barkstead's regiments; in the ensuing mêlée five or six petitioners were killed and a great many wounded. Lieutenant-Colonel Ralph Cobbett, bleeding from his wounds, went at once to the bar of the House of Commons to report on the episode.[21]

Despite the skirmish with the Surrey petitioners, Fairfax found himself compelled to withdraw Rich's, Barkstead's and Tichborne's regiments from London to deal with the rising in Kent. He was able to do this because the London militia was now controlled by the politically reliable Major-General Skippon.[22]

Maidstone

After Horton's victory in Wales (see above, p. 112), the royalists in Kent decided to wait for the Scottish invasion before unleashing their rebellion. But they were pre-empted by the wave of indignation that swept the county when the Christmas rioters were put on trial on 10 May at Canterbury. As insurgents overran one town after another, a panicky Derby House Committee ordered Fairfax to send more cavalry into the county. On the 22nd, armed men rallied at Rochester, shut the city's gates and declared their support for the king. Thanks to the revolt of naval ships in the Downs, the insurgents were successful in seizing county magazines and coastal castles. The Commons tried to defuse the anger of the revolting ships by replacing Rainborowe as vice-admiral with Robert Rich, second earl of Warwick. What gave the parliamentarians nightmares was the prospect that the royalist mobilisation in Kent would become the springboard for an assault on London. That is why they did not flinch when Fairfax took the three London-based regiments, as well as four others and a few companies of Ingoldsby's, into Kent.[23]

A combination of calculated concessions and a determined show of strength had the desired effect of sowing disunity among the insurgents' ranks. Once Fairfax had marshalled his forces, a little over 4,000 strong, on Blackheath on 30 May, the more fainthearted among the royalists began to retreat to their homes, while the others fell back to Rochester.[24]

The same day, Fairfax advanced the main body of his brigade towards Maidstone by a circuitous route. Hidden by thick woods of hazel, yew and whitebeam, he was able to keep the rebels guessing until, late in the evening of 31 May, the people of Maidstone discovered parliamentarian troops encamped 4 miles to the west. Fairfax continued to circle the town the next day, reaching it at 7 p.m.[25]

He resolved to attack the following morning, but his advance guard of dragoons, hearing the townsmen shout 'For God, King Charles and Kent!', impetuously attacked at once, undeterred by a heavy downpour of rain. Their onslaught was violent and furious, but the veterans of the New Model ran into resolute resistance from troops that had been recruited scarcely ten days before. Pitched fighting began a mile outside the town, and it took two hours to drive the defenders from hedge to hedge back inside their fortress. Once Fairfax's men surmounted the barricades, they had to fight from street to street, as the royalists exacted a heavy price for every foot of ground they gave up. In the narrow streets they deployed their cannon to deadly effect, cutting down thirty men of the New Model. Fairfax held a large part of his brigade in reserve, pouring them in at critical junctures throughout the evening. He personally led his men through the greatest danger on horseback, all the while fighting back excruciating pain from gout. It was almost 1 a.m. by the time the defenders were overpowered and the town was still.[26]

Maidstone was a critical victory for Parliament. It was won partly by Fairfax's careful planning and personal valour, and partly by the seasoned quality of his troops. His one failure was in neglecting to follow up his victory with an effective pursuit. Still, the day after their defeat, the majority of royalists opted to desert. Those who stuck with their leader, George Goring, first earl of Norwich (the father of Lord Goring), trudged over Rochester Bridge, eluded their pursuers, and made it to Blackheath.[27]

For all that Fairfax had won a sparkling victory in Kent, there was now great anxiety in the Derby House Committee lest the City throw its support behind the royalists and their project of a general rising in Surrey and Essex. All ferryboats across the Thames were stopped, while Skippon supervised the fortification of London Bridge. Norwich managed to spirit only 1,500 of his remaining forces back across the river into Essex, some by swimming, others on horseback.[28]

With Kent pacified, Essex now became the main theatre of conflict. There were no grounds for parliamentary complacency. Norwich was increasing in strength in Essex; half a dozen other counties in East Anglia and the Midlands were aflame with revolt; Poyer was keeping Cromwell and 8,000 men pinned down at Pembroke; unfriendly petitions were streaming in from Sussex and Dorset. Another worry was the threat of revolting ships of the navy spearheading an invasion of the Isle of Wight to rescue the king.[29]

For the next two months the political and military situation in the metropolis was highly volatile. Munition trains on their way to Fairfax's forces were attacked and overturned by royalist apprentices. From then on, New Model supply wagons had to give the City a wide berth on their way to Essex. A petition to bring the king to London attracted wide support, and on 7 August the Common Council publicly backed the royalist programme recently announced by the prince of Wales. The chief reason why a royalist counter-revolution did not carry the day in London in the summer of 1648 was that Major-General Skippon remained in charge of the trained bands, with the added authority to recruit a regiment of cavalry. Skippon not only kept the City under control, he also strangled the flow of men and matériel to the earl of Norwich at Colchester.[30]

In spite of Fairfax's recent success in Kent, therefore, it is hardly surprising that the minutes of the Derby House Committee reveal not a sense of inevitable triumph, but one of barely controlled panic.[31]

Because London could no longer be relied upon, the New Model's resources had to be spread very thinly. The looming danger in Surrey compelled the withdrawal in early July of the guard of horse at Bow Bridge. Skippon was asked to send 100 of his newly raised cavalry to Kingston to help break up the royalist concentration there. The Hertfordshire militia and Sir Michael Livesey, having returned to his radical beliefs, were also enlisted to link up with small detachments from Rich's and Ireton's regiments. In Surrey, the earl of Holland and George Villiers, second duke of Buckingham were rallying royalists from the southern counties. Their hope was to rendezvous with the prince of Wales, who was daily expected to sail up the Thames. Together they would launch the counter-revolution in the metropolis. But before the prince of Wales could arrive, the fortunes of battle turned against the royalists. Parliament's motley force met and defeated them at Kingston, killing Buckingham's brother in the process. Taken prisoner, Holland was incarcerated in Warwick Castle.[32]

The Siege of Colchester

Of all the theatres of war in 1648, Colchester occupied the attention of the Derby House Committee most. So obsessed were they by the danger posed to the capital by the earl of Norwich and his 5,000 hard-bitten men, a mere two-days march away from London, that never during the eleven-week siege did they dare suggest to Fairfax a storm of the town, even after its starving defenders had spent their ammunition.

A few days after arriving in the county, Norwich met Sir Charles Lucas, the royalist general for Essex. Together they marched to Chelmsford, where they were joined by Lord Arthur Capel, first Baron Capel, former commissioner of array for Hertfordshire, a soldier of fortune called Sir George Lisle, an Italian, Sir Bernard Gascoigne, and 'divers gentlemen of quality' from a number of counties. Shadowed at a safe distance by Whalley and 1,000 cavalry, they made their way to Colchester, Lucas's native town. Whalley was not inclined to cross swords with an enemy who was 'like a snowball increasing'. Instead he linked up with Sir Thomas Honywood's 1,200 Essex horse and foot, and waited for Fairfax to arrive with reinforcements. In his main strategic object – heading off an attack on London by Norwich – Whalley was successful.[33]

On the morning of Sunday 11 June, after hearing a sermon at Gravesend, Fairfax brought his brigade across the Thames at Tilbury Fort. Racked with gout, he still advanced with lightning speed, picking up Honywood and Whalley on the way, and pushing on to the outskirts of Colchester by the evening of the 12th. With the road to London now secured, the Derby House Committee fretted that Norwich might break out of Colchester, head north, and join Langdale and the Scottish invaders. Their apprehension was well grounded, as Colchester was quite unsuitable for withstanding a siege.[34]

The town was oblong in shape, and its walls had only one salient bastion from which the defenders could fire on assailants in the flank. By contrast, the suburbs, which spread ribbon-like along the roads, furnished cover to an assailant who approached near enough to make use of them. Yet there were disadvantages for the besieger as well. If he approached from the London side, as Fairfax did, he had to get past Lucas's house which stood as a royalist outpost on high ground, a short distance beyond the south wall. That wall was itself commanded by a battery placed on the south-western angle in St Mary's churchyard.[35]

Colchester was anything but a royalist town. When the royalists arrived many clothworkers fled and threw in their lot with Fairfax. On Tuesday the

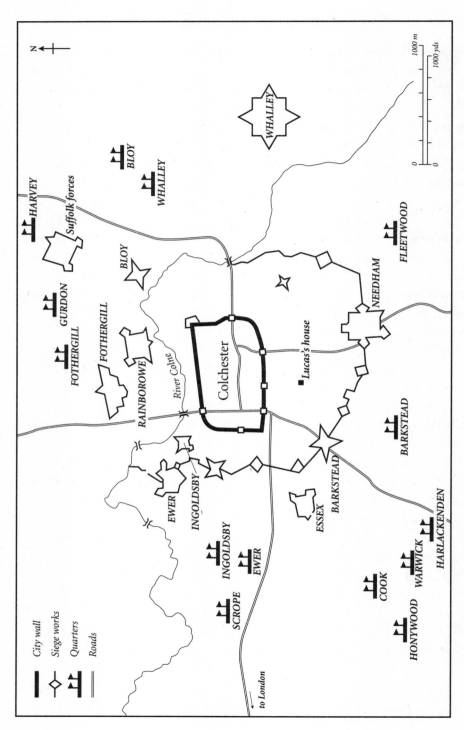

2. The siege of Colchester, 13 July–26 August 1648

13th the royalist invaders paid the price for lax intelligence when they woke up to find the besiegers within musket-shot of the suburbs. They met Fairfax's summons to surrender with characteristic bravado. Alluding to Fairfax's gout, Norwich asked the trumpeter who had brought the summons to tell his master not to worry, for he 'would cure him of all diseases'. The New Model soldiers were enraged by this mockery of their commander's frailty. Norwich's violation of the etiquette surrounding the communication between opposing forces set the ill-tempered tone of all future exchanges at Colchester.[36]

Having contemptuously rejected the summons to surrender, the royalists hastily drew up their men in battle order across the London road and prepared to meet their enemy head on. Fairfax hurled his troops at this target, expecting a victory as quick and telling as the one he had gained at Maidstone. To his dismay, Colonel Barkstead's foot, who spearheaded the attack, were repulsed three times. In the end the royalists fell back behind the town walls. Pursuing them into the town, the parliamentary vanguard fell into the trap Lucas had set for them. The royalists charged from two directions and drove Barkstead's men back through the gate. The fighting went on for almost eight hours – till nearly midnight – with royalist losses totalling between 150 and 500, while Fairfax lost perhaps 500 dead and wounded.[37]

Fairfax now had to face the disagreeable fact that Colchester would not be an easy nut to crack. Because a storm, if unsuccessful, would place London in jeopardy, he had no choice but to settle down for a long siege. His soldiers spent most of the next eleven weeks investing the town with a line of trenches and stockades punctuated with star- and square-shaped forts. The result was 'probably the most sophisticated set of siege lines of either civil war'. The defenders for their part busily repaired the town's decaying walls, but their main hardship was an ever-dwindling food supply, while the besiegers were sorely tested by having to camp out of doors in the midst of a miserably cold, wet summer. Besides his own troops, numbering perhaps 5,000, Fairfax profited from a major infusion of strength from the county regiments of Essex (2,000) and Suffolk (2,400). His total numbers reached at least 9,000. Midway through the siege his army was further swelled by 1,500 men recruited by Major-General Skippon in London. Norwich's forces by contrast shrank steadily from 5,000–6,000 to 4,000. A high percentage of them were not properly armed.[38]

The siege of Colchester was the bitterest episode of either Civil War. Its sheer length deepened the boundless contempt that each side felt towards the other. There was great property destruction – 300 houses, mainly in the suburbs. The object on the one hand was to prevent the besiegers from using the houses as cover to approach the town's walls; on the other to give the besieged a clear field of fire against their enemy. Whole streets were reduced to ashes. Besides the horrors of fire, with their echoes of the Thirty Years' War, there were other alleged atrocities, including the maltreatment of civilians, and the use of starvation as a weapon of war. Fairfax choked off the town's profitable trade with London, cut its water supply, and stopped civilians from fleeing, which accelerated the depletion of the town's food stocks. When Norwich drove a large number of women and children outside the town walls, Fairfax heartlessly drove them back again, as he had every right to do according to the laws of war, then as now. Yet he offered generous terms to any soldiers who would desert their officers.[39]

The siege of Colchester, because it was so long and so bitter, provoked accusations of atrocity from both sides. For example, chewed or poisoned bullets were strictly in violation of the laws of war, but the royalists were accused of using both.[40]

By 19 August the royalists knew the game was up. During eleven weeks of stubborn resistance no one had come to their aid except a trickle of apprentices, butchers, watermen and others from London. The news of Cromwell's victory at Preston five days later (see below, pp. 121–6), dashed all hope. The officers had no choice but to accept Fairfax's stringent requirement that they surrender, not to quarter, but to 'mercy'. Even though the town had been reduced to desolation by parliamentary bombardment its humiliation was not over. In order to escape a sacking by Fairfax's soldiers it had to pay a fine of £14,000.[41]

When the royalist officers surrendered to 'mercy' they gave Fairfax the right to do with them as he pleased.[42] He chose to sentence Sir Charles Lucas and Sir George Lisle to be shot to death by firing squad. Norwich, Capel and Hastings, being peers, he turned over to the judgement of Parliament.

The two executions have long been the subject of controversy, Fairfax's severity at Colchester being contrasted with Cromwell's mildness after Preston. It has been suggested that Fairfax was manipulated by the Iago-like figure of Ireton. There is no need to accept such speculation. Fairfax never shrank from severity when he thought it was called for. Two days before the royalists capitulated he wrote that 'justice must be done on such exemplary offenders who have embroiled the kingdom in a second bloody war'. The record shows that he enjoyed solid support from his Council of War.

THE SECOND CIVIL WAR

Parliament too betrayed no flicker of doubt as to the justice of the executions. They were vindicated on two counts. First, according to the code of war at the time, officers who caused unnecessary bloodshed by continuing to hold an untenable position forfeited their right to quarter. Second, an officer taken prisoner and then released was guilty of breaking his parole if he took up arms again against the enemy who had released him. This was the charge against Sir Charles Lucas, who had been taken prisoner at Marston Moor and released in 1644.[43]

The political legacy of Colchester was a deepened conviction on the part of most of the higher officers that the king, as the ultimate author of the bloodshed that they and their comrades had suffered, must be brought to account for his crimes. Their bitterness stemmed in part from the fact that the victory was extremely costly. Colchester had become a rallying point for royalist diehards, Londoners in particular. The royalist strategy of pinning down almost half of Parliament's mobile forces had worked for nearly three months. Parliament's appreciation of the supreme importance of the siege is signalled by the Committee for the Army's taking up residence at Colchester. The gritty perseverance of Norwich's men handed the northern royalists and Scots invaders a matchless opportunity. That they made so little of it testifies to their divided counsel and military incompetence.

The Battle of Preston

A great conflict had just concluded in the north. It had been delayed so long owing to difficulties on both sides. Colonel John Lambert, with only 3,000 effectives, had no choice but to play for time until Cromwell could be spared from Wales to bolster him. Cromwell and Horton finally combined their forces at the end of May, bringing them to 8,000 at Pembroke where they confronted Colonel John Poyer.[44]

The key to toppling Poyer, however, was not men but artillery. The wet weather did not let up, and during one storm the heavy guns of the siege train were dumped in the mud at the mouth of the Severn. It took until 4 July to dig them out. On that day Cromwell swung into action and Poyer surrendered within the week. Cromwell was now ready to embark on his first campaign as general in command of a marching army.[45]

Cromwell's victory in Wales came none too soon, for the duke of Hamilton had already crossed the border into England at the head of 9,000 men. He had been preceded more than two months earlier by the English royalists Sir Marmaduke Langdale and Sir Philip Musgrave, who with breathtaking ease had overrun Berwick, Carlisle and Pontefract.[46]

Lambert meanwhile patiently augmented his numbers, at the same time playing cat and mouse with the royalists. By the end of June he had added Colonel Edward Ashton's 1,500 Lancashire troops to his own 3,000, and was more and more taking the offensive in his engagements with Langdale. In this way he laid an excellent foundation for Cromwell's stunning successes in August.[47]

The Scottish invaders were doomed from the start. Their alliance with the English royalists had brought together people who neither liked nor trusted one another. They were already several weeks too late to help the risings in England and Wales, and they were commanded by a second-rate general. Hamilton's mediocrity fuelled dissension among his subordinates, which ultimately destroyed the army as an effective fighting force. The Scots were a demoralised force from the start, reduced to plundering the English countryside to feed themselves.[48]

They were also plagued throughout their adventure by 'constant rainy, stormy and tempestuous weather'. Rivers and streams that were easy to ford in normal years turned into raging floods; roads became quagmires; match and powder were soaked; and life for the rank and file, shivering in their sodden clothes while sleeping beneath the sky, was hellish. The English suffered in the same way, but they at least were fighting on home ground.[49] Because of the scarcity of forage in England, Hamilton was powerless to prevent his cavalry from enlarging their quarters and advancing ahead of the foot. At the height of the struggle his troops, strung out along a thin, 20-mile line, were in no position to deliver a concentrated blow against their enemy.[50]

Cromwell had set out from Pembroke with 4,200 men to join Lambert on 14 July. The 1,000 infantry and 2,400 horse that he had already sent had swelled Lambert's forces to 9,000. Hamilton had now lost his numerical superiority. He timidly opted to stay at Kendal, allowing Lambert and Cromwell to combine their forces at their leisure. Cromwell paused at Nottingham to collect the 2,500 pairs of boots and stockings that he had previously ordered from Northampton and Coventry shoemakers. Similarly, when he reached Doncaster on 8 August he waited for three days until the artillery arrived from Hull. At every step of the way we see Cromwell sticking to his policy of never rushing unprepared into battle.[51]

On 13 August he finally rendezvoused with Lambert at Ripon. While waiting for Cromwell, Lambert used the time profitably to seal off Yorkshire from Scottish incursions. Langdale responded by marshalling his forces and directing them to Preston, where he expected to combine with the Scots.[52]

We are not sure of the size of Cromwell and Lambert's combined army. Cromwell informed Speaker Lenthall that it was 8,600. Whatever their numbers, an observer in Lancashire reported on their vastly superior morale: being 'most gallantly resolved, formed and accoutred'.[53]

By 16 August Cromwell was marching 'where the knotted muscles of the high Pennines relax into the pastoral slopes and fertile closes of the lower Ribble'. That day, at a council of war, he decided that they should fall on the enemy on the north side of the River Ribble. The less daring policy would have been to cross the Ribble and block Hamilton's way south as he quit Preston. This would have left the way open for him to retreat to Scotland. By staying on the north side Cromwell made sure that the encounter would be decisive.[54]

Langdale and the Scots had no inkling of their peril. Most of Hamilton's cavalry had advanced south to Wigan, leaving only a small rearguard to protect the infantry, which was strung out along a line 20 miles to their north. Langdale was 6 miles to the east of this line with his compact force of 3,600.[55]

By the night of the 16th, Langdale at last realised how close Cromwell was, and began hurriedly to pull back towards Preston. Knowing that a battle could not be avoided, he took up a defensive position across the road leading to the town. The site was inhospitable to cavalry, as the road was waterlogged and lined on either side with enclosures and ditches. Outnumbering Langdale three to one, Cromwell placed two of his crack horse regiments – Harrison's and his own – on the lane running through the middle of Langdale's position. Another horse regiment he kept in reserve. The two forward regiments were sandwiched between infantry, while Colonel Ashton stayed back with the Lancashire infantry in reserve. These two layers of infantry were in turn hemmed in by horse regiments on left and right.[56]

Langdale now spurred his horse for Preston, where he met Hamilton and James Livingston, first earl of Callendar, with most of the Scottish foot. They did not believe what they heard about the nearness of Cromwell's army, did not recall their horse from Wigan, and – incredibly – told him they intended

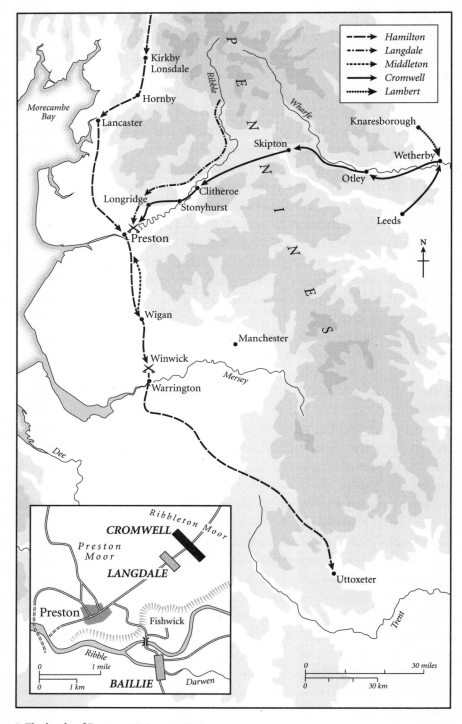

–––▶	*Hamilton*
–·–▶	*Langdale*
····▶	*Middleton*
——▶	*Cromwell*
●●●●▶	*Lambert*

3. The battle of Preston, 17 August 1648

to continue marching south with the foot. At the very moment when Cromwell attacked Langdale's force, the Scottish foot were tramping in the opposite direction, over the bridge across the Ribble.

By the time Langdale rode back to re-join his troops Cromwell had sent a 'forlorn hope' of 600 to probe his outer defences. One of Langdale's newly raised companies opened fire on them, but Captain John Hodgson, the puritan diarist, could tell that they had already lost heart: 'They shot at the skies, which did so encourage our men, that they were willing to venture upon any attempt . . . and we came up to the hedge end, and the enemy, many of them, threw down their arms, and ran to their party, where was their stand of pikes.'[57]

This skirmish gave Cromwell time to bring up his whole army from 4 miles off. The two sides were now engaged in a struggle that lasted around five hours. Given the cramped terrain, it was the infantry who bore the brunt of the fighting. On the right wing, Cromwell's cavalry worsted Langdale's after two charges. Having driven them from the field, they then wheeled around and rushed to the aid of the infantry on the left, who were in danger of being overrun. The ground had now been contested tenaciously for two hours; at the height of the battle, Hodgson tells us, 'there was nothing but fire and smoke', and 'the bullets flew freely'. Seeing the trouble the left wing was in, Lambert ordered Hodgson to fetch the Lancashire reserves. Their intervention, along with the cavalry's, was decisive. Hodgson, himself a man of considerable personal courage, was awed by the bravery and determination he witnessed around him, 'and how God hid from us the fears and dangers we were exposed to.'[58]

Most of Langdale's cavalry scattered northward in the direction of Lancaster, hoping to unite with the brigade of George Monro, first of Newmore, which had seen no action. Most of the infantry were taken prisoner. The great bulk of Hamilton's army, having sat immobile on the south side of the Ribble, were still unscathed. But they were profoundly depressed by the news from Preston, and by the realisation that, thanks to their leaders' incompetence, they had done nothing to head off the catastrophe.

Cromwell had effectively divided the enemy in two, and now prepared to press his advantage. He sent Colonel Ralph Assheton, commander of the Lancashire brigade, to attack the bridge over the Ribble. Assheton masterminded a highly unusual charge of massed pikes straight into 'the mouths of the [enemy's] muskets'. This bravery cleared the bridge. The dispirited Hamilton now opted to retreat southwards to the cavalry of John Middleton, first earl of Middleton, even though it meant abandoning his ammunition wagons, and shifting a shivering, hungry, exhausted body of infantry through mud-clogged lanes in a wet black night. During that night of horror almost half his infantry fell away. Cromwell, meanwhile, in hot pursuit at the head of 5,500 troops, caught up with Hamilton at Winwick. There was a desperate struggle, in which 1,000 Scots were slaughtered and several times that number taken prisoner.[59]

Yet for all its losses, Hamilton's army still slightly outnumbered Cromwell's. Numerical superiority was of little consequence, however, given the helpless and discouraged condition of the invaders. Following the disaster at Winwick, Callander persuaded Hamilton to abandon the foot so that the cavalry could either return to Scotland or make themselves useful to the English royalists. The result: 4,000–5,000 more Scottish infantry passed into Cromwell's hands.[60]

Cromwell was now burdened with 10,000 prisoners, and his men were almost as worn out as the cavalry they were pursuing. If only he had a thousand fresh horse, he mused, he could make quick work of them, 'but truly we are so harassed and haggled out in this business, that we are not able to do more than walk an easy pace after them'. Confident of his ability to fight on two fronts, Cromwell now divided his cavalry, dispatching Lambert southward to round up the remnant of Hamilton's force, while he headed northward with the rest to deal with Monro. With the help of county militias Lambert easily obtained Hamilton's surrender at Uttoxeter on 22 August.[61]

Owing to the utter royalist defeat at Preston, Scotland in 1648 was 'a dog that bit itself'.[62] Besides divided and incompetent leadership, the Scots were stymied by the failure of the inhabitants of northern England to rally to the royalist standard. The suspicion and hostility of the English towards the Scots outweighed any desire they nursed to see Charles I recover his throne. Preston was also a personal triumph for Cromwell and Lambert, and showcased the bravery of their men – New Model veterans and county troops alike. The commanders deployed their forces to the best advantage by concentrating them at one single point after another, at the same time exploiting the personal and geographical dividedness of their foes.

All that remained to Cromwell in the north was a mopping-up operation. He easily retook Berwick and Carlisle. A trickier assignment was to extinguish the royalist base of operations north of the border. The collapse of the Engager army had been the signal for civil war to erupt in Scotland. Cromwell marched into the fray with five regiments of horse and a sizeable contingent of foot. Once there he had to deal with Archibald Campbell, first marquess of Argyll, his supposed ally, who did everything he could to get him out of the country. Cromwell did not budge until he had overseen the removal of all who had supported the Engagement with the king. Then, leaving Argyll in control, he set out for Pontefract Castle, still occupied by the royalists.[63] They held out for another five months, during which time a political revolution was consummated at Westminster, rendering their resistance pointless. We now turn to that revolution.

CHAPTER EIGHT

'THAT MAN OF BLOOD': THE ARMY AND THE REGICIDE, SEPTEMBER 1648 TO MAY 1649

> . . . attending and acting the providence of God.
>
> Sir Thomas Fairfax to Speaker Lenthall, 29 November 1648[1]

After the wet summer of 1648 came an even wetter autumn. Disastrous harvests heightened the sense of unease on all sides. Mirroring popular sentiment, which craved only an end to civil strife, Parliament opted to resume talks with the twice-defeated king. This alarmed the army grandees, who were at a loss to comprehend why the 'author of the late troubles' should be offered anything except an imposed settlement.[2]

The aftermath of the Second Civil War would witness the forging of that alliance so ardently sought by the Levellers in 1647, but thwarted by the army high command. In building this alliance the key role was played by Ireton, with the counsel and approval of Cromwell, his father-in-law.

This time the Levellers were much more solicitous of the army's interests than they had been in the spring of 1647. They now petitioned for regular pay, and indemnity for any illegal acts committed by soldiers while in uniform. They also condemned further negotiations with the king, and called for justice upon 'the capital authors of the late wars'. A few days later the army issued a list of demands that was almost identical to the Levellers' large petition of 11 September.[3]

During the next two months, Ireton's attitude shifted from defeatism to determination. At the end of September he handed in a long letter of resignation, but the letter was rejected, which seems to have prompted a change of heart. In the Commons he declared that it was 'high time' to 'clear the House again . . . with a new purge of impeachment'. To achieve this he had to change Fairfax's thinking. Army militants combined with Levellers to orchestrate an influx of petitions from regiments and garrisons across England with this objective. Between 10 October 1648 and the adoption of the army's *Remonstrance* on 18 November (see below, pp. 130–2), nine army petitions were laid at Fairfax's door. Five of them explicitly endorsed the Leveller programme. Between 19 November and the end of December, Fairfax received another twenty-one petitions from thirteen regiments, twenty-five garrisons, the Northern Brigade and the county forces of Northumberland. In all, thirty petitions are known to have reached army headquarters during the last three months of 1648, of which seventeen explicitly backed the Leveller programme.[4]

In vain Fairfax tried to damp down the fires of political discontent by promoting the army's material demands – 'constant pay', an end to free quarter, and a watertight statute of indemnity for illegal acts committed during the Civil Wars. He worked diligently with Robert Scawen, chairman of the Army Committee, to document the army's financial claims. Many officers were convinced that the army was being deliberately starved of cash in order to throw it back on free quarter, and render it even more unpopular with people. The circle of moderates from whom Fairfax took counsel was becoming increasingly discredited. Meanwhile, the Leveller leaders promised to 'live and die, and stand and fall [with the army] . . . against all opposition whatsoever'.[5]

Most regiments were in a dangerous political condition by late October. Numerous anonymous and unauthorised pamphlets were being published in the name of the army, often apocalyptic in tone and implacable in their hatred of the king. The fires of revolutionary conviction were also stoked by pamphlets issuing from civilian pens in London and various counties.[6]

The Death of Colonel Rainborowe

Thomas Rainborowe and his regiment had been sent north to assist in the siege of Pontefract. Having reached Doncaster, on the night of 29 October he retired to bed, leaving Captain-Lieutenant John Smith in charge of the guard. Smith, however, did not report for duty, being either sick (as he later claimed), or occupied in the local whorehouse (as *The Moderate* indignantly alleged). Royalist assassins already had Rainborowe in their sights. Twenty-two of them rode to Doncaster, where they surprised his guards. Only Rainborowe himself offered resistance, one of his captors trying to drag him down by his waistcoat. In the struggle Rainborowe managed to seize his captor's sword, while his lieutenant got hold of a pistol, but the royalists overpowered them both. Rainborowe was thrown to the ground and stabbed in the throat, while his lieutenant was killed. A second time he broke free, brandishing his sword at his assailants, but one of them thrust him through the body and he fell down dead. The royalist attackers then returned to Pontefract unchallenged.[7]

The repercussions of Rainborowe's killing were instantaneous. Parliamentarians and soldiers alike saw it as the deliberate murder of one of the king's most outspoken antagonists. From that moment onwards, most regimental petitions included a fresh demand: vengeance against Rainborowe's murderers.

The body of the fallen hero was brought to London a fortnight later. His funeral procession, numbering nearly 3,000, wound its way through the City, and ended at Wapping, where he was buried beside his father.[8]

The Remonstrance of the Army

In this volatile situation, Fairfax summoned the Council of Officers on 7 November. Twenty officers assembled in the abbey church of St Alban for prayers and a sermon. They then turned to review a number of regimental petitions calling for the prosecution of the king. The officers were still far from a consensus about what to do with him. When Ireton presented a first draft of what was to become *The Remonstrance of the Army*, no immediate decision was taken. However, attendance at the next meeting rose dramatically to forty-eight, including militant revolutionaries such as Colonels Harrison, Ewer, Pride and Tomlinson.[9]

Held at the Bull-head Tavern in St Albans, the meeting culminated in the adoption of Ireton's *Remonstrance* with its implicit call for capital punishment on the king. Ireton was assisted by events in Westminster. Parliamentary appeasement of the king brought almost all the officers around to Ireton's way of thinking within the next two days.[10]

In London, the Leveller leaders were already meeting with a group of 'gentleman Independents' at the Nag's Head Tavern to discuss strategy. Before proceeding they resolved to speak with 'the steer-man' of the army himself, so they rode to Windsor and confronted Ireton along with several other officers at the Garter Inn. There was a loud argument over liberty of conscience, and whether Parliament should have the power to punish where no visible law is transgressed. Ireton would not budge on either point. The second one would become crucial if Parliament proceeded to a trial of the king. To break the impasse, John Lilburne proposed a committee of sixteen, representing the four parties equally: Levellers, army, London Independents, and the 'honest party' (meaning reliable revolutionaries) in Parliament. Because of the army's haste to get to London and purge the House of Commons, the committee did little before December.[11]

The Leveller intervention had its desired impact. The demand that the king be brought to trial was not watered down, but phrases directly offensive to the Levellers were removed; the 11 September petition was endorsed; and a new constitution based on an Agreement of the People was proposed. According to Fairfax the *Remonstrance* was approved unanimously.[12]

The army's manifesto was laid before the House of Commons on Monday 20 November. It took the clerk four hours to read its 25,000 words. Once finished, the radicals were on their feet moving a vote of thanks to the army. Their opponents were almost as quick to inveigh against the army's 'insolency'. The *Remonstrance* was put aside for a week. Stung by the Commons' refusal to accept their blueprint for settlement, the officers, who had been hovering all day at the door, chased the hostile MPs down the stairs, threatening that if the *Remonstrance* was not 'debated out of hand . . . the House might take what followed'.[13]

The *Remonstrance* was the masterplan for the army's actions in December 1648 and January 1649, and it furnishes the chief theoretical justification for their coup d'état. It therefore merits close attention.[14]

More than any of his contemporaries, Ireton 'saw the need to strike a balance between natural and positive law, between the demands of *salus populi* and the constraints of the existing constitution, between necessity and the need for agreements'.[15] Accordingly, the *Remonstrance* opened with an appeal to the principle that the public safety is the highest law. It then reminded the MPs of their Vote of No Addresses passed the previous January, which had united the parliamentary side, enabling it to wage a successful war against the king. Why then had Parliament provoked division among its own supporters, and given aid and comfort to the enemy by reopening negotiations when the king had been utterly defeated on the battlefield?

Instead of chasing the will-o'-the-wisp of reconciliation with the king, Parliament should be upholding the public interest. The present political system should be replaced by a 'supreme council or parliament' elected frequently 'with as much equality as may be'. This council should have exclusive responsibility for 'making laws . . . war or peace, the safety and welfare of the people, and all civil things whatsoever.'[16] It would have the sole right to define the public interest, and call offenders to account, even if they had broken no existing law: 'And if they find the offence, though not particularly provided against by particular laws, yet against the general law of reason or nations and the vindication of the public interest to require justice; . . . in such case no person whatsoever may be exempt from . . . punishment.'[17]

The king's great crime had been breaking his covenant to protect the people's rights and liberties. He had thereby absolved the people from their covenant with him.[18] More to the point, if the king, having been defeated in his attempts to overthrow the public interest, should resume that struggle, causing bloodshed and desolation, 'we may justly say he is guilty of all the innocent blood spilt thereby'.[19] In such a case the wrath of God cannot be appeased unless judgement is executed against him.

In a startling admission of the king's popularity, the *Remonstrance* signalled the danger of permitting him to return to London: 'The king comes in with the reputation among the people of having long graciously sought peace'. Worse still, should the re-enthroned king threaten a new war, the people 'will surely be more apt to join unanimously with him or let him have what he will, that there may be no war, than join with [Parliament] to maintain another war'.[20] To sum up, the king had committed treason against his people and must be brought to judgement for his crimes. Negotiating with this tyrant would be the height of folly, both because of his untrustworthiness and his popularity.

Pride's Purge

Convinced that Parliament had no intention of listening to their opinions, and that the king would shortly be brought to London amidst popular rejoicing, the officers took emergency action to avert political catastrophe. Cromwell wrote to the king's gaoler, Colonel Hammond, cautioning him to 'beware of men', and labelling the king 'this man against whom the Lord hath witnessed'.[21]

When Hammond remained unconvinced, the grandees ordered him to come to army headquarters, leaving Major Edmund Rolphe and two others in charge of the king. They dispatched another two trusty officers, Lieutenant-Colonel Ralph Cobbett and Captain John Merriman, to take Charles into custody. Despite his later denials (see below, pp. 151–2), Fairfax continued to go along with the momentum of revolution. Because of Parliament's insulting treatment of its manifesto, he wrote, the army was coming to London 'attending and acting the providence of God for the gaining of such ends as we have proposed in our . . . *Remonstrance*'.[22]

The officers now girded their loins for a climactic struggle. Their initial intention was to dissolve Parliament by force, but their parliamentary friends persuaded them only to purge it. Lord Grey of Groby, a radical parliamentary friend of the New Model, visited St Albans on 23 November, probably in order to advise about the list of MPs slated for exclusion.[23]

On the 25th, the army shifted its headquarters from St Albans to Windsor, where Ireton had been living since late September. The grandees now found themselves in one of the strongest castles in England, situated on the edge of the Thames, and perched atop a substantial arsenal. It constituted an ideal prison in which to guard the king.

At once the grandees wrote to every regiment, informing it of Parliament's inaction over the *Remonstrance*, and suggesting a letter-writing campaign to reassure Fairfax of its support. A high-level steering committee was named 'to consider of such things as may be of concernment for the present affairs, and to make transaction thereof'. The militant character of the committee points to Ireton's control of the army's political strategy.[24]

The day after their arrival at Windsor, the grandees convened a prayer meeting. Fairfax's officers were never more politically dangerous than when they wrestled with God. For eight hours they 'sought God earnestly for a blessing upon their councils and to direct them in the way they should walk'. Uppermost in many minds was the question: were they right to challenge 'visible authority'? But since the purpose of the day was 'only to wait upon God for his direction', that debate was suppressed.[25]

Fortified by prayer, the officers returned to politics on Tuesday the 28th. They agreed to advance on Parliament and quarter in or about the City. Ireton, Constable, Tomlinson, Barkstead, Kelsey and Packer were selected as the army's nominees, four of whom were to sit on the committee of sixteen charged with drafting a new version of the *Agreement of the People*.[26]

On 30 November the Commons again refused to debate the *Remonstrance*. The same day the army hinted that it would replace them by 'a more orderly and equal judicature of men in a just Representative according to our *Remonstrance*'. They announced that they would shortly occupy London, 'there to follow Providence as God shall clear our way'. The next day, 7,000 troops mustered in Hyde Park, and marched to Westminster. The City was ordered to hurry up and pay its assessment arrears, or else have soldiers quartered within its walls.[27]

While the City trembled, and the Commons majority continued their defiance, the regiments took up their positions in Westminster. A number of officers with their parliamentary allies occupied Whitehall Palace.[28]

As late as 4 December the Council of Officers had still not decided exactly what to do with Parliament. They continued to cherish the unrealistic hope that the House of Commons would purge itself of 'corrupt and apostatised members'. Meanwhile, on the bitterly cold night of 30 November, amidst high winds and sheets of falling rain, a New Model detachment arrived at Carisbrooke Castle, and awakened Charles with a loud knocking on his bedroom door. Before he could get out of bed several officers rushed into his chamber and ordered him to get ready for removal to Hurst Castle. Charles asked Lieutenant-Colonel Cobbett whether his instructions were from Parliament or the general of the army. Cobbett told him they were from neither. In reality they were from Ireton.[29]

When word of this reached Westminster on 4 December, the Commons moved 'that the removal of the king . . . was without the knowledge or consent of this House'.[30] By this time night had fallen, yet they still had to deal with the main item on their agenda: the king's answer to their propositions at the treaty of Newport the previous September. Not till 8 a.m. on the 5th, crushed with fatigue, did they approve the resolution that the king's answer was 'a ground . . . for the settlement of the peace of the kingdom'.[31]

The army reacted swiftly to this snubbing of its *Remonstrance*. The City's trained bands were ordered to hand over the guarding of Parliament to Colonel Rich's horse and Colonel Pride's foot regiments. The officers for their part now prepared to purge the House. Between eighty and ninety MPs were marked out for arrest. Ireton then went back to headquarters to inform Fairfax 'of the necessity of this extraordinary way of proceeding'.[32]

Which individuals hammered out the details of the purge? We can be sure that they included Ireton and Edmund Ludlow. Harrison, who was at the centre of affairs during this period, was probably another, while Sir William Constable, the most senior member of the Council of Officers' steering committee, may have been the fourth officer. The MPs, in addition to Ludlow, were very likely Lord Grey of Groby, who stood at Colonel Pride's elbow the next morning to identify his colleagues, and radical war-party MP Cornelius Holland.[33]

The regiments were on duty at seven o'clock on the morning of 6 December. Standing in the lobby of the House of Commons, Colonel Pride, assisted by one of the doorkeepers and Lord Grey of Groby, arrested those

MPs on the committee's list who were brave or unlucky enough to turn up that morning. Forty-one were seized, while many more, hearing what was afoot, stayed away.[34]

A few MPs obtained an audience with Fairfax. His vague answers to their pointed questions are eloquent testimony to his anguished confusion at being thrust into the centre of an affair not of his making. He put off the MPs with a statement signed by the army secretary John Rushworth. It demanded that that the eleven members whose impeachment was launched in June 1647 (see above, pp. 82–3) should at once be brought to trial, and Major-General Richard Browne, sheriff of London, should be added to their number on account of his role in inviting the Scots to invade England the previous summer. An additional ninety or more MPs who opposed the vote declaring the Scots enemies should be excluded from the House. The officers hoped the House would then proceed to 'the execution of justice, to set a short period to your own power, [and] to provide for a speedy succession of equal Representatives according to our late *Remonstrance*'.[35]

Later that day Oliver Cromwell arrived from the north and lodged himself in one of the king's bedrooms in Whitehall. About the purge he commented that 'he had not been acquainted with this design; yet since it was done, he was glad of it, and would endeavour to maintain it'.[36] This and other enigmatic statements by Cromwell have given rise to a variety of interpretations of his role in the events leading up to the trial and execution of the king. When did he make up his mind that the king must die? Why did he stay in the north during the critical months from September to December, when the most far-reaching decisions were being taken at army headquarters? Was he a moderate or a revolutionary?

The first thing to note is that Cromwell kept open his lines of communication with both radicals and moderates. When Lilburne came north in September the two men met, and they stayed in touch with each other throughout the autumn. Cromwell gave his implicit support to the Levellers' 'large petition' of 11 September. He also advised on the negotiations over the *Agreement of the People*. In his letter to the king's gaoler Colonel Robert Hammond, he made a gesture of reconciliation by reassuring Hammond that a peaceful settlement was desirable, but that 'peace is only good when we receive it out of our Father's hand . . . War is good when led to by our Father.' Light is shed on these enigmatic words by the answer Cromwell sent to Lilburne when he asked if Cromwell agreed that the sole end of the Civil Wars was to establish the people's rights and freedoms under a just government, The Independents, who were negotiating with the Levellers at the Nag's Head Tavern in London, told the Levellers that the army's desire was 'to cut off the king's head . . . and force and thoroughly purge, if not dissolve the Parliament'. Two weeks later, Cromwell wrote a covering letter to Fairfax, commending his regiment's pro-Leveller petition. He added, 'I find . . . in them all a very great zeal to have impartial justice done upon offenders; and . . . I do . . . from my heart, concur with them'. When the army presented its *Remonstrance* to the House of Commons on 20 November, Cromwell wrote to Hammond commending it: the people of God could not expect any good from Charles Stuart.[37]

On 28 November, Fairfax wrote to Cromwell instructing him to come to headquarters soon in order to help with 'the very great business now in agitation'. Cromwell left almost immediately, transferring command of the north to Major-General John Lambert.[38]

The allegation that Cromwell stayed in the north because his mind was not made up about purging Parliament and trying the king for capital crimes, that he loitered after being ordered southward by Fairfax, that he deliberately arrived in the capital after the dirty work had been done by his friends and subordinates, does not stand up. He had been at the meeting of the army officers on the eve of the Second Civil War that had branded Charles 'a Man of Blood', and despite his distance from the capital in the autumn of 1648 he continued to be known as Charles's greatest adversary. The north was a challenging military assignment. He was there to direct military operations in the last major theatre of the Second Civil War. Equally important was the duty of organising Scotland and the north politically. It is likely, too, that Cromwell kept in close touch with his son-in-law Henry Ireton about political developments at army headquarters and at Westminster, although no letters between them survive. His statement on the evening of 6 December that he was not acquainted with the plans for Pride's Purge does not disprove this assumption. All along Ireton had hoped for a dissolution or a voluntary separation of the minority in the Commons from the 'corrupt' majority. Only when these hopes were disappointed on the morning of 5 December did Ireton and the grandees finally agree to the purge that their parliamentary friends had been insisting on for over a week.[39]

Cromwell's political behaviour was of a piece before and after his arrival in London. He supported the release of sixteen of the purged MPs, not because he was a 'softliner', but because he knew the importance of having as many MPs as possible backing the king's trial. More significant than

Cromwell's solemn pretence of 'join[ing] counsels for the public good' was his lolling on one of the king's rich beds during an interview with Bulstrode Whitelocke and Sir Thomas Widdrington.[40]

The Agreement of the People *and the Whitehall Debates*

Between December and the end of January two great dramas were choreographed for the political stage; one was thwarted, the other was brought successfully to its climax. They were, first, the hammering out of a new constitution and, second, the overthrow and beheading of the king.

After Lilburne had secured the army's assent to a committee of sixteen to re-draft an *Agreement of the People*, little progress was made before Pride's Purge. But once the army was in town it was easy for the sixteen to get together, and so several meetings were held at Whitehall. The Levellers found it hard to bring Ireton to their way of thinking on two issues: liberty of conscience, and whether Parliament had the right to punish for acts that were not against the law. It was 'a long and tedious tug', the meetings sometimes lasting through the night. To Lilburne, Ireton was 'very angry and lordly', and we may imagine what Ireton thought of his long-winded, conceited adversary. At the end of the week the draft was ready for submission to the Council of Officers. That it was only a draft is proved by the fact that none of the committee of sixteen or their clergy supporters made any objection when the officers proceeded to subject the *Agreement* to meticulous scrutiny.[41]

By early December the officers had already met several times and approved most of the *Agreement*. The great stumbling block was religion. They debated the subject for five days, in addition to several more days spent in committee meetings between 14 December and 13 January. At least 160 officers and civilians (including over thirty clergy) spoke, served on committees or attended the debates on the *Agreement*. All participants, including the recording secretary William Clarke and his assistants, seemed to share the conviction that they were taking part in deliberations of the highest historical importance. They were sure that they had been handed an unrepeatable opportunity to shape the political and spiritual destiny of their country.

The document on the table before them assumed the abolition of monarchy and House of Lords. It stipulated that the Long Parliament would dissolve on or before the last day of April 1649. Future parliaments – 'representatives' – would consist of 300 members chosen according to a radically redrawn electoral map reflecting up-to-date demographic realities.

Eligible electors would be male householders assessed for poor relief who were not royalists, servants or wage-earners, and who had signed the *Agreement*. At the heart of the *Agreement* was a list of powers reserved by the people to themselves. The Representative would wield no power over religion, no power to conscript for military service, no power to question people for their actions during the Civil War, no power to violate the principle of equality before the law, and no power to punish in the absence of an existing law. The *Agreement* also abolished the excise, imprisonment for debt, capital punishment (except for murder), and tithes.[42]

On 14 December a room in Whitehall became the scene of a momentous debate on freedom of conscience. Attended by sixty-eight officers, radical clergy and a sprinkling of Levellers and Independents, the debate produced classic statements of the case for unfettered religious freedom, and the contrary case for the magistrate's exercising control in the interest of public peace and order. It produced unanswerable appeals to principle that were countered by equally unanswerable appeals to political reality. The fruit of the debate was victory for neither side, but a genuine compromise.[43]

Some lower officers had already underlined their attachment to liberty of conscience in their published *Articles and Charges* of 8 December, in which they begged Fairfax not to permit the consciences of men to be cruelly shipwrecked. On 14 December these officers and their civilian supporters went on the offensive. They had already published an unauthorised statement endorsing the whole Leveller programme and promising not to disband until it had been implemented.[44]

The debate opened with several speakers defending liberty of conscience. It was left to Ireton to present a trenchant counter-argument against absolute religious liberty. Refuting the Leveller John Wildman's statement that the Civil War had been about the power of the magistrate, he reminded his hearers that the issue had been about whether only the king should exercise that power. If all that mattered was liberty, then there was no need for a commonwealth in the first place. But peace also mattered, so the question must be, what powers did the magistrate need in order to preserve civil peace? Ireton made a further telling point. If the *Agreement* was meant to embrace as many of the well-affected people as possible, it should contain no clause that would prevent such people from signing it. The reserve on religion, which denied all power to the magistrate, was such a clause.[45] Colonel Whalley reminded his listeners that the reserve on religion had already divided the army. Think how it would divide the kingdom. What was the sense of imposing liberty upon the people against their will? 'How can we term that an *Agreement of the People* which is neither an agreement of the major part of the people, and truly for anything I can perceive, not an agreement of the major part of the honest party of the kingdom?'[46] Sir Hardress Waller and Hugh Peters joined Whalley in speaking up for moderation.

Captain John Clarke of Skippon's regiment urged that the army must strike while the iron was hot. At this historic moment they had an unrepeatable opportunity to bring about fundamental change. The army was especially qualified for the task, since it had for three years 'been a shelter to honest people that had otherwise been hammered to dust'.[47]

Ireton, who was at all times animated by the vision of a godly commonwealth, would have nothing to do with the religious libertarianism of the radicals. It had, he insisted, been the magistrate's duty to restrain sin in ancient times, and that duty continued in the Christian era.[48] After several hours of debate Fairfax, perhaps feeling unwell, vacated the chair.[49]

Ireton's frequent and lengthy interventions show that he took the *Agreement* seriously. If the debate had been merely a sop to the radicals, a 'children's rattle' to distract them while the grandees got on with the more serious business of cutting off the king's head, why did the commissary-general spend so much time and intellectual energy trying to make sure that the *Agreement* said what he wanted it to say? The record contradicts Lilburne's accusation that Ireton behaved like 'an absolute king, if not an emperor, against whose will no man must dispute'.[50] Yet his stubbornness paid off. The revised version of the *Agreement* contained an article (no. 9) that reflected Ireton's thinking, with the stipulation that Christianity would be 'held forth and recommended, as the public profession in this nation'. A preaching ministry would be maintained out of the public Treasury – not by tithes. Featuring limited toleration and a loosely structured national church, this revised – or officers' – *Agreement* foreshadowed the Cromwellian church of the 1650s.

Nothing else in the *Agreement* provoked as much debate. The second reserve, prohibiting military conscription, was passed on 16 December. The original reserve had been absolute, but now only conscription for foreign service was prohibited.[51]

On 18 December there was a horrified royalist witness to the day's proceedings. The diarist John Evelyn, unable to restrain his curiosity about the debate that was currently the talk of the town, donned a disguise and smuggled himself into the officers' meeting room. The draft *Agreement* lay before them in the form of a large scroll, with Ireton in the chair, Fairfax being absent that day. Evelyn was shocked to see such 'young, raw and ill-spoken men' arguing constitutional law. He was certain that the disrespectful, free-wheeling manner of the lower officers was nothing but 'disorder and irreverence', while Ireton practised 'palpable cozenage [deception]' in the way he drove the business on.[52]

Again the discussion centred on the heart of the *Agreement*: the reserved powers. The third reserve – that no one except royalists and those who had handled public money should be questioned for their actions in the Civil Wars, passed without dissent.[53] The fourth reserve, guaranteeing equality before the law and implicitly attacking the House of Lords, was 'laid aside'; it would mysteriously reappear when the officers brought the *Agreement* to the House of Commons on 20 January. The fifth reserve, similar in content, was also set aside, and did not reappear in the final version presented to Parliament. Although none is recorded, there must have been intense debate on the sixth reserve: 'That the Representatives intermeddle not with the execution of laws, nor give judgement upon any man's person or estate where no law hath been before provided.' Ireton was evidently worried that this reserve might be used to block the trial of the king, but the attempt to delete the sixth reserve was narrowly defeated. This was a victory for the lower officers against the grandees.[54]

The 19 December was kept as a day of humiliation, and on the 21st the council reassembled to address the thorny question of how to define the sovereign powers of the Representative, apart from those that were explicitly reserved to the people. In a stunning endorsement of Leveller libertarianism, the officers voted that while the Representative should have 'highest and final judgement concerning all natural and civil things', it should have no jurisdiction over moral questions. Again the grandees were voted down by the more numerous junior officers.[55]

The rest of the *Agreement* was agreed to without dissent. On 6 January the termination of the present Parliament was debated. Ireton argued that the date for Parliament's dissolution – 30 April 1649 – should be embedded in the text of the *Agreement*. His reasoning showed that for him the *Agreement* was a key pillar of the constitution that would be adopted following the abolition of monarchy. He perceived that because the majority of people still favoured the king, the only hope of preventing the return of monarchy after the soldiers laid down their arms was through the adoption of the *Agreement*.[56]

It is only a slight exaggeration to say that the *Agreement of the People* would have ushered in something closer to a dictatorship of the godly than a golden age of democracy. True, electoral boundaries would have been redrawn on the principle of representation by population. The vote would have been extended to male householders. But it would have been denied to all enemies of the revolutionary regime. The Levellers would have barred all who refused to sign the *Agreement*. In the officers' version, this restriction was relaxed, but in both versions the vote was withheld for seven years from those who had supported the king or who opposed the *Agreement*. The qualifications for election to the new Representative were far more stringent. Excluded from the first and second representatives were any who had aided the king, signed the London Engagement of the summer of 1647 calling for a personal treaty with the king, petitioned for a truce with the Scottish invaders in the summer of 1648, or cooperated in any way with the rebels in the Second Civil War. Bearing in mind the extensive support enjoyed by the royalists in 1648, we can appreciate that these provisions, combined with the exclusion of servants and wage-earners, would have disenfranchised not only all women, but much of the adult male population of England for several years, and prevented all but a minority from standing for election. These facts have been overlooked by most historians, but they were not missed at the time. Unfriendly critics attacked the *Agreement* for its restrictiveness, while friends of the Levellers, such as the editor of *The Moderate*, recognised that the *Agreement* would initially disenfranchise a large segment of the people.[57]

A delegation of officers led by Lieutenant-General Thomas Hammond brought the finished version of the *Agreement*, inscribed on parchment, to the Commons on 20 January 1649. After listening to Hammond, the Commons ordered it printed. The Commons promised to consider it as soon as 'the present weighty and urgent affairs will permit'. They never did, and the officers never reminded them of their promise. Why did the officers acquiesce in the neglect of the *Agreement*? Their immediate reason may have been their preoccupation with the king's trial. It was also undeniable that hardly anyone was passionately attached to the *Agreement*. Even the Levellers were less concerned with government structures than with decentralising authority and liberalising the laws. The *Agreement* evoked little public support from the quarters that might have been expected to become zealous for it. The gathered churches were more anxious to establish the reign of Christ than fashion a new constitution. As for the purged Parliament, apart from an understandable reluctance to sign its own death warrant, many of the members were convinced, when they gauged the unpopularity of the king's trial, that the time was not ripe for a radical transformation of the machinery of government. Nor was there any noticeable groundswell of support from the army rank and file. The most insistent pressure for the *Agreement* came from the lower officers. Yet their repeated triumphs in the Council of Officers over Ireton and the grandees may have caused the latter to become cool towards the *Agreement,* which up to that moment they had taken so seriously. Whatever the case, when the Commons kicked the *Agreement* into the long grass, it was soon forgotten by everyone except John Lilburne.[58]

The Trial of Charles I

From Pride's Purge onwards the army kept a tight grip on Parliament, the City of London and the king. After releasing two of the arrested MPs, Sir Thomas Fairfax had the remaining thirty-nine carted off in coaches to a nearby alehouse known as Hell.[59]

Many MPs stayed away from the House that day, and for many days to come. A radical remnant of forty or fifty – the 'fierce party' – continued to sit, and started undoing Parliament's work of the previous four months. Steps were also taken to bring in the last six months' assessment for the army, now greatly in arrears.[60]

The boycott of the House by large numbers of moderate MPs caused attendance to dip perilously close to the quorum of forty, and there were often delays in beginning the sittings. On 14, 19 and 20 December Colonel Pride allowed a number of the excluded MPs to re-enter the House. The House asked Fairfax to explain the exclusion of MPs. He temporised, but had sixteen of the imprisoned members brought to him for an interview. They were kept waiting for two or three hours, until Ireton, Whalley and Rich emerged to tell them that Fairfax had suddenly fallen ill and could not see them. However, they were told they were free to go, provided they stayed out of trouble. The release of imprisoned MPs was an olive branch extended to moderates. The officers did it because they saw the need to rally as much support as possible to their cause, or at least to neutralise opposition to it.[61]

That is why Cromwell devoted time to meetings with moderate lawyer-MPs Bulstrode Whitelocke and Sir Thomas Widdrington. Three times in late December he had lengthy chats with the two men in which he asked them to draw up proposals for the settlement of the kingdom. Flattered by the attention lavished on them, Whitelocke and Widdrington set to work at once. They believed, as Cromwell intended they should, that they were helping keep the army from falling into the hands of extremists. His agenda was different: to give them a feeling of importance and to keep them harmlessly busy while the army got on with eliminating the king. Nothing more was heard of Whitelocke's and Widdrington's proposals. More important for Cromwell were his several meetings with the duke of Hamilton in his prison cell at Windsor Castle. The object was to induce him to confess that he had been invited by the king himself to invade England the previous summer. Such a confession would have made for an open-and-shut case for the king's treason against his own people. Had Cromwell not already made up his mind about the king's trial, it is unlikely that he would have gone to all this trouble.[62]

The few peers who were amenable to persuasion were also courted. Not only were their clients in the Commons, such as Sir Benjamin Rudyerd and Nathaniel Fiennes released, but Michael Oldisworth, the patronage secretary of Philip Herbert, fourth earl of Pembroke, even though he was an active promoter of the treaty of Newport, was left off the list of MPs to be imprisoned. Around the same time, four peers visited Fairfax to assure him of their support of the army's position with respect to the House of Lords. On 15 December a delegation of senior army officers waited on the earl of Warwick at Warwick House upon his return from sea. They were relieved when Warwick and his officers threw their weight behind the purge. Yet he later clarified that he was not in favour of trying the king, much less executing him. On 18 December, Pembroke was appointed constable of Windsor Castle, making him officially the king's gaoler. On 19 December the earl of Denbigh led a delegation, which included the earls of Pembroke, Salisbury and Northumberland, to parley with the Council of Officers. A few days later when the second earl of Middlesex dumped a full chamber pot onto the heads of some of Colonel Rich's troopers in Friday Street, he was brought before the Council of Officers but let off with just a warning.[63]

All the time they were conciliating or neutralising moderates, the grandees tightened their grip on the king and on their enemies in Parliament and in the City. Hugh Peters's statement that the army would not prove so unreasonable as some men imagined may have been designed to lull the fears of moderates, or falsely raise the hopes of royalists. Certainly royalists welcomed any crumb of hope that fed their craving to believe that the army was divided, and that Cromwell was working to save the king's life. It was wishful thinking. On 15 December the officers ordered Charles brought from Hurst Castle to Windsor.[64]

Around the same time several regiments marched into London, and demanded the City's £40,000 in overdue assessment. The Common Council tried to appease the soldiers with a hundred barrels of 'good strong beer' and two cartloads of the best bread, butter and cheese, but the officers no longer had patience for such gestures. Tired of seeing their men sleep on bare boards, they wheeled artillery into position at Blackfriars, while companies of foot occupied St Martin's Church near Ludgate, St Paul's Cathedral, Cheapside, Lombard Street, and the heart of the City. Colonels Richard Deane and John Hewson raided the treasuries at Goldsmiths', Weavers' and Haberdashers' Halls. In St Paul's, the men of Skippon's foot regiment warmed themselves at great fires on the cathedral floor, fuelled by carved timber, scaffolding and other materials which they found at hand. When the City fathers implored Fairfax, who was enjoying a brief spell of good health, to remove the troops, he sardonically informed them that the continued presence of his troops would facilitate the work of collection.[65]

Seeing the approaching political climax, London Presbyterian ministers held protest meetings at the beginning of January, accompanied by prayer and fasting. Alert to the power of these spiritual practices, Cromwell, Ireton and Peters went about the City visiting the ministers and trying to subdue them with threats of military force. Prayer rose in a crescendo on both sides. The soldiers were kept continually on their knees except when they were on duty. Their religious exercises wound them up to a high pitch of tension and fortified them against the hatred of the urban population. Hugh Peters's rhetoric contributed more than a little to stiffening the soldiers' and officers' conviction of their own righteousness.[66]

While those MPs who promised not to cause trouble were let go, others thought to be still dangerous were placed under closer confinement. In early January the Council of Officers issued a lengthy indictment of them and nine others as a danger to the Commonwealth.[67]

The army now felt confident enough to move against the king. The municipal elections of 21 December had produced a revolutionary Common Council dominated by radical militia officers who backed the army to the hilt. The purged Commons, for its part, had annulled all the previous year's votes to which the army objected, and resolved to resurrect the trials of the eleven members impeached by the army. A day or two before Christmas the army was emboldened to publish its charge against the king and call for his trial. He had, they alleged, devoured the people's liberties, flouted Parliament and waged war against the kingdom, reducing it to desolation. Consequently, 'this capital and grand offender and author of our troubles, the person of the king, . . . is guilty of all the trouble, loss, hazard and expense of the blood and mischiefs that have happened by the late wars in this kingdom'.[68]

Marching in step with the army, the purged Commons voted to consider precisely 'how to proceed in a way of justice against the king and other capital offenders'. A large committee was appointed to look into the question. Besides Philip Skippon, Henry Marten and the usual array of radicals, Bulstrode Whitelocke and Sir Thomas Widdrington were named, because of their legal expertise.[69] Cromwell's omission from the committee can only have been because at this juncture he judged that he was needed for more sensitive political work than debating the legal ins and outs of the king's trial.

On 23 December the king arrived at Windsor in drenching rain. Once he was lodged there they took the greatest care to ensure that he did not escape. Troops from Harrison's horse regiment, which had escorted the king to Windsor, were stationed at the castle. The foot guards that were placed in and about the rooms where the king and his servants were kept were instructed to read all his letters and be present at all his conversations. While he was being toasted in the town's taverns, preparations were going ahead rapidly to try him. There was debate in both the army and the House of Commons: should he be executed or merely deposed? Should he be replaced by one of his children, or should there be no king at all? The Council of Officers devoted precious time on two separate days to hearing and cross-examining a prophetess from Abingdon. Elizabeth Poole's vision revealed that the army could try, and even depose the king, but they ought not to shed his blood. After listening respectfully to her words, several militant officers, led by Ireton, wanted to know how she could prove that her vision was from God. No one expressed hostility towards this remarkable woman, while senior officers like Harrison, Ireton and Rich made a point of showing her respect. Her views and her piety corresponded closely to those of Fairfax, but neither he nor Cromwell attended either session where she spoke.[70]

In the Commons the debate on whether to try the king for his life was launched the day after Christmas. Cromwell rose and spoke delphically: 'if any man whatsoever had carried on this design of deposing the king and disinheriting his posterity, or if any had yet such a design, he should be the greatest traitor and rebel in the world. But since the providence of God hath cast this upon us, I cannot but submit to providence, though I am not yet provided to give you my advice.'[71]

Public business was suspended on the 27th for the monthly fast day. MPs and officers spent most of it in St Margaret's Church, Westminster. On the 28th the charge against the king was read on the floor of the House. It was a comprehensive indictment, broadly similar to the one published by the army four days earlier.[72]

The ordinance for erecting a High Court of Justice to try the king was ready and was sent to the Lords. The peers threw it out, as they did the Commons resolution that 'by the fundamental laws of this kingdom it is treason in the king of England to levy war against the parliament and kingdom of England'. The Commons retaliated by repassing their motions, and adding that the people were 'under God, the original of all just power', that the Commons, as representatives of the people, possessed supreme power, and that whatever they decided had the force of law, even without the assent of king or lords.[73]

Efforts to ensure that the High Court was broadly representative of the social and legal elite of England were a failure. None of the half-dozen peers named, nor any of the lord chief justices, would attend a single sitting. The business of the court was driven on by a cabal of army officers and revolutionary MPs. Twenty-nine of the 135 commissioners were serving army officers; several of them however would have a spotty attendance record and, when the time came, would decline to sign the death warrant. Fairfax, whose attendance would have been most highly prized, came only to the first meeting (on 8 January), and would not even sit down. Skippon, although he was in London, attended few sittings, as did Colonels Lambert, Overton, Sidney, Tomlinson, Ingoldsby and Fenwick. Some had legitimate reasons for their absence. Colonel Tomlinson was preoccupied with guarding the king. Overton, as governor of Hull, was responsible for the second greatest arsenal in the kingdom. Algernon Sidney, governor of Dover, attended the court's planning meetings, but threw cold water on the proceedings, insisting that the king could be tried by no court, and no one could be tried by *this* court. This provoked Cromwell's crushing riposte: 'I tell you, we will cut off his head with the crown upon it.'[74] John Disbrowe, governor of Yarmouth, could have attended had he wished. So too could Ingoldsby, governor of Oxford, though he did sign the king's death warrant.

In the twelve days before the trial opened, the commissioners were busy with a host of questions. Assuming that Charles was to be found guilty, would he be sentenced to death or merely deposed? If condemned to die, where would the scaffold be erected? Who would do the beheading? How would they prevent a riot or a rescue attempt? While the commissioners grappled with these and other questions that had no precedent they must have been discouraged by the chronic absence of nearly half their number. A knot of men who had banished all their doubts hounded the rest and made them stick to their work. Some of them were soldiers (Cromwell, Ireton and Harrison); some were parliamentarians (Henry Marten, Thomas Scot, Viscount Saye, John Lisle); and one was the redoubtable Hugh Peters, who, alternating between bouts of manic frenzy and melancholic sickness, dashed to and fro between Westminster and the City, inciting his colleagues and confuting his foes.[75]

On 13 January it was decided that the trial would be held in Westminster Hall, the great mediaeval edifice adjacent to the House of Commons where the high courts held their sittings. Colonel Francis Hacker and a company of guards would secure the king, while a large contingent of soldiers under Lieutenant-Colonel Daniel Axtell would be stationed between the king and the crowd to prevent a disturbance.

As the king's life approached its dénouement, royalists were paralysed with disbelief at what they witnessed. The London Presbyterian clergy demanded and got a meeting with the officers to dispute the legality of the trial. Several of them trudged to Fairfax's lodgings on the afternoon of 11 January. The following week, forty-seven of them publicly exhorted the army to search its heart and repent before it was too late. The army's defenders made up for the smallness of their numbers by the forcefulness of their arguments. John Goodwin set the tone with a vigorous address to the Council of War, buttressing the case for prosecuting the 'warfare of heaven' with texts scriptural and classical. Cromwell, Ireton and Peters worked relentlessly to confound the opponents of regicide. The recently elected Common Council of London, under the leadership of Colonel Robert Tichborne, also played a part in silencing the disaffected. On 15 January it framed a petition 'against all grand and capital actors in the late war against the Parliament'. There was also pressure from the forces outside London for the purged Commons and the Council of Officers not to falter in their resolve.[76]

Besides taming their opponents, the grandees also had to curb the zeal of those who wanted the instant enactment of the full revolutionary agenda. Cromwell, conscious of the debt of gratitude he owed the Saye–Wharton group for past support, opposed the radical attempt to abolish the House of Lords before the king was out of the way. Another step towards the appeasement of moderates was the release of the angry Presbyterian William Prynne and most of the other imprisoned MPs during the week of 10 January.[77] Their release removed a source of indignation against a flagrant violation of the law, leaving the grandees to get on with another more flagrant one.

A younger group of historians has recently argued that neither the purged Parliament, nor the army, nor the High Court of Justice wanted the king's death. His indictment for treason and other high crimes was a bargaining ploy. It was the intention of his prosecutors that if he showed remorse and 'a full and free yielding', and in particular if he pleaded guilty, he need not die. Regicide was 'the accidental outcome of a trial undertaken to quite opposite ends'.[78]

The new interpreters of the regicide emphasise that powerful forces were arrayed against killing the king: Scotland and Ireland almost unanimously, the great majority of the English public, virtually the whole aristocracy including the entire House of Lords, the vociferous Presbyterian clergy of London, every foreign power that mattered, the navy led by the earl of Warwick, and the great majority of elected MPs. This is why the army grandees held back for so long – in Cromwell's words 'the sons of Zeruiah', meaning criminals too powerful to be punished, were initially too strong for them. That is why, it is alleged, the General Council of the Army voted by a simple majority against the king's execution on 21 December, and on 25 December to spare his life by a margin of six to one if he accepted the terms put to him by the earl of Denbigh. It is also claimed that the grandees made behind-the-scenes approaches to the king in December and early January. They strove unsuccessfully to get Charles to instruct James Butler, marquess of Ormond to call off his projected invasion of England at the head of a Catholic Irish army. At the same time they curried favour with key peers: the earl of Warwick, whom they attended upon his return from his latest naval campaign, and Denbigh, Speaker of the House of Lords. It was only when all attempts at negotiation ran into the brick wall of the king's intransigence that the army grandees and their allies in the purged House of Commons concluded that they had no alternative but to bring him to the block.[79]

Adherents of this interpretation also point to the evidence of dividedness among the officers, to ambiguity in Cromwell's mind, to the fact that none of the army documents – including the *Remonstrance* – explicitly demands the king's death. They point, too, to the many delays in bringing Charles to the scaffold.[80] This protracted, agonising process, almost two months from beginning to end, suggests hesitation, fear and indecision, rather than an iron determination to have the king dead.

Recently, however, a number of scholars have rejected this revisionist interpretation. They have pointed out that the evidence for the Denbigh peace mission is very slender or non-existent, based on a passing comment by the Sieur de Grignon, the French agent in London, who in any case regarded the whole scheme as a typical piece of persiflage perpetrated by Oliver Cromwell. Furthermore, the revisionist interpretation leans heavily on shaky royalist sources which, rather than relaying hard evidence, more often betray wishful thinking – that the General Council of the Army was divided, that it would not be as implacable as people feared, that it voted against bringing the king to the scaffold. There is little evidence from army sources to support these assertions.[81]

As for Cromwell, since the beginning of 1648 he spoke of the king as 'a man whose heart God has hardened'. This could only mean the end of Charles I. Through Colonel Tichborne he told Lilburne that the army was determined to cut off the king's head. He said the same to Algernon Sidney. In contrast to the wishful thinking of the London royalist newsbooks we have the sombre statement of a newswriter to Ormond on 8 January 1649: 'the king's accusers have decided that he will shortly be executed'. This was twelve days before the trial had even begun. It is true that the army officers listened to the prophetess Elizabeth Poole, who advised them not kill the king. But at the end of the day what animated the grandees was 'consternation at Charles's wickedness in defying providence and in defiling the land with innocent blood'. After respectfully considering Poole's testimony, 'they now believed themselves endowed with authority to match the power they had claimed in purging parliament and initiating proceedings against the king. From this point onwards, might and right were indeed well met.'[82]

One group gave no cause for worry in January: the Levellers. Adopting the *Agreement of the People* was not the only action the grandees took to head off trouble from them. They also piloted a bill through Parliament to grant John Lilburne the £3,000 that he had been claiming for almost a decade as damages for his sufferings at the hands of Star Chamber. Because there was no ready cash in the Treasury, Lilburne was advised to recover his money from the sale of timber on the estates of royalist delinquents in his native Durham. He immediately quit the capital and headed north, not to return until after Charles had been beheaded.[83]

On the eve of Charles's trial, the Lords found themselves marginalised; the Presbyterian clergy were fuming but impotent; disaffected MPs had been neutralised then conciliated; the Scots and foreign representatives were politely ignored; the Levellers were quiescent; and the royalists dumb with disbelief. There were still many details of the trial to be thrashed out. Ireton, Cromwell, Harrison and Peters met day and night, sometimes in rooms near Westminster Hall, sometimes in taverns like the Star in Coleman Street, occasionally in Ireton's lodgings in Windsor.[84]

The trial opened on Saturday 20 January. The mild wet weather of autumn had given way to a bitter frost. The week of the trial would witness the freezing-over of the Thames, and a 'horrid tempest of winds' would sweep the metropolis. Just before two o'clock, sixty-eight commissioners formed in procession for their entry into Westminster Hall. When the clerk read the roll-call of commissioners the first name he pronounced was Fairfax's. 'He has more wit than to be here' shouted Lady Fairfax from behind her mask in one of the galleries. Lieutenant-Colonel Axtell turned abruptly in her direction and commanded his men to shoot 'if they speak one word more'. His men's muskets pointing at the gallery produced a sudden hush.[85]

Now the king appeared, tightly escorted by twelve halberdiers. The prosecuting attorney John Cook recited the charge. As king of England, Charles had been 'trusted with a limited power to govern by, and according to, the laws of the land, and not otherwise'. Yet he had engineered 'a wicked design to erect and uphold in himself an unlimited and tyrannical power to rule according to his will, and to overthrow the rights and liberties of the people'. In prosecuting this design, he had 'traitorously and maliciously levied war against the present parliament and the people therein represented'. He was therefore worthy to be impeached as a 'tyrant, traitor and murderer, and a public and implacable enemy to the people of England'. Charles stood up and answered the charge with a question: by what *lawful* authority had he been summoned before them? John Bradshaw, President of the High Court of Justice, only reiterated the substance of the charge and ordered the king to answer 'in the name of the people of England, of which you are *elected* king'. Charles pounced on this piece of novel constitutional theory: 'England was never an elective kingdom, but a hereditary kingdom for near these thousand years.' Moreover, 'I do stand more for the liberty of my people than any here that come to be my pretended judges.' Rattled by the king's unexpected eloquence, Bradshaw quickly brought the proceedings to a halt and ordered the prisoner removed. As if on cue, Axtell's soldiers cried 'Justice! Justice!' A few who were near the king sprinkled gunpowder on their palms, lit it, and blew it into his face. Some spectators joined the cry for 'justice', but others shouted 'God save the king!'[86]

On the next day, Sunday, the commissioners fasted and heard three sermons, two by chaplains from the army. Ioshua Sprigge preached on the text 'He that sheds blood, by man shall his blood be shed'.[87] Hugh Peters took his text from Psalm 149: 'I will bind their kings in chains and their nobles in fetters of iron'. Remarkably, only one other clergyman besides Peters – John Goodwin, minister of the large Independent congregation at St Stephen Coleman Street – had publicly declared his support for the army since its invasion of London in December.

On the afternoon of Monday the 22nd, seventy commissioners assembled as the king was brought in for the second time. Again Charles refused to recognise the court's competence to try him, and again Bradshaw ordered him removed. The third public sitting of the court was held early in the afternoon of Tuesday 23 January. The proceedings were essentially a repetition of the previous day, with the king even more boldly rejecting the commissioners' competence to try him. Amidst the confusion that erupted as the king was hustled away, the court crier shouted out 'God bless the kingdom of England!', striving to drown out those again shouting a shorter slogan: 'God save the king!'[88]

At the end of this episode the commissioners went directly into secret session in the Painted Chamber to deal with their own crisis of self-confidence. Not sure of what to do next, they decided to call witnesses against the king, hoping to rally the waverers. The same night steps were taken to round up notable absentees, chief among them Sir Thomas Fairfax. He was 'baited with fresh dogs . . . to bring him into the hall on the morrow', but he would not budge.[89]

This time marked the low point of Fairfax's public life. A soldier first and a politician second, he had none the less cooperated fully with the army's revolutionary acts until at least December. He was easily the most popular of all the officers, caring deeply for his men's welfare, working tirelessly to keep them properly clothed, equipped and lodged, and writing countless letters demanding the pay that was due to them. He had not shrunk from chairing their revolutionary council from July to October 1647. Willingly he had led invasions of London in August 1647, and again in December 1648. While Cromwell and Ireton assumed a steadily higher political profile Fairfax retained control of appointments and promotions, on occasion vetoing promotions for prominent radicals. No friend to the Levellers, he had also resisted the adoption of the November 1648 *Remonstrance* for as long as he could, yet he made no attempt to prevent Pride's Purge. Nominated to the High Court of Justice, his cameo appearance at the first meeting decidedly enhanced the court's prestige. By failing to insist on having his name removed from the list of commissioners, he compromised his moral authority when the time came to ponder resistance. Perhaps he hoped that their threats to kill the king were only intended to intimidate Charles into unconditional surrender or abdication. Not until the first session in the Painted Chamber did the truth hit home that his comrades were in deadly earnest. His silent withdrawal then signified the collapse of his personal influence among the officers. Torn between their implacable determination and his wife's bitter hostility to the trial, he resigned himself to political impotence.[90]

On Wednesday the 24th, the court held a closed session in the Painted Chamber where the commissioners resolved to sentence Charles to death. Ireton and Harrison were part of the seven-man committee named to draw up the sentence.[91]

At the next public session, in the afternoon of Saturday the 27th, Bradshaw opened his remarks 'in the name of the people of England'. A masked lady in the gallery called out 'Not half, not a quarter of the people of England. Oliver Cromwell is a traitor.' Lieutenant-Colonel Axtell ordered the guards to turn their muskets in her direction. Lady Fairfax – for she it was – was quickly hustled out.[92] Once Bradshaw had completed his remarks Charles was permitted to speak. He had one request: prior to sentencing he wished to address the Lords and Commons in the Painted Chamber.

Bradshaw rejected the king's request, and called upon the clerk to pronounce sentence. The sixty-seven commissioners present then stood up to show their assent. The king was shattered, not so much by the sentence of death, for which he had long prepared himself, as by the characterisation of himself as 'tyrant, traitor and murderer'. He asked to be heard, but Bradshaw refused, and ordered the guards to remove him. His exit was punctuated by Lieutenant-Colonel Axtell's soldiers crying 'Execution! Justice! Execution!'

As he descended the stairs they blew smoke in his face and rolled their pipes in his way to trip him.[93]

Sunday provided a brief pause in the hastening tragedy. It was kept as a fast day by soldiers, clergy and the pious on both sides. At St James's the soldiers were treated to a homiletic extravaganza by Hugh Peters. The grandees were absorbed with a last-minute appeal from the Dutch ambassadors to save the king's life. Early on Monday the 29th, Fairfax summoned a council of war, at which he strove to persuade his comrades to postpone the execution. They turned a deaf ear to their commander-in-chief.[94]

Meanwhile the commissioners had finally approved the time and place of the execution. It was to be outside the Banqueting House in Whitehall, designed by Inigo Jones for Charles at the beginning of his reign. The death warrant had already been drawn up; some commissioners had signed as early as the 26th and 27th. On Monday morning Cromwell stood at the door of the Commons, intending to add to the total. Some MPs slipped by him, but he pursued them into the House, crying, 'those that are gone in shall set their hands, I will have their hands now'. On the same day, the warrant lay on a table in the Painted Chamber, waiting for those who might yet be brought to sign. To break the intolerable tension, Cromwell took the pen and marked up Henry Marten's face, and Marten did the same to Cromwell.[95]

Many commissioners managed to avoid signing. Colonel Tomlinson, the officer in charge of the king, had excused himself from most meetings because of his duties. Other officers who avoided signing were Fairfax, Major-General Skippon, Colonel Lambert, Colonel Fleetwood and Major Disbrowe. There is no need to believe Colonel Richard Ingoldsby's story after the Restoration that Cromwell dragged him to the table, held his hand, and forced him to sign. The firmness of his signature falsifies his claim. By the end of the day eighteen of the fifty-nine signatures belonged to army officers in current service: Oliver Cromwell, Edward Whalley, John Okey, Henry Ireton, Sir Hardress Waller, William Goffe, Thomas Pride, Thomas Harrison, John Hewson, Richard Deane, Adrian Scrope, William Constable, Richard Ingoldsby, John Barkstead, Isaac Ewer, Valentine Wauton, Thomas Horton and Robert Lilburne. Former officers who signed were Sir Michael Livesey, Thomas Mauleverer, John Hutchinson, Owen Rowe, Edmund Ludlow, Henry Marten and John Jones.[96]

Although they numbered fewer than half the signatories, army officers played a pre-eminent role in bringing the king to the scaffold. But on the day of the execution they would be strangely absent.

Charles was escorted from St James's to Whitehall at half past ten on the bitterly cold morning of Tuesday 30 January. His execution did not occur till after two o'clock. Why the delay? There was no trouble finding an executioner. The common hangman, Richard Brandon, may have had scruples about cutting off the king's head, but he was almost certainly one of the two who were on the scaffold. The other was a sergeant in Colonel Hewson's regiment, William Hewlet. A dispute among the officers supervising the proceedings may have held up the execution. No one wanted to sign the order for the actual beheading, so Huncks, Phayre and Hacker appealed to Cromwell, whom they found lying in bed with Colonel Harrison. Cromwell instructed Huncks to write out and sign the order for the execution. Huncks refused. Lieutenant-Colonel Axtell, who had come to the door, berated Huncks for his cowardice, but Huncks was immovable. Impatient at the delay, Cromwell seized pen and paper, scribbled out the order, and handed it to Colonel Hacker, who stooped and signed it.[97]

There was another hold-up: they still needed a law against anyone proclaiming a new king. An emergency bill was read twice, committed during the midday break, then read a third time and passed.[98]

The Dutch ambassadors used the delay to make a last-minute appeal to Fairfax to block the execution. Fairfax had already spent much of the night trying to do what they were now asking. He promised to go directly to the Commons and prevail upon them to postpone the execution, but he shrank from an open confrontation with the officers. The only high-ranking officers whom he might have counted upon were Philip Skippon, major-general of the infantry, and perhaps Colonel Nathaniel Rich.[99] Other opponents of the execution such as Colonels John Lambert and Charles Fleetwood and Major John Disbrowe were stationed far away from London. Arrayed against Fairfax would have been the incomparably abler Cromwell and Ireton, who could count on the almost unanimous backing of the lower officers, and probably most of the rank and file stationed in London. The private soldiers, furious at the king for dragging them through a second civil war and trying to launch a third, impatient at the lack of pay, stirred up by Peters's preaching, and in a foul temper because of the intense cold and lack of decent accommodation, were hardly inclined to support clemency for the 'grand author' of their misery.

While Fairfax did not attempt a coup against his officers on 30 January, he did go and talk to them. Thomas Herbert ran into him in the Long Gallery, coming from Colonel Harrison's apartment, where he had been in prayer or conversation with the other officers. They were willing enough to converse with their commander-in-chief so long as he did not interfere with the events unfolding in the street below. Knowing there was nothing left that he could do, Fairfax allowed himself to be distracted.[100]

Just before two o'clock, Colonel Hacker knocked on the door to summon the king. Together they walked along the corridors and across the Banqueting Hall beneath Rubens's awe-inspiring portrayal of James I's ascent to heaven. Through one of the windows Charles stepped onto the raised scaffold draped in black. Crowded into that small space were Colonels Tomlinson and Hacker, the two executioners (masked and heavily disguised), Bishop William Juxon, Thomas Herbert, several guards and two or three scribes. The leading scribe was the army's secretary William Clarke. Gifted with a canny intuition for memorable historical moments, he and his assistants had already recorded the army's debates at Putney and Whitehall on the franchise, religious liberty and the *Agreement of the People*. Clarke attracted the king's attention on the scaffold. As he pressed closer to catch Charles's last words his cloak brushed against the 'bright execution axe'. Noticing this, Charles twice turned and asked him to 'hurt not the axe that may hurt me'.[101]

Casting his eyes across the sea of faces below him, Charles saw that he was separated from the populace by densely packed ranks of mounted troopers. The adjacent streets were also thick with soldiers. It was unlikely that his words would reach the non-military audience. So he addressed himself to the soldiers and scribes surrounding him on the platform. He proclaimed his innocence and affirmed that he was dying 'a Christian according to the profession of the Church of England'. Then, laying his head upon the block, he was beheaded with one stroke. The second executioner picked up the severed head and displayed it with the traditional words: 'Behold the head of a traitor.' The throng were now hushed, but at the moment the axe fell they had involuntarily given out a deep heart-rending groan, expressive of their horror at the unprecedented act of regicide.[102]

Almost immediately, a troop of horse stationed at Charing Cross swept down Whitehall, while another approached from King Street in the opposite direction. Within minutes the people were scattered and the streets empty.[103]

There is one aspect of the execution that few have remarked on. The officers and MPs directly responsible were not there. The Commons were busy until a few minutes before the beheading, passing a law against proclaiming a new king. The army grandees congregated in Colonel Harrison's apartment at the end of the Long Gallery in Whitehall Palace, where they prayed and conversed. They had to make do without the eloquence of Hugh Peters, who spent the day sick in bed. Colonel Robert Lilburne also retired to his own chamber. The highest-ranking officer to witness the execution was Colonel Tomlinson, who, though he had not signed the warrant, had stood up with the other commissioners to show his approval of the sentence. At the Restoration he would successfully appeal for clemency on the grounds of his civil behaviour towards the king during his last days. Colonel Hacker and Lieutenant-Colonel Axtell, who could not make a similar claim, were not spared.[104]

Bishop Juxon and Thomas Herbert took the king's body back to the palace. On their way they ran into Fairfax in the Long Gallery. To their amazement he enquired 'how the king did', and 'seemed much surprised' to learn that he was already dead. A few seconds later they encountered Cromwell, who drily informed the two men that 'they should have orders for the king's burial speedily'.[105]

The nation was in shock at the king's death. A parliamentary journalist reported that it did not rain on 30 January, 'yet it was a very wet day . . . in and about the City of London by reason of the abundance of affliction that fell from many eyes for the death of the king'.[106] The new rulers acted resolutely to consolidate their power. On 1 February the remnant of the House of Commons, soon to be labelled the 'Rump' by its detractors, decided that no one who had voted on 5 December that the king's offers were a ground for settlement, or had been absent when the vote was given, should be allowed to sit until he had recorded his dissent from that motion. Five days later they voted to abolish the House of Lords as 'useless and dangerous'. On the 7th, the office of king was also eradicated. At the same time, the chief executive body of the previous two years, the Derby House Committee, was replaced by a larger Council of State, with authority inferior only to Parliament. A small committee was asked to draw up a list of nominees for this new council. After a week they submitted a slate including peers and army officers as well as MPs. Some MPs took alarm at the number of active army officers on the slate. At the end of the day two of the most prominent officers – Henry Ireton and Thomas Harrison – were rejected. Of the remaining thirty-nine nominees, six were in active military service: Fairfax, Cromwell, Skippon, Hesilrige, Wauton and Constable. Another seven had served in the war or would do so in the near future: Anthony Stapley, John Hutchinson, Henry Marten, Alexander Popham, William Purefoy, John Jones and Edmund Ludlow. Fully a third of the new council had military associations, but the exclusion of Ireton and Harrison, two of the steersmen of recent events, was a stinging rebuke to their political aspirations.

Only days before, Ireton had sketched the outline of the 'Engagement' that would be required of all members of the Council of State. They were to declare their approval of the High Court of Justice, of the trial and execution of the king, and of the abolition of monarchy and House of Lords. Many balked at giving retroactive approval to illegal acts; by the 19th, twenty-two nominees were still holding out against the Engagement. They included Sidney, Fairfax and the five peers. Cromwell now intervened to bring about a compromise. New members of the council were only required to recognise the republican form of government 'for the future'. Over half the councillors, including Fairfax, continued to hold out against even this modified oath. In order to bring him on side, the revolutionaries let him write his own version of the Engagement in which he uttered no support for what had been done, but merely promised to defend the present government 'without king and House of Peers'.[107]

By mid-February the ship of state appeared to be on a steady course. Officers and MPs accordingly began preparing for the long-deferred invasion of Ireland. It was from there that the main threat to the republic now emanated. A second cause of conflict, universally acknowledged, was the obligation to avenge the massacres of Protestants in 1641. But no invasion could take place unless soldiers were willing. After several months of having their own concerns ignored, the rank and file were seething with anger. In addition, John Lilburne had returned from the north, intent on stirring up more political discontent. The conjunction of Leveller agitation and rank-and-file anger in the late winter and spring of 1649 would present the grandees with the most dangerous internal threat they had yet faced. How they handled this threat is the theme of the next chapter.

CHAPTER NINE

THE ARMY AND THE LEVELLERS, FEBRUARY TO SEPTEMBER 1649

As soon as the great drama of the scaffold was over, the discontents that had been simmering in the army since the end of the Second Civil War bubbled up to the surface. Again the principal grievance was arrears of pay. The knowledge that many of them would soon be shipped off to Ireland only deepened the soldiers' anxiety. Their mood was not improved by the recently experienced hostility of the London populace, or having slept on bare boards in unheated rooms. A poor harvest – the third in a row – added to a bitterly cold winter, sharpened their discomfort.

The previous autumn the soldiers' anger had been directed against Parliament. But now that the officers had become part of the new political establishment, they too became a target of rank-and-file resentment. As an awareness of how well these officers were providing for themselves perco-lated down through the ranks, the sense of grievance spread. Controlling the army was not made easier by the swelling of its numbers since the outbreak of the Second Civil War. Most of the newly enlisted men were Londoners, and many were radicals. The situation was exacerbated by the Commons' ill-considered permission to the radicals Henry Marten and John Reynolds to enlarge their rogue regiments.

The civilian Levellers soon started stirring the pot again. John Lilburne returned from Durham in early February; within days troopers were posting up his pamphlets and petitions, and urging an alliance of soldiers and people against their oppressors. When the Council of Officers met to consider what to do about the mounting dissatisfaction in the ranks they decided on a programme combining reform and repression. While approving a moderate petition from Fairfax's own horse regiment, they decided to suppress outside agitators. 'Clandestine contrivances or private meetings' were to stop. All petitions were to be channelled through regimental officers who would then submit them to Fairfax. He in turn would lay them before Parliament. When one officer suggested that these outside agitators might better be prosecuted in the civil courts than by martial law, Colonel Hewson fumed 'we have had trial enough of civil courts; we can hang twenty before they will hang one'.[1]

Two leading figures in the armed struggle between February and May 1649 were Corporal William Thompson and Colonel William Eyre. Thompson, formerly of Whalley's regiment, had been cashiered in September 1647 for his part in a tavern brawl. Almost immediately he tried to raise a mutiny in Fleetwood's regiment. Court-martialled and imprisoned, he made friends with John Lilburne, and published *England's Freedom Souldiers Rights*, possibly with Lilburne's help. Allowed out on parole, he soon fell to stirring up sedition in London, for which he was imprisoned and sentenced to death. Fairfax reprieved him. Eyre had already been arrested for inciting soldiers to mutiny at Corkbush Field in November 1647. Yet neither he nor Thompson was tried by a court-martial for his offences, because neither was any longer a member of the army.[2]

According to Lilburne it was the repressive policies of the Council of Officers that obliged him to spring into action once more. Within four days of the officers' meeting he had framed, circulated, published and submitted to Parliament a major statement taking the officers to task for their many sins.[3] He first upbraided them for the compromises they had incorporated into their version of the *Agreement of the People*. Ever since the army's *Solemne Engagement* of 5 June 1647 (see above, pp. 80–1), the officers' conduct had been a sorry tale of broken promises and oppression of the rank and file. What was needed was nothing less than a purge of the high command. Parliament should set up a committee to settle all disputes between officers and soldiers, and should temper the martial law.

At the end of February, Lilburne and several of his comrades presented *England's New Chains* to Parliament. Ushered in by the sergeant-at-arms, he would never again enjoy such respectful treatment. His repeated, reckless attacks on the army leadership would drive an irreparable breach between him and them.

On the same day that Lilburne published his diatribe, anonymous radicals within the army brought their own petition before the House. In it they called for liberty of conscience, the abolition of tithes, the freeing of prisoners for debt, and the relaxing of the existing code of martial law 'as being too severe and tyrannous for any army of freeborn Englishmen'. Reaching out to England's rural poor, they also urged 'that speedy provision be made for the continual supply of the necessities of the poor of this nation, whose miseries cry aloud in our ears for redress'. Along the same lines, they suggested that regular pay for the army would obviate the deplorable practice of free quarter. Parliament ignored the petition.[4]

Within the army the new rules for petitioning sparked angry resentment. On 1 March at the weekly meeting of the Council of Officers Fairfax tabled a petition from eight troopers demanding the democratisation of the army: 'The strength of the officer doth consist in the arm of the soldier. Is it not the soldier that endureth the heat and burden of the day, and performeth that work whereof the officers beareth the glory and name?' The troopers were court-martialled and sentenced to ride the wooden horse with their faces to the tail, to have their swords broken over their heads, and to be cashiered from the army. Fashioned from a crude, thin piece of wood, the wooden horse was designed both to inflict humiliation and the maximum pain – even to the point of drawing blood – on the genitals of its unfortunate victim. While suffering this penalty the convicted men had their swords, which had been nearly cut through by a blacksmith, smashed over their heads. When the ordeal was over, all eight repaired in coaches to a Leveller tavern where they were fêted for their heroism.[5]

A fortnight later the five cashiered men published their defiant answer to their tormentors. The powerful eloquence of *The Hunting of the Foxes* points towards Richard Overton's authorship. With its denunciation of all the institutions of the new republic and its vitriolic attack on the grandees, the Leveller leaders now effectively foreclosed any possibility of rapprochement. The grandees' original sin, in their eyes, was the abolition of the General Council of the Army. Their behaviour had been nothing less than that of 'apostates . . . Jesuits and traitors to the people'. Even more repellent was their religious hypocrisy: 'Did ever men pretend to an higher degree of holiness, religion, and zeal to God and their country than these? . . . You shall scarce speak to Cromwell about any thing, but he will lay his hand on his breast, elevate his eyes, and call God to record, he will weep, howl and repent, even while he doth smite you under the first rib.'[6] The radicals wanted the immediate re-institution of the General Council of the Army as the sovereign power in the army – power which it had never in fact exercised in its heyday of 1647. Officers were to be subject to their men – who were the essential part of the army. It was a quixotic and inherently anarchic vision. (On one occasion when it was implemented – in the popular republican militias during the Spanish Civil War of the 1930s – it was of short-lived and doubtful effectiveness.)[7]

This contemptuous animosity towards the leaders of the republic was a grave blunder on the Levellers' part. Several of their army friends now began to desert them. Major Francis White and John Reynolds, now a colonel, who had been among their prominent advocates in 1647, decided to back the grandees. The haemorrhaging of Leveller support was remarkably sudden. In December and January a majority of the officers had compelled the grandees to adopt an *Agreement of the People* very similar to what the Levellers wanted. By April the only two officers of note to maintain their radical allegiance were Major John Cobbett of Skippon's regiment and John Jubbes, formerly lieutenant-colonel of Hewson's regiment. With superlative bad timing as far as the grandees were concerned, Jubbes published an attack on the army leadership at the beginning of May.[8]

Among the junior officers there were a few who stuck with the Levellers. William Bray, captain-lieutenant in Colonel John Reynolds's new regiment, backed the five troopers' right to petition in early March. Thrown out of the Council of Officers, he appealed to Parliament in a long pamphlet calling Fairfax as greedy as William the Conqueror and as cruel as the emperor Tiberius. He was locked up in Windsor Castle for his pains. His troop was almost certainly one of those which joined the armed resistance in May.[9]

The vitriol of Richard Overton in *The Hunting of the Foxes* was matched by the hot-headedness of John Lilburne in *The Second Part of Englands New-Chaines Discovered*.[10] It was nothing less than a declaration of war against the grandees. They were responsible for the outbreak of the Second Civil War. They had deliberately sent Colonel Thomas Rainborowe to his death. These 'monstrously wicked' men were guilty of 'vile apostasy' and bore direct responsibility for the bitterness, division and famine that presently stalked the land. What was the remedy for this sorry state of affairs? Nothing less than a new parliament, the restoration of the agitators to the army's General Council and the enactment of the full Leveller programme of socio-economic reform, contained in their version of the *Agreement of the People*. The tract summed up all the helpless anger felt by Lilburne and his friends at the betrayal of their vision of the Revolution.

The Second Part of Englands New-Chaines was debated in the Commons for three hours on 27 March and voted 'highly seditious'. Lilburne and the other three Leveller leaders – Walwyn, Overton and Thomas Prince – were hauled before the Council of State the next morning to answer for their alleged treason.[11] After cooling their heels all day outside the council chamber, they were brought in one by one for cross-examination. While they were

waiting Lilburne crept up to the door and put his ear to the keyhole. He heard
Cromwell shouting as he thumped the table, 'I tell you sir, you have no other
way to deal with these men but to break them in pieces . . . I tell you again,
you are necessitated to break them.' They were then sent to the Tower, where
to their good fortune their custodian was Captain John Jenkins, 'an old and
familiar acquaintance' of Lilburne from Durham. He greeted them warmly
and sent them all home to their wives in exchange for a promise to meet him
the following morning at the Angel Tavern near the Tower, which they did.

The kindly treatment meted out by his gaoler did little to appease
Lilburne's anger. Conceding that he was perhaps 'of an hasty and choleric
temper', he warned 'I will fire it [the Tower] and burn it down to the ground',
and ended by calling for an insurrection by people and soldiers against the
'mock parliament'.

Throughout the month of April Lilburne and Overton strained every
sinew to incite the rank and file to take over the army and implement the
Leveller agenda. The second prong of their insurrectionary strategy was to
send agents into the countryside of southern England, Wales and Lancashire
to stir up the rural poor and align them with the soldiers. The strategy came
to grief for two reasons. First, the rural poor saw little identity of interest
between themselves, in a state of near-starvation at the end of a third nightmarish winter, and rebellious troops who could only survive by exacting
free quarter. Second, the mutinous regiments, dispersed across several
counties, could not be brought together quickly enough to form the critical
mass required to bring down the grandees. But the grandees could not know
in advance that the projected insurrection was futile, and so they suffered
many sleepless nights between the beginning of April and the middle of
May 1649.

By accelerating their agitation in London, in the army, and in the provinces, the Levellers kept the pot bubbling ever more furiously. In response to
the mounting unrest, Fairfax reissued his January order for all officers to
repair to their charges. No officer was to leave his post for above twenty-four
hours unless upon business at headquarters.[12]

In London the Levellers stepped up their propagandising of the regiments
in the capital. In mid-April, several hundred women besieged the door of the
Commons with a petition bearing 10,000 signatures calling for a jury trial for
the prisoners in the Tower and the implementation of the *Agreement of the
People*. The troops guarding the House showed them no gallantry, pointing
loaded pistols at the women's breasts and throwing squibs among them. One

MP told them to go home and wash their dishes. Galvanised by this and other insults they returned three more times with fresh petitions. The last was prefaced with a ringing statement of their equality with men: 'Since we are assured of our creation in the image of God, [and] of an interest in Christ equal unto men . . . we cannot but wonder and grieve that we should appear so despicable in your eyes as to be thought unworthy to petition or represent our grievances to this honourable House.'[13]

Efforts to propagandise the army intensified as Levellers distributed pamphlets among the troops. A trooper named Sawyer was arrested for this seditious activity, and immediately joined the Leveller pantheon of martyr-heroes. A broadsheet was scattered about the streets of London calling on men in the army to resist their officers and elect a council of agitators. A new, partisan newsbook also hit the streets. Bearing the title *Mercurius Militaris*, it was bitterly hostile to the grandees. It accused them of attempting to manipulate the choice of regiments for the Irish expedition, and of attempting to infiltrate and undermine the Leveller organisation.[14]

The Diggers

Among the many disturbances that beset the new regime in the spring of 1649, was one stirred up by a band of agrarian radicals a few miles south of the capital. In the middle of April the Council of State received word that a new group of 'Levellers' were digging up the common at St George's Hill near Oatlands, Surrey, and sowing it with parsnips, carrots and beans. It was the first of several experiments in voluntary, agrarian communism. Jerrard Winstanley, the leader of this group of 'True Levellers' or 'Diggers', as they soon came to be known, produced a large and eloquent volume of writings denouncing the existing socio-economic system based on the 'cheating art of buying and selling', and calling for its replacement by a new system recognising the earth as the common Treasury of mankind. Only the abolition of private property, he argued, could bring an end to the tyranny and bloodshed that had plagued Europe for centuries.[15]

At another time the Council of State might have ignored Winstanley and his little group, but it was the Diggers' misfortune to come to official attention when rural disturbances were seen as a danger to the security of the fragile republic. That was why the authorities instructed Fairfax to disperse them. The next day the two Digger leaders came to army headquarters to explain their actions. They assured Fairfax that they did not intend to

trespass on private property, but only to occupy what was common and
untilled. They would not take up arms or even defend themselves.

Fairfax listened patiently to the two men, although his staff were offended
by their refusal to remove their hats. For the moment he left them alone, but
at the end of November, apparently yielding to demands from local landowners, the Council of State again ordered a crackdown, and Fairfax sent a
detachment to disperse the commune. The Diggers' poignant appeal to be
allowed 'to conquer them with love' fell on deaf dears. Brought to court in
Kingston, they were convicted of trespass and fined, while Winstanley's
cows were beaten.[16]

Mutiny in Whalley's Regiment

In late April 1649 the army grandees were far more absorbed with the political
scene in London than what was happening in the Surrey countryside. Extreme
instability in the capital prompted them to remove some troops to the outskirts,
where they would be less subject to Leveller subversion. There was already
considerable unrest in Whalley's regiment over Parliament's refusal to release
the four Leveller leaders from the Tower. In was not surprising, therefore, that
when Captain John Savage's men were assigned new quarters in Essex they
balked.[17] Seizing the troop's colours, they carried them to the Bull Inn near
Bishopsgate, a radical meeting place in the City. Their commanding officer
then went to report this insubordination to his colonel. Whalley along with
Major Robert Swallow and other officers rode to the Bull, where they ordered
the soldiers to come out. Shouts of 'No, no!' were the response. A crowd had by
now gathered in the courtyard of the Bull and the street. The commanders
feared that a conjunction between an unruly crowd and a troop of mutinous
soldiers could easily flare into a full-scale urban uprising against the shaky
regime. In the event, troops loyal to Whalley were able to drive off the crowd
and quell the mutiny. At that moment Fairfax and Cromwell stormed onto the
scene, 'furiously breathing nothing but death to them all'. The fifteen who had
been arrested were marched to Whitehall and tried by court-martial. Five were
sentenced to ride the wooden horse with a carbine at each heel and cashiered,
while the six judged to be ringleaders were sentenced to death.

When they abjectly apologised, Cromwell was for pardoning them, but
Fairfax insisted that one must die. Robert Lockyer was deemed the most
guilty and was denied clemency. In the speech he gave before his execution
he regretted that he should lose his life for a dispute over pay rather than for

the freedom and liberties of the nation which he had fought for since 1642. Disdaining the proffered blindfold, he stared at the musketeers appointed to shoot him, and urged them to spare him. Then, after praying he gave the appointed signal by raising both arms. Seconds later he crumpled under a rain of bullets.

Lockyer's funeral was one of the most impressive that Londoners could remember. Led by six trumpeters, about 4,000 people accompanied his corpse. Many wore ribbons, black for mourning and sea-green (Colonel Rainborowe's colour) for their political allegiance. Most alarming to the authorities, several hundred soldiers joined the procession. After hearing eulogies in the Moorfields churchyard the crowd dispersed. Some witnesses thought Lockyer had more mourners than King Charles.[18]

Resistance to the Irish Expedition

During and after the Lockyer affair, radical agitation in the regiments and among the rural poor continued. Inside the army, discontent was particularly acute in the horse regiments designated for Ireland – Scrope's, Ireton's and Horton's – but this spilled over into Harrison's, Cromwell's, the regiments stationed in London, and the new regiments of Reynolds and Marten.[19] The few infantry regiments touched by discontent included Skippon's in Bristol and Ingoldsby's in Oxford. Among the garrisons and local troops were Captain Bamber's in Lancaster, Portsmouth garrison, those in Somerset, and Captain John Smith's country troop in Oxfordshire. Potentially there were several thousand men ready to rise up against their commanding officers. The challenge facing the radicals was how to foster cooperation among these disparate groups of horse, foot, field-army, local and garrison troops, and, more difficult, how to weld them into a critical mass weighty enough to overawe the troops loyal to the grandees.

What converted the grumbling normal to any army into active mutiny was the project of Ireland. When the regiments were selected there was resentment among the rank and file. Labelling it the 'cut-throat expedition', they made it clear that the throats they objected to being cut were their own, not those of the Irish. The radicals also put it about that the real motive for sending men to Ireland was to purge the army of dissident elements. Many officers and men melted away from the designated regiments, and tried to transfer into regiments that were staying in England. Fairfax quickly ordered that no such transfers should be allowed.[20]

Leveller agents appealed eloquently to the soldiers to reject the Irish service: 'will you go on still to kill, slay and murther men, to make [your officers] absolute lords and masters over Ireland . . . [and] to fill their prisons with poor disabled prisoners [and] their land with swarms of beggars . . . ?'[21] Besides their sympathy for the plight of the Irish, the Levellers were also worried that their hopes for the Revolution would be dashed if a large part of the army was sent to Ireland before fundamental social change had been achieved in England.[22]

A few soldiers were touched by Leveller idealism. An anonymous writer in Bristol, where Skippon's foot regiment was stationed, published one of the most eloquent pamphlets of the revolutionary era. It was scathing in its indictment of the Irish project: 'What have we to do with Ireland, to fight and murther a people and nation . . . which have done us no harm, only deeper to put our hands in blood with [the officers'] own? We have waded too far in that crimson stream (already) of innocent and Christian blood.'[23] The characterisation of the Irish as innocent and Christian was extraordinary, challenging as it did the common belief that they were both the followers of Antichrist (the Pope), and the murderers of thousands of innocent English settlers.

Far more representative of the views of the English soldiery was the statement of the rebellious troops of Colonel Scrope's regiment. Disclaiming any desire 'to hinder or retard the service of Ireland', they vowed that as soon as their material grievances were satisfied and liberty established in England 'we shall to the utmost of our abilities engage ourselves in the service of that land'.[24]

The Mutiny at Burford

By the beginning of May agitators were active again in every regiment.[25] Disaffection was most acute among four troops of Scrope's cavalry regiment in Salisbury. Around the first of May, Scrope marshalled them and broke the news that they had been selected to go to Ireland. The men calmly informed their officers that they would not go. To their surprise they were treated to angry threats and accusations of mutiny. At this provocation they marched off with the regimental colours in the direction of Bristol. Only about eighty men, mainly officers, remained with Scrope. His other two troops, at Malmesbury, had already expelled their officers and rendezvoused with the rebellious men of Ireton's regiment, who were also on their way to Bristol.

They doubtless knew of the discontent in Skippon's regiment over the death of Robert Lockyer and the imprisonment of the four Leveller leaders.

The mutineers explained themselves in a pamphlet published in London under the title *The Resolutions of the Private Souldiery of Colonel Scrope's Regiment of Horse*. Recalling their *Engagement* of 5 June 1647 not to disband or allow themselves to be disbanded, they called to mind their officers' oft-repeated promise that after the war the people should have 'freedom, peace and happiness', and the soldiers their arrears. Neither promise had been kept 'and yet you would have us to engage, to give you power over another land'. At the same time, troopers were having to pay more than double their daily pay just for lodgings and food for themselves and their horses – horses they had purchased out of their own pocket. What other choice did they have but to oppress the people by resorting to free quarter?[26]

These *Resolutions* were soon taken up and endorsed by some of the men in Ireton's regiment. Three of the six troops bent their steps towards Bristol to rendezvous with Scrope's men. But on the way 150 men melted away and returned to obedience. In the end the regiment produced no more than ninety mutineers.[27] The two groups joined forces at Old Sarum, near Salisbury, where they chose new officers and issued a declaration explaining their actions.

In London meanwhile the authorities scrambled to contain the mutiny. The Council of State reinforced the guards of the imprisoned Leveller leaders in the Tower of London with 400 infantry from Pride's and Hewson's regiments. The lieutenant of the Tower was instructed to keep Lilburne under strict surveillance, without pen, ink or paper, and with no more day passes to visit his wife or friends.[28]

Fairfax and Cromwell knew that prompt action was essential to extinguish the revolt. The infantry were as yet untouched; in fact some regiments were openly hostile to the mutiny. But among the horse the discontent had spread even to Cromwell's own regiment. Agitators travelled between regiments, trying to convince each that all the others had thrown in their lot with the mutineers. In addition to Bristol and Banbury, the product of Leveller organising was seen in Portsmouth, the Isle of Wight, Somerset, Lancaster and Oxford.[29]

Having made sure that London was not rebellious, the grandees decided to move a large force to the epicentre of discontent, Bristol. First they mustered their five most trustworthy regiments – Cromwell's and Fairfax's horse, plus Fairfax's, Hewson's and Ewer's foot. Cromwell addressed the troops, promising them that Parliament was looking out for the best interests of both nation and army. Those who wished to quit the army were free to do so. A few troopers who dared to wear the sea-green Leveller colours had them pulled from their hats.[30]

This force, just shy of 4,000, then set out. By Friday 11 May they reached Alton in Hampshire, where they were joined by Colonel Scrope with the eighty officers and men who had remained loyal. On the same day the rest of Scrope's regiment and the three half-troops from Ireton's held a rendez-vous at Old Sarum. There they vented their indignation at the treatment of those who declined to enlist for Ireland, and voiced the familiar demand for the restoration of the General Council of the Army with two rank-and-file agitators per regiment. If this were done, 'we shall willingly show ourselves (many of us) in the van for Ireland'. To the people the mutineers promised that 'we seek not your disturbance but your ease; not the rifling of your houses or seizing of your goods, or levelling of your estates ... but your freedom from the intolerable burthens lying upon your shoulders'. They asked the people's forgiveness for having to take free quarter.[31]

Fairfax answered the soldiers, accusing them of giving aid and comfort to the Cavaliers and denying that there was any compulsion to join the Irish service. In words that must have been written for him, he declared that Parliament had begun by bringing the king to the scaffold, 'that great act of justice, which was by good men so called for, and was indeed so necessary a duty to take off the pollution of innocent blood, wherewith the land was defiled'. Now Parliament was preparing to relieve Ireland and provide for soldiers' arrears with the best security possible: the crown lands. The people had been relieved of free quarter, unless 'you now again begin it'. The rest of the *Agreement*'s provisions were well in hand. If the rebellious regiments returned at once to obedience they would be pardoned; if not the conse-quences would be dire.[32]

It was a tough, shrewdly written piece of propaganda. Although it bore Fairfax's name, the Cromwellian authorship is clear in the justification of the king's beheading. Its unvarnished threat to use force caused wavering among some of the mutineers, most of whom still cherished profound respect for their commander-in-chief.

As the mutineers took stock, they must have been troubled by their limited success in mobilising support. Their core comprised the bulk of Scrope's regiment – perhaps 450 men – and the three half-troops from Ireton's regiment, numbering probably not more than 120. At Bristol not one soldier had come forward from Skippon's old regiment. The money promised from London had not arrived, while the necessity of taking free quarter from a hungry populace meant that the project of an insurrectionary union of rural poor and radical soldiery was stillborn.

The mutineers' only hope now was to bolster their strength by teaming up with Harrison's regiment in Buckinghamshire and Horton's in the west. They headed north, reaching Marlborough, Wiltshire on the 11th. In a last-ditch effort to win popular support, they spread word through the country-side that their objective was only to restore 'magistracy, liberty and freedom . . . under fair pretence for Charles the Second'.[33]

The grandees had their own reasons for anxiety. The mutineers were still attracting recruits, and there was no way of knowing on which side Harrison's or Horton's regiment would come down. Equally worrying, the mettle of Fairfax's and Cromwell's horse regiments had not yet been tested. If push came to shove, would they be willing to draw their swords against friends with whom they had fought shoulder to shoulder so often in the past?[34]

On 12 May Fairfax and Cromwell summoned a rendezvous at Andover. Cromwell rode to the head of each regiment and told the men he was confi-dent they would follow him to subdue the Levellers and bring the ring-leaders to exemplary punishment. Many expressed their support, but others were heard to mutter that they would not fight against their comrades.[35]

That evening, Fairfax sent a delegation headed by Major Francis White to negotiate with the mutineers at Marlborough. Shortly after he departed, Fairfax received a conciliatory letter from the eight agitators of Scrope's and Ireton's regiments. Pleased to have been assured that the Irish service was not compulsory, they undertook 'to put our lives in our hands for that service'. If he would honour the army's *Solemne Engagement* they would guarantee him perpetual obedience. This was the great stumbling block; at no time was Fairfax prepared to yield to the Leveller demand for the General Council to exercise sovereign power in the army.[36]

When he heard of the Levellers' advance to Wantage, Fairfax decided that the time for talk had ended. They had to be headed off before their meeting with Harrison's and Horton's regiments doubled their strength. He left Andover on the 13th, arriving at Theale, near Reading, the same day.[37]

Meanwhile Major White stuck with the Levellers and tried for a reconcil-iation right up until shots were being fired. Through White the Levellers told the general that by failing to honour the Engagement of 5 June 1647 'you keep not covenant with us'. Only when the General Council of the

Army had been revived would they return to obedience. Otherwise 'we must lay at your door all the misery, bloodshed and ruin that will fall upon this nation and army'. White's willingness to include this language in his document testifies to the enduring tug of his previous Leveller attachments and the lengths to which he was willing to go to conciliate them.[38]

By now the mutineers from Scrope's and Ireton's regiments had met up with two troops from Harrison's regiment. Their combined strength was eleven troops, plus the Leveller Colonel William Eyre with a few soldiers and citizen volunteers from London.[39] Their confidence was bolstered by this fresh accession of strength, but soberer heads wondered why only two of Harrison's six troops had thrown in their lot with the mutiny. At this point they turned west in the hope of picking up Horton's regiment, thought to be in Gloucestershire. Crossing the Thames, they got as far as Burford by nine o'clock, where they settled for the night, having been assured by Major White that Fairfax would not attack them.

Fairfax, however, had concluded that the mutineers had to be crushed before their numbers swelled any further. He justified himself with the thought that he had already put them on notice that if they failed to return to obedience they would be attacked. They could hardly claim that they had not been warned, while their refusal to halt when talks were in progress proved their bad faith.

The general and his little army now advanced rapidly up the Thames Valley. By the late afternoon his men had marched an astonishing 35 miles, and it was now almost dark, but Fairfax saw that if they could cover another 10 miles they stood a good chance of pouncing on the mutineers in their beds. The twin advantages of surprise and superior numbers might reward them with a bloodless victory. When Fairfax canvassed his men about their willingness to keep going they responded with 'great alacrity' and 'resolvedness'. The final stage of the operation he turned over to Cromwell. The two generals agreed that if the mutineers did not resist they would be offered mercy; otherwise they would be treated as enemies. Because speed was of the essence, and because they wanted to avoid a pitched battle, Cromwell set off with the cavalry regiments and a detachment of Okey's dragoons. They reached Burford after midnight.[40]

Suspecting nothing, Major White and Cornet Henry Denne were at that moment perfecting the final draft of their paper for Fairfax. Denne, a Cambridge graduate, had been ordained a priest and later become a Baptist, preaching universal grace. The two men's labours were interrupted by the alarm that Fairfax and Cromwell were at the entrance to Burford with a large force of dragoons. What had happened was that Cromwell's forlorn hope had run into the Levellers' scouts outside the town. Rather than wheeling back to headquarters they stuck with the scouts as the latter raced back to raise the alarm. They thus achieved complete surprise by riding into Burford at the same moment as the scouts. They then charged down the main street lined with the handsome stone houses of the town's wool merchants. Following close behind was the main party of cavalry under Colonel Okey, along with another cavalry regiment from Buckinghamshire. Fairfax held back with a party in reserve, while Colonel Scrope commanded another detachment in the rear. Captain Fisher led a smaller party that circled west to enter the town at the opposite end. There he ran into two Leveller troops already mounted with swords drawn and pistols cocked, ready to charge. Fortunately they accepted his offer of quarter, and no blood was shed.[41]

At the first alarm, White, dismayed at appearing a liar in the eyes of the mutineers, ran into the street in his slippers, seeking Fairfax to beg him to call off the attack. His quest was futile. Colonel Okey and the other officers had shouted offers of mercy to the sleeping men if they surrendered at once. In their dazed condition most did, but in one house the occupants fired out the windows, wounding a few of their attackers. Okey, who was in the thick of this confused scene, narrowly escaped with his life. After these men were subdued another party led by Colonel Eyre barricaded themselves in the Crown Inn where, with muskets blazing, they held off the besieging troops for several minutes. One man was killed on each side, and several wounded in the most serious exchange of the night. Of the roughly 900 mutineers, 340 were taken prisoner and locked in the parish church. The rest escaped on foot into the night.[42]

The next day Fairfax's Council of War resolved that all the mutineers were equally liable to the penalty of death. When this judgement was conveyed to the prisoners they were reduced to terror and remorse. Copious tears were shed, 'and indeed', noted Fairfax, 'it is hardly to be believed how many of them did melt into a noble and Christian sorrow'. In this mood all 340 confessed 'the odious wickedness' of what they had done. This was just what the officers wanted to hear; they accordingly chose to limit the death penalty to the four ringleaders.[43]

Cornets Thomson and Denne were full of remorse, while Corporals Perkins and Church remained defiant till the last. Denne's submission was the most extravagant. On 17 May the four condemned men were brought to the churchyard for execution by firing squad, as the other prisoners watched. Thomson died first, 'contrite and in great terror'. Perkins and Church both carried themselves with courage. The last to die should have been Cornet Denne, but Fairfax, impressed by his contrition, lifted the sentence of death moments before he was to be shot. 'I am not worthy of such a mercy,' he cried, and wept bitterly. After escorting him into the church, Cromwell mounted the pulpit to inform the tightly packed throng that they were reprieved. Many of their grievances, he conceded, were justified, and would be remedied. Then he turned the pulpit over to Denne who, 'howling and weeping like a crocodile', confessed the unlawfulness of everything he and the mutineers had done.[44]

The Burford mutiny was the most serious internal challenge faced by the republican regime until 1659. While the number of men routed on the night of 14–15 May was under 1,000, there were several times that many disaffected soldiers in the area bounded by Portsmouth in the south, Lancaster in the north, London in the east and Bristol in the west. Geographic dispersion, as well as the inability to stage simultaneous uprisings in diverse centres, was what condemned the Levellers to military failure. Still, the number who actually took up arms against their commanders was impressive. Watching the various troop movements with the keenest interest were the 1,000 men of Ingoldsby's radical regiment in Oxford. If they hadn't waited till September to stage their own revolt but had united with the others in May they might have created a major headache for Fairfax and Cromwell.

The total number of men involved in Leveller-inspired mutinies between the spring and autumn of 1649 was over 2,500. The expeditionary force dispatched from London was well under twice that size. Starting out with fewer than 4,000 men, Fairfax picked up another 800 along the way. On the night of 14–15 May, with his three infantry regiments several miles to the rear, Fairfax would have barely outnumbered his foes. Telling in his favour was the advantage of surprise and the absence of any serving officer above the rank of cornet on the mutineers' side. A final factor in his favour was the reluctance of New Model cavalry troopers to sheathe their swords in one another's bowels.

After Burford, all that remained was for the officers to snuff out the last embers of radical disaffection, and then receive the accolades of the intellectual and business elites for a job well done. William Thompson was still at large, wandering through the Northamptonshire countryside. It was Colonel Reynolds who in the end hunted him down. Formerly considered a friend of the Levellers, Reynolds had done more frontline work in suppressing their revolt than any other officer. Eliminating Thompson was his final accomplishment. He caught up with Thompson in the woods near Wellingborough, where his corporal 'gave Thompson his death wounds'.[45]

By now there remained only one centre of Leveller discontent, the garrison at Oxford. The mutiny that finally broke out there in September came too late to inspire risings elsewhere, and was soon quelled.[46]

By the beginning of June, with the loose ends mostly tied up, the army commanders could bask in the plaudits of the political nation. Already the clerks of Oxford University had concocted a special ceremony to bestow honorary degrees on them. Handsomely entertained at a feast in Magdelen College, they proceeded to the schools to receive their degrees. Fairfax and Cromwell wore the scarlet gowns of doctors of civil law, while Harrison, Hewson, Okey and other leading officers were clothed in the more sober garb of masters of arts. Engulfed by pageantry, jubilation and flattery, they momentarily forgot the royalist hostility of the city's inhabitants, and the Leveller sympathies of their own garrison there.[47]

The Lessons of Burford

Once back in London they were greeted with unrestrained rejoicing. MPs, monied men and magistrates heaved a huge sigh of relief that the limits of the Revolution had been decisively set. Tithes would not be abolished. Monopolies would remain untouched. Parliament would not be dissolved. The *Agreement of the People* would not be imposed. The invasion of Ireland would go ahead as planned, and the Irish Adventurers could look forward, they were sure, to an early return on their investment. Social and religious conservatives could now sleep peacefully, secure in the knowledge that Fairfax and Cromwell wielded unchallenged authority over the army. There was much to be happy about, and so the House of Commons named Thursday 7 June a day of national thanksgiving for the Levellers' defeat.

What lessons had been learned from the Leveller insurrection and its suppression? To Cromwell the victory at Burford was like waking up from a bad dream. Had it continued, he feared, England might soon have been overrun by an alliance of 'discontented persons, servants, reformadoes [and] beggars'. This motley rabble would have 'cast off all government and chosen amongst themselves to have made new laws'. They would have murdered all lawyers as well as Presbyterian and Episcopalian ministers, abolished private property and instituted communal ownership of the land.[48]

The lessons that Fairfax drew from these same events were very different. Although he had been incensed by the soldiers' insubordination, he understood their frustration and recognised the justice of many of their demands. To him the victory of Burford was another of God's mercies towards Parliament, but instead of lapsing into complacency they should all use the opportunity that had been won for them to get back on track with the unfinished agenda of reform. Only by 'settl[ing] this poor nation upon foundations of justice and righteousness' would they rally the poor to their side.[49]

Regardless of these contrasting views among the leaders of the New Model Army, England was now politically quiescent. Its rulers could at last address the troublesome and long-deferred business of Ireland.

CHAPTER TEN

THE CONQUEST AND OCCUPATION OF IRELAND, 1649–60

The conquest of Ireland was high on the Commonwealth's agenda. Less than a month after the king's execution a powerful committee led by Cromwell was directed to organise the expedition. They soon agreed that it would take an army of 12,000 to subdue the nation. Why Ireland had to be conquered was not a subject for debate. Had it not belonged to England since the Middle Ages? Was not vengeance required for the slaughter of thousands of English settlers in the revolt of 1641? Unless Ireland were brought under control, would it not become a dangerous base of operations against the fragile Commonwealth? Even John Lilburne, who exploited rank-and-file disaffection with the 'cut-throat expedition', did not for the most part question these assumptions.[1]

Recruitment

The question of who should lead the expedition remained up in the air. Everyone looked to Cromwell, but he did not relish the prospect. He knew that while he was absent he would have little influence on policy in England. He therefore resolved that he would only lead the expedition if stringent conditions were met. His army must be well equipped, well provisioned and well financed. As commander-in-chief he must have plenary powers, civil as well as military. He must also be assured that the Irish project would continue to have top priority at Westminster.

When he met his fellow officers on 22 March he launched into a long speech reviewing the perils facing the Commonwealth. First there were the Scots, who harboured 'a very angry hateful spirit' against them. But a far greater threat came from the Irish: 'I had rather be overrun by a Cavalierish interest [than] of a Scotch interest; I had rather be overrun with a Scotch interest than an Irish interest; and I think of all this is the most dangerous.'[2] Still, he refused to commit himself. The officers screwed up the pressure by naming a large committee to meet the following morning to seek God.

On the 24th, after fasting and praying all day, the committee approved Colonel Whalley's proposal that the commander-in-chief must have full power to treat with the enemy and must not be tied by harsh terms 'as either to eradicate the natives, or to divest them of their estates'. It is a pity that this humanitarian guideline was soon forgotten. There followed a vehement debate on the selection of regiments. In the end it was decided to adopt the example of the New Testament and cast lots. This, they believed, would have the double merit of handing the decision to God and short-circuiting the political infighting over who should go and who should stay.[3]

The casting of lots was done by placing fourteen pieces of paper, ten blank and four bearing the word Ireland, into a hat. The papers were then drawn out by a child. The four horse regiments that drew the word Ireland were Ireton's, Scrope's, Lambert's and Horton's. The foot were Ewer's, Deane's, Cooke's and Hewson's. Half of Okey's dragoon regiment was also selected. The regiments selected were from a broad political spectrum; there was no discrimination against radical regiments. Yet many in the designated regiments refused to go. That is why the pressing of men had to go on unabated.[4]

Financing and Outfitting the Expedition

Manning the expedition was hard enough. Paying for it posed an even greater challenge. Soldiers could be pressed, but monied men had to be coaxed. Cromwell devoted more attention to money and matériel than to manpower. Between April and July he got the City to advance £150,000 towards the cause. In May he hectored Parliament and won £400,000 from the future receipts of the excise. Then, in an extraordinary act of high-handedness, he seized a consignment of £10,000 that was on its way to Bristol for the navy's use.[5]

On 9 July Cromwell left London for the west coast. His departure was attended with great pomp – blaring trumpets, six Flanders mares drawing his coach, and eighty gentlemen as a personal lifeguard. He spent the next month in Bristol, mustering his regiments, waiting for a favourable wind, and writing to the Irish governors of the ports on the Munster coast offering money if they would open their gates to him.[6]

No matter how favourable the wind, Cromwell would not depart until he had £100,000 in his pocket to pay his troops, cover his salary of £13,000 per year as commander-in-chief and lord-lieutenant of Ireland, and bribe the forces in the Munster ports to desert to Parliament. When the Council of State realised that Cromwell could not be budged from the full amount it scrambled to raise the cash, even though it meant robbing the navy again to do so.[7]

Despite having to play second fiddle to the land force, the navy was crucial to Cromwell's success. Colonels William Blake, Richard Deane and Alexander Popham were given the vital task of keeping the sea lanes clear between the south coast and the Irish sea. In addition, some 130 ships were commandeered to transport soldiers, arms, ammunition and supplies. During the summer vast quantities of biscuit, salt, wheat and beer were loaded onto ships in Milford Haven, Chester and Bristol. Lesser quantities of rye, oats, peas, barley and cheese were also taken aboard, besides 274 barrels of raisins and 230 bags of rice – rice pudding evidently forming part of the military diet. An even greater logistical challenge was shipping the artillery train accompanied by 600 barrels of powder and large quantities of iron, timbers, steel and tools, as well as 900 carriage- and draft-horses. Each of the four largest ('whole') cannon needed eighteen oxen to move it overland. Saltpetre (potassium nitrate), an essential ingredient of gunpowder, was supplied by the East India Company, now under the control of the Irish Adventurers, who thereby became even more important to the Irish project.[8]

Initially it had been thought that Ireland could be conquered quickly on a budget of £20,000 a month. Seven years later the cost of subjugating the kingdom had come to £6.8 million. Until late 1650 the money for the expedition was raised exclusively in England, but as soon as a territorial foothold was established, Ireland was made to pay for its own conquest. By 1656 close to half the money spent in Ireland had been raised there.[9]

There was another dimension to Cromwell's preparations: diplomacy. During the spring and summer of 1649 he directed his considerable political talent to sabotaging the royalist coalition that was being erected against him by the marquess of Ormond, the Catholics of the Kilkenny Confederation, now governing Ireland, the Munster Protestants under Lord Inchiquin, and Sir George Monro's Scottish Protestant army in the north. Meanwhile, the new king, Charles II, sent his cousin Prince Rupert with a small fleet to Kinsale on the Munster coast.[10]

Fortunately for the republic, three of its key commanders – Lieutenant-General Michael Jones in Dublin, Sir Charles Coote at Londonderry and Colonel George Monck at Dundalk – remained loyal to the regime. Monck achieved a three-month cessation of hostilities with Owen Roe O'Neill, leader

of the Catholics in Ulster and Connacht. In return for O'Neill's promise
to uphold the interests of Parliament, Monck agreed to support liberty of
conscience for O'Neill's followers, oblivion for all acts committed since 1641,
and a commission for O'Neill in the parliamentary army.[11]

Monck wrote to Cromwell that because of this cessation O'Neill and
Ormond were now pitted against each other. He also reported that O'Neill
was ready for serious talks with Parliament. When Cromwell informed the
Council of State of the cessation it neither ratified nor condemned it.[12]

If Parliament had made the détente with O'Neill permanent it might well
have crushed the royalist coalition in the egg. But the price was high. It
meant abandoning the quest to avenge the 1641–42 massacres of Protestants,
agreeing to tolerate Catholicism, and compromising on the land question.
The Rump would have none of it. Once Monck's cessation had expired and
its tactical advantages been exploited to the full, Parliament hypocritically
repudiated it. They then summoned Monck to Westminster and reassured
him that he would not be blamed for his error. The majority of MPs believed
they were being clever 'thus to beat him, and afterwards to stroke him'. But
Monck did not forget his humiliation.[13]

Cromwell's rapprochement with Roger Boyle, first Lord Broghill (son of
Ireland's wealthiest landowner), over the execution of Charles I bore fruit
that was more enduring than Monck's cessation with Owen Roe O'Neill.
Broghill was to be instrumental in securing the surrender of several Munster
towns – Youghal, Kinsale, Bandon and Dungarvon. Cromwell rewarded
him richly, and eventually he was made lieutenant-general of the Ordnance
in Ireland. Cromwell's talent for friendship came into play once again when
he prevailed on a number of officers to postpone their desertions from
Inchiquin's army, in effect keeping them as money in the bank to be drawn
when he needed it most.[14]

Rathmines

Now that everything possible had been done to ensure his success, on
13 August Cromwell at last quit England, accompanied by 10,000 men,
nearly 4,000 horses, and ammunition, supplies and artillery. He was violently
seasick on the crossing, but his spirits were buoyed by the news of a sensa-
tional victory won by Michael Jones against Ormond's main army outside
Dublin just ten days before. Rathmines was a stupendous reversal of royalist
fortunes, which had incalculable psychological and strategic consequences.

From the parliamentary perspective, 'there was never any day in Ireland like this'. Irish royalists would never again confront the English in a battle of this magnitude.[15] Had Jones *not* won, Cromwell would have had nowhere to land, and the invasion of Ireland might have been postponed indefinitely.

Ormond salvaged what he could from the disaster by reinforcing nearby Drogheda with the aim of holding out at all costs.

Drogheda

One of Cromwell's first acts upon arriving in Dublin was to issue strict orders to his soldiers against taking free quarter or plunder. He also promised the peasantry that if they brought goods or provisions for sale they would be paid in cash.[16] These policies only lasted a few months, but they served to win much of the populace to his side at the beginning. Cromwell's strategic plan was to take as many coastal ports as he could, beginning with Drogheda in the north, and ending with Cork in the south, before moving inland. Everything he needed to execute this plan – men, money, arms, supplies – he had to hand.

Ormond by contrast was desperately short of everything, and he also faced the daunting challenge of somehow repairing the shattered morale of his troops. Unfortunately almost every royalist and Catholic commander found a good reason why he could not come to Ormond's aid. His garrison also continued to be short of money, match and shot. Despite these overwhelming drawbacks, Ormond was determined to make a stand. Yet his new governor of Drogheda, Sir Arthur Aston, can have been under few illusions about his chances of repelling Cromwell.[17]

As Cromwell approached Drogheda, a party of Inchiquin's Irish horse rode over from Ormond's camp to join him. It was the first of many defections. Even with 12,000 soldiers, however, Cromwell could not hope to command all the approaches to the town. Straddling the deep channel of the Boyne, Drogheda boasted only a single bridge linking its two halves. Cromwell chose to besiege it from the south, where its ancient wall was 20 feet high and 4–6 feet thick.[18] Below the south-east portion of the wall was a steep ravine, a formidable obstacle to any storming operation. The advantage was that on its far side Cromwell was able to station his heavy guns exactly on a level with the wall. Because his artillery was late arriving from sea he was not ready until 9 September. All together he had eleven siege guns and twelve field pieces.

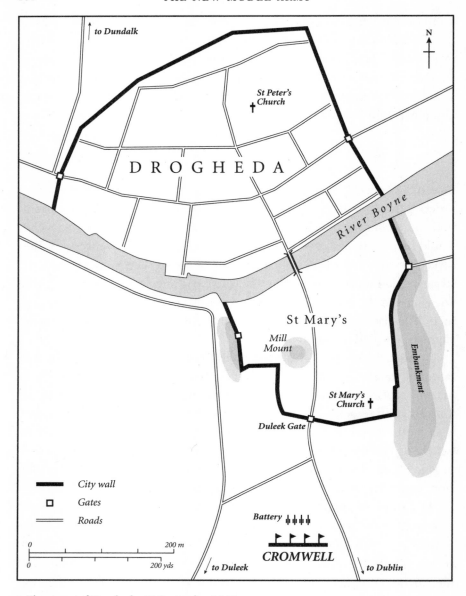

4. The storm of Drogheda, 10 September 1649

Early on the morning of the 10th Cromwell launched his bombardment in earnest, and by evening had blasted a large hole in the southern wall. By the next day he had opened a second breach. Neither was low enough to permit cavalry to enter, so Cromwell ordered three infantry regiments – Castle's, Hewson's and Ewer's – to lead the attack. Castle's men, who were

1. 'One-eyed cobbler John Hewson', infantry colonel and Westminster shoemaker. Known for his extreme anti-royalism, he sat on the High Court of Justice and signed the king's death warrant. He participated in the storm of Drogheda, but subsequently, as governor of Drogheda, was a remarkably even-handed president of the Dublin court martial. Back in London, he ruthlessly put down a demonstration in favour of a free parliament in December 1659. At the Restoration he escaped punishment by fleeing to the continent.

2. Thomas Rainborowe, infantry colonel, vice-admiral in the navy and Leveller spokesman. At the Putney debates (October 1647) he argued that 'the poorest he that is in England hath a life to live as the greatest he'. Assassinated by royalists in October 1648, his London funeral attracted a large crowd of mourners.

3. Hugh Peters, 'strenuous puritan' and chaplain to Sir Thomas Fairfax. In his writings and preaching he was an energetic propagandist for the New Model Army. During the weeks leading up to the king's trial he dashed to and fro between various parties frenetically promoting the regicide. A manic-depressive, however, he retreated to his sickbed on the day of the king's execution.

4. Commissary-General Henry Ireton. Cromwell's son-in-law and the army's leading political theorist. An adversary of the Levellers, he opposed extending the franchise, and upheld the role of the magistrate in maintaining a state religion. In November 1648 he authored the *Remonstrance of the Army*, which made the intellectual case for bringing the king to trial on capital charges. He and Cromwell may have had a falling out in 1648–9 over the regicide.

5. Philip Skippon, major-general of the infantry. A zealous puritan, he published several religious tracts, and was known as 'the Christian Centurion'. Badly wounded at Naseby, he was greeted rapturously by the soldiers on his return to the army fifteen months later.

6. 'The religious, successful and truly valliant lieutenant-genrall', Oliver Cromwell. He wore his religious heart on his sleeve, and often shed copious tears. Commander-in-chief of the New Model after Sir Thomas Fairfax's resignation in 1649, and lord protector from December 1653 until his death in September 1658. As commander of the invasion of Ireland he led the storm of Drogheda in September 1649. His order of 'no quarter' to the defenders permanently blackened his reputation in Ireland.

7. Sir Thomas Fairfax, captain-general of the New Model. Beloved by his troops, he was an inspired battlefield commander, and a man of deep, providentialist piety, known variously as 'Black Tom' and 'England's fortress'. While he gave brilliant leadership to the New Model in the two civil wars, he found himself out of his depth in the political struggles that followed. In 1650 he resigned his command rather than lead the invasion of Scotland.

8. The battlefield at Naseby in Northamptonshire. Site of the New Model Army's first great victory over the royalists, 14 June 1645. One of the keys to the victory was Cromwell's right wing of cavalry, three lines deep, in contrast to Ireton's two lines on the left. Another key was the stationing of Colonel Okey's crack regiment of dragoons behind the hedges on the far left.

9. The New Model's brief experiment in democratic self-rule. General Fairfax presiding over a session of the General Council of the Army (1647). The Council comprised four agitators from each regiment – two elected by the rank and file, and two by the officers – as well as the members of the general staff. The Council's debates in Putney Church in November–December 1647 resulted in the army's adoption of most of the Leveller programme.

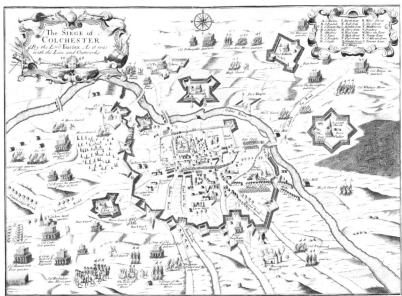

10. The siege of Colchester in the summer of 1648. One of the bitterest episodes of the civil wars, over a period of eleven weeks it reduced both civilians and soldiers to a state of virtual starvation. Fairfax was widely criticised for the execution of two of the royalist officers, but he was vindicated by the laws of war, which stipulated that officers who continued to hold an untenable position, thereby causing unnecessary bloodshed, forfeited their right to quarter.

11. Westminster Hall, seat of justice and venue for the trial of Charles I in January 1649. The public thronged to witness their monarch's trial, which was disrupted on two occasions by Lady Fairfax's shouted denunciations from the gallery. The trial was also prolonged by Charles's refusal to recognise the court's legality, and by his steadfast refusal to enter a plea of guilty or not guilty.

12. 'O horrable murder'. The beheading of Charles I outside his own Banqueting Hall, 30 January 1649. While the officers were absent from the event that they had engineered, the packed crowd who were present gave up a deep involuntary groan as the axe severed the king's head from his body. A contemporary journalist recorded that that day was the wettest in London's history, thanks to the copious tears that were shed by the populace for their king.

13. Cromwell's siege and storm of Drogheda, 10 September 1649. Cromwell led the assault in person; nearly 3,000 royalist soldiers were killed, as well as many inhabitants, and every priest and friar who could be found. The final death toll was about 3,500, earning Cromwell a nefarious reputation in Ireland from that day until this.

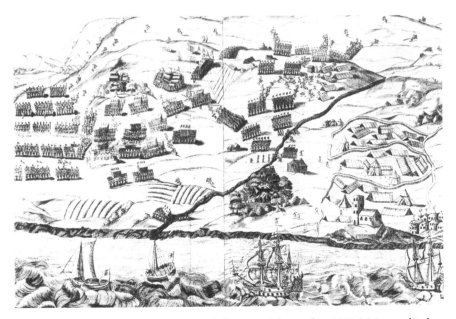

14. Dunbar, Scotland. Cromwell's most one-sided victory, 3 September 1650. Major credit also belongs to General John Lambert, who perceived the weakness in the Scottish position, and suggested crossing in front of their army under cover of darkness in order to attack their right flank at dawn. Though outnumbered two to one, the New Model crushed Leslie's army while suffering scarcely any casualties.

15. 'A Common wealth ruleing with a standing Army'. A dragon devours all property, laws and institutions, while defecating taxes and the excise. Inside its belly sits a docile parliament; below, the English people are bound in chains. The unpopularity of army rule led to its overthrow, and the restoration of monarchy, engineered (ironically) by the New Model Army itself.

16. General George Monck. The army's second most gifted commander after Cromwell. Some contemporaries had a low opinion of him as 'a dull heavy man' and 'a thick-skulled fellow', but they drastically underestimated him. Thanks to his deftness and consummate sense of political timing, Monck was able to engineer the restoration of monarchy in the face of deep unease within the New Model. What made this achievement all the more impressive was that he effected it without a drop of blood being shed.

the first through the breach, ran into unexpectedly bitter resistance. The defenders had not been idle during the bombardment, but had dug three lines of earthworks arching back from St Mary's Church to Duleek Gate, and from the church to the eastern wall. After quarter of an hour of furious combat Colonel Castle was killed by a shot to the head, and his men fell back in fear and confusion, tumbling through the breach and down the steep ravine below.

Cromwell then fired a cannonade of half-pound shot to clear the royalist horse from the breaches. Swelling the three regiments with reserves from Venables's and Farre's, he and Hewson accompanied the men on foot for a second assault. As the last daylight ebbed away they overran the enemy's entrenchments, took possession of St Mary's Church, and opened the nearby gate to their own cavalry. Aston personally made a stand on a high mound of earth known as Mill Mount. Others, hearing the offer of quarter shouted by Cromwell's men, surrendered and were taken prisoner. Spying the royalists still resisting on Mill Mount, Cromwell ordered them all put to the sword, 'and indeed, being in the heat of action, I forbade them to spare any that were in arms in the town'.[19]

Some soldiers and officers, dismayed by Cromwell's order, let their prisoners escape, but their isolated acts of mercy scarcely redeemed the night of terror. As the soldiers clattered over the bridge in pursuit of Aston's panic-stricken men they trapped many of them inside the steeple of another church – St Peter's – and two towers in the northern and western walls. They set the steeple on fire, and butchered the men as they tried to escape. Thirty refugees from the towers were spared and later shipped to Barbados.[20]

In understanding the slaughter of Drogheda, we should note that it was mostly perpetrated in the heat of battle. According to the international laws of war at the time, if a besieged town refused to surrender, was stormed and overrun, it was legitimate not only to sack and plunder it, but also to kill all those within, both soldiers and civilians. There was precedent for this in the First and Second English Civil Wars, but on nothing like the same scale. Some of the killing continued the following day when most of the royalist officers were massacred in cold blood. Sir Edmund Verney was removed from Cromwell's presence and stabbed to death. The story is told that Aston was clubbed to death with his own wooden leg by Castle's soldiers, enraged at the loss of their commander.[21]

There were 3,100 soldiers in the town, of whom 2,800 were killed, as well as many inhabitants, including every friar who could be found. Though an effort was made to spare the town's Protestant inhabitants, New Model troops deliberately attacked non-combatant Catholics in their homes. The final toll may have been about 3,500 soldiers, civilians and clergy. Parliamentary losses were about 150.[22]

After he had recovered from the shock of this second disaster, Ormond mournfully construed it as God's punishment for royalist sins. Cromwell too was convinced that God had been involved, but he was not so ebullient about the slaughter he had authorised: 'I am persuaded that this is a righteous judgement of God upon these barbarous wretches, who have imbrued their hands in so much innocent blood, and that it will tend to prevent the effusion of blood for the future, which are satisfactory grounds to such actions which otherwise cannot but work remorse and regret.' It used to be thought that Cromwell was referring to the Irish Catholics who were guilty of the massacres of English Protestants in 1641–42. But he knew as well as anyone that the garrison consisted mainly of English royalist troops, none of whom could have taken any part in the massacres. The blood guilt he was referring belonged to those who refused to accept the judgement of God in the First Civil War. By launching the Second Civil War, they had incurred direct responsibility for all the thousands of deaths in 1648. The reports of the Drogheda massacre established Cromwell's reputation for cruelty in Ireland.[23] As a practical man, he hoped that the terrible example he had set would bring Irish resistance to a speedy end and produce a net saving of lives. Subsequent events were to prove him wrong.

The shock of Drogheda continues to reverberate to the present day. At the time it was merely experienced as a second hammer-blow to royalist morale. Ormond told the king that 'it is not to be imagined how great the terror is that . . . the rebels have struck into this people'. Royalist strength continued to be sapped by desertions. Cromwell, with the magnetism of success, the power of money and the promise of protection, drew soldiers and civilians to him. A cynical royalist commented on Cromwell and his army's excellent public relations: 'So slyly the rogues allure [the countryfolk] by speaking that they are for the liberty of the commoners and . . . by hanging troopers for taking three herrings.'[24]

Wexford

Without these additions to his strength Cromwell would have found himself sorely stretched. Directly after overrunning Drogheda he sent Colonels

Robert Venables and Theophilus Jones with 5,000 troops to subdue the region north of the town. By the end of November the only coastal town in Ulster still in royalist hands was Carrickfergus. After resting his main army for a few days, Cromwell left Dublin for Wexford, collecting garrisons as he went. His conquests drank up men, for, as he explained to Parliament, each new garrison needed between a few dozen and a few hundred men to defend it. The shrinkage of his field army was accelerated by the ravages of dysentery – the 'country sickness' or 'bloody flux', as it was variously known. By the end of September, 4,000 of his men had fallen ill. On 3 November a large part of the army, under attack by Inchiquin's army at Glascarrig, was forced to fight with their breeches down because of the 'flux'. Cromwell would lose two of his most valued officers to dysentery: Colonel Thomas Horton in October and Lieutenant-General Michael Jones in December.[25]

Speaker Lenthall responded to Cromwell's appeal with an assurance that fresh recruits would soon be on their way. But by the following February recruitment was still far short of the targeted 5,000.[26]

Wexford had long been a base for privateering raids against English commerce. The town also stood out in English minds for its fervent Catholicism. Its rulers stipulated to Ormond that he send them only Catholic reinforcements.[27]

On 29 September, in advance of the army, Colonel Deane arrived in Wexford harbour with his squadron bearing food, siege guns and ammunition. For a whole week violent storms prevented him from landing them, but otherwise he met with no resistance. On 2 October Cromwell appeared before the town with his main force, now less than 8,000 strong. His summons to surrender was parried with a delaying answer from the governor, David Sinnott, who hoped that Ormond would soon relieve him. Ormond's way however was blocked by Lieutenant-General Michael Jones.[28] The besiegers were given another boost by the news that two of Lord Inchiquin's regiments had cast off their officers and seized the nearby garrison of Youghal. Cromwell was none the less anxious. The heavy winds and rain, food shortages and relentless attacks of dysentery had in a matter of days further reduced his effective numbers to 6,000. Sinnott's demands for liberty of worship and the maintenance of clerical privileges only aggravated Cromwell's impatience, and on the 11th he started his bombardment. He had soon blasted a hole through the castle's walls. The townsfolk began to flee by boat, the defenders quailed, and the magistrates sent out a message that they wished to negotiate a surrender.

While negotiations were underway, however, the Catholic governor unilaterally yielded up the castle. The parliamentary soldiers lost no time, but immediately seized the castle's guns and turned them on the town. Recognising the disaster now overtaking them, the town's defenders promptly fled. With the collapse of the town's defences, the men occupying the castle did not wait for orders, but at once launched an assault. Hoisting themselves up with pikes and scaling ladders, they took possession of the town within half an hour. Some of the enemy made a stand in the market place, but were soon overcome and killed on the spot. Another 300 who tried to escape across the harbour drowned when their boats sank. Any priests or friars unfortunate enough to cross the attackers' path were butchered without mercy.

Cromwell estimated the death toll at Wexford at around 2,000 on the royalist side and less than twenty on his own. What is appalling is that the slaughter was more or less accidental. The garrison had been on the point of surrender, and there was no order from Cromwell to put anyone to the sword. On the other hand, his men carried out what they believed from previous practice to be his policy, and he did not rebuke them for it. The Wexford slaughter, unlike that at Drogheda, occurred in the midst of negotiations for the town's surrender. For this there could be no appeal to the laws of war.[29]

Cromwell's own hope had been that they could take the town peacefully, 'Yet God would not have it so; but by an unexpected providence, in His righteous justice, brought a just judgement upon them, causing them to become a prey to the soldier'.[30] After Wexford Cromwell's effective force was down to 5,600 men, of whom some would be left behind to garrison the town. With men, money and supplies arriving very slowly from England, and with his soldiers now on half-pay, the standard of conduct in the New Model deteriorated sharply. His situation would have been desperate but for the near-collapse of his foes.[31]

Ormond's shaky coalition was disintegrating. His immediate problem after the loss of Wexford was the betrayal, within the space of a month, of five Munster towns. These betrayals had been engineered by Lord Broghill at Cromwell's instigation. The fall of four more Munster towns was not long in coming. The loss of Kinsale meant that Prince Rupert with his royalist fleet had to make a hasty getaway. By the middle of November Inchiquin had lost virtually all his army and Ormond was in disgrace in Catholic Irish eyes.[32]

Waterford

Cromwell's next major target was a further 35 miles down the coast. On 17 October he was before New Ross, which guarded the approaches to Waterford, and summoned the governor, Major Lucas Taaffe. Several townsmen had already let him know that they welcomed his arrival. When Taaffe asked for liberty of conscience in exchange for surrender Cromwell set him straight on the English understanding of this concept: 'I meddle not with any man's conscience, but if by liberty of conscience you mean a liberty to exercise the mass, I judge it best to use plain dealing, and to let you know [that] where the parliament of England have power, that will not be allowed of.' He then unleashed his cannon; Taaffe yielded at once, and 500 of his soldiers crossed over to the parliamentary side.[33]

Cromwell spent the next several weeks preparing to assault Waterford. As he told Speaker Lenthall, 'a considerable part of your army is fitter for a hospital than the field'. By the time he arrived before Waterford his troops numbered barely 6,500, even counting the large numbers who had crossed over from Inchiquin's army.[34]

The second city in Ireland, Waterford's Catholic citizenry had made of it a thriving commercial centre next only to Dublin in both population and wealth.[35] Defensively it was well situated on the River Suir, its ample harbour guarded by two forts: Duncannon on the east and Passage on the west. The royalists had to hold the harbour if Cromwell was to be stopped from bringing in heavy artillery by sea. Ormond placed James Tuchet, third earl of Castlehaven in charge of Passage, and Colonel Edward Wogan in charge of Duncannon. Wogan was the turncoat captain of dragoons who had quit the New Model Army in 1647. A brilliant tactician, as well as a man of extraordinary personal magnetism, Wogan was a born fighter. When he saw Lieutenant-General Michael Jones's 2,000 men investing his garrison he realised that his only hope lay in a ruse. He arranged for Castlehaven to ferry eighty cavalry from across the harbour at Passage. When he threw these troops into his next sortie, Jones, believing that Wogan himself had no cavalry, jumped to the conclusion that Ormond must have just arrived with the field army. This prompted him to withdraw in disorder.[36]

This setback was most unwelcome to Cromwell. 'Crazy in my health', he admitted to Parliament, and with his army demanding to retire to winter quarters, he called off his intended assault against Waterford. With ten men being carried off every night by disease, his numbers were now down to barely 3,000 troops fit for action. And so, on 2 December he quit Waterford, under pelting rain, 'it being as terrible a day as ever I marched in, all my life'. The cost of defeat was high. Not only were his men demoralised, but he had lost two valued officers – his kinsman Major Philip Cromwell and Lieutenant-General Jones – to disease.[37]

Waterford was the only Irish city that successfully resisted a siege by Oliver Cromwell. It is noteworthy that at Waterford alone Cromwell was deprived of his artillery. The wretched weather made the ground 'so moist and rotten' that he could not haul the heavy guns overland. Wogan's brilliant defence of Duncannon meant that he could not bring them by sea either. The resistance at Waterford showed that the terror of Drogheda and Wexford had already worn off. Far from preventing further bloodshed, these atrocities sharpened the resolve of royalists and Catholics alike to resist the invader with every ounce of their strength.

Apart from this one setback, Cromwell could now contemplate with satisfaction what he had accomplished during his short stay in Ireland. With the fall of Carrickfergus to Sir Charles Coote on 6 December, his control of the entire Irish eastern and southern coastline was broken only at Waterford. The Munster towns betrayed by Inchiquin's soldiers gave comfortable winter quarters for his army. In comparison with his enemy Cromwell continued to be richly endowed with arms, ammunition and money, and he knew that Sir Hardress Waller would soon be on his way from England with an infusion of 3,000 recruits. More important in the short term were the seasoned troops he detached from Inchiquin and other commanders. Their familiarity with the country made them far less susceptible to disease.[38] Cromwell knew there was a lot more to be accomplished before he could pronounce Ireland conquered. Had he known that at that moment Parliament was planning to recall him to England, he would have been profoundly dissatisfied at leaving a job half done.

The aura of defeat had fatally undermined Catholic Irish confidence in Ormond. Increasingly the Irish were heard to say they could trust no one who did not go to Mass. In a bid to halt the corrosion of trust within the royalist alliance, the bishops met at Clonmacnoise and issued a call for Irish unity. They reminded their people that Cromwell was a mortal enemy, from whom they could expect neither toleration nor mercy.[39]

The bishops' appeal for unity drew from Cromwell a ferocious counter blast. His 'Declaration for the Undeceiving of Deluded and Seduced People' slammed the clergy for greed, pride, cruelty and ambition. They had kept the people ignorant and plunged the country into a terrible rebellion: 'Your covenant is with death and hell . . . You are a part of Antichrist . . . and ere it be long, you must all of you have blood to drink; even the dregs of the cup of the fury and the wrath of God.' In a gross distortion of history he lectured the bishops that their country had prospered under English rule. He denied any intention to 'massacre, banish and destroy the Catholic inhabitants' of Ireland, unless they took up arms against him. The purpose of the parliamentary army was 'to ask an account of the innocent blood that hath been shed'. Nevertheless, 'if this people shall headily run on after the counsels of their prelates and clergy and other leaders, I . . . shall rejoice to exercise utmost severity against them'.[40] Cromwell had been in Parliament in 1641, when he had heard Pym's exhaustive indictment of Strafford's misgovernment of Ireland. He therefore had an inkling of the grievances of the native population against their English overlords.

Kilkenny

The Irish were not given long to digest the significance of Cromwell's Declaration. The mild winter permitted him to resume his military campaign on 29 January. He was determined to make quick work of it. By mid-March, apart from the province of Connacht, only Limerick, Waterford, Kilkenny and Clonmel still resisted. But time was running out. In March and again in April Parliament sent him urgent instructions to return home. Preoccupied with his sieges, he attempted to block out the unwelcome messages from England. In March he was engaged with Hewson and Ireton in a pincer movement against Kilkenny. Under Cromwell's instructions, Hewson marched from Dublin through Kildare, to rendezvous with his commanders at Gowran Castle. The threat of artillery fire brought the defenders to their knees, after which all but one of the officers were shot and a priest hanged, while the soldiers who were English crossed to Cromwell's side.[41]

On 22 March they were before Kilkenny. The handsome headquarters of the Catholic Confederation, it was also the chief inland town of Ireland. Standing on the banks of the River Nore, it was divided into two parts, Kilkenny proper and Irishtown, and would not be easily overrun.[42] However, it was now experiencing its own agony. The plague, which had begun at Galway the previous summer, had spread rapidly inland, and now was raging within Kilkenny's walls. Despite the hopelessness of his situation, the town's governor, Sir Walter Butler, refused to surrender. Cromwell opened fire with his artillery at 9 a.m. on 25 March, and by noon had made a breach in the town wall. The counter-measures taken by the town's defenders revealed that the Irish were now becoming adept at neutralising Cromwell's heavy guns. Around the area where the hole was blasted they had thrown up two counterworks of earth, strongly palisaded. To create a diversion Cromwell sent Colonel Ewer across the river with 1,000 foot to possess Irishtown. When Cromwell flung his men into the breach under the leadership of Axtell and Hewson, the Irish, who were more than ready, poured withering fire on them from the safety of their palisades. Cromwell did not acknowledge the ingeniousness of the defence, but blamed his men for not performing 'with usual courage nor success'. They were beaten off with the loss of a captain and twenty to thirty men killed or wounded.

A second attempt was also abortive, and after each assault the defences were repaired A third order to attack was disobeyed, while losses continued to mount. By now, however, Ewer had taken Irishtown, and Butler could see that the end was in sight, so he reopened negotiations. Cromwell, in a hurry to get to Clonmel, granted generous terms, leaving Lieutenant-Colonel Axtell behind as governor.[43]

Clonmel

The siege of Clonmel a month later demonstrated afresh the maturing Irish ability to withstand the shock of parliamentary heavy guns.[44] Clonmel was a populous, well-fortified town about 25 miles upstream from Waterford on the River Suir. By April the size of its garrison had grown to over 2,000. Cromwell encamped before the town for three weeks before he deployed his heavy artillery. At the point where the breach was being opened, the governor, Hugh Dubh O'Neill, enlisted every available person within to build a twin set of makeshift walls out of rubbish, stones, timber and mortar, running back 80 yards from either side of the breach. At the end of the lane this created he dug a deep ditch and planted his own guns behind it. As fortune would have it there was a row of houses running just behind one of the walls where the breach was appearing. The upper storeys of these houses he filled with soldiers, in order that they could fire on the invaders when they charged through the breach.

Not suspecting any of these arrangements, Cromwell ordered the storm to begin at eight o'clock on the morning of 16 May.[45] The town was eerily quiet as Colonel Arthur Culme led the men into the breach, singing a hymn. In contrast to most assaults on city walls, this one included a sizeable contingent of horse, because the foot had insisted that the cavalry should run the same hazards as them. By the time those at the front realised they were in a trap, the whole lane was crammed with troops. In vain they cried to those behind them to halt. The men entering the breach, hearing them shout, thought the defenders of the garrison were on the run, and jubilantly cried 'Advance! Advance!' In the confusion no one was able to budge. At that moment a party of O'Neill's pikemen and musketeers ran to the breach and sealed it off. His main force then fell on those trapped in the lane, with muskets, pikes, scythes and stones. They also threw long timber posts among the helpless invaders, and let loose with their two artillery pieces from the end of the lane, cutting the invaders between the knees and the stomach with chained bullets. In the space of an hour 1,000 men were piled dead on top of one another.

In the meantime Cromwell had ridden with his guard to the town gate, expecting it to be opened for him. His first clue that something had gone wrong was the sound of cannon going off within the town. Unaccustomed to defeat, Cromwell determined that they must attack again. For four hours he poured men through the deadly breach, but they were continually mowed down, At the end of the day he had lost 1,500 men and still failed to break the town's resistance.[46]

Later that night, however, O'Neill and his Ulster regiment slipped out of the town in the direction of Waterford. Their ammunition had run out and they knew they could expect no relief. At midnight the townsmen sent a message asking to treat for surrender. Cromwell quickly granted the town easy terms. Only after making the agreement did he discover the deception. Angry as he was he stuck to his terms, and when his men entered the town they did no damage.[47]

A week later, after barely nine months in Ireland, Cromwell left. He had come expecting a quick conquest. His deliberate policy had been to spread terror by shedding blood, in order to save it later. But it had not worked out as he intended. As his campaign wore on he found the Irish did not terrify easily, and his victories became ever more costly.[48]

In principle the war should now have been largely a mopping-up operation. The provinces of Ulster and Leinster were firmly under parliamentary control, while in Munster the Irish held only Waterford, Duncannon, Limerick and the fastnesses of Kerry. The only province they could still call their own was the poorest, Connacht. Bubonic plague was now raging across the breadth of the country, with neither side being spared its devastation.[49]

Upon the death of Owen Roe O'Neill in November 1649, the provincial assembly of Ulster commissioned Emer McMahon, bishop of Clogher, as his successor. He led his 6,000-strong army to Letterkenny. There Sir Charles Coote's forces wiped out the precious army he had inherited from Owen Roe. Bishop McMahon was captured the next day, hanged and quartered, and his head set on the gate at Londonderry.[50]

Thanks to the impetuosity and inexperience of its clerical leader, the main Catholic army in Ireland had been lost. Most of the remaining garrisons in Leinster and Munster tumbled into Parliament's lap that summer. Those still bent on resistance withdrew to Connacht and the fastnesses of Kerry in western Munster. In December Ormond quit Ireland. The news of Cromwell's triumph in Scotland and Charles II's treaty with the Scottish Presbyterians (see below, pp. 205, 209ff.) clinched the discrediting of the royalist cause in Ireland.[51]

In reality the Irish would have been happy to negotiate an end to the killing and destruction of their country but for one stumbling block: England's refusal to let them practise the Catholic religion. Cromwell's Declaration in January 1650 had made it brutally clear that the price of maintaining their religion would be a struggle to the death. The instructions issued to the parliamentary commissioners for Ireland in November of the same year, calling for the 'suppression of idolatry, popery, superstition and profaneness', demonstrated that Cromwell's policy was still in force. Yet a few months after their arrival in January 1651 the parliamentary commissioners, backed by Henry Ireton, wrote to the Council of State proposing a more tolerant and compassionate approach than their instructions permitted. Otherwise, they said, the soil would go untilled, flocks untended, and the war prolonged indefinitely. The financial burden to England would be incalculable. The Council of State and the Rump referred their statesmanlike proposal back and forth without taking any action, and Ireland descended ever deeper into the maelstrom of violence.[52]

When Cromwell left Ireland in May 1650, Henry Ireton took charge, with the title of lord deputy. Other commanders had shown greater military flair: Sir Charles Coote, Commissary-General Reynolds, Lord Broghill, Colonel John Hewson, but none matched Cromwell's political and religious outlook as closely as his own son-in-law. A month later Edmund Ludlow joined Ireton as lieutenant-general of horse. For the remainder of the summer their main obstacle was the pestilence, which ravaged Irish and parliamentary troops alike. Ireton, resolving to combat this foe with divine weapons, proclaimed an eight-day fast on 6 August. Four days later Thomas Preston surrendered Waterford after Ireton offered generous terms: the soldiers marched out with their weapons, luggage, horses and colours, while the citizens stayed, unmolested.[53]

Limerick

Limerick was a large, well-defended city sitting athwart the River Shannon where it divides, its sturdy walls shaped like an hourglass. Ireton was confident he could exploit the bitter factionalism that smouldered within the city and force its surrender before another winter set in. By mid-October, however, Limerick was still holding out, and Ireton withdrew to winter quarters. If at any time in the preceding months he had made a vigorous attack the city would almost certainly have toppled. It was out of ammunition.[54]

In May 1651 Ireton led his army once more against Limerick. By the time he arrived there was already a flotilla of parliamentary ships in the mouth of the Shannon. The ships blocked the estuary, kept the army supplied with provisions, and later brought up the heavy guns for siege operations.[55]

On 14 June Ireton launched a bombardment of the castle. Two days later the defenders sued for peace, but the talks foundered on Ireton's refusal to promise any tolerance for the Catholic religion. Inconclusively the siege dragged on through the summer and into the autumn, with the daunting prospect that the besiegers might have to go through a third year before Limerick surrendered. Ireton was kept supplied with food, munitions and money in quantities that the Irish could only dream of, yet he seemed incapable of bringing the city to its knees. During the spring and summer of 1651, Parliament sent an additional 9,000 troops to Ireland, but disease, frost, hard marching and enemy attack 'considerably wasted them'. By the end of October, 2,000 had been lost at Limerick alone.[56]

Had Cromwell been in charge the siege would have been over much sooner. But Ireton lacked Cromwell's decisiveness. For almost four months he relied on starvation to win the city for him. Not until 27 October did he identify a sector of the city wall that lacked an earthen backing. As soon as he unleashed his battery against it the masonry collapsed. As the storming party prepared to hurl itself into the breach, the defenders abandoned their insistence on religious freedom, and surrendered under the articles that Ireton had offered them several months earlier. Twenty-two notables were excluded from mercy including the governor, Hugh Dubh O'Neill. The Council of

War found itself divided over his fate. He had impressed the parliamentary officers by his courteous and cooperative behaviour after the surrender.

Ireton however was obsessed with the humiliation that O'Neill had inflicted on the parliamentary troops at Clonmel. Three times he compelled the Council of War to vote on O'Neill's death. Finally he yielded to the majority, who wished to spare O'Neill's life. The incident sheds light on the officers' sense of honour as well as their admiration for O'Neill. It also shines a spotlight on Ireton's harshness, but also on his ability to listen and change his mind.[57]

The five-month siege of Limerick cost Ireton his life. A few days after it was over he came down with a bad cold. Yet he refused to relax his pace of work. He rode through a storm to Clare, where his cold turned into a fever, but he insisted on carrying on. By 26 November he was dead. With his death the New Model lost its leading intellectual theoretician and politician. His genius lay in his ability to articulate with his pen a coherent vision of godly republicanism. Through his voluminous writings and political realism in action he forged a unity of purpose in the New Model Army between 1647 and 1649. To Ireton as much as any individual belongs the credit for calling monarchy to account and erecting the English republic on its ruins.

Guerrilla Warfare, 1651–52

At the time of Ireton's death the war had already entered into a new phase. Soon virtually all of the nearly 400 forts and garrisons in Ireland were in parliamentary hands. Control of the garrisons ironically weakened Parliament's grip on the country. Pinned down in them, the soldiers found their freedom of movement reduced. The enemy, by contrast, were free to roam at large, wreaking havoc when and where they pleased. Defeated in the field, and deprived of urban strongholds, the Irish adopted the classic tactic of guerrilla warfare against the occupying power.[58]

Before the end of 1650 the three provinces of Munster, Leinster and Ulster were already 'much infested with tories', as the dispossessed native outlaws were called. Characteristically they conducted lightning raids, and then retreated to bogs, woods or mountains where the cavalry could not venture. They captured the arms and munitions they needed from their enemy. Violence and disorder seemed endless. According to the parliamentary commissioners the root of the problem was Parliament's refusal to give the Irish security for their estates. The result was the economic near-collapse of the country. The stock of cattle was reduced to almost zero, while four-fifths of fertile land lay waste and uninhabited. Bubonic plague was everywhere; many starved to death, while others kept themselves alive by feeding on 'those very bodies of men who had a little before perished for famine'. This was a very recent development. As late as 1650 food was so plentiful in Ireland that it was cheaper than in England. A year later it was the opposite: the price of bread was much higher in Ireland and starvation stalked the land.[59]

Between the summer of 1651, when the parliamentary commissioners wrote their doleful report on the condition of Ireland, and the passage of the Act of Settlement, thirteen months later, the situation only worsened. The army grew to over 33,000 – nearly three times the number Cromwell had brought over. Yet a third of the recruits Parliament had sent the previous year were now dead. One of the ironies of the occupation is that increasingly the New Model Army had to rely on native Catholic Irish recruits to fill its empty ranks. In February 1652 the commissioners had to admit that great stretches of the country were still under enemy control in all four provinces. Two and a half years after Cromwell's arrival in Ireland, Parliament was still engaged in an unremitting war against the native population. At the end of 1651 there were said to be 30,000 men in arms against Parliament 'besides the people generally ready to join with them upon any occasion'. As late as the summer of 1652 the parliamentary commissioners were still engaging enemy armies larger than their own.[60]

In this guerrilla phase the parliamentary commanders tried to imitate the tactics of their enemies, by denying the tories food and rendering them hateful to the rural population. By 1652 every vestige of the earlier enlightened attitudes of Whalley, Ireton and Ludlow had vanished. In April a joint meeting of army officers and parliamentary commissioners at Kilkenny declared that it was their own leniency and weakness that had encouraged the obstinacy of the Irish. Indicting the whole nation for 'blood-guiltiness', they professed to be 'deeply . . . affected with the barbarous wickedness of . . . these cruel murthers and massacres'. The commissioners' loathing for the Irish was reinforced in May, when they read Scoutmaster-General Henry Jones's lengthy abstract of several thousand depositions concerning barbarous cruelty to Protestants in 1641 and after. Colonel John Jones believed that because the Irish were a 'cursed people', Christ had had to fetch instruments from farther off to save the country, and that he was one of these instruments.[61]

Formally speaking, resistance came to an end in May 1652 with the signing of the Kilkenny articles between the parliamentarians and the Irish in Leinster. The forces there agreed to lay down their arms by 1 June, and a few days later in the other three provinces. Yet at the end of the year it was reported that 11,000 men still kept up the resistance against Parliament.[62]

The Land Settlement

If the Irish were a cursed people, then it was justifiable to replace them with a new population. The name of this policy was plantation or transplantation, and its chief architect had been Henry Ireton. In the beginning the towns of the south-east such as Waterford were to be colonised with soldier-settlers from England to take the place of the Catholic Irish inhabitants. This would not only free up garrison troops, but also keep the towns from collapsing economically from depopulation. In February 1651 Parliament had approved the scheme and Ireton had made ready to remove the citizens of Waterford.[63]

Initially he had planned to remove the entire Catholic population from the three provinces of Munster, Leinster and Ulster and resettle them in Connacht. This promised the security that the Adventurers craved, but it had quickly become apparent that denuding the country of most of its native population would quickly lead to the collapse of food production and the evaporation of tax revenues. It didn't take the four parliamentary commissioners long to change their minds about the need for wholesale transplantation. Exemptions were granted for ploughing, sowing and harvesting crops. In March 1655 Colonel Richard Lawrence explained that transplantation only applied to those who had served in the armies of the Catholic regime, and to landowners. Parliament had been trying to square the circle. On the one hand it needed the native Irish population to till the soil and prevent economic collapse. On the other hand the new settlers would not feel secure unless the land was cleansed of its native population. Not only that, the new regime needed every inch of Irish land it could lay its hands on to meet its obligations to the Irish Adventurers of 1641–42 – a group of merchants, financiers and MPs who had invested over £1 million in the invasion of Ireland – and to its soldiers. To honour the pledge to the Adventurers would require about 1 million acres. By 1652 no less than £1.75 million was owed to the soldiers for their back pay. So in theory, under the terms of the Act for the Settlement of Ireland (12 August 1652), more than half the landmass of Ireland was transferred to Adventurers and soldiers, and all Catholic landowners and soldiers were transplanted to Connacht and County Clare. However, many exemptions were granted. Another difficulty in the way of transplantation was the numerous surrender articles signed by the parliamentary commanders with the Catholic and royalist Irish troops. In order to bring a speedier end to the fighting, these articles often allowed the Irish most of their land and freedom of worship. For example, in return for their surrender in April 1652, Sir Charles Coote had granted the townsmen of Galway two-thirds of their lands. The parliamentary commissioners in Dublin, supported by the Council of State in London, tried to overthrow these lenient terms and deprive the townsmen of their lands, but in the end the commissioners accepted the validity of Coote's original articles.[64]

By July 1655, transplantation had already effectively come to a halt. While Adventurers and soldiers both proclaimed that they wanted a tough line on transplantation, the soldiers soon wanted to retain their Catholic tenants. There was a scheme for the Protestant settlement of five southeastern counties. All Catholics were to be shipped out of these counties to Connacht. It didn't work. By 1659 in County Kildare, for example, Catholics outnumbered Protestants by fifteen to one. In County Wicklow the Catholics not only remained but also kept their weapons.[65]

Dr William Petty's accurate estimate in the 1670s was that 700,000 acres in Connacht had been assigned to transplanters in the 1650s. They in their turn had been displaced from at least 2 million profitable acres elsewhere in Ireland. This was a revolution in landownership. Catholics had owned 61 per cent of the land in 1641; by 1678 their share had shrunk to less than 21 per cent. In one Irish county – Fermanagh – Protestants had entirely replaced native Irish landholders by the Restoration.[66]

This revolution was made possible by Petty. Arriving in Ireland in 1652 as physician to the Cromwellian army, within two short years he had wrested control of the surveying of Catholic-held lands from the civil authorities. He promised to complete the survey in thirteen months, and kept his promise. Under his supervision 1,000 soldier-surveyors, working parish by parish, set out to measure all the forfeited lands of Ireland. The result was 'the most epic and monumental transformation of Irish life, property and landscape that the island has ever known'. The emergence of the Protestant ascendancy class, which would dominate Ireland until the reforms of the nineteenth century, was made possible by the Down Survey, designed by Petty and carried out by the soldiers of the New Model Army. A committee of officers monitored all the work. Yet in the end, such was the cost of maintaining the army of occupation that the lands reserved for them only covered two-thirds of their arrears. To the civilian administrators and the population at large the army was a great monster into whose insatiable maw money was endlessly poured.[67]

While the measuring was going on, the population of the country continued its precipitous decline. According to the best modern estimate, Ireland lost 15–20 per cent of its population, or about 300,000 people, between 1641 and the Restoration, with the bulk of the deaths concentrated between 1649 and 1652. It was by far the largest loss of life in the three nations during the English Revolution. This nightmare could have been largely avoided had the parliamentarians been willing to grant the Irish their land and the practice of their religion. In a dignified statement in August 1652, Sir Phelim O'Neill and sixteen other Irish leaders declared their willingness even to give up their lands if they could be allowed the free practice of their religion. Failing that 'we beseech the omnipotent God to protect us from the violence of such as thirst after Catholic blood and our extirpation'.[68] Three years later, guerrilla war was continuing almost unabated, and the three provinces assigned to the English still swarmed with tories.

Spreading the Gospel

A number of zealous New Model officers regarded conquered Ireland as a blank slate, a white sheet of paper on which a 'Christian' (meaning Protestant) commonwealth could be inscribed. Colonel John Jones, a parliamentary commissioner until 1654, believed that they had been led by God 'into a strange land and to act in as strange a work, a work that neither we nor our forefathers knew or heard of: the framing or forming of a commonwealth out of a corrupt rude mass'. Encouraged by Cromwell's son-in-law, Lieutenant-General Charles Fleetwood, who became lord deputy of Ireland in August 1652, they strained every muscle to turn their millennial visions into reality.[69]

Oliver Cromwell and three military chaplains, Hugh Peters, John Owen and Jenkin Lloyd, were the driving force behind the 'Ordinance for the Propagation of the Gospel in Ireland', passed in March 1650. The arrival of Lord Deputy Fleetwood in September 1652 opened the doors to religious separatism. In the name of religious freedom for Protestants, soldiers preached, and Ireland was subjected to a kind of religious extremism and oppression that it had never before experienced.[70]

Baptists were dominant in the early 1650s, promoted by Lieutenant-General Ludlow and Adjutant-General William Allen. Tours of duty by Baptist soldiers fostered the evangelisation of the country. Notable converts were the military governors of Waterford and Kilkenny, Colonel Richard Lawrence and Lieutenant-Colonel Daniel Axtell. But outside the garrisons converts were few.

After Oliver Cromwell's son Henry replaced Fleetwood in 1655 the Baptists' political power declined, only to be replaced by a new radical religious threat: Quakerism. Officers such as Lieutenant-Colonel Robert Phaire, the governor of Cork, and Major Richard Hodden, the governor of Kinsale, were convinced that the Quakers would accomplish Ireland's long-delayed reformation. 'We look for a new heaven and a new earth', wrote Hodden.[71] Few soldiers and even fewer native Irish were won over. Alert to the political danger of Quakerism in the army, Henry Cromwell took ruthless steps to extinguish it. Quaker officers were cashiered and military discipline was restored.

Late in the day (April 1658), Henry Cromwell came to an agreement with the Presbyterians for a state church supported by tithes. In doing so he turned his back on the Independents, and angered Hugh Peters, who reminded him that 'your father died as he lived, an Independent'.[72]

Much as the parliamentary authorities yearned to eradicate Catholicism, the goal was beyond their reach. Two-thirds of the soldiers sold the debentures they had been issued for their arrears to their officers, and no more than 12,000 settled in Ireland. Nor did they stay long: barely 2,000 remained after 1660. As in England, the debentures of the rank and file were heavily discounted when they were sold to the officers for the purchase of confiscated land. Soldiers received anywhere from 20 to 60 per cent of the face value of their debentures. The reluctance of most of the rank and file to sink roots in an unfriendly land effectively sabotaged the vision of a Protestant yeomanry tilling the soil of Ireland.[73]

Running the Country

On the other hand, New Model Army officers made an active and telling contribution to the administration of Ireland during the decade of the Commonwealth and Protectorate. Besides Lord Deputy Fleetwood, two of the first four parliamentary commissioners – Lieutenant-General Edmund Ludlow and Colonel John Jones – were New Model officers. When the commissioners were replaced by an Irish Council, two of its four members were military – Colonels Miles Corbet and Matthew Tomlinson. When Henry Cromwell arrived in the late summer of 1655 they became his vociferous enemies. Yet among Henry's closest advisers were another two army men: Colonel Sir John Reynolds and Major Dr Anthony Morgan. Colonel Sir Hardress Waller, an old Irish Protestant with a large landed estate, was entrusted by his fellow officers in 1653 to represent them in London. Three out the six men sent from Ireland to Barebone's Parliament (see below, pp. 253–6) were army officers: Colonels Henry Cromwell, John Hewson and John Clarke. Before the arrival of Dr William Petty, the chief surveyors for the project of transplantation were army officers: Dr Henry Jones, Colonel Edward Doyly and Major Miles Symnes.[74]

In the judicial sphere, New Model Army officers wielded immense influence. Out of twenty named to the Commission of the Peace for Leinster, eight were English army officers. Colonel John Hewson, assisted by the entire officer corps stationed in Dublin, presided over the court-martial that mediated relations between the soldiers of Dublin garrison and the civilian population of the city. Many soldiers were punished for theft and drunkenness, and ordered to pay restitution to their victims. Meeting weekly, the court inflicted punishments that were chiefly corporal – whippings, running the gauntlet, riding the wooden horse, being tied neck and heels together, being compelled to wear a sign identifying the nature of the offence, being gagged, tied to the gallows or forced to stand on a stool. One soldier had his tongue drawn out with pincers and bored with a red-hot iron for swearing, drunkenness and neglect of duty. Other punishments were less gruesome: fines, cashiering or demotion. The Dublin court-martial appears to have been successful at maintaining relatively high standards of conduct among the military. We don't hear of Dublin's landlords, shopkeepers or women suffering outrageous abuse or exploitation at the hands of soldiers. On the other hand, it is doubtful if all the exertions of the Dublin court-martial won the army many friends among the civilian population.[75]

Civilians too were hauled before the court-martial. The leading charge against them was spying or communicating with tories. Five of the forty-three charged with this offence were either acquitted or had their convictions suspended, while another two had their trials postponed pending further investigation.[76]

Army officers were also a strong presence on the High Court of Justice. Astonishingly, it pardoned some 41 per cent of those brought before it. This was a much higher rate of acquittal than in the English high courts in the same period. As Jennifer Wells has written, 'law and legal process served as languages of legitimation to consolidate power and authority in the wake of violent conquest in both the domestic and the imperial spheres'. Five of the sixty-two commissioners were New Model officers, some of whom had been connected with the High Court of Justice that tried Charles I – Colonels Hewson, Waller, Reynolds and Venables, as well as Henry Cromwell. The Irish court was well ahead of courts in England in reducing the frequency of the death penalty, providing legal aid and counsel for defendants and permitting witnesses for the defence as well as for the prosecution, and in its high ratio of acquittals.[77]

The Political Influence of the Officers in Ireland

Not only did the New Model officers play a leading role in running Ireland during the 1650s, they also had a lot to say about politics at Westminster. When John Weaver, their arch-enemy among the parliamentary commissioners, returned to London in 1652, he made it his business to thwart the New Model and cut it down to size at every turn. His motives? Reducing the strain on the Commonwealth's Treasury, and upholding parliamentary rule against the threat of military dictatorship. It was he who mobilised the Rump in May 1652 to abolish – for a time – the posts of lord-lieutenant and lord deputy of Ireland. This was not only a blow against Oliver Cromwell – one of many – but also against Lambert (among the ablest and most intelligent of the officers), who had been promised the latter position, and, indeed, a blow against the army as a whole. There were more provocations to come, which incensed the officers in Ireland. The numerous articles of surrender that had brought an end to the war ran directly counter to the draconian Act of Settlement of August 1652, which specified the death penalty for countless thousands of Catholic Irish. The surrender articles promised much milder treatment, and the officers felt passionately that their honour was at stake in upholding them in the face of the punitive Act of Settlement.[78]

Yet the officers themselves were torn between their reverence for the surrender articles, and their low opinion of the Irish. They could not get the massacres of 1641–42 out of their heads. A collective letter to the Speaker of the Commons about a meeting between the civilian authorities and a number of senior officers referred to the 'blood-guiltiness of this people', and expressed the fear that 'our behaviour towards this people may never sufficiently avenge the same'. That is why they ordered several Irish cities and towns cleared of their inhabitants – Limerick, Galway, Clonmel and Lackagh among others. That is why, too, soldiers were strictly forbidden to marry papist Irishwomen, and why in 1655 1,000 Irish girls were conscripted and sent to newly conquered Jamaica 'for their own good'. It is why 35,000–40,000 Irish soldiers were either allowed or encouraged to go off and serve the king of Spain or other continental rulers, and why 15,000–25,000 priests and schoolmasters, as well as ordinary men, women and children, were shipped as slaves to work on the sugar plantations of Barbados and Virginia.[79]

The radical, mainly Baptist, officers had a constant friend in Lieutenant-General Fleetwood, who by marrying Cromwell's daughter Bridget (Henry Ireton's widow), obtained direct access to the future lord protector. The Baptist officers regarded themselves as torchbearers for the 'Good Old Cause' (see below, p. 258), and kept a close watch on Westminster politics. Along with their counterparts in England and Scotland, Baptist officers aligned themselves with the Three Colonels' Petition of 1654 (see below, pp. 258–9). Adjutant-General Allen took up the torch for Colonel Alured's cause, as did Lieutenant-General Ludlow, who was caught circulating the petition in January 1655, and Colonel Hierome (or Jerome) Sankey, who also had close links with the radical John Wildman. The government appears to have been more effective at keeping the lid on dissension in England.[80]

Mid-way through the Interregnum there was a big debate between the radicals and their critics on how best to run Ireland. It took the form of a pamphlet war between Vincent Gookin, an old Irish Protestant, and the governor of Waterford Colonel Richard Lawrence, a radical Baptist. Gookin questioned the policy of transplantation, and gave reasons why it was unnecessary. First of all, there was nothing to fear from mutual contact between Protestants and papists. It was far more likely that the papists would convert to Protestantism than vice-versa. Second, since only a minority of the Irish were guilty of shedding English blood, it was wrong to punish the whole nation. Third, England's punitive treatment of the native Irish was turning them into thieves, and driving them into the hands of the tories. The economic arguments against transplantation were if anything more telling. The native Irish were far more skilled than the English adventurers and soldiers at farming, clothmaking and house-building. Removing them to the province of Connacht would deprive the rest of the country of their skills, and devastate the state's tax revenues. More than that, concentrating them into one province would make it easier for them to organise themselves for rebellion.

Gookin ended by underlining the cruelty practised by the army of occupation: 'the violence and oppression by some of the soldiers ... is incredible; and by the injured people's just fear to complain, many horrible facts of this nature go daily unpunished.'[81]

Speaking for the army, Richard Lawrence struck back with an unabashed defence of transplantation. First was the argument of security. Transplantation would eliminate future rebellions, and the expense of suppressing them. It would also 'be a means to preserve the English from degenerating and learning Irish customs and manners'. As for the economic argument, a great part of the country was so wasted and depopulated that it paid hardly any tax anyway. Citing the remarkable success of the Anglo-Irish Protestant Richard Boyle, second earl of Cork, Lawrence was confident that the arrival of English Protestant settlers would soon make the soil of Ireland far more productive than it was under their previous Catholic owners and tenants. Elsewhere he admitted that Irish agricultural techniques were not so inefficient after all. Irish farmers would be able to undersell the English settlers in the marketplace if the English were not granted tax breaks and subsidies. The reason why so many English settlers had recently returned with 'discouragement and loss' is that they came with unrealistic expectations into a country still at war and ruined by plague and famine. Finally, transplantation, by increasing security, would enable the disbandment of a large part of the army, and bring about large tax savings.[82]

The arrival of Henry Cromwell in July 1655 as commander of the army and chief administrator shifted the argument decisively in favour of the moderates and against the army radicals. Henry was passionately supported by the Old Protestants – such as Lord Broghill, Vincent Gookin, Sir Charles Coote and Sir Hardress Waller, whose families had arrived before the 1640s – and by a minority of serving army officers. The majority, however, harboured an inveterate suspicion of Oliver's younger son, and were a continual thorn in his flesh, not least because they were consistently supported by Lieutenant-General Fleetwood, who undermined Henry's authority at every turn, even though he was now in London. Matters were not helped by the ambivalence displayed by Oliver Cromwell, now lord protector (see below, p. 203), who felt the enduring emotional tug of his old comrades in the army, and who did more than a little to weaken his son's struggle against the radicals. Matters were made worse for Henry when Colonel John Jones, one of his bitterest critics, married Oliver's widowed sister. This marriage made him politically invulnerable. Henry, who had been trying to get rid of Jones, because he was 'more dangerous and prejudicial to the public' than anyone, now had to draw in his horns. 'I did not know that he was likely to be my uncle,' he lamented.[83]

Henry's biggest obstacle to reducing the influence of the army was the presence in London of Lieutenant-General Charles Fleetwood, the lord protector's son-in-law and ally. As lord deputy of Ireland, Fleetwood was superior in rank to Henry. He was also a friend to the army radicals who were a constant thorn in Henry's side.

During the four years that he was in power, Henry saw with blinding clarity that the only way to balance the budget and reduce the influence of the army was to shave its numbers – drastically. His predecessors, the parliamentary commissioners, had in 1653 persuaded the army to disband 8,000 of its 32,000 soldiers and turn them into settlers. Henry, shortly after his arrival in July 1655, was able to persuade the officers to disband a further 5,000. Some of the regiments were dissolved for political reasons. Lieutenant-General Ludlow lost his because he was refusing to cooperate with the regime, and was a bitter critic of the Protectorate. Colonels Pretty and Axtell were also politically suspect, although they were staunchly loyal to Lord Deputy Fleetwood. Axtell's regiment and a number of other soldiers totalling 1,500 were conscripted for Colonel Robert Venables's expedition to Hispaniola (see below, pp. 261–7).[84]

The army of occupation, now below 20,000, was still too great a burden for the ravaged Irish economy. The Protectorate could promise no more than £8,000 a month, and even this derisory sum arrived in fits and starts, and fell more and more in arrears. To cope with financial reality Henry promoted the idea of disbanding most of the regular army and replacing it with a voluntary militia that would only be active – and therefore only paid – in times of emergency. Unsurprisingly the officers fought him tooth and nail. They could not see that their continuance entailed the bankruptcy and ultimate collapse of the Protectorate, and that this would seal their own fate. Henry's other chief policy, almost as unpopular as disbanding the army, was to bring back compulsory tithes for a state-sponsored church. The church he had in mind was something very like the Scottish Presbyterian Kirk. In pursuing these two policies he cemented his friendship with the Old Protestants and completed his alienation from the army.[85]

Failing in his effort to disband the army, Henry next tried to thin out the officer corps while retaining most of the rank and file. Not only would this save substantial sums of money, it would facilitate the weeding out of turbulent and factious officers. Fleetwood and his allies in London thwarted him.

The protectoral government chose to impose the more expensive policy – retaining most of the officers while disbanding most of the rank and file.[86]

Henry became so discouraged by the unrelenting hostility of the army from Fleetwood down, and by the mixed signals from his father, that he wrote several resignation letters in the early summer of 1656. His requests to resign were denied, leaving him no choice but to carry on.[87]

In spite of the large number of officers who dominated both the government and the judiciary, and in spite of the large number who worked actively to sabotage his policies, Henry could claim some solid victories. The steady pressure he exerted against the Baptist allies of Fleetwood bore fruit in the elections to the second Protectoral Parliament in September 1656. Out of the thirty MPs from Ireland, only three could be counted as Fleetwood's radical supporters. The rest were either Old Protestants who had settled in Ireland before the Cromwellian reconquest, or allies of Henry Cromwell. In short, the election was a catastrophe for the Baptist faction. Four of its most prominent members – Adjutant-General William Allen, Quartermaster-General John Vernon, Colonel Daniel Axtell and Colonel Robert Barrow – resigned from the army later that year.[88]

They did not leave, however, before firing a final shot against those who were campaigning to convert Oliver Cromwell into a hereditary monarch. This campaign re-ignited the radicals' will to fight. Allen, Vernon, Hewson, Lawrence, Brayfield and others bitterly opposed the Humble Petition and Advice, with its offer of the crown to Oliver (see below, pp. 281–2). For Henry Cromwell this posed a security concern, since Dublin Castle, the regime's arsenal, was under the command of Colonels Henry Jones and Richard Lawrence. Colonel Hewson was father-in-law to both these men. Henry wrote to his father that there were frequent meetings between Allen, Vernon and 'that party whose very spirit is legible in this libellous declaration'.[89]

Yet for all his seditious activity Hewson enjoyed the unqualified support of Fleetwood. Vouching for his 'faithfulness and integrity', Fleetwood wrote: 'I am sorry to understand there is any occasion for a misunderstanding twixt yourself and Colonel Hewson.' Henry's suspicions of Hewson were amply confirmed when, together with Lawrence, he promoted a letter from the army in Ireland expressing relief and joy at the news of his father's rejection of the crown. The letter was endorsed by fifteen officers. Like other moderates, Henry was dismayed by his father's refusal to found a new royal dynasty, which he believed was the only way to guarantee the long-term stability of the three nations. He could not understand why all of the top army grandees – Fleetwood, Disbrowe and Lambert – and the great majority of lower officers were so adamantly opposed to Oliver's acceptance of the crown. He was disgusted by the smugness of the radicals in Ireland when Oliver turned it down. 'These busybodies creep about like snakes in the warm sun,' he wrote to Secretary Thurloe.[90]

Henry's next setback was the rumour, in the summer of 1657, that Fleetwood was to become lord-lieutenant of Ireland, and that he, Henry, was to serve under him as lord deputy. 'How can I continue in this condition?', he moaned to Lord Broghill. He was also dismayed that half the new Irish Council would consist of his enemies: William Steele and Colonels Miles Corbet and Matthew Tomlinson. In the event Fleetwood did not become lord-lieutenant, and after Henry was appointed lord deputy in November he was able to govern Ireland without too much interference.[91]

Henry spent his remaining months in Ireland wrestling with the impossible challenge of disbanding soldiers when there was no money to pay them off. He could expect no help from England, because, as Fleetwood reminded him, the government there was essentially bankrupt – unable to pay either the army or the navy. There was another even greater problem: religion. In June 1657 Parliament passed an Act for Convicting, Discovering and Repressing Popish Recusants, requiring anyone suspected of being a papist to swear an Oath of Abjuration, explicitly denying transubstantiation, purgatory and the pope's authority. The Irish were 'much troubled' by this new law, and increasingly avoided any contact with the English and Scottish settlers. The requirement to abandon their religion immediately became a greater grievance even than the confiscation of their property. As one of the administrators in Galway observed to Henry, 'the general grievance of the Irish is not the transplantation, for now they account sending into Connacht and losing their estates nothing in comparison of this oath'.[92]

The end of the Protectorate lay just around the corner; Ireland's problems remained as intractable as ever.

CHAPTER ELEVEN

THE CONQUEST AND RULE OF SCOTLAND, 1650–59

By 1650 the Long Parliament had built up many grudges against its former allies in Scotland. Seven years earlier the Scots had sent an army to help Parliament defeat the king. In return Parliament had promised to adopt Presbyterianism in England. Each side then disappointed the other. Except at Marston Moor (see above, p. 2), the Scots' military contribution was lacklustre. For its part, Parliament dragged its feet about imposing Presbyterianism upon England. In 1645 the founding of the New Model Army had led several high-ranking Scottish officers to quit the parliamentary cause. From that point the Scots grew more and more disenchanted by what they heard of the religious and social radicalism within the army. Led by the duke of Hamilton, Engagers signed a secret agreement with Charles I, and invaded England in the summer of 1648. After beating the invaders at Preston, Cromwell took the New Model into Scotland, where he was cordially received by the Covenanters, who had held aloof from any alliance with the king. Upon his departure a month later, Cromwell left about 1,500 troops to help the Covenanters maintain their ascendancy over the Engagers.[1]

The execution of Charles I precipitated a counter-revolutionary realignment of forces in Scotland. A majority of Covenanters – the 'Kirk party'– joined with Engagers to resist the New Model. Charles II for his part was obliged to swear loyalty to the Covenant, which, as the politically active merchant Alexander Jaffray wrote, 'we knew from clear and demonstrable reasons, that he hated in his heart'.[2]

Fairfax's Resignation

This alarming transformation, which saw Scottish Presbyterians turn into militant defenders of the monarchy, is what had prompted the Rump to recall Cromwell from Ireland early in 1650. When he reluctantly came home at the end of May, it was to a heartfelt welcome from the republican establishment. With Charles II proclaimed king of all three nations by the Scots, and now about to land in his northern kingdom to 'all signs of joy' from the people, members of the Rump were in no doubt that war was just around the corner. Grasping the nettle, the Council of State resolved on a preemptive invasion of Scotland. Parliament hoped that Fairfax and Cromwell would jointly lead the invasion, but Fairfax had scruples about going to war against an old ally, and refused. This was a grave blow to the regime; yet the prospect of becoming commander-in-chief must have appealed to Cromwell. His main concern was not to change Fairfax's mind, but to control the political damage caused by his retirement. This goal was achieved by having Fairfax cite health reasons for bowing out.[3]

Preparations for Invasion: Propaganda and Logistical Support

Soon after being named sole commander, Cromwell set off for the north. By early July he was in Newcastle, organising the expedition, holding a fast with his officers and hearing sermons from five preachers. As he waited for men, money and matériel, Cromwell used the time to write to key political figures, striving to undermine their allegiance to the king. Much of this work was carried on in secret, but for public consumption he penned two army declarations, one 'to the people of Scotland', the other 'to all that are saints and partakers of the faith of God's elect in Scotland'. To the people he merely promised that they had nothing to fear from the army. To the saints he expressed 'tenderness . . . as our brethren', but taxed them for their adherence to a completely untrustworthy king. On religion he implored them to soften their rigidity: 'Are we to be dealt with as enemies because we come not to your way? Is all religion wrapped up in that or any one form? . . . We think not so.'[4] The next few months would demonstrate Cromwell's skill in planting doubts in sincere minds, and weaning many Scots from their attachment to Charles II.

Important though the work of political subversion was, the primary task that summer was logistical. Collecting the soldiers was easy: by mid-July over 16,000 men had been assembled at Newcastle. However, the Scottish general David Leslie reportedly commanded at least twice as many.

Logistical support was the key to offsetting Cromwell's inferior numbers during their twelve-month campaign. A fleet of 140 ships transported arms, ammunition, food and supplies from London, Harwich, Lynn and Newcastle.

Flatboats were also built in Lynn and Newcastle and shipped to Scotland to transport troops and supplies on the Forth. The artillery train numbered over fifty pieces. At least 1,300 draught horses were required to haul the gun carriages and wagons that transported them.[5]

In the face of Leslie's systematic evacuation of people and livestock, and his destruction of all food in the path of the invading army, virtually all foodstuffs had to be imported from England or Holland. Every soldier carried several days' supply on his back. A day's ration consisted of just under a pound of biscuit, half a pound of cheese and a pint of small beer. Most of this food was supplied by London merchants, but at least some cheese was shipped from Holland and Hamburg. Food also included animal provender, since for several months the Scots denied the English access to grazing land.[6]

The system did not always run smoothly. The soldiers were frequently short of food and drink, and for a time had to do without tents. Bad food ('corrupt bread') and short measure were chronic complaints. Overall, however, the equipping and provisioning of the army were an impressive achievement, which reflected Cromwell's able generalship. As he had done during the Irish expedition, Cromwell kept in constant touch with the highest authorities in the government to ensure that the needs of his army were attended to diligently. It was this support that made victory with fewer numbers in another country possible. By enabling Cromwell to keep his forces concentrated, it denied the Scots the chance to weaken them by picking off small parties of foraging and looting soldiers.[7]

Less important than food, arms and supplies was pay, since there was often nothing for the soldiers to spend their money on. Yet the Treasurers at War doled out £1,210,000 to the Scottish expeditionary soldiers between May 1650 and December 1651. It was never enough; on occasion officers borrowed money to pay their men. There was only one exception to this pattern of haphazard remuneration: Oliver Cromwell received his £10 a day as commander-in-chief punctually and usually in advance. For the rest of the army, erratic pay produced a lot of grumbling in the ranks and, in the spring of 1651, a good deal of desertion.[8]

Preliminary Engagements: Musselburgh and the Pentland Hills

When the New Model Army crossed the border into Scotland on 22 July it surveyed a deserted country. Leslie had stripped the border region between the River Tweed and Edinburgh of its food and population. He had also entrenched his immense army behind a fortified line running between Edinburgh and Leith. Any attempt by the English to outflank Leslie by marching west of Edinburgh ran the risk that they would be attacked in the flank or have their supply lines cut.[9]

By the end of July the New Model had occupied Dunbar, Musselburgh and Haddington, the vanguard taking up positions just 6 miles from Scottish outposts. Some provisions were unloaded at Dunbar, but hardship increased when armed country people suddenly appeared and cut off supplies coming by road from Northumberland.[10]

Brushing aside these setbacks, Cromwell pushed his army to the outskirts of Leith. With the support of four men-of-war he subjected the port to intense bombardment. Torrential rain prevented the soldiers from pressing home their offensive, however, and the Scots refused to be drawn outside the walls. All night long the soldiers stood in battle order. By the morning, having subsisted on bread and water for six days, they were in a sorry state, and Cromwell decided to withdraw. They arrived tired and dirty at their camp in Musselburgh, but were able to take little rest. That night the Scots sent 800 of the cream of their cavalry to fall upon the sleeping army. They succeeded in breaking past the guards and four bodies of horse before Fleetwood's and Lambert's regiments drove them off.[11]

After this bruising encounter, Cromwell decided to suspend military activity for a while and resume the battle for his adversaries' hearts and minds. As a goodwill gesture he released sixty wounded prisoners, lending his own coach to ferry them back. Then he wrote to the General Assembly of the Kirk, reproaching them for censorship and intolerance, and excoriating them for their alliance with Charles II: 'a covenant made with death and hell'. 'Is it therefore infallibly agreeable to the Word of God, all that you say? I beseech you, in the bowels of Christ, think it possible you may be mistaken.' The Covenanters replied caustically: 'Would you have us to be sceptics in our religion?'[12]

Cromwell's next move as he awaited the tardy supply ships was to stir up his men spiritually. Much time was spent in the early days of August in 'preaching, praying and heavenly communion with God'.[13] At last the desperately needed supplies arrived, and with morale restored Cromwell embarked on another foray. Taking his army from Dunbar to the Pentland Hills south of Edinburgh, he thought he might be able to provoke a battle by outflanking the Scottish army and cutting it off from its rich hinterland. On 20 August, Leslie stationed a strong force on Corstorphine Hill to protect the Stirling road and block English access to the sea, but he declined to let his main army be drawn out.

By now Cromwell's supplies were running short again, and he was in danger of being isolated from his base. He had no choice but to hurry back to Musselburgh. Only the stormy weather prevented the Scots from mauling the English on their retreat: 'trees ... were blown down, and the rain fell with that force it made my face smart, and so dark we could scarce see our way'.[14]

And so the English fell back to Dunbar, 'the provisions of our army being once more near exhausted and gone, the nights cold, the ground wet, the bloody flux and other diseases prevailing in the army, and the Scots hitherto refusing to fight'.[15] It looked as if Cromwell had been out-generalled. Not only had he failed to tempt Leslie into a decisive engagement, he had suffered heavy losses – at first from disease, now more and more from desertion. By 1 September his 'poor, shattered, hungry, discouraged army' numbered only 11,000 'sound men'. Within a month his expeditionary force had been reduced by one-third. Small wonder that a despairing Council of War opted for calling off the invasion. The only question was, could they get back to England alive?

The Battle of Dunbar

The invaders now busied themselves putting 500 of the sickest men into waiting ships, fortifying the town and establishing a storage depot. This intense activity did not hide the fact that Cromwell was at a loss what to do. Encamped in the midst of bogs and swamps, and with their backs to the sea, it seemed that his army were about to be encircled and devoured by a force more than twice their size. Yet his officer corps continued to display 'unparalleled unity'. They worked to keep morale high by unleashing a torrent of prayer and God-seeking. In the midst of these spiritual exercises they were also conscious of being borne up by the prayers of the faithful in England.[16]

On 1 September the Scottish army occupied a commanding position on Doon Hill overlooking Dunbar. In reality the English position was less precarious and the Scottish more vulnerable than first appeared. On each side of Dunbar there flowed a little stream, Spott Burn. On the south-east it descended through a narrow glen about 40 feet deep, which protected the English from a surprise attack by the Scots on the other side. The English camp was also out of range of the Scottish artillery. The only way Leslie could attack would be to come down the hill to the plain south-east of the town on the other side of Spott Burn. His army's situation was far from pleasant. The high ground overlooking the sea exposed the Scots much more than the English to wind, cold and wet.[17]

When Cromwell evacuated those of his men with dysentery, Leslie thought that he had commenced a wholesale retreat. Confident that he had them on the run, he brought the Scottish army down the hill on the morning of Monday 2 September. The manoeuvre involved transferring two-thirds of the left wing of his cavalry – about 2,000 men – to the right. This caused the existing right wing to edge down towards the sea. His army was now strung along a mile-long front. His intention was to fall upon the flank or rear of the English cavalry as they tried to make good their escape along the coast road.[18]

Leslie's move down Doon Hill was not so foolish as is often alleged. By preparing to attack the English before they had time to fortify their position he retained the initiative. He also saved his army from further attrition from sickness and desertion, which would have been inevitable had he stayed on the bleak hilltop. With his overwhelming numerical superiority he can be forgiven for believing that an easy victory was within his grasp. He can hardly have thought when he moved off the hill that the English would turn and attack.[19]

That they did so was thanks to the careful reconnoitring work of the New Model commanders, Lambert in particular. The major-general spent most of 2 September on horseback observing the Scots' troop movements, and noting the new posture in which they were drawn up. Through their experienced eyes, Lambert and Cromwell both spotted the same weakness in the arrangement of the Scottish army. Their left wing was crowded against the steep slope of Spott Burn Glen. Given the superior quality of the English soldiers, they agreed that a surprise attack on Leslie's right wing would not allow the left time to rally to its assistance.[20]

In order to concentrate his forces against the right wing, Cromwell had to get the bulk of his army past the front of the Scots line. At five o'clock that afternoon he held a council of war on horseback, so that all the officers could scrutinise the Scottish position. After sundown the discussion continued indoors. Several of the colonels still wanted to ship the foot, and leave the cavalry to cut their way through the Scottish army. But with Cromwell's backing Lambert presented the case for going on the offensive. There was no time to evacuate the foot, and in any event the ships could not hold more

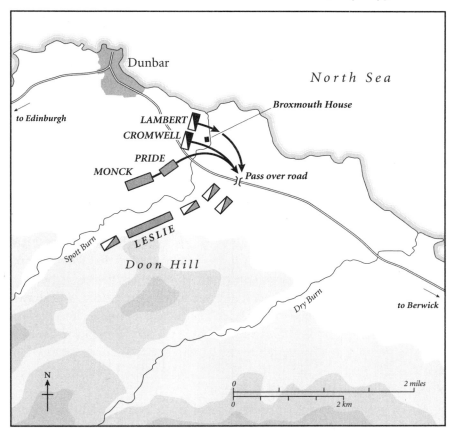

5. The battle of Dunbar, 3 September 1650

than a fraction of them. If they were able to get the better of the Scottish right wing, Leslie's whole army would be imperilled. Hemmed in by the hill and the ravine, the Scots would not be able to wheel around quickly enough to meet an attack on their flank. The English could also discharge their heavy guns at the left wing while charging the right. The discussion in the Council of War was wide ranging, but in the end Lambert carried the day, as Cromwell intended he should. When one officer stepped forward to propose that Lambert should lead the attack next morning, Cromwell freely granted the request.[21]

Both generals ordered their armies to be in battle order throughout the night. In contrast to the Scots, the New Model was on the move for most of the night. Cromwell personally supervised the arrangements, riding from one regiment to another by torchlight 'upon a little Scots nag, biting his lips till the blood had run down his chin without his perceiving it, his thoughts being busily employed to be ready for the action now at hand'. For a time hail and heavy rain screened the English movements from Scottish eyes and ears. During their march Captain Hodgson came across a cornet praying aloud. Exalted by what he heard, he returned to his own company and encouraged them with an impromptu sermon. The men needed encouragement from whatever quarter they could get it: 'our bodies enfeebled with fluxes, our strength wasted with watchings, want of drink, wet and cold being our continual companions'.[22] Yet the prospect of battle did much to re-animate their spirits after six weeks of frustration.

By 4 a.m. the troop movements were nearly complete, and Cromwell was impatient to be underway. The Scots had now caught wind of what the English were up to and were sounding the trumpets to rouse their men. Lambert took up his position at the head of the vanguard that was to spearhead the attack. This brigade, consisting of three regiments of horse – Lambert's, Whalley's and Robert Lilburne's – and two of foot, was drawn back and taken across lower Spott Burn near where it empties into the sea. Lambert led it along low ground out of sight of the Scottish army to the pass over the Berwick road guarded by an enemy detachment. Capturing the pass was the first step to clearing the way for the main body of the New Model to fall upon the Scottish right flank.[23]

There was a fierce clash under moonlight, during which both sides discharged their artillery. After an hour Lambert's men wrested control of the pass from its defenders, and the brigade passed over to confront the main body of the Scottish army.[24]

They were met with a resolute charge by Scottish cavalry armed with lances. The New Model troops recoiled a little under the shock, but quickly rallied. With the help of Cromwell's own horse regiment under Major Packer they fell upon the Scottish flank, while the foot behind them charged the enemy home. Cromwell himself rode up behind Lambert's foot regiment and ordered it to incline more to the left in order to give him a clear run at the Scottish infantry. It was now just before 6 a.m. and at that moment the full sun appeared over the sea. Echoing the psalmist, Cromwell cried 'Now let God arise and his enemies shall be scattered'. The horse and foot were quickly engaged all over the field. Panic soon gripped the Scottish ranks; Captain Hodgson heard Cromwell exult, 'I profess they run!' After a second combined charge by the cavalry regiments of Lambert, Fleetwood, Whalley and Twisleton, and the foot regiments of Cromwell and Pride, the Scottish right wing collapsed. Like the horse, the foot had at first been repulsed, but after regrouping they engaged the Scots' crack regiments 'at push of pike' and overwhelmed them. This main action lasted barely an hour – the battle was over by 7 a.m. As Hodgson observed, 'they routed one another after we had done their work on their right wing.'[25]

Seeing the cavalry and the cream of the infantry bested, the Scottish artillery now deserted their station. The rest of the foot then flung down their weapons, and scattered, terrified by the remorseless advance of their New Model counterparts. The New Model cavalry then rode among these panic-stricken men, who became, in Cromwell's words, 'stubble to their swords'. Rushworth, who was an eyewitness, testified that 'I never beheld a more terrible charge of foot than was given by our army, our foot alone making the Scots foot give ground for three-quarters of a mile together.'[26]

Now, having crossed the full breadth of the battlefield, trampling the enemy commanders' tents as they went, the cavalry encircled the left wing of the Scottish cavalry, which until now had not struck a blow. For the triumphant Ironsides it was short work to cut through these demoralised men. Finally they came to Leslie's own lifeguard, who bravely stood their ground for a time, but were eventually sent packing. The cavalry now wheeled about and returned the way they had come, charging and mowing down fleeing bodies of the enemy as they rode.

The English could scarcely believe their good fortune at seeing an enemy more than twice their size crumble before their eyes. It was noted at the time that Cromwell 'was carried on with a divine impulse; he did laugh so excessively as if he had been drunk; his eyes sparkled with spirits'. According to his usual practice, Cromwell sent his men after the fleeing soldiers for several miles, but not before halting his horsemen to give thanks for the victory. Together they sang Psalm 117.[27]

Tactically the key to the victory was Lambert and Cromwell's perception of the weakness of Leslie's position once his troops had descended Doon Hill. Their brilliance lay in their willingness to act on this perception by attacking with much smaller numbers, rather than waiting for Leslie to attack them. Cromwell once again demonstrated his ability as a field commander by massing tremendous force at a single point. His daring stroke was made possible by the superior quality of the New Model troops. The victory also was the product of England's superior economic might. Mastery of the sea enabled Cromwell to keep his army well fed and supplied.[28] He never had to disperse them in search for food and shelter.

Dunbar was Cromwell's most one-sided victory. The Scottish dead numbered 3,000, while almost 10,000 were taken prisoner.[29] If we can believe Cromwell, the New Model slain were no more than twenty, all of whom perished in the struggle for the pass. Not a single English soldier was killed during the main battle.

Dunbar had far-reaching strategic and political consequences. Having lost almost half his army, Leslie could no longer hold his heavily fortified line from Edinburgh to Leith. Both the capital and the port fell to Cromwell. Leslie withdrew to Stirling hoping to repair his shattered force. The defeat was also a blow to the Kirk party who had pressured Leslie into attacking the New Model against his better judgement.[30]

Religious Warfare

Cromwell knew the war was far from over. Immediately after Dunbar he requested troop reinforcements from England. The Council of State paid him the compliment of producing 6,000 fresh soldiers over the next several weeks. While he waited for them to arrive, Cromwell renewed his theological offensive. One of his converts was Alexander Jaffray of the Committee of Estates (Scotland's executive council), who had been wounded and imprisoned at Dunbar. After his conversion to republicanism and religious toleration, Jaffray travelled up and down the country trying to win others to the same view. English preaching seems occasionally to have struck an emotional chord. One congregation responded to a sermon by Colonel Stapilton 'in their usual way of groans'.[31]

While Cromwell did not get very far with his effort to unyoke the Committee of Estates in Stirling from their alliance with the king, he met with an altogether different reception from the Kirk party in Glasgow, when he visited the city accompanied by 9,000 soldiers in October. Patiently he attended a lengthy Presbyterian sermon in the high church, but then overwhelmed the hapless minister with a prayer of two to three hours' duration. Cromwell also took advantage of the opportunity to cultivate Colonel Archibald Strachan, who was increasingly disillusioned with Presbyterian rigidity. One effect of this theological offensive was that Strachan and Gilbert Ker, both moderate Covenanters, published a 'Remonstrance' against fighting for Charles when he had still not repented his ways or abandoned the 'malignants'. A number of moderate, anti-royalist officers in the Glasgow-based Western Army went farther, and were not ashamed to call themselves Independents. For his part

Cromwell demonstrated goodwill towards the Presbyterians by purging a Captain Covell from his own regiment for denying the divinity of Christ, and by holding a day of humiliation for the sins of the army.[32]

By late November Cromwell had grown impatient at the slowness of negotiations with the western Covenanters, irritated by the attacks of 'moss-troopers' (bands of marauding ex-soldiers, roughly equivalent to Irish tories), and exasperated at the refusal of Edinburgh Castle to capitulate. Hankering for a fresh military exploit, he ordered Whalley and Lambert to rendezvous with him at Hamilton in order to bring the Western Army to heel. When Lambert and Whalley routed the Western Army there on 1 December without Cromwell's help, their victory revived the apprehension of the extreme Covenanters that in resisting Cromwell they were resisting the will of God.[33]

One of their number was Sir Walter Dundas, governor of Edinburgh Castle. Cromwell knew that Dundas was leaning towards Independency, and since September had been cultivating him assiduously. In his second letter he scolded the Presbyterian clergy for their denial of Christian liberty, their welcoming Charles II 'like fire into your bosoms', and their prohibition of lay preaching: 'Are you troubled that Christ is preached? . . . Your pretended fear lest error should step in, is like the man that would keep all the wine out of the country lest men should be drunk.' Cromwell made little headway before the beginning of December, when great siege guns and mortar pieces arrived at Leith from England. Four days of bombardment from land and sea were enough to bring Dundas to his knees. On Christmas Eve 1650 he surrendered.[34]

Cromwell's Illnesses, February to May 1651

By the end of 1650, through a combination of military action, ideological warfare and espionage, Cromwell had for all purposes reduced the Kirk party and its army to ruins. Royalists and Engagers were by no means displeased with this turn of events. At the same time that Cromwell was undermining the Covenanters, Charles was marshalling his energies to become the dominant political force in Scotland. Willingly he submitted to the self-abasement needed to get himself crowned at Scone on New Year's Day 1651. He then carried out a vigorous recruitment campaign to rebuild Leslie's army and shape it into an instrument loyal to himself.

Meanwhile, following the capitulation of Edinburgh Castle, the English war effort in Scotland stalled for over half a year. A major reason was the health of the commander-in-chief. On the day after Dunbar Cromwell confided to his wife: 'I assure thee, I grow an old man, and feel infirmities of age marvellously stealing upon me.' At the beginning of February 1651 he set out on an ill-advised expedition to overrun Fife, the breadbasket of Scotland, but was forced to turn back by wind, hail, snow and rain. As he retraced his steps to Edinburgh he fell ill from exposure. Once back he also succumbed to dysentery. A few weeks later he acknowledged 'I thought I should have died of this fit of sickness'. Not until early June were his physicians able to report that he was restored to health.[35]

These prolonged illnesses and relapses, with the idleness they enforced on the army, dampened the soldiers' morale. There was grumbling over lack of pay, while desertion and drunkenness increased. While they waited for Cromwell to get better, and for the grass to grow and provide fresh fodder for the horses, the English officers could only think of one way of bolstering their spirits: religious exercises. On 3 March they kept a day of humiliation for the army's sins; in April they spent another whole day in prayer; in May there was a fast, and in June another. Between relapses, Cromwell kept trying to win his enemies 'by love', attending Presbyterian sermons in Glasgow and Edinburgh, then arguing scripture with clerical and lay opponents.[36]

One of the debilitating effects of his illness was that Cromwell became indecisive about military strategy. In May he dithered over whether to invade corn-rich Fife in order to cut off Charles's food supplies, or to besiege Leslie in his stronghold at Stirling. His indecision lasted until late July, when he summoned Major-General Harrison from the north of England to confer. A new strategy emerged from this parley. Harrison was allotted 3,000 men to take south and guard against a royalist invasion, while Cromwell began to concentrate his forces at Queensferry.[37]

Inverkeithing

By July the size of the New Model Army in Scotland had swelled to over 21,000. It was now the Scots who were outnumbered. While conducting a number of skirmishes and reconnoitring moves towards the west, Cromwell proceeded to implement the contingency plans that had been held in reserve since the previous autumn. On flatboats constructed for the purpose he transported 4,000 men across the Firth of Forth under Lambert and Overton's leadership. Cromwell himself stayed at Torwood with the remainder of the army.

Cromwell's forays into the west during July were a blind, designed to divert attention from the east, while Lambert and Overton crossed the Firth of Forth. The strategy worked, and the Scots were taken by surprise, giving the English three days before the Scottish commanders Major-General James Holborne of Menstrie and Sir John Brown could hasten from Stirling towards Queensferry. Cromwell now responded by advancing with his forces on Stirling. This prompted the major part of the Scottish army to turn back to that stronghold. Seeing his opportunity, Lambert, though outnumbered, went on the attack against the Scottish rear at Inverkeithing. By his boldness – he led from the front, as he had at Dunbar – he inflicted a devastating defeat, slaughtering 2,000 Scots and taking a further 1,400 prisoner. He claimed to have lost only eight of his own men. Once again Lambert covered himself with glory, but it was Cromwell who provided the protection that made the victory possible.[38]

Cromwell now hastened back to Edinburgh to reinforce Lambert. By the end of July he was in Fife with two-thirds of the New Model Army, leaving only eight regiments south of the Forth. On 1 August he appeared before Perth, obtaining a bloodless victory the next day. Within the space of two weeks he and Lambert had transformed the military situation. They had fooled the Scots as to their intentions, and by establishing themselves in Perth, had cut them off from all hopes of reinforcements and supplies from the north. The results of Inverkeithing were therefore even more decisive than those of Dunbar. The risk that the Scots in Stirling would profit from the opportunity to invade England was one they had taken with their eyes open. Cromwell's paramount objective had been to force the Scots into the field; when they quit Stirling they were fulfilling his intention. If Cromwell was to be believed, this extraordinary turn of events had come about because he had waited upon the Lord, 'not knowing what course to take'.[39] We may accept the sincerity of this profession of ignorance; yet he *had* commissioned the flatboats the previous winter. Like a capable general he was ready for more than one eventuality.

Worcester

With the benefit of hindsight we know that Charles and the Scots were facing imminent annihilation. We may wonder why they imagined they had anything to gain from invading England. They had in fact some reason to hope for success. With the Commonwealth's ablest troops and officers behind them, they might, as they marched southward, plausibly expect to gather strength and to exploit the disillusionment of much of the population with republican rule. However, as the duke of Hamilton candidly admitted to a friend, 'I cannot tell you whether our hopes or fears are greatest: but we have one stout argument, despair.'[40]

The intuition of Hamilton and others was correct: the invasion was doomed from the start. Once they left the safety of Stirling, their soldiers deserted by the thousand. The invasion force was ill provided and ill armed. In England hardly anyone reported to Charles's standard after he crossed the border at the beginning of August.[41]

None the less, at the news that they had crossed the border the Council of State swept into a whirlwind of activity. In collaboration with Cromwell, Lambert, Fleetwood and Harrison they concerted a three-pronged strategy to break the invasion. First, troops were raised in every region to guard against royalist insurrection. Second, Harrison and Lambert, each with 3,000 or 4,000 horse and dragoons, were sent to harass Charles's rear, Harrison in the vanguard, and Lambert behind him. They were to shepherd the king towards the west and away from London. Third, Cromwell was to bring his mounted regiments of horse and foot, together with a light artillery train – 10,000 troops in all – swiftly south in forced marches to rendezvous with Lambert and Harrison. Once the three commanders had combined their forces and supplemented them with county militias, they were to hunt down and destroy Charles's army before it could get near the capital.[42]

In the north-east, Sir Thomas Fairfax organised Yorkshire, taking control of Hull in Overton's absence. The Yorkshire Committee set about mobilising 2,400 foot. To the west, infantry from the Cheshire and Staffordshire militias were sent to assist Harrison. Late in August four great military rendezvous were held in southern England – at Northampton, Gloucester, St Albans and Barnet (London). The rallying of so many men to the Commonwealth's defence shows that, however unpopular the republic may have been, the Scottish invaders were more unpopular still.[43]

In mid-August Cromwell entered Yorkshire, where he was joined by Fairfax, who rode with him for 3 miles in his coach. By 22 August he was in Nottinghamshire, and on the 24th he rendezvoused with Lambert and Harrison at Warwick. With Colonel Robert Lilburne standing guard in Lancashire, and Fleetwood's brigade stationed at Upton Bridge on the River Severn, Charles was hemmed in on every side. On the 27th Cromwell stopped at Evesham. By the time the Essex and Suffolk militias arrived a few days later, his army had swollen to 31,000, in addition to several thousand local levies. The king no longer had the remotest chance of reaching London.[44]

On 25 August Charles was dealt another hammer blow. The earl of Derby's contingent of 1,500 men was annihilated by Lilburne's horse regiment, assisted by three companies of Cheshire infantry at Wigan.[45]

Charles had now halted at Worcester, which he turned into his headquarters and fortified. He set fire to the suburbs beyond the walls and broke down several bridges leading to the city.[46]

Cromwell arrived outside Worcester on 28 August. His army, already two-and-a-half times bigger than Charles's, continued to grow until the day of battle as county militia regiments streamed in from many parts of the country.[47]

The abundance of manpower at his disposal relieved Cromwell of the need to waste time on a siege. The city of Worcester, lying in the level fields on the east bank of the Severn, was connected to the west bank by a bridge to the suburb of St Johns. On the land side it was encircled with walls fortified by an outwork, Fort Royal, which was connected to the south-east wall. Now in possession of the bridges across the Severn, both at Bewdley, 15 miles to the north, and at Upton, 9 miles to the south, the Commonwealth forces could cross the river at will. A mile and a half south of St Johns, the River Teme flowed into the Severn and was spanned by Powick Bridge, which had been dismantled by the Scots. Cromwell's numerical superiority enabled him to divide his army and threaten a pincer movement against the enemy. As soon as Lambert had captured and restored Upton Bridge, Cromwell transferred 11,000 men to the west bank of the Severn under Fleetwood's command. The main body of his army he kept at Perry Wood in a low range of hills near Spetchley.[48]

By the morning of Tuesday 2 September the English arrangements were complete. Boats had been collected to make temporary bridges across the rivers Severn and Teme at their junction, while Major-General Deane with two regiments of foot and two of horse had joined Fleetwood at Upton. Cromwell's plan was not to storm Worcester's fortifications, which had been strengthened 'beyond imagination', but to force the Scots to come out and meet him in the fields west of the Severn, or wait to be attacked on the weaker, west side of the city. The battle could have begun that day, but Oliver chose to put it off until the 3rd, the anniversary of Dunbar.[49]

Between five and six o'clock on the morning of 3 September, Fleetwood's brigade set out from Upton along the west bank of the Severn. The speed of

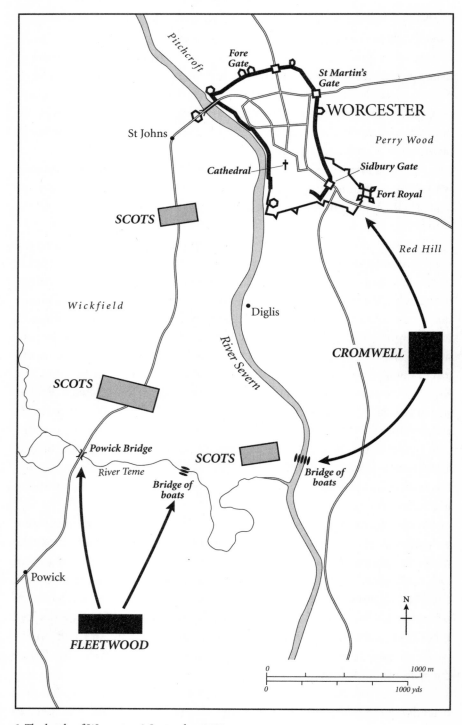

6. The battle of Worcester, 3 September 1651

his advance was limited by the need to stay abreast of the boats that were being brought slowly up the Severn to form the two bridges over which the soldiers would cross the Severn and the Teme. The 8-mile trip to the River Teme took him till one o'clock in the afternoon. When he arrived there, Fleetwood split his regiments, sending the left wing to cross the broken bridge at Powick, and the right wing to run over the bridge of boats next to the Severn. Simultaneously, Cromwell brought about a third of his remaining forces across the bridge of boats to link up with Fleetwood.

Over the bridge they poured, the first to set foot on the battleground being Cromwell himself, leading his men in their battle cry, 'The Lord of Hosts', as they engaged the defenders.[50]

The king in person led the royalist charge against Fleetwood's left wing where they were trying to cross at Powick Bridge. At first he was successful, but when he returned to the main body, who were struggling with Fleetwood's right wing and Cromwell's reinforcements, he found them in disorder. The Scottish foot fought manfully at first, using the thick hedges for cover, and fighting from field to field. But, when the English musketeers fired a second salvo, they 'gave back violently and forced the king to retreat into the town'.[51]

Defeated on the west side of the Severn, the royalists regrouped on the east side, and late in the afternoon the second phase of the battle began. While Cromwell and Fleetwood were still preoccupied on the west side, Charles seized the opportunity to attack the force that Cromwell had left near Perry Wood. The king could still call upon Leslie's cavalry at Pitch Croft, which so far had taken no part in the fighting. The royalist horse and most of the foot thus thundered out of the St Martin's and Sidbury gates for an attack on Red Hill, where Lambert and Harrison were stationed with the regiments of Whalley, Disbrowe, Pride, Cooper, Tomlinson, Cobbett and the militias. Leslie himself was of little help, but Charles, with his own and Hamilton's regiments of horse, broke an enemy regiment of foot, and forced back a considerable body of horse. His success was short-lived, for Cromwell was able to lead his troops back and turn the tide of battle. There were three more hours of close fighting in which the Surrey, Essex and Cheshire militias played a notable part. Their bravery was most memorable as they chased their foe right up to the mouth of the cannon planted upon the mount and works of Fort Royal. Cromwell himself tried to halt the butchery, by riding up and down the ranks of the royalist infantry, offering them quarter, 'whereto they returned no answer but shot'. He then poured one reserve after another into the battle until the royalists were pushed back into Fort Royal and then behind the city walls.[52]

Now, after sundown, began the third phase of the battle, the struggle for Worcester itself. Cromwell hurled all his troops against the city, holding back no reserves. The Essex militia took Fort Royal, and at once turned the guns against the royalists. Within the walls there was bitter and bloody street-to-street fighting. Before long the Scottish foot had thrown down their arms and fled. The cavalry under the king's own command still disputed the streets after everyone else had given up. Royalist witnesses testified afterwards to the king's suicidal courage. Time and again he led his troops against the enemy, evidently preferring death to imprisonment in the hopeless struggle. In the end he could find no one to obey him, and so after a hurried conference he fled with an improvised lifeguard of sixty mounted men. The battle was over by 8 p.m.[53] The only remaining task for Cromwell's troops was to herd the last bodies of royalist resisters down to the quay, where they were taken prisoner and locked in the cathedral.[54]

On Thursday morning Worcester and its environs were a scene of carnage and desolation. Dead bodies strewed the ground from Powick to the bridge at St Johns, and from Sidbury Gate to Perry Wood. Within the walls, streets and buildings were choked with corpses. Soldiers 'plucked lords, knights and gentlemen out of holes'. The stench of death was everywhere. The slain numbered between 2,000 and 3,000 royalists and fewer than 200 republicans. Prisoners numbered between 6,000 and 7,000, while perhaps 3,000 cavalry escaped northward. Charles, following a series of fabulous adventures, eventually reached the south coast, where he boarded a ship for France. The men he left behind did not fare so well. If they straggled, or fell asleep from exhaustion on their horses, 'we might hear by their cry what the bloody country people were doing with them'.[55]

This popular antagonism to the Scottish invaders shows how little support Charles had mustered for the project of reclaiming his kingdom. Loudly as they may have groaned under the financial burdens of the republic, and keenly as they may have resented the dominance of new men in local government, the English people in 1651 had no wish to see their country overrun by a foreign army. The contrast with 1639 is striking. In that year people had reacted either passively or with enthusiasm when a Scottish army had humiliated Charles by occupying the northern counties. The anger shown in 1651 to the alien soldiers, together with the massive outpouring of militia support at the battle of Worcester, testifies to the widespread if temporary favour enjoyed by the Commonwealth. Parliament shortly attempted to consolidate its unaccustomed popularity by reducing the size of the military establishment and cutting its outlay by over £420,000 a year.[56]

On 12 September Cromwell arrived in London to a hero's welcome. As he rode into Westminster, the Council of State, members of Parliament, the London magistrates and the City militia escorted him in pomp. The streets were lined with shouting crowds, while cannon and musketry saluted his arrival in Whitehall. The following day 4,000 of the prisoners taken at Worcester were paraded through the capital. The government then meted out punishments to the defeated. Lord Derby and four others were executed. Leading figures, such as John Maitland, first duke of Lauderdale, and David Leslie were kept in confinement till the Restoration, though Edward Massie and the earl of Middleton managed to escape. By this time so many high-ranking prisoners had been taken that the parliamentary editor Marchamont Needham scoffingly pronounced that 'the nobility of Scotland that are at liberty may sit about a joint-stool'.[57]

Some of the common prisoners were sent to Ireland and Bermuda, while the rest, if they had not already died in England, were eventually sent home.[58]

The Political Settlement

The battle of Worcester shattered Scottish morale, as well as the reputation of the Presbyterian Kirk. When Cromwell quit the country he left behind one of his ablest lieutenants, George Monck, with 5,000–6,000 troops to complete the country's subjugation. Monck accomplished the task with his usual efficiency. The last stronghold he tackled was Dundee. The garrison was obstinate, so Monck opted for a storm. After half an hour of fierce fighting the town was overrun, with between 400 and 800 soldiers and townsfolk put to the sword. The surviving population were plundered, 'even to ruin', for a fortnight. Their punishment was prolonged by having two foot regiments quartered on them, 'to the great impoverishment of the town'.[59]

The evidence from the court-martial that Monck convened shortly after storming Dundee points to the officers' desire to protect the local population from predatory troops. As Major-General Deane privately conceded, 'divers offences and misdemeanours are daily committed by the soldiers in Scotland'. The officers' approach to disputes between soldiers and civilians was remarkably even-handed. Corporal punishments such as tying head to heels (excruciatingly painful) and whipping were imposed for minor acts of plunder as well as for fornication. There was one recorded instance of attempted rape, based on the information of two Scottish women. The guilty soldier was sentenced to be whipped through the streets with sixty lashes and then imprisoned 'during the lieutenant-general's pleasure'. Punishments imposed by other courts-martial included running a gauntlet of one's fellow soldiers, riding the wooden horse with muskets tied about one's feet, being ducked in the sea several times, and standing for several hours with a paper on one's breast publicising one's crime. At least one soldier was hanged in Edinburgh for robbing a butcher.[60]

Under the terms of Parliament's *Declaration . . . Concerning the Settlement of Scotland* there was to be: 1. religious toleration; 2. political union with England; 3. reparations paid out of the estates of the crown and leading Scottish royalist landowners; and 4. amnesty for most tenants and vassals. It also included a 'war-guilt' clause which placed the onus, not on the Scottish nation as a whole, but on its social and political leaders. In contrast to the Irish policy of repression and punishment, the Declaration extended the hand of friendship to the mass of the people, hoping thereby to safeguard the Revolution in England.[61]

The conquerors still faced a number of daunting problems. After the east coast up to Aberdeen had been subdued, Monck fell gravely ill, while the Highlands remained untamed. In December Major-Generals Deane and Lambert came to his aid. Another phenomenon that had been plaguing the country since the beginning of the English Civil War came to the forefront once more: moss-troopers. The Scots generally were viewed as 'ignorant of soap to a quite terrible extent', and 'sullen, suspicious and unremittingly hostile'.[62]

To bring this hostile country to heel it was saddled with an unapologetically military government. Six of the eight commissioners appointed to rule it were New Model Army officers. In December 1651, attempting to improve public relations with the civilian population, they replaced free quarter with a heavy assessment of £10,000 a month.[63]

A committee of officers was to sit at Leith and dispense justice. One of the first issues they tackled was the prosecution of witches. At that time many witches were being brought to trial and burnt. Innocent women were being tortured. The commissioners determined to investigate. Before long a jury of soldiers at Stirling had freed several accused witches. That was in 1652. After that the soldiers sadly seem to have lost interest in defending witches, and at least twenty-seven more were tried and burnt in Edinburgh alone during the later 1650s.[64]

More than one observer commented on the good discipline that characterised the army of occupation. This did not, however, reconcile the Scots to Commonwealth rule.[65]

Still less did they take kindly to heavy-handed campaigns by New Model soldiers to remould Scottish religious practice so as to resemble their own Independent, Congregationalist theology and church government. The first thing the soldiers aimed to suppress was the common Presbyterian clerical practice of praying for the king. They also took aim at the Calvinist emphasis on sin by pulling down stools of repentance in whatever church they found them, or mockingly sitting on them. They interrupted sermons and debated with Presbyterian clergy in front of their congregations. At other times they commandeered pulpits and preached; sometimes they erected an internal wall to split a church into two congregations. Here and there a small number of Scots were attracted to the New Model Army's congregationalism. In Inverness and Sutherland 'a very precious people' who 'seek the face of God' came to private houses to meet officers and soldiers. More typically the soldiers' activities were coercive. For example, they broke up meetings of the Kirk assembly, both local and general. In the later 1650s the soldiers were blamed for the increase in 'that damnable sect of Quakers', especially in Edinburgh. Before the end of the decade Quakers seemed to be everywhere, 'sent in here in the army to infect and mislead the people'. It didn't matter that the higher officers found them just as offensive as the Presbyterian clergy did. Monck was determined to hound them out of the army.[66]

While Major-General George Monck was put in overall charge of Scotland, he was soon seconded to the navy as one of the generals at sea to fight the Dutch. Major-Generals Richard Deane and John Lambert thus served briefly as the effective rulers of Scotland. Their achievement was to remove free quarter throughout the Lowlands, replacing it with a regular assessment. They also began to appoint regular magistrates, such as assessment commissioners who were mostly army officers. An army officer was also appointed as a second sheriff in each shire. In fact the restoration of normal civil order to a war-torn Scotland was mainly the army's doing. By their participation in the day-to-day administration of justice, they won the plaudits of native observers who said that they 'proceeded more equitably and conscientiously than our own Scots magistrates', and settled cases a lot more quickly.[67]

General Robert Lilburne's Governance

Sometime in 1652 Lambert was recalled to England; next Deane left, to be replaced by Major-General Robert Lilburne, who held the post of commander-in-chief from December 1652 till April 1654. Lilburne was nothing if not conscientious, but he hated his job almost from the beginning. For all his efforts to enforce strict military discipline and cultivate good relations with the civilian population, he was acutely conscious of their 'deadly antipathy' towards the army. The people were a blank wall when it came to passing on intelligence about royalist activity; they were constantly stealing horses for the enemy, and were ready at the least encouragement to throw in their lot with the king's forces. He was especially mistrustful of the Presbyterian clergy as a force for sedition. So dangerous did he consider them that in late July 1653 he sent a troop of horse and a company of foot to dissolve a meeting of the General Assembly of the Kirk in Edinburgh – 'an engine so formidable' – and ordered them to leave the city by the next day.[68]

Lilburne faced excruciating problems as he tried to rule Scotland. Not only was he up against the incorrigible animus of the people against his army, the regime in London never sent him enough resources to carry out his work. He had only three men-of-war to patrol the east coast; he needed at least two more. The soldiers' pay was chronically in arrears; for much of the time they had nothing to eat but hard biscuit and cheese. Combined with the frequent lack of pay, and the necessity for some of them to sleep in the open, many fell sick. He lacked the manpower to overawe the Highlands. From garrisons all over the country he sent out patrols daily trying to hunt down the enemy, 'but such is the inveterate malignancy of the country that (through want of intelligence) we can never meet with them.'[69]

He knew that repression alone wouldn't work. Near the end of 1653 he sent proposals to London that he thought might reconcile the Scots to English rule: 1. Lift sequestrations and forfeitures of estates except for five or six 'grand offenders', accompanied by a 'free pardon and Act of Oblivion' to all who would lay down their arms; 2. Give liberty to any Scotsman 'to transport regiments to foreign princes in amity with us'; 3.. Moderate the sentences handed out by the Court of Justice, and allow more time for the settling of debts 'to save men from being driven to extremity by caption, and thereby forced to fly to the enemy; which is conceived is a very great cause of the present troubles'.[70]

No answer to these enlightened proposals is recorded from London. By now Lilburne was wearying of his responsibilities and realising that the job was also beyond his capabilities. Without the least hint of resentment or envy he asked to be allowed to resign in favour of Monck: 'Methinks Monck's spirit would do well amongst [the people here].' In this he echoed the opinion of the army secretary William Clarke, who saw Monck as 'a very precious instrument'.[71]

General Monck: the Smack of Firm Government

On 8 April 1654, Cromwell commissioned Monck as commander-in-chief of all the forces in Scotland, with powers to collect taxes, fine and imprison at will, and issue proclamations. This made him effective dictator of the country with an authority greater than that given to any previous republican general. He was also given about 3,000 more soldiers and promised £50,000 with which to quell royalist risings.[72]

Monck continued to manifest a strong personal loyalty to, and affection for, the lord protector. When Cromwell died in September 1658 he transferred that loyalty to Oliver's son and successor, Richard, having him proclaimed lord protector throughout Scotland, obtaining an address of recognition for him from the army, and working to ensure that supporters of the regime were elected to represent Scotland in the parliament called for January 1659. He also sent Richard a private letter of advice, which reveals him as part of the faction which favoured more conservative or reactionary policies. He advocated strengthening the Church of England by favouring moderate Presbyterian ministers and calling an 'assembly of divines' (a clerical synod) to achieve greater unity within the church and find a means of attracting separatist groups back into it. He hinted that the prevailing tolerance of such groups should be curtailed. In political affairs he advised the young lord protector to favour the more conservative advisers bequeathed by his father, such as Broghill, and to reorganise the army in England so as to get rid of 'some insolent spirits', meaning radicals.[73]

Glencairn's Rising

By the time Lilburne was relieved as commander-in-chief in April 1654 the only major challenge to the republican regime was already half over. Despite several crushing defeats, the royalists had never thrown in the towel. From Highland redoubts they carried on what amounted to a guerrilla war, living off the population, stealing horses, recruiting forces and conducting occasional raids against the occupying power. They pinned their hopes on external help. The outbreak of the First Anglo-Dutch War in 1652 raised the chances of a successful financial and military challenge to the English republic. The earl of Middleton was thought to be raising large numbers of troops on the Continent, along with large quantities of weapons, ammunition, supplies and money to bolster the home-grown royalist revolt. The king, it was promised, would soon leave the comfort and safety of his exile court in Paris to lead the revolt in person.

A major problem for Lilburne as he faced a swelling wave of royalism was the absence of most of his officers in England. 'Often', he wrote to Cromwell, 'I can hardly get a field officer to confer with.'[74] Fortunately he had one extremely able commander who did not desert him: Colonel Thomas Morgan. In January 1654 Morgan took fourteen companies of foot and eight troops of horse and dragoons marching from Aberdeen towards the royalists. He kept them off balance with several small skirmishes, in one of which the English royalist Colonel Edward Wogan was killed. This was a severe blow to Scottish royalist morale. On 8 February Morgan forced Lords Glencairn and Kenmore with their roughly 4,000 troops to fight a major battle. The royalists were in a rendezvous at the head of Cromar. After 'a little dispute', Morgan totally routed their combined army, before demolishing the royalist garrison at Kildrummy. A few days later Colonel William Daniel took 1,000 horse, dragoons and foot from Dundee and St Johnstons to Dunkeld, where he captured, without the loss of a single man, over 120 prisoners and twenty horses, 'and when he had done, blew up the house'. The large number of prisoners was a burden, and so Lilburne asked for permission to ship them off to serve 'some foreign prince in amity with us'.[75]

Lilburne and his colonels had effectively broken the back of Glencairn's rising. Yet the royalists had not absorbed the reality of their defeat, and volunteers continued to flock to their standard. When Monck arrived at army headquarters on 22 April he at once recognised that the population mostly supported the insurrection and were assisting the insurgents as much as they dared. The long drought, which lasted through most of May, prevented him from moving aggressively against the royalists, owing to the lack of grass for his horses.[76]

With Monck's appointment as commander-in-chief the Council of State began taking Scotland much more seriously. William Clarke, secretary to the army in Scotland, bluntly told him that 'it will be of absolute necessity that your Honour get a considerable supply of money', because both the

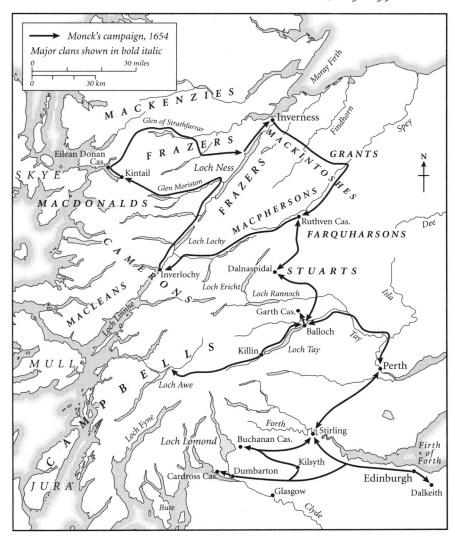

7. Glencairn's rising, 1654

horse and foot were half a year behind in their pay, and many were now sick. Monck took Clarke's message to heart. By March he got the Council of State to send the promised £50,000 to Scotland. Colonel William Brayne was ordered to bring 1,000 troops from the north of Ireland to the isles of Lewis and Mull; another 100 troops came from Pride's regiment, and seven companies from Constable's. The naval force patrolling the east coast of Scotland was raised from four to ten men-of-war.[77]

By the middle of May Monck was ready to take the field. On the 18th he set out with two regiments of horse and three and a half of foot. He did not waste time. One night his secretary William Clarke, who accompanied him taking daily notes and sending dispatches to Secretary Thurloe, had to sleep in his clothes in the fields. Heavy summer rains and high winds succeeded the spring drought. One day the winds were so violent that they blew down many tents. In late June the men shivered through 'great frosts' that brought many cattle and sheep down the hillside. In August there were more storms and flooding.[78] In preparation for the decisive encounter Monck did everything in his power to disperse the royalist forces, burn their strongholds, capture their cattle and destroy their crops. The royalists did what they could to wreak equivalent destruction on the marquess of Argyll's lands to punish him for supporting Parliament. Colonel Morgan and his brigade met Monck in Moriston at the south end of Loch Ness on 24 June. Middleton had now returned from the Continent. Their coordinated strategy was to deprive him of food, wear out his forces with repeated marches and counter-marches, and then trap him between their forces, and compel him to fight one or the other, preferably Morgan's, since his were fresher. At their second meeting on 1 July, Monck ordered Morgan to take his brigade to Caithness and waste and burn the surrounding country to make it incapable of supporting any military presence through the winter. To exhaust his enemy Monck followed a zig-zag route, starting from Edinburgh (Dalkeith), marching east to Dunbarton, back to Kilsyth, up to Loch Lomond, back and northward through Stirling and Perth, east along the River Tay to Loch Awe, then retracing his steps past Killin, Lawers on Loch Tay, Garth Castle and Wemyss Castle, up to Ruthven Castle, east to Inverlochy, north to Loch Ness, east to Glen Moriston and Kintail, around in a semi-circle and back to Loch Ness, then up to Inverness, south-east across the River Spey, back to Ruthven Castle, and then to Loch Garry again, and down to Kinnell at the west end of Loch Tay.[79]

By mid-July, after nearly two months of relentless pursuit, Monck had reduced Middleton's horse from 3,000 to 1,200. By then Middleton was so desperate to avoid Monck that he neglected to scout the whereabouts of Morgan's brigade. He seemed unaware that when Monck herded him towards a narrow pass at Dalnaspidal beside Loch Garry, he was heading straight into Morgan's hands. On 19 July, at the head of 2,000 foot and seventeen troops of horse and dragoons – about 3,500 in all – Morgan carried out his assignment. In fact he seems to have been favoured by more than an element of good luck, since, as he acknowledged, he lighted upon Middleton's horse 'unawares' in a narrow passage 'where they could march but two or three abreast'. However, he quickly took advantage of his good fortune to go on the offensive. Personally leading his forlorn hope, he totally routed Middleton's force, capturing 300 horses. Middleton himself only narrowly escaped by twice changing horses during his flight. The foot, who were 4 miles away, contributed nothing to the battle and fled to Lochaber. Morgan lost four wounded and none killed. In the aftermath of the battle Lord Atholl's portmanteau containing important papers was captured. The royalist rank and file were in disarray, 'all of them full of terror', and deserting en masse. Monck sent many of the prisoners to Barbados, a fate they would have done almost anything to avoid.[80]

Though enjoying virtually universal popular support in Scotland, the royalists had just endured another humiliating defeat, a decisive one. Why? Partly because of the superior generalship of Monck and Morgan, but also because of the latter's greatly superior numbers. Between them they commanded well over 8,000 well-equipped, well-disciplined troops, while the royalists never mustered more than 5,000 mostly ragged, ill-equipped men, who had shrunk to 2,000 or fewer by the time Middleton faced Morgan. 'English gold was not sparing' to woo royalist recruits from their colours. In spite of the constant complaining of Lilburne and Monck, the New Model soldiers were exceptionally well armed, clothed and fed in comparison to their royalist counterparts. At the beginning of the rising the royalists were counting heavily on European, especially Dutch, support. Virtually none materialised. The signing of peace between England and the United Provinces of the Netherlands in April 1654 at once deflated royalist visions of a Dutch-led invasion of Scotland. As Middleton later put it, 'that peace did strike all [of us] dead'. The ending of the First Anglo-Dutch War meant that Monck could be re-assigned from the navy to the army and Scotland. It also released additional ships to patrol the Scottish east coast. Another factor sapping royalist morale was the failure of Charles, despite frequent promises, to turn up and lead the rising in person. Understandably, he held back until other parties gave tangible evidence of the men, money, arms, ammunition and supplies they would commit to the cause. Finally, there was the incessant quarrelling among the royalist leadership.[81] There was no quarrelling among the New Model high command.

By now most of the population were weary of the conflict. The historian and bishop Gilbert Burnet, who lived through these years, reflected later on the suppression of Glencairn's rising:

there was an universal joy at the dispersing of that little unruly army.
After this the country was kept in great order: . . . The Highlands were
kept in better order than during the usurpation . . . The pay of the army
brought so much money into the kingdom that it continued all that while
in a very flourishing state . . . There was good justice done, and vice was
suppressed and punished, so that we always reckon those eight years . . .
a time of great peace and prosperity.[82]

After Monck's victory the authorities in Westminster again became inat-
tentive to the needs of the army in Scotland, and its hardship became acute
once more. As late as March 1655 Colonel Morgan had received nothing for
the forces who had won the stellar victory of July 1654. Monck became so
depressed that he submitted his resignation five times, giving for reasons his
lameness and his need to settle family affairs. He would even have preferred
a command in the West Indies to continuing to serve in Scotland.[83] His
request was each time ignored. He would not forget his second shabby treatment, this time at the hands of the Protectorate.

By the summer of 1655 the army's arrears had mounted up to £152,000,
and Monck was warning that they would soon be driven to take free quarter,
which would profoundly alienate the population. The country had been
so devastated that the Scottish 'cess' or monthly assessment could produce
no more than £6,000 a month. The officers were already lending their
men money to buy clothes. As a partial solution Monck suggested an excise
upon all commodities except victuals, small beer and bread. This he thought
would bring in between £10,000 and £20,000 a month. His suggestion was
adopted that October.[84]

Monck knew that the permanent solution was to reduce military costs by
making drastic cuts in the army payroll. But he was in a double bind because
he lacked the money to pay off the disbanded men. Still, by a superhuman
effort he was able to effect significant cuts and bring military expenditure
more in line with revenue. Immediately after putting down Glencairn's
rising he shaved £3,500 a month off army spending. In part he was able to
do this by making local communities responsible for the conduct of their
members, in part by allowing trusted Scots to participate in the suppression
of disorder. He also went to bat for indebted lairds and noblemen against the
severe application of Scottish law by Scottish judges. Like Henry Cromwell
in Ireland, he was critical of army headquarters in London for wanting to

preserve officers' jobs while shedding rank and file. The real way to save money, he knew, was to dismiss officers.[85]

By the summer of 1655 the army had a tighter grip on the country than at any time since 1652. It had penetrated almost all aspects of Scottish life. It had bent the church to its will. When Lord Broghill became first president of the Scottish Council, Monck appeared to take a back seat in running the country, but army officers were at all times a strong presence on the council. Monck had seen to it that there were army officers doubling as justices of the peace in every shire, and that every shire also had a second sheriff who was an army officer. The elections to the Protectoral Parliament of 1656 saw six serving officers among the thirty members elected from Scotland. In February 1656 a Captain Hill wrote from Ruthven Castle in the Highlands that, thanks to the new regime of JPs, peace and civility now reigned in the Highlands: 'Fornicators are startled at the punishment some have received, and drunkards begin to look towards sobriety, and swearers to speak more deliberately'.[86]

Monck left nothing to chance. He exploited a network of spies to keep himself constantly informed of suspicious movements. Throughout Scotland he enforced a system of passes by which persons travelling from one district to another, or from Scotland to England, had to obtain permits signed by the general or his officers. Permits were required to carry fire-arms. Chiefs were held responsible for the conduct of their clansmen.[87]

Vital to military security were the five great garrisons plus a multitude of smaller garrisons that carpeted the country, but which were concentrated in the Highlands. The four great Highland garrisons were Inverlochy, Inverness, Ayre and St Johnstons (Perth). Most important was Inverlochy, whose first governor was Colonel William Brayne. Thanks to his efforts, crime was greatly reduced in the region.[88] Next was Inverness, whose citadel was planned and begun by Major-General Deane in 1652. Most impressive was the great citadel constructed at army headquarters in Leith, next door to Edinburgh. Fully accessible by sea and virtually impregnable, it was a source of great pride to Monck. A later commentator wrote that it was

> one of the best fortifications that ever we beheld, passing fair and sump-tuous . . . The works round about are faced with freestone . . . and withal thick and substantial. Below are very pleasant, convenient, and well-built houses for the governor, officers, and soldiers, and for magazines and

stores; . . . the piazza or void space within, as large as Trinity College (in Cambridge) great court.[89]

After Lord Broghill became president of the Scottish Council in the spring of 1655 he conceived an immediate dislike to the man Monck had been leaning on to keep the Highlands under control – the marquess of Argyll. He based his dislike on information passed onto him by Thurloe's intelligence network, but it took him two years to persuade Monck that Argyll was playing a double game. By early 1659 Monck too had become Argyll's sworn enemy, and in 1661 he would be instrumental in having the marquess executed.[90]

Unrest in the Army

The army's enemies were not only external; there was also subversion from within. The first ripple on the surface of the Scottish army's calm was created by the Three Colonels' Petition. Two of its three signatories – John Okey and Thomas Sanders – had connections to Scotland. In November 1654 Monck alerted Cromwell that the petition was being circulated to a Captain Cleare of Okey's regiment, and that it had also found its way to Captain William Giffen from a member of Mr Feake's Fifth Monarchist church in London. Far from being a Fifth Monarchist petition, however, its thrust was towards Leveller republicanism.[91]

The first internal challenge to Monck's authority came from the alleged plot of Colonel Robert Overton. In December 1654 a cadre of nine discontented officers in the Aberdeen garrison wrote to sympathisers in other garrisons announcing a meeting at the Green Dragon Tavern in Canny-gate, Edinburgh on 1 January to discuss whether all the blood that had been spilt, the treasure spent, the prayers put up to heaven and the tears poured out, 'call upon us seriously to consider whether we have attained our end, or whether the guilt of the blood of so many thousands, [and] the miseries of a wasted commonwealth . . . will not lie heavy upon our consciences'. Overton did not sign the letter, but the regimental chaplain Samuel Oates said that nothing was done without his 'privity and concession'; furthermore, Overton hosted a meeting of the dissident officers in his own quarters. He was already under surveillance owing to the doubts he had admitted to Cromwell before leaving London, and to the fact that he had met with John Wildman, a notable enemy of the Protectorate. Nor did Overton inform Monck of the political dissension that was brewing among his officers in Aberdeen. Monck nipped the plot in the bud: he summoned Overton to headquarters to explain himself and had several officers of Colonel Rich's former regiment arrested, as well as Majors John Bramston and Henry Hedworth, whom he sent to London, and the chaplain Samuel Oates. He also sent Overton to London, from where he was transported to the Isle of Jersey, to be held in custody for more than four years without trial. It is entirely possible that had Overton not been so formidably talented, both intellectually and administratively, he might have escaped imprisonment. Cromwell had a lively respect for his potential appeal as an opposition leader.[92]

But was there actually a plot? According to a seaman from the *Constant Warwick*, one Dallington, there was. In December he had come ashore from the fleet with instructions to see how much support he could organise for a seamen's petition along roughly the same lines as the Three Colonels' Petition. It soon developed into a seditious conspiracy to send 3,000 foot supported by a contingent of horse into England to challenge the Protectorate. Once there they would be joined by forces raised by John Bradshaw and Admiral John Lawson. They would advance on London, arrest Cromwell and 'set us upon new courses'. They would twist Overton's arm in order to get him to take on the leadership of the conspiracy.[93]

One of the key figures in Overton's plot was Miles Sindercombe, a private in Colonel Thomlinson's troop. He was 'as [Monck was] credibly informed, one who was first employed as an agent to several regiments in Scotland'. Monck didn't know the details about Sindercombe's political agitation, 'yet [had] discharged him [from] the troop as a busy and suspicious person, and one who was forward to promote such ill designs'. Sindercombe fled to Flanders, where he joined the agitator Edward Sexby in a plot against Cromwell's life. Sexby provided him with money, weapons and ammunition, and upon his return to London in 1656 Sindercombe engaged in several attempts to kill the Protector. He was finally arrested, convicted of treason and sentenced to be hanged, drawn and quartered. He avoided this gruesome fate by killing himself with poison in his prison cell on 13 February 1657.[94]

That was not the end of unrest in the Scottish army. In late January 1655, Monck wrote to Cromwell that an address had just been brought to him by Major Thomas Reade and other officers on behalf of themselves and several of the re-baptised churches of St Johnstons (Perth), Leith and Edinburgh. However, they distanced themselves from the 'recent plot of some officers here against your Highness and present government', and their agitation seems to have petered out. Monck was then able to govern for more than three years without further challenges to his authority.[95]

He used that time to promote harmony between the army and Scottish society. He also maintained a high standard of military discipline by punishing severely any offences against the civilian population such as the unauthorised taking of free quarter. But he was also vigilant in punishing theft and illegal possession of firearms, particularly in the Highlands. The army acted as a police force, and operated a network of spies and informers which neutralised royalist efforts to stir up trouble.[96]

The critical importance of the army to Scottish affairs was seen vividly in January 1657. Colonel Scrope was 'laid low by the gout', and, because of his absence from the council in Edinburgh, government business virtually ground to a halt. None the less, by the beginning of June 1659 Monck was able to report with satisfaction, 'all is quiet here'.[97]

During the same period he concentrated on reducing the colossal expense of the military occupation of Scotland. By the end of 1657 he had got the army down to five horse regiments comprising 1,440 men, eleven foot regiments, comprising 7,770, and four companies of dragoons comprising 192, for a total of 9,402 men, not counting officers or the train of artillery. The cost of the army dropped from £36,000 to £21,000 per month. Of this only £6,000 a month came from the Scottish 'cess'. Almost twice that sum – £11,400 – came from the monthly assessment in England. The balance was made up from the recently introduced Scottish excise. Yet with all these financial infusions the army's pay continued to fall deeper into arrears. Almost until the very end Monck had hardly any more success than the leaders in the other two kingdoms in keeping the ship of state afloat against the weight of indebtedness that was inexorably pulling it down.[98]

CHAPTER TWELVE

THE ARMY AND THE EXPULSION OF THE RUMP PARLIAMENT, SEPTEMBER 1651 TO APRIL 1653

The Reform Agenda, from Burford to Worcester

The conquest of Ireland and Scotland distracted the army from political affairs until the autumn of 1651. After the crushing of the Leveller mutinies in May and September 1649 (see above, pp. 166–72) the army's rank and file never found their political voice again. During the next decade the army's political consciousness would reside almost entirely in the officer corps.

Upon the establishment of the Commonwealth in February 1649, the officers lost neither their religious ardour nor their impatience with the shortcomings of English society. Five New Model officers gained election to the Commonwealth's first Council of State: Fairfax, Cromwell, Skippon, Constable and John Jones. But Harrison and Ireton, both strongly identified with Pride's Purge, were defeated.[1] The officers were not backward in making their wishes known to the purged Parliament (soon to be called the Rump), but until their return from the battle of Worcester their tone was respectful. Their petition of March 1649, for example, confined itself to the army's material needs. Before embarking for Ireland the officers authored two more manifestoes demonstrating their continuing zeal for godly reformation, the abolition of tithes and religious liberty.[2]

In fact the army's disillusionment set in quite early. Captain William Siddall spoke for many when he condemned Parliament for being slow to act for the welfare of the kingdom. It was an accusation that would be made with rising impatience over the next three years. During that time Cromwell also strove to keep fences mended with the Commonwealth's radical critics. Right after his return from Ireland in June 1650, for example, he delivered to Parliament a petition for John Lilburne. The following month, on his way to Scotland, he invited Lilburne and his friends to ride and sup with him. At their parting Cromwell embraced them all and promised 'to make the people of England the most absolute free nation on the earth'. He reassured Ludlow of his commitment to 'thorough reformation', but cautioned him that 'the sons of Zeruiah are yet too strong for us'.[3]

Cromwell took advantage of his glittering triumph at Dunbar to recommend to Parliament a broad programme of social and legal reform. Colonel Pride expressed similar views more bluntly and aggressively. During the winter of 1650–51, as economic hardship worsened, the army became more acutely conscious of its unpopularity, particularly in London. Embarrassed by the immiseration of the people, it tried to recover lost ground by taking up radical demands for the abolition of tithes and the excise, and by supporting separatist congregations in the midst of their tribulations. In the summer of 1651 Cromwell again exploited a military victory – Lambert's at Inverkeithing – to press his argument for social justice. Robert Lilburne capitalised on his victory at Wigan to deliver a similar message. After the delirium of Worcester – 'for aught I know a crowning mercy' – Cromwell pleaded with the Rump 'that justice, righteousness, mercy and truth may flow from you, as a thankful return to our gracious God'. Major-General Thomas Harrison lectured his political masters in the same vein. The Rump should open 'a wider door to the publishing the everlasting gospel of our only Lord and Saviour . . . [so that] all his enemies shall be made his footstool'.[4]

From the Aftermath of Worcester to the Petition of August 1652

For all the religious exaltation that he felt in the autumn of 1651, Cromwell's political agenda was a moderate one. He had three objectives: 1. the dissolution of the Rump and the election of a new parliament; 2. an Act of Oblivion for most royalists in order to broaden the Commonwealth's base of support; and 3. systematic law reform that would give the people impartial justice. The problem with this agenda was that it was too extreme for the Rump, but too insipid for most of the officers. Their long hazardous campaigns had radicalised them, while their victories had made them surer than ever that the Lord was with them and that they were the humble instruments of some tremendous purpose for which England had been singled out. Men who had gone through the fire of battle were estranged from backroom politics, power-broking, compromises and deals, which now only aroused their disgust. Cromwell aimed to harness their militancy and win support from across the political spectrum through a generous Act of Oblivion, fresh elections, and a reformed monarchy. He believed that the regime should now profit from its unaccustomed popularity to stage the long-overdue national elections. It was a tribute to his sway over Parliament that on the day he resumed his Commons seat the bill for new elections was 'briskly revived'.[5]

Euphoria over their recent battlefield triumphs did not blind Cromwell and the officers to the reality that such elections would have to be carefully guided. Since the time of the second *Agreement of the People* (December 1648) the officers had known perfectly well that for the achievement of godly reformation, the 'ungodly' (meaning the anti-revolutionaries) would have to be weeded from the electorate. That is what Cromwell had in mind when he secured the Rump's assent to a motion for a new representative with 'fit rules qualifications, [and] proportions'. The same motion also stipulated that a date should be set for Parliament's dissolution. Parliament debated the bill repeatedly for nearly two months before it fixed the time for its dissolution – 3 November 1654. This allowed the members a further three years to contemplate their demise. Parliament had effectively emasculated Cromwell's initiative. Its next rebuff to the army came at the 1651 elections to the Council of State. Cromwell as usual stood at the top of the poll, and was joined by military colleagues Fleetwood, Constable and Wauton. But two key military men – Skippon and Harrison – were defeated.[6]

Undaunted by these setbacks, Cromwell pushed ahead with his strategy of radicalism in public and conservatism behind the scenes. In December he brought together leading army officers and MPs to discuss what political system would best suit England. At the meeting he tipped his hand. Constitutional change was 'a business of more than ordinary difficulty', he conceded, but 'if it may be done with safety and preservation of our rights both as Englishmen and as Christians, [then] a settlement of somewhat with monarchical power in it would be very effectual'.[7]

By the end of 1651 the Rump was blocking all reform initiatives. Colonel Pride's appearance at the door of the House on 26 December was a none too subtle reminder to the MPs of what might happen to them if they continued to obstruct the army's programme. Yet the MPs seemed unable to shake off the grip of their collective death wish. On the one hand they assented to the establishment of the celebrated Hale Commission on law reform, and nominated several officers and associates of the army to it. On the other hand they refused to implement a single one of the commission's reasoned and practical proposals.[8]

More provoking than its deafness to the cry for law reform was the Rump's vindictive treatment of John Lilburne in 1652, when it sentenced him to banishment from England. Early in the new year Commissary-General Whalley laid a petition before Parliament appealing the sentence against Lilburne, but the House ducked the issue, and never allowed the petition to be debated.[9]

In February one of the key items on Cromwell's agenda of reconciliation was an Act of Oblivion for all except the regime's worst enemies. Fierce debates ensued day after day until the bill passed its third reading on the 24th. But by the time it reached the statute book the act was so hobbled with exceptions that the objective of reconciling royalists was nullified.[10]

Besides turning its back on reform, the Rump succeeded in alienating one of the most powerful men in the army, Major-General John Lambert. A tolerant and enlightened man, Lambert was Cromwell's ablest general. Having shown early promise in the Northern Army, he had recently covered himself with glory in the Scottish campaign at Dunbar, Hamilton and Inverkeithing. Nor were his talents confined to the battlefield. Trained at the Inns of Court, he was, as Whitelocke observed, a man 'of a subtle and working brain': he had helped Ireton draft the army's manifestoes in 1647. With Ireton's death Lambert became the foremost intellect on the Council of Officers. Fourteen years younger than Cromwell, he had plenty of ambition, and doubtless considered it only just recognition of his talents when the Council of State recommended him to succeed Ireton as deputy lieutenant of Ireland. Leaving Scotland, he went to considerable expense to outfit himself for his new post. The diarist Lucy Hutchinson (wife of Colonel John) reported that he treated the MPs to whom he owed his advancement as 'underlings, and such as were scarce worth the great man's nod'. In May, to save money, and as a slap against Cromwell, Parliament abolished the posts of lord-lieutenant and deputy lieutenant and reduced Cromwell to commander-in-chief in Ireland. Lambert was so insulted that he turned down the lesser commission as Cromwell's second-in-command, which was then given to Cromwell's new son-in-law, Charles Fleetwood, who had just married Bridget Ireton. Lambert was further antagonised when the Council of State attempted (without success) to send him back to Scotland in April 1653.[11]

The lack of progress on reform, mounting concern about the Dutch war and impatience over the Rump's refusal to dissolve itself all played a part in spurring the officers to launch a second major political offensive in August 1652. They began with a petition. The officers who took it to Parliament were loyal Cromwellians: Whalley, Hacker, Barkstead, Okey, Goffe and Worsley. They prefaced their demands with a reference to the several meetings they had held 'to seek the Lord, and to speak of the great things God hath done for this Commonwealth'. The wording of the demand for a new parliament was in line with the second *Agreement of the People*: 'That . . . qualifications for future and successive parliaments [should] tend to the election only of such as are pious and faithful to the interest of the Commonwealth, to sit and serve as members in the said parliament'. Publicly the petitioners were thanked, but privately there was much resentment among the MPs, who saw it as 'improper if not arrogant' for the officers to engage in political lobbying. Yet the MPs deferred to the army by ordering a committee report on the petition within a month.[12]

From Petition to Prayer Meeting, August 1652 to January 1653

For the next two months Parliament continued to throw conciliatory crumbs in the army's direction. To handle the many petitions with which it was inundated it set up a committee, to which it appointed Cromwell, Harrison, Fleetwood and Rich. Excluded were the army's enemies, Sir Henry Vane and Sir Arthur Hesilrige. Yet the gulf of distrust that had opened up between the Rump and the grandees continued to widen. Captain Edmund Chillenden hinted broadly to his friend William Clarke, the army's secretary in Scotland, that the day was not far off when the army would be rid of Parliament.[13]

Another nail was driven into the coffin of the Rump by its protracted debate on the Act of Articles. Since the beginning of the Civil Wars parliamentary commanders had negotiated many treaties of surrender with royalist field armies and garrisons. Normally these treaties were submitted to Parliament for ratification. To every commander, from Fairfax down, it was of the utmost importance that the terms which they granted to their defeated foes should be upheld by Parliament and the courts. Anything less would be highly destructive of military self-respect. Parliament had yielded to military pressure in 1649 when it passed the first Act of Articles. The act's declared purpose was to protect the army's good name, recognising 'how much it concerneth them in justice and honour that the [articles] may be made good'. Yet the act lapsed the following year.[14]

Not till the spring of 1652 did Parliament get round to hearing a motion to renew the Act of Articles. The motion was referred to the Indemnity Committee and Colonel Rich instructed to take care of it. For the next half year a bill meandered through committee hearings where it was subjected to repeated amendment. The Rump spoilt the goodwill it might have won from the army by vetoing the nomination of Colonel Pride as one of the commissioners for articles. Before the bill was read a third time it was muti-lated by a number of last-minute provisos. The most drastic stipulated that a resolution of Parliament could override any articles negotiated by the army. The new act, which reached the statute book in September 1652, did almost nothing to assuage the army's offended sense of honour. The cup was made more bitter in November by the inclusion of a rider that the act did not apply to the additional bill for sale of lands forfeited for treason. Many royalists who had surrendered on the understanding that they could keep their estates were now stripped of the protection that Fairfax and other offi-cers had promised them. The vehemence with which the officers resented Parliament's emasculation of the act is shown by their behaviour in June 1653. With the Rump out of the way a committee of officers took over the administration of the act and restored several royalists to their estates.[15]

The mood of the officers had by now turned ugly. Over a period of several weeks from October 1652, Cromwell held ten or twelve meetings with MPs, arguing that Parliament was no longer capable of undertaking a programme of reform, and must therefore be eliminated.[16]

Whitelocke relates a conversation he had with Cromwell around this time. On a fine autumn evening as he was walking in St James's Park, the general saluted him and began to unburden himself of his worries about the 'jarrings and animosities' currently plaguing the government. The root of the problem, he was sure, was that the MPs were accountable to no supe-rior power. Then abruptly he asked, 'what if a man should take upon him to be king?' Alarmed, Whitelocke tried to puncture Cromwell's ambition with the rejoinder, 'I think that remedy would be worse than the disease.'[17]

Meanwhile, the Rump seemed oblivious to the peril it was in. Insouciantly it moved to knock Cromwell down a peg by selling off Hampton Court, where he had resided since his triumphal return from Worcester. The capital was rife with rumours that he was soon to lose his command.[18]

The Council of State elections later that month produced a mixed result for the army. Among the twenty-two councillors whose mandate was renewed, only two were serving officers: Cromwell and Wauton. Fleetwood was defeated. On the other hand, two officers who had been defeated the year before – Skippon and Harrison – were elected, as was Colonel Richard Ingoldsby. The slightly improved military representation in government did little to cool the molten rhetoric that was now pouring from radical City pulpits and Fifth Monarchist strongholds such as All Hallows the Great and Blackfriars. Harrison, along with 'many precious ones', was confident, as he wrote to his friend John Jones, that 'our blessed Lord will shortly work with eminence'.[19]

Additional signs of the Rump's hostility to the army at this time were troop reductions, pay cuts and mounting arrears. At the time of Worcester there had been 45,000 troops on the payroll in England and a further 8,000 in Scotland. By December 1652 the army had been cut to 31,500 in the two nations, costing £111,000 a month. During the autumn Cromwell, Lambert, Ingoldsby and Goffe had all seen their regiments sharply pared. Another option the Rump debated was a decrease in the pay of troopers and foot soldiers by 20–25 per cent. Not surprisingly, the prospect of lower pay angered the rank and file. Yet, thanks to these belt-tightening measures, the army received regular pay for three years after Worcester.[20]

The Rump's whittling away of the army's numbers continued almost until the moment it was expelled. Most disturbing to Cromwell must have been the order in April to send half the men from both his and his close ally Barkstead's regiments to the navy. This measure convinced the officers that Parliament was bent on their destruction.[21]

Preparations for the Suppression of the Rump, January to April 1653

In this atmosphere of escalating paranoia, the officers met at the end of December 1652 in St James's for a protracted series of prayer meetings. Every day during the first week of January they waited on God, confessing their sins to one another and hearing sermons. Two miles to the east soldiers were gathering at All Hallows the Great in Thames Street, to pray for a new representative.[22]

Almost no public notice was paid to the officers' prayer meetings, but inside the army they generated much turbulence. Flowing from this turbulence was a letter that headquarters circulated to all the regiments in England, Scotland and Ireland, and also made public in London. The army must repent, it declared, but the corruption in Parliament could not be healed. The present

MPs must be replaced by successive parliaments consisting of 'men of truth, fearing God and hating covetousness'. There must also be law reform, liberty of worship and publicly sponsored evangelisation. Few responses to the call from headquarters survive; one which did reflected back with almost equal intensity the fervour of the Whitehall grandees. Reproaching themselves for their coldness 'in promoting the glorious things of Jesus Christ, and his precious people', they pronounced their dismay that 'floods of ungodly men are ready to break over the banks which the Lord hath raised for the defence of his own inheritance'. This perfervid chiliasm did not pour from the lips of men who were marginalised or oppressed, but from the self-confident leaders of an undefeated army, impatient for the new age to begin.[23]

A new representative was now front and centre among the army's concerns. Ever since Worcester, if not before, military impatience at the longevity of the Long Parliament had been simmering. From September 1651 Cromwell had been exhorting Parliament to set a date for new elections, and frame qualifications for voters and candidates.[24]

By January 1653, evidently frightened at the intensity of the army's anger, the House turned over responsibility for the bill for a new representative to Major-General Harrison, with instructions to him to bring it before the House 'with speed'. Implicit in this move was an acknowledgement that Parliament's mere existence had become one of the grandees' core grievances. Here was an extraordinary opportunity for the Fifth Monarchist major-general to shape his country's political future. Inexplicably, however, he fumbled the ball. As far as we can tell he did nothing. Perhaps he already thought parliaments were useless and preferred the simpler option of a hand-picked Sanhedrin or assembly on the Jewish model. Whatever the explanation for Harrison's failure to act, it was Hesilrige, the army's arch foe, who on 23 February reported the amendments to the bill for a new representative. The text of these amendments has not survived, but we know that they were unacceptable to the grandees, who stepped up their agitation for new elections.[25]

Cromwell laboured to avoid an open breach, but the officers, meeting at St James's, resolved on 11 March to turn out the Rump. Cromwell tried to dampen their fervour. Backed by Disbrowe, he challenged them to think, 'if they destroyed that parliament, what they should call themselves. A state they could not be. They answered that they would call a new parliament. Then, says the general, the parliament is not the supreme power, but that is the supreme power that calls it.'[26]

The Rump was not blind to this deadly threat. It hatched plans to dismiss Cromwell and reappoint Fairfax. Meanwhile, more and more senior officers, including some from Ireland and Scotland, congregated in London. Not all of them supported a forcible dissolution, but the doubters comprised a small minority. Overwhelmingly the officers saw eye to eye on the necessity of sweeping away what they regarded as a hopelessly reactionary and corrupt regime. Cromwell was by now well positioned to repel any attempt by Parliament to dislodge him. Surrounded by his leading officers and their trustworthy troops, his base of operations was the Cockpit, a few steps away from the House. He had seen to it that his own regiment of foot was appointed to guard the House. There appeared, at least for the time being, a fundamental harmony of purpose between the Cromwellians, who included Fleetwood, Disbrowe, Whalley, Barkstead and Goffe, and the militant radicals under Harrison. Lambert, who at this juncture led no faction, was a moderate constitutionalist, more or less in the mould of Ireton. Like Harrison, Cromwell absented himself from the Council of State and the House of Commons for most of March and April, showing that he had already written off these institutions.[27]

Cromwell advertised his alienation from Parliament in other ways. Apart from boycotting its meetings and taking steps to defend himself, he seems to have sanctioned a new petition hammered out by the officers in mid-March, demanding that the Rump convert its promise to dissolve not later than November 1654 into a statute. More portentous was the report of a conference held by Cromwell near the end of March with leading City divines, at which he proposed the forcible dissolution of Parliament. The London cleric Edmund Calamy denounced the scheme as unlawful and impracticable. 'Why impracticable?' asked Cromwell. 'Oh,' replied Calamy, ''tis against the voice of the nation; there will be nine in ten against you.' 'Very well,' said Cromwell, 'but what if I should disarm the nine, and put a sword into the tenth man's hand; would not that do the business?' A perceptive royalist noted that although Cromwell was distancing himself from the militants in public, in private he was very thick with them.[28]

A new representative, while it was the chief issue in army–Parliament relations, was only one of many. The grandees had made known a number of times their solicitude for the poor. In mid-February, however, the Rump gratuitously insulted their sensibilities by refusing to hear a bill for poor relief. Law reform was another question close to the grandees' hearts. Yet after resolving to dedicate every Thursday to the subject, the MPs forgot about it altogether, and law reform was never heard of again before the next Parliament.[29]

As we have seen, religion loomed large in the grandees' mental landscape. Several times they pronounced themselves in favour of replacing tithes with a more equitable system of church taxation. However, tithes had by the mid-seventeenth century become a kind of lay property no less than a source of church revenue. It is hardly surprising that Parliament always refused to contemplate their abolition. The officers were also much more avid for the promotion of Christianity than were the MPs. Early in 1652 Whalley, Okey and Goffe signed a petition for a religious settlement. Their scheme would have provided for an established church surrounded by self-supporting, officially tolerated nonconformist churches. Recognising the officers' zeal for evangelisation, the Rump appointed six of their number – Whalley, Harrison, Okey, Goffe, Francis White and John Blackwell – to a committee for the propagation of the gospel.[30]

It took a full year before the Rump got around to hearing their report. Once again it succeeded in treading on army sensibilities. On the issue of lay preaching, the officers had stoutly defended the right of anyone who believed he had received spiritual gifts to preach, regardless of his formal qualifications. The MPs could not stomach so much religious liberty. They hedged in the clause on lay preaching to read 'that persons of godliness and gifts, of the universities and others, though not ordained, *that shall be approved* shall receive the public maintenance for preaching the gospel'.[31]

Another major clash occurred over the propagation of the gospel in Wales. The principality had long been regarded by Puritans as one of the 'dark corners of the land'. In 1650 when the commission was established to promote the gospel there it came as no surprise that a large number of serving army officers were nominated to it.[32]

In company with the fiery preacher Vavasour Powell, Harrison and the others set about energetically to root out the malignant and scandalous clergy and plant a preaching ministry in their place. In late 1652 the commissioners orchestrated a shower of letters describing their good stewardship of the revenues and enthusing over the flourishing state of preaching and education throughout the length and breadth of Wales. On 25 March the House voted that the original act of 1650 should be brought forward for renewal on 1 April. But when that day came it declined to proceed with the act, and 'ordered a moderate clergy to be put in their places'. It was a disastrously ill-timed decision. More than any other, save the refusal to act on the question of a new representative, it sealed the Rump's fate.[33]

The Rump's waiving of the scheduled debate on a new representative on 6 April was virtually the last straw. Privately Cromwell told Whitelocke that the time had come to be done with Parliament. On 7 April the army submitted a fresh petition demanding that the House should proceed with the bill, while taking care to define the qualifications that would exclude improper persons from future parliaments. In its previous debate on 30 March, the House had ignored the army's concern to sift the electorate by passing a motion that 'all persons' possessing property worth £200 should have the vote. This motion, had it stood, would have practically guaranteed the election of a royalist parliament. A week later the House complied with the army's request by adding a requirement that members of the new House would only be allowed to take their seats if they were 'such as are persons of known integrity, fearing God, and not scandalous in their conversation'. The question now was, who was to judge? It was perhaps to resolve that very question that Cromwell broke his month-long boycott and attended the House on 14 April. There, he ran into a wall of hostility. It is high time, shouted one of the parliamentary leaders, to choose a new general. Cromwell traded angry words with his attacker, and Members of the House had to intervene to restore order.[34]

The chances of avoiding a violent breach with Parliament had by now almost vanished. To prepare for the coming showdown Cromwell consolidated his position in the army. Summoning the Council of Officers, he offered to resign as general. Not surprisingly this was rejected. At the same meeting the officers 'resolved very speedily to pull . . . down the parliament'.[35]

In the absence of any copy of the Rump's bill for a new representative, we can only infer why the army was so angry with it. Critical seems to have been its dissatisfaction over who was to judge the qualifications of the newly elected MPs. The bill stipulated that during the interval between parliaments the country was to be governed by a council of state chosen by Parliament. The existing council was dominated by anti-army republicans such as Hesilrige and Scot, who could be counted on to keep the officers away from the levers of political power. In fact the French ambassador reported that the Rump was planning to exclude all army officers from the new representative.[36]

Extra-parliamentary developments contributed to the gathering sense of crisis. For many weeks the coal fleet had been bottled up by the Dutch at

Scarborough. Londoners shivered in unheated houses, while cooks and brewers closed up shop because they could not afford to fire their ovens. Members of the Council of State walked in fear of their lives, two of them being recently assaulted in Smithfield. While people murmured and preachers ranted against Parliament, a petition made the rounds in the City condemning corruption in high places and implicitly calling upon the army to end the Rump's sitting. By mid-April the air was thick with the odour of panic.[37]

In this charged atmosphere Cromwell summoned his officers and several MPs to his lodgings in Whitehall for a marathon meeting on the night of 19 April. On the table was a proposal that a committee of forty MPs and officers, to be nominated by the Rump, should run the country until the next Parliament met. All the officers and some of the MPs, notably Oliver St John, lined up behind the general. A majority of the MPs were strongly opposed. After all opinions had been aired, the meeting trailed on until the early hours of the morning. Finally, collapsing with fatigue, the remaining participants agreed to go home and reconvene the following afternoon. The MPs who had not already left said they would do their best to postpone the parliamentary debate scheduled for tomorrow until Cromwell's ad hoc committee had exhausted all possible avenues to a compromise.[38]

The Violence against Parliament and Its Aftermath, 20 April to 4 July

About 100 members of the Long Parliament assembled on the morning of 20 April. It was odd of Cromwell to believe that this institution would do his bidding without his even being there to explain why it should. Confident perhaps in their large numbers, the MPs refused to bow to the general's request, and called for the bill. Oblivious to this development, Cromwell was at that moment conversing with Ingoldsby and a few other officers and MPs in his lodgings. They were interrupted by a messenger with the news that Parliament was in the final stages of its debate on the controversial bill. The MPs present immediately left for the House, where they found their colleagues debating 'an act, the which would . . . prolong their sitting'.[39]

Enraged by what he presumed to be a betrayal of trust, Cromwell got ready to go to the House. He was not dressed for the occasion; his outfit was plain black, with grey worsted stockings. While his junior officers marshalled a party of soldiers to accompany him, he addressed the others at the Cockpit, telling them that reformation could not be expected from the present parliament, and that if they should put the people to elect a new parliament it would but tempt God. Therefore his opinion was that God did intend to save and deliver this nation by few; and that five or six men, or few more, setting themselves to the work, might do more in one day than the parliament had or would do in one hundred days, for . . . the burdens are continued still on the people, injustice aboundeth, the law is not regulated; they intend nothing but to seek themselves, and to perpetuate themselves . . .[40]

Cromwell then marched his soldiers to the House. Most of them he placed at the door and in the lobby. He also took in with him a file of thirty musketeers, leaving them at the entrance to the chamber. Cromwell slipped into his usual place, where he sat quietly for a time. Then, just as the MPs were about to vote on the bill, he leaned over to Harrison and whispered, 'This is the time I must do it.' It was about midday when he stood up to speak. At first he commended the Rump for all it had done for the public good. But shortly his tone changed and he began to upbraid the MPs for delaying justice, and other failings. Suddenly his language became barbed and personal. Leaving his place he put his hat on and walked to the open floor in the middle of the chamber. From this vantage point he berated them collectively and singly. 'You are no parliament, I say you are no parliament, I will put an end to your sitting.' Then he stamped his foot to give the pre-arranged signal for the musketeers to enter the House. The soldiers seem to have missed their cue, for he had to shout, 'call them in'. As Lieutenant-Colonel Worsley ushered in the thirty armed men of his own regiment, Cromwell informed the MPs that 'the Lord had done with them, and had chosen other instruments for the carrying on his work that were more worthy'. Then, pointing to Speaker Lenthall, he ordered Harrison to fetch him down from his seat. The Speaker at first resisted until Harrison gently said 'Sir, I will lend you my hand.' Most of the MPs beat a quick retreat, and as they streamed past him Cromwell reproached them in injured tones: 'It's you that have forced me to this, for I have sought the Lord night and day, that he would rather slay me than put me upon the doing of this work'. When a few protested against their expulsion he turned vengeful again. Some of them were whoremasters, he fulminated, looking straight at Henry Marten and Peter Wentworth. 'Others of them [like Chaloner] were drunkards, and some corrupt and unjust men, and scandalous to the profession of the gospel.' The elder Sir Henry Vane was a 'juggler' and his son a 'cheat'. Henry

Marten was both atheist and adulterer. Sir Henry Mildmay, Francis Allein and Thomas Scot were embezzlers of public money. As if these jibes were not enough, the MPs also had to endure the taunts of the musketeers as they left the chamber. It was too much for the younger Vane, who expostulated 'this is not honest, yea it is against morality and common honesty', at which Cromwell lashed out: 'O Sir Henry Vane, Sir Henry Vane, the Lord deliver me from Sir Henry Vane'. Then his eye lighted upon the mace, symbol of the Commons' authority. 'Take away that fool's bauble', he barked to one of the soldiers. Not until every other MP was out did Cromwell leave the House. Then he saw to it that the door was locked, entrusting the key to Colonel Okey and the mace to Lieutenant-Colonel Worsley.[41]

In the early afternoon Cromwell returned to the Cockpit, where he met his officers again. He told them that his act had been unpremeditated, 'that when he went into the House he intended not to do it; but the spirit was so upon him, that he was over-ruled by it: and that he consulted not with flesh and blood at all, nor did he premeditate the doing thereof'.[42] It is quite believable that by his own lights Cromwell had not consciously planned what he would do on 20 April, even though he had been determined for several months that the Rump had to go.

Public reaction to the disappearance of the Long Parliament was muted. By the end of the day a wag had hung a sign on the door reading, 'This house to be let, now unfurnished'. Soon two new ballads were heard in the streets of London celebrating Cromwell's action. The Venetian ambassador confirmed that people were happy at the Rump's demise. Tacitly conceding their unpopularity, the MPs voiced no protest. Warm expressions of support came from the navy, as well as from officers in Scotland and the north. *The Humble Petition of the Churches of Christ* hailed Cromwell as 'our Moses', while others urged him to put the crown on his own head.[43]

What happened on 20 April 1653 and the popular reaction to it are clear. Less clear is why the army chose to act the way it did, and, more precisely, what it was about the Rump's bill for a new representative that was so unacceptable. In the days after the expulsion the grandees repeatedly accused the Rump of intending merely to recruit itself without holding general elections.[44]

There was more to the army's objections than that. Ever since the autumn of 1648 it had known that, if the Revolution was to be safe, the godly would have to govern for the foreseeable future. The rules for electoral eligibility would have to be carefully drafted so as to exclude all but 'persons of known integrity, fearing God and not scandalous in their conversation'. Cromwell later charged that the Rump made no provision for enforcing its qualifications for election, and no one ever contradicted him.[45]

The chasm of suspicion dividing the officers and the parliamentary majority was so wide that neither side could trust the other with the judging of qualifications. That is why at the last moment the Council of Officers had launched an intensive round of negotiations with the parliamentary leaders designed to postpone the elections and set up an interim government of about forty godly men – half officers and half MPs. Exercising supreme authority, the proposed executive would be

> the most hopeful way to encourage and countenance all God's people, reform the law, and administer justice impartially; hoping thereby the people might forget monarchy, and, understanding their true interest in the election of successive parliaments, may have the government settled upon a true basis, without hazard to this glorious cause, or necessitating to keep up armies for the defence of the same . . .

On the morning of 20 April, however, the MPs rejected Cromwell's plan and proceeded with a scheme that would have barred the officers from participation in running the country. Even worse, the Rump's bill would have fired Cromwell as commander-in-chief. Apparently it would have put the army command into commission, just as the restored Rump would do in 1659.[46]

An officer-inspired report explaining the dissolution affirmed that, had the Rump's bill passed, the nation would have been 'in a sad condition, and involved in a labyrinth of new troubles'. The 'several things . . . of dangerous consequence' in the bill included a reduction in the army's budget to £31,000 a month, which would have hardly paid the wages of 14,000 soldiers. The army's depletion and exclusion from the new representative would have generated a power vacuum that would have provided a tempting opportunity for royalists to stage a coup d'état.[47]

Thus the army's expulsion of the Rump was not only a last-ditch resort to forestall the accession to power of the ungodly, it was also a desperate act of self-preservation from the Rump's clear intention to destroy it. It was something more as well. The officers' *Declaration of the Grounds and Reasons for Dissolving the Parliament* (22 April) opened with an indictment of the Rump for failing to provide good government and for being dilatory about reform. For twenty months they had exhorted it to address the pressing issues of law reform, financial probity, and the spreading of the gospel. As the officers wrote to their comrades in Ireland, they had to take action because of 'the ill management of affairs by the late parliament'.[48]

A further reason why Cromwell dissolved the Rump was his personal drive for power. It is clear from his conversations with Whitelocke and Calamy that he had been meditating a seizure of power for his own purposes. It was entirely natural that he should have such thoughts. An undefeated general, he had a secure power base among his troops. By risking their lives time and again for almost a decade, he and his officers had surely won the moral right to be listened to on political affairs. Yet since returning from Worcester they had been blocked at every turn. As Cromwell contemplated the men who thwarted him, the thought would have crossed his mind that he could do a better job at the helm of government than any of them. No one in Parliament could match his military prowess, and when it came to political subtlety and effectiveness he outdid the best of them. It was galling for Oliver to see his dreams of godly reformation and political settlement frustrated week after week by men of such blinkered vision. It exasperated him that they were more troubled by the threat of usurpation by soldiers and sectarians than by a resurgent Presbyterianism, and its potential ally, the House of Stuart. He therefore decided that 'the Lord had done' with these men, and that he, Cromwell, would wipe the slate clean of them. While he did not aspire to be a military dictator, he unquestionably wanted to be at the centre of political decision-making in England.[49]

CHAPTER THIRTEEN

BAREBONE'S PARLIAMENT AND
THE PROTECTORATE, 1653–56

The Summoning of Barebone's

After the expulsion of the Rump, Cromwell and the officers appeared to be in a daze, irresolute and unprepared. They soon issued a declaration justifying the coup, which they sent to all the regiments outside London. Their promised aim was to call to the next Parliament 'persons of approved fidelity and honesty' An executive council of ten was created, of whom six were army officers. Almost the first thing they did was to instruct the mayor of London and the rest of the justices in the capital to cancel all hangings for theft, or any other crime except murder.[1]

Only then did discussions begin as to what form of government should replace the Rump. Harrison was president of the council during its third week. It was at this time that he attained the zenith of his political influence. In the debate over how to reshape the sovereign power in the wake of the Long Parliament's demise, he argued for an assembly of seventy, on the Old Testament model of the Jewish Sanhedrin. In the event the officers opted to summon a body twice that large, consisting of 'men fearing God and of approved fidelity', to form an interim government until England should be ready to hold normal elections once again. Every officer had an equal vote in the selection of the nominees. Not only did Cromwell wish to avoid one-man rule, he was equally determined not to usher in a collective military dictatorship. That is why he persuaded his Council of Officers not to name any serving officers to the new assembly. He and the Council of Officers also listened when the minor officers piped up demanding another restriction: no one should be nominated who had handled public money since the Civil War. At the end of May the officers sat with Cromwell for several days going over the names. It took almost two weeks to select 140 godly nominees from England, Ireland, Scotland and

Wales. As soon as it met the assembly added to its number by co-opting five officers: Cromwell, Disbrowe, Harrison, Lambert and Tomlinson. In the end sixteen officers and former officers sat in the assembly.[2]

Besides being co-opted to the assembly, Harrison was also instrumental in the nomination of several Welsh saints (committed Protestants) and four members of his own Fifth Monarchist sect, as well as getting himself elected to the new Council of State, both in July and December.

In the meantime, Lambert was made president of the interim Council of State for a week, a move that demonstrated both his support for the regime and Cromwell's confidence in him. Also at the peak of his influence in the army, he continued to play a full part in the interim government. The council speedily adopted a number of progressive measures, including an inquiry into the state of the Post Office, an investigation of the debtors' prison of the Court of Upper Bench, a scheme for the better management of the treasuries, and the suppression of bear- and bull-baiting.[3]

Nevertheless, there was resentment among many officers when they realised that the small Council of State and not the Council of Officers was the effective locus of decision-making. The sense of alienation felt by officers found a parallel in the umbrage taken by the rank and file at being 'cozened out of their debentures by the insinuation of the superior officers'. One report had it that there was also a momentary rekindling of democratic aspirations among the soldiery. Military agitators were said to have presented a remonstrance to the Council of Officers, claiming for every soldier 'an equal voice in electing the members of the forthcoming new representative'. To quell this restlessness the grandees placed the forces in and about London on a diet of prayer and preaching for two or three hours each day.[4]

When the assembly gathered for the first time on a very hot day in July 1653 Cromwell addressed it in the most exalted terms. Calling the occasion 'a day of the power of Christ', he told the nominees he expected them to bring in measures that would turn England into a spiritual new Jerusalem. The draft constitution under which the assembly was governed was drawn up by the Council of Officers, who kept a close watch on its proceedings. The assembly soon acquired the mocking nickname 'Barebone's Parliament', after one of its members, Praise-God Barebone, a godly leather seller in Fleet Street.

It lost no time in grappling with several of Thomas Harrison's favourite issues: tithes, law reform, the excise tax, and the war with the Netherlands. He pressed for the immediate abolition of tithes, but was unable to prevent the question being shunted into a committee. In August the House passed resolutions for the abolition of the Court of Chancery and the framing of a completely new body of law. Harrison was appointed to the committee to embody these resolutions into statutes, but no statutes materialised. He was also named to the excise committee, in the expectation that the tax would soon be eliminated, but the expectation was never fulfilled. There are several reasons for the failure of the radical agenda in Barebone's Parliament, but among them must be counted Harrison's lack of political aptitude, his impatience with committee work, and his reluctance to undertake the hard slogging required to accomplish significant change. His record of attendance, in both the Council of State and Parliament, was spotty. More exciting to him than tedious parliamentary debates seemed to be the Monday prayer meetings at St Ann Blackfriars, where the fiery preaching of Christopher Feake and John Rogers furnished heady inspiration. More appealing than boring meetings of the Council of State were the Fifth Monarchist gatherings at Arthur Squibb's house in Fleet Street. Inflamed by the millenarian vision of the imminent overthrow of Antichrist, Harrison and his friends campaigned for the continued prosecution of the war against the Dutch: 'the Dutch must be destroyed; and we shall have an heaven upon earth'.[5] By adopting this position he collided with Cromwell, who was seeking peace with the Netherlands. By late November 1653 the two were near to an open breach.

Harrison fiercely opposed the decision by the moderate majority in Barebone's to surrender its authority to Cromwell. Barebone's dissolution also marked the effective end of Harrison's political career. Before the end of December 1653 he had been stripped of his military commission. In mid-January, Cromwell granted him an interview that lasted four or five hours, but with no resolution of the issues separating them. A few weeks later he was ordered to retire to Staffordshire. Harrison's eclipse accelerated the continuing rise of John Lambert's star.[6]

There were other reasons than Harrison's ineptitude for the failure of Barebone's, notably the resistance of entrenched interests. The attempt to abolish the corrupt Court of Chancery and codify the law ran into fierce opposition from the legal profession, even though it was not represented in the assembly. The attack on tithes posed a threat to landowners. Another source of alarm was the increasingly extravagant claim of the saints to rule simply as saints. Cromwell in exasperation confided to a friend that he was 'more troubled now with the fool than with the knave'. He and the officers soon became irked by the assembly's carelessness over army pay. Calls were heard within it for the abolition of both the excise and the monthly assessment, cornerstone of army finance. Some nominees suggested that senior officers should serve for a year without pay. The last straw was the rejection of the surrender articles that the army had signed with the royalist Sir John Stawell at the close of the Civil War. A careless attitude towards the army's financial welfare, combined with indifference to the army's honour led moderates, with covert support from the army, to pull the plug on Barebone's Parliament.[7]

Who was the guiding force behind the dissolution? 'The finger points . . . irresistibly at Lambert.' Carrying out his will were several officers: Colonels John Disbrowe, William Sydenham, Philip Jones, John Hewson and John Clarke. The first three were also members of the current Council of State. Arriving early on the morning of Monday 12 December, while many radicals were still in bed, they moved to dissolve the assembly. The Speaker did not put the motion to a vote; he simply got up and left, followed by about eighty members, leaving thirty-five or fewer behind. Some time later Colonel Goffe and Lieutenant-Colonel White arrived with a file of musketeers and 'entreated [the remaining members] earnestly to go out'. Seeing the musketeers they left quietly, though they later protested against their forcible expulsion.[8]

Waiting in the wings with his draft of a new constitution named the Instrument of Government was John Lambert. With the help of James Berry, William Goffe and perhaps three or four others, he had been working on it ever since October, when the attacks had begun on the renewal of the excise and the monthly assessment. He presented it to the Council of Officers as a *fait accompli*. There followed some delicate negotiations with Cromwell which culminated in his agreeing to accept limitations on the absolute power that he now exercised as effective military dictator. Having rejected the title of king, he was named lord protector. He and the elected members of Parliament would exercise supreme legislative authority. The vote was limited to those whose property was worth at least £200, who were not Roman Catholic and had not in any way supported the Irish rebellion of 1641, nor taken any part in the war against Parliament. Parliaments were to be triennial. The council, whose first members were named in the Instrument itself, was to control the lord protector, and, in the event of his death, to elect his successor. No tax was to be levied without Parliament's consent. On the other hand, another article guaranteed the lord protector a yearly revenue adequate to maintain an army of 30,000, a navy capable of guarding the seas, and £200,000 for civil expenses, to be raised out of the customs. The lord protector was allowed a maximum of twenty days in which to veto parliamentary legislation; otherwise, it would automatically become law. Christianity was to be the official religion, maintained at public expense, but people were allowed to practise whatever form of Christianity they chose except for 'Popery or Prelacy [Anglicanism]'. In due time tithes would be replaced by a more appropriate form of public maintenance for the church. All surrender articles made by the army with the enemy were to be upheld by the government, thus resolving the army's longstanding grievance against previous regimes.[9]

Cromwell, accompanied by his lifeguard and all the chief officers of the army, was installed as lord protector on 16 December. He was dressed in a black suit and cloak rather than his captain-general's uniform, in an effort to emphasise the non-military character of the new government. Later that month, with his council and officers, he held a day of fast and humiliation. At the end of the day, after a lot of arm-twisting, fifteen officers endorsed an engagement of loyalty which all regiments and garrisons were asked to sign. More than a few officers were opposed to Cromwell's elevation, including the major of his own foot regiment, John Wigan, who resigned his commission. Around the same time, Cornet Caithness of Cromwell's own lifeguard also resigned. Another officer accused him of having 'traitorously assumed to himself regal power'. Some officers were won over by Cromwell's promise to abolish tithes before September of that year. In the event they were to be bitterly disappointed. So anxious was the regime about the army's response to the Instrument that it took seventeen days after Cromwell's installation to get it published. Particularly concerning to the government was the reaction of Thomas Harrison. Over the long run what doomed the Instrument of Government was 'its abiding and insuperable defect', namely that it was an illegal decree, never to be recognised or adopted by Parliament. Nevertheless most of the officers, including those in Ireland and Scotland, accepted its creation, the Protectorate, despite all its shortcomings. They were acutely conscious of being islands of revolutionary conviction surrounded by a sea of popular hostility. They also respected Cromwell for his godliness. Typical of many was the deeply pious Colonel Robert Bennett, a sectary and garrison commander in Cornwall, who wrote to Cromwell, 'I am persuaded that . . . our God hath placed your Highness over us.'[10]

The First Protectoral Parliament

There were two major instances of early military opposition to the Protectorate: the Three Colonels' Petition and the so-called 'Overton's Plot'. In May 1654 Cromwell was informed that Colonel Matthew Alured in Ireland had 'evil intentions' towards the government. He was promptly relieved of his command and called to London. According to General Fleetwood, Colonels Okey, Thomas Saunders and Francis Hacker, as well as Vice-Admiral John Lawson and some other officers were plotting with John Wildman. Okey, Saunders and Wildman had all been elected to Parliament, but were excluded after they refused to sign the 'Recognition of Government' imposed by Cromwell. The outcome of the three men's collaboration was adoption of a petition that Wildman had drafted. The petition was further discussed at secret meetings at his house and in the Blue Boar's Head Tavern in King Street and the Dolphin Tavern in Tower Street. Captain John Bishop took one version and ran it by the republican John Bradshaw, former president of the High Court of Justice. Other civilian radicals were also implicated in the plot. The plan was to circulate the petition, once perfected, among army officers in all three nations. However, Thurloe's intelligence service was several steps ahead of the conspirators, and before he could disseminate it, Alured had been imprisoned and the petition, bearing as yet only three signatures – his own, Okey's and Saunders's – taken from his chamber.[11]

On 18 October someone, presumably Wildman, published the petition. It is likely that many officers, given the chance, would have added their names to it. Already it was well known that a significant number of officers were much less enthusiastic about the establishment of the Protectorate than they had been about the expulsion of the Rump. In fact nostalgia was growing for the 'Good Old Cause'. This resonant phrase, originated by Sir Henry Vane, would be invoked more and more often during the later 1650s. It stood for an unsystematic summation of what was thought to be the army's programme: religious liberty (for sectarian Protestants), the reformation of manners, law reform, justice for the poor, the abolition of tithes, and a broader franchise based on the *Agreement of the People*. With great poignancy the three signatories expressed anguish that 'the blood of many thousands hath been . . . shed by our means'. They went on: 'we tremble and fear before the Lord, [because of the] account, we must render for all that precious blood if we should by silence give away the freedom purchased for our country at so dear a rate'. They denounced the Protectorate as a betrayal of that freedom and called for the implementation of the *Agreement of the People*.[12] Copies of the petition were dispatched to army units in England, Scotland and Ireland. They were accompanied by copies of a pamphlet, probably also by Wildman, entitled *Some Memento's for the Officers and Souldiers of the Army from Some Sober Christians*. This was a bitter attack on Cromwell, characterising him as he who 'claims all these powers and maintains all those principles of tyranny against which you fought'. In fact he was a worse tyrant than Charles I. The tract ended with a clarion call to the army to stand up for the people's rights and freedoms, through 'free and successive parliaments . . . under an authority justly derived'.[13]

The radical protest movement among the officers was covertly supported by no less an authority than General Fleetwood, who wrote to Secretary Thurloe that if Colonel Alured were to suffer capital punishment for his political activity, 'it would sadly wound me'. Adjutant-General Allen took up the torch for the cause, as did Lieutenant-General Ludlow, who was caught circulating the petition in January 1655, Colonel Hierome Sankey, who also had close links with Wildman, Lieutenant-Colonel Alexander Brayfield, Captain Thomas Walcott and others. Yet for all the support it attracted, the programme of Wildman and the Three Colonels was intellectually incoherent. Had Cromwell permitted the free elections they demanded, the result could only have been the return of the royalists to power – as would also have happened in 1649 with free elections. It was disingenuous to advocate a freely elected parliament as the guarantor of liberty of conscience when Cromwell personally favoured a broader religious freedom than any parliament of the Interregnum.[14]

The petitioners mustered more support in Ireland and Scotland than in England. The ease with which their movement was snuffed out testifies to the shallowness of soldierly disenchantment with the Protectorate. The whole episode is also another example of Cromwell's political skill. Alured was convicted of mutiny and imprisoned for over a year. Okey was acquitted of treason by a court-martial, and, after surrendering his commission, Cromwell gave him his liberty. Saunders does not appear to have been detained at all, but was ordered to surrender his commission. The differentiation of punishments shows Cromwell's magnanimity and wisdom.[15]

When Major-General Ludlow, who had already withheld his approval for the Protectorate, was finally recalled to England for distributing copies of the Three Colonels' Petition and other subversive literature, he was brought before Cromwell and the council. Grilled by Cromwell and Lambert as to why he thought he could oppose the government, he offered only a weak reply. Dismissed from his command, he attracted virtually no support from the other officers. Major-General Thomas Kelsey summed up army sentiment when he assured Cromwell in 1656 that he and his comrades would stand by the lord protector to maintain 'the interest of God's people with life and fortune, which is to be preferred before 1,000 parliaments'. Kelsey was not alone in his disenchantment with Parliament. An 'intense distrust of parliaments' runs through the Instrument of Government. The army's view that the people should be governed for their own good rather than according to the popular will, and educated in right religion and virtue, was one that they shared with Milton.[16]

Despite the wish to share power with the civilian population, the military complexion of the Protectorate was plain for all to see. Of the fifteen members of the first Protectoral Council, six were or had been army officers: Lambert, Disbrowe, Skippon, Colonel Philip Jones, Colonel William Sydenham and Sir Anthony Ashley Cooper. The later nomination of the former colonel Nathaniel Fiennes brought the total to seven, in addition to Cromwell.[17]

Perhaps the most contentious issue in the first Protectoral Parliament was the size of the armed forces. According to the Instrument of Government, the lord protector was to command an army of 30,000 spread over the three nations. The actual size of the army in the autumn of 1654 was 57,000. Strident demands were heard in Parliament for the army to be reduced to its authorised number, and for the monthly assessment to be cut from £90,000 (it had previously been as high as £120,000) to £30,000. This reduction would have crippled the army. The council attempted to meet Parliament half-way by reducing the assessment to £60,000 a month. Parliament also moved to strip the lord protector of his sole authority over the standing army, a power that had been enjoyed by none of his monarchical predecessors. To deprive the lord protector of the power of the sword, his supporters shot back, would be to give up 'that eminent and glorious cause, which had been so much and so long contended; for such parliaments might hereafter be chosen as would betray the glorious cause of the people of God'. The attacks on the army prompted the great majority of officers to rally behind Cromwell.[18]

The army petition addressed to Cromwell in December 1654, calling for reform but reiterating undying support for him was much more representative of army opinion than the Three Colonels' Petition. The substance of the petition was almost a rehash of the promises embodied in the Instrument of Government: liberty of conscience in public worship (but not for papists), removal of tithes, law reform, compulsory payment of debts by those who could afford to pay them, setting the poor to work, recognition of the amnesty granted to people under the articles of war, and the payment of all public debts. Cromwell received it 'with much respect' and promised to do his best to meet their demands.[19] But his mind at that moment was much more preoccupied with the so-called 'Western Design', and imminent war against Spain in the Caribbean.

The Expedition to the West Indies

In June 1649, musing on foreign policy, Cromwell had pronounced to his Council of Officers, 'the Spaniard is your great enemy' – great because of never-ending Spanish raids on English shipping in the Caribbean, and great also because Spain was the strongest supporter of Antichrist (the pope). Delivering a body blow to the Spanish Empire would weaken popish power and advance the cause of international Protestantism. A raid against Spanish possessions also offered the tantalising prospect of scooping up some of the fabulous treasure that crossed the Atlantic every year in the form of gold and silver plate. This, it was hoped, would rescue the republic from bankruptcy. Besides, peace having recently been signed with the Dutch, England now had 160 well-equipped ships and a surplus of troops with little to do.[20]

The only member of the lord protector's council with the courage to speak out against the proposed expedition was Lambert. 'The work', he said, was 'improbable', the target too far away, the scheme unlikely to advance the Protestant cause, and the cost 'not well considered'. There would be many casualties, not least from disease, and people would not flock to settle Hispaniola even if it were conquered. Better to concentrate on settling Ireland. Lambert however was overruled, and planning for a raid against the Spanish empire began in earnest in the summer of 1654.[21]

Robert Venables, colonel of a regiment in Ireland, was selected to head the expedition and advanced to the rank of general, while General William Penn was appointed to command the fleet. Both had honourable military records.[22] Cromwell gave each man equal authority. Three civilian commissioners were also named, and these five together exercised overall command of the expedition. This arrangement led to divided counsel, with unfortunate results.

By late December a large invading force had been put together: six regiments of foot, a troop of sixty cavalry, a fifty-man artillery train, and a company of 120 firelocks, totalling 2,500. In addition there was a full regiment of seamen under Vice-Admiral William Goodson. It would perform better than all the other regiments put together. The problem with the latter was that they included very few seasoned soldiers, having been collected randomly from here and there. Few of them knew one another, and they lacked regimental *esprit de corps*. Venables would later complain bitterly that they were raw, undisciplined men, many of them the offscourings of the streets and prisons of London. They showed little enthusiasm for their mission. General Disbrowe with a squadron of cavalry had to herd them aboard the thirty-eight ships on which they set sail at the end of December.[23]

They were also badly equipped and under-provisioned. Of those who had arms, half were 'defective and altogether unserviceable'. When they got to Barbados they lost valuable time manufacturing 10-foot long 'half-pikes' for the men without arms. On the eve of the rainy season they all lacked tents, and no one thought to supply them with water bottles. A number of the store ships that were meant to accompany the expedition were detained in English ports by bad weather, and did not catch up with the fleet until after it arrived in Jamaica. What food they had allegedly went mouldy (biscuit) or rotten (salted meat) before they reached the West Indies. By the time they got to Hispaniola they were living on half-rations, eked out by slaughtered dogs and horses.[24]

The sea was calm and the crossing to Barbados uneventful. The flotilla arrived on 29 January. On the way they picked up another 1,000 volunteers at Saint Kitts, and a handful more at Monserrat and Nevis. Barbados yielded a further 3,000–4,000 men. Together with the sea regiment, and 700 or so officers, the invading force had reached close to 9,000, with the fleet now numbering sixty ships. The size of the invading force turned out to be more of a hindrance than an asset. They were now short of provisions, arms and ammunition. Devoid of military experience, the West Indian recruits were of even poorer quality than the refuse scraped up from the London streets – 'the very scum of scums and mere dregs of corruption' in the words of one witness. The removal of so many Barbadians from their place of work had a negative effect on the island's economy, provoking anger from planters who were hard hit by the loss of labour.[25]

Cromwell had left it to Venables's discretion how many additional troops he should recruit in the Caribbean, and also whether he should first attack

Hispaniola or Cuba or Puerto Rico (Saint John's Island). In the event the commanders settled upon Hispaniola, and on Saturday 31 March the fleet set sail from Barbados, arriving at Santo Domingo harbour a week later.[26]

Before a blow was ever struck in anger the army was severely demoralised by Cromwell's order forbidding all plunder. His reasoning was that, since it was intended to settle the conquered territory, it would not do to subject it to economic ruin. Venables promised the men six weeks' pay in lieu of plunder, but this pay was not forthcoming. For many men the sole attraction of the expedition had been the glittering prospect of Spanish plunder. Led by the seamen, they staged a brief strike against the prohibition by laying down their arms.[27]

Rather than charge right into Santo Domingo against the high prevailing winds and risk being cut to pieces by Spanish artillery, General Penn chose to land the main part of the fleet 30 miles west of the capital, on the other side of the Haina River. The next morning they began their march, 'our men . . . being in good heart and cheerful'. The mood was not to last. They marched hard all day long and into the night. The heat was so intense that the sand scorched their feet through their shoes. Under the blazing tropical sun they quickly became thirsty. Having no water, they became dehydrated and before the day was out were collapsing from thirst. Some men in desperation drank their own urine or begged their comrades to urinate into their mouths. Others gorged themselves on the oranges and limes hanging from the trees under which they passed, and soon began to suffer violent dysentery.[28]

The rest of the army landed 9 miles west of Santo Domingo. They advanced towards it, but stricken by thirst, they fell back. To compound the troops' misery the rainy season began that very night. Camping outside without tents over their heads, and with heavy rains beating down on them, they suffered terribly from cold. The extreme wet triggered savage dysentery (the 'bloody flux'), and a variety of fevers. The men complained bitterly of the lack of brandy – another oversight on the part of the provisioners.[29]

Venables soon joined his regiments with the main part of the army. Now refreshed at the river, they advanced on the capital. When they were 3 miles from it their vanguard was ambushed by a small party of Spaniards. Both the vanguard and the next regiment under Venables were put to flight. Their guide was killed, a major setback. The regiment of seamen put a stop to the flight. At this point the Spaniards retreated into a small fort – a plain brick wall with nothing on the flanks, but furnished with nine cannon. Unprovided

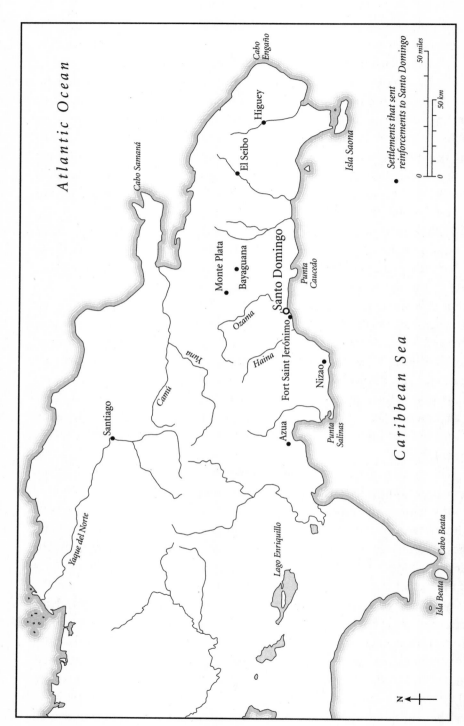

8. The expedition to Hispaniola, 1655

with scaling ladders, Venables decided not to attack the fort, but to go around it and head directly for the town.

Not knowing the way, and feeling the need for time to recover from the ambush, in spite of the soldiers' desire to march on, Venables insisted on stopping for a whole week before setting off again for the town. Without their guide they lost their way. Adjutant-General Thomas Jackson was put in charge of the vanguard, but he ignored the order to sweep the woods on either side of their march for a possible ambush. Before they knew it, the vanguard was under attack again – in exactly the same place as before. After waiting for the English to empty all their muskets in one volley, the Spanish fell on them with their lances. They scattered Jackson's vanguard (he hid ignominiously behind a bush), and then came upon Major-General Haynes's regiment. They performed no better. Almost all of them fled, leaving Haynes and two companions to fight against perhaps 400 enemy troops. He and one companion were killed, after which the Spanish drove half Venables's army before them, slaughtering 600 or more until they were, in the words of several witnesses 'weary of killing'.[30] It was not just being ambushed in a strange country that terrified the English soldiers. The Spanish lance was only 12 feet long, but as it was used for cutting sugar, and steel tipped, it was much heavier than the even shorter English half-pike, made in Barbados out of inferior cabbage wood. Such was the collapse of morale on the English side that the men threw away their arms, ammunition and food in their headlong retreat. The Spanish fighters were mostly negro slaves and mulattoes who had been spurred on by the promise of emancipation if they fought successfully for Spain. Once again it was the regiment of seamen who stood their ground and finally brought the Spanish attack to a halt.

After the great humiliation of the second ambush, Venables wanted to recover the army's honour by storming the fort and its few hundred defenders the next morning. A small mortar-piece and two drakes (small cannon) were brought ashore, along with three days' provisions. But it was no use: the 'men's spirits were so cowed' that they would flee in terror if they spotted a single enemy soldier. The sound of crabs clicking their claws in the night threw them into a panic.[31]

Faced with the utter demoralisation of their men, Venables and his officers concluded that a third attempt on Santo Domingo was out of the question. After a quick consultation they agreed that Jamaica would be their next objective. Jamaica was smaller and assumed to be less well defended. It lay astride the route of the returning treasure fleet, and was reputed to be endowed with fertile soil, the potential for rich crops of tobacco, sugar and chocolate, and many thousands of cattle, both domesticated and wild.[32] The whole army, now at 1,000 less because of losses in battle and from disease, embarked from Hispaniola on 2–3 May, and arrived in sight of the Jamaican coast on the 9th.

The island was thinly populated – perhaps 2,000–3,000 Spaniards at the most, besides 3,000 slaves. At the first sighting of the fleet the property-owners fled into the woods and mountains with all their moveable goods and slaves. Venables, who had been violently sick with dysentery for almost three weeks, did not venture ashore. Reduced to a near-skeleton, he could only stand up when supported by two soldiers. The condition of the island governor was hardly better. He was so eaten up by venereal disease ('the pox') that the Spanish were 'ashamed that we should see him'. They surrendered almost immediately, articles were signed, and Jamaica remained a British colony for the next 300 years.[33]

It was not just the leaders who were ravaged by disease. After killing and consuming several hundred cattle the army was again thrown back on substandard provisions, which the navy was increasingly unwilling to supply. Before long they were living again off horse, dog and asses' meat, and their health deteriorated to the point where they lost more men than they had in Hispaniola. Within a few months of landing in Jamaica their numbers were down to less than 4,000 from 'bloody flux, rheum, ague [and] fever'. Half of those still alive lay sick and helpless.[34]

Is it any surprise that during this nightmarish adventure bitter conflict broke out among the officers? Penn and Venables exchanged 'high words'. Venables suspected the navy of withholding supplies from the army, while saving the best for themselves. Penn made no secret of his contempt for Venables's competence. The sailors mocked the soldiers for their cowardice. Penn became so fed up with the whole mission that he decided to sail back to England, taking the greater part of the fleet with him. When he got back he was upbraided for returning without orders. Cromwell accused him of desertion. Furious too that he had made no attempt to capture some of the Spanish treasure ships, he threw Penn into the Tower of London for a month.[35]

Venables also returned without permission, on the pretext that he was too ill to be of any use in the West Indies, and that his officers had authorised him to leave in order to present the army's side of the story.[36] By the time he reached Portsmouth his health had improved, and he was able to make the final leg of the trip under his own steam. Cromwell, equally unsympathetic to his story, meted out the same punishment – imprisonment in the Tower for a month. Neither man would be employed again under the Protectorate.

The Cromwellian expedition to the West Indies was an unmitigated disaster. What explains this sorry state of affairs? Robert Venables was the familiar example of an individual promoted to his level of incompetence. An able regimental commander, he proved not to be up to the challenge of shepherding 9,000 men across the Atlantic and leading them in an attack on the Spanish Empire. From the beginning he was dealt a poor hand. His request for seasoned soldiers was ignored, and all the colonels who were ordered to turn over part of their regiments to him scraped from the bottom of their barrel. Impressment agents in London and the West Indies provided men devoid of military experience. More were recruited than necessary, the consequence being that from the start they were short of arms, equipment, ammunition and food. As we have seen, it occurred to no one that the soldiers might need water bottles in the scorching heat, or tents for the torrential rain, and, whether through corruption or negligence, much of the food was mouldy or rotten. Saddled with divided command, a greater man than Venables would have found it hard to assert his authority. Admiral Penn soon expressed open contempt for him, and the seamen were quick to imitate their admiral's example, not only against Venables but against the land soldiers as a whole. These factors combined led to severe demoralisation, ending in an utter collapse of spirit into panic and terror, so that a few dozen of the enemy could send several thousand English soldiers into heedless flight. Every general since Julius Caesar has understood that in war the spiritual – morale in other words – is far more important than the material.[37] It is sobering to reflect that Santo Domingo was so lightly defended that if only one or two things had been different the expedition might have ended in success. For example, if high winds had not prevented Penn from attacking the capital directly, or if the army's guide had not been killed in the first ambush, or if Venables had not declined Penn's offer to bombard the capital after the second ambush. Yet had they taken Hispaniola, one has to wonder if the Spanish would not simply have sent a larger expedition the following year to take it back.

The Experiment with Direct Military Rule, 1655–56

The failure of the 'Western Design' was one of several catalysts of a new system of military rule in England. When the defeated soldiers crept home from the Caribbean the country's finances were in more of a shambles than ever. The Protectorate was running an annual deficit of £700,000, yet the government felt compelled to maintain a standing army of over 50,000 men in the three nations. Most of the Council of State favoured a reduction in these numbers, but Cromwell was opposed. 'The condition of the people [is] such as the major part, . . . are persons disaffected and engaged against us.' This disaffection had been demonstrated by a number of assassination attempts against the lord protector, and also by a recent royalist uprising.[38]

On the night of 11 March 1655, John Penruddock, a West Country gentleman, led several hundred cavalry to a rendezvous at Clarendon Park, Wiltshire. From there they rode into Salisbury, where they arrested the sheriff of Wiltshire, hoping to trigger a general royalist uprising. Their rebellion was a laughable failure, quickly snuffed out by local government troops. Yet it threw such a scare into the rulers of the republic that it impelled them to search for ways of strengthening internal security.

There was another catalyst behind the new system, in the person of John Lambert. Besides tackling the financial crisis and improving military security, he wanted to take the godly minorities, who were the core of the regime's popular support, into a fuller partnership. The government had been impressed by the vital part played by its Puritan supporters in putting down the recent rebellion. Journalists commented on the raising of 500 horse in Leicestershire, and how the royalists had also been resisted in Gloucester by 'honest men, most of them of the congregational way'.[39]

Lambert's scheme divided England into eleven (later twelve) regional associations, placing each of them under the overall command of a prominent New Model officer, elevated to the rank of major-general. At the end of October 1655 the government published a Declaration justifying the new system. Royalists had obstinately refused to reconcile themselves to the fall of monarchy and establishment of the Commonwealth. By their implacable opposition they had generated the need for enhanced national security.[40] It was only fair that they should bear the financial burden of these necessary measures. The Declaration ended with an offer to exempt from the new tax any royalists who were prepared to give proof of their change of heart.

Nearly two months after their appointment, the major-generals were at last issued a set of 'Instructions', also drafted by Lambert. They were to suppress 'all tumults, insurrections, rebellion, or other unlawful assemblies . . . as also all invasions from abroad'. They were to disarm 'all papists and others who have been in arms against the Parliament'. They were to apprehend all 'thieves,

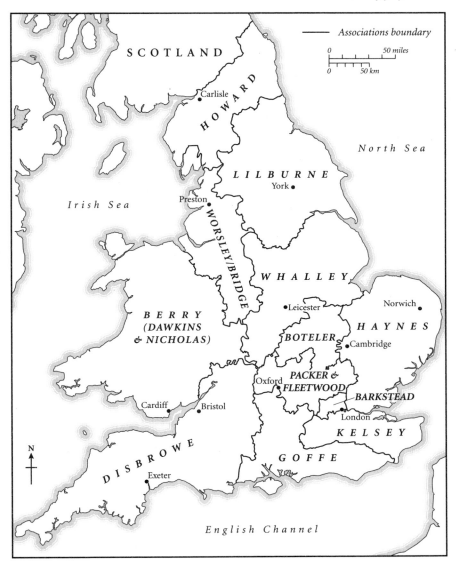

9. The twelve English provinces and their major-generals, 1655–56

robbers, highway-men and other dangerous persons'. As part of their remit to keep 'a strict eye' upon all disaffected persons they were to suppress all 'horse-racings, cockfightings, bear-baitings, [and] stage-plays'. Why? Because 'treason and rebellion is usually hatched and contrived against the state upon such occasions and much evil and wickedness committed'.

State security was not to be their only concern. They were to apprehend all 'idle and loose people . . . who have no visible way of livelihood', and 'compel them to work or be sent out of the Commonwealth'. They were also to consider 'how the poor and impotent may be employed and better provided for than now they are', and either put them to work or transport them out of the country. Besides improving the lot of the poor, they were also to

> encourage and promote godliness and virtue, and discourage and discountenance all 'profaneness and ungodliness; and . . . endeavour . . . that the laws against drunkenness, blaspheming, and taking of the name of God in vain, by swearing and cursing, plays and interludes, and profaning the Lord's day . . . be put in more effectual execution than they have been hitherto.

Finally, they were to work closely with justices of the peace, ministers and other local officials to enforce the ordinance 'for ejecting of ignorant, insufficient and scandalous ministers [and] schoolmasters'.[41]

Who were the men charged with this heavy responsibility of preserving the nation from royalist subversion while bringing about its moral and spiritual reformation? Most of them were young – under forty years old – and from modest, even lowly social backgrounds. Four of them had started out in Cromwell's original regiments of Ironsides, five were regicides, and all were thoroughgoing Puritans. Several of them were zealous in their Puritanism. Charles Worsley was sure 'the finger of God' was with them in Lancashire. William Boteler boasted, 'I cannot but please myself to think how greedily we shall put down profaneness'. Proclaiming his commitment to godly reformation, Edward Whalley reported from the Midlands that 'we have many plows agoing, . . . ejecting scandalous ministers, . . . providing for the poor, depressing alehouses'. Commenting on his recent successes in East Anglia, Hezekiah Haynes knew that 'every tongue must confess it was of the Lord, who is a righteous God in the execution of his judgements'. Thomas Kelsey confided that 'the Lord hath vouchsafe[d] to me more of his presence and comfort in this uncouth employment than I could expect'. James Berry cared deeply for the spiritual welfare of the Welsh, but had to acknowledge that 'Reformation hath many enemies [here]'.[42] William Goffe was well known for his piety, but did not express it in his letters to Thurloe. Nor did the other major-generals.

The twelve major-generals were supported administratively by about a thousand Commissioners for Securing the Peace of the Commonwealth, many of whom were soldiers. Far from being 'the dregs of the people', according to a royalist slur, many commissioners were minor landowners, and a few were merchants. A large proportion were noted for their godliness or religious and political radicalism. Each county's commission was seasoned with a handful of the powerful local magnate gentry. The great majority of them were chosen by the Council of State, the remainder being added by the major-generals upon taking up their appointments. While godliness is the thread connecting most of these appointees, it is clear that a few accepted the position out of a desire to exercise local power and influence, and to look out for their royalist friends and neighbours. Others were drawn to their position by the excellent opportunity it offered to punish royalist enemies. More positively, these godly activists welcomed the chance to reduce the power of royalism, purge the ministry and curb the pervasive ungodliness of their local communities.[43]

Along with the major-generals and commissioners went a new national or 'select' militia of 6,250 men. It was hoped that their creation would reduce the costs of the regular army. These mounted troops were intended to provide the muscle for each major-general to impose his will. A number of their officers were old New Model Army men, and they were all conspicuous supporters of the regime. They comprised sixty-two cavalry troops, and two infantry companies distributed across all the English and Welsh counties. However, their effectiveness would be greatly reduced by the regime's failure to pay them regularly.

The Decimation Tax

The new system of running the country was expected to cost £80,000 a year. It was to be paid for by a new levy of 10 per cent on the income of the regime's enemies. This 'Decimation' tax was probably another brainchild of John Lambert. Both he and Cromwell saw eye to eye on the fundamental principle that 'security and reformation were indivisible goals, and that just as godly reform would only be realised once the regime was fully secure, so real security would only be established once godly reformation had taken firm root'. Only royalists whose annual income was over £100 had to pay, but the Decimation stirred up great resentment, and receipts fell far short of what was expected. It was also resented more generally as an illegal, unparliamentary tax.[44] Enforcing and collecting it would consume an inordinate amount of the major-generals' time.

Besides being subjected to a special tax, royalists were also punished with mass disarming. Bonds for good behaviour were imposed on over 14,000 royalist suspects, as well as miscellaneous radical republicans, Anabaptists, Fifth Monarchists and Quakers. The revenue from the Decimation came in patchily, which in turn was a reflection of the widely varying number of royalists in each county. In the West Country and the north-west receipts more than covered the cost of the new militia, but in East Anglia, the Midlands, Wales, Kent, Hampshire and Sussex, revenues always fell short. In June 1656 the government decided that, rather than let the tax be collected and spent locally, the Committee for the Army would collect and distribute it centrally. Underfunding still continued at all levels; indeed, the major-generals themselves never received more than a fraction of their own salaries. Yet with all its shortcomings, the new system was completely successful in eliminating the royalist threat until the end of the decade.[45]

Not surprisingly, the Decimation Tax, along with security, was the most time-consuming of the major-generals' duties. It fell unevenly across the twelve provinces and, except in Worsley's, which was heavily populated with royalists, never raised enough to pay the militia. There were simply not enough royalists worth over £100 a year to generate the needed revenue. Furthermore, Cromwell vitiated the whole scheme by granting many exemptions as part of his policy of 'healing and settling'. Most of the major-generals had no sympathy for this policy, complaining that the lord protector's indulgence was making their job very difficult. The only solution they could offer, apart from limiting the exemptions, was to cast the financial net more widely by lowering the floor for the tax to £50 or even £40. Goffe also proposed to smooth out the discrepancies between provinces by having all receipts from the Decimation paid into a central Treasury, and re-distributed equitably. Only Whalley opposed lowering the floor from £100. He foresaw that an already unpopular tax would be hated even more if its floor were lowered to include a higher percentage of royalists. Whalley also noted that the enormous amount of time spent collecting the Decimation distracted the major-generals from their higher calling of promoting godly reformation.[46]

At all times security remained their number one concern. Horse-racing was perceived as a major threat. In December Worsley broke up a race in Lancashire and confiscated the horses. In the Midlands Whalley handled the question with more tact. When the fourth earl of Exeter asked him if he would permit Lady Grantham's Cup to be run in Lincolnshire, 'I assured him it was not your Highness' intention in the suppressing of horse races, to abridge gentlemen of that sport, but to prevent the great confluences of irreconcilable enemies'. In July Colonel Barkstead informed the government that 150 horsemen were staging races between Hackney Bridge and Essex.[47]

The major-generals also kept a close watch on 'dangerous' towns, among them Chelmsford, Colchester and Bristol. They did not hesitate to interfere in local government. Disbrowe 'discreetly' removed several 'malignant' officers from Gloucester and other corporations. Berry showed no compunction about throwing his weight around in Wales, where 'men will rule if they be not ruled'. In Lancashire Worsley announced his intention of replacing 'bad officers with good' in several corporations. Whalley conceded that in Lincoln corporation 'I was forced . . . to assume a little more power than I think belonged to me'. Boteler too acknowledged that he 'exceeded the bounds of my power' almost every day, for example when he forced the resignation of the mayor of Bedford and four common councilmen. William Packer, new on the job, wrote that there were 'some very bad men in corporations under my power', and asked if he had the right to dismiss them 'and get good men chosen in their places'.[48]

Religious Reform

A supposedly important part of their remit was removing scandalous ministers and schoolmasters. Worsely, Whalley and to a lesser extent Boteler and Berry took the matter seriously. In Lancashire Worsley cast out five ministers in March. A month later he expelled a second batch. Whalley took the bull by the horns, cheerfully expelling scandalous or ignorant ministers in three cities: Leicester, Nottingham and Lincoln. Boteler removed six in his four counties. Disbrowe said that he had been inactive in his province because there were not enough active commissioners to do the legwork. In Wales, Berry reported that scandalous ministers were not the problem, rather 'a great evil . . . which I know not how to remedy': a lack of preachers. If something was not done, 'these people will some of them become heathens'. The other seven major-generals evinced no interest in ejecting scandalous ministers and schoolmasters, perhaps because the job had mostly been completed before they assumed office, or perhaps because they were aware of how unpopular the practice was. The total ejections under their watch numbered 120, and served to augment the odium under which the Cromwellian regime laboured.[49]

Several major-generals became much more worked up by the stubborn refusal of Fifth Monarchists and Quakers to cooperate with the regime. The Fifth Monarchists offended by their militancy in seeking to hasten the return of Christ to rule the earth. Quakers offended by their disruptive behaviour in churches, their refusal to pay tithes and their rejection of the Trinity. Most troubling was their steady growth in numbers during the 1650s. Although the Protectorate prided itself on upholding liberty of conscience for Protestants, these two sects were not welcomed into the tent of toleration. At Bury St Edmunds, according to Haynes, 'we are plagued with [Quakers] and the gaol is full of them, and the town swarms with those who come to visit them'. As if that were not headache enough, the number of Fifth Monarchists of North Walsham was also 'exceedingly high'. Other major-generals who were troubled by Quakers were Worsley, Goffe, Disbrowe and Whalley. Disbrowe had no compunction about confiscating their literature. Only Berry showed them any sympathy. Aligning himself with Cromwell, he wrote of the nine Quakers imprisoned at Evesham, 'I cannot understand . . . either their faults or their fines'.[50]

Reforming the English People

When it came to godliness and the reformation of manners, their greatest exponent was the indefatigable Whalley. In a long letter of 18 January 1656, he outlined the programme that he was carrying out: in addition to enforcing the Decimation tax, he was suppressing

> all base books, . . . gathering up idle and dangerous persons, . . . casting out scandalous and ignorant ministers, suppressing alehouses, taking order that the poor in all places under our charge may be set a work, and beggars suppressed . . . It's the best way that ere as yet was devised for the peace and safety of the nation. You cannot imagine what awe it hath struck into the spirits of wicked men, what encouragement it is to the godly . . .

For Whalley social justice was an indispensable element in godly reformation. Enclosure of arable land had to be resisted because it further impoverished the poor. Justice Hale was praiseworthy for 'taking care of poor men in their causes'. Whalley was proud of the progress he had made in the Midlands. 'You may ride over all Nottinghamshire and not see a beggar or wandering rogue,' he boasted, 'and I hope suddenly to have it so in all the counties under my charge'. A bold advocate of prison reform, he also proposed emptying the gaols by pardoning lesser criminals, and sending hardened ones beyond the seas. For none did he advocate capital punishment.[51]

Several other major-generals also relished the challenge of turning England into a godly nation. They saw it as central to their mission. By mid-November 1655 Charles Worsley had already toured the major towns of the north-west, encouraging the 'best people' within them to punish drunkards, swearers and those who profaned the Sabbath. He found that 'God hath already put into his people a praying spirit for this great and good work'. The mayors and aldermen of several towns were cooperating in the execution of laws against 'drunkenness, swearing, profaning the Lord's Day and other wickednesses'. He took special aim at Sabbath-breakers in Cheshire. Boteler revealed that he had gaoled people in Northampton, Huntingdon, Okeham and Bedford for drunkenness, vagrancy, brewing without a licence, swearing and brawling. Of course the campaign to instill godliness had been in full swing ever since the Commonwealth's beginning in 1649. John Barkstead in London and Middlesex, keenly supported by Colonel Thomas Pride, sheriff of Middlesex, rose to the renewed challenge with special zeal. Barkstead made a dramatic attack on illicit sexuality when he ordered the arrest of several 'loose wenches' and prostitutes and their transportation to Jamaica. The two men worked together to close down the popular bear garden in Bankside, killing all the bears, dogs and cocks that had performed there before London crowds. Three times as many moral transgressions were brought before the Middlesex JPs in 1655 as in 1652. Other suppressed activities included horse races, unauthorised fairs and markets, card-playing, dancing, worshipping with the Book of Common Prayer, and scoffing at 'strict professors of religion or godliness'.[52]

Worsley had a special animus against alehouses, 'the very womb . . . of wickedness'. That was why he ordered over 200 of them put down in Blackburn, Lancashire alone. He followed five criteria for suppressing them: 1. those whose owners had been in arms against Parliament; 2. those whose owners 'have good trades' (and therefore did not need the income); 3. those that 'stand in . . . dark corners and go by the name of blind alehouses'; 4. those whose owners 'are persons of bad name and repute . . . and keep disorder';

5. 'All houses reputed for bawdry.' Haynes shared this animus, boasting that he was very busy travelling around his province of East Anglia, 'principally regarding inns and alehouses'. Whalley, with his usual energy, instructed the JPs of his counties to suppress all alehouses 'judged unnecessary', and to send him lists of the ones they had closed and the ones they had allowed to stay open. As a result of his chivvying, the justices in Nottinghamshire instructed the high constables and grand jurymen of the county to draw up a list of alehouses suitable to be retained, and to suppress all the rest. At the same time the justices in Warwickshire decided to suppress one-third of the county's alehouses, instructing their high constables to bring in lists of those they recommended for closure. At Whalley's urging the Corporation of Coventry ordered twenty-seven alehouses to close in that city. In London and Middlesex John Barkstead warned alehouse keepers that they would be shut down if 'they were convicted for profane cursing or swearing or drunkenness, suffering disorders in their houses, or playing at billiard-tables, shovelboard tables, dice, cards, tables, nine-pins, pigeonholes, bowling-alley or bowling-green or any other unlawful game', or of failure to provide accommodation for soldiers, labourers or travellers. Yet for all the zeal of the major-generals, the hundreds of alehouses closed under their watch were only a small fraction of the tens of thousands of drinking places in England and Wales. Whalley was undoutedly more realistic than his colleagues when he reflected that in Lincoln and Coventry godly magistrates 'no sooner suppress alehouses but they are set up again'. What progress there was was admittedly 'slow and bumpy', yet the major-generals seem to have contributed a 'significant lurch forward' in the tighter and tighter regulation of alehouses over the following two centuries.[53]

Cromwell certainly praised their work – at least in public. Thanks to the major-generals, he claimed, the whole country had grown 'stronger in virtue'. Six months later, in his opening address to Parliament, he asserted that the major-generals had been 'more effectual towards the discountenancing of vice and settling religion than anything done these fifty years . . . notwithstanding the envy and slander of foolish men . . . and a great deal of grudging in the nation that we cannot have our horse races, cock-fightings and the like!'[54]

In reality, their achievements were modest, while their campaign for moral reform has been judged 'a clear failure'. This was partly because of the onerous nature of their other duties. Also, their ten-month tenure was too short to achieve lasting change. On the other hand, they and all the other campaigners for godly reformation who came before and after them may have had more success than most historians have allowed. It is surely significant that the decade of Puritan rule – the 1650s – was also the decade when the recorded rate of bastardy, meaning out-of-wedlock births, sank to its lowest point ever.[55] Less bastardy suggests less fornication, which in turn suggests less drunkenness. The Puritan campaign for godly reformation may have changed more lives than we once thought.

A New Parliament

Cromwell summoned the major-generals to meet with him and his council in the middle of May. Their discussions lasted for almost a month. After considering many alternatives the major-generals' preferred option of calling a parliament was adopted. The government was so short of money that Cromwell, though initially opposed, was persuaded that people would be more willing to open their purses if the levy had been sanctioned by their elected representatives. The major-generals were optimistic that they could manage the outcome and promised to deliver Cromwell a 'godly parliament'. They then returned to their counties to campaign for the candidates who supported the Protectorate, and against the numerous republicans who opposed it. Royalists were denied the vote. The major-generals soon ran into heavy weather. In early August Cromwell wrote to each one of them expressing his deep misgivings about the current political climate. Most of them had come to share his disquiet about the people's 'inveterate and implacable malice', but their interpretation of its causes were different from his.[56]

Even in the Puritan heartland of East Anglia, Haynes was pessimistic about the prospects for protectoral candidates. In Norfolk it was hard to get 'honest men' to run. He was even gloomier about the outlook in Suffolk, on account of a malignant grand jury, and an equally malignant high sheriff. 'Honest men' will do their utmost, he assured Thurloe, 'but will be compelled to take in with the Presbyterian to keep out the malignant'. It would be a great help, he thought, if the militia troops could be mustered, to put on a show of strength before the election. But in order to do that they would have to be paid, and by now it was too late.[57]

Goffe was almost as pessimistic. The godly in Abingdon wanted to nominate him, but he was sure that 'all the rabble of the town' would prevent his election. In Winchester the prospects seemed equally bleak, as 'the unquiet spirit of discontented men doth begin to show itself'. In the event he was elected for the more prestigious county seat of Hampshire.

In the north-east Lilburne believed there was a concerted campaign managed by Sir Arthur Hesilrige to keep any friend of the government out of Parliament. In Durham and Northumberland there was a potent slogan circulating: 'no swordsmen, no decimator, or any that receives salary from the state, to serve in Parliament'. In York he feared the power of 'perverse spirits [who] labour to set up some new interest'.[58] In the south-west, Disbrowe reported 'great opposition', which he was doing his best to counter by encouraging the 'honest sober people' in his province. By dint of strenuous exertion Tobias Bridge managed to get the arch-republican John Bradshaw taken off the ballot for Cheshire, but confessed that in Lancashire he expected 'much thwarting . . . through the peevishness of some and disaffection of others'. In Dover, Kelsey was certain that 'the rabble of this town' would succeed in electing the malignant Mr Cony, and that the government's only recourse would be to exclude him from sitting.[59]

Only one major-general, Edward Whalley, was not gripped by alarm as election day approached. In late July he described the view from Nottingham: 'the general temper of men's spirits are to have a settlement. I trust in the Lord we shall have a good parliament.' As late as 11 August he maintained this sunny outlook. 'The heart [of the people] is sound.' They knew they must pay their taxes. Confident of his ability to prevent the anti-Cromwellian Colonel Hutchinson from being elected, he was equally sure that the candidacy of another anti-Cromwellian, Sir Henry Vane, would go nowhere. In the event he was right.[60]

The outcome was not quite as bad as the pessimists had feared. All but one of the major-generals were elected, but they were outnumbered by many others who had been sharply critical of Cromwell's government. Their next self-appointed task was to draft lists of enemies of the Protectorate who should be barred from sitting. In the end, guided by the major-generals, Cromwell excluded 112 of the 400 elected. The perceived necessity to deny over a quarter of the elected members their right to sit was an implicit rebuke to the major-generals and their godly allies.[61]

CHAPTER FOURTEEN

THE ARMY AND THE END OF THE PARLIAMENTARY RULE, 1656–59

For ten months the major-generals had worked flat out to defuse the royalist threat and to bring about Cromwell's vision of a godly nation. Constantly in the saddle as they rode from one county to the next, their efforts had exhausted them and taken a toll on their health. As early as late November 1655, Haynes confessed that he was 'not . . . in perfect health'. The nervous Goffe complained of profound fatigue due to overwork and the chronic lack of money. In May, Worsley, having ridden relentlessly through his three counties over the previous month, was feeling unwell. A month later he was dead at the age of thirty-four.[1]

Every one of the major-generals except George Fleetwood was elected in August to the second Protectoral Parliament, but they failed in their promise to deliver Cromwell a godly parliament. A quarter of the MPs had to be excluded because of their hostility to the Protectorate. More army officers were elected in 1656 than in the first or third Protectoral Parliaments.[2] Yet a large majority of the other MPs found the major-generals and their regime odious.

Nevertheless, in his speech at the opening of Parliament, Cromwell continued to express his unqualified support of the major-generals. Regarding the unparliamentary Decimation tax he was unrepentant. 'If nothing should "ever" be done but what is according to law, the throat of the nation may be cut while we send for some to make a law!'[3]

In private, however, Cromwell was scathing towards the major-generals for having misread the temper of the country and talked him into calling an unnecessary election. Their next blunder was to seek to legalise the Decimation tax, which had been imposed by protectoral fiat.

Instead of letting sleeping dogs lie, Disbrowe introduced a bill on Christmas Day to make the tax lawful. Most of the more conservative MPs had gone home to celebrate the holiday, so the bill easily passed first reading. But when in January it was brought back for second reading, Parliament decisively rejected it. The vote was a clear verdict on the record of the major-generals. Many feared that by attempting to legalise the Decimation, John Disbrowe, backed by John Lambert, was seeking to make their rule permanent and that their long-term aim was to prepare Lambert to succeed Cromwell after his death. While Cromwell stood by indecisively, the conservative, anti-army group led by Lord Broghill, Henry Cromwell, John Thurloe, Marchamont Nedham and Vincent Gookin worked to bring down the major-generals and re-introduce monarchy.[4]

In sum, the brevity of the experiment in military rule was due in part to people's resentment against the high taxes which it entailed. In part it was due to their sympathy for persecuted royalists. In part it was alienation from army rule, and antipathy to the major-generals' 'strident godly fundamentalism'.[5] In part it was also due to the activity of a well-organised anti-army faction in Parliament who wanted Cromwell to cut his ties with the army and assume the crown. Yet there was a significant minority who were sorry to see the end of the major-generals, 'under whom the Lord's people had comfortable protection'.[6]

The Offer of the Crown

More alarming to the officers than the rejection of the Decimation were the behind-the-scenes machinations to bring about a restoration of monarchy. Spearheading them were members of the so-called 'Court party' – Lord Broghill, John Thurloe, and Cromwell's younger son Henry among the most prominent. These courtiers were the ones who drafted the *Remonstrance* of February 1657, which tried to re-establish the 'ancient [three-part] constitution' of king, lords and commons. They wanted to make Cromwell king, but not an absolute one. Reluctantly they had already accepted his rejection of the hereditary principle. If he became king he would be required to uphold the law, though he would enjoy the right to veto parliamentary legislation. Most of the powers of the Council of State, given back its old name of Privy Council, would be transferred to the king. Parliament would meet every three years, and the Commons would control taxation. Royalists would be allowed back into the political fold if they renounced Charles Stuart. Religious toleration would be extended to all except Roman Catholics and 'such who publish horrible blasphemies or practise . . . licentiousness or profaneness under the profession of Christ'. The bottom line was that Parliament, not the king, would be supreme.[7]

For a time the civilian Cromwellians seemed to have the lord protector's ear. In January and February 1657 he entertained them with unbuttoned ease in his apartments at Whitehall, while seeing less of his officers. Thurloe attempted to neutralise the officers by distracting them with fabricated reports of an imminent royalist invasion and insurrection during the period when the *Remonstrance* was before the House.[8]

To the army's dismay the *Remonstrance* attracted majority support in Parliament. That support did not include the lord protector himself, however. So, a month later it was reformulated and reintroduced with a new name, *The Humble Petition and Advice*. The *Petition* was little different from the *Remonstrance*, except that it dropped the contentious title 'king' in favour of the more familiar 'lord protector'. It was harsher on royalists, making them incapable of any office or public trust, and excluding forever from the franchise any who had been in arms against Parliament since 1642. Its religious articles leaned more towards Presbyterianism, and it was more restrictive when it came to liberty of conscience.[9]

Realising that they had lost the battle in Parliament, the grandees strove with might and main to persuade Cromwell to refuse the offer of the crown. Led by Lambert, a delegation of 100 officers confronted him the day after the *Remonstrance* was laid before the House. They urged him not to accept the crown, and voiced their opposition to the creation of an upper house. Cromwell met them with unconcealed anger, telling them self pityingly 'that they had made him their drudge upon all occasions'. He called them out for their political blunders of the past several months, most notably their insistence on calling a new parliament against his better judgement, and their unnecessary introduction of a bill to legalise the Decimation. The nation, he said, was 'tired of major-generalcies'. He shrugged off the title of king as 'a feather in a man's hat', without telling them definitely that he would refuse it. However, the new upper chamber was vital. Only such an institution could protect 'civil liberties' and 'your liberties in religion' against an intolerant majority. He then cut short the discussion and bade them good night. The officers left the meeting with their tails between their legs, their militancy quite deflated. When a month later Colonel Pride and his second-in-command John Mason mustered twenty-six or twenty-seven signatures on a petition against kingship, Fleetwood and Disbrowe prevailed on the House to lay it aside.[10]

The officers were joined in their campaign by representatives of the Independent and Baptist churches, who addressed heartfelt pleas to the Protector not to forsake the Good Old Cause. They need not have worried. The Council of State, with its solid block of officers, had Cromwell's ear on a daily basis. Even though the *Humble Petition and Advice* commanded majority support in Parliament, it failed ultimately to win Cromwell over. The debate shone a harsh light on the civilian–military split regarding England's political future. While a handful of officers supported the document, the overwhelming majority were opposed. The three highest ranked – Fleetwood, Disbrowe and Lambert – let Cromwell know that if he accepted the crown they would not publicly oppose him but they would quit the army. They too need not have worried. On 13 April Cromwell revealed to the Committee for the *Humble Petition* that experience had chastened his ambitions: 'I am ready to serve not as a king but as a constable.' After all, hadn't God already indicated his displeasure with monarchy? 'I will not seek to set up that, that Providence hath destroyed and laid in the dust. I would not build Jericho again.' Finally, on 8 May, he bluntly stated, 'I cannot undertake this government with that title of king, and that is my answer to this great weighty business.'[11] It was not the officers who stopped Cromwell from accepting the title of king; he himself had no desire for it in the first place.

What he did want, however, was an upper or 'other' house, appointed by himself to act as a buffer between him and the lower house. This the civilian Cromwellians were only too willing to grant him, and his officers had to make the best of it.

The Humble Petition and Advice, modified by the removal of the title of king, became the new constitution, and Cromwell was installed again as lord protector. Once installed he quickly got down to the business of the 'other' house, appointing sixty-three members. To his dismay, fully a third of them declined his invitation, while only two of the seven nobles whom he named took their seats. A further complication was that many of those whom he elevated were among his strongest supporters in the Commons, thus draining Cromwellian support from the lower house.[12]

All army officers were required to swear fidelity to the lord protector. However, there was continuing opposition within the army to rule by a single person, even though Cromwell had refused the crown. It was General Lambert's unwillingness to swear the oath of fidelity that led to his dismissal in July 1657. Up to that point he had been seen universally as the second most powerful officer in the army. There was general astonishment, then, when his departure produced not so much as a murmur of protest. The explanation for this is that Lambert had not developed a personal following either in the Council of State, or in the army. He was known to be hostile to the new constitution, to the additional power it gave to the lord protector, and to the establishment of an upper house. He was also the chief symbol of the military domination of England that the new constitution was meant to end. 'Never was any man less pitied or lamented after . . . he was all for himself; he hoped to be next protector.' Once again Cromwell demonstrated that he was the undisputed master of the army.[13]

Unlike Lambert, Cromwell at all times commanded a great reservoir of affection among the mass of both officers and rank and file. This originated in his brilliant military record and the fact that soldiers felt safe when he led them into battle, confident that he would not carelessly sacrifice their lives. He never forgot their material wants. 'His Highness's great care of the army doth much indulge both officers and soldiers,' wrote one commentator.[14] When the battles were over he held the reins of discipline loosely in his hands. He did not attempt to prevent the officers from meeting, he absorbed their criticisms, and he rarely retaliated against them. He did not push radicals out of the army: William Allen rose to the rank of adjutant-general, resigning of his own accord from the army and faithfully serving the Protectorate. Colonel John Jones, the regicide and close ally of fellow regicide Major-General Thomas Harrison (who finally lost his commission at the end of 1653 on account of his zeal for Fifth Monarchism), was recalled from his Irish posting on suspicion of subverting the Protectorate in 1655. But within a year he had married Cromwell's sister, and returned to Ireland. In 1657 he was appointed to the new upper house. The Baptist Colonel Robert Bennett was taken to task by his godly friends for holding office under the Protectorate, but he testified to his high opinion of Cromwell. 'Many good men,' he added, were of the same mind.[15]

Even if Cromwell did not satisfy all their expectations, the officers were keenly aware of the need to preserve unity in the face of a largely hostile nation. They knew that if they fell to quarrelling among themselves a royalist takeover would be the likely consequence. A number of high-ranking officers left or were dismissed from the army between 1653 and 1658, but their departures provoked little reaction from their comrades, and none of them showed any inclination to take up arms against the government. Cromwell repaid the army's trust in him by treating it with respect and managing it with skill. For example, Monday evenings were reserved for dining with senior officers in London. In addition he was always available to meet with an officer who had a grievance. His chief secretary and director of intelligence, John Thurloe was sure that 'His Highness need[s] no help to govern his army.'[16]

The last major challenge to Cromwell's authority came in February 1658, just after he had dissolved his second parliament. The major of his own horse regiment, William Packer, and all five troop captains voiced their unhappiness with the lord protector's high handedness, and with the new constitution: 'They told him that he had left them and not they him.'[17]

Cromwell strove to head off the mounting discontent by inviting 200 of the officers in and around London to a feast. Many bottles of wine were emptied, and Cromwell delivered a speech that went on for two hours. The officers responded to him enthusiastically, promising to 'stand, live and fall with my lord protector'. 'Deal plainly and freely with me,' he replied, 'if any of you cannot in conscience conform to the new government, let him speak.'[18]

He followed this up with a series of meetings with his six regimental officers. When they refused to withdraw their accusation that he had abandoned the Good Old Cause, he dismissed all six of them. Further dismissals in England and Scotland followed. This purge triggered no reaction from the rest of the officer corps. Although observers commented on his declining mental powers, Cromwell's control was still absolute: as Packer later lamented, 'without any trial or appeal, with the breath of his nostrils I was outed'.[19]

Fifth Monarchists tried to stir up mutiny by scattering pamphlets in London and among the soldiers, appealing to them to rise up, but they aroused no response. At the instigation of General Monck, addresses flowed in from regiments and garrisons in Scotland expressing their confidence in Cromwell and his government. Near the end of March all the general and field officers in the vicinity of London were summoned to Whitehall. General Fleetwood addressed them briefly about the necessity to remain united, and read out the draft of an address promising loyalty to the lord protector. He then invited discussion, and urged those who agreed with the address to sign it. There was no discussion, and every one of the 224 present put his name to it. Fleetwood then brought it to Cromwell, expressing the hope that 'you will run and not be weary in that race God hath set you in . . . And in all your actings tending thereto we do freely and heartily engage . . . to stand by your Highness with our lives.' The officers in Dublin sent a similar address.[20] From then until the time of his death there was no challenge to Cromwell's authority from within the army.

Cromwell's regime has often been called a military dictatorship. Was it? Superficially, yes, in that Cromwell was both head of state and commander-in-chief of the army. But he was never a pure dictator. He always functioned under a written constitution, even if the Instrument of Government was devised by a small group of army officers, and was in effect a decree without legal status. His aim was always to broaden the basis of his regime to include as much of the political nation as possible. His acceptance of the *Humble Petition and Advice* marked an important step on the road to parliamentary government, though Cromwell died before it could be put to the test.

It is noteworthy that the Protectorate took very few political prisoners. No one was put to death for his political activities unless he had actively plotted to overthrow the regime or assassinate the lord protector. Judicial torture, which had been employed under Charles I, was never inflicted by Cromwell. There was a generous liberty of conscience. Even though the Book of Common Prayer was still under a formal ban, a blind eye was turned to the widespread practice of Anglican worship. Censorship was much less rigid than it would become after the Restoration; several hundred pamphlets poured from the presses each year, many of them critical of the regime. When Cromwell's son Richard came to power in the autumn of 1658, he inherited a system in which Parliament played a central role. One thing is clear: the protectoral regime bore little resemblance to modern military dictatorships.[21]

The End of the Protectorate

Oliver Cromwell died in his bed of a fever at the age of fifty-nine in the afternoon of 3 September 1658, the anniversary of two of his greatest battlefield victories: Dunbar and Worcester. Richard, his eldest son, was immediately proclaimed his successor as lord protector. Richard inherited his father's intelligence and quick temper, but little else. He also inherited a national debt of £2 million, which left him very little financial room for manoeuvre.[22] Lacking military experience and without political training, he was regarded with apprehension by the grandees.

After a decent interval all the officers who were present in London gathered at Whitehall where they unanimously adopted an address to the new lord protector on 18 September. Prepared by Major-General James Berry, Colonel William Sydenham and Colonel John Hewson, it envisaged a tripartite government of lord protector, Privy Council and army to ensure that the army's interests were never forgotten. It bore 276 signatures, and for all its outward appearance of obedience and respect, it carried a menacing undertone. If Richard did not safeguard the Good Old Cause as his father had done, implied the officers, they would look for an alternative form of government. By contrast, the officers in Ireland and Scotland, under the tutelage of Henry Cromwell and General George Monck, circulated loyalty addresses, which all the officers dutifully signed.[23]

Meanwhile in London the officers worked themselves up into an extreme state of anxiety – 'monstrous high' as one observer put it. This despite their playing a full part in the administrative work of the Council of State throughout the rest of the year. While the senior officers met regularly at Fleetwood's grand residence, Wallingford House, the junior officers congregated at St James's Palace on Friday mornings for prayer and Bible study. They were gradually coalescing into a group with a clear-cut political agenda. Early in October, 300 of them threw their support behind a petition for Fleetwood to be general of all the forces of the three nations, with the exclusive right to commission all but field officers. Fleetwood submitted their petition to the lord protector, who adamantly refused to surrender the power of appointing officers. Fleetwood and several other grandees then warned the junior officers of the 'dangerous consequence' of such petitions, urged them to preserve the unity of the army, and recommended trust in Richard's pledge to uphold the Good Old Cause. With oil thus poured on troubled waters, the meeting broke up in a spirit of sweetness and light. Or so it appeared.[24]

Richard was not content to let the matter lie, but took it upon himself to clarify why he could not surrender the power to appoint officers to anyone. Quite simply it would be a violation of the *Humble Petition and Advice*, which was effectively the nation's constitution. He made this point in a major speech on 18 October. He followed it up with several mollifying gestures that served to preserve the army's outward calm for the next several months. Behind the scenes his chief adviser Lord Broghill worked to defuse the political power of the army.[25]

Despite Richard's solemn promise to wipe out the army's arrears in England, they stood at £300,000 by the time his newly elected Parliament met in January. Arrears in Ireland would soon reach £371,000. Among the elected members were a few officers, but the civilian members numbered few friends of the army, and its financial needs were quickly overlooked. Efforts to save money by shrinking the size of the army ran into a brick wall:

disbanding soldiers was impossible until there was money to pay them off. Collectors of the excise on beer lagged in their payments, which meant that the army as a whole went unpaid. Officers had to dig into their own pockets to stave off starvation among their men, who themselves 'extended to the utmost' their credits with victuallers.[26] By January 1659 rumblings of discontent were being heard once again from the junior officers.

Besides its neglect of the army's financial needs, the other great sin of Richard's Parliament, in the army's eyes, was its opposition to religious liberty. The conservative majority were itching to place curbs on the radical religious sects so beloved by most of the officers from Fleetwood down. By mid-February another petition was circulating in the army. When Richard got wind of it he rode in person to Wallingford House and had it stopped, admonishing the officers against interfering in politics.[27]

Meanwhile, political divisions were beginning to wrench the army apart. By the late winter three identifiable groups had emerged: the Junto–supporting Lieutenant-General Fleetwood that met at Wallingford House – initially comprising Lord Disbrowe and most of the senior officers in London; the lower officers who by and large prided themselves on their godliness, republicanism and faithfulness to the Good Old Cause, who met and prayed at St James's Palace; and, smallest of the three, those who stood by Richard Cromwell and the Protectorate. The lower officers were joined by a number of senior officers who considered themselves 'Commonwealthsmen' and backers of the Good Old Cause: Colonels Hacker, Wauton, Twisleton and most of the officers in their regiments, as well as Edmund Ludlow and the former colonels Okey, Alured, Saunders and Morley.[28]

Ominously for Richard's hopes of controlling the army, in February Dr John Owen, formerly one of his father's chaplains, 'gathered a church in the Independent way' among the grandees. They were chiefly members of the Wallingford House Junto, a small ruling oligarchy: Lords Fleetwood and Disbrowe, Major-Generals John Lambert, James Berry and William Goffe, Colonel William Sydenham, 'and divers others'. This new religious grouping was 'not very well liked at Whitehall'.[29]

The lower officers began to trumpet the political creed of republicanism more stridently than ever. Amidst mounting worry over the threat of royalism, they named a committee to draft a petition to Parliament. None of its members belonged to the Wallingford House Junto. Their petition came to the lord protector's attention on 6 April. It reminded him of their 'crying necessities for want of pay'. Professing themselves 'living monuments of patience and mercy', they sounded the alarm over the mounting tide of royalism that they claimed to witness on every side, making them fear for the future of the Good Old Cause. Reaffirming their commitment to 'the reformation of law and manners . . . [and] encouraging the ways of holiness', they exhorted him to issue a public statement vindicating the trial and execution of Charles I. Richard received the petition courteously, but inwardly he seethed with fury. The petition was 'much disrelished' by him and most of his parliament.[30]

The junior officers had no intention of letting the matter drop. They prevailed upon their superiors to summon a meeting of all the officers for prayer and fasting at Wallingford House the following week. The backdrop to this meeting was a report by the Commons Committee on Public Revenue that the government was now nearly £2.5 million in debt, and that it owed the army £727,000.[31]

It was common knowledge that when the officers engaged in collective prayer major political changes were on the way. The mood at the prayer meeting was angry, and there was copious muttering against Richard's parliament. Electrifying preaching by Hugh Peters and John Owen helped to stiffen the officers' resolve. The next day (14 April) over 500 officers attended the General Council of the Army. What, we may wonder, were so many officers doing in London, away from their regiments? When John Disbrowe moved that every officer should reaffirm his loyalty by making an 'attestation' that the execution of Charles I had been just and lawful, there were shouts of approval. They drew up a Declaration 'against Charles Stuart and his interest', urging the lord protector and Parliament to protect all those who were involved in the death of Charles's father.[32]

The army was throwing its weight around, brazenly claiming the right to interfere in politics. This was not least because, while they constituted around 40 per cent of the 'Other House' (the republican equivalent to the House of Lords), they were unable to bend it to their will. The army's growing militancy could only lead to a showdown with Parliament. On the 18th, the House of Commons voted that there should be no meeting of the General Council of Officers at Wallingford House without the permission of the lord protector and both houses of Parliament. At a stormy meeting Richard ordered the officers to cease their meetings and return to their regiments. Disbrowe and Ashfield defied him to his face. Parliament voted Richard general of all the armies, and he prepared to arrest Fleetwood and Disbrowe.[33]

A trial of strength was now unavoidable. Late on the night of the 21st, Fleetwood summoned a general rendezvous of the regiments about the capital to St James's. Londoners were roused by the thundering hooves and marching boots as thousands of soldiers from the capital and its outskirts converged on the centre. Richard countered by calling out his lifeguard and ordering a counter-rendezvous at Whitehall, but only two troops of horse and three companies of foot answered his call. The officers who remained loyal – Thomas Belasyse, first earl Fauconberg, and Colonels Howard, Goffe, Whalley, Ingoldsby and a few others – could not get their men to obey them. During the night Disbrowe presented the lord protector with an ultimatum: throw yourself on the officers and dissolve Parliament. After some agonised consultations with his advisers, Richard caved in. The next day the MPs, cowering behind a locked door, suffered the humiliation of having the Black Rod broken against the other side of that door 'in testimony of their disso-lution'.[34]

The Army Strives to Control Events

The General Council of the Army, sitting at Wallingford House, now took over the government of the country. For a while the grandees were at a loss as to what to do next. Seeking help from someone with a modicum of polit-ical intelligence, they invited Major-General John Lambert into their coun-cils. Sir Arthur Hesilrige and Sir Henry Vane were welcomed into the meetings of the junior officers at St James's. The latter were both more numerous, and had a much clearer idea of what they wanted: the restoration of the purged Long Parliament (the Rump). They weakened the authority of the Wallingford House Junto by campaigning for the reappointment of long-standing republicans ('Commonwealthsmen'), including Major-General Robert Overton, and Colonels Nathaniel Rich, John Okey, Matthew Alured and Thomas Saunders, Major William Packer and Captain John Gladman, to command in their old regiments. In addition, the arch-republican Sir Arthur Hesilrige was given back his colonelcy and the regiment of the disgraced protectoral colonel Charles Howard. With every passing day pres-sure mounted from below for the recall of the Rump, which had been in a state of suspended animation since its expulsion in April 1653.[35]

Finally the lower officers got their way. After two weeks of political vacuum, at the end of the first week of May Richard was sent into early retirement and the Rump was called back. As all the officers would soon realise, they had gone from the frying pan into the fire. In the short run, though, there was unalloyed joy at the return of so many officers who had been expelled under the rule of Oliver and his son. The most jubilant reception was reserved for Major-General Overton, who received a hero's welcome when he entered London after his four-year exile on Jersey. The Rump voted that he should be given a command in the army 'as becomes his merit', and that his old friend Colonel Alured should be given a regiment of horse. Overton was awarded the governorship of Hull, the second most important fortress in the nation, with a regiment of foot.[36]

In Ireland, Henry Cromwell was dismissed and replaced by a commission of five. Three of them were radical Baptist republican regicides: Colonel John Jones, John Corbet and William Steele. Together with Major-General Ludlow, who soon arrived from England, they set about undoing Henry's appointments of moderate officers and replacing them with radical Baptist republicans, men such as Colonels Hierome Sankey, William Allen and Daniel Axtell, Lieutenant-Colonel Alexander Brayfield and Major Henry Pretty. Close to half the Irish officers were replaced or transferred. The rest, including Sir Hardress Waller, pragmatically accepted the authority of the restored Rump. The Irish officers in London meanwhile petitioned Parliament for Ludlow to be made lieutenant-general of horse and commander-in-chief of the Irish forces. Hesilrige moved his appointment, and the Rump approved it at the beginning of July.[37]

On 8 May eight officers, including Fleetwood, Lambert and Disbrowe, were charged with the responsibility of framing a new constitution for the three nations. They never finished their assignment, but some of what they had in mind is found in a petition they submitted to Parliament on 13 May. They sought to entrench the power of the Wallingford House Junto by having Fleetwood appointed 'commander-in-chief of the land forces of this Commonwealth'. They exhorted Parliament to carry on the work of reformation, 'without a single person, kingship or a House of Peers'. By reformation they meant freedom of conscience for professing (Protestant, non-Anglican) Christians, law reform, an Act of Oblivion, and that 'the persons who are chiefly entrusted with the management and exercise of the government [shall be those] most eminent for godliness, faithfulness and constancy to the Good Cause, and interests of these nations'. Recognising that bringing back the Rump was only a temporary solution, they grappled with how to restore full parliamentary government while protecting the gains of the Revolution, and in particular hedging in the army's role as guarantor of the

Good Old Cause. Their solution was to allow for an elected House of Commons 'chosen by the people', but overseen by a 'select senate', co-ordinate in power, of 'able and faithful persons, eminent for godliness, and such as continue adhering to this cause'. How this senate was to be selected and by whom was not specified, but contemporary observers reported that it was either to consist of army officers, or to be chosen by them.[38] The idea of an army-controlled upper house with veto power over the legislation of the popularly elected lower house was to be central to the Junto's constitutional proposals for the next eight months, until they were overwhelmed by events beyond their control.

The petition was presented to Parliament by a delegation of eighteen officers, with Lambert as their spokesman. The Rump ignored the petition, insisting instead that in the future all army commissions be issued by the Commons Speaker, and naming seven commissioners to recommend the names of new officers. The Junto soon became deeply unhappy as the Rump proceeded to dismiss 160 of their number. Many of them were Cromwellians, such as the former major-generals Edward Whalley and William Boteler, Colonel John Barkstead and Captain Thomas Pride, whom it proceeded to replace with officers of unimpeachable republican credentials. After a few days the remaining officers buckled under and traipsed to the House to receive their renewed commissions from the Speaker. Many of their new, republican colleagues were displeasing to the Wallingford Junto: men such as Colonels Nathaniel Rich, Matthew Alured, Tobias Bridge, John Mason, Robert Overton, Daniel Axtell, John Clarke and Thomas Fitch. Other displeasing nominations would follow during the rest of the summer.[39]

Most ill-judged on the Rump's part was its tampering with General Monck's regiments in Scotland. On 18 June he wrote respectfully to the Speaker assuring him that he had no desire to meddle in politics, 'having had my education in a Commonwealth [the United Provinces of the Netherlands] where soldiers received and observed demands but gave none'. In light of his conduct a mere four months later, when he held the political destiny of the nation in his hands, this statement is deeply ironic. His request was that there be no interference in the make-up of his regiments, because they were all loyal to the Rump. A brusque reply came back that 'such things are known to the parliament that are not to yourself'. The Rump then went ahead and made fresh appointments to his own horse and foot regiments. Perhaps most offensive to Monck was the intrusion of Colonel Ralph Cobbett's Leveller brother, Major Robert Cobbett. The Rump also tampered with the regiment of Monck's trusted colonel, Thomas Talbot. Monck would long remember the affronts he suffered at the hands of the Rump. It had blatantly politicised army appointments by large-scale dismissal of Cromwellian officers in favour of republican luminaries. Even though the Committee for the Nomination of Officers contained a majority of officers, if the Rump did not like the committee's recommendations it simply rejected them in favour of reliable republicans. For example, when the famous Cromwellian, the former major-general Edward Whalley, was nominated for a regiment, the House narrowly rejected him and voted in the less distinguished, but reliably republican Matthew Alured.[40]

This systematic interference in military appointments undermined army unity, discipline, and the all-important relationship between officers and men. It inflicted grave damage on regimental morale. After the purges the army found itself in a state of uncertainty and disorgansation from which it never recovered.[41]

Booth's Rebellion

The only bright spot for the army in that dismal summer was provided by a minor royalist-Presbyterian uprising in the north-west. Sir George Booth, a Cheshire gentleman, managed to raise about 4,000 armed men in August, ostensibly to fight for a 'free parliament', which was the code phrase for restoring the king. The rising was meant to be coordinated with several other risings in England, but in the event Booth's was the only one that got off the ground. Here was a chance for the New Model to show its mettle once again. Lambert was given command of the brigade sent to crush the rising – three regiments of horse, one of dragoons, three of foot and a train of artillery. By early August Booth was said to be at the head of 7,000 or 8,000 troops, so major reinforcements were sent for – four regiments from Scotland, three out of Flanders, and a regiment of horse and another of foot out of Ireland (1,500 troops in all) under the command of Hierome Sankey and Daniel Axtell. Was it significant that General Monck refused to send any of his troops to help suppress Booth's rebellion? Whatever the case, Lambert did not need them. By 13 August Booth was reported to be down to 1,000 horse and an unknown number of foot. Lambert caught up with these demoralised troops and forced them to fight at Northwich. After a short, sharp engagement at Winnington Bridge 'the enemy fell into disorder'. Lambert had suppressed the rebellion at the cost of only thirty lives. Booth fled the field and made his way to Newport Pagnell disguised as a woman. The landlord of the Red Lion Inn was not fooled, and made him remove his female attire, after which he was taken into custody and lodged in the Tower of London.[42]

This easy victory over the royalists did wonders for army morale, and temporarily reminded the members of the Rump of their dependence on the military to defend them against an increasingly alienated populace. It also enhanced the prestige of John Lambert, the only person in the regime who combined the talents of first-rate soldier, statesman and administrator. This was not the last time that he would be called upon to deploy his talents.[43]

The army's triumph in Cheshire did little to solve the regime's more deep-seated problems, which were disunity, political conflict with the Wallingford House Junto, and inability to generate enough tax revenue to support an increasingly bloated army. In early 1659 the army in England numbered 14,000 and the assessment was down to £35,000 a month, from a high of £120,000 eight years previously. The mounting royalist threat forced the recruitment of 8,000 more troops within the space of three months, raising the army's size to 22,000. This, on top of about 16,000 in Ireland (down from 33,000 a few years before), besides an unknown number in fifty-seven garrisons, and 10,000 or 12,000 in Scotland, yielded a total military establishment of at least 48,000–50,000. The Rump tried to meet the cost of its large army by raising the assessment first to £70,000 then £100,000. Given the people's greater and greater unwillingness to pay, it was never enough; arrears continued to swell, and before the year was out the army would hugely increase its unpopularity by falling back on free quarter.[44]

In the wake of the triumph over Booth, General Fleetwood moved that Lambert be restored to the rank of major-general. The motion was blocked by Hesilrige, who commanded a majority in the House. As a consolation prize Lambert was voted £1,000 to buy himself a jewel. He used the money instead to cement the loyalty of his men by dividing it among them.[45]

The Derby Petition

While they rested at Derby his troops occupied themselves by framing yet another petition to Parliament. Lambert was allegedly behind it, and he was indeed present in Derby at the time. Yet he seems to have stayed in the background. The petition was the fruit of discussions among fifty officers, and was prepared by Hierome Sankey, commander of the Irish brigade, Colonel

William Mitchell and Major Richard Creed among others. It prayed that the *Humble Petition* of 13 May 'may not be laid asleep, but may have fresh life given unto it'; that Fleetwood be confirmed as commander-in-chief of the armies; that 'the footsteps of monarchy may be rooted out'; and that those who stirred up the late insurrections 'may be proceeded against'. It further demanded alterations in the army's senior command. After Fleetwood, Lambert should be second-in-command with the rank of major-general, John Disbrowe chief of the cavalry, and Monck (because he was too important to be left out) commander of the infantry.[46]

Though addressed to Parliament, the petition was first sent to Fleetwood for consideration by the General Council of Officers. Fleetwood passed it onto Sir Arthur Hesilrige, who would soon have seen it anyway, as a recently restored colonel with his own regiment. Hesilrige immediately laid it before the House, which, irritated by repeated hectoring from the army, voted that to have any more generals would be 'chargeable and dangerous to the Commonwealth', and instructed Fleetwood to communicate this decision to the officers. He did so the next day at a meeting at Wallingford House. Lambert himself disclaimed the Derby Petition and dramatically offered to resign for the sake of peace. The rest of the officers agreed to drop the petition and accepted Fleetwood's suggestion to replace it with a more moderate one.[47]

That, however, is not what happened. The committee charged with the task departed from their brief and brought in a draft that was *less* moderate than the first. It deeply split the General Council of Officers, with the recently appointed republicans opposing, and the adherents of the Junto supporting it. Fleetwood, indecisive as usual, urged both sides to sleep on it, but in the end the republicans were steam-rollered by the still substantial majority of Junto officers. No fewer than 230 of them put their names to the provocative text. Clearly Fleetwood was no longer in control of his officers. Rather than he, it was Colonel Disbrowe who delivered it to the House the next day (5 October). Bearing the title *The Humble Representation and Petition of the Officers of the Army to the Parliament of the Commonwealth of England*, it was anything but humble. Essentially it was a vindication of the Derby petitioners, attacking the Rump for its proceedings against Lambert's brigade. The officers reiterated their opposition to 'setting up any single person with supreme authority'. While reaffirming their fidelity to Parliament, they asserted their right to petition it. They drew attention once again to 'the necessitous condition of the poor soldiers of your armies'. Finally they demanded that the army, not

Parliament should make all military appointments, and that any dismissals or cashierings be carried out solely within the army, by court-martial.[48]

Hesilrige, donning his hat as a newly restored colonel of foot, had attended the fiery meetings at which the petition was debated. As both the majority leader in the Rump and a senior officer of the New Model, he acted as a conduit of military information for his fellow parliamentary republicans. Never one to seek peace and reconciliation, he seemed to take pleasure in provoking conflict. His sheer intelligence and dynamism had vaulted him into a leadership role, to which he was partially suited on account of his 'rectitude and sincerity of . . . intentions'. But he lacked several key qualities of an effective leader. As a fellow republican pointed out, he was 'a man of disobliging carriage, sour and morose of temper, liable to be transported with passion, and to whom liberality seemed to be a vice'. Utterly lacking personal magnetism, he was prickly in his interpersonal relations, even with like-minded people. In September he had had a violent falling-out with Sir Henry Vane the younger for example, a person of similar principles, but of a far more generous, tolerant temper. The one person that he was careful to stay on the right side of, General George Monck, would soon betray him utterly.[49]

When he heard that the *Representation and Petition* was also being circulated among the rank and file of the army Hesilrige became almost hysterical. Dreading a coup, he went straight to the House, got the members to lock the doors, and 'after long, brisk debate' pass a bill declaring that all legislation enacted since the Rump had been expelled in April 1653 was null and void unless confirmed by the Rump, and that from 11 October it would be treason to raise money in any form without parliamentary consent. As if these votes were not inflammatory enough, the next day the House moved to cashier all but one of the Wallingford House Junto ringleaders: Lambert, Disbrowe, Berry, Kelsey, Ashfield, Cobbett, Creed, Packer and Barrow. Fleetwood, the only one not cashiered, was replaced as commander-in-chief by a commission consisting of himself and six others: Hesilrige, Monck, Ludlow, and Colonels Wauton, Morley and Overton. The newly appointed parliamentary commissioners now mobilised their troops.[50]

The Military Takeover

Hesilrige had thrown down the gauntlet; the Junto were not slow to take it up. They mustered the troops in and around London, then, under Lambert's command they surrounded Westminster. At the gate of Scotland Yard the Horse Guards barred the way. Showing impressive personal courage, Lambert dismounted, walked forward and ordered Major Arthur Evelin, the commander of the Guards, also to dismount. Evelin hesitated – after all Lambert had just been dismissed and therefore had no legal right to be issuing commands. Nevertheless, such was Lambert's personal authority that Evelin gave in and did as he was told, at which point his men crossed over to Lambert's side. A scant five months after it had unlocked the House of Commons, the army locked it again. Later the same day, Lambert rode through the files of Colonel Moss's regiment which had earlier opposed him, but which now, 'in the acknowledgement of so brave a soldier, did salute him with several volleys of shot'.[51]

In Ireland the officers under Colonel John Jones, after initially supporting the coup, drew back and adopted a wait-and-see attitude. Among the officers there was great 'searching of hearts'. Ludlow sailed to England, with the purpose of effecting a reconciliation between the Rump and the army.[52]

CHAPTER FIFTEEN

THE ARMY BRINGS BACK THE KING,
1659–60

The Two Months of Army Rule

England was once again in the hands of a naked military dictatorship. Less than ever, however, did the Junto know what to do. One of their few decisive actions was to relieve thirteen prominent republican officers of their commands. For the next two and a half months, striving to govern a sullen and resentful populace, they would flounder under inept leadership. As Monck's emissary observed shortly after the army took power, 'the officers themselves can scarce tell which way to move'. Not least among their problems was the fact that the financial cupboard was almost bare. Increasingly they would find themselves plagued by conflict with the officers in Scotland and Ireland, and by divisions among the officers in London, with the grandees meeting at Fleetwood's Wallingford House, and the junior officers at St James's Palace. There were also divisions within the Wallingford House Junto that would sabotage the leadership's efforts to present a united front to a hostile world. Typical of the disunity within the army was a pamphlet, full of exalted, chiliastic language, issued shortly after the second expulsion of the Rump. *The Armies Vindication of This Last Change* boldly justified their recent action. Because the Commons had ceased to be of use to the nation 'they were gently laid aside'. The army did not merely represent the people, they '*are* the people in an active body . . . It was not man but God that raised up his people into an army.' Under it, 'we are upon our march from Egypt to Canaan, from a land of bondage and darkness, to a land of liberty & rest . . . so that while the Lord leads us in a troublesome wilderness, in dark and rough paths, amidst wild beasts, and enemies on every side, how comfortable is it to all good people, to be led by the hand of an army, in the ways of justice and freedom'. In conclusion the author advised the army to construct a firm alliance with the people of God: 'fill the land with righteousness . . . and the Lord your God will go before you, He will fight for you, according to all that He did for you in Egypt'. Extreme religious language such as this was an embarrassment to the Junto, who were striving to present a moderate face to the world. In addition to the wild forces on the religious left, there were political elements actively working to undermine the Junto. On 12 October, Sir Arthur Hesilrige received from General Monck in Leith a secret message directed, through Thomas Clarges, to him, Valentine Wauton and Thomas Scot. It promised that 'if the parliament would be resolute in asserting their own authority against the army, he would assist them in it'. This encouraged the republican leaders to take a hard line against the army. That same day Monck, in a letter to Speaker Lenthall, urged him to 'hasten the settlement of the government of these nations . . . with successive parliaments so to be regulated in elections'. Did Monck know the implications of dispensing with the Rump in favour of successive, elected parliaments? I believe he did.[1]

For the moment the Irish officers continued to stick with the Junto, in letters of 26 October signed by Sir Hardress Waller and others, and on 4 November, signed by Colonel John Jones, Sir William Waller and others. They accused Monck of dividing the army and 'opening . . . a door for the common enemy to come in'. The façade of unity would soon crack, however. Monck had already been secretly assured that Sir Charles Coote, Sir Theophilus Jones 'and a very considerable part of the army were resolved to assist him', and that they were confident of gaining Sir Hardress Waller's support.[2]

Monck's Challenge to the Junto

For the next seven months General Monck would be at the centre of the whirlwind changes that shaped the political destiny of England. He gained this position by deploying political skill of a far higher order than any of his counterparts in England. Many people at the time regarded him with suspicion and hostility. Samuel Pepys thought he seemed 'a dull, heavy man'. Sir Edward Montagu confided in Pepys more than once that he considered Monck 'but a thick-skulled fellow'. Bishop Gilbert Burnet shared this low opinion, adding that he was guilty of 'inexcusable baseness'. These and other contemporary observers drastically underestimated Monck's deftness, as well as his consummate sense of political timing. They had also forgotten, if they ever knew of it, his distinguished military career after joining the parliamentary army in 1647 following his earlier capture by them. His record in both Ireland and Scotland showed him to be the second most gifted military leader after Oliver Cromwell, perhaps on a par with John Lambert. His brief career as general at sea in the Dutch war (1652–54) established him as 'one of the ablest and most significant of seventeenth-century naval leaders'.[3]

When he learned that the Wallingford House Junto had sent the Rump packing, Monck decided to act. He was fed up with the power that religious radicals exercised over the London officers, and was determined to save the English church from such fanatics. In fact his appeal against religious 'fanatics', Quakers in particular, struck a responsive chord. That sect had become more and more aggressive in promoting itself, and there was a corresponding popular pushback. All over the country there were attacks on Quakers in 1659–60. The French ambassador noted that the dread of sectaries and other religious radicals was a crucial factor in the increasing popular desire for Restoration. Monck toured all the garrisons in Scotland, arresting unreliable officers and replacing them with men he trusted. He then wrote to Fleetwood and Lambert denouncing their action, and putting them on notice that he intended to restore the Rump to power. He still needed time before embarking on this ambitious and risky endeavour. First, he had to amass a war chest sufficient to finance his expeditionary force for several months. Fortunately the Council of State had just sent him a large sum, and he was able to raise additional funds from sympathetic Scots. Soon he had accumulated £50,000, as well as an impressive stock of arms and ammunition. Next he had to ensure the absolute loyalty of his troops, both the ones he took with him into England, and the ones he left behind in Scotland. He began by ordering a day of fasting and humiliation 'to seek the Lord for His blessing in this great affair'. Around the same time, he wrote to two civilians, perhaps Presbyterian ministers, stating: 'I look upon the liberty of the churches and the maintenance of a gospel ministry as my grand motive to this work.' He then set about purging his army. By the beginning of November he had eliminated over 150 commissioned and non-commissioned officers either by dismissal or forced resignation. He then summoned a number of the ones loyal to him to Greyfriars Church in Edinburgh, where he told them that he was 'resolved to make the military power subservient to the civil'. As expected, they 'unanimously declared to live and die with him'. Next he convened a meeting of the nobles and lairds of the shires – the Scottish Assembly – in Edinburgh on 15 November. He did not object when they elected William Cunningham, ninth earl of Glencairn, leader of the royalist rising five years earlier, as their president. His only requirement was that they oppose any attempt to communicate with Charles Stuart.[4]

As soon as he went public with his support for the Rump and his defiance of the Wallingford House Junto, Monck was widely accused of playing into the king's hands. From York, Colonel Robert Lilburne wrote to his friend William Clarke, who was now Monck's secretary, commiserating with him for having 'to play Charles Stuart's game' in the service of Monck. After converting this explosive letter into shorthand so that no one else could read it, Clarke destroyed the original. Lilburne was not the only one who thought he understood Monck's agenda. From London General Fleetwood wrote that Monck's action was nothing less than 'a way to bring Charles Stuart amongst us again'. Religious radicals in London were in no doubt that Monck 'intends to bring in the king of Scots, and that he hath put out all the godly'. From Hull, Colonel Overton accused him of being 'under a bad influence', while several of the leading officers in Ireland – Colonels John Jones, Sir Hardress Waller, Thomas Cooper, Richard Lawrence and others – echoed this accusation. From Newcastle Lambert and his officers were sure that Monck's conduct would only serve the interests of 'the common enemy'. From London Monck's commissioners, Timothy Wilkes and John Clobery reported to him that in light of the recent selection of Glencairn as president of the Scottish Assembly there were 'great jealousies here that your Lordship hath a farther design than is contained in your Declaration.'[5]

Against the testimony of all these people who were in no doubt that Monck was either working to bring back the king, or at the minimum, creating an opportunity for the royalists, we have Monck's repeated denials: his intention was merely to put an end to military dictatorship by restoring the supremacy of Parliament. He assured Colonel John Jones of his 'resolution to be true and faithful to the Parliament, and to oppose to the death the setting up of a king, single person or House of Lords'. To Dr John Owen in London he wrote: 'As to the Cavaliers' interest, . . . it hath not a greater enemy in the three nations than myself.' In late January 1660 he wrote that Lord Fairfax 'assured me in a private conference that he would join me to the opposing of Charles Stuart's family'. Statements like these poured continually from his pen; as late as early March 1660, he was still voicing his opposition to a Stuart restoration.[6]

Do all these declarations in support of Parliament and the Commonwealth mean that he really was opposed to the Restoration until the very last minute?

My view is that Monck, not later than October 1659, could tell that all three nations were overwhelmingly hostile to the army, suspicious of the Rump, lukewarm about the restoration of the unpurged Long Parliament, and increasingly supportive of a Stuart restoration. True, Presbyterians allied with royalists in calling for 'a full and free parliament', but basically they were being manipulated in the service of the royalist cause. In one county after another it was understood that 'the gentry commitment to a free parliament [meant] a restoration of monarchy'. For his part, Monck chose to flow with the current rather than buck it. However, in order to avoid a mutiny by large numbers of the officers, particularly those in London who were identified with the Wallingford House Junto, and the more radical junior officers who were passionate in their attachment to the Good Old Cause, he had to maintain a public stance in favour of the Commonwealth. His professions of repugnance towards monarchy wore increasingly thin, but by the time republicans such as Hesilrige, Okey and Rich came to the realisation that Monck was playing a deep game in favour of the king, the ground had been cut from under their feet and further resistance was futile.[7]

Lambert and Fleetwood were not fooled by Monck's public stance in favour of the Commonwealth, and told him so. Monck ignored Lambert, but wrote the bluntest of ripostes to Fleetwood, accusing the Junto of contempt of Parliament 'such as the greatest tyrants amongst us never openly pretended to'. Monck's accusation was vindicated by the *Declaration of the General Council of Officers*. Rehearsing all their grievances against the Rump, the Wallingford House Junto announced that the recent legislation of that body cancelling all acts passed after it had been expelled in 1653 and prohibiting the raising of money without its authority was 'invalid, null and void'. This was the first time in England's history that an army or any other body had ever presumed to cancel an Act of Parliament. It was an unprecedented exercise of military power. Not only that, the Junto went on to assure their radical godly friends that they would soon undertake 'a full and thorough reformation of the law' and abolish tithes, at the same time professing 'no aim . . . to set up a military or arbitrary government'. The Committee of Safety they had just created would shortly draft a new constitution 'as may best suit . . . a free state and commonwealth'.[8]

This executive body, charged with running the country, was chaired by a civilian, Sir Archibald Johnston of Wariston, and it exercised essentially the same powers as the Council of State of the previous Parliament. Ten out of its twenty-three members were officers, but not every nominee agreed to serve – Ludlow, Vane and Richard Salwey (a member of the previous Council of State) declining the invitation. Bulstrode Whitelocke was in an agony of indecision over whether to serve until a high-level delegation led by Disbrowe persuaded him that he was desperately needed as a counterweight to the radicals who 'had a design to overthrow magistracy, ministry and law'. By 3 November no more than nine or ten out of the twenty-three had actually sat down together. Although officers comprised only a minority, the Committee of Safety was still under the thumb of the army, since it was required to consult with the General Council of Officers, and to exercise whatever authority the officers delegated to it.[9]

Meanwhile the General Council of Officers talked much but did little. By mid-November they had agreed on nothing more than that the new constitution would not be adopted without the consent of the General Council of the Army and Navy. Monck's three emissaries put their names to this agreement, but their word signified little. To keep their radical constituency onside, the Junto leaked a rumour that they were on the verge of abolishing both tithes and the Court of Chancery. Meanwhile the committee tasked with drawing up a new constitution struggled with the problem of how to cope with the election of a parliament that would almost certainly turn against the army. The idea of a select senate controlled by the army, with veto power over legislation, had gone nowhere. The next idea was to put the army at one more remove, by setting up a committee of twenty-one 'Conservators of Liberty', army officers who would oversee the elected parliament. These Conservators would enforce several fundamental principles: 1. the government by Commonwealth should not be altered by setting up a king, single person, or House of Peers; 2. no violation of 'the consciences of those that fear God'; 3. the army should not be reduced, its leadership altered, nor its pay lessened without the consent of the Conservators; 4. the legislative and executive powers should be distinct; 5. 'That both the assemblies of the parliament shall be elected by the people of this Commonwealth duly qualified'.

The brainchild of General Edmund Ludlow, the scheme of twenty-one Conservators was eagerly embraced by the officers as a lifeline to pull them out of their morass of indecision. The list of principles, however, bore signs of haste and confusion. There were to be two chambers, both elected, but no House of Peers. The last word would lie with the Conservators of Liberty, implying that the army would still be the ultimate authority in the state. The proposal was stillborn because it was anathema to a large segment of the English population.[10]

In response to intolerable pressure to end the military dictatorship, the General Council of the Army announced that a new parliament would meet before February, even though no decision had yet been taken on the crucial question of who would be eligible to vote, and how the two houses were to be distinguished, one from the other. Leaving these matters up in the air, the General Council of Officers instructed the Committee of Safety to issue writs for parliamentary elections. Hesilrige, leader of the Rump, dismissed this move as 'a mere delusion to amuse the people now the Scotch army is advancing'.[11]

Monck meanwhile wrote a conciliatory letter to Lambert accepting his offer of mediation, and sending Colonel Wilkes, Lieutenant-Colonel Clobery and Major Knight to treat with the Junto. In reality he was playing for time to complete his preparations to invade England. He was encouraged by news from London that 'woeful divisions increase daily' in the army.[12]

Finally, in early November, leaving his reliable and supremely competent second-in-command, Major-General Thomas Morgan, in charge of Scotland, Monck set out for England. The latest news was that Lambert was coming north to block his way, but that his force was 'very much divided, and vows that they will not strike a stroke against General Monck'. Another report assured him that 'the private soldiers, both horse and foot . . . would not fight General Monck in this quarrel', but counselled him to wait another month or two before crossing the border, in order to allow the Wallingford House Junto to complete its self-immolation.[13]

Meanwhile in Ireland there had been a decisive shift in Monck's favour. On 13 December, a majority of the Irish officers, led by Sir Charles Coote and Lord Broghill, carried out a coup d'état, seizing Dublin Castle, surprising and dismissing Colonel John Jones and two other commissioners for being leading representatives of the Anabaptist, republican wing. They won over Sir Hardress Waller, who, though a regicide, was a time-server, tempted by the promise of becoming commander-in-chief. For the moment they continued to profess loyalty to the absent Ludlow as their commander-in-chief, but soon he would come under suspicion for cooperating too closely with Wallingford House. The citizens of Dublin 'all made bonfires and offered their assistance', while declaring their opposition to 'the interest of any single person whatsoever'. A few days later the officers wrote to Monck regretting that they had not been able to join him earlier in the defence of Parliament, and praising 'the good cause that you and we are now asserting', and boasting that they had carried out their coup with 'not one drop of blood spilt'. In another letter they indicted the Wallingford House Junto for setting up 'Anabaptists, Quakers and other sectaries' and bringing the country to the brink of ruin. Calling for the readmission of the MPs excluded in 1648, they thought it necessary to purge Lieutenant-General Ludlow from the army and charge him with high treason – along with Corbet, Jones and Thomlinson – for favouring 'fanatic spirits'. The letter was signed by Coote, Sir Theophilus Jones, Colonel Henry Ingoldsby and fifty-two more officers.[14]

These fifty-five officers backed up their endorsement of Monck with an offer to raise up to 4,000 troops for Parliament, while continuing to condemn the 'fanatic spirits' who had almost destroyed Ireland.[15]

Despite this backing from Ireland, it was still not smooth sailing for Monck. The citadels at Ayre and Berwick submitted to him, but then he ran into rough weather. The garrison at Carlisle refused him entry. He sent a much larger squadron to surprise Newcastle, but they were turned back. At York, Colonel Robert Lilburne, formerly a trusted subordinate, had become his bitter enemy and drawn all his officers into an association sworn to resist the invasion from Scotland.[16]

Halting on the Scottish side of the border, Monck consolidated his forces, while engaging in a propaganda war against the Junto and their adherents. Declaring 'the great grief of our hearts [caused by] the interrupting of the members of Parliament', he pledged to establish 'the government of a free state or commonwealth'. In an address to the churches in the three nations, he promised 'to secure the just liberties of all the churches'. At the same time he emphasised 'that we own and assert the authority of this present Parliament which is now through sad mistakes and misapprehensions inter-rupted'. In another letter he warned the Junto that 'the nation of England will not endure any arbitrary power, neither will any true Englishman in the army'.[17]

Despite a full Treasury and excellent morale among his troops, Monck postponed his entry into England until the coldest, iciest time of year. Why? A major reason for his delay was the lack of a response from Speaker Lenthall, the Council of State, or any members of the Rump to his letters asking for confirmation that they did indeed wish him to intervene in their defence. He did not hear from them until well into December.[18]

The delay was propitious because the political wind was steadily shifting in Monck's direction. In London the Junto were in a state of near paralysis, torn between the demands of the lower officers and their godly votaries for implementation of the Good Old Cause, and their growing awareness of the loathing of the general public towards them. Floundering helplessly, Fleetwood abdicated his leadership role. Decisiveness had never been his forte. His father-in-law Oliver Cromwell had once angrily dismissed him as a 'milksop'. Archibald Johnston, while chairing the Committee of Safety in November to December 1659, told him to his face that he had three faults which rendered him unfit for leadership: 'No good friend and no ill foe; slow to come to a determination and suddenly to break it; and do things by private suggestions.' The Venetian ambassador found him a man of 'unexampled frigidity', while Edmund Ludlow saw him as 'extremely disturbed' by the realisation that the cause to which he had dedicated his life was now on the brink of collapse.[19]

By mid-December his trusted adviser Bulstrode Whitelocke could read the writing on the wall. He went to Fleetwood and in the course of a long conversation explained to him why he was certain that Monck's intention was to bring in the king, which would ruin them all. Monck had misled Hesilrige and others with his proclamations that he wanted a republic based on the recall of the Rump. Therefore 'it was more prudence for Fleetwood and his friends to be the instruments of bringing [the king] in than leave it to Monck'. Fleetwood was initially won over by Whitelocke's analysis, and told him to get ready for a diplomatic mission to the king. As Whitelocke was leaving he ran into Sir Henry Vane, General John Disbrowe and General James Berry who were coming in to speak with Fleetwood. Fleetwood asked Whitelocke to wait outside. Within a quarter of an hour he burst from the room, 'and in much passion said . . . "I cannot do it, I cannot do it." ' When Whitelocke asked him why, Fleetwood responded that he had been reminded that 'I am engaged not to do any such thing without my Lord Lambert's consent'. Whitelocke replied that Lambert was too far away, and the time for action was now. 'Fleetwood again said "I cannot do it without him" ', to which Whitelocke answered 'you will ruin yourself and your friends' Fleetwood responded 'I cannot help it', at which point Whitelocke gave up and left.[20]

The next day Fleetwood signalled his total surrender to Monck and the republicans. He confessed to Speaker Lenthall that 'the Lord hath blasted them and spit in their faces', and handed over the keys to the Parliament House. On the same day a large contingent of soldiers marched down Chancery Lane to Speaker Lenthall's house, where he stood in his robes of office flanked by two republicans, Sir James Harrington and Colonel Thompson. Colonel John Okey, speaking for the troops, delivered a short speech comparing their return to obedience to Parliament to the humble return of the prodigal son in the gospel parable, hoping for the same forgiveness. Lenthall welcomed their submission, to which the soldiers responded with 'many volleys of shot with joy'.[21]

Monck Makes His Move

In the north Monck had not been idle. Showing that he regarded the recall of the Rump as only a temporary solution, he wrote confidentially to Speaker Lenthall urging him 'to hasten the settlement of the government of these nations now into a commonwealth with successive parliaments so to be regulated in elections'. He must have known that such elections would result in the return of many MPs hostile to the army and favourable to the king. At the beginning of November he confided to his agent Dr Thomas Clarges that he favoured not only the recall of the Rump, but all the members who had been 'secluded' –expelled – at Pride's Purge in December 1648. Having said this, 'he conjured Clarges to secrecy'. He must also have known that readmitting the secluded members would have brought a strongly Presbyterian and royalist complexion to the restored Parliament. Yet he assured the regicide Colonel John Jones of his affection for the Commonwealth, and he kept up a constant correspondence with Sir Arthur Hesilrige, repeatedly expressing his 'zeal for a Commonwealth government'.[22]

On 3 November Lambert headed north, intending to confront and defeat Monck before he could set foot in England. He was, however, hobbled by lack of money, obliging his troops to survive on free quarter. Many of them were heard vowing 'that they will not strike a stroke against General Monck'. Although Lambert comfortably outnumbered his antagonist's 5,800 soldiers, the morale on Monck's side was high. That more than made up for his inferiority in numbers.[23]

Stationed at Coldstream near Berwick, he awaited the auspicious moment. With each passing day events continued to unfold in his favour. In November Monck was in touch with Thomas, Lord Fairfax, who told him that he and the Yorkshire gentry were unhappy with his pledges to restore only the Rump, without the members secluded in 1648. Monck replied that his published declarations did not reveal his whole mind. To keep the army onside he had to make them believe that he was not working for the king's restoration. For the next three months Monck would walk a tightrope as he tried to follow public opinion while not alarming the New Model. At the beginning of December the garrison of Portsmouth, the third most important stronghold in England, declared for the Rump, after Hesilrige, with Colonels Morley and Wauton, brought two regiments and convinced their governor, Colonel Whetham, and his garrison to repudiate the Wallingford House Junto and come out for Monck. The troops sent by the Junto to recapture the garrison instead seized their officers and joined the rebel garrison. A few days later, the fleet under the command of Admiral John Lawson unanimously declared for the restitution of Parliament, throwing the senior officers at Wallingford House 'into confusion'.[24] Hesilrige and Lawson still appeared not to realise that by hitching their star to General Monck they were dooming the republic.

In an ominous development, the Committee of Safety dispatched the deposed Parliament's serjeant-at-arms with a squadron of cavalry to the Exchange in the heart of London to read a new proclamation forbidding circulation of petitions for a 'free' (code for 'royalist') parliament. A crowd of hostile apprentices climbed onto the roofs of adjacent houses from where they tore tiles, and great pieces of ice out of the gutters, and hurled them onto the heads of the troopers below. The soldiers retreated, but returned that afternoon (5 December) in greater numbers under Colonel Hewson, a regicide and former Westminster shoemaker known for his ruthlessness. As he approached the Exchange, his men's swords drawn and their pistols cocked, derisive shouts of 'a cobbler, a cobbler' greeted him along the way. The apprentices then began throwing stones, goading the soldiers into opening fire. They killed two or more of their tormentors, while suffering five casualties on their own side. This shedding of civilian blood was a public relations disaster for the army, causing 'a great heart burning in the City'. From then on individual soldiers did not dare set foot in London: 'The soldiers here are so vilified, scorned, and hissed that they are ashamed to march, and many officers, when they go into the City dare not wear their swords for fear of affronts, and thus . . . they are become vile in the eyes of the people.' Just over two weeks later (21 December) the London municipal elections returned a strongly royalist Common Council, and there was a widespread threat of a tax strike unless the military government resigned.[25]

From his base at Coldstream Monck watched and waited as the Wallingford House Junto and their followers endured one hammer blow after another. He wrote secretly to Speaker Lenthall and to the deposed members of the Rump's Council of State to begin raising troops in the south, 'which will not be difficult for you to do', given what he had already accomplished in undermining the Junto. After Portsmouth and the fleet had thrown in their lot with him, Taunton, Plymouth, Bristol, Arundel, Colchester and Chester also defected. In Kent, Sir Michael Livesey raised two regiments for Monck. The Junto were 'in so great a consternation' that they countermanded their recent call for new elections and prepared to capitulate to the Rump. By the end of the year the garrisons in Windsor Castle and the Tower of London had also deserted to the Rump. From Ireland came the news that the great majority of the officers had declared for the Rump, and against Lieutenant-General Ludlow, Colonel John Jones and others identified with the Junto, whom they indicted for treason. They also offered to send over 3,000 or 4,000 men 'for the service of Parliament'. Monck wrote to Sir Hardress Waller, who had led the coup against Jones, commending 'this noble act of yours'. He reassured him that there was 'little ground . . . to fear that either the Scots or Cavaliers should gain any advantage by our late transactions'.[26]

With messages of support streaming in from all sides, the time now seemed right for Monck to roll the dice. On New Year's Day 1660 he crossed the Tweed at Coldstream, proclaiming his mission's purpose as the defence of the rights and liberties of Parliament, 'and the government of these nations by a free state and commonwealth'. The only remaining organised opposition was Lambert's brigade, whose numbers were evaporating so rapidly that Monck let the officers in Dublin know that he no longer needed the horse regiment he had earlier requested from them. Most of the brigade had already arrived, however, and met Lord Fairfax on Marston Moor at the beginning of January. Some of them were worried that Monck was part of a 'Cavalier design', and presented Fairfax with a paper declaring against any government by a single person, while their colonel, Hierome Sankey, conferred with Lambert. Not shrinking from the challenge, Fairfax tore up their statement before their faces and prepared to fight. The men from Ireland quailed at the prospect and the crisis blew over. A day or two later Fairfax met Monck and told him that there would be no peace in England 'but by a free parliament, and upon the old foundation of monarchy'.[27]

Robert Overton's Resistance

As he made his slow progress southwards Monck was hailed almost universally as the saviour of England. The main exception was Colonel Overton, governor of Hull, who kept up a pretence of studied neutrality. Monck overlooked Overton's past as a radical icon, and chose not to scrutinise too closely his dubious claim that he had 'all along declared for the

Parliament'. He airily dismissed Overton with the reflection that he was glad to have any previous misunderstandings cleared up, demanding only that he make a 'declaration of your obedience to Parliament in their present constitution'. Overton cheekily replied, 'I am very glad to hear that you adhere to this parliament in their present constitution, against the readmission of the secluded members, a free parliament or single person, one of which hath been continually charged upon you, as the common cry of your army'.[28]

Upon resuming its sittings at the end of December, the Rump wasted little time avenging itself on the Wallingford House Junto. Helped by Monck and its three army commissioners – Hesilrige, Colonel Herbert Morley and Colonel Valentine Wauton – it purged over 500, or 40 per cent, of the officer corps. The once proud army was reduced to a shadow of its former self. The purges continued right up until the Rump's own overthrow in early February and beyond. The new commanders of the army were reliable republicans: Colonels John Okey, Matthew Alured, Henry Markham and Thompson; as well as the MPs Anthony Ashley Cooper and Thomas Scot.[29]

At the end of the first week of January 1660 Speaker Lenthall wrote Monck exhorting him to march speedily to London in order to prevent any further trouble from the Junto. Monck was no longer worried about them. Rather than hurry to London he accepted an invitation from Lord Fairfax to visit him at Nun Appleton, his family seat near York. Upon his arrival, Fairfax received him with 'expressions of joy and affection' and threw a lavish party. After inspecting his army, Fairfax paid him the compliment 'that he never saw a completer and better disciplined body of men'. Far from being a burden to the country, they 'pay for every pennyworth'.[30]

Monck's triumphal descent from the north took him another month. At one stop after another he was greeted with the ringing of bells, the plaudits of the people, 'and all the testimonies of joy that could possibly be expressed'. During his leisurely progress he was writing constantly – to his officers in Scotland, to his allies in Dublin, to Speaker Lenthall and Sir Arthur Hesilrige, to the London City fathers, and to supporters in England. Part of his effort was devoted to reining in the enthusiasm of his royalist supporters. In a letter to the gentry of Devon for example, he reaffirmed his commitment to a commonwealth, and abhorrence of monarchy. He repeated this commitment in his frequent letters to Hesilrige. Yet a Mr Courtney, his tongue loosened by drink, boasted to Ludlow that his cousin General Monck 'would do great things for the king'.[31]

Monck's Entry into London

On Friday 3 February Monck brought his army from Barnet, a few miles north of London, into Whitehall. There was no ringing of bells or popular jubilation at his arrival, just people crying out for a free parliament. As far as Londoners were concerned his public backing of the Rump was a black mark against his name. For the moment, however, his main task was to show the Rump that he – not they – was in charge of the country. On Monday 5 February he went to the Parliament House, where he was greeted effusively by Speaker Lenthall. Standing bareheaded he declined Lenthall's invitation to be seated on a plush chair. Then he addressed the small group of assembled parliamentarians. There was steel beneath the velvet glove of deferential respect. He would not swear the oath against the Stuarts as a condition of being appointed to the Council of State, and urged the Rump to revoke the oath entirely. He opined that 'the less oaths and engagements are imposed . . . your settlement will be the sooner attained to'. He also suggested that they quickly augment their pathetically small numbers by holding fresh elections to fill the many vacancies. These aspects of his speech 'troubled and amused some of his masters of the Parliament'.[32]

Monck's supporters in the Rump were a minority and his pretended cordiality towards the majority soon wore thin. Alarmed that London had become a hotbed of royalism, the republican majority ordered him to demolish the City's chains, posts, portcullises and gates. This put Monck in a dilemma. He had been cultivating good relations with the City authorities, yet he was not ready to defy openly his political masters in Westminster. Reluctantly he marched into the City, and began gingerly removing the chains and posts while leaving intact the portcullises and gates. He let the Council of State know that the operation was distasteful both to the City and to his own soldiers, and conferred with the mayor and aldermen at Guildhall, doubtless letting them know how hateful he found this assault on the City's defences. When the parliamentary majority saw how lukewarmly Monck had obeyed them, they angrily repeated their order for the total dismantling of the City's defences.[33]

Monck's Overthrow of the Rump

This was the breaking point for Monck. On 11 February he sent a bombshell letter to the Commons, reminding them that he and his army had been instrumental in restoring them to power just a few weeks before. And yet they were guilty of 'signal indulgence to late notorious offenders', notably John Lambert. He ordered them to 'fill up your number' within seven days. He finished by informing them that he had accepted the invitation of the mayor and aldermen to take up residence in the City, and quarter the bulk of his troops just outside the walls in Finsbury where they would be fed and accommodated. 'This in truth,' wrote Richard Baxter years later, 'was the act that turned the scales and brought in the king.'[34]

And yet, still clinging to power, the Rump reacted with suicidal folly by introducing an act vesting supreme military authority in a commission of five, of which Monck was but one member, and not even part of the quorum.[35]

Delighted by Monck's defiance, the City fathers threw a sumptuous banquet the same afternoon for him and his officers. All the bells of the City rang out, and 'everywhere shouts and acclamations and bonfires . . . and several sums of money given by the citizens amongst the soldiery'. It turned into the wildest celebration in London's history, for which we have Samuel Pepys's unforgettable eye-witness account:

And indeed I saw many people give the soldiers drink and money, and all along in the streets cried, 'God bless them' and extraordinary good words . . . And so we went to the Star Tavern . . . where we drank . . . In Cheapside there was a great many bonfires . . . and all the bells in all the churches as we went home were a-ringing. Hence we went homewards, it being about ten o'clock. But the common joy that was everywhere to be seen! The number of bonfires, there being fourteen between St Dunstan's and Temple-Bar. And at Strand Bridge I could at one view tell 31 fires. In King-street, seven or eight; and all along burning and roasting and drinking for rumps – there being rumps tied upon sticks and carried up and down. The butchers at the maypole in the Strand rang a peal with their knives when they were going to sacrifice their rump. On Ludgate Hill there was one turning of the spit, that had a rump tied upon it, and another basting of it. Indeed, it was past imagination, both the greatness and the suddenness of it. At one end of the street there was a whole lane of fire, and so hot that we were fain to keep still on the further side merely for the heat.[36]

The Return of the Unpurged Long Parliament

From that day on Monck had very little to do with the Rump. Revelling in his new-found popularity with Londoners, he was feasted in the coming weeks by one City company after another. Letting down his guard, he toler-ated expressions of Cavalierish sentiments, and allowed himself to get 'drunk as a beast'. Remaining in the City, he also kept the Council of State at arm's length, but conferred with several of the secluded members. He also consulted with his officers about whether they were willing to have the secluded members sit. Warily they said yes, on condition that the members should declare for a commonwealth government and agree to dissolve within a short time. The secluded members assented to these conditions, promising to dissolve themselves and call new elections within a month.[37]

They arrived at Whitehall on 20 February, and demanded admission to the Commons the next day. There were seventy-three of them, more than enough to outvote the Rump, which by now had shrunk to a skeleton of its former self. After assuring the officers that he would not, Monck allowed them to sit, with the warning that monarchy could only be re-established on the ruins of the people. They proceeded to elect a new Council of State, showing that they knew which side their bread was buttered on by voting Monck at the top of the poll. Yet the enduring affection of many of his offi-cers for the Commonwealth and the Good Old Cause continued to vex the general for another two months. Once again he promised Hesilrige that he would not bring back the king, and repeated that promise to the immovably republican Colonel Okey.[38]

The New Model's Lingering Attachment to the 'Good Old Cause'

In spite of the massive purges of the previous two months there were still many officers wedded to the Commonwealth. Because of their unease over the direction of events, a number of them came together at the beginning of March to draft a remonstrance against monarchy. Colonel Okey opened with a long speech on the evils of government by a single person, and on how they were facing an inundation of evils that threatened to swamp their religious and civil liberties. They asked Monck to present these views on their behalf to Parliament. He put off his answer to the following day, when he refused their request and said that 'nothing was more injurious to disci-pline than their meeting in military councils to interpose in civil things'. He spoke harshly to the militants, and told them to stop their political meetings. This diktat he enforced by ordering the officers to go back to their regi-ments, but softened the blow by arranging a meeting between ten officers and ten MPs. At this meeting the officers demanded a watertight Act of Indemnity for everything they had done while in the army, confirmation of the sales of confiscated land, and (perhaps as an afterthought) a guarantee of no king or House of Lords. The MPs refused to promise anything, simply referring them to the next Parliament, soon to be elected. With that they had to be satisfied.[39]

Hesilrige and a few others then came privately to Monck and confided to him that they knew 'a commonwealth government was not agreeable with the disposition of the people, who are always bad judges of what is best for themselves, and therefore since a single person was necessary, there could not be one fitter than he for that office'. Monck at once quashed the idea, vowing that 'he would rather be drawn in pieces with wild horses than be so treacherous to the nation'.[40]

By this point any republican with a grasp of political reality knew the jig was up. When a friend came to visit Sir Arthur Hesilrige he found him with his head in his hands, moaning 'we are undone, we are undone'.[41]

All political avenues were now closed to the republicans, but in the next few weeks there were three armed attempts to breathe life into the dying embers of the Commonwealth. With the readmission of the secluded members on 21 February, the highly regarded republican colonel Nathaniel Rich decided to act. He left London for East Anglia, hoping to stir up his regiment against the almost certain return of the king. His attempt to organise military resistance to the forces of royalism suffered a fatal disability: the regiment was no longer his. Monck had already replaced him with another respected colonel, Richard Ingoldsby, a regicide who had just repudiated his radical past. Unwilling to take up arms against their comrades, the men sided with their new colonel, giving Rich no choice but to surrender, which he did on the last day of February.[42]

The second, and most serious attempt to resist Monck originated with Major-General Overton from his base at Hull. He wrote a widely circulated letter to Colonels Hugh Bethell, Charles Fairfax and George Smithson lamenting that 'the abandoned interest of Charles Stuart doth seem so to shine in the face of public transactions'. Unfortunately for Overton the three colonels were staunch friends of Monck, whom they promptly informed. Whether his own officers supported Overton, his men definitely did not. Monck wrote to him pointing out that there was no discontent in any regiment of the army 'except part of Colonel Rich's'. Overton accepted that for the Commonwealth the game was over, and promised to obey his commander's order to report to London. When his replacement, Colonel Charles Fairfax, arrived at Hull, the soldiers greeted him with 'a volley, after which the great guns were fired'. As soon as Overton was gone 'the bells began to ring'.[43]

In April Major-General John Lambert launched the last, most desperate attempt to reverse the inexorable tide of royalism. Monck had already imprisoned him in the Tower as a man too dangerous to be on the loose. A brilliant military and political strategist, Lambert was the most highly regarded of Cromwell's generals. His ingenuity did not desert him in the Tower. On the night of 10 April he charmed the maid who tended his chamber into putting on his nightcap and crawling into his bed, so as to deceive the guards until morning. (We can only guess at what motivated the maid, or what her fate was when her treachery was discovered.) Lambert then slid down a rope into a waiting boat on the Thames. Once at large he put out a call for soldiers loyal to the Commonwealth to meet him at Edgehill. Men from at least six horse regiments rode to the rendezvous. The Good Old Cause was to breathe its last gasp on the field where it had begun nearly eighteen years before. Some of the most famous republicans turned up: Colonels Okey, Axtell, Cobbett and Creed, but only a few troops of horse joined them. Monck, with his usual decisiveness, sent Colonel Ingoldsby with a squadron to nip the rising in the bud. Lambert was captured and brought to London where he suffered the humiliation of having to stand beneath the Tyburn gallows. He was then returned to his cell. He would remain a prisoner for the rest of his life – he did not die until 1684.[44]

These risings demonstrate that there was still a strain of militant republicanism in the army. During the weeks in which he cleared the way for the king's return, Monck kept a close watch on his officers, disguising his true intentions until it was too late for them to take effective action against him.

He was now in negotiation with Charles Stuart. On 17 March his kinsman William Morice arranged a vital meeting with the king's emissary Sir John Grenville. Through him Monck advised Charles to leave Spanish territory (Flanders) for Breda in the Dutch provinces. He also laid out conditions that would clear the way for him to come back to England. These were: 1. 'a free and general pardon to all his subjects'; 2. 'his consent to any act or acts of Parliament . . . for the settlement of public sales and dispositions of lands, to officers, soldiers and others'; 3. 'the payment of the soldiers' arrears'; 4. 'toleration or liberty of conscience to all his subjects'. These four points formed the substance of the Declaration of Breda that Charles duly published at the beginning of April.[45]

It is often thought that Monck did not begin actively working for the king's restoration until this time. Yet there had been intimations of his disengagement from the Commonwealth as early as the previous August when he refused to send troops to help with the suppression of Booth's rebellion. His denunciation of the Wallingford House Junto's expulsion of Parliament in October alerted astute political observers to the royalist implications of his actions from that point onwards. Still, as late as the end of March he was keeping his options open by refusing to make a treaty with Charles until the new Parliament met. After all, his lodestar had always been the supremacy of the civil over the military power. By 9 April he was sure enough of himself to impose a *Humble Remonstrance and Address* on all his officers that they would,

> instructed by your example and discipline, . . . obey and not dispute the orders of our superiors . . . and freely and readily observe such commands as we shall receive from your Excellency or the Council of State, or the parliament when assembled. And in particular, we shall . . . decline any meeting . . . for the contriving or carrying on of any Declaration or subscriptions concerning affairs of state . . .[46]

Signatures to the *Humble Remonstrance* streamed in from garrisons and regiments all over the country in the coming days. Yet this was not the end of the story.

Radical agitators were moving among the regiments, handing out pamphlets, and trying to muster support for one last fling of the Good Old Cause. The soldier-author of *Eye-Salve for the English Armie* demanded: 'has the blood of thousands which you . . . have shed in that just and righteous cause' been all in vain? 'God knows we take up arms in judgement and for conscience' sake, not to serve the arbitrary lusts and will of any whatsoever.' He concluded with a call to arms: 'let us now resolve to take the field with our swords in our hands . . . we will not disband . . . until we see our liberties, both civil and religious, asserted and secured, in a free state and commonwealth, and our arrears fully paid'.

The anonymous author – not a soldier – of *An Alarum to the Officers and Souldiers of the Armies of England, Scotland, and Ireland* warned the soldiers that, once back, Charles would hang many of them and banish others as rebels and traitors. To avoid this dread fate they should come together and elect agitators as they did in 1647, get their officers onside, and then 'make an Engagment not to be disbanded or divided until the Commonwealth is re-established without a king, single person or House of Lords'.[47]

Republican Officers Quit the Army on Principle

Reacting to this agitation Monck issued an order that the *Humble Remonstrance* should be tendered to the rank and file as well as the officers. This was more than many of them could stomach. In a striking demonstration of their hatred of monarchy and enduring loyalty to the Commonwealth, many left the army. Ludlow estimated the defections at 90 per cent of the soldiery. This was wishful thinking, but a royalist source conceded that up to 30 per cent of many horse regiments did quit. In other words, a significant proportion of the cavalry, if not the infantry, chose to give up any hope of receiving their very sizeable arrears of pay rather than betray their republican principles. This impressive act of conscience made it that much easier for the king to fulfil his promise to pay the army's arrears in full.[48]

After these last efforts to rescue something from the wreckage of the Good Old Cause, everyone in the army except Monck fell silent. On 2 May he wrote to the regimental commanders enclosing the king's letter, the Declaration of Breda, and the *Humble Address of the Officers*, with orders that every officer should subscribe. The initial signatories numbered ninety-two, but there were soon many more. In it they supposedly welcomed the Declaration of Breda, and committed themselves to 'the preservation of the true Protestant religion, the honour and dignity of the king, the privileges of Parliament, the liberty and property of the subject, and the fundamental laws of the land'. The army was now firmly under the thumb of its general.[49]

Monck Meets the King

With this documentary proof of the army's obedience in hand, Monck prepared to meet Charles Stuart. Thanks to his unfailing sense of timing, and his careful neutralisation of all opposition, he was able to win virtually sole credit for accomplishing the peaceful return of monarchy. For this he would soon be richly rewarded. He gave Charles the green light to sail across the Channel, and marched to Dover to greet him. There he enacted what everyone knew to be a charade. As a contrite subject he knelt before his sovereign and begged forgiveness for his and the nation's sins. For his part, Charles, after graciously pronouncing absolution and embracing Monck as the saviour of monarchy, embarked on his triumphal procession to the capital accompanied by Monck and his guards. It took four days for the entourage to cover the 77 miles from Dover to London. The army that overthrew and executed Charles I now ushered his son back onto the throne, without anyone suffering so much as a bloody nose.[50]

EPILOGUE

That an army that had conquered three such kingdoms, and brought
so many armies to destruction, cut off the king, pulled down the
Parliament, and set up and pulled down others at their pleasure, that
had conquered so many cities and castles, that were so united by
principles and interest and guilt, and so deeply engaged as much as
their estates, and honour, and lives came to, to have stood it out to the
very utmost, that had professed so much of their wisdom and reli-
giousness; and had declared such high resolutions against monarchy:
I say, that such an army should have one commander among themselves, whom they accounted not religious, that should march against
them without resistance, and that they should all stand still, and let
him come on and restore the Parliament, and bring in the king and
disband themselves, and all this without one bloody nose! Let any
man that hath the use of his understanding judge whether this were
not enough to prove that there is a God that governeth the world . . .
Richard Baxter, Reliquiae Baxterianae[1]

Three questions have long engaged the attention of people interested in the
epochal events of mid-seventeenth-century Britain and Ireland. First, why
was the Restoration so quick and so peaceful? Second, when precisely did
George Monck decide to abandon the cause of the republic and make it his
business to bring back the king? Finally, how did he ensure at every step of
the way that no violence broke out among the warring factions, so that he
gained virtually the entire credit for this monumental achievement? To
anyone who has thrilled to the exploits of the New Model Army, both on the
battlefield and in the political arena, its demise in 1659–60 can only be a
disappointment. How did it come about that this nearly invincible army,

widely admired as the terror of tyrants, tamely submitted to the return of the
son of the tyrant they had vanquished only eleven years before?

To deal with the second question first, I have argued that Monck's conversion to the cause of monarchy occurred sooner than most historians have
allowed. Charles Stuart approached him through an intermediary in July
1659, offering a rich reward if he would assist him back onto the throne.[2]
Monck did not reply to the invitation. However, he did not lift a finger
against the Presbyterian–royalist uprising the following month. When he
announced in October that he was bringing several regiments to London to
restore the recently expelled Rump Parliament to power, he was bitterly
attacked for promoting the royalist cause. As time went on it became
increasingly clear, to those who had eyes to see, that this was exactly what he
was doing. That was why, as he marched south on his stated mission to
restore the Rump to power, he was greeted jubilantly on all sides by crowds
of people who detested the Rump. That is why Londoners spontaneously
erupted with the greatest celebration in their history when he defied the
Rump and ordered the re-admission of the members secluded at Pride's
Purge. That is why there was suspicion, unhappiness and discontent in the
New Model Army that lasted until the moment in March 1660 when any
possibility of protest had been rendered impossible.

Monck's consummate management of a potentially rebellious and violent
army earned him the extravagant bounty of a profoundly grateful monarch.
In addition to keeping his posts as commander-in-chief and general at sea,
he was showered with money and lands, and elevated to a dukedom.

To answer the first, and more important question, it is important to recall
that the body of men whom Monck skilfully guided towards acquiescence
in the restoration of monarchy were not the same New Model Army, fired
by revolutionary zeal, that had purged the Long Parliament, abolished the
House of Lords and overthrown the Stuart monarchy. But they were still the
army of Parliament, and they were still haunted by the ideals of a republican
commonwealth: religious liberty (only, it is true, for the Protestant sects
outside the previously Established Church), law reform (abolishing hanging
for theft and – in Scotland – the persecution of witches, and replacing Latin
with English in the courts), a broader franchise, and promoting with great
sincerity what they called godly reformation.

By the mid-1650s, however, it had become a very different army. From
being a heroic instrument of war that scarcely lost a skirmish between 1645
and 1652, it had become a guarantor of peace. The officers in particular settled

into a comfortable routine. There was less turnover, and therefore fewer prospects for promotion. Many officers were absent from their commands for months at a time. Morale inevitably sagged among the privates and non-commissioned officers who rarely saw their captains and field officers. There was an ongoing awareness that several hundred officers had enriched themselves and become substantial landowners. They had accomplished this by purchasing their men's arrears debentures at a fraction – typically 15–25 per cent – of their face value, and exchanging them for confiscated crown and church lands. This awareness that many officers had turned themselves into great landowners did not help morale. As one pamphleteer rhetorically asked the rank and file: the officers 'have something to say for their perseverance; they have got wealth and something like honour; but what benefit accrues to you?' Another complained of 'self-seeking men ... who by our means were raised from the meanest mechanics to lord-like inheritances'. Following the example of many of their superiors, the rank and file looked more and more to their own interests. Finally, the pathetic and indecisive leadership of the Wallingford House Junto under Fleetwood, Lambert and Disbrowe, in contrast to the decisive and highly skilled leadership exercised by George Monck, was a significant factor in the army's collapse.[3]

There is also the external factor of public opinion. During the years after its greatest victories the New Model incurred steadily increasing popular hostility. Ralph Josselin, the Essex Puritan clergyman, not an unsympathetic observer, commented in May 1659 that the army was divided. 'This self-seeking, deceitful crew are likely to receive the recompence of their deceits wherein they have sported themselves', he thought. People resented the suppression of traditional festive culture – Morris dancing, Christmas celebrations, Sabbath sports, bear-baiting, cockfighting, horse-racing, the theatre and alehouses. More seriously, they fiercely resented the ballooning expense of an increasingly bloated army. In 1645 the New Model Army had started with a strength of 21,000. With the conquest of Scotland and Ireland the army's size had risen to 12,000 and 33,000 in these two nations respectively, just to keep them under permanent occupation. The army in England was reduced to 14,000, but in 1659, amidst the growing royalist threat, rose to 22,000. Between January and February 1660 its numbers soared again to over 36,000. The occupying force in Scotland had meanwhile shrunk to under 9,000, while the army in Ireland was down to about 10,000. In Jamaica the force had shrunk from a high of 9,000 to 1,600. There were also the troops in Flanders numbering 6,600, for a grand total of about 63,000 in 1659–60. The cost of maintaining so many men under arms had become insupportable. Arrears mushroomed, and the army in England fell back on free quarter, which further exasperated the civilian population. The two months of direct military rule (late October to late December 1659) outraged people by its illegality, and provoked a tax strike. In the end the Commonwealth was bankrupt, and few people were ready to bail it out. By the end of 1659 soldiers were mocked, hissed and attacked in the streets. Witnessing this unpopularity from Scotland, George Monck knew that if he played his cards right he could soon bring this once redoubtable army to heel.[4]

When the army finally did lay down its arms it was rewarded with full payment of the arrears that no earlier parliament had been able to satisfy, as well as a far-reaching Act of Indemnity for everything it had done during the years of armed conflict. The only soldiers not indemnified were the ones who had signed the king's death warrant, and a few others. Several of them were already dead: Oliver Cromwell, Henry Ireton and Thomas Pride. To slake its thirst for revenge the Cavalier Parliament ordered their corpses exhumed, hanged in their shrouds, drawn and quartered, and their skulls stuck on spikes in Westminster Hall.[5] Of the remaining regicides some escaped and two were pardoned – Colonel Richard Ingoldsby after an abject and tearful apology, and General George Fleetwood. Colonels Whalley and Goffe fled to New England, Hewson, Ludlow and others to the Continent. In the end only four regicide colonels – Harrison, Okey, John Jones and Barkstead – went to the scaffold, in addition to Colonels Axtell and Hacker, who had commanded the guards at Charles I's trial. The many officers who had bought crown and church lands saw them confiscated (a betrayal of the Declaration of Breda).

In later centuries the New Model Army would be admired for having tamed absolute monarchy, advanced the cause of democracy and begun the long process of law reform. The other aspect of its legacy would be an enduring popular suspicion of standing armies, and an aversion to Puritanism.[6]

NOTES

ABBREVIATIONS

AA	Clement Walker, *Anarchia Anglicana, or the History of Independency Second Part* (London: no publisher, 1649)
A&O	C.H. Firth and R.S. Rait (eds), *The Acts and Ordinances of the Interregnum, 1642–1660*, 3 vols (London: HMSO, 1911)
Abbott	Wilbur Cortez Abbott (ed.), *The Writings and Speeches of Oliver Cromwell*, 4 vols (Cambridge, MA: Harvard University Press, 1937–47)
Add. MS	British Library, Additional Manuscripts
Baillie	Robert Baillie, *Letters and Journals*, ed. David Laing, 3 vols, Bannatyne Club, vols 72, 73, 77 (1841)
Battles	Austin Woolrych, *Battles of the English Civil War* (London: Batsford, 1961)
Bell	Robert Bell (ed.), *Memorials of the Civil War*, 2 vols (London: Richard Bentley, 1849)
BIHR	*Bulletin of the Institute of Historical Research*
BL	British Library
Bodl. Lib.	Bodleian Library, Oxford
C&P	S.R. Gardiner, *History of the Commonwealth and Protectorate 1649–1656*, 4 vols (London: Longmans, Green, 1903)
MS Carte	Bodleian Library, Correspondence of the marquess of Ormonde
Carte, *Coll.*	Thomas Carte, *A Collection of Original Letters and Papers . . . 1641–1660. Found among the Duke of Ormonde's Papers*, 2 vols (London: A. Millar, 1739)
Cary	Henry Cary (ed.), *Memorials of the Great Civil War in England from 1646 to 1652*, 2 vols (London: Henry Colburn, 1842)
CCJ	Corporation of London Records Office, Journal of the Common Council of London
CCSP	O. Ogle, W.H. Bliss and W.D. Macray (eds), *Calendar of the Clarendon State Papers*, 5 vols (Oxford: Clarendon Press, 1869–1970)
CJ	*Journal of the House of Commons*
Clarendon, *History*	Edward, earl of Clarendon, *The History of the Rebellion and Civil Wars in England*, ed. W.D. Macray, 6 vols (Oxford: Clarendon Press, 1888)
CLRO	Corporation of London Records Office
Codr. Lib.	Codrington Library, All Souls College, Oxford

Const. Docs	S.R. Gardiner (ed.), *The Constitutional Documents of the Puritan Revolution, 1625–1660*, 3rd edn (Oxford: Clarendon Press, 1906)
CP	*The Clarke Papers*, ed. C.H. Firth, 4 vols, Camden Society, new ser., vols 44, 54, 60, 62 (1891–1901); vol. 5, ed. Frances Henderson, Camden Society, 5th ser., vol. 27 (2005)
Crom. Army	C.H. Firth, *Cromwell's Army*, 4th edn (London: Methuen, 1962)
Crom. Navy	B.S. Capp, *Cromwell's Navy: The Fleet and the English Revolution, 1648–1660* (Oxford: Clarendon Press, 1989)
CSPD	*Calendar of State Papers, Domestic Series*
CSPI	*Calendar of State Papers, Irish Series*
CSPV	*Calendar of State Papers Relating to English Affairs in the Archives of Venice*
C to P	Austin Woolrych, *Commonwealth to Protectorate* (Oxford: Clarendon Press, 1982)
Donagan, *War*	Barbara Donagan, *War in England 1642–1649* (Oxford: Oxford University Press, 2008)
Dow	F.D. Dow, *Cromwellian Scotland, 1651–1660* (Edinburgh: Donald, 1979)
Duffy	Christopher Duffy, *Siege Warfare* (London: Routledge & Kegan Paul, 1979)
Dyve	*The Tower of London Letterbook of Sir Lewis Dyve*, ed. H.G. Tibbutt, Bedfordshire Historical Record Society, vol. 38 (1958)
TT	British Library, Thomason Tracts
Edwards, *Gang.*	Thomas Edwards, *Gangraena*, 3 vols (London: Ralph Smith, 1646)
EHR	*English Historical Review*
Evelyn, *D&C*	John Evelyn, *Diary and Correspondence*, ed. William Bray, 4 vols (London: G. Bell, 1887–89)
Evelyn, *Diary*	John Evelyn, *Diary*, ed. E.S. de Beer, 6 vols (Oxford: Clarendon Press, 1955)
Fairfax Correspondence	George W. Johnson and Robert Bell (eds), *The Fairfax Correspondence*, 4 vols (London: Richard Bentley, 1848–49)
GCW	S.R. Gardiner, *History of the Great Civil War, 1642–1649*, 4 vols (London: Longmans, Green, 1893)
Haller & Davies	William Haller and Godfrey Davies (eds), *The Leveller Tracts, 1647–1653* (New York: Columbia Press, 1944)
Harl. MS	British Library, Harley Manuscripts
HJ	*Historical Journal*
HLRO	House of Lords Record Office
HMC	Royal Commission on Historical Manuscripts
HMSO	His/Her Majesty's Stationery Office
Hodgson	*Original Memoirs Written during the Great Civil War; Being the Life of Sir Henry Slingsby and Memoirs of Capt. Hodgson* (Edinburgh: Constable, 1806)
Holles	Denzil Holles, *Memoirs* (London: T. Goodwin, 1699)
HS	*Historical Society*
Hughes, *Gang.*	Ann Hughes, *Gangraena and the Struggle for the English Revolution* (Oxford: Oxford University Press, 2004)
Hutchinson	Lucy Hutchinson, *Memoirs of the Life of Colonel Hutchinson*, ed. James Sutherland (London: Oxford University Press, 1973)
Intell.	*Intelligencer*
JEH	*Journal of Ecclesiastical History*
JSAHR	*Journal of the Society for Army Historical Research*

Juxon, *Journal*	*The Journal of Thomas Juxon*, ed. Keith Lindley and David Scott, Camden Society, 5th ser., vol. 13 (1999)
Kishlansky, *Rise*	Mark Kishlansky, *The Rise of the New Model Army* (Cambridge: Cambridge University Press, 1979)
Lanc. Tracts	*Tracts Relating to Military Proceedings in Lancashire during the Great Civil War*, vol. 2 (Manchester: Chetham Society, 1844)
LJ	*Journal of the House of Lords*
Lomas–Carlyle	*The Letters and Speeches of Oliver Cromwell with Elucidations by Thomas Carlyle*, ed. S.C. Lomas, 3 vols (London: Methuen, 1904)
Ludlow, *Memoirs*	Edmund Ludlow, *Memoirs*, ed. C.H. Firth, 2 vols (Oxford: Clarendon Press, 1894)
Ludlow, *Voyce*	Edmund Ludlow, *A Voyce from the Watch Tower, Part Five: 1660–1662*, ed. A.B. Worden, Camden Society, 4th ser., vol. 21 (1978)
Massarella	Derek Massarella, 'The Politics of the Army, 1647–1660' (unpublished PhD thesis, University of York, 1978)
Merc.	*Mercurius*
Montereul	*Diplomatic Correspondence of Jean de Montereul . . . 1645–48*, ed. J.G. Fotheringham, vols 24–30 (Edinburgh: Scottish History Society, 1989–89)
MS	manuscript
MS Clar.	Bodleian Library, Clarendon Manuscript
MS Tanner	Bodleian Library, Tanner Manuscripts
NA	National Archives
Nickolls	John Nickolls (ed.), *Originall Letters and Papers of State Addressed to Oliver Cromwell . . . MDCXLIX to MDCLVIII. Found among the Political Collections of John Milton* (London: Whiston, 1743)
Nicoll, *Diary*	John Nicoll, *A Diary of Public Transactions and Other Occurrences, Chiefly in Scotland, from January 1650 to June 1667*, ed. David Laing, Bannatyne Club, vol. 52 (1836)
NLW	National Library of Wales
NMA	Ian Gentles, *The New Model Army in England, Ireland and Scotland, 1645–1653* (Oxford: Blackwell, 1992)
ODNB	*Oxford Dictionary of National Biography*, 60 vols (Oxford: Oxford University Press, 2004)
OPH	*The Parliamentary or Constitutional History of England* (also known as *The Old Parliamentary History*), 2nd edn, 24 vols (London: J. & R. Tonson, 1762–63)
P&P	*Past & Present*
Parl.	*Parliamentary*
Perf.	*Perfect*
Procs	*Proceedings*
Quarrel	*The Quarrel between the Earl of Manchester and Oliver Cromwell*, ed. David Masson, Camden Society, new ser., vol. 12 (1875)
Reece	Henry Reece, *The Army in Cromwellian England, 1646–1660* (Oxford: Oxford University Press, 2013)
Reg. Hist.	Sir Charles Firth and Godfrey Davies, *The Regimental History of Cromwell's Army*, 2 vols (Oxford: Clarendon Press, 1940)
RO	Record Office
Rushworth	John Rushworth, *Historical Collections*, 8 vols (London: D. Browne, 1721–22)
S&P	C.H. Firth (ed.), *Scotland and the Protectorate: Letters and Papers Relating to the Military Government of Scotland from*

	January 1654 to June 1659, Publications of the Scottish History Society, vol. 31 (Edinburgh: T. and A. Constable, 1899)
S&S	Austin Woolrych, Soldiers and Statesmen: The General Council and Its Debates 1647–1648 (Oxford: Clarendon Press, 1987)
SHS	Scottish History Society
Sloane MS	British Library, Sloane Manuscripts
Soc.	Society
SP	National Archives, State Papers
Sprigge	Ioshua Sprigge, Anglia Rediviva, England's Recovery (London: John Partridge, 1647)
Stevenson	David Stevenson, Revolution and Counter-Revolution in Scotland 1644–1651 (London: Royal Historical Society, 1977)
Sydney Papers	Sydney Papers, Consisting of a Journal of the Earl of Leicester, 1646–1661, ed. R.W. Blencowe (London: John Murray, 1825)
TRHS	Transactions of the Royal Historical Society
TSP	A Collection of the State Papers of John Thurloe, 7 vols (London: Woodward, 1742)
TT	British Library, Thomason Tracts
Whitelocke	Bulstrode Whitelocke, Memorials of English Affairs, 4 vols (Oxford: Oxford University Press, 1853)
Whitelocke, Diary	The Diary of Bulstrode Whitelocke 1605–1675, ed. Ruth Spalding (Oxford: Oxford University Press for the British Academy, 1990)
Wolfe	Don M. Wolfe (ed.), Leveller Manifestoes of the Puritan Revolution (New York: Thomas Nelson, 1944; repr. London: Frank Cass, 1967)
Worc. Coll.	Worcester College, Oxford
Worc. MS	Worcester College, Oxford, Clarke Papers
Worden, Rump	Blair Worden, The Rump Parliament, 1648–1653 (Cambridge: Cambridge University Press, 1974)

PROLOGUE

1. Only about a sixth of the deaths were in England: Charles Carlton, Going to the Wars: The Experience of the British Civil Wars, 1638–1651 (London: Routledge, 1992), pp. 204, 214; Pádraigh Lenihan, 'War and population, 1649–52', Irish Economic and Social History, vol. 24 (1997): 1–21, pp. 9–11, 18, 19–21.
2. Three Petitions . . . Brought by Many Thousands of the County of Essex (London: Benjamin Allen, 1642), TT E.134[13], pp. 2, 6; The Humble Petition of Many Thousands of the Inhabitants of Norwich (London: George Tomlinson and R.C., 16 July 1642), TT 669.f.6[54].
3. The phrase is E.P. Thompson's.
4. Thomas Crawshaw, 'Military Finance and the Earl of Essex's Regular Army, 1642–1644' (unpublished PhD thesis, York University, Toronto, 2013), documents the striking initial success of the Long Parliament in funding the earl of Essex's army.
5. The Solemn League and Covenant, printed in Const. Docs, pp. 270–1.
6. Lomas–Carlyle, i.176.
7. CCSP, ii.155.
8. Quarrel, p. 93.

1 THE FOUNDING OF THE NEW MODEL ARMY

1. Ian Gentles, The English Revolution and the Wars in the Three Kingdoms, 1638–1652 (Harlow: Pearson Longman, 2007), p. 100; Malcolm Wanklyn and Frank Jones, A Military History of the English Civil War, 1642–1646 (Harlow: Pearson and Longman, 2005), p. 136.

2. Ibid., pp. xx, xxii, xxiv, xxv, xi; Baillie, ii.208–9, 211, 218, 229–30; *Battles*, p. 88.

3. Ibid., p. 82.

4. Clive Holmes, *The Eastern Association in the English Civil War* (Cambridge: Cambridge University Press, 1974), pp. 199, 204.

5. NA, Baschet's Transcripts of the Correspondence of the French Ambassador, PRO31/3/75, fos 195, 199, 201; 'Defence of the Earl of Manchester' [1643/64], BL, Loan MS 29/123/Misc. 31, unfol.; Juxon, *Journal*, p. 63; *Quarrel*, p. 69; untitled broadside ([9 Dec.] 1644), TT E.21[9]; Malcolm Wanklyn, *The Warrior Generals: Winning the British Civil Wars, 1642–1652* (London: Yale University Press, 2010), pp. 138–40; Wanklyn and Jones, *A Military History of the English Civil War*, pp. 205–9; Gentles, *English Revolution*, pp. 240–6.

6. BL, Loan MS 29/123/Misc. 31, unfol.; *LJ*, vii.79; Rushworth, v.733–6; Simeon Ashe, *A True Relation of the Most Chiefe Occurrences at, and since the Late Battell at Newbery* (n.d.), TT E.22[10], p. 6.

7. MS Tanner 61, fos 205^v–6; NA, PRO31/3/75, fos 204–5.

8. *Perf. Occurrences*, 22–29 Nov. 1644, TT E.256[42], sig. Q1^v–2; *Quarrel*, p. 69; A.N.B. Cotton, 'Cromwell and the Self-Denying Ordinance', *History*, vol. 62 (1977): 211–31, pp. 218–19. Manchester himself admitted that London public opinion blamed him for the Newbury–Donnington fiasco: NA, PRO31/3/75, fo. 201; J.S.A. Adamson, 'Oliver Cromwell and the Long Parliament', in John Morrill (ed.), *Oliver Cromwell* (London: Longman, 1990), p. 62, n. 48.

9. Whitelocke, i. 343–8; Baillie, ii.244–5.

10. *Quarrel*, pp. 96–9; Baillie, ii.246.

11. Rushworth, vi.1–3; Juxon, *Journal*, pp. 69–70; Add. MS 31116 (Lawrence Whitacre's diary), fo. 188; Lomas–Carlyle, i.187.

12. *CJ*, iii.718; L. Kaplan, *Politics and Religion during the English Revolution* (New York: New York University Press, 1976), pp. 86–7; Violet A. Rowe, *Sir Henry Vane the Younger* (London: Athlone Press, 1970), p. 57.

13. Sloane MS 1519, fo. 37: John Lambert to Sir Thomas Fairfax; Baillie, ii.247; *Perf. Occurrences*, 6–13 Dec. 1644, TT E.258[1], sig. S2–2^v; *Parliament Scout*, 5–12 Dec. 1644, TT E.21[15], pp. 617–18; *Merc. Britanicus*, 9–16 Dec. 1644, TT E.21[23], pp. 482–3; untitled broadside ([9 Dec.] 1644), TT E.21[9]; *Kingdomes Weekly Intell.*, 10–17 Dec. 1644, TT E.21[25], pp. 681–2.

14. *CJ*, iii.723, 726; *Perf. Passages*, 11–18 Dec. 1644, TT E.21[26], p. 68; *Perf. Diurnall*, 16–23 Dec. 1644, TT E.258[5], p. 579; Sloane MS 1519, fo. 39–9^v; Whitelocke, i.349.

15. Ibid., i.355.

16. *LJ*, vii.117, 122, 129; NA, HLRO, House of Lords Minute Book, 3 Jan. 1645, unfol..

17. *CJ*, iv.13, 14; Rushworth, vi.7; *LJ*, vii.134.

18. *CJ*, iv.14, 16; Lotte Mulligan, 'Peace negotiations and the Committee of Both Kingdoms, 1644–1646', *HJ*, vol. 12 (1969): 3–22.

19. The appointment of moderates may have been a kind of window dressing to impress the Lords. They were John Maynard, Thomas Lane and Lawrence Whitacre: *CJ*, iv.18; *Kingdomes Weekly Intell.*, 7–14 Jan. 1645, TT E.24[18], p. 706. The quarrel soon petered out as the Commons found themselves preoccupied with the more constructive task of creating a new army: *Quarrel*, pp. xc–xci, xciii; *LJ*, vii.141.

20. *Merc. Civicus*, 16–23 Jan. 1645, TT E.25[21], p. 795; Sir Thomas and his father's chief correspondents on political affairs in this period were the earl of Northumberland, Lord Wharton, James Chaloner, Thomas Widdrington and John Lambert: Bell, i.142, 145, 156, 162; *CJ*, iv.26; Malcolm Wanklyn, 'Choosing officers for the New Model Army, February to April 1645', *JSAHR*, vol. 92 (2014): 109–25, p. 120; Sloane MS 1519, fos 37, 39; J.S.A. Adamson, 'The baronial context of the English Civil War', *TRHS*, 5th ser., vol. 40 (1990): 93–120, p. 116.

21. *CJ*, iv.26.

22. *CJ*, iv.28, 30, 31, 36, 37; *Perf. Diurnall*, 20–27 Jan. 1645, TT E.258[17], pp. 621–2; *LJ*, vii.159, 164, 166, 169, 175; Juxon, *Journal*, p. 74; NA, HLRO, Main Papers, 4 Feb. 1645, fo. 87–7^v.

23. For diametrically opposed petitions, see *CJ*, iv.37; *Perf. Diurnall*, 27 Jan.–3 Feb. 1645, TT E.258[19], p. 628; *LJ*, vii.178, 180. See also the comments of journalists: *London Post*, 4 Feb. 1645, TT E.27[10], p. 2; *Scotish Dove*, 31 Jan.–7 Feb. 1645, TT E.269[3], p. 529. On 31 January Kentish petitioners supporting the Self-Denying Ordinance were received with exaggerated courtesy by the Commons, who referred their petition to a large committee. Five days later an opposing petition signed by members of the country committees of the Eastern Association arrived at the House of Lords. The petitioners expressed their 'sad apprehension' that the proposed alterations would destroy their association. The Lords referred the letter to the Commons, with a request for answers to the objections of the Eastern Association. These diametrically opposed petitions both showed an awareness that great changes were implied in the move to remodel Parliament's armies.

24. *True Informer*, 1–8 Feb. 1645, TT E.269[4], p. 495; *CJ*, iv.43, 44; *LJ*, vii.187, 190, 192; *Perf. Diurnall*, 3–10 Feb. 1645, TT E.258[22], p. 638; *Weekly Account*, 5–12 Feb. 1645, TT E.269[12], sig. Ffff4–4ᵛ.

25. *LJ*, vii.166, 160, 192; *CJ*, iv.46–7, 48; Whitelocke, i.372.

26. *CJ*, iv.48; Harl. MS 166 (Sir Simonds d'Ewes's diary), fo. 177ᵛ; Kaplan, *Politics and Religion*, p. 110.

27. *LJ*, vii.204–9; Malcolm Wanklyn, *Reconstructing the New Model Army: Volume 1, Regimental Lists April 1645 to May 1649* (Solihull: Helion, 2015), p. 24.

28. *CJ*, vii.51–2, 53–4; *Perf. Diurnall*, 17–24 Feb. 1645, TT E.258[27], p. 649; Bell, i.161.

29. Hull RO, BRL333: Pelham to Denham; NA, PRO31/3/76, fos 98, 99, 102.

30. *CJ*, iv.64; Ian Gentles, 'The choosing of officers for the New Model Army', *BIHR*, vol. 67 (1994): 264–85, pp. 266–7.

31. David Brown, *Empire and Enterprise: Money, Power and the Adventurers for Irish Land during the British Civil Wars* (Manchester: Manchester University Press, 2020), p. 144; NA, HLRO, Main Papers, 10 Mar. 1645, fos 145–8. The document has been printed in Robert K.G. Temple, 'The original officer list of the New Model Army', *BIHR*, vol. 59 (1986): 50–77, pp. 54–77.

32. Wanklyn, 'Choosing officers for the New Model', p. 120; Temple, 'Original officer list', p. 53; the italics are Temple's. Cf. Mark Kishlansky, 'The case of the army truly stated: The creation of the New Model Army', *P&P*, no. 81 (1978): 51–74, p. 68. The MP was the radical Peregrine Pelham: Hull RO, BRL342; Juxon, *Journal*, p. 75.

33. NA, PRO31/3/76, fo. 119ᵛ. The French ambassador's account is corroborated by Juxon, *Journal*, p. 75. Cf. Wanklyn, *Reconstructing the New Model Army: Volume 1*, p. 24, n. 5; Juxon, *Journal*, p. 76; Harl. MS 166 (d'Ewes's diary), fo. 184ᵛ; Add. MS 31116 (Whitacre's diary), fo. 198ᵛ; *LJ*, vii.274.

34. *LJ*, vii.274, 277. John Adamson informs me that the one lord who opposed Fairfax's list but did not enter his dissent must have been Warwick.

35. *CJ*, iv.82, 88–91; *LJ*, vii.289.

36. NA, PRO31/3/76, fo. 141ᵛ; Kaplan, *Politics and Religion*, pp. 111–12. The figure 300 is the French ambassador's, and must have included non-commissioned as well as commissioned officers.

37. *CJ*, iv.91, 93, 94; *LJ*, vii.293.

38. *CJ*, iv.94; *LJ*, vii.298–9, 300; NA, PRO31/3/76, fo. 150ᵛ.

39. Juxon, *Journal*, p. 76; *LJ*, vii.298–9; NA, PRO31/3/76, fo. 150ᵛ. Juxon wrongly gives the margin as thirteen to nine, and erroneously assigns the vote to Monday instead of Tuesday.

40. *LJ*, vii.300; *CJ*, iv.97; Bell, i.142, 156; Sloane MS 1519, fo. 39.

41. *LJ*, vii.310. The five lords who withdrew from the committee were Northumberland, Kent, Pembroke, North and Howard: MS Tanner 60, fo. 73.

42. *CSPD, 1644–45*, p. 445; *CJ*, iv.138; *LJ*, vii.365; Whitelocke, i.432.

43. Abbott, i.339; *Perf. Occurrences*, 2–9 May 1645, TT E.260[33], sig. T4–4ᵛ. Cromwell was not the only commander reappointed after being discharged under the Self-Denying Ordinance. *CJ*, iv.138–9, 147, 166; Whitelocke, i.433.

44. *CSPD, 1644–45*, pp. 526, 553, 558; *LJ*, vii.408, 411–12, 414–15, 419, 420, 424.
45. *LJ*, vii.421, 433; Rushworth, vi.39; *CJ*, iv.176.

2 RECRUITMENT, PROVISIONING AND PAY

1. John Adamson, 'Of armies and architecture: The employments of Robert Scawen', in Ian Gentles, John Morrill and Blair Worden (eds), *Soldiers, Writers and Statesmen of the English Revolution* (Cambridge: Cambridge University Press, 1998), p. 55. I am also grateful to Stephen Roberts of the History of Parliament Trust for permission to read the unpublished article by David Scott on Robert Scawen and the Committee for the Army, p. 16.
2. NA, Exchequer, Treasurers at War Accounts, 28 Mar. 1645–25 Dec. 1651, E.351/302, fos 1–6, printed in Ian Gentles, 'The arrears of pay of the parliamentary army at the end of the First Civil War', *BIHR*, vol. 48 (1975): 52–63, pp. 62–3.
3. NA, Exchequer, E351/302, fo. 1; *CJ*, iv.90.
4. Ibid., iv.265; HMC, *Portland*, i.267; *Moderate Intell.*, 25 Sept.–2 Oct. 1645, TT E.303[31], p. 147; Sprigge, p. 127. By 1651 over 31 per cent of the army's revenue had come from sources other than the monthly assessment: NA, Exchequer, Treasurers at War Accounts, 28 Mar. 1645–25 Dec. 1651, E.351/302, fos 1–6, printed in Gentles, 'Arrears of pay', pp. 62–3.
5. Add. MS 31116 (Whitacre's diary), fo. 304; *CJ*, v.396; NA, Exchequer, E101/67/11A, fos 68–85. Thanks to protracted resistance from the Lords, the ordinance for the new twelve-month assessment, scheduled to begin on 25 March 1647, did not pass until 23 June. Parliament's neglecting to name the Treasurers at War to receive the assessment until 23 September doubtless had much to do with its failure to generate revenue for the first nine months: *CJ*, v.114, 119, 130; *LJ*, ix.288; *A&O*, i.958, 1,015; SP 28/41, fos 359, 234.
6. *CJ*, iv.51, 56; *LJ*, vii.256.
7. *CJ*, iv.75–6; *LJ*, vii.269; Harl. MS 166 (d'Ewes's diary), fo. 183; Rushworth, vi.17–18; Whitelocke, i.418; *Merc. Civicus*, 3–10 Apr. 1645, TT E.277[12], pp. 882–3; MS Tanner 60, fo. 73; 'An Historicall Diarie of the Militarie Proceedings of . . . Sir Thomas Fairfax . . . by John Rushworth', Harl. MS 252, fo. 33; *Scotish Dove*, 25 Apr.–2 May 1645, TT E.281[10], p. 632; HMC, *Portland*, i.215; John Adair, *Roundhead General: A Military Biography of Sir William Waller* (London: Macdonald, 1969), p. 185.
8. *CJ*, iv.85.
9. *CSPD, 1644–45*, pp. 381, 411, 420, 426, 437, 444; *Perf. Occurrences*, 11–18 Apr. 1645, TT E.260[17], sigs Q2ᵛ–Q3. The newsbook completely glosses over the mutinous behaviour of these conscripts: MS Tanner 60, fos 101, 138.
10. *LJ*, vii.334–5, 461.
11. *Perf. Diurnall*, 23–30 June 1645, TT E.262[14], p. 795; *Scotish Dove*, 27 June–4 July 1645, TT E.292[5], p. 702; *Perf. Passages*, 3–10 Dec. 1645, TT E.266[26], p. 468; *Moderate Intell.*, 16–23 Apr. 1646, TT E.334[2], p. 402.
12. Ibid., 16 June–3 July 1645, TT E.292[3], p. 139; *LJ*, vii.268. Venn's complaint was echoed by the *Moderate Intell.*, normally effusive in its praise of the New Model. It damned the new recruits as 'the vilest rogues and cowards that ever breathed'; some of them were also shameless royalists: *Moderate Intell.*, 16–23 Apr. 1646, TT E.334[2], p. 404; 23–30 Apr. 1646, TT E.334[18], p. 410.
13. After Naseby 102 prisoners were absorbed into the army. After Torrington 200 royalists signed on, with many dozens trickling in later. As Lord Hopton's army disintegrated at the end of February 1646, 300–400 men changed sides, while a further 1,000 declared their willingness to serve Parliament in Ireland: SP 28/34, fo. 464ᵛ; Sprigge, pp. 192, 195, 196; *Cities Weekly Post*, 24 Feb.–3 Mar. 1646, TT E.325[19], p. 5; *LJ*, viii.230; John Rushworth, *A More Full and Exact Relation . . . of the Several Treaties between Sir Thomas Fairfax and Sir Ralph Hopton* (London: Edward Husband, 1646), TT E.328[15], pp. 4–5; *CSPD, 1645–47*, p. 128; Bell, i.249; Sprigge, p. 99; *Perf. Occurrences*, 12–19 Sept. 1645, TT E.264[17], sig. Qq3ᵛ.

14. MS Tanner 60, fos 128, 132^v; *LJ*, vii.565, 570; *CJ*, iv.262.

15. SP 28/43, fos 528, 536; vol. 246, unfol.; vol. 34, fos 463–4; *LJ*, viii.170. Cf. *Moderate Intell.*, 12–18 Feb. 1646, TT E.322[35], p. 304.

16. London's early disenchantment with the New Model is shown both in its almost complete failure to produce recruits in Sept. 1645, and in the sharply reduced quota assigned to it the following Jan.: *CJ*, iv.299; *CSPD, 1645–47*, p. 319. The Eastern Association was at the same time ordered to raise an additional 2,000 troops to stop the king's forces from breaking through to London: MS Tanner 60, fo. 244. For recruitment in the west, see *CJ*, iv.418; *CSPD, 1645–47*, p. 319.

17. HMC, *Portland*, i.215. Since service in the cavalry was so attractive that former officers volunteered to serve as troopers, there can be little doubt that this target was easily reached. Nor was recourse ever had subsequently to impressment for the cavalry: *CSPD, 1644–45*, pp. 358–9.

18. *Merc. Civicus*, 24 Apr.–1 May 1645, TT E.281[4], p. 910; *Perf. Occurrences*, 2–9 May 1645, TT E.260[33], sig. T4r; *Kingdomes Weekly Intell.*, 6–13 May 1645, TT E.284[2], p. 792.

19. A brigade of 4,000 had been dispatched north under Colonel Bartholomew Vermuyden to assist the Scots; perhaps 5,000 were still under Oliver Cromwell, and a small force of perhaps 500 had been stationed at Boarstall, Oxfordshire.

20. The gruelling 78-mile march to Witchampton near Taunton, and the slower march back to Oxfordshire, resulted in a loss of at least 3,000 infantry: *Parliaments Post*, 6–13 May 1645, TT E.284[1], p. 3; 3–10 June 1645, TT E.287[5], p. 6; *Weekly Account*, 21–27 May 1645, TT E.285[19], sig. Yyyy1^v; *Perf. Passages*, 4–11 June 1645, TT E.262[6], p. 264; Sprigge, p. 29; *Exchange Intell.*, 4–11 June 1645, TT E.288[3], p. 29. Baillie, ii.276 reports the army's total strength on the eve of Naseby as 14,000. He had a political motivation for underestimating the army's strength: he wished to establish that the exclusion of the Scots had been a disastrous mistake which had irreparably damaged Parliament's military effort in 1645. His estimate is also belied by the precise figures supplied by the *Scotish Dove* for the 5 June muster before the arrival of Cromwell's and Vermuyden's forces: 7,031 foot and 3,014 horse: *Scotish Dove*, 6–13 June 1645, TT E.288[11], p. 678; Glenn Foard, *Naseby: The Decisive Campaign* (Whitstable: Pryor, 1995), pp. 200, 203; Austin Woolrych, *Britain in Revolution 1625–1660* (Oxford: Oxford University Press, 2002), p. 316.

21. *CSPD, 1644–45*, pp. 600, 603, 625–6. A week before Naseby the Eastern Association had been 1,515 below its quota: *LJ*, vii.414; *Scotish Dove*, 27 June–4 July 1645, TT E.292[5], p. 702.

22. Ibid., 27 June–4 July 1645, TT E.292[5], p. 702; *Perf. Diurnall*, 23–30 June 1645, TT E.262[14], p. 795; *LJ*, vii.463. The 2,000 new foot dwindled to 1,300 on the journey from Reading to Sherborne: *Perf. Occurrences*, 8–15 Aug. 1645, TT E.262[44], sig. Ii2^{r-v}; *Perf. Passages*, 13–20 Aug. 1645, TT E.262[46], p. 341.

23. *CJ*, iv. 264, 277, 299, 307, 402; *LJ*, viii.267–8, 571–2; Bell, i.249; *CSPD, 1645–47*, pp. 118, 121, 130, 152, 170.

24. *Perf. Passages*, 3–10 Dec. 1645, TT E.266[26], p. 468. For the stringent measures taken to deter and punish desertion, see *CJ*, iv.383 and *LJ*, viii.102.

25. *CSPD, 1645–47*, p. 319; *Moderate Intell.*, 26 Feb.–5 Mar. 1646, TT E.327[2], p. 319; 12–19 Mar. 1646, TT E.328[21], p. 341; 16–23 Apr. 1646, TT E.334[2], p. 402; *LJ*, viii.230, 268; *Scotish Dove*, 11–18 Mar. 1646, TT E.328[18], p. 599. The 3,000 foot and horse mentioned in this source include Ireton's regiment of 700 horse, who were not recruits, but armed escorts; cf. *Moderate Intell.*, 12–19 Mar. 1646, TT E.328[21], p. 341.

26. Wanklyn, *Reconstructing the New Model Army: Volume 1*, pp. 33, 35. I accept Wanklyn's figure, which is higher than the one I arrived at in my article, 'The New Model officer corps in 1647: A collective portrait', *Social History*, vol. 22 (1997): 127–44, p. 130.

27. The wastage rate discovered by Hughes for the Warwickshire forces was similarly high, except that the losses were greater in the horse than the foot, evidently because it was the horse who did most of the actual fighting: Anne Hughes, *Politics, Society and Civil War in Warwickshire* (Cambridge: Cambridge University Press, 1987), pp. 199–202. In

Caesar's Due (London: Royal HS, 1983), Joyce Malcolm documents the king's difficulties in raising troops. However, her less thorough knowledge of Parliament's difficulties in mobilising the New Model leads her to exaggerate the contrast between the two.

28. *CJ*, iv.78. The six contractors were parliamentary heavyweights Sir Walter Erle, Anthony Nicoll, Thomas Hodges, Robert Scawen, Sir John Evelyn Senior and Thomas Pury Senior.

29. Thus members of the Cutlers Company contracted on 31 March 1645 to supply 9,200 swords and belts. The cutlers met their contract and were paid in full within sixteen days. Again, Daniel Judd contracted to supply 20 tons of English match on 4 October 1645. He made two deliveries and was paid in two instalments. Likewise, thirteen shoemakers signed contracts on 24 February 1646 to deliver 8,000 pairs of shoes 'of good neat leather'. They met their contracts and four weeks later were paid in full. The gunmakers occupied workshops mostly in the Minories or East Smithfield, the streets adjoining the Tower of London, to which they made their deliveries: Walter M. Stern, 'Gunmaking in seventeenth-century London', *Journal of the Arms and Armour Soc.*, vol. 1 (1954): 55–100, pp. 61, 80. Joan Thirsk points out that provisions merchants placed their orders in specialist farming regions: Suffolk for butter and Cheshire for cheese, for example: Joan Thirsk (ed.) *Agrarian History of England and Wales*, vol. 5, part 2 (Cambridge: Cambridge University Press, 1985), pp. 302–3; 'New Model Army Contract Book, 1645–46', London Museum, 46–78/709, fos 114, 36, 58 (printed in G.I. Mungeam, 'Contracts for the supply of equipment to the "New Model" Army in 1645', *Journal of the Arms and Armour Soc.*, vol. 6 (1968–70): 60–115; SP 28/29, fos 207–8, 226; vol. 33, fos 168, 208; vol. 37, fos 355–7. The Scottish army, the Northern Association army, Massie's Western Brigade and the numerous garrisons were all penalised by the favouritism shown to the New Model.

30. Thomas Andrewes, linen draper and future Commonwealth lord mayor, supplied 4.5 tons of Flemish match. A consortium of cloth merchants – Stephen Estwick, Thomas Player, Maurice Gething, Tempest Milner and John Pocock – furnished several thousand coats, breeches and pairs of stockings. All but Pocock are known to have been active in City government and in the London trained bands. The cutler Alexander Normington, a political Independent in 1647, supplied swords to the New Model in 1646. The future regicide Colonel Owen Rowe, who was to dominate the Common Council from 1649 onwards, supplied 1,000 suits of armour and 1,000 pikes. Thomas Prince, Leveller and cheesemonger, was one of a group of three who sold the army almost nine hundred-weight of cheese. Two officers in the army itself also acted as suppliers: Thomas Hammond, lieutenant-general of the Ordnance, and Christopher Mercer, captain in John Okey's dragoon regiment. The political attitudes of most suppliers are unknown, assuming they had any. One or two, however, were unsympathetic to the war or even crypto-royalist in their leanings. Colonel Lawrence Bromfield, who sold the army 1,500 swords and belts in 1645 and 1646, emerged in 1647 as a militant Presbyterian, hostile to the army. Charles I's gunfounder, John Browne, also supplied the army with cannon. Based in Kent, at London's southern edge, he was prevented from helping the king once the war got under way. Always regarded with suspicion, he was at least once accused of trying to sabotage Fairfax's army by underfilling orders. Valerie Pearl, *London and the Outbreak of the Puritan Revolution* (Oxford: Oxford University Press, 1961), pp. 144, 315, 323–4; Ian Roy (ed.), *The Royalist Ordnance Papers, 1642–1646*, 2 parts (Oxfordshire Record Soc., 1963–64 and 1971–73), part 1, pp. 8, 14; Andrewes: SP 28/33, fo. 164; Estwick et al.: SP 28/36, fos 188–9; vol. 37, fos 407, 413; Rowe: SP 28/352, fos 55–8; Normington: SP 28/36, fo. 181; Prince: SP 28/30, fos 363, 375; Hammond: SP 28/352, fos 180–1; Mercer: SP 28/36, fo. 658; Bromfield: SP 28/30, fo. 374; vol. 37, fo. 345; Browne: SP 28/29, fo. 137; vol. 30, fo. 294; vol. 32, fo. 376; vol. 33, fo. 165; *CSPD, 1644–45*, pp. 606–8, 619.

31. In contrast to the hapless Northamptonshire shoemakers, obliged to wait six years to be paid for the shoes they had furnished to Essex's army: SP 28/305, unfol.

32. *CJ*, iv.386, 388. The supply warrants for the first year of the New Model's operations are found in SP 28/29–33, and vols 36, 37 and 352. Testimony to the fullness and accuracy of

this archive is provided in the account book of horses delivered to Sir Thomas Fairfax's army, 3 Apr. 1645–25 Aug. 1646 (SP 28/140, part 7). For the twelve-month period ending 2 Apr. 1646 the account book shows 4,739 horses being delivered to the army. For the twelve months ending 31 March 1646 the supply warrants show 4,660 horses were paid for. The slight discrepancy may be entirely due to the two extra days covered by the account book.

33. SP 28/31, fo. 547.

34. *Perf. Passages*, 30 Apr.–7 May 1645, TT E.260[32], p. 218.

35. *CJ*, iv.85; SP 28/29–30, *passim*; *CSPD, 1644–45*, p. 594; *Colonel Weldon's Taking of Inch House* (London: Matthew Walbancke, 1646), TT E.330[5], p. 6; SP 28/140, part 7.

36. 'The New Model Army Contract Book', London Museum, 46–78/709, fo. 27ᵛ. Red coats faced with blue were worn throughout the army, except that the firelocks who guarded the artillery train wore tawny coats: *Perf. Passages*, 30 Apr.–7 May 1645, TT E.260[32], p. 218. Once a campaign was underway, coats were not always replaced in the same colour: Geoffrey Parker, *The Military Revolution* (Cambridge: Cambridge University Press, 1977), pp. 71–2; Keith Roberts, *Cromwell's War Machine: The New Model Army 1645–1660* (Barnsley: Pen & Sword, 2005), p. 50.

37. Almost 90,000 pounds of Suffolk and other cheeses and 1,503 hundredweight of biscuit were distributed during the first two months: Aryeh J.S. Nusbacher, 'Civil supply in the Civil War: Supply of victuals to the New Model Army on the Naseby campaign, 1–14 June 1645', *EHR*, vol. 115 (2000): 145–60, pp. 156, 159–60; *Merc. Civicus*, 28 Aug.–4 Sept. 1645, TT E.299[7], p. 1,049; 7–14 May 1646, TT E.337[21], p. 2,241; *A Continuation of Certain Speciall and Remarkable Passages*, 23–30 Jan. 1646, TT E.319[21], p. 7; *Weekly Account*, 27 May–3 June 1646, TT E.339[14], sig. Z4ᵛ; *Kingdomes Weekly Intell.*, 23–30 June 1646, TT E.342[6], p. 151.

38. *A Diary, or an Exact Iovrnall*, 12–18 Feb. 1646, TT E.322[36], p. 7.

39. SP 28/29–31, *passim*.

40. SP 25/136, fo. 51; vols 171–3 (Northants), 182–6 (Warwicks), *passim*. For Kineton, vol. 182, unfol.; for Stretton under Fosse, vol. 185, unfol.

41. *Moderate Intell.*, 6–13 Nov. 1645, TT E.309[11], p. 195.

42. *Weekly Account*, 27 May–3 June 1646, TT E.339[14], sig. Z4ᵛ; *Perf. Occurrences*, 22–29 May, TT E.339[5], sig. Y1–1ᵛ.

43. *LJ*, ix.66–71.

44. *A Diary or an Exact Iovrnall*, 2–9 Oct. 1645, TT E.304[13], sig. Yyyy3; *CSPD, 1645–47*, p. 196.

45. *CJ*, v.126; SP 28/33, 36, 37.

46. *LJ*, x.66–71; SP 28/52, fo. 135; vol. 53, fos 325, 349; SP 28/50–7.

47. Rushworth, vii.1,383; *A&O*, ii.24–57. The authors of the ordinance admitted that £120,000 was the sum the army really needed, but conceded that the country could not bear such a tax burden. For much in this and the following paragraphs I am indebted to Reece, chapter 5. The monthly assessment stood at £120,000 for the entire year 1651: ibid., ii.456, 511; *CJ*, vi.501, 561; vii.10.

48. Field soldiers went down from 10d to 9d, garrison soldiers from 9d to 8d, and horse troopers from 2s 6d to 2s a day: *S&P*, p. 221; *CP*, iii.39.

49. *Perf. Occurrences*, 10–17 Oct. 1645, TT E.266[3], sig. Yy1ᵛ; Bell, i.235–318, *passim*; *Continuation of Certain Speciall and Remarkable Passages*, 7–14 Nov. 1645, TT E.309[15], p. 5; Gentles, *English Revolution*, p. 107 and n. 30.

3 THE YEAR OF VICTORIES, 1645–46

1. Rushworth, vi.17–18; *CSPD, 1644–45*, pp. 453, 461; *Moderate Intell.*, 8–15 May 1645, TT E.284[6], p. 88; *Perf. Diurnall*, 28 Apr.–5 May 1645, TT E.260[29], p. 729.

2. *CSPD, 1644–45*, pp. 502–54, *passim*; pp. 578–9.

3. *CJ*, iv.169–70; Sprigge, p. 32.

4. This and other royal letters ended up in the hands of Scoutmaster-General Leonard Watson, who brought them to Fairfax. Cromwell and Ireton prevailed on him to conquer his scruples and open the king's mail. What they read convinced them of the necessity of fighting the king at once, and then moving quickly to smash Goring at Taunton: Rushworth, vi.49; MS Tanner 59, fo. 750.

5. Peter Young estimated the size of the royalist army as 9,590–9,690 men; In his *Briefe Relation*, Lord Belasyse estimated the New Model at 15,000: Peter Young, *Naseby 1645* (London: Century, 1985), pp. 118, 133, 182, 237, 245, 321. Cf. Foard, *Naseby*, pp. 200, 203, 233, 236, 239, 246.

6. Ibid., p. 256.

7. *A More Particvlar and Exact Relation* . . . ([19 June] 1645), TT E.288[38], p. 2; Young, *Naseby 1645*, pp. 218, 245; Foard, *Naseby*, pp. 263–5. Skippon was out of action for the better part of a year. For the first-class medical treatment he received, see Ismini Pells, ' "Stout Skippon hath a wound": The medical treatment of Parliament's infantry commander following the battle of Naseby', in David J. Appleby and Andrew Hopper (eds), *Battle-scarred: Mortality, Medical and Military Welfare in the British Civil Wars* (Manchester: Manchester University Press, 2018), pp. 78–94, pp. 80–5.

8. *A Trve Relation of a Victory* . . . *[at] Nasiby* . . . *1645*, TT E.288[22], sigs A3ᵛ–4; 'The copie of a letter sent from a gentleman of publike employment in the late service neere Knaseby', in *An Ordinance . . . for a Day of Thanksgiving . . . 1645*, TT E.288[26], p. 3.

9. *CSPD, 1644–45*, p. 594; Sprigge, p. 40; *A Trve Relation of a Victory*, sig. A3ᵛ; *A More Exact and Perfect Relation of the Great Victory in Naisby Field* (1645), TT E.288[28], p. 5; 'The copie of a letter sent from a gentleman of publike employment', p. 4; Mark Stoyle, 'The road to Farndon Field: Explaining the massacre of the royalist women at Naseby', *EHR*, vol. 123 (2008): 895–923, pp. 896, 922–3.

10. *LJ*, vii.484–5; John Lilburne, *A More Full Relation of the Great Battle Fought between Sir Thomas Fairfax and Goring* (1645), TT E.292[3], p. 8; John Blackwell, *A More Exact Relation of the Great Defeat Given to Goring's Army by Sir Thomas Fairfax* (1645), TT E.293[8], p. 7; D.E. Underdown, *Somerset in the Civil War and Interregnum* (Newton Abbot: David & Charles, 1973), pp. 104, 106; Whitelocke, i.480; *Sir Thomas Fairfax Entering Bridgwater by Storming* (1645), TT E.293[27], p. 4; *A Letter Concerning the Routing of Colonel Goring's Army near Bridgewater* (1645), TT E.293[17], p. 8; NA, HLRO, Nalson MS, iv (13), fos 1,241–2; G.D. Aylmer, 'Collective mentalities in mid seventeenth century England: IV. Crosscurrents: Neutrals, trimmers and others', *TRHS*, 5th ser., vol. 39 (1989): 1–22, p. 8.

11. *Two Great Victories* (1645), TT E.296[6]; *Two Letters* (1645), TT E.296[7]; *Procs of the Army*, 1–7 Aug. 1645, TT E.296[14], pp. 3–5; Abbott, i.368; *Moderate Intell.*, 7–15 Aug. 1645, TT E.296[27], p. 187.

12. Sprigge, pp. 91, 99; Underdown, *Somerset*, p. 113; *Mr Peters Report from Bristol* (1645), TT E.301[4], p. 3; Bell, i.250; *Merc. Civicus*, 4–11 Sept. 1645, TT E.300[19], p. 1,058; *A True Relation of the Storming of Bristol* (1645), TT E.301[5], p. 20.

13. Sprigge, pp. 332–3; *Procs of the Army*, 1–6 July 1645, TT E.292[16], p. 8; *CSPD, 1644–45*, pp. 617, 626; see also above, p. 23.

14. Alfred H. Burne and Peter Young, *The Great Civil War: A Military History of the First Civil War, 1642–1646* (London: Eyre & Spottiswoode, 1959), pp. 209–15; Abbott, i.364–6; Underdown, *Somerset*, pp. 100–4; *GCW*, ii.267–73; Sprigge, pp. 60–6; Whitelocke, i.475; *LJ*, vii.496; Rushworth, vi.55; *The Coppie of a Letter . . . concerning the Great Battle . . . at Langport* (1645), TT E.261[4]; *Procs of the Army*, 6–11 July 1645, TT E.292[28], pp. 5–6; *A Trve Relation of a Victory . . . neer Langport* (1645), TT E.292[30]; Lilburne, *A More Full Relation*, pp. 5–6; Blackwell, *A More Exact Relation*, pp. 2–3.

15. For a detailed account of these conquests, see *NMA*, pp. 61–84.

16. Edward Walker, *Historical Discourses upon Several Occasions*, ed. H. Clopton (London: Samuel Keble, 1705), p. 137, quoted in Roy (ed.), *Royalist Ordnance Papers*, part 2, p. 46; Clarendon, *History*, iv.93; *CJ*, iv.272; Sprigge, p. 118; Rushworth, vi.88. An identical letter went to the Lords over Fairfax's signature, omitting the appeal for religious toleration: *LJ*, vii.584–6.

17. Sprigge, pp. 243-6; *Merc. Civicus*, 23-30 Apr. 1646, TT E.335[3], pp. 2,219-20.
18. *Kingdomes Weekly Intell.*, 28 Apr.-5 May 1646, TT E.336[1], p. 89; Whitelocke, ii.23; *LJ*, viii.374.
19. Sprigge, pp. 262, 273.
20. Ibid., pp. 313-15.

4 RELIGION AND MORALE

1. Sprigge, p. 323.
2. Napoleon and Xenophon quoted in F.M. Richardson, *Fighting Spirit: A Study of Psychological Factors in War* (London: Cooper, 1978), pp. 1, 3; S.L.A. Marshall, *Men against Fire: The Problem of Battle Command in Future War* (Washington: Infantry Journal, 1947), p. 158.
3. *CSPD, 1648-49*, p. 210; *CSPD, 1649-50*, pp. 239, 245-6, 257, 281-3; *Lieutenant Generall Cromwell His Declaration* ([18 Aug.] 1648), TT E.459[24], sig. A2^v.
4. Elmar Dinter, *Hero or Coward: Pressures Facing the Soldier in Battle* (London: Frank Cass, 1985), p. 50; Ian Gentles, 'Why men fought in the British Civil Wars, 1639-1652', *History Teacher*, vol. 26 (1993): 407-18, pp. 414-16.
5. William McNeill, *The Pursuit of Power* (Oxford: Blackwell, 1978), pp. 117, 131.
6. Lomas-Carlyle, i.154.
7. Edwards, *Gang.*, i.123; ii.6-7, 152-3, 154; iii.18, 22, 107, 250-1, 260. The debate on *Gangraena*'s worth as historical evidence goes on. Most historians consider it quite reliable, while Colin Davis dismisses it as wholly unreliable: Hughes, *Gang.*, pp. 5, 143-4, 386; Christopher Hill, 'Irreligion in the Puritan Revolution', in J.F. McGregor and B. Reay (eds), *Radical Religion in the English Revolution* (Oxford: Oxford University Press,1984), p. 206; J.C. Davis, *Fear, Myth and History: The Ranters and the Historians* (Cambridge: Cambridge University Press, 1986), p. 126; Murray Tolmie, *Triumph of the Saints: The Separate Churches of London, 1616-1649* (Cambridge: Cambridge University Press, 1977), p. 134; W. Lamont, review of Tolmie, *Times Literary Supplement*, 11 Aug. 1978.
8. The army's Laws and Ordinances are printed in *Crom. Army*, p. 400. Sarah Mortimer has argued that the doctrine of the Holy Trinity was debated strenuously during the English Revolution, and that Puritan parliamentarians tended to be more zealous in their trinitarianism than many royalists: Sarah Mortimer, *Reason and Religion in the English Revolution: The Challenge of Socinianism* (Cambridge: Cambridge University Press, 2010), pp. 91, 190-4, 208-11; Whitelocke, iii.110.
9. NLW, MS 11440D (letterbook of Colonel John Jones), p. 151; B.S. Capp, *The Fifth Monarchy Men* (London: Faber, 1972), p. 80; McGregor and Reay (eds), *Radical Religion*, pp. 153-5; Reece, pp. 133-7; Kate Peters, 'Quakers and the politics of the army in the crisis of 1659', *P&P*, no. 231 (May 2016): 97-128.
10. Sprigge, pp. 321, 322, 88, 112; Bell, i.279, 284, 251. For more detailed accounts of Fairfax's religion, see 'Fairfax, Sir Thomas', *ODNB*; Andrew Hopper, *'Black Tom': Sir Thomas Fairfax and the English Revolution* (Manchester: Manchester University Press, 2007), pp. 155-68.
11. Whitelocke, i.191; *Crom. Army*, p. 327; NA, Wills, PROB11/300, fos 257-63^v (21 Feb. 1660). For more on Skippon's religion, see also 'Skippon, Philip', *ODNB*; Ismini Pells, *Philip Skippon and the British Civil Wars: The 'Christian Centurion'* (New York: Routledge, 2020).
12. Lomas-Carlyle, i.246.
13. Colin Davis, 'Cromwell's religion', in Morrill (ed.), *Oliver Cromwell*, p. 207; Lomas-Carlyle, i.204, 217, 385, 387; iii.247.
14. Blair Worden, 'Oliver Cromwell and the sin of Achan', in David Smith (ed.), *Cromwell and the Interregnum: The Essential Readings* (Oxford: Blackwell, 2003), pp. 49-54.
15. For references to expressions of religious fervour by individual officers, see *NMA*, p. 467, n. 40; *A Religious Retreat Sounded to a Religious Army* ([27 Aug.] 1647), TT E.404[34], p. 9; William Dell, *The Building and Glory of the Truely Spiritual Christian Church* (1646),

TT E.343[5], 'To the reader', sig. A5ᵛ; *England's Remembrancer*, [14 Jan.] 1646, TT E.513[33], p. 7; *Memoirs of the Life of Ambrose Barnes*, Surtees Soc., vol. 50 (1867), p. 107. The story, if true, points to the low velocity of seventeenth-century musket balls!

16. *Perf. Occurrences*, 22–29 May 1646, TT E.339[5], sig. X2ᵛ. For further evidence of the soldiers' appetite for sermons see Robert Bacon, *A Taste of the Spirit of God* ([6 July] 1652), TT 669[13], p. 27. The officers of the navy shared that conviction: *Crom. Navy*, p. 298. The episode at Dartmouth was meant to remind readers of the 'miraculous draught of fishes' in Luke 5:4–11: Hugh Peters, *Narration of the Taking of Dartmouth* (1646), TT E.318[6], pp. 3, 4; *Mr Peters Last Report of the English Wars* ([27 Aug.] 1646), TT E.351[12], pp. 4–5; Dell, *The Building and Glory*, sigs A4ᵛ–6ᵛ

17. Kishlansky, *Rise*, pp. 70–5; Anne Laurence, 'The Parliamentary Army Chaplains, 1642–1651' (DPhil thesis, Oxford University, 1982), pp. 54, 78, 84, 86–7; R.P. Stearns, *Strenuous Puritan: Hugh Peter, 1598–1660* (Champaign: University of Illinois Press, 1954), p. 249.

18. *Perf. Passages*, 16–23 Jul. 1645, TT E.262[27], p., 307; *Moderate Intell.*, 3–10 Jul. 1645, TT E.292[21], p. 149; *A Bloody Plot Discovered against the Independents* ([21 Jan.] 1647), TT E.371[18], sig. a1ᵛ; John Pounset, *Certaine Scruples from the Army* (1647), Bodl. Lib., Fairfax Deposit, pp. 1–2; *Perf. Diurnall . . . of the Armies*, 19–26 May 1651, TT E.785[31], p. 1,046; *The Humble Desires and Proposals of the Private Agitators of Colonel Hewsons Regiment* (1647), Codr. Lib., vx, 2.1/29, pp. 1–2.

19. Ian Gentles, 'The iconography of revolution: England 1642–1649', in Gentles, Morrill and Worden (eds), *Soldiers, Writers and Statesmen*, pp. 102–7; Kevin Sharpe, *Image Wars: Promoting Kings and Commonwealths in England 1603–1660* (New Haven and London: Yale University Press, 2010), pp. 364–9.

20. *Merc. Militaris*, 17–24 Apr. 1649, TT E.551[13], p. 15.

21. BL, Stowe MS 189, fo. 40. For an equally ardent letter from Thomas Margetts, secretary of the Northern Army, see Worc. MS 114, fo. 163; *Perf. Occurrences*, 28 Sept.–4 Oct. 1649, TT E.533[15], p. 1,276; MS Clar. 34, fo. 34; *Diary of Sir Archibald Johnston of Wariston*, ed. D.H. Fleming, SHS, 2nd ser., vol. 18 (1919), p. 59; NLW, MS 11440D, p. 43; Worc. MS 18, fos 8–8ᵛ, 9ᵛ.

22. Abbott, i.365; *Mr Peters Report from the Army to Parliament* [re Bridgwater] (26 July 1645), TT E.261[7], pp. 11–12; Sprigge, pp. 323, 212; Abbott, ii.378; *Perf. Diurnall*, 25 Dec. 1648–1 Jan. 1649, TT E.527[1], p. 2,276; *The Christian Soldiers Great Engine, or the Mysterious and Mighty Workings of Faith* (Oxford, 20 May 1649), TT E.531[31], pp. 5, 7, 18–19, 27.

23. Untitled broadside (28 Jan. 1653), Worc. Coll. pamphlet LR.8.58; Abbott, ii.153.

24. *GCW*, ii.192–3; *CJ*, iv.192–3; *LJ*, vii.337.

25. *The Letter Books of Sir Samuel Luke*, ed. H.G. Tibbutt, Bedfordshire Hist. Rec. Soc. (1963), p. 324; Edwards, *Gang.*, i.121–4, 215–16; ii.20; iii.41, 95, 96, 107, 174, 250, 251–2. For other examples, see *NMA*, pp. 101–2. W.G., *A Just Apologie for an Abused Armie* ([29 Jan.] 1646), TT E.372[22]; Edmund Chillenden, *Preaching without Ordination* ([2 Sept.] 1647), TT E.405[10], p. 6.

26. *Moderate Intell.*, 3–10 Jul. 1645, TT E.292[21], p. 147; *Mr Peters Message . . . to Parliament . . . of the Taking of Dartmouth* (1646), TT E.318[6], p. 5; Abbott, i.377; Edwards, *Gang.*, iii.45; *CP*, i.256.

27. Sprigge, pp. 19, 20, 65, 70, 80, 111 106–7, 126.

28. Ibid., p. 130; *Perf. Diurnall*, 3–10 Aug. 1646, TT E.511[29], p. 1,270; *Perf. Occurrences*, 10–17 Oct. 1645, TT E.266[3], sig. Vn1ᵛ; Reece, p. 35.

29. NLW, MS 11440D, pp. 89, 145; Richard Baxter, *Reliquiae Baxterianae*, ed. Matthew Sylvester (London: T. Parkhurst, 1696), p. 51; Sir William Brereton, *Cheshire's Success* (1643), Cambridge University Library, syn. 7.64.236.63: I thank John Morrill for this reference; Eric C. Walker, *William Dell: Master Puritan* (Cambridge: Heffer, 1970), p. 60; *Perf. Diurnall . . . of the Armies*, 8–15 Dec. 1651, TT E.791[27], pp. 1,506–8; ibid., 5–12 Jan. 1652, TT E.793[9], pp. 1,571–2; Worc. MS 18, fos 7–11ᵛ; untitled broadside (1650), Worc. Coll. pamphlet AA.8.3(127).

30. *CP*, i.254; Nickolls, p. 74. Ten signatories, but probably composed by Henry Ireton; see below, p. xxx.

31. Abbott, i.387; John Goodwin, *Right and Might Well Met* ([2 Jan.] 1649), TT E.536[28], p. 44; Sprigge, pp. 76. 84, 107, 144.

32. Ibid., p. 15; *Moderate Intell.*, 15–22 May 1645, TT E.285[7], p. 93; *A Narration of the Expedition to Taunton* (1645), TT E.285[10], p. 83; *Perf. Occurrences*, 4–11 Jul. 1645, TT E.262[20], sig. Ee4ᵛ; ibid., 16 Jan. 1646, TT E.506[1], sig. C3ᵛ. For other examples of blasphemy, see *NMA*, p. 470, n. 115. For the punishment of sexual offences, see also ibid., p. 470, n. 116; Heather MacLean, Ian Gentles and Micheál Ó Siochrú, 'Minutes of courts martial held in Dublin in the years 1651–3', *Archivium Hibernicum*, vol. 64 (2011): 56–164, p. 63; 'Dundee court-martial records, 1651', ed. Godfrey Davies, SHS, 2nd ser., vol. 19 (1919): 3–70, p. 33.

33. *Perf. Occurrences*, 30 May–6 June 1645, TT E.262[3], sig. Z1. The army chaplains naturally concurred in this high estimate of the army's conduct, but so did the neutral observer Ralph Josselin: *The Diary of Ralph Josselin 1616–1683*, ed. Alan Macfarlane, British Academy, Records of Social and Economic History, new ser., vol. 3 (1976), p. 91; *Scotish Dove*, 18–26 Feb. 1646, TT E.325[11], p. 572; *Perf. Occurrences*, 16 Jan. 1646, TT E.506[1], sig. C3ᵛ.

34. In addition, much iconoclasm had actually occurred a century earlier under Edward VI. Margaret Aston, *England's Iconoclasts, Volume I: Laws against Images* (Oxford: Clarendon Press, 1988), pp. 66–7; John R. Phillips, *The Reformation of Images* (Berkeley: University of California Press, 1973), p. 195; G.E. Aylmer and R. Cant (eds), *A History of York Minster* (Oxford: Clarendon Press, 1977), p. 439; V. Staley, *Hierurgia Anglicana*, revised edn, 3 vols (London: De La More Press, 1902–4), i.100, 185–6; G.B. Tatham, *The Puritans in Power* (Cambridge: Cambridge University Press, 1913), pp. 259–61; J.G. Cheshire, 'William Dowsing's destructions in Cambridgeshire', *Transactions of the Cambridgeshire and Huntingdonshire Archaeological Soc.*, vol. 3 (1914): 77–91, pp. 78, 81; Alexandra Walsham, *The Reformation of the Landscape: Religion, Identity, and Memory in Early Modern Britain and Ireland* (Oxford: Oxford University Press, 2011), p. 123.

35. *Notes and Queries*, vol. 12 (1867), p. 490; Keith Thomas, *Man and the Natural World* (London: Allen Lane, 1983), p. 109; Edwards, *Gang.*, ii.253; *Merc. Aulicus*, 10 May 1644, p. 977; ibid., 5 Oct. 1644, p. 1,187; Sir William Dugdale, *The Life, Diary and Correspondence of Sir William Dugdale*, ed. W. Hamper (London: Harding, Lepard and Co., 1827), p. 566.

36. Aston, *England's Iconoclasts*, pp. 63–5, 68–9, 71–3, 84–92; Bruno Ryves, *Mercurius Rusticus: or, the Country's Complaint* (London: R. Royston, 1685 edn), pp. 136–7, 139, 154; *Merc. Aulicus*, 21 Sept. 1644. p. 1,168; Dugdale, *Life*, pp. 557, 559, 566; *Notes and Queries*, vol. 18 (1873), p. 207; *CJ*, iii.583; HMC, *Lechmere*, pp. 46, 48; *The Victoria History of the County of Northampton* (London: Archibald Constable, 1902), vol. i.446, 449, 454; Aylmer and Cant (eds), *York Minster*, pp. 439–40.

37. Tatham, *Puritans in Power*, pp. 257–8; CLRO, Repertories, 59, fos 322ᵛ–3; *CSPD, 1641–43*, p. 372; *The Victoria History of the County of Gloucester* (London: Constable, 1907), vol. i.37. For additional references to military iconoclasm, see *NMA*, pp. 471–2, n. 132.

38. *Perf. Diurnall . . . of the Armies*, 17–24 Dec. 1649, TT E.533[31], p. 18; *Moderate Intell.*, 11–18 May 1648, TT E.443[21], p. 1,319; Hutchinson, p. 206; Roger Howell, 'The army and the English Revolution: The case of Robert Lilburne', *Archaeologia Aeliana*, 5th ser., vol. 9 (1981): 299–315, p. 310; idem, *Newcastle upon Tyne in the English Revolution* (London: Oxford University Press, 1967), pp. 232–3; Reece, pp. 141–2; John Lamont, *The Diary of Mr John Lamont of Newton* (Edinburgh, 1830), p. 47.

39. Reece, pp. 142, 168; Ian Gentles, 'London Levellers and the English Revolution: The Chidleys and their circle', *JEH*, vol. 29 (1978): 281–309, p. 287; *Perf. Occurrences*, 4–11 May 1649, TT E.530[1], p. 1,030; 1–8 June 1649, TT E.530[32], p. 1,088; *Merc. Politicus*, 20–27 June 1650, TT E.604[6], pp. 39–40; Howell, 'Robert Lilburne', p. 310.

40. *Perf. Diurnall . . . of the Armies*, 14–21 Oct. 1650, TT E.780[23], pp. 561, 565; Reece, pp. 117–18; John Musgrave, *A True and Exact Relation* (1650), TT E.619[10], p. 22; Bacon, *A Taste of the Spirit of God*, pp. 32–4; *Perf. Diurnall*, 18–25 Apr. 1653, TT E.211[22], p. 2,660.

41. Reece, p. 116; *A Letter from His Excellency Sir Thomas Fairfax ... conceraing* [sic] *the Abuses and Injuries Done to Certain Godly Ministers* (26 Aug. 1647), TT E.404[27]; *Hinc Illae Lachrymae* ([23 Dec.] 1647), TT E.421[6], pp. 11–13; *Man in the Moon*, 9–16 Jan. 1650, TT E.589[15], p. 302; *Kingdomes Faithfull and Impartiall Scout*, 2–9 Feb. 1649, TT E.542[2], p. 12.

42. Reece, pp. 123–9, 133–7; Ralph Farmer, *Sathan Inthron'd* (1656), TT E.897[2]; George Bishop et al., *The Cry of Blood* (1656), TT E.884[3]; Howell, 'Robert Lilburne', p. 303; *Moderate Intell.*, 6–13 Sept. 1649, TT E.575[19], p. 2,254; *Severall Procs in Parliament*, 29 Apr.–6 May 1652, TT E.794[33], pp. 2,123–4; ibid., 15–21 May 1651, TT E.785[28], p. 1,308.

43. Ludlow, *Voyce*, pp. 149–50.

44. NLW, MS 11440D, p. 22; T. Pape, *Newcastle-under-Lyme in Tudor and Early Stuart Times* (Manchester: Manchester University Press, 1938), p. 173; Bell, i.251; Abbott, i.429.

45. Ibid., i.371; Lomas–Carlyle, i.248.

46. Nickolls, p. 72; untitled broadside (28 Jan. 1653), Worc. Coll. pamphlet LR.8.58; *CP*, iv.220.

47. Christopher Hill, *The Experience of Defeat: Milton and Some Contemporaries* (London: Faber, 1984), pp. 70–8, especially p. 71; C.H. Firth, 'Memoir of Major-General Thomas Harrison', *Procs of the American Antiquarian Soc.*, new ser., vol. 8 (1893): 390–464, p. 442.

48. Ludlow, *Voyce*, pp. 248–50, 149; Hill, *Experience of Defeat*, pp. 77–8.

5 THE POLITICAL WARS, 1646–48 – PART I: FROM THE KING'S SURRENDER TO THE ASSAULT ON PARLIAMENT

1. *Perf. Passages*, 19–25 Nov. 1645, TT E.366[22], p. 450; *Perf. Occurrences*, 31 Oct.–7 Nov. 1645, TT E.266[14], sig. Yy1ᵛ; CCJ 40, fos 178ᵛ–82ᵛ.

2. *Plain English: or, the Sectaries Anatomized* ([17 Aug.] 1646), TT E.350[11], pp. 10–11; *Mr Peters Last Report of the English Wars*.

3. *LJ*, viii.425; Montereul, i.272; Kishlansky, *Rise*, p. 117; *CJ*, iv. 631–2; Ludlow, *Memoirs*, i.141.

4. Zachary Grey, *Impartial Examination* (London: Bettesworth and Hitch, 1737), appendix, pp. 26–46; MS Tanner 59 (Lenthall Papers), fo. 428.

5. Holles, p. 70, 45; David Evans, 'The Civil War Career of Major-General Edward Massie (1642–1647)' (PhD thesis, University of London, 1995); Cary, i.101; *Scotish Dove*, 24 June–1 July 1645, TT E.342[11], p. 711; *CJ*, iv.581, 652; Baxter, *Reliquiae Baxterianae*, p. 59; Juxon, *Journal*, p. 135; Montereul, i.251, 259, 267–8, 317.

6. MS Clar. 29, fo. 72ᵛ.

7. Juxon, *Journal*, p. 140; Ian Gentles, 'The sales of bishops' lands in the English Revolution, 1646–60', *EHR*, vol. 95 (1980): 573–96, pp. 574–5, 591.

8. CCJ 40, fos 200, 204; *Plain English: or, the Sectaries Anatomized*, p. 10; *A Copy of a Letter Written from Northampton Containing a True Relation of the Souldier's Preaching and Murdering a Woman* (28 Jan. 1647), Worc. Coll. pamphlet BB.8.16/14; *Perf. Diurnall*, 11–18 Jan. 1647, TT E.513[34], p. 1,453; *A Bloody Plot Discovered; Englands Remembrancer* ([14 Jan.] 1647), TT E.513[33], p. 3; Montereul, i.372; MS Clar. 29, fo. 161ᵛ.

9. Ibid.; *CJ*, v.25. A payment of £150 to a Mr Partridge 'for the losses he sustained by *Anglia Rediviva*' indicates that the book found few readers in London: Chequers Court, Bucks, Chequers MS 782, fo. 42ᵛ.

10. NA, PRO31/3/82, fo. 4ᵛ; MS Clar. 29, fos 67ᵛ, 68ᵛ; Richard Lawrence, *The Anti-Christian Presbyter: or, Antichrist Transformed* ([9 Jan.] 1647), TT E.370[22].

11. *Nicholas Papers, Volume I: 1641–1652*, ed. George F. Warner, Camden Soc., new ser., vol. 9 (1886), p. 75; MS Clar. 29, fo. 97; Gentles, 'Arrears of pay', pp. 52–63; HMC, *Portland*, i.447.

12. NA, PRO31/3/82, fo. 124ᵛ; MS Tanner 59, fo. 786; Add. MS 19399 (Original Letters, 1646–1768), fo. 1; *CP*, i.58; *Reg. Hist.*, pp. 104, 129, 293; *CJ*, v.91, 107–8.

13. CCJ 40, fo. 207; Wolfe, p. 138.

14. *An Apollogie of the Souldiers* (26 Mar. 1647), TT E.381[18], pp. 1–2; Polly Ha, 'Revolutionizing the New Model Army: Ecclesiastical independence, social justice, and political legitimacy', *Journal of the History of Ideas*, vol. 81 (2021): 531–53, pp. 543, 546, 548. I am grateful to Dr Ha for letting me read this article in advance of publication. *The Petition of the Officers and Souldiers . . . [of] Sir Thomas Fairfax* (2 Apr. 1647), TT E.383[12], sig. A2r–v; Michael A. Norris, 'Edward Sexby, John Reynolds and Edmund Chillenden: Agitators, "sectarian grandees" and the relations of the New Model Army with London in the spring of 1647', *BIHR*, vol. 76 (2003): 30–53, p. 45.
15. *The Petition of the Officers and Souldiers . . . [of] Sir Thomas Fairfax*, sig. A3.
16. *Kingdomes Weekly Intell.*, 23–30 Mar. 1647, TT E.383[2], p. 475; *Army Book of Declarations*, TT E.409[25], p. 5; MS Tanner 58, fo. 28; *CJ*, v.127; *OPH*, xv.344–5; Ludlow, *Memoirs*, i.149–50; Sir William Waller, *Vindication* (London: J. Debrett, 1793), p. 62; *S&S*, pp. 37–8.
17. MS Clar. 29, fo. 165ᵛ; HMC, *Egmont*, i.384, 389; *NMA*, p. 481, n. 83.
18. A member of neither the New Model nor the London militia, his military background is obscure. He was a continental soldier, who would by July 1647 be appointed adjutant-general of the New Model horse, a position that he held only briefly: *Moderate Intell.*, 23–30 Oct. 1645, TT E.307[22], p. 175; Worc. MS 41, fo. 158. Tulidah had been relieved of his post by Nov. 1647 if not earlier: Worc. MS 67, fo. 27; SP 28/48, fo. 402; Chequers MS 782, fo. 45; *CSPD, 1650*, p. 565.
19. HMC, *Portland*, iii.156; *CP*, i.5n.
20. *NMA*, p. 153; *S&S*, pp. 69–71.
21. *Perf. Diurnall*, 12–19 Apr. 1647, TT E.515[8], p. 1,558.
22. *CP*, i.6; BL, Loan MS 29/175, fos 52ᵛ-3; *Weekly Account*, 21–9 Apr. 1647, TT E.385[10], sig. R2ᵛ.
23. *S&S*, p. 54.
24. Lawrence Nagel, 'The Militia of London, 1641–1649' (PhD thesis, University of London, 1982), pp. 241–5; Juxon, *Journal*, pp. 152–3, 156–7; CCJ 40, fos 200, 207ᵛ, 215ᵛ; *A&O*, i.928; John Lilburne, *Rash Oaths Unwarrantable* (3 May 1647), TT E.393[39], p. 45; *Army Book of Declarations*, p. 91.
25. *The Apologie of the Common Souldiers* (3 May 1647), TT E.385[18], pp. 2–4.
26. *A Second Apologie of All the Private Souldiers* (n.d.), TT E.385[18], pp. 5, 7–8; Ha, 'Revolutionizing the New Model Army', p. 542.
27. *The Petition and Vindication of the Officers . . . to the House of Commons* (27 Apr. 1647), TT E.385[19], p. 1; *CJ*, v.154–5; *A New Found Stratagem Framed in the Old Forge of Machivilisme . . . to Destroy the Army* (4 Apr. 1647), TT E.384[11]; *S&S*, pp. 56–7; HMC, *House of Lords 1644–47*, p. 171; *LJ*, ix.152; NA, HLRO, Main Papers, 27 April 1647, fo. 61.
28. *A Plea for the Late Agents of the Army* (1647), Worc. Coll. pamphlet AA.1.19/147.
29. Norris, 'Edward Sexby', pp. 46–8.
30. *CP*, i.430–1; *Perf. Weekly Account*, 28 Apr.–5 May 1647, no. 18, TT E.386[3], sig. 2ʳ; Holles, p. 89.
31. *Perf. Diurnall*, 26 Apr.–3 May 1647, TT E.515[10], p. 1,569; Worc. MS 41, fo.18–18ᵛ; John Lilburne, *Ionah's Cry out of the Whale's Belly* (26 July 1647), TT E.400[5], p. 9.
32. *CP*, i.22–4; John Rees, *The Leveller Revolution: Radical Political Organisation in England, 1640–1650* (London: Verso, 2016), p. 181. On 30 August Lieutenant Chillenden was paid £78 17s 'for Mr Coe's printing press'; it had probably been acquired some months earlier: Chequers MS 782, fo. 43ᵛ.
33. *Perf. Occurrences*, 7–14 May 1647, TT E.387[5], p. 152; Worc. MS 41, fo. 113.
34. Ibid., fos 120, 124; *CP*, i.36–8, 42–3; *Perf. Diurnall*, 10–27 May 1647, TT E.515[12], p. 1,588. The editor, Samuel Pecke, was fed his information by Secretary Rushworth: *NMA*, p. 405, n. 177.
35. For the importance of honour to the army, see Kishlansky, *Rise*, pp. 212–15. *A Perfect and True Copy of the Severall Grievances of the Army* (16 May 1647), TT E.390[3]; *Army Book of Declarations*, pp. 17–21.
36. *CP*, i.58, 72, 76–7, 96–9; Juxon, *Journal*, p. 157.
37. Worc. MS 41, fo. 131ᵛ; *Moderate Intell.*, 13–20 May 1647, TT E.388[13], p. 1,079.

38. *LJ*, ix.245–6; Montereul, ii.160.
39. *Perf. Diurnall*, 17–24 May 1647, TT E.515[14], p. 1,598; MS Clar. 29, fo. 227. For the history of the three radical London petitions, see William Walwyn, *Gold Tried in Fire* (1647), printed in Jack R. McMichael and Barbara Taft (eds), *The Writings of William Walwyn* (Athens, GA and London: University of Georgia Press, 1989), pp. 276–93; Worc. MS 41, fo. 132ᵛ.
40. SP 21/26, fos 72–3; Worc. MS 41, fo. 132ᵛ; *Perf. Diurnall*, 17–24 May 1647, TT E.515[14], p. 1,598; MS Clar. 29, fo. 229.
41. *CJ*, v.183, 188; *LJ*, ix.207–8; Add. MS 10114 (Harington's diary), fo. 25; Waller, *Vindication*, pp. 64–5, 67; *CJ*, v.207; *CP*, i.168–9; Montereul, ii.164; *Perf. Diurnall*, 7–14 June 1647, TT E.515[19], p. 1,622; *CSPI, 1647–60*, pp. 753, 754; SP 28/124, fo. 337ᵛ, Holles, p. 121; *CSPD Addenda, 1625–49*, pp. 709–11; Add. MS 37344 (Whitelocke's annals), fos 92, 93ᵛ; Valerie Pearl, 'London's counter-revolution', in G.E. Aylmer (ed.), *The Interregnum: The Quest for Settlement, 1646–1660* (London: Macmillan, 1972), pp. 29–56, pp. 44–56.
42. *A Vindication of a Hundred Sixty Seven Officers that Are Come Off from the Army* ([26 June] 1647), TT E.394[3]; MS Tanner 58, fo. 153; Juxon, *Journal*, p. 161; *NMA*, pp. 167–8; *Perf. Diurnall*, 24–31 May 1647, TT E.515[15], p. 1,603; MS Clar. 29, fos 229–9ᵛ; Holles, pp. 95–6; *Perf. Diurnall*, 31 May–7 June 1647, TT E.515[17], p. 1,608.
43. McMichael and Taft (eds), *Walwyn*, p. 392; Rees, *Leveller Revolution*, p. 183; John Harris, *The Grand Designe* (8 Dec. 1647), TT E.419[15], p. 3; *Windsor Projects and Westminster Practices* ([15 May] 1648), TT E.442[10], p. 2.
44. *Perf. Diurnall*, 31 May–7 June 1647, TT E.515[17], p. 1,617; *S&S*, pp. 106–9.
45. Add. MS 31116 (Whitacre's diary), fo. 312ᵛ.
46. Rushworth, vi.516; *OPH*, xv.416–19; HMC, *De L'Isle and Dudley*, vi.567; *A True and Impartial Narration Concerning the Armies Preservation of the King* ([4 June] 1647), TT E.393[1].
47. Rushworth, vi.516–17; *S&S*, p. 114.
48. *CP*, i.125; *A Narrative of the Causes of the Late Lord General's Anger against Lieutenant-Colonel Joyce* (1659), TT 669.f.21[50].
49. Clarendon, *History*, iv.223; Harris, *The Grand Designe*, p. 3; Holles, p. 246. It is implicit in Rushworth's letter of 9 June to Ferdinando, Lord Fairfax that the seizure of the king was carried out with the full support of the army high command: Add. MS 18979, fo. 238.
50. T. Fairfax, *Short Memorials of Thomas Lord Fairfax* (London: Ri. Chiswell, 1699), pp. 103–19, 125.
51. Montereul, ii.160; Holles, p. 160; Add. MS 37344 (Whitelocke's annals), fo.88ᵛ; Add. MS 34253 (Civil War papers), fo. 59.
52. Robert Harley is an example of one who distanced himself from the Presbyterian leaders: BL, Loan MS 29/122, fo. 16; I owe this reference to Michael Mahoney. CCJ 40, fo. 224; Worc. MS 41, fos 79–9ᵛ, 96ᵛ.
53. Pearl, 'London's counter-revolution', pp. 44–8; Waller, *Vindication*, p. 162; CCJ 40, fos 231ᵛ–2ᵛ.
54. Cary, i.293; *CP*, i.168; Add. MS 37344, fo. 105ᵛ.
55. *CP*, i.428–9; Nickolls, p. 52; Montereul, ii.168; Add. MS 37344, fos 96, 98; *Perf. Diurnall*, 12–19 July 1647, TT E.518[6], p. 1,663; Stevenson, pp. 89–91; *LJ*, ix.246, 247–8; *CJ*, v.197, 202; Juxon, *Journal*, pp. 198–9.
56. *A Plea for the Late Agents of the Army*, p. 4; *The Humble Representation* (4 June) and the *Solemne Engagement* (5 June) were published together: E.392[9].
57. Ha, 'Revolutionizing the New Model Army', p. 548.
58. In addition, members of Fairfax's Council of War would attend the Reading and Putney debates and take part in their deliberations. I owe a debt of gratitude to the late Austin Woolrych for discussion on this point.
59. *The Copy of a Letter Printed at Newcastle, July the 6, 1647*, TT E.398[16], pp. 2–3. See also *A Copie of that Letter . . . to the Souldiery of Lancashire* ([13 July] 1647), TT E.398[7]; Add. MS 18789, fos 242–4; Cary, i.282–4; Bell, i. 363–4.
60. Rolphe, who acted as a paymaster to the agitators, received £150 in two instalments. A payment of £30 to the agitators who arrested Colonel Poynts showed that this action was

approved by headquarters. Over a five-month period (June–Nov.) the agitators received over £1,000 for their expenses: Thoresby Soc., Leeds, William Clarke's Account Book, MS SD ix, unfol. I am indebted to Henry Reece for drawing my attention to this source, and to the librarian, Mrs J. Mary D. Foster, for permission to cite it. It has also been printed – with a number of errors – in Thoresby Soc., vol. 11 (1902). A contemporary transcript exists at Chequers MS 782. It is less useful than the original because it does not reproduce the word 'agitator(s)', which has been crossed out in several entries in the original.

61. *S&S*, p. 130; *A Charge Delivered in the Name of the Army* (14 June 1647), TT E.393[5]; Montereul, ii.179; Juxon, *Journal*, p. 161; Bell, i.359; MS Clar. 29, fo. 249; BL, Egerton MS 1048, fos 51–80, printed in *Army Book of Declarations*, pp. 79–94, and in TT E.397[17].
62. *S&S*, p. 124; Montereul, ii.164; *Severall Letters Sent from … Sir Thomas Fairfax … to London* ([26 June] 1647), TT E.394[3], pp. 2–3; *Perf. Diurnall*, 7–14 June 1647, TT E.525[19]; *CSPI, 1647–60*, pp. 753–4; MS Clar. 29, fo. 236; *LJ*, ix.279; CCJ 40, fo. 224; Worc. MS 41, fos 43, 79, 96ᵛ.
63. *Army Book of Declarations*, TT E.409[25], p. 39.
64. Ibid., pp. 40–6; *S&S*, pp. 126–30; *The Remonstrance of the Representations of the Army* ([21 June] 1647), TT E.393[17]; *An Humble Remonstrance from … the Army* (23 June 1647), TT E.393[36], pp. 11–15.
65. *CJ*, v.226; *Army Book of Declarations*, p. 71. For other conciliatory gestures, see *A Letter from … a Councel of War at Uxbridge* (29 June 1647), TT E.396[4]; *LJ*, ix.313.
66. *CJ*, v.248; *LJ*, ix.339; Bell, i.368.
67. *CP*, i.170–5, 205.
68. Ibid., i.202, 205, 209.
69. David Como, 'Making "the Heads of the Proposals"': The king, the army, the Levellers and the roads to Putney', *EHR*, vol. 135 (2020): 1,387–432, pp. 1,387, 1,390: I am grateful to David Como for permission to read and cite his article in advance of publication. J.S.A. Adamson, 'The English nobility and the projected settlement of 1647', *HJ*, vol. 30 (1987): 567–602, pp. 571–9, 601. Rushworth tells us that the Heads were prepared, not by Saye, Wharton et al., but by the army: Bell, i.368; see also *S&S*, p. 152.
70. *Const. Docs*, pp. 316–26. Ironically they also 'failed ignominiously and comprehensively' because they satisfied no one – Parliament, king, most of the army, and the army's radical friends in London: Como, 'Making "the Heads of the Proposals"', p. 1,422.
71. *S&S*, p. 164, n. 81; Como, 'Making "the Heads of the Proposals"'; William Walwyn, *Walwyns Just Defence* (1649), printed in McMichael and Taft (eds), *Walwyn*, pp. 423–4, 430; Rachel Foxley, *The Levellers: Radical Political Thought in the English Revolution* (Manchester: Manchester University Press, 2013), pp. 154, 157, 185, n. 21; Rees, *Leveller Revolution*, pp. 187–91.
72. Ludlow, *Memoirs*, i.151.
73. Adamson, 'The English nobility and the projected settlement of 1647', pp. 555–8; *S&S*, p. 179.
74. *CP*, i.151 ff; Worc. MS 41, fo. 176; Dyve, p. 68.
75. *CJ*, v. 254; Rushworth, vi. 634–5; MS Clar. 30, fo. 12; Juxon, *Journal*, p. 162.
76. *Perf. Summary*, 26 July–2 August 1647, E518[13], pp. 12–13; Ludlow, *Memoirs*, i.161; Bell, i.381; Waller, *Vindication*, pp. 182–3; Add. MS 37344, fo. 100.
77. Pearl, 'London's counter-revolution', p. 51; Kishlansky, *Rise*, pp. 267–8; Adamson, 'The English nobility and the projected settlement of 1647', pp. 567–8, 576; *S&S*, pp. 168–72; *Sydney Papers*, pp. 15–16; Dyve, p. 72; *NMA*, p. 188; Holles, pp. 152, 153–4; Add. MS, 37344, fo. 101.

6 THE POLITICAL WARS, 1646–48 – PART II: FROM THE OCCUPATION OF LONDON TO THE SECOND CIVIL WAR

1. According to one report, London militia officers were issued secret commissions to 'force, kill, slay and destroy', in order to keep the New Model at bay: Grey, *Impartial Examination*, pp. 124–5; Worc. MS 110, unfol. *NMA*, pp. 190–1.

2. CCJ 40, fo. 243ᵛ.

3. *NMA*, p. 494, nn. 16–18; Juxon, *Journal*, p. 167; MS Clar. 30, fo. 24; *Perf. Diurnall*, 2–9 Aug. 1647, TT E.518[16], p. 1,685.

4. Tatton Park, Cheshire, Diary of Nehemiah Wallington, 1644–48, MS 104, p. 536; Holles, p. 159; Add. MS 37344, fo. 103; CCJ 40, fo. 250ᵛ.

5. The figure of 15,000, given by Bellièvre, is if anything too high: NA, PRO31/3/84, fo. 72. Cf. *GCW*, iii.344; *NMA*, p. 494, n. 24. BL, microfilm 330 (Duke of Northumberland, Alnwick MS 548), fo. 1; Gloucestershire RO, microfilm 285, Barwick MS 33b (I owe this reference to David Evans); *Perf. Diurnall*, 2–9 Aug. 1647, TT E.518[16], p. 1,691; *Moderne Intell.*, 19–26 Aug. 1647, TT E.404[28], p. 10; *A Speedy Hue and Crie after Generall Massie, Col. Poyntz, Sir Robert Pye, William Pryn, and Many Other New-modelled Reformadoes* ([10 Aug.] 1647), TT E.401[20].

6. *A Paire of Spectacles for the Cities* ([4 Dec.] 1647), TT E.419[9], p. 8; NA, HLRO, Main Papers, 21, 23 Aug. 1647, fos 86–8; Adamson, 'The English nobility and the projected settlement of 1647', p. 578; MS Clar. 30, fo. 33.

7. In the words of a hostile royalist witness, 'Yea, and the common people through the whole City filling the streets . . . admiring and applauding with the highest panegyrics that their greedily-gazing eyes could manifest . . .': *Perf. Summary*, 2–9 Aug. 1647, TT E.518[15], p. 24; Juxon, *Journal*, p. 168; Wallington, MS Diary, pp. 539–40; MS Clar. 30, fo. 33; *Seria Exercitus* ([4 Dec.] 1647), TT E.419[6], p. 30.

8. The speaker of the Lords, the earl of Manchester, invited Fairfax to dine at his house in Chelsea with several other peers, presumably of the Saye–Wharton group: *Two Speeches Made by the Speakers of Both Houses of Parliament to His Excellency Sir Thomas Fairfax Generall* ([9 Aug.] 1647), TT E.401[15], pp. 3–4; Worc. MS 67, p. 13; Juxon, *Journal*, p. 169; CCJ 40, fos 251, 252ᵛ; *A Continuation of Certain Speciall and Remarkable Passages*, 14–21 Aug. 1647, TT E.404[5], sig. H4ᵛ.

9. MS Clar. 30, fo. 33ᵛ; *LJ*, ix.375; *CJ*, v.269–70, 271, 273, 275, 279; HMC, *Egmont*, i.443–4; *S&S*, pp. 184–5; Adamson, 'The English nobility and the projected settlement of 1647', pp. 579–80; idem, 'Politics and the nobility in civil war England', *HJ*, vol. 34 (1991): 231–55, pp. 246–7.

10. *The Humble Address of the Agitators . . . on the 5 of this Instant August* ([14 Aug.] 1647), TT E.402[8]; *S&S*, p. 193; *Two Letters from His Excellency Sir Thomas Fairfax with . . . a Remonstrance of . . . the Army* (20 Aug. 1647), TT E.402[28], pp. 23–4; *The Machivilian Cromwellist and Hypocritical Perfidious New Statist* (1648), Bodl. Lib., Fairfax Deposit, Tracts 38/21, p. 6; *Perf. Occurrences*, 5–12 Nov. 1647, TT E.520[4], p. 305.

11. Ibid., 24 Sept.–1 Oct. 1647, TT E.518[39], pp. 266–7; *A Charge and Impeachment of High Treason against Sir John Geyer, Lord Major of London [et al.]* (1647), Bodl. Lib., Fairfax Deposit, Wing E2536+; *The Impeachment by the House of Commons against the Lord Major of the City of London and Divers Other[s] . . .* [1647], Bodl. Lib., Fairfax Deposit, Wing E2587+; Ian Gentles, 'The struggle for London in the Second Civil War', *HJ*, vol. 26 (1983): 277–305, p. 284; CCJ 40, fos 254, 255–255ᵛ; NA, Exchequer, E101/67/11A, fo. 112.

12. *Perf. Diurnall*, 16–23 Aug. 1647, TT E.518[21], p. 1,716; *Perf. Occurrences*, 27 Aug.–3 Sept. 1647, TT E.517[26], p. 235; *A Second Letter from the Agitators* ([July] 1647), Codr. Lib., xv, 2.3/26, p. 2; Richard Overton, *Eighteene Reasons Propounded to the Soldiers . . . Why They Ought to Continue the Several Adjutators* (11 Aug. 1647), BL, 534.d.10; William Walwyn, *Walwyns Just Defence* (1649), printed in McMichael and Taft (eds), *Walwyn*, pp. 392–3; John Lilburne, *The Ivst Mans Ivstification* ([18 Sept.] 1647), TT E.407[26]. Wildman played an active role in the Putney debates of Oct.–Nov.: Foxley, *Levellers*, p. 154; Rees, *Leveller Revolution*, pp. 178–91; *A Religious Retreat Sounded to a Religious Army* ([27 Aug.] 1647), TT E.404[34], p. 12; *The Army Brought to the Barre* ([17 Sept.] 1647), TT E.407[22], p. 8; Worc. MS 66 (Minute Book of the Committee of General Officers), fo. 1.

13. The members of the Committee of General Officers were Cromwell, Thomas Hammond, Henry Ireton, Colonels Thomas Rainborowe, Charles Fleetwood, Robert Hammond, Sir

Hardress Waller, Nathaniel Rich, Dr William Stane, Scoutmaster-General Leonard Watson, Quartermaster-General Thomas Ireton and Adjutant-General Richard Deane: Worc. MS 66, fos 6, 12, 15ᵛ. The extent of radical influence is seen in the recommendations that Cornet Joyce be promoted captain in Fleetwood's regiment, that Captain Reynolds become governor of Weymouth and Melcombe Fort, Dorset, that John Wildman be made governor of Poole and Brownsea Castle, and that Major Alexander Tulidah be commissioned governor of Hereford Castle. Fairfax later agreed to Joyce's commission as governor of Southsea Castle and captain of a company in Portsmouth: Worc. MS 66, fos 13ᵛ, 16ᵛ. Dyve, pp. 84–5, 89.

14. A month's wages had been paid in Aug., but nothing in Sept.: SP 28/47, fos 281–480. Another month's pay was received in Oct.: SP 28/48, fos 90, 155, *et passim*; John Lilburne, *The Ivglers Discovered* (8 Sept. 1647), TT E.409[22], pp. 10–11; Dyve, pp. 85–6.

15. Rushworth, vii.859–60; *A Copy of a Letter Sent by the Agents of Severall Regiments . . . to all the Souldiers . . .* (11 Nov. 1647), TT E.413[18]. Ireton's regiment found civilians willing to represent Hampshire, and also set about organising the western garrisons between Bristol and Southampton: *A Copy of a Letter from the Com. Gen. Regiment to the Convention of Agents Residing in London* (11 Nov. 1647), Worc. Coll. pamphlet AA.1.19/145; *NMA*, p. 199 and nn. 76–8. Lists of the new agents can be found in TT E.411[9], TT E.412[21], TT E.413[18], and in Worc. Coll. pamphlet AA.1.19/145.

16. When the men of Captain Cannon's troop in Whalley's regiment wrote to one agent (William Russell, 'cleric'), ordering him to leave London and re-join the other agitators at headquarters, they accused him of acting 'contrary to our intentions *when we made choice of you*' (my emphasis): *A Copy of a Letter from the Com. Gen. Regiment*; *Perf. Weekly Account*, 10–17 Nov. 1647, TT E.416[2], sig. V3ᵛ.

17. *S&S*, p. 200; *Perf. Diurnall*, 11–18 Oct. 1647, TT E.518[45], p. 1,768; *Proposalls from . . . the Councell of the Army, by Way of Address to the Parliament* (17 Oct. 1647), TT E.411[5].

18. *The Case of the Armie Truly Stated*, in Wolfe, pp. 206–7, 220. I agree with John Morrill and Philip Baker that the likeliest author of the *Case* was Edward Sexby. Michael Mendle (ed.), *The Putney Debates of 1647: The Army, the Levellers and the English State* (Cambridge: Cambridge University Press, 2001), pp. 103–24.

19. *The Case of the Armie*, pp. 199–218.

20. I owe this point about the anti-army subtext of the Leveller message to John Morrill's brilliant article, 'The army revolt of 1647', in his *Nature of the English Revolution*, pp. 308–9, 320, 326–9.

21. *Propositions of the Adjutators of the Five Regiments* ([20 Oct.] 1647), TT E.411[13]; *CP*, i.342–3; Philip Baker, ' "A despicable contemptible generation of men"?: Cromwell and the Levellers', in Patrick Little (ed.), *Oliver Cromwell: New Perspectives* (Basingstoke: Palgrave Macmillan, 2009), p. 101; Rushworth, vii.150; *Papers from the Armie* (22 Oct. 1647), TT E.411[19], p. 4.

22. Wolfe, p. 234; Elliot Vernon and Philip Baker, 'What was the first *Agreement of the People*?', *HJ*, vol. 53 (2010): 39–59, pp. 56–8; D.E. Underdown, 'The parliamentary diary of John Boys, 1647–8', *BIHR*, vol. 39 (1966): 141–64, p. 152.

23. *S&S*, p. 213.

24. Rushworth, vii.857. The four were Matthew Wealey, William Russell, Richard Seale and William Sampson: *NMA*, p. 499, n. 99.

25. *CP*, i.236–7.

26. Ibid., i.244–7.

27. Ibid., i.254.

28. Other conciliatory words were spoken by Nicholas Lockyer, Captain John Merriman, Captain Robert Everard and the extremely pious Lieutenant Edmund Chillenden: ibid., i.277–8.

29. Goffe's texts were Revelation 17–20 and Numbers 14: ibid., i.280, 281–5, 287.

30. Ibid., i.297.

31. Ibid., i.301–2; Derek Hirst, *The Representative of the People? Voters and Voting in England under the Early Stuarts* (Cambridge: Cambridge University Press, 1975), pp. 22, 63, 96.

32. *CP*, i.304, 305, 309, 318, 320, 323.

33. Ibid., i.333–4, 342; *NMA*, p. 501, nn. 134–5; McMichael and Taft (eds), *Walwyn*, pp. 31, 34; Keith Thomas, 'The Levellers and the franchise', in Aylmer (ed.), *The Interregnum*, pp. 57–78; Como, 'Making "the Heads of the Proposals"', p. 1,424.

34. *CP*, i.359–61; *Perf. Occurrences*, 29 Oct.–5 Nov. 1647, TT E.520[2], p. 306; *A Copy of a Letter Sent by the Agents*, pp. 1–2; *S&S*, pp. 243–4.

35. *CP*, i.363–7, 407–11; *S&S*, p. 247.

36. *CP*, i.367–71. Oliver was citing Saint Paul (Philippians 3:8).

37. Sexby was joined by John Jubbs, Leveller sympathiser and lieutenant-colonel of Hewson's regiment, who suggested obliquely that the king was 'guilty of all the bloodshed, vast expense of treasure and ruin that hath been occasioned by all the wars both of England and Ireland'. Lieutenant-Colonel William Goffe, always respectful of Cromwell, diffidently revealed that 'a voice from heaven' had informed him that 'we have sinned against the Lord in tampering with his enemies': ibid., i.372–3, 374, 377, 383; SP 28/257, unfol.; *Apology unto the Officers of the Lord General's Army* ([4 May] 1649), TT E.552[28].

38. Rushworth, vii.861.

39. Ibid., vii.863; *Perf. Diurnall*, 1–8 Nov. 1647, TT E.520[3], pp. 1,774–5; *CP*, i.414n; *S&S*, p. 260; *A Call to All the Souldiers of the Army* ([29 Oct.] 1647), TT E.412[10], p. 7 (italics in the original); *An Alarum to the Headquarters* ([9 Nov.] 1647), TT E.413[10], p. 4; Dyve, p. 95; *Perf. Occurrences*, 5–12 Nov. 1647, TT E.520[4], p. 305. This report, from one of the more reliable newsbooks, about Lilburne walking freely in London, is not mentioned by Michael Braddick in his recent biography of Lilburne, *The Common Freedom of the People: John Lilburne and the English Revolution* (Oxford: Oxford University Press, 2018).

40. Wolfe, p. 225; *The Humble Remonstrance and Desires of [Hewson's Regiment]* (4 Nov. 1647), TT E.413[6], pp. 2–3. The petition to Fairfax, which does not survive, was later referred to by Cornet Henry Denne in *The Levellers Designe* ([24 May] 1649), TT E.556[11], p. 4. In 1649 the defeated Levellers also implicitly admitted that the members of the five horse regiments who had first chosen new agents had petitioned to have them sent back: *Sea Green and Blue* ([6 June] 1649), TT E.559[1], p. 11; *CJ*, v.353; *CP*, i.413–14.

41. Ibid., i.417; HMC, *Portland*, i.441; *OPH*, xvi.328; Edward Whalley, *A More Full Relation of the Manner and Circumstances of His Majesties Departure from Hampton Court* ([22 Nov.] 1647), TT E.416[23], p. 6; *Perf. Occurrences*, 12–19 Nov. 1647, TT E.520[6], p. 313.

42. *NMA*, 503, n. 180; Grey, *Impartial Examination*, appendix, p. 130; *A New Declaration from Eight Regiments in the Army* (22 Nov. 1647), TT E.416[35], p. 3.

43. *A Copy of a Letter Sent by the Agents*, pp. 2–3. In the end only three horse regiments and one of foot were won over – Harrison's, Ireton's, Twisleton's, and Lilburne's.

44. *S&S*, pp. 228–9; *The Iustice of the Army Vindicated against Evildoers* (5 June 1649), TT E.558[14], pp. 1–3; [John Canne], *The Discoverer . . . the Second Part* ([13 July] 1649), TT E.564[9], pp. 52–4; *Perf. Occurrences*, 12–19 Nov. 1647, TT E.520[6], p. 313; Mark Kishlansky, 'What Happened at Ware?', *HJ*, vol. 25 (1982): 827–39, pp. 833–4.

45. *A Full Relation of the Proceedings at the Rendezvous in Corkbush Field* (15 Nov. 1647), TT E.414[13], pp. 4–5; *LJ*, ix.528; *A Full Relation . . . of Corkbush Field*, p. 6; Rushworth, vii.876; *CJ*, v.378; Worc. MS 41, fo. 167, and MS 110, unfol. (30 Nov. 1647). Other arrests included Jeremy Ives, an agitator from Waller's regiment, and three London agents: Samuel Chidley, William Larner and Captain Taylor (perhaps from the Southwark trained bands): Gentles, 'London Levellers and the English Revolution', p. 291; *Merc. Pragmaticus*, 16–22 Nov. 1647, TT E.416[19], p. 73; *Perf. Occurrences*, 12–19 Nov. 1647, TT E.520[6], p. 318; *Merc. Anti-Pragmaticus*, 18–25 Nov. 1647, TT E.416[38], p. 4.

46. *NMA*, p. 504, n. 195; *S&S*, p. 282; *A Full Relation . . . of Corkbush Field*, p. 6; *A Remonstrance from His Excellency Sir Thomas Fairfax and His Councell of Warre* (15 Nov. 1647), TT E.414[14]; John Wildman, *Putney Proiects* ([30 Dec.] 1647), TT E.421[19], p. 97.

47. *The Iustice of the Army Vindicated*, p. 6; *NMA*, p. 504, n. 201.

48. [Canne], *The Discoverer . . . the Second Part*, p. 55; *LJ*, ix.528.

49. Underdown, 'Parliamentary diary of John Boys', pp. 152–3.

50. *A Letter from His Excellency Sir Thomas Fairfax to . . . the City of London* ([19 Nov.] 1647), TT E.416[18]; Rushworth, vii.921.

51. *LJ*, ix.556–63, 605–10; *A&O*, i.1,048–56; SP 28/50, fo. 16; vol. 54, fo. 14.

52. *Wonderful Predictions . . . by John Saltmarsh* ([29 Dec.] 1647, TT E.421[16], p. 5; *Perf. Diurnall*, 20–27 Dec. 1647, TT E.520[19], p. 1,856; *S&S*, p. 296; *Perf. Diurnall*, 13–20 Dec. 1647, TT E.520[17], p. 1,848.

53. Massarella, p. 105; Rushworth, vii.943; *Perf. Diurnall*, 20–27 Dec. 1647, TT E.520[19], p. 1,855. Rainborowe's submission was evidently his part of the bargain by which the officers campaigned for him to be made vice-admiral: *CJ*, v.378; *LJ*, ix.615; *Kingdomes Weekly Intell.*, 21–28 Dec. 1647, TT E.548[16], pp. 780, 782.

54. They included Kempson's, Eyre's, Herbert's, Gray's, Morgan's, Laugharne's and Mitton's foot regiments, and Birch's and Cooke's troops of horse: *NMA*, p. 506, nn. 237–8.

55. MS Clar. 29, fo. 134–4ᵛ; *Merc. Elencticus*, 23 Feb.–1 Mar. 1648. E.430[3], p. 106; SP 28/51, fos 134–6; *Kingdomes Weekly Intell.*, 22–29 Feb. 1648, TT E.429[11], pp. 853–4.

56. SP 28/50-1. The regiments retained from the Northern army were Colonel Bright's, Mauleverer's and Charles Fairfax's foot, and Major-General Lambert's and Colonel Robert Lilburne's horse: SP 25/52, fos 217, 219, 188; Add. MS 21417, fos 127, 155. Rushworth gives an incomplete summary of the great disbandment in *A True Relation of Disbanding the Supernumerary Forces in the Several Counties of this Kingdom and the Dominion of Wales, Amounting to Twenty Thousand Horse and Foot* (28 Feb. 1648), TT E.429[10].

57. *LJ*, x.69–71; *CJ*, v.459; Worc. MS 110, unfol. (9 Feb. 1648); Rushworth, vii.993–6.

58. These included, besides the five regiments from the Northern Army, Colonel Francis Thornhaugh's horse in Notts, Robert Duckenfield's in Cheshire, Robert Tichborne's in the Tower of London, Valentine Wauton's in East Anglia, and divers companies belonging to Colonel Robert Bennett in Cornwall, Colonel Philip Jones in Swansea, Colonels Thomas Mason and John Carter in Caernarvonshire, Lieutenant-Colonel George Twisleton in Denbigh Castle, Colonel Edward Prichard in Cardiff, Colonel Hugh Price in Red Castle, and Colonel Thomas Bettesworth in Portsmouth: SP 28/50, fos 70, 131, 144, 292; vol. 51, fos 20, 42, 46, 48, 50, 52, 355; vol. 52, fos 80, 219, 288.

59. Ibid. 28/52, fos 137–9, 149; Worc. MS 110, unfol. (28 Feb. 1648), *Kingdomes Weekly Post*, 22 Feb.–1 Mar. 1648, TT E.430[6], p. 72. The three condemned men were Henry Gittings (one of the regiment's agitators), Thomas Latham and John Mallosse. For evidence of Gittings' survival, see NA, Exchequer, E315/5/153.

7 THE SECOND CIVIL WAR

1. Ludlow, *Memoirs*, i.175–6; Abbott, i.569.

2. Ibid., i.564–5; *CJ*, v.378, 391, 403, 413; *LJ*, ix. 567, 615–16.

3. MS Clar. 30, fo. 211; *Perf. Occurrences*, 10–17 Dec. 1647, TT E.520[16], p. 348; *CJ*, v.391; Abbott, i.574.

4. Ibid., i.575–6, 566–7; Clement Walker, *The Compleat History of Independency*, 4 parts in 1 vol. (London: R. Royston, 1661), part 1, pp. 70–2; Cromwell was paraphrasing Job 34:30; *CJ*, v.416; *CSPD, 1648–49*, pp. 5 ff.

5. Stevenson, p. 98; Gentles, 'Struggle for London', pp. 287–9; MS Clar. 31, fo. 42.

6. Gentles, 'Struggle for London', pp. 287–9; SP 25/54, fo. 350.

7. *NMA*, pp. 508–9, nn. 22–3.

8. MS Tanner 58, fo. 653; *CJ*, v.410; *Perf. Weekly Account*, 28 Dec.–5 Jan. 1647–48, TT E.421[33], sig. A1ᵛ; Alan Everitt, *The Community of Kent and the Great Rebellion, 1640–60* (Leicester: Leicester University Press, 1966), pp. 231–4.

9. BL, Stowe MS 361, fo. 100, for an anonymous protest against free quarter from early 1648. 1648 pay warrants are in SP 28/50-7. See also the petition adopted by the Essex grand jury at Chelmsford calling for total disbandment and a personal treaty with the king. It was brought to Westminster by 2,000 men on 4 May: Rushworth, vii.1,101; *CJ*,

v.551; *LJ*, x.244; Brian Lyndon, 'Essex and the king's cause in 1648', *HJ*, vol. 29 (1986): 17–39, p. 24.

10. Whitelocke, ii.304; *CJ*, v.553; vi.294; Cary, i.399, 402; David Underdown, *Pride's Purge: Politics in the Puritan Revolution* (Oxford: Clarendon Press, 1971), p. 91.

11. Worc. MS 114, fo.11ᵛ; *OPH*, xvii.254; Rushworth, vii.1,112, 1,119; *LJ*, ix.302.

12. *The Hamilton Papers*, ed. S.R. Gardiner, Camden Soc., new ser., vol. 27 (1880), p. 182; *OPH*, xvii.159–61; Worc. MS 114, fos 26–7ᵛ.

13. Hutchinson, p. 177; *CJ*, v.585, 594, 614, 617; *CSPD, 1648–49*, pp. 105–6, 108, 146, 148, 152; Whitelocke, ii.330; *CP*, ii.28; John Morrill, *The Revolt of the Provinces* (London: Allen and Unwin, 1976), p. 207; Rushworth, vii.1,175. For the student brawl in Cambridge: BL, Loan MS 29/176, fo. 24.

14. Poyer turned to royalist agents, who gave him a ready welcome. Laugharne played his cards more coolly. Obtaining a letter of support from Fairfax, he and his men petitioned the Commons for their arrears and distanced themselves from Poyer. The Committee for the Army rewarded Laugharne's loyalty with £2,500 in February and March: Whitelocke, ii.265; Worc. MS 110, unfol. (22 Feb. 1648); MS Tanner 58, fos 721, 724; Morrill, *Revolt of the Provinces*, pp. 129–30; MS Tanner 58, fos 733, 735; SP 28/50, fos 233–7ᵛ, 255–7ᵛ.

15. Whitelocke, ii.286–7, 288–9, 298, 306; Rushworth, vii.1,036–7, 1,065, 1,098; Worc. MS 114, fos 1, 8ᵛ; Morrill, *Revolt of the Provinces*, pp. 202–3; *CSPD, 1648–49*, p. 53.

16. Rushworth, vii.1,110; Whitelocke, ii.311; Ludlow, *Memoirs*, i.192; Bell, ii.22–5; *LJ*, x.253–4; MS Clar. 31, fo. 83; *CP*, ii.6–7.

17. Ludlow, *Memoirs*, i.184–5; Abbott, i.583–4; MS Clar. 29, fo. 134 (perhaps a garbled account of this meeting).

18. *Sir Philip Musgrave's Relation*, SHS, vol. 44 (1904), p. 303; *OPH*, xvii.107; *CSPD, 1648–49*, p. 29; Abbott, i.593–4; *CP*, ii.23–4; Rushworth, vii.1,060; *Hamilton Papers*, pp. 174, 178, 189; *The Armies Petition* ([3 May] 1648), TT E.438[1]; *Windsor Projects*; *Perf. Weekly Account*, 26 Apr.–3 May 1648, TT E.438[8], pp. 58–9; Massarella, p. 121.

19. Lomas–Carlyle, i.308; William Allen, *A Faithful Memorial of that Remarkable Meeting of Many Officers of the Army in England at Windsor Castle, in the Year 1648* ([27 Apr.] 1659), TT E.979[3], pp. 2–5. I believe Allen's account is basically trustworthy, even though he published it more than a decade later. It was plainly one of the most vivid and meaningful experiences of his life, and he may well have jotted down notes on it shortly after it occurred. Cf. *S&S*, pp. 332–5; Underdown, *Pride's Purge*, p. 96.

20. *CSPD, 1648–49*, p. 53; Abbott, i.599–601.

21. MS Tanner 57, fo. 27; Underdown, 'Parliamentary diary of John Boys', p. 164; Evelyn, *Diary*, iii.18; Ludlow, *Memoirs*, i.188–9; Gentles, 'Struggle for London', pp. 289–90.

22. MS Tanner 57, fo. 27; *CJ*, v.549, 574; SP 21/24, pp. 61, 75–8; Gentles, 'Struggle for London', p. 292; Pells, *Philip Skippon*, pp. 187–90.

23. Worc. MS 114, fo. 19; Cary, i.421–2; Everitt, *Kent*, pp. 247–8; Matthew Carter, *A Most True and Exact Relation of That as Honourable as Unfortunate Expedition of Kent, Essex and Colchester* (London, 1650), pp. 76–7; *CP*, ii.15–18; *CJ*, v.572; Everitt, *Kent*, p. 255; *CSPD, 1648–49*, pp. 79–80; SP 21/24, pp. 75–8; MS Clar.31, fo. 92; Whitelocke, ii.320; Gentles, 'Struggle for London', p. 292.

24. Everitt, *Kent*, p. 261n. See also *NMA*, p. 511, n. 61. I am not persuaded by Wanklyn's estimate of 5,000: Wanklyn, *Warrior Generals*, p. 282, n. 32.

25. Cary, i.437–8; Whitelocke, ii.322; Rushworth, vii.1,136; Everitt, *Kent*, p. 261.

26. Carter, *A Most True and Exact Relation,* pp. 88–91; HMC, *De L'Isle and Dudley*, vi.572; Rushworth, vii.1137; *LJ*, x.301, 304; *Perf. Occurrences*, 2–9 June 1648, TT E.522[37], pp. 543, 546; R. Temple, 'Discovery of a manuscript eye-witness account of the battle of Maidstone', *Archaeologia Cantiana*, vol. 97 (1981): 209–20, pp. 210–11; Whitelocke, ii.323–4; Ludlow, *Memoirs*, i.193–4; Everitt, *Kent*, pp. 261–3.

27. Wanklyn, *Warrior Generals*, p. 197; *LJ*, x.304; Whitelocke, ii.324.

28. *CSPD, 1648–49*, pp. 92–3; Rushworth, vii.1,138 (corrected pag.), *Perf. Occurrences*, 2–9 June 1648, TT E.522[37], p. 543; Everitt, *Kent*, p. 265; *An Impartiall Narration of the Management of the Late Kentish Petition* ([21 July] 1648), TT E.453[37], p. 3.

29. Rushworth, vii.1,143 (corrected pag.), 1,149–50; *CSPD, 1648–49*, pp. 105–6, 108–9, 111; Worc. MS 114, fo. 38ᵛ; *Hamilton Papers*, p. 211; Bell, ii.8–9.

30. Lyndon, 'Essex and the king's cause', p. 35; Gentles, 'Struggle for London', pp. 293–9; *CSPD, 1648–49*, p. 185.

31. Ibid., pp. 105–6, 108–9, 111.

32. SP 21/24, fos 182, 184; *CSPD, 1648–49*, pp. 167, 169; Whitelocke, ii.351, 354–5; HMC, *De L'Isle and Dudley*, vi.573; *Perf. Diurnall*, 3–10 July 1648, TT E.525[4], p. 2,079; Rushworth, vii.1,183.

33. Lyndon, 'Essex and the king's cause', pp. 26–7; *GCW*, iv.149, 150–1; *CP*, ii.26–7.

34. *GCW*, iv.150–1; *CSPD, 1648–49*, pp. 120–1.

35. *GCW*, iv.151.

36. John Walter, *Understanding Popular Violence in the English Revolution: The Colchester Plunderers* (Cambridge: Cambridge University Press, 1999), pp. 285, 287, 292, 319; Donagan, *War*, pp. 350–1.

37. HMC, *Beaufort*, pp. 23–5; *Hamilton Papers*, p. 215; Carter, *A Most True and Exact Relation*, pp. 131–3; Whitelocke, ii.332; Rushworth, vii.1,155; *GCW*, iv.151–3.

38. Carter, *A Most True and Exact Relation*, pp. 141, 146; *CP*, ii.27; *OPH*, xvii.152; Rushworth, vii.1,150, 1,153; HMC, *Beaufort*, p. 22; Whitelocke, ii.330, 339; Brian Lyndon, 'The Parliament's army in Essex, 1648', *JSAHR*, vol. 59 (1981), p. 145; *Merc. Melancholicus*, 17–24 July 1648, TT E.453[43], p. 127 (for Skippon's numbers); Pells, *Philip Skippon*, p. 188; Donagan, *War*, pp. 318, 323. Fairfax's own troops included the regular foot regiments of Needham (Tower of London), Barkstead, Ingoldsby and Ewer, and the horse regiments of Fleetwood, Scrope, Whalley, Ireton, plus his own.

39. Stephen Porter, *Destruction in the English Civil Wars* (Stroud: Sutton, 1994), pp. 68, 120; Donagan, *War*, pp. 330, 333, 341; Rushworth, vii.1,166–7, 1,196–232; Whitelocke, ii.365; Worc. MS 114, fo. 56ᵛ; Carter, *A Most True and Exact Relation*, p. 163.

40. Donagan, *War*, pp. 330, 338–42. Chewed bullets were believed to cause much more lethal wounds.

41. Rushworth, vii.1,242 (29 Aug. 1648); Harl. MS 7001, fo. 189ᵛ.

42. Barbara Donagan, 'Atrocity, war crime, and treason in the English Civil War', *American Historical Review*, vol. 99 (1994): 1,137–66, p. 1,150.

43. Hopper, *'Black Tom'*, p. 88; Donagan, *War*, pp. 158, 285–8; Abbott, i.642–3; Sir James Turner, *Memoirs*, Bannatyne Club, vol. 28 (1829), p. 70; Worc. MS 114, fo. 74ᵛ; *CJ*, v.695; Bell, ii.66–7; *CP*, ii.34–9; Ludlow, *Memoirs*, i.95–6.

44. *A Declaration of Lieut.-General Cromwell* (8 May 1648), TT E.441[16], p. 3; Abbott, i.606, 608, 611, 613, 618–19; Whitelocke, ii.311, 334; *CJ*, v.576; *CSPD, 1648–49*, pp. 101–2. Before they could come to Lambert's assistance, the foot regiment was diverted to Colchester to assist Fairfax: Abbott, i.612.

45. Wanklyn, *Warrior Generals*, p. 197.

46. For a discussion of the varying estimates of the Scottish army, see *NMA*, p. 513, n. 94. 'The relation of Sir Philip Musgrave', ed. C.H. Firth, *Miscellany II*, SHS, vol. 44 (1904), pp. 304–5; *CP*, ii.25–6; Cary, i.397, 407, 410–11, 419; Rushworth, vii.1,106, 1,113, 1,122, 1,127. To the gloomy eye of Thomas Margetts (Colonel John Lambert's secretary), Cavaliers outnumbered Roundheads twenty to one in the north-east: *CP*, ii.9, 26 (Margetts); *Moderate Intell.*, 11–18 May 1648, TT E.443[21], p. 1,327

47. Rushworth, vii.1,122, 1,127, 1,148, 1,157, 1,177; Whitelocke, ii.313, 334, 337; *LJ*, x.267; 'The relation of Sir Philip Musgrave', pp. 306, 308; *CSPD, 1648–49*, p. 130.

48. *Hamilton Papers*, pp. 233–4; Rushworth, vii.1,141 (corrected pag.); 'The relation of Sir Philip Musgrave', p. 292; Gilbert Burnet, *The Memoires of the Lives and Actions of James and William, Dukes of Hamilton and Castleherald* (London: R. Royston, 1677), pp. 354–5; Turner, *Memoirs*, p. 62; Stevenson, p. 113; Laura A.M. Stewart, *Rethinking the Scottish Revolution: Covenanted Scotland, 1637–1651* (Oxford: Oxford University Press, 2016), pp. 264–5, 284–5, 291, 295–301.

49. Turner, *Memoirs*, p. 78.

50. Burnet, *Memoires*, p. 358; Turner, *Memoirs*, p. 62.

51. *CSPD, 1648–49*, p. 210; Rushworth, vii.1,211; *GCW*, iv.178–80; Abbott, i.628, 634; *The Declaration of Lieut. Genll. Cromwell* ([18 Aug.] 1648), TT E.459[24], pp. 1–2; *The Bloudy Battel at Preston* (22 Aug. 1648), TT E.460[20], p. 3.
52. *GCW*, iv.180, 182.
53. On the other hand we have a reliable report from Lambert's quarters that Cromwell's force numbered 14,000. Perhaps the two sides at Preston were more nearly equal than previously thought: Abbott, i.638; Hodgson, p. 114; Rushworth, vii.1,211; William Thornton to Richard Richardson, Bolton Abbey MSS, box 2, no. 173. I am grateful to David Scott for this reference.
54. *Battles*, p. 166; Abbott, i.634.
55. *A Letter from Holland* (The Hague [12 Oct.] 1648), E.467[21], pp. 3–4; Abbott, i.361; Burnet, *Memoires*, p. 358.
56. *Battles*, p. 167; Abbott, i.635.
57. Hodgson, p. 116.
58. *Bloudy Battel at Preston*, pp. 4–5; Hodgson, pp. 116, 119; Abbott, i.635–6; Burnet, *Memoires*, pp. 358–60; *Lanc. Tracts*, pp. 267–9; *Battles*, pp. 168–71.
59. Burnet, *Memoires*, pp. 360–1; Turner, *Memoirs*, pp. 63–5; Hodgson, p. 120; *Letter from Holland*, pp. 4–6; *Moderate Intell.*, 17–24 Aug. 1648, TT E.460[35], p. 1,503; Wanklyn, *Warrior Generals*, p. 202; Abbott, i.636; *Battles*, pp. 172–3.
60. Hodgson, p. 122; Abbott, i.637; Turner, *Memoirs*, pp. 66–7; Baillie, iii.457.
61. Abbott, i.637; Burnet, *Memoires*, pp. 362–3; *Letter from Holland*, pp. 8–10.
62. Stewart, *Rethinking the Scottish Revolution*, p. 266.
63. Wanklyn, *Warrior Generals*, p. 204; *CSPD, 1648–49*, pp. 255–6; HMC, *Braye*, pp. 169–72; *Battles*, pp. 177–8; Stevenson, pp. 115–18.

8 'THAT MAN OF BLOOD': THE ARMY AND THE REGICIDE, SEPTEMBER 1648 TO MAY 1649

1. Worc. MS 114, fo. 115.
2. Ludlow, *Memoirs*, i.203–4.
3. *To the Right Honourable the Commons of England . . . the Humble Petition of Divers Wel Affected Persons* (1648), TT E.464[5], also printed in Wolfe, pp. 279–90; *Merc. Pragmaticus*, 12–19 Sept. 1648, TT E.464[12], sig. Ii2-ᵛ. According to this source the 'large petition' was drafted by the MP Henry Marten. *The Demands, Resolutions and Intentions of the Army* ([26 Sept.] 1648), TT E.464[41].
4. Worc. MS 114, fo. 80; *Merc. Pragmaticus*, 26 Sept.–1 Oct. 1648, TT E.465[19], sig. Nn2. The regiments, with the Thomason pressmarks of their petitions, were Constable's (E.467[34]), Ireton's (E.468[18]), Fleetwood's (E.468[32]), Fleetwood's, Whalley's and Barkstead's (E.470[32]), Rainborowe's and Overton's (E.473[1]), Cromwell's and Harrison's (E.474[5]), Ingoldsby's (E.526[25]), the Northern Brigade (E.472[6]), and 'several regiments' in the west (E.470[23]): *NMA*, p. 515, n. 11.
5. Rushworth, vii.1,297–8, 1,320, 1,324; Worc. MS 16, fo. 1; Abbott, i.324; Adamson, 'The English nobility and the projected settlement of 1647', pp. 572–4, n. 51; *True Informer*, 7 Oct.–8 Nov. 1648, TT E.526[28], pp. 5, 8. An anonymous pamphlet, calling itself *The Declaration of the Armie* ([5 Oct.] 1648), TT E.465[38], threatened on its title page that, if the royalist party in the City were not suppressed, the soldiers would 'put hundreds of them to the sword, and hang their quarters upon the gates, and set their heads upon the spires of the steeples'. A friendlier letter from the army addressed its friends in the City, thanking them for their support and encouragement, and promising to return the compliment: *His Majesties Gracious Message . . . [and] A Letter from the Army, to the Citizens of London* (10 Oct. 1648), TT E.467[6], pp. 5–6. Chief among Fairfax's moderate advisers was Dr William Stane, commissary-general of musters and a go-between in the correspondence between the Saye–Northumberland group in the House of Lords and the higher officers. A doctor of physic, Stane was the second son of a minor Essex gentleman:

Essex RO, Wills, D/DC q. E1. I owe this reference to Jeremy Ives. The moderates would soon be drowned out by the rising chorus of voices in favour of decisive action against Parliament: *The Declaration and Resolution of Many Thousand Citizens of London concerning the Army* ([12 Oct.] 1648), TT E.467[18], p. 6.

6. Agitators reappeared in Fleetwood's and Ireton's regiments: TT E.468[32, 18]. The Thomason Tracts pressmarks for the pamphlets published in the name of the army are E.464[41], E.465[38], E.467[6], E.468[13, 23, 28], and E.470[34]. See the Devon petition in *Packets of Letters from Severall Parts of England* . . . (10 Nov. 1648), TT E.472[[9], pp. 4–5. From Oxfordshire came a call for innocent blood to be avenged: *The Moderate*, 26 Sept.–3 Oct. 1648, TT E.465[25], sig. M3. An elitist London Leveller deplored the inconstancy of 'the rude multitude . . . [who] are sometimes for the king, and sometimes for Parliament, and sometimes for both'. The army, he wrote, represented the only hope for carrying through a genuine revolution: *Fruitfull England Like to Become a Barren Wilderness through the Wickednes of the Inhabitants* . . . ([17 Oct.] 1648), TT E.467[36], pp. 7–8.

7. *The Moderate*, 31 Oct.–7 Nov. 1648, TT E.472[15], sig. R4-ᵛ; *A Full and Exact Relation of the Horrid Murder Committed upon the Body of Col. Rainsborough* ([3 Nov.] 1648); *The Innocent Cleared: or the Vindication of Captaine John Smith* (13 Nov. 1648), TT E.472[25]; MS Clar. 34, fos 27ᵛ–8ᵛ; Nathan Drake, *A Journal of the First and Second Sieges of Pontefract Castle, 1644–5* . . . *with an Appendix of Evidence Relating to the Third Siege*, Surtees Soc., vol. 37 (1861), pp. 96–8.

8. *Merc. Militaris*, 14–21 Nov. 1648, TT E.473[8], p. 37; *Merc. Melancholicus*, 14–21 Nov. 1648, TT E.472[26], sig. A2ᵛ–3; *Merc. Elencticus*, 15–22 Nov. 1648, TT E.473[9], pp. 503–4. An even larger crowd would honour the body of another Leveller hero, Private Robert Lockyer, the following April: Ian Gentles, 'Political funerals during the English Revolution', in Stephen Porter (ed.), *London and the Civil War* (Basingstoke: Macmillan, 1996), pp. 205–24, pp. 216–20.

9. *The Representations and Consultations of the Generall Councell of the Armie at St Albans* ([14 Nov.] 1648), TT E.472[3], p. 3; Worc. MS 16, fo. 1ᵛ; *A Declaration of the Armie* ([9 Nov.] 1648), TT E.470[23], pp. 2–3; *A Letter from the Head-quarters, at St Albanes* (10 Nov. 1648), TT E.470[34]; *CP*, ii, appendix D, pp. 270–81.

10. On the 15th the peace party carried a motion 'that the king shall be settled in a condition of honour, freedom and safety, agreeable to the laws of the land': *CJ*, vi.76–7, 122.

11. John Lilburne, *The Legall Fundamentall Liberties of the People of England* (1649), TT E.560[14], pp. 29–34; Underdown, *Pride's Purge*, p. 122. I agree with Barbara Taft in rejecting Lilburne's claim that the officers undertook not to alter the version of the *Agreement of the People* drawn up by the committee of sixteen: Barbara Taft, 'The Council of Officers' *Agreement of the People*, 1648/9', *HJ*, vol. 28 (1985): 169–85, p. 173. For Ireton's lengthy residence at Windsor, see *A Complete Collection of State Trials for High Treason*, ed. Francis Hargrave, 4th edn, 11 vols (London: Bathurst, etc., 1776–81), ii.359.

12. *A Remonstrance of His Excellency Thomas Lord Fairfax . . . and of the Generall Councell of Officers Held at St Albans the 16 of Nov., 1648*, TT E.473[11], p. 71.

13. *The Moderate*, 14–21 Nov. 1648, TT E.473[1], p. 164; Whitelocke, ii.457; *Merc. Pragmaticus*, 21–28 Nov. 1648, TT E.473[46], sig. Bbbᵛ–Bbb2ᵛ; *OPH*, xviii.238–9.

14. The original printed version of the *Remonstrance* is in TT E.473[11]. In the discussion below, page references are to the version found in *OPH*, xviii.161–238.

15. Sarah Mortimer, 'Henry Ireton and the limits of radicalism, 1647–1649', in George Southcombe and Grant Tapsell (eds), *Revolutionary England, c. 1630–c. 1660: Essays for Clive Holmes* (Abingdon: Routledge, 2017), pp. 69–70.

16. *OPH*, xviii.174.
17. Ibid., xviii.175.
18. Ibid., xviii.182.
19. Ibid., xviii.183–4.
20. Ibid., xviii.198.

21. *Letters between Col. Robert Hammond and the Committee of Lords and Commons at Derby House . . . Relating to King Charles I* (London: Robert Horsfield, 1764), pp. 87–8, 95–101; Abbott, i.696–9.

22. MS Tanner 57, fos 425, 428; *CJ*, vi.87, 88; *LJ*, x.614–15, 616; Worc. MS 114, fos 110, 115 (29 Nov. 1648). See also *NMA*, p. 518, n. 65; Sir Thomas Herbert, *Memoirs of the Two Last Years of the Reign of King Charles I* (London: G. & W. Nicol, 1813), p. 117. Fairfax also put his name to the letter explaining the army's disobedience as a natural consequence of Parliament's refusal to deal with the *Remonstrance*: *The Demands of His Excellency Thomas Lord Fairfax and the Generall Councell of the Army* ([5 Dec.] 1648), TT E.475[10].

23. Ludlow, *Memoirs*, i.206; *Merc. Pragmaticus*, 21–28 Nov. 1648, TT E.473[35], sig. Bbb3ᵛ; Whitelocke, ii.461.

24. Worc. MS 114, fo. 104; besides Ireton, its members included Thomas Hammond, lieutenant-general of the Ordnance, cavalry colonels Sir William Constable, Thomas Harrison, Edward Whalley and Matthew Tomlinson, and Colonel Christopher Whichcote, governor of Windsor Castle: CP, ii.56. See also *NMA*, pp. 518–19, n. 71.

25. Worc. MS 114, fo. 111; *Reg. Hist.*, p. 374; *CP*, ii.58–9.

26. Ibid., ii.58–9.

27. *The Declaration of His Excellency and the General Council of Officers* (30 Nov. 1648), in Rushworth, vii.1,341–3; *CJ*, vi.91; *The Moderate*, 28 Nov.–5 Dec. 1648, TT E.475[8], p. 187; *CP*, ii.65; *LJ*, ix.618; *A Warning, or a Word of Advice to the City of London . . .* ([30 Nov.] 1648), TT E.474[6], p. 5.

28. *Merc. Pragmaticus*, 5–12 Dec. 1648, TT E.476[2], sig. Ccc2–2ᵛ; Harl. MS 4898, fos 9ᵛ, 12–12ᵛ, 14, 189, 193, 280; J.S.A. Adamson, 'The Peerage in Politics, 1645–1649' (PhD thesis, Cambridge University, 1986), pp. 17, 262.

29. *The Demands of His Excellency Thomas Lord Fairfax and the Generall Councell of the Army*, pp. 4–6; Rushworth, vii.1,345, 1,348; MS Tanner 57, fo. 450; C.W. Firebrace, *Honest Harry, Being a Biography of Sir Henry Firebrace, Knight (1619–1691)* (London: John Murray, 1932), pp. 165–81 (Colonel Edward Cooke's narrative).

30. *CJ*, vi.93.

31. *Merc. Pragmaticus*, 5–12 Dec. 1648, TT E.476[2], sigs Ccc2–3; *The Parliament under the Power of the Sword* ([11 Dec.] 1648), TT E.476[1], pp. 6–7; *CJ*, vi.93.

32. Rushworth, vii.1,353; *Perf. Occurrences*, 1–8 Dec. 1648, TT E.526[38], p. 755; *CJ*, v.666; vi.94; Worc. MS 114, fo. 128; *The Articles and Charge of the Armie against Fourscore and Odd of the Parliament Men Who Have Acted Contrary to the Trust Reposed in Them by the People . . .* ([8 Dec.] 1648), TT E.475[30]; Ludlow, *Memoirs*, i.209.

33. *CP*, ii.156; Underdown, *Pride's Purge*, pp. 141–2.

34. My account of the events of 6 Dec. is based on ibid., chapter 6, unless otherwise noted. Hutchinson, p. 188; Whitelocke, ii.472.

35. *CJ*, vi.93–4; *The Humble Proposals and Desires of His Excellency Lord Fairfax and of the General Councel of Officers . . .* (6 Dec. 1648), TT E.475[25], pp. 4–8.

36. Ludlow, *Memoirs*, i.211–12.

37. Massarella, p. 149; *Merc. Elencticus*, 14–21 Oct. 1648, TT E.469[15], p. 400; Whitelocke, ii.431; Lilburne, *Legall Fundamentall Liberties*, p. 29. The words about cutting off the king's head are not explicitly attributed to Cromwell, but the linkage is apparent. Lilburne's account, however, must be treated with caution. *Severall Petitions Presented to His Excellency the Lord Fairfax* ([30 Nov.] 1648), TT E.474[5], pp. 3–4; Abbott, i.676–8, 690, 698–9.

38. *CP*, ii.63; Abbott, i.707; Worc. MS 114, fo. 124; *Moderate Intell.*, 30 Nov.–7 Dec. 1648, TT E.475[26], p. 1,776.

39. *NMA*, p. 521, nn. 113–14; *Packets of Letters* ([15 Nov.] 1648), TT E.472[9], p. 4; *Perf. Diurnall*, 27 Nov.–4 Dec. 1648, TT E.526[36], p. 2,242; *The Resolution of the Armie* ([28 Nov.] 1648], TT E.473[36], p. 5. For the last-minute character of the decision to purge rather than dissolve Parliament, see *CP*, ii.67.

40. Whitelocke, ii.477; Abbott, i.710.

41. In June 1649 Lilburne maintained that the document produced by the committee of sixteen was meant to be final and unalterable: Lilburne, *Legall Fundamentall Liberties*, p. 35. If this was so, he could have raised the point at the 24 Dec. meeting, which he did not: *CP*, ii.78. Nor did he make the claim of unalterability in the pamphlet he and fifteen other Levellers published on 28 Dec.: *A Plea for Common Right and Freedom* (1648), TT E.536[22]. Taft, 'The Council of Officers' *Agreement of the People*, 1648/9', esp. p. 173. I am indebted to this article, as well as to conversations with Barbara Taft, and her article, 'Voting lists of the Council of Officers, December 1648', *BIHR*, vol. 52 (1979): 138–54. See also the important chapter by Frances Henderson, 'Drafting the officers' *Agreement of the People*, 1648–49: A reappraisal', in Philip Baker and Elliot Vernon (eds), *The Agreements of the People, the Levellers and the Constitutional Crisis of the English Revolution* (Basingstoke: Palgrave Macmillan, 2010), pp. 163–94.

42. Rushworth, vii.1,358–61.

43. *CP*, ii.73–132; page numbers in the following paragraphs refer to this source.

44. *The Articles and Charges of the Armie* ([8 Dec.] 1648), TT E.575[30], pp. 3–4; *The Resolution of the Army* ([13 Dec.] 1648), TT E.476[16], pp. 1–3. The printer of this tract, Nehemiah Wilson, was not used by the army for any of its official publications.

45. *CP*, ii.79–83.

46. Ibid., ii.84.

47. Ibid., ii.94–5.

48. Ibid., ii.112–14, 122, 128–30.

49. Ireton, who adjourned the debate, was in the chair before the end of the day: ibid., ii.131. After p. 107 the speakers stop referring to the chairman as 'your Lordship' and 'your Excellency', and either call him 'Sir' or address him by no title at all.

50. Lilburne, *Legall Fundamentall Liberties*, p. 35.

51. Rushworth, vii.1,360; Wolfe, p. 347. Two days later another anonymous pamphlet appeared, pretending to be from the army, summarising the *Agreement of the People*, and pointedly referring to the scheduled date of the dissolution of the Long Paliament – 30 April 1649. Ignoring the compromise on religion, it baldly declared that the *Agreement* would guarantee complete freedom of conscience. The pamphlet, bearing no printer's name, perhaps testifies to the sustained pressure of the lower officers to get the *Agreement* passed without modification. Alternatively, it may have come from the Levellers. In either case it conveyed the impression that the *Agreement* was the army's own document: *A Declaration to the City and Kingdome . . . Likewise a New Covenant and Agreement from the Army, to be Tendered to All Free-born Englishmen . . .* ([18 Dec.] 1648), TT E.476[33], p. 6.

52. Evelyn, *D&C*, iii.34–5.

53. *CP*, ii.135.

54. Wolfe, p. 348. The fifth reserve would have abolished all privileges and exemptions from the laws. Wolfe, p. 300; Rushworth, vii.1,360; Taft, 'Voting lists of the Council of Officers', p. 147. On the 26th, the Council returned to the sixth reserve. Again it was upheld by a large margin against the solid opposition of the grandees: ibid., p. 148.

55. Ibid., p. 149. In the officers' Agreement of 20 Jan. 1649 this reserve appears as no. 5: Wolfe, p. 348.

56. *CP*, ii.170–1.

57. Ironically, the Levellers had lost the support of most of the sects, and the godly, 'well-affected' people of the nation by early 1649: Tolmie, *Triumph of the Saints*, pp. 180–3; John Vernon, *The Sword's Abuse Asserted* (1648), TT E.477[3], p. 17; *AA*, pp. 22, 24, 41–2; *The Moderate*, 14–21 Nov. 1648, TT E.473[1], p. 154. See also *A Warning, or a Word of Advice to the City of London*, p. 3, for an admission that 'the major party are not to have any vote'. See also Ian Gentles, 'The *Agreements of the People* and their political contexts, 1647–1649', in Mendle, *Putney Debates*, p. 162.

58. *CJ*, vi.122; Taft, 'The Council of Officers' *Agreement of the People*, 1648/9', pp. 179–85.

59. Whitelocke, ii.467; *A True and Ful Relation of the Officers and Armies Forcible Seising of Divers Eminent Members of the Commons House . . .* ([13 Dec.] 1648), TT E.476[14],

pp. 4–6; *Parliament under the Power of the Sword*, p. 3. The two MPs released were Sir Benjamin Rudyerd and Nathaniel Fiennes.

60. Whitelocke, ii.480; *CJ*, vi.96–7.

61. Evelyn, *D&C*, iii.33; *Merc. Pragmaticus*, 12–19 Dec. 1648, TT E.476[35], sig. Ddd3; 19–26 Dec., TT E.477[30], sigs Eee1ᵛ–2, 2ᵛ, 3-3ᵛ; *The Second Part of the Narrative Concerning the Armies Force and Violence upon the Commons* ... ([23 Dec.] 1648), TT E.477[19], p. 8; MS Clar. 34, fo. 12.

62. Whitelocke, ii.477, 479; Rushworth, vii.1,363; *Merc. Pragmaticus*, 12–19 Dec. 1648, TT E.476[35], sigs Ddd3-3ᵛ, 4–4ᵛ; *Kingdomes Weekly Intell.*, 12–19 Dec. 1648, TT E.476[39], p. 1,192.

63. Adamson, 'The peerage in politics', pp. 260–1. The four peers who visited Fairfax were Pembroke, Denbigh, Mulgrave and Lord Grey of Warke: Worc. MS 114, fo. 129; *CJ*, vi.100–1. Their meeting with Fairfax took place about 10 Dec. The king's real gaoler was of course the governor of the castle, Colonel Christopher Whichcote: John Adamson, 'The frighted junto: Perceptions of Ireland, and the last attempts at settlement with Charles I', in Jason Peacey (ed.), *The Regicides and the Execution of Charles I* (Basingstoke: Palgrave, 2001), pp. 36–70, pp. 40, 42, 43; MS Clar. 34, fo. 12; *Merc. Pragmaticus*, 19–26 Dec. 1648, TT E.477[30], sig. Eee2ᵛ; *The Joynt Resolution and Declaration of the Parliament and Counsell of the Army* ... ([11 Jan.] 1649, TT E.538[1*], pp. 1–2.

64. *Merc. Pragmaticus*, 5–12 Dec. 1648, TT E.476[2], sig. 4ᵛ; Underdown, *Pride's Purge*, pp. 144–5; Worc. MS 16, fo. 61.

65. Gentles, 'Struggle for London', pp. 301–2; *The Moderate*, 5–12 Dec. 1648, TT E.476[5], p. 199.

66. Abbott, i.732–3; Gilbert Burnet, *History of His Own Time*, 2 vols (London, 1724–34), i.79. In his two-to-three-hour fast-day address at St Margaret's Westminster, Peters called for the rooting out of monarchy in England and throughout Christendom. He likened the army leaders to Moses leading the Israelites out of Egypt. The citizens of London he compared to the Jerusalem crowd crying for the release of Barabbas (Charles I) and the crucifixion of Christ (the New Model soldiers): *Merc. Pragmaticus*, 19–26 Dec. 1648, TT E.477[30], sig. Eee4; *State Trials*, ii.362.

67. *The Declaration and Proposals of the Citizens of London* ([12 Dec.] 1648), TT E.476[6], p. 4; *Perf. Occurrences*, 8–15 Dec. 1648, TT E.526[40], p. 745; *The Joynt Resolution and Declaration of the Parliament and Counsell of the Army*, pp. 2–5. The five placed under closer confinement were Sir William Waller, Major-General Edward Massie, Colonel Copley, the sheriff of London, Major-General Richard Browne, and William Prynne.

68. *Heads of the Charge against the King* ... *by the Generall Councell of the Armie* ... ([24 Dec.] 1648), TT E.477[25], pp. 4–6.

69. *CJ*, vi.102–3.

70. Abbott, i.713–15; *CP*, ii.146n. Cromwell alone is known to have opposed the last instruction, perhaps because it obstructed last-minute negotiations for the king's abdication. MS Tanner 57, fo. 474; Whitelocke, ii.480; *CP*, ii.150–4, 163–70.

71. MS Clar 34, fo. 72. Cf Abbott, i.719 for a slightly different version.

72. Rushworth, vii.1,376.

73. *CJ*, vi.107, 110–11; *LJ*, x. 641–2.

74. Massarella, pp. 192–3. This figure excludes officers not in present service – Colonels Robert Tichborne, Edmund Ludlow, Robert Duckenfield and John Hutchinson. Rushworth, vii.1,386; *Sydney Papers*, p. 282.

75. For a fuller narrative of the trial, see the matchless account in C.V. Wedgwood, *The Trial of Charles I* (London: World Books, 1964); Rushworth, vii.1,390; Evelyn, *Diary*, ii.547; *State Trials*, ii.364.

76. *The Moderate*, 9–16 Jan. 1649, TT E.538[5], p. 257; *A Serious and Faithful Representation of the Judgement of Ministers* ... *within the Province of London* ... *to the Generall and his Councell of Warre* (18 Jan. 1649), TT E.538[25]. For another denunciation of regicide, see the anonymous *Vindication of the Army* ([22 Jan.] 1649), TT E.538[29]; Goodwin, *Right and Might Well Met*, pp. 6–7, 20, 35, 43–4. Abbott, i.732–3; Burnet, *History of His Own*

Time, i.63. See the petitions from the south-coast garrisons to the army and Parliament in Rushworth, vii,1,388–9, 1,391; *CJ*, vi.120. See also Thomas Margetts's letter expressing the puzzlement of the northern officers at the release of most of the imprisoned MPs: Worc. MS 114, fo. 163.

77. MS Clar. 34, fo. 73ᵛ; *CJ*, vi.132, 168; Underdown, *Pride's Purge*, pp. 194–5.
78. Michael Braddick, *God's Fury, England's Fire: A New History of the English Civil War* (London: Penguin, 2008), p. 556; Sean Kelsey, 'The death of Charles I', *HJ*, vol. 45 (2002): 727–54, pp. 748, 754.
79. John Morrill and Philip Baker, 'Oliver Cromwell, the regicide and the sons of Zeruiah', in Peacey (ed.), *Regicides*, pp. 14–35, pp. 22, 32; Adamson, 'The frighted junto', pp. 40–2, 48, 52.
80. Philip Baker, 'The regicide', in Michael J. Braddick (ed.), *The Oxford Handbook of the English Revolution* (Oxford: Oxford University Press, 2015), p. 165.
81. Mark Kishlansky, 'Mission impossible: Charles I, Oliver Cromwell and the regicide', *EHR*, vol. 125 (2010), pp. 844–74; Clive Holmes, 'The trial and execution of Charles I', *HJ*, vol. 53 (2010): 289–316, pp. 296–7, 315; idem, 'The *Remonstrance of the Army* and the execution of Charles I', *History*, vol. 104 (2019): 585–605, p. 587.
82. Morrill and Baker, 'Oliver Cromwell, the regicide and the sons of Zeruiah', p. 23; Lilburne, *Legall Fundamentall Liberties*, p. 412; *Sydney Papers*, p. 54, cited in Holmes, 'Trial and execution of Charles I', p. 303; MS Carte 23, fo. 425; David Scott, 'Motives for king-killing', in Peacey (ed.), *Regicides*, pp. 138–60, p. 147. Scott's phrase is applied to the eight regicide MPs from the northern counties, but it is just as apt a description of the motivation of the majority of the army grandees; Carolyn Polizzotto, 'Speaking truth to power: The problem of authority in the Whitehall debates of 1648–9', *EHR*, vol. 131 (2016): 31–63, p. 59. See also Andrew Hopper, 'Reluctant Regicides? The trial of Charles I revisited', National Archives podcast series, 2014: available online at http://media.nationalarchives. gov.uk/index.php/reluctant-regicides (accessed 25 June 2021).
83. *A New-years Gift* ([1 Jan.] 1649), TT E.536[24]; *A Declaration of the Lords and Commons . . . [and the] Resolution of the Army . . .* ([3 Jan.] 1649), TT E.536[36]; *CJ*, vi.102; *LJ*, x.637; Wedgwood, *Trial of Charles I*, p. 74, n. 28; Tolmie, *Triumph of the Saints*, pp. 180–1; Pauline Gregg, *Free-Born John: A Biography of John Lilburne* (London: Harrap, 1961), pp. 258–61.
84. *State Trials*, ii.317, 359, 392.
85. Evelyn, *Diary*, ii.547; Clarendon, *History*, iv.486; Rushworth, vii.1395; *State Trials*, ii.371, 378.
86. Rushworth, vii.1,396–8; *The King's Tryal . . . on Saturday, January 20 1648*, TT E.538[26], p. 4; *State Trials*, ii.371.
87. Genesis 9:6; Matthew 7:1; *The Moderate*, 16–23 Jan. 1649, TT E.539[7], p. 271.
88. Wedgwood, *Trial of Charles I*, p. 145.
89. MS Clar. 34, fo. 88.
90. For perceptive discussion of Fairfax's position in 1648–49, see Wedgwood, *Trial of Charles I*, pp. 27–9, 71–4, 89–90, 104–7; Underdown, *Pride's Purge*, pp. 189–93; and Hopper, 'Black Tom', pp. 94–105. Worc. MS 66, fos 26, 13ᵛ, 26ᵛ.
91. *State Trials*, i.1,027, 1,034; Rushworth, vii.1,411.
92. Wedgwood, *Trial of Charles I*, p. 155.
93. Only fifty-nine signed the death warrant, but the total number of regicides, including those who stood up but did not sign, as well as those who signed but were not present when sentence was pronounced, is sixty-nine: A.W. McIntosh, 'The numbers of the English regicides', *History*, vol. 67 (1982): 195–216, p. 197; *State Trials*, i.1,037, 1,041; Rushworth, vii.1,425.
94. John Winthrop, *Papers 1598–1649*, Massachusetts HS, 5 vols (1929–47), v.438; Wedgwood, *Trial of Charles I*, p. 166; *Moderate Intell.*, 25 Jan.–1 Feb. 1649, TT E.541[4], p. 1,869; *Kingdomes Faithfull and Impartiall Scout*, 26 Jan.–2 Feb. 1649, TT E.541[5], p. 3; François Guizot, *History of the English Revolution of 1640* (London: Bohn, 1856), appendix, pp. 460–1.

95. *State Trials*, ii.392, 400.
96. Hutchinson, p. 190; 'Ingoldsby, Sir Richard', *ODNB*. For a full list of the signatories to the death warrant, see *GCW*, iv.309.
97. *State Trials*, ii.386, 389–90; Rushworth, vii.1,425.
98. *CJ*, vi.125.
99. The evidence for Rich is ambiguous. In November he was said to have opposed the army's *Remonstrance* with its demand for justice upon the king: *Merc. Militaris*, 14–21 Nov. 1648, TT E.473[8], p. 40. He was not named to the High Court of Justice, yet at the Restoration he was alleged to have been a close confidant of Cromwell, Ireton and Peters during the weeks leading up to the regicide. However, the evidence for this is shaky: *State Trials*, ii.359; Guizot, *History of the English Revolution*, p. 461.
100. Herbert, *Memoirs*, p. 194.
101. *Moderate Intell.*, 25 Jan.–1 Feb. 1649, TT E.541[4], p. 1,872; *King Charls His Speech Made upon the Scaffold* (30 Jan. 1649), p. 9. In the Worcester College copy of this pamphlet (AA.2.4/11), pp. 9, 12, the two incidents to do with the axe have been asterisked in ink, and a contemporary hand has written 'W.C.' in the margin. I am very grateful to the late Worcester College librarian, Lesley Le Claire, for drawing this evidence for William Clarke's presence on the scaffold to my attention.
102. *Diaries and Letters of Philip Henry, 1631–1696*, ed. Matthew Henry Lee (London: Kegan Paul, 1882), p. 12.
103. *State Trials*, i.1,044.
104. *CJ*, vi.125; Whitelocke, ii.516; McIntosh, 'The numbers of the English regicides', p. 197; *State Trials*, ii.364, 374, 383–4, 395.
105. Herbert, *Memoirs*, pp. 194–5.
106. *Kingdomes Weekly Intell.*, 30 Jan.–6 Feb. 1649, TT E.541[17], p. 1,241. I am grateful to Nicole Greenspan for this reference. Besides this parliamentary source we have the testimony of the Puritan clergyman Ralph Josselin that his tears were 'not restrained' when he learned of Charles's death: *Diary*, p. 155. Lady Fairfax also asserted that 'not a quarter' of the people of England supported his trial.
107. *CSPD, 1648–49*, p. 340; *CJ*, vi.129, 132–3, 140–1; *C&P*, i.4, 6–7; Worden, *Rump*, pp. 180–1.

9 THE ARMY AND THE LEVELLERS, FEBRUARY TO SEPTEMBER 1649

1. Untitled MS ([4 Jan.] 1649), TT E.537[8]; *The Petition of the General Council of Officers . . . to . . . the Commons of England* (3 Mar. 1649), TT E.545[30], pp. 6–10; *Perf. Diurnall*, 26 Feb.–5 Mar. 1649, TT E.527[29], p. 1,346; *CJ*, vi.153; *CP*, ii. 200n; John Lilburne, *The Hunting of the Foxes from New-Market and Triploe-Heath to White-Hall* ([21 Mar.] 1649), TT E.548[7], also printed in Wolfe, pp. 355–83. Since Hewson's words were reported by Lilburne they are to be treated with caution.
2. *CP*, ii. 190–2; *The Humble Petition of the Officers and Soldiers of His Excellency's Regiment of Horse* ([22 Feb.] 1649, TT E.545[17], pp. 21–2; Lilburne, *Legall Fundamentall Liberties*, p. 74; Lilburne, *The Hunting of the Foxes*, in Wolfe, p. 368. While William Thompson called himself a captain in 1649, his New Model rank had never been higher than corporal.
3. *England's New Chains Discovered*, in Haller & Davies, pp. 157–68.
4. *[To the] Svpreme Entrvsted Avthority of this Nation . . . the Humble Petition of Divers of the Well-Affected Officers and Souldiers of the Army . . .* (1649), Worc. Coll. pamphlet BB.8.7/189; also printed in *OPH*, xix.50–1.
5. *The Hunting of the Foxes*, in Wolfe, pp. 373–4; *Perf. Diurnall*, 26 Feb.–5 Mar. 1649, TT E.527[29], pp. 1,345, 1,347; *Perf. Occurrences*, 2–9 Mar. 1649, TT E.527[31], p. 886; *Certain Occurrences of Parliament*, 2–9 Mar. 1649, TT E.527[32], p. 43; *Kingdomes Weekly Intell.*, 6–13 Mar. 1649, TT E.546[19], pp. 1,282–3; H.N. Brailsford, *The Levellers and the English Revolution* (London: Cresset Press, 1961), p. 475.

6. *The Hunting of the Foxes*, in Wolfe, p. 370.
7. For a sympathetic account see George Orwell, *Homage to Catalonia* (London: Secker and Warburg, 1951), pp. 26–8, 57.
8. John Jubbes, *An Apology unto the Lord Generals Army* (1649), TT E.552[28].
9. William Bray, *An Appeal in the Humble Claim of Justice against Thomas Lord Fairfax* ([19 Mar.] 1649), TT E.546[30]; CJ, vi.167; *The Moderate*, 13–20 Mar. 1649, TT E.548[2], pp. 371–2.
10. In Haller & Davies, pp. 171–89.
11. John Lilburne, *The Picture of the Councel of State*, in Haller & Davies, pp. 191–246. The quotations below are taken from this source. See also William Walwyn, *The Fountain of Slaunder Discovered* [30 May] 1649, printed in McMichael and Taft (eds), *Walwyn*, pp. 362–6.
12. *NMA*, p. 323 and nn. 36–8; *Perf. Occurrences*, 6–13 Apr. 1649, TT E.529[10], pp. 966–7.
13. *The Humble Petition of Divers Well-Affected Women* ([5 May] 1649), TT 669.f.14[27].
14. Untitled pamphlet, TT E.551[21]. The first issue of *Merc. Militaris*, 17–24 Apr., reported the incident as having occurred on 23 Apr: E.551[13], p. 14.
15. *CSPD, 1649–50*, p. 95; Whitelocke, iii.17; *CP*, ii.210; *The Collected Writings of Gerrard Winstanley*, ed. George H. Sabine (Ithaca, NY: Cornell University Press, 1941), pp. 188, 197, 529–34.
16. William Everard, *The Declaration and Standard of the Levellers of England* (23 Apr. 1649), TT E.551[11]; Jerrard Winstanley, *A Letter to the Lord Fairfax and his Councell of War* ([13 June] 1649), TT E.560[1]; BL, Egerton MS 2618, fo. 38; *CP*, ii.215–20.
17. The two most detailed accounts of the mutiny in Whalley's regiment are *A True Narrative of the Late Mutiny by Several Troopers of Captain Savage's Troop in Col: Whaley's Regiment . . .* (1 May 1649), TT E.552[18], and *The Army's Martyr* ([7 May] 1649), TT E.554[6].
18. *The Moderate*, 24 Apr.–1 May 1649, TT E.552[20], p. 483, and *Perf. Diurnall*, 30 Apr.–7 May 1649, TT E.529[34], p. 2,469. Gentles, 'Political funerals during the English Revolution', pp. 218–21. There were more mourners for Lockyer than for Rainborowe the previous autumn.
19. In the immediate aftermath of the regicide, Marten had been authorised to recruit his troop to a full regiment: CJ, vi.129. In May many of them would join the Leveller mutiny at Burford: *Perf. Occurrences*, 4–11 May 1649, TT E.530[1], p. 1,031.
20. *Merc. Pragmaticus*, 24 Apr.–1 May 1649, TT E.552[15], p. 14; *Perf. Diurnall*, 30 Apr.–7 May 1649, TT E.529[34], p. 2,469.
21. *The English Souldiers Standard*, [5 Apr.] 1649, E.550[1], p. 9.
22. John Price, *Walwins Wiles*, 10 May 1649, in Haller & Davies, pp. 288–9. The Leveller pamphlet *Eighteen Queries* does not survive, but it was reproduced in the five issues of the *Moderate Intell.* for May 1649, and is reprinted in Brailsford, *The Levellers*, pp. 501–2. N. Carlin, 'The Levellers and the Conquest of Ireland in 1649', *HJ*, vol. 30 (1987): 269–88, pp. 271–2.
23. *The Souldiers Demand* (Bristol, [18 May] 1649), TT E.555[29], pp. 12–13. Major John Cobbett, who was based in Bristol, was cashiered on 18 June 1649, and it seems reasonable to conjecture that his dismissal was connected with the publication of *The Souldiers Demand*.
24. *The Moderate*, 1–8 May 1649, TT E.554[15], sig. Vv2ᵛ.
25. *Modest Narrative*, 5–12 May 1649, TT E.555[8], p. 45.
26. Printed in *The Moderate*, 1–8 May 1649, TT E.554[15], sig. Vv2–2ᵛ.
27. *Moderate Intell.*, 2–10 May 1649, TT E.555[3], p. 2,034; *Perf. Diurnall*, 7–14 May 1649, TT E.530[6], pp. 2,498–9; Worc. MS 16, fos 103–9.
28. *Perf. Weekly Account*, 9–16 May 1649, TT E.530[7], p. 478.
29. *Impartiall Intell.*, 16–23 May 1649, TT E.530[15], p. 96; *A Moderate Intelligence*, 17–24 May 1649, TT E.556[13], sig. A4; Whitelocke, iii.38, 43; *Moderate*, 22–29 May 1649, TT E.556[31], p. 529; *Perf. Occurrences*, 4–11 May 1649, TT E.539[1], p. 1,032.
30. Ibid., 4–11 May 1649, TT E.530[1], pp. 1,030–1; Worc. MS 16, fo. 93.

31. *The Unanimous Declaration of Colonel Scroope's and Commissary Gen. Ireton's Regiments* . . . *11 of May 1649*, TT E.555[4], pp. 5, 6, 7.
32. *A Declaration from His Excellencie* . . . *Aulton, Hamshire* (12 May 1649), TT E.555[6].
33. *The Declaration of the Levellers concerning Prince Charles*, 17 May 1649, E.555[26], p. 3.
34. *Impartiall Intell.*, 9–16 May 1649, TT E.530[8], p. 188.
35. Abbott, ii.68; *The Declaration of Lieutenant-Generall Cromwell Concerning the Levellers* (14 May 1649), TT E.555[12], pp. 1–2.
36. Worc. MS 181, unfol. (12 May 1649). I use the term 'Leveller' advisedly. Although there is no positive proof that the London Levellers organised the mutiny by Scrope's, Ireton's and Harrison's men, the mutineers' programme was clearly Leveller inspired. Their suppression at Burford was bitterly denounced in Leveller circles. The Burford mutiny, moreover, was commonly referred to as 'the Leveller rising'. SP 24/25, fos 12–12ᵛ; Add. MS 21417, fo. 134; *Perf. Occurrences*, 4–11 May 1649, TT E.530[1], p. 1,031; Massarella, p. 221; Rees, *Leveller Revolution*, pp. 297–9.
37. *A Declaration of the Proceedings of His Excellency the Lord Fairfax in the Reducing of the Revolted Troops* (23 May 1649), TT E.556[1], pp. 7–8.
38. *The Levellers (Falsly So Called) Vindicated*, 20 Aug. 1649, E.571[11], p. 6; *England's Moderate Messenger*, 14–21 May 1649, TT E.530[13], pp. 27–8. See also Francis White, *A True Relation of the Proceedings in the Businesse of Burford* (17 Sept. 1649), TT E.574[26], p. 6; A.L. Morton (ed.), *Freedom in Arms* (Berlin: Seven Seas, 1975), pp. 304–6.
39. *Declaration of the Proceedings*, p. 8.
40. *Moderate Intell.*, 10–17 May 1649, TT E.555[25], p. 2,048; *Declaration of the Proceedings*, p. 9.
41. Laurence, *Army Chaplains*, pp. 326–7; *Full Narrative of All the Proceedings between His Excellency the Lord Fairfax and the Mutineers* . . . ([18 May] 1649), TT E.555[27], p. 3; R.H. Gretton, *Burford Records* (Oxford: Clarendon Press, 1920), p. 243; *Perf. Summary*, 14–21 May 1649, TT E.530[12], pp. 150–1.
42. *Full Narrative of All the Proceedings*, p. 3; Gretton, *Burford Records*, p. 255.
43. *Declaration of the Proceedings*, pp. 10–11; *The Declaration and Speeches of Cornet Thomson and the Rest of the Levellers* (22 May 1649), TT E.556[7], p. 4.
44. *Kingdomes Weekly Intell.*, 15–22 May 1649, TT E.556[6], p. 1,363; *Moderate*, 15–22 May 1649, TT E.556[3], pp. 516–17; *The Levellers (Falsly So Called) Vindicated*, pp. 7–8.
45. Worc. MS 16, fos 100–100ᵛ; *Impartiall Intell.*, 16–23 May 1649, TT E.530[15], p. 96. For further detail, see *NMA*, p. 347.
46. *A Full Narrative of All the Proceedings*, pp. 12–13. The Oxford mutiny is covered in detail by C.H. Firth in *Procs of the Oxford Architectural and HS*, new ser. 4 (1884), pp. 235–46, and by Rees, *Leveller Revolution*, pp. 300–3.
47. *C&P*, i.54; Anthony à Wood, *The History and Antiquities of the University of Oxford [Annals]*, ed. John Gutch, 2 vols (Oxford, 1792–96), ii.619–21; Worc. MS 16, fo. 101.
48. *Perf. Occurrences*, 25 May–1 June 1649, TT E.530[25], p. 1,054 (Cromwell's report to the House of Commons, 26 May).
49. *A Full Narrative of All the Proceedings*, p. 2.

10 THE CONQUEST AND OCCUPATION OF IRELAND, 1649–60

1. *CSPD, 1649–50*, pp. 22, 28; John Lilburne, *An Impeachment of High Treason against Oliver Cromwell* ([20 Aug.] 1649), TT E.568[20], p. 4.
2. *CP*, ii.205.
3. Ibid., ii.208–9. The apostles cast lots to select the replacement for Judas: Acts 1:26.
4. *Perf. Passages*, 22 Apr.–4 May 1649, TT E.529[30], p. 19; *Great Britaines Paine-Full Messenger*, 9–16 Aug. 1649, TT E.569[18], p. 4; MS Clar. 38, fo. 7ᵛ; Whitelocke, iii.87; *Moderate Intell.*, 16 Aug. 1649, TT E.569[19], p. 2,212.
5. Ibid., 12–18 Apr. 1649, TT E.551[1], p. 1,989; Abbott, ii.67, 93; *CSPD, 1649–50*, pp. 132, 134.

6. *Sydney Papers*, p. 76; *C&P*, i.197.

7. Ibid., i.97; *CSPD, 1649–50*, pp. xlv, 229, 239, 245–6, 257, 581–3.

8. Richard J. Blackmore and Elaine Murphy, *The British Civil Wars at Sea, 1638–1653* (Woodbridge: Boydell, 2018), pp. 157–61; N.A.M. Rodger, *The Command of the Ocean: A Naval History of Britain 1649–1815* (London: Penguin, 2005), pp. 3–4; Whitelocke, iii.87; *Crom. Navy*, pp. 61–4; Council of State, Charges for the War in Ireland, 1 Mar. 1649–16 Feb. 1650, SP 25/118, pp. 55–65; James Scott Wheeler, 'English Army Finance and Logistics 1642–1660' (PhD thesis, University of California, Berkeley, 1980), p, 221; Brown, *Empire and Enterprise*, p. 169. J.G. Simms, *War and Politics in Ireland 1649–1730* (London: Hambledon, 1986), p. 2; MS Carte 25, fo. 624.

9. Wheeler, 'English army finance', pp. 205, 211–12.

10. Carte, *Coll.*, ii.369, 379, 382; Simms, *War and Politics*, p. 1.

11. *C&P*, i.73–5; *CSPI, 1647–60*, p. 365.

12. The knock-on effects of the cessation were extensive. Later in May O'Neill signed a similar agreement with Sir Charles Coote, parliamentary commander in Londonderry. In June O'Neill and Colonel Jones came to an understanding not to disturb one another's quarters, while later that summer O'Neill actually relieved Coote in Londonderry. This halted the royalist sweep through Ulster: John T. Gilbert (ed.), *Contemporary History of Affairs in Ireland from 1641 to 1652*, 3 vols (Dublin: Irish Archaeological and Celtic Soc., 1879–80), ii.221–2; *C&P*, i.78, 83; Whitelocke, iii.356; Clarendon, Edward Hyde, first Earl of, *A History of the Rebellion and Civil Wars in Ireland* (Dublin: Patrick Dugan, 1719–20), p. 98.

13. *CJ*, vi.277; Whitelocke, iii.84.

14. *OPH*, xix.486; Patrick Little, *Lord Broghill and the Cromwellian Union with Ireland and Scotland*, Irish Historical Monographs (Rochester, NY: Boydell, 2004), pp. 59–64; Abbott, ii.88.

15. HMC, *Leyborne-Popham*, p. 35; *Moderate*, 14–21 Aug. 1649, TT E.571[7], p. 675; Abbott, ii.104. An additional 2,600 men had already sailed in July to bolster Colonel Michael Jones's defence of Dublin. *C&P*, i.105; MS Carte 25, fo. 193, Ormond to Clanricarde. Clarendon reflected that on that day Ormond's troops contracted a great fear of the enemy, a fear that they never overcame: Clarendon, *Rebellion and Civil Wars in Ireland*, p. 93; Whitelocke, iii.85; *Merc. Elencticus*, 13–20 Aug. 1649, TT E.471[1], p. 129.

16. Abbott, ii.111–12.

17. MS Carte 25, fos 212, 274, 319, 341, 353, 362, 367, 397, 471, 486.

18. Abbott, ii.119.

19. Ibid., ii.126.

20. MS Clar., 38, fo. 24^v (Inchiquin to Ormond). This startling testimony to the humanity of some of Cromwell's troops at Drogheda was previously unnoticed by historians. Cf. Carte, *Coll.*, ii.412. *Perf. Occurrences*, 28 Sept.–4 Oct. 1649, TT E.533[15], p. 1,276.

21. J.G. Simms, 'Cromwell at Drogheda, 1649', *Irish Sword*, vol. 11 (1973–74): 212–21, p. 220; *C&P*, i.119; Donagan, 'Atrocity, war crime, and treason', pp. 1,144, 1,146.

22. Micheál Ó Siochrú, *God's Executioner: Oliver Cromwell and the Conquest of Ireland* (London: Faber, 2008), p. 89; *Letters from Ireland Relating . . . to the Taking of Drogheda . . .* (2 Oct. 1649), TT E.575[7], pp. 12, 13 (corrected pag.); *Perf. Occurrences*, 28 Sept.–4 Oct. 1649, TT E.533[15], p. 1,276.

23. Carte, *Coll.*, ii.412; Abbott, ii.127; John Morrill, 'The Drogheda massacre in Cromwellian context', in David Edwards, Pádraig Lenihan and Clodagh Tait (eds), *Age of Atrocity: Violence and Political Conflict in Early Modern Ireland* (Dublin: Four Courts Press, 2007), pp. 258–9; Micheál Ó Siochrú, 'Oliver Cromwell and the massacre at Drogheda', in ibid., p. 281.

24. See the balanced account in Ó Siochrú, *God's Executioner*, chapter 4 and pp. 247–50; Carte, *Coll.*, ii.398; MS Carte 25, fo. 624; Dyve, p. 41.

25. *Letters from Ireland*, p. 15; *A Very Full and Particular Relation of the Great Progress . . . toward the Reducing of Ireland* ([31 Oct.] 1649), TT E.576[6]; *AA*, p. 255; Abbott, ii.128, 130; *Perf. Diurnall*, 5–12 Nov. 1649, TT E.533[23], p. 2,834; Ludlow, *Memoirs*, i.235, 239.

26. Abbott, ii.133; SP 25/118, pp. 138–40, 143–4; *CSPD, 1649–50*, p. 50; MS Carte 25, fos 553, 585, 689, 712; HMC, *Leyborne-Popham*, p. 45.

27. C&P, i.126, 128; A Very Full and Particular Relation, p. 50; Clarendon, A History of the Rebellion, p. 96; MS Carte 25, fo. 676.
28. HMC, Leyborne-Popham, p. 47; A Very Full and Particular Relation, p. 51. Gardiner says Cromwell's besieging force was 9,000 strong, but does not take sufficient account of his various losses along the way: C&P, i.127; Gilbert (ed.), Contemporary History, ii.288; Abbott, ii.141, 143.
29. C&P, i.133; T.W. Moody, F.X. Martin and F.J. Byrne (eds), A New History of Ireland, Volume III: Early Modern Ireland, 1534–1691 (Oxford: Clarendon Press, 1976), p. 341; Donagan, 'Atrocity, war crime, and treason', pp. 1,149–50.
30. Apart from Cromwell's letters, the best accounts of the taking of Wexford are Colonel Deanes's narration in HMC, Leyborne-Popham, p. 47, and the two anonymous reports in A Very Full and Particular Relation, pp. 50–2, 56; Abbott, ii.141, 142–3.
31. MS Carte 25, fo. 757; Abbott, ii.154–5.
32. MS Carte 26, fos 23, 45, 300ᵛ; Gilbert (ed.), Contemporary History, ii.56, 322; Little, Lord Broghill, pp. 59–62; Moody, Martin and Byrne (eds), New History, p. 342; Cary, ii.186.
33. MS Carte 25, fo. 738; Abbott ii.146, 153.
34. Ibid., ii.163, 173; MS Clar. 38, fo. 146ᵛ.
35. Simms, War and Politics, p. 11.
36. MS Carte 26, fos 7, 14, 21; Diarmuid Murtagh, 'Colonel Edward Wogan', Irish Sword, vol. 2 (1954–56): 43–54, p. 47; Simms, War and Politics, pp. 13–14.
37. Abbott, ii.160, 176.
38. SP 25/118, pp. 143, 145; MS Clar. 39, fo. 40ᵛ.
39. MS Clar. 38, fos 155, 282; Calendar of the Clarendon State Papers, ed. O. Ogle et al., 4 vols (Oxford: Clarendon Press, 1869–1932), ii.33.
40. He seems to have derived this and other convictions about the Irish from reading Sir John Temple, The Irish Rebellion (1646). T.C. Barnard, 'Crises of Identity among Irish Protestants, 1641–1685', P&P, no. 127 (1990): 39–83, pp. 52–9; Abbott, ii.197–9, 201, 203–5.
41. Ibid., ii.221; CSPD, 1650, p. 90; MS Tanner 56, fo. 182; MS Carte 67, fo. 195.
42. Gilbert (ed.), Contemporary History, ii.388.
43. Abbott, ii.223–40; Whitelocke, iii.176–7; MS Carte 67, fo. 195; Gilbert (ed.), Contemporary History, ii.388.
44. MS Carte 26, fos 170, 238, 534; Gilbert (ed.), Contemporary History, ii.504.
45. Perf. Diurnall, 20–27 May 1650, TT E.777[5], p. 278 (corrected pag.); 27 May–6 June 1650, TT E.777[8], p. 272 (sic); Abbott, ii.250.
46. Gilbert (ed.), Contemporary History, ii.417.
47. Ibid., ii.408–17; Severall Procs in Parliament, 23–30 May 1650, E777[6], pp. 504–5; Perf. Diurnall, 27 May–3 June 1650, TT E.777[8], p. 2; Whitelocke, iii.196; Cromwelliana, ed. Michael Stace (London: George Smeeton, 1810), p. 81.
48. Dyve, p. 50.
49. In Dublin by August the death toll had reached 797 a week: Whitelocke, iii.200, 212, 231–2.
50. MS Carte 27, fo. 602; Gilbert (ed.), Contemporary History, ii.70, 390, 84–8, iii.148–9; Whitelocke, iii.203, 215–17; Clarendon, A History of the Rebellion, pp. 133–4; Ludlow, Memoirs, i.255.
51. Edmund Borlase, The History of the Execrable Irish Rebellion (Dublin: Oli Nelson and Charles Connor, 1743), p. 314; Ludlow, Memoirs, i.251; Gilbert (ed.), Contemporary History, ii.100, 179; MS Carte 28, fo. 584; Carte, Coll., ii.453–5, 460; Clarendon, A History of the Rebellion, pp. 146, 163–4, 183; HMC, Leyborne-Popham, p. 75.
52. Whitelocke, iii.174; BL, Egerton MS 1048, fo. 192; MS Tanner 56, fo. 253; CSPD, 1651, pp. 147, 175.
53. Ludlow, Memoirs, i.250; Whitelocke, iii.233; MS Clar. 41, fo. 55; Perf. Diurnall, 26 Aug.–2 Sept. 1650, TT E.780[1], pp. 454–5.
54. Carte, Coll., ii.426; MS Carte 28, fos 432, 459; Clarendon, A History of the Rebellion, p. 130; Simms, War and Politics, pp. 22–3.

55. MS Clar. 42, fos 198–204, 208.
56. Ibid., fos 217–18, 222; Ludlow, *Memoirs*, i.275, 278, n. 1; *CSPD, 1651*, p. 171; *Perf. Diurnall*, 23–30 June 1651, TT E.786[11], pp. 1,121–2; Robert Dunlop, *Ireland under the Commonwealth*, 2 vols (Manchester: Manchester University Press, 1913), i.69, 74, 27–8; NA, Exchequer, E101/67/11B, fo. 141ᵛ.
57. Ludlow, *Memoirs*, i.287–8; MS Clar. 42, fos 233–4.
58. Ludlow, *Memoirs*, i.290–1, 308; MS Carte 67, fo. 238; MS Clar. 42, fos 223–4; MS Tanner 53, fos 4, 31; HMC, *Egmont*, i.508; NLW, MS 11440D, p. 62; J. Mayer, 'Inedited Letters of Cromwell, Colonel Jones, Bradshaw and other regicides', *Transactions of the Historic Soc. of Lancashire and Cheshire*, new ser., vol. 1 (1860–61), p. 234; Whitelocke, iii.461.
59. Ibid., iii.205; MS Carte 67, fos 202, 223ᵛ; Ludlow, *Memoirs*, i.491; MS Tanner 55, fo. 73; Cary, ii.280–1; *CSPD, 1650*, pp. 427, 60; W. McCarthy, 'The royalist collapse in Munster, 1650–1652', *Irish Sword*, vol. 6 (1963–64): 171–9, pp. 171–2, 176; Gilbert (ed.), *Contemporary History*, iii.167; Whitelocke, iii.317; *Severall Procs in Parliament*, 8–15 Jan. 1652, TT E.793[11], p. 1,856; Dunlop, *Ireland under the Commonwealth*, i.6–7, 113, 189, 239; ii.511.
60. MS Tanner 55, fos 99, 133; vol. 53, fos 24–5, 69, 74; Dunlop, *Ireland under the Commonwealth*, i.113, 130, 133, 248–9; Micheál Ó Siochrú, 'English military intelligence in Ireland during the Wars of the Three Kingdoms', in Eunan O'Halpin, Robert Armstrong and Jane Ohlmeyer (eds), *Intelligence, Statecraft and International Power: Papers Read before the 27th Conference of Irish Historians, Trinity College Dublin 19–21 May 2005* (Dublin: Irish Academic Press, 2005), pp. 48–64, pp. 53–6; MS Carte 67, fos 248, 266; Ludlow, *Memoirs*, i.317–18, 320–2; D. Bryan, 'Colonel Richard Grace, 1651–1652', *Irish Sword*, vol. 4 (1959–60): 43–51, p. 47; Moody, Martin and Byrne (eds), *New History*, 362; William J. Smyth, *Map-making, Landscapes and Memory: A Geography of Colonial and Early Modern Ireland, c. 1630–1750* (Cork: Cork University Press, 2006), p. 160.
61. Cary, ii.281, 419–20; MS Clar 42, fo. 241ᵛ; Ludlow, *Memoirs*, i.302, 509; NLW, MS 11440D, pp. 42, 47–8, 54, 75, 105; MS Carte 67, fo. 238; HMC, *Egmont*, i.508; MS Tanner 53, fos 20–1; Karl S. Bottigheimer, *English Money and Irish Land* (Oxford: Clarendon Press, 1971), p. 127.
62. *Severall Procs in Parliament*, 20–27 May 1652, TT E.795[8], pp. 2m171–4; Dunlop, *Ireland under the Commonwealth*, i.236; Gilbert (ed.), *Contemporary History*, iii.348; MS Clar. 44, fo. 137–7ᵛ.
63. John Cunningham, *Conquest and Land in Ireland: The Transplantation to Connacht, 1649–1680* (Woodbridge: Boydell for the Royal HS, 2011), p. 16; *CJ*, vi.540–2.
64. Ludlow, *Memoirs*, i.301; NLW, 11440D, p. 85; A&O, ii.598–63; Bottigheimer, *English Money and Irish Land*, pp. 117, 139–40; Moody, Martin and Byrne (eds), *New History*, 359–61, 369; Cunningham, *Conquest and Land in Ireland*, pp. 39–43, 57, 62–3.
65. Ibid., pp. 43, 47, 76, 78.
66. Ibid., pp. 88, 90, 100. Micheál Ó Siochrú and David Brown point out that the Down Survey estimated Catholic and Protestant landownership in 1641 at 54 per cent and 46 per cent respectively: 'The Down Survey and the Cromwellian Land Settlement', in Jane Ohlmeyher, ed., *The Cambridge History of Ireland, Volume II: 1550–1730* (Cambridge: Cambridge University Press, 2018), pp. 584–607, p. 605; Charlene McCoy, 'War and Revolution: County Fermanagh and Its Borders, c. 1640–c. 1666' (unpublished PhD thesis, Trinity College Dublin, 2007), p. 356.
67. Ted McCormick, *William Petty and the Ambitions of Political Arithmetic* (Oxford: Oxford University Press, 2009), pp. 97, 101, 113; Smyth, *Map-making, Landscapes and Memory*, pp. 173, 175, 196; Ó Siochrú and Brown, 'The Down Survey and the Cromwellian Land Settlement', p. 600; Caitlin Higgins Ní Chinnéide, 'The Political Influence of the Cromwellian Army in Ireland, 1649–1659' (unpublished PhD thesis, Trinity College Dublin, 2013), p. 152. Between July 1649 and November 1656 the army in Ireland was paid £3.5 million, of which £1.5 million came from England: Trinity College Dublin, MS 650/7, unfol., cited in Ní Chinnéide, 'Political Influence of the Cromwellian Army', p. 204. See also Dunlop, *Ireland under the Commonwealth*, ii.545.

68. Lenihan, 'War and population, 1649–52', pp. 19, 21; Gentles, *English Revolution*, p. 436; MS Tanner 53, fo. 101.

69. T.C. Barnard, *Cromwellian Ireland: English Government and Reform in Ireland 1649–1660* (Oxford: Oxford University Press, 2000), p. 14. This and the following paragraphs owe much to Barnard's work.

70. Ibid., pp. 97–8, 100.

71. Quoted in idem, *Cromwellian Ireland*, p. 110.

72. *The Correspondence of Henry Cromwell 1655–1659*, ed. Peter Gaunt, Camden Soc., 5th ser., vol. 31 (Cambridge: Cambridge University Press for the Royal HS, 2007), p. 416.

73. Moody, Martin and Byrne (eds), *New History*, p. 273; Ní Chinnéide, 'Political Influence of the Cromwellian Army', p. 170; Ian Gentles, 'The sales of crown lands during the English Revolution', *Economic History Review*, 2nd ser., vol. 26 (1973): 614–35, p. 618; Public RO of Northern Ireland, Dartry Papers, D 3053; National Library of Ireland, MS 768; King's Inns Library, Dublin, Prendergast Papers, ii.787; iv.887; Kevin McKenny, *The Laggan Army in Ireland, 1640–1685* (Dublin: Four Courts Press, 2005), p. 131.

74. Patrick Little (ed.), *The Cromwellian Protectorate* (Woodbridge: Boydell, 2007), pp. 129–30, 132; John Cunningham, 'Politics, 1641–1660', in Ohlmeyer (ed.), *Cambridge History of Ireland, Volume II*, pp. 72–95, p. 92; Ní Chinnéide, 'Political Influence of the Cromwellian Army', p. 103; King's Inns Library, Dublin, Prendergast Papers, i.162.

75. Trinity College Dublin, MS 844, fo. 110 (4 Nov. 1651); MacLean, Gentles and Ó Siochrú, 'Minutes of courts martial', pp. 60–3.

76. Ibid., p. 60.

77. Jennifer Wells, 'English law, Irish trials and Cromwellian state building in the 1650s', *P&P*, no. 227 (May 2015): 77–119; idem, 'Proceedings at the High Court of Justice at Dublin and Cork 1652–1654', *Archivium Hibernicum*, vol. 66 (2013): 63–260, p. 67.

78. Cunningham, 'Politics, 1641–1660', p. 91; John Morrill, 'Cromwell, Parliament, Ireland and a commonwealth in crisis: 1652 revisited', *Parliamentary History*, vol. 30 (2011): 193–214, pp. 194–5, 196, 199.

79. King's Inns Library, Dublin, Prendergast Papers, i.73 (May 1652), 276 (Limerick), 360 (Lackagh, Co. Kildare), 467 (Galway); ii.217, 493–4, 516–17, 643; v.29; *TSP*, iv.404 (27 June 1654); Brid McGrath, 'Booting out, settling out: The Cromwellian takeover of Clonmel', unpublished paper, North American Conference on British Studies, Providence, RI, 27 Oct. 2018; Patricia Stapilton, 'The Merchant Community of Dublin in the Early Seventeenth Century: A Social, Economic and Political Study' (unpublished PhD thesis, Trinity College Dublin, 2008), p. 263. In theory all towns east of the Shannon were cleared of their Catholic inhabitants: Patrick J. Corish, 'The Cromwellian regime, 1650–60', in Moody, Martin and Byrne (eds), *New History*, pp. 353–86, pp. 373–4; Raymond Gillespie, *The Transformation of the Irish Economy, 1550–1700*, Studies in Irish Economic and Social History, no. 6 (Dundalk: Dundalgan Press, 1991), pp. 39–40; Carla Gardina Pestana, *The English Conquest of Jamaica: Oliver Cromwell's Bid for Empire* (Cambridge, MA: Harvard University Press, 2017), p. 217 for the recruitment of women for Jamaica; Smyth, *Map-making, Landscapes and Memory*, p. 160.

80. *To His Highness the Lord Protector, &c. and Our General. The Humble Petition of Several Colonels of the Army* (London, 1654), TT 669.f.19[21]; *TSP*, ii.733; Ní Chinnéide, 'Political Influence of the Cromwellian Army', pp. 175, 180, 182; Massarella, p. 364; Gentles, '*Agreements of the People*', pp. 160–2.

81. Vincent Gookin, *The Great Case of Transplantation in Ireland Discussed, or Certain Considerations* (London: I.C., 1655), TT E.234[6], pp. 3, 7, 15, 17, 22, 24.

82. Richard Lawrence, *England's Great Interest in the Well Planting of Ireland with English People Discussed*, 2nd edn (Dublin: Wil. Bladen, 1656), pp. 3, 29, 31–3, 37, 42–3. Gookin answered Lawrence in a second pamphlet which largely reiterated the arguments of his first: *The Author and Case of Transplanting the Irish into Connaught Vindicated, from the Unjust Aspersions of Col. Richard Laurence* (London: I. C., [12 May]1655), TT E.838[7].

83. *Correspondence of Henry Cromwell*, p. 115; *TSP*, iv.606, 672.

84. Ibid., iii.715, 728, 744 (15, 22, 29 Aug. 1655); Ní Chinnéide, 'Political Influence of the Cromwellian Army', pp. 100, 158–9.
85. Ibid., p. 203.
86. Ibid., pp. 215–16; *Correspondence of Henry Cromwell*, p. 314.
87. Ibid., p. 155, n. 201; *TSP*, v.150, 176, 177, 196–7, 213–14.
88. Ní Chinnéide, 'Political Influence of the Cromwellian Army', pp. 198–200.
89. He was referring to a recent Fifth Monarchy tract denouncing the Protectorate.
90. *Correspondence of Henry Cromwell*, p. 275; Add. MS 4157, fo. 182, cited in *Correspondence of Henry Cromwell*, p. 285.
91. Ibid., pp. 311–12, n. 325, pp. 341, 345.
92. *A&O*, ii.1,170–80; *Correspondence of Henry Cromwell*, p. 347.

11 THE CONQUEST AND RULE OF SCOTLAND, 1650-59

1. Dow, p. 6.
2. Stevenson, p. 314; Carte, *Coll.*, i.373–4; *Diary of Alexander Jaffray*, ed. John Barclay, 3rd edn (Aberdeen: George and Robert King, 1856), p. 55.
3. *Perf. Diurnall*, 27 May–3 June 1650, TT E.377[8], p. 280; Nicoll, *Diary*, p. 16; *CSPD, 1650*, p. 210 (20 June 1650); Whitelocke, iii.211.
4. *Cromwelliana*, p. 82; *CSPD, 1650*, p. 267; Stevenson, p. 175; *OPH*, xix.298–312; Abbott, ii.285.
5. *Perf. Diurnall*, 5–12 Aug. 1650, TT E.778[18], p. 409; Wheeler, 'English army finance', pp. 246–7; Nickolls, p. 41.
6. Wheeler, 'English army finance', pp. 236, 243, 243, 247–8; *A Brief Relation*, 13–20 Aug. 1651, TT E.609[17], p. 802. For information about the size of daily rations, see *CSPD, 1650*, p. 464; *Perf. Diurnall*, 8–15. Dec. 1651, TT E.791[27], p. 1,502. Beer was brewed in Newcastle for the expeditionary force just after its departure at the end of July 1650: Nickolls, pp. 11–12; Nicoll, *Diary*, p. 55. During the invasion 2,800 tons of oats and about 10,700 tons of hay, mostly from East Anglia, Surrey and Kent, were shipped to Scotland for the New Model. For information about suppliers, see Wheeler, p. 145; *CSPD, 1650*, p. 464; *Merc. Politicus*, 20–27 Feb. 1651, TT E.625[6], pp. 514, 622.
7. *Perf. Diurnall*, 22–29 July 1650, TT E.778[7], p. 391; *CSPD, 1650*, p. 478; *CJ*, vi.483; Nickolls, p. 41 (letter from Sir Henry Vane, 28 Dec. 1650); Wheeler, 'English army finance', pp. 233, 250.
8. In fact the expeditionary army was paid much less faithfully than the forces stationed in England during the same period. At home the soldiers were paid month by month with almost clockwork regularity. In Scotland, during the sixty-four weeks of active service, the foot and artillery were paid just over three-quarters of the time, while the horse and dragoons got just over half what was due to them: NA, Exchequer, Treasurers at War Accounts, 28 Mar. 1645–25 Dec. 1651, E351/302, fo. 5ᵛ; SP 28/69–80, *passim*. See also *NMA*, p. 389; Add. MS 21419, fo. 271; Reece, p. 93; Add. MS, 21420, fos 131, 157; *Perf. Diurnall*, 19–26 May 1651, TT E.785[31], p. 1,058.
9. Stevenson, p. 173.
10. *Perf. Diurnall*, 5–12 Aug. 1650, TT E.778[18], p. 409; Abbott, ii.297.
11. *Perf. Diurnall*, 5–12 Aug. 1650, TT E.778[18], p. 410; Hodgson, pp. 215–20, 236–40; *Merc. Politicus*, 1–8 Aug. 1650, TT E.609[5], p. 142; *Perf. Diurnall*, 5–12 Aug. 1650, TT E.778[18], p. 411; Johnston, *Diary*, ii.6; *Cromwelliana*, p. 87; Nicoll, *Diary*, p. 22; Balfour, *Historical Works*, iv.87; Abbott, ii.300.
12. *C&P*, i.275; Abbott, ii.303, 305–6.
13. *Merc. Politicus*, 15–22 Aug. 1650, TT E.610[3], p. 165; *Perf. Diurnall*, 12–19 Aug. 1650, TT E.778[20], p. 440; *Severall Procs in Parliament*, 15–22 Aug. 1650, TT E.778[21], p. 692.
14. *Perf. Diurnall*, 2–9 Sept. 1650, TT E.780[4], p. 486; W.S. Douglas, *Cromwell's Scotch Campaigns: 1650–51* (London: E. Stock, 1898), pp. 89–90.

15. *Perf. Passages*, 9–13 Sept. 1650, TT E.780[6], p. 71.
16. Abbott, ii.314, 322; Hodgson, p. 267; *Severall Procs in Parliament*, 15–22 Aug. 1650, TT E.778[21], p. 692; *Perf. Diurnall*, 26 Aug.–2 Sept. 1650, TT E.780[1], p. 470; Nickolls, p. 18.
17. *Perf. Passages*, 9–13 Sept. 1650, TT E.780[6], p. 77; *A True Relation of the Routing of the Scotish Army, near Dunbar* (9 Sept. 1650), TT E.612[9], p. 4; Abbott, ii.314, 322.
18. *OPH*, xix.341; C.H. Firth, 'The battle of Dunbar', *TRHS*, new ser., vol. 14 (1900): 19–52, p. 36n.; Abbott, ii.316, 323; Hodgson, pp. 144–6; Carte, *Coll.*, i.381.
19. Stevenson, p. 178.
20. Abbott, ii.316; *C&P*, i.290.
21. Cadwell's account in Carte, *Coll.*, i.382; Hodgson, pp. 144–5.
22. Rushworth's report in *OPH*, xix.341; *Correspondence of Sir Robert Ker, First Earl of Ancram, and His Son William*, ed. David Laing, 2 vols (Edinburgh: R. & R. Clark, 1875), ii.298; Firth, 'The battle of Dunbar', p. 41; Walker, *Historical Discourses*, p. 180; *Memoirs of the Life of Ambrose Barnes*, p. 111; *Merc. Politicus*, 12–19 Sept. 1650, TT E.613[1], pp. 227–8; Hodgson, p. 146.
23. Ibid., pp. 146–7; Abbott, ii.317, 323; *A Brief Narrative of the Great Victorie ... near Dunbar* (7 Sept. 1650), TT E.612[7], p. 2; *Merc. Politicus*, 5–12 Sept. 1650, TT E.612[14], p. 218; *A True Relation of the Routing of the Scotish Army*, p. 4; James Heath, *Flagellum: or the Life and Death, Birth and Burial of Oliver Cromwell, the Late Usurper* (London: L.R., 1663), pp. 98–9; Douglas, *Cromwell's Scotch Campaigns*, p. 109.
24. *Perf. Passages*, 9–13 Sept. 1650, TT E.780[6], p. 72; *A Brief Narrative*, p. 2.
25. Cadwell in Carte, *Coll.*, i.383; Hodgson, pp. 147–8, 279; *C&P*, i.292, n. 3; *A Brief Narrative*, pp. 2–3; Abbott, ii.324
26. Ibid., ii.324; *OPH*, xix.341.
27. John Aubrey, *Miscellanies upon Various Subjects* (London: W. Ottridge, 1784), pp. 160–1; Hodgson, p. 147.
28. *Crom. Navy*, p. 67.
29. *Cromwelliana*, p. 91.
30. Stevenson, p. 181; Clarendon, *History*, v.149; *Merc. Politicus*, 12–19 Sept. 1650, TT E.613[1], p. 259; Hodgson, p. 147; Dow, pp. 8–9, Nickolls, p. 24.
31. Abbott, ii.327, 331–2; *CSPD, 1650*, pp. 333, 339, 348–50, 352, 363, 394; Nickolls, p. 19; Jaffray, *Diary*, pp. 58–60; *Cromwelliana*, p. 92.
32. Abbott, ii.354–5, 357; Baillie, iii.119; Dow, p. 9; Ancram, *Correspondence*, ii.335n; Stevenson, p. 195; Baillie, iii.125; *Merc. Politicus*, 24–31 Oct. 1650, TT E.615[10], p. 337; *Cromwelliana*, p. 92; Hodgson, p. 336.
33. Abbott, ii.363; *Merc. Politicus*, 12–19 Dec. 1650, TT E.620[8], p. 467; 19–26 Dec. 1650, TT E.620[12], p. 483.
34. Ibid., 19–26 Dec. 1650, TT E.620[12], pp. 473, 477; 26 Dec. 1650–1 Jan. 1651, TT E.621[4], pp. 494, 497; Duffy, p. 156; Baillie, iii.125; Nicoll, *Diary*, p. 37; Heath, *Flagellum*, p. 107; Abbott, ii.335–6, 338–9, 369–72, 373; Douglas, *Cromwell's Scotch Campaigns*, pp. 203n., 206.
35. Abbott, ii.329, 393–5, 400, 403, 419; *Faithful Scout*, 14–21 Feb. 1651, TT E.784[12], p. 72; *Cromwelliana*, pp. 100, 102; Add. MS 21419, fo. 333; Carte, *Coll.*, i.426; John Yonge Akerman (ed.), *Letters from Roundhead Officers, Written from Scotland, and Chiefly Addressed to Captain Adam Baynes July MDCL–June MDCLX*, Bannatyne Club, vol. 108 (1823), pp. 10, 12, 24; *Faithful Scout*, 23–30 May 1651, TT E.785[34], p. 183; *CSPD, 1651*, pp. 91, 218; Johnston, *Diary*, ii.54–5; *CJ*, vi.579; Whitelocke, iii.308.
36. Ibid., iii.293, 300–1, 306, 310, 313; Add. MS 21420, fos 114, 122; Akerman (ed.), *Letters from Roundhead Officers*, p. 31; Abbott, ii.408, 415, 420, 424; *CSPD, 1651*, pp. 84, 98–9; *Perf. Diurnall*, 19–26 May 1651, TT E.785[31], p. 1,046; Johnston, *Diary*, ii.59; Nicoll, *Diary*, p. 50.
37. Johnston, *Diary*, ii.53; *OPH*, xix.480; *C&P*, ii.29; Abbott, ii.434–5; *Merc. Politicus*, 24–31 July 1651, TT E.638[10], p. 957.
38. Stevenson, p. 205; Abbott, ii.430; Johnston, *Diary*, ii.85; *Merc. Politicus*, 24–31 July 1651, TT E.638[10], p. 953; Whitelocke, iii.321–3; Akerman (ed.), *Letters from Roundhead*

Officers, pp. 34–5; David Farr, *John Lambert, Parliamentary Soldier and Cromwellian Major-General, 1619–1684* (Woodbridge: Boydell, 2003), pp. 87–9.

39. Stevenson, p. 206; Abbott, ii.431–2; Farr, *John Lambert*, p. 86.
40. Abbott, ii.441; *C&P*, ii.34; Cary, ii.305.
41. Stevenson, pp. 206–7; Cary, ii.305; *Merc. Politicus*, 14–21 Aug. 1651, TT E.640[14], p. 1,012; 21–28 Aug., TT E.640[23], p. 1,024; D.E. Underdown, *Royalist Conspiracy in England, 1649–1660* (New Haven: Yale University Press, 1960), pp. 42–7.
42. Nickolls, pp. 78–9; Cary, ii.295, 297–302; *CSPD, 1651*, pp. 307–8; Abbott, ii.446–8; HMC, *De L'Isle and Dudley*, vi.603.
43. MS Tanner 55, fo. 8; *CSPD, 1651*, pp. 327–8, 340, 344, 346; Whitelocke, iii.355; *C&P*, ii.35.
44. Abbott, ii.450–2; *Merc. Politicus*, 21–28 Aug. 1651, TT E.640[23], p. 1,019; Cary, ii.327; *C&P*, ii.41, 43.
45. MS Tanner 55, fos 2, 4; Hodgson, p. 152; *Merc. Politicus*, 28 Aug.–4 Sept. 1651, TT E.641[4], p. 1,038; Whitelocke, iii.338, 343; *Two Letters from Col. Robert Lilburne* ([30 Aug.] 1651), TT E.640[26], printed in Cary, ii.339–41, 343–4; *A Great Victory . . . Near Wigon* ([29 Aug.] 1651), TT E.640[27].
46. MS Clar 42, fo. 151ᵛ; MS Tanner 55, fo. 50; *Merc. Politicus*, 21–28 Aug. 1651, TT E.640[23], p. 1,019; 28 Aug.–4 Sept. 1651, TT E.641[4], pp. 1,041–2; Whitelocke, iii.335–6, 340, 344; *Severall Procs in Parliament*, 28 Aug.–4 Sept.1651, TT E.787[12], pp. 1,557–8; HMC, *Lechmere*, p. 299; Abbott, ii.455; Duffy, p. 157; P. Styles, *Studies in Seventeenth Century West Midland History* (Kineton: Roundwood Press, 1978), p. 249; *Faithful Scout*, 29 Aug.–5 Sept.1651, TT E.787[13], p. 256; *Perf. Passages*, 29 Aug.–5 Sept. 1651, TT E.787[14], p. 370; *Weekly Intell.*, 26 Aug.–2 Sept. 1651, TT E.641[2], p. 272.
47. Abbott, ii.455; MS Tanner 55, fo. 23; *Merc. Politicus*, 28 Aug.–4 Sept. 1651, TT E.641[4], pp. 1,042–4; Whitelocke, iii.337–8.
48. Abbott, ii.456.
49. Ibid., ii.458; Styles, *Studies*, p. 249.
50. *Perf. Diurnall*, 8–15 Sept. 1651, TT E.787[19], p. 1,203; *Severall Procs in Parliament*, 4–11 Sept. 1651, TT E.787[16], p. 1,566; HMC, *Lechmere*, p. 299; *Merc. Politicus*, 4–11 Sept. 1651, TT E.641[12], p. 1,052.
51. MS Clar. 42, fos 151ᵛ–2; MS Tanner 55, fo. 37–7ᵛ; Abbott, ii.459; Cary, ii.463.
52. MS Tanner 55, fos 37ᵛ–8; Whitelocke, ii.346, following the newsbooks, mistranscribes 'mount and works' as 'mountain works'. For Cromwell's bravery, see *Merc. Politicus*, 4–11 Sept. 1651, TT E.641[12], pp. 1,053–4; MS Clar. 42, fos 149ᵛ, 167; Cary ii.363.
53. MS Clar. 42, fo. 152ᵛ; NA, HLRO, Braye MS 3, fo. 34 (printed in HMC, *Braye*, p. 175); MS Clar. 42, fo. 149ᵛ; *Weekly Intell.*, 2–9 Sept. 1651, TT E.641[11], p. 278; Heath, *Flagellum*, pp. 121–2.
54. Abbott, ii.461; MS Tanner 55, fo. 50; *Faithful Scout*, 5–12 Sept. 1651, TT E.787[18], p. 258; Cary, ii.354; Ronald Hutton, *Charles II* (Oxford: Clarendon Press, 1989), pp. 64–7.
55. *Perf. Diurnall*, 8–15 Sept. 1651, TT E.787[19], pp. 1,293–6; Abbott, ii.464; NA, HLRO, Braye MS 3, fo. 34; Hutton, *Charles II*, pp. 67–70; *C&P*, ii.52–6; MS Clar. 42, fo. 150; Whitelocke, iii.349; *Merc. Politicus*, 4–11 Sept. 1651, TT E.641[12], pp. 1,057–8.
56. *CJ*, viii.24–5.
57. *Merc. Politicus*, 11–18 Sept. 1651, TT E.641[20], p. 1,076.
58. Whitelocke, iii.352; Abbott, ii.472, 474, 476; *CJ*, vii.46; *C&P*, ii.62–5.
59. Worc. MS 22, fos 18ᵛ, 35ᵛ.
60. Ibid., fo. 35; 'Dundee court-martial records, 1651', pp. 13, 14, 16, 17, 21, 59–60, 33. See also MacLean, Gentles and Ó Siochrú, 'Minutes of courts martial'; Nicoll, *Diary*, pp. 33, 66.
61. *CJ*, vii.56.
62. Lesley Smith, 'Scotland and Cromwell: A Study in Early Modern Government' (DPhil thesis, University of Oxford, 1979), pp. 31–2; Carlyle, *Cromwell*, ii.81, citing Whitelocke.
63. The military commissioners were Major-Generals Monck, Deane and Lambert, Colonels Robert Tichborne and George Fenwick, and Major Richard Salwey. The non-military commissioners were Sir Henry Vane and Oliver St John: Smith, 'Scotland and Cromwell', p. 58; Dow, p. 24.

64. Lamont, *Diary*, pp. 6, 47; C.H. Firth (ed.), *Scotland and the Commonwealth: Letters and Papers Relating to the Military Government of Scotland, from August 1651 to December 1653*, SHS, vol. 18 (1895), p. 368; Nicoll, *Diary*, pp. 174, 175, 202, 213–14, 216, 228, 233. The burnings continued after the Restoration.
65. Ibid., p. 33
66. For the religious and cultural significance of the stool of repentance, see Margo Todd, *The Culture of Protestantism in Early Modern Scotland* (New Haven and London: Yale University Press, 2002), pp. 168–82, and Stewart, *Rethinking the Scottish Revolution*, p. 1. Worc. MS 22, fo. 8; Lamont, *Diary*, pp. 44, 56, 86–7; John Gwynne, *Military Memoirs of the Great Civil War* (Edinburgh: Archibald Constable, 1822), p. 199; Nicoll, *Diary*, pp. 68, 147, 174, 250.
67. 'Monck, George, first duke of Albemarle', *ODNB*; Firth (ed.), *Scotland and the Commonwealth*, pp. 174–9; Dow, p. 55; Smith, 'Scotland and Cromwell', pp. 31, 38, 45; Nicoll, *Diary*, p. 65.
68. Firth (ed.), *Scotland and the Commonwealth*, pp. xxxi, 62, 162, 164–5, 262, 265, 271, 274; *Merc. Politicus*, 21–28 July 1653, TT E.708[2], p. 2,612.
69. *CP*, v.95; Firth (ed.), *Scotland and the Commonwealth*, pp. 149, 164, 271, 273, 276, 283; *Merc. Politicus*, 9–16 Dec. 1653, TT E.724[8], p. 3,026.
70. Firth (ed.), *Scotland and the Commonwealth*, pp. 295–6.
71. Ibid., pp. 307, 323.
72. 'Monck, George', *ODNB*; Firth, *Scotland and the Protectorate*, vol. 31, pp. 76–9.
73. *TSP*, vii.37.
74. Firth (ed.), *Scotland and the Commonwealth*, p. 265.
75. Gwynne, *Military Memoirs*, pp. 242, 244–5; *S&P*, pp. 43, 46; *TSP*, ii.95; *CP*, v.155.
76. *S&P*, pp. xix, 105, 107, 108.
77. *CP*, v.145; *CSPD, 1654*, pp. 57, 76, 102, 113–14.
78. Clarke MS 26, fos 76ᵛ, 89ᵛ, 93ᵛ, 109ᵛ, 118. I am most grateful to Frances Henderson for making available to me her recent decipherment of William Clarke's journal of the army's movements and actions in Scotland in 1654.
79. Clarke MS 26, fos 72ᵛ–103; *C&P*, iii.108.
80. *Reg. Hist.*, pp. 537–8; *S&P*, pp. xx, 138, 145, 154, 172, 401–2; *TSP*, ii.475, 483; Clarke MS 26, fos 99ᵛ–107, 109–10; *Merc. Politicus*, 27 Jul.–3 Aug. 1654, TT E.806[13], pp. 3,654, 3,662–3; 3–10 Aug. 1654, TT E.808[7], pp. 3, 669–70; 10–17 Aug. 1654, TT E.808[17], pp. 3,695–700. Monck himself claimed that he had reduced Middleton's army from 3,000 to 1,200: *S&P*, p. 145. Another reliable source said that he wore down Middleton's force from 4,000 to 2,000 before the two ever crossed swords. *Merc. Politicus*, 10–17 Aug. 1654, TT E.808[17], p. 1,699; Clarke MS 26, fo. 106ᵛ.
81. The earl of Glencairn could not get along with Lieutenant-General Sir George Monro and fought a duel with him. The marquess of Argyll's royalist son Lord Lorne quarrelled with the marquess of Huntly, the earl of Glencairn, Viscount Kenmure, Lord Balcarres, the young Montrose and the laird of Glengarry. Lord Atholl and Glengarry wanted to fight a duel but were prevented. *TSP*, ii.18; Nicoll, *Diary*, p. 136; Gwynne, *Military Memoirs*, pp. 98, 163–4, 176, 180, 229, 250; *S&P*, pp. 23, 126, 196; *C&P*, iii.94.
82. Burnet, *History of His Own Time*, i.108–9.
83. *S&P*, pp. 157, 161, 162, 173, 184, 295; *CP*, v.210–11.
84. *S&P*, pp. 253, 259, 260, 266, 288; Nicoll, *Diary*, p. 167; Dow, p. 111.
85. *CSPD, 1654*, p. 310; Dow, pp. 143, 155; *S&P*, pp. 290, 305.
86. Little, *Lord Broghill*, chapter 4. Four of the first nine members of the Scottish Council were military: General Monck and Colonels Charles Howard, Adrian Scrope and Thomas Cooper: *CSPD, 1655*, p. 152; *TSP*, iii.323–4. Dow, p. 185. For a list of JPs, sheriffs and commissaries of shires for the years 1656–57, see *S&P*, pp. 308–18. Four of the six military MPs were colonels: Thomas Fitch, governor of Inverness, William Mitchell, Stephen Winthrop, Edward Salmon. The other two were Advocate-General Henry Whalley and Scoutmaster-General George Downing. Charles Sanford Terry, *The Cromwellian Union* (Edinburgh: Scottish History Society, 1902), pp. lxii–lxiii; *S&P*, p. 321.

87. Ibid., pp. xxxiii, xxxvi.
88. Ibid., p. xliii. Brayne 'hath done more in settling the peace in the Highlands and in Lochaber, where there was nothing but barbarities, that now there is not one robbery all this year' (J. Drummond, 8 Jan. 1656); *TSP*, iv.401.
89. *S&P*, p. 360 (Monck to lord protector, 11 Jul. 1657); *Memorials of John Ray*, ed. Edwin Lankester (London: Ray Soc., 1846), p. 156.
90. Little, *Lord Broghill*, pp. 116, 120; *S&P*, p. 411; *TSP*, v. 604; vi.295, 306.
91. *S&P*, pp. 213, 215–16.
92. *TSP*, iii.29–30, 45–6; 'Overton, Robert', *ODNB*. The officers were Captain Henry Hedworth of Sir William Constable's regiment, Lieutenant John Braman, Cornet John Toomes and Private John Loveland of Captain Merryman's troop, Rich's regiment; Lieutenant Francis Rawson, Quarter Master John Waltredge, of Captain Babington's troop, Rich's regiment; Quarter Master William Barford of Colonel Rich's troop; Quarter Master John Gregory of Major Husband's troop, Rich's regiment; and Chaplain Samuel Oates of Colonel Pride's regiment; *CP*, v.240; Barbara Taft, '*The Humble Petition of Several Colonels of the Army*: Causes, Character, and Results of Military Opposition to Cromwell's Protectorate', *Huntington Library Quarterly*, vol. 42 (1978): 15–41, p. 38.
93. *C to P*, iii.226, 231–2; *Merc. Politicus*, 11–18 Jan. 1655, TT E.825[4], pp. 5,051–2; *TSP*, iii.147.
94. *S&P*, p. 243; 'Sindercombe, Miles', *ODNB*.
95. *S&P*, p. liii.
96. Dow, pp. 187–8.
97. *S&P*, pp. 349, 350, 362, 416; *TSP*, iv.136, 145, 162, 167, 208, 215, 241.
98. Ibid., pp. 366–7, 370, 373–7; *CJ*, vii.628; *CSPD, 1657–58*, p. 316. By April 1659 the Scottish excise was raising £14,174 per month: *CJ*, vii.628. By then it was too late.

12 THE ARMY AND THE EXPULSION OF THE RUMP PARLIAMENT, SEPTEMBER 1651 TO APRIL 1653

1. Ibid., vi.141.
2. Ibid., vi.153; Whitelocke, iii.66–7; *The Petition of the General Council of Officers*; MS Tanner 56, fos 91–2ᵛ; *The Petition of Thomas Lord Fairfax and His Councel of Officers for the Recalling of All Penal Laws Made against Private Meetings, the Punishing of Prophaneness, &c.* (16 Aug. 1649), TT E.569[22].
3. Add. MS 21418, fo. 286; John Lilburne, *Apologetical Narration* (Amsterdam: L.I., 1652), TT E.659[30], pp. 12–13; Ludlow, *Memoirs*, i.246. Cromwell was quoting 2 Samuel 3:39: Morrill and Baker, 'Oliver Cromwell, the regicide and the sons of Zeruiah'.
4. Abbott, ii.325, 433, 463; Worc. MS 181, unfol., 29 Oct. 1650, cited in Massarella, p. 269; Cary, ii.344, 375–6.
5. Worden, *Rump*, pp. 265, 275, 278; *C to P*, p. 9; *OPH*, xx.57.
6. The second *Agreement* would have excluded well over half the adult males from the franchise. See above, p. 141. *CJ*, vii.20, 36–7; HMC, *De L'Isle and Dudley*, vi.609; Abbott, ii.501.
7. Worden, *Rump*, pp. 276, 278; *C to P*, pp. 29–30; Abbott, ii.499; *CJ*, vii.38–9; Massarella, p. 278; Whitelocke, iii.372–5.
8. Mary Cotterell, 'Interregnum law reform: The Hale Commission of 1652', *EHR*, vol. 83 (1968): 689–704, pp. 694, 703; Worden, *Rump*, pp. 271, 280; Massarella, p. 281. The army's representatives on the commission were Disbrowe, Tomlinson, Packer, Peters and Rushworth: *CJ*, vii.74.
9. Worden, *Rump*, p. 282; *CJ*, vii.55, 71–5, 77, 80, 101, 104; Lilburne, *Apologetical Narration*, pp. 19–20; *Faithful Scout*, 23–30 Jan. 1652, TT E.793[20], pp. 418–21. According to ibid. the officers were divided over Lilburne.
10. Worden, *Rump*, pp. 269–70; Abbott, ii.515; *CJ*, vii.84–7, 147–51, *et passim*; Whitelocke, iii.392.

11. *CJ*, vii.77, 79, 133–4, 142; Abbott, ii.517; Hutchinson, p. 204; Whitelocke, iii.438; *CSPD, 1652–53*, pp. 242, 260, 263; Farr, *John Lambert*.

12. *A Declaration of the Armie to His Excellency the Lord General Cromwell* ([10 Aug.] 1652), TT E.673[13]; *The Humble Petition of the Officers of the Army* ([14 Aug.] 1652), TT 669.f.16[62]; *Weekly Intell.*, 10–17 Aug. 1652, TT E.674[3], p. 561; *CJ*, vii.164, 175, 178; Whitelocke, iii.446; Worden, *Rump*, p. 309; *C to P*, p. 41, n. 36.

13. *CJ*, vi. 171; Worden, *Rump*, p. 309; HMC, *Leyborne-Popham*, p. 104; *Nicholas Papers, Volume I*, ed. G.F. Warner, Camden Soc., new ser., vol. 40 (1886), p. 310.

14. Parliamentary and royalist officers shared the same chivalric sense of honour. It had little to do with Puritan principles and much to do with the code of the feudal warrior, as mediated by mediaeval theology and sixteenth-century humanism: M. E. James, 'English politics and the concept of honour', in idem, *Society, Politics and Culture* (Cambridge: Cambridge University Press, 1986), pp. 341, 345, 389; Maurice Keen, *Chivalry* (New Haven: Yale University Press, 1984), p. 177; *A&O*, ii.148–51.

15. *CJ*, vii.110, 130, 140, 186–7; Worden, *Rump*, p. 284; *C to P*, p. 38; *A&O*, ii.618–20; MS Clar. 45, fos 356, 485.

16. Ludlow, *Memoirs*, i.345–6, 350–1; Abbott, iii.55.

17. Whitelocke, iii.468–73; Whitelocke, *Diary*, pp. 281–2.

18. Ludlow, *Memoirs*, i.347; *C to P*, p. 47.

19. Mayer, 'Inedited letters', pp. 214, 218; *C to P*, p. 47; Capp, *The Fifth Monarchy Men*, pp. 57, 59; William Erbury, *The Bishop of London* ([8 Jan.] 1653), TT E.684[26], pp. 1–2; Worden, *Rump*, pp. 315–16.

20. *CJ*, vii.128, 224, 241–2; *CSPD, 1651–52*, pp. 424, 432, and *1652–53*, p. 95; Reece, pp. 93–4.

21. *CSPD, 1652–53*, pp. 261, 266, 291, 297.

22. Erbury, *Bishop of London*, pp. 1, 2, 7; C.H. Firth, 'Cromwell and the expulsion of the Long Parliament in 1653', *EHR*, vol. 8 (1893): 526–34, p. 527; Worden, *Rump*, pp. 317–18.

23. The Bodleian Library has a specimen of the circular letter bearing the signature of Thomas Margetts: Bodl. Lib., Fairfax Deposit, Smith. newsb.a.3/5. It is also reproduced in *Merc. Politicus*, 3–10 Feb. 1653, TT E.686[12], pp. 2,113–16. For the answer of the Edinburgh artillery officers, see *Perf. Diurnall*, 28 Mar.–4 Apr. 1653, TT E.211[11], pp. 2,605–7. Similar chiliastic responses were recorded from Robert Lilburne's and Anthony Morgan's regiments in Scotland: Massarella, pp. 295–6.

24. As we have seen above (p. 141), the Levellers and the Council of Officers were quite prepared in 1648–49 to bar more than half the adult male population from the franchise.

25. *CJ*, vii.244; *C to P*, pp. 54–5.

26. Worden, *Rump*, p. 331; MS Clar. 45, fo. 204, printed in Firth, 'Cromwell and the expulsion of the Long Parliament', p. 527.

27. Ibid., p. 530; Heath, *Flagellum*, pp. 133–4; Ludlow, *Memoirs*, i.356; HMC, *Portland*, iii.201.

28. Ludlow, *Memoirs*, i.348–9; *C to P*, pp. 56–7; Abbott, ii.626; MS Clar. 45, fo. 270ᵛ.

29. *CJ*, vii.258–9.

30. *C&P*, ii.98–100; Abbott, ii.520; *CJ*, vii.258–9.

31. Ibid. (my emphasis); *OPH*, xx.125; *C to P*, pp. 53–4.

32. They were Thomas Harrison, John Jones, William Packer, William Boteler, Rowland Dawkins, Wroth Rogers, Stephen Winthrop, Robert Duckenfield, Humphrey Mackworth, and several other commanders of local garrisons: *A&O*, ii.342–8; Christopher Hill, 'Puritans and "the dark corners of the land" ', in idem, *Change and Continuity in Seventeenth-Century England* (London: Weidenfeld & Nicolson, 1974), pp. 32–8; Massarella, p. 263.

33. *C&P*, ii.249, 251–2; Whitelocke, ii.252–3; MS Clar. 45, fo. 269; *C to P*, pp. 58, 60–1; Thomas Richards, *History of the Puritan Movement in Wales* (London: National Eisteddfod Association, 1920), pp. 271–2; Abbott, iii.57; Worden, *Rump*, p. 328.

34. Firth, 'Cromwell and the expulsion of the Long Parliament', p. 529; Whitelocke, iv.2; Whitelocke, *Diary*, p. 285; *CJ*, vii.273, 277–8. The contents of the army petition were reported by the French ambassador Bordeaux: NA, PRO30/3/90, fo. 653; *C&P*, ii.252–3; *C to P*, p. 61.

35. *C&P*, ii.255; MS Clar. 45, fo. 292^v; *C to P*, p. 80.

36. Ludlow, *Memoirs*, i.351; *C to P*, p. 80.

37. *CSPD, 1652–53*, pp. 205, 274; MS Clar. 45, fos 292, 270, 223; *Humble Remonstrance of Many Thousands* ([21 Apr.] 1653), TT E.692[4], pp. 6–7.

38. Whitelocke, iv.4–5; Firth, 'Cromwell and the expulsion of the Long Parliament', pp. 531–2; *C&P*, ii.258; *C to P*, pp. 63–4; Abbott, iii.59.

39. Whitelocke, iv.5.

40. John Streater, *Secret Reasons of State* ([23 May] 1659), TT E.983[24], pp. 2–3. The best accounts of the dissolution of the Rump on 20 April 1653 are by eye witnesses: Whitelocke, iv.4–6; Whitelocke, *Diary*, pp. 285–6; Algernon Sidney as told to his father the earl of Leicester, HMC, *De L'Isle and Dudley*, vi.615–16, and the Genoese ambassador's, printed in C.H. Firth, 'The expulsion of the Long Parliament', *History*, new ser., vol. 2 (1917–18), pp. 135–6.

41. Ludlow, *Memoirs*, i.352; *The Moderate Publisher*, 15–22 Apr. 1653, TT E.211[21], p. 813; Worden, *Rump*, p. 336; Firth, 'The expulsion of the Long Parliament', p. 194.

42. Streater, *Secret Reasons of State*, p. 3.

43. *Severall Procs in Parliament*, 21–8 Apr. 1653, TT E.211[24], p. 2,945; 28 Apr.–5 May 1653, TT E.213[2], p. 2,959; *Rump Songs* (London: H. Brome & H. Marsh, 1662), part 1, pp. 305, 320; *CSPV, 1653–54*, pp. 64–5; MS Clar. 45, fos 326^v, 358; Whitelocke, iv.9; *OPH*, xx.145–7; Massarella, pp. 309–10; MS Tanner 52, fo. 13.

44. Worden, *Rump*, pp. 345, 363; *C to P*, pp. 80–1.

45. Abbott, iii.60; *C to P*, p. 89.

46. *Declaration of the Grounds and Reasons for Dissolving the Parliament* (22 Apr. 1653), *OPH*, xx.140; Worden, *Rump*, p. 348; Streater, *Secret Reasons of State*, p. 4; Hutchinson, p. 205; *C to P*, pp. 69–71, 85–90; Abbott, iii.56.

47. *Another Declaration . . . by the Lord Generall and His Council of Officers* (26 May 1653), TT E.693[17], pp. 4, 6; *A Letter to a Gentleman in the Country* (3 May 1653), TT E.697[2], pp. 10–11; John Spittlehouse, *The Army Vindicated* ([24 Apr.] 1653), TT E.693[1]; Austin Woolrych, 'The calling of Barebone's Parliament', *EHR*, vol. 80 (1965): 492–513, p. 495n.; Worden, *Rump*, p. 353; *C to P*, p. 52, n. 62.

48. *Declaration of the Grounds*, *OPH*, xx.137–43; MS Tanner 52, fo. 13; *The Fifth Monarchy . . . Asserted* ([28 Aug.] 1659), TT E.993[31], p. 22.

49. *C to P*, pp. 101–2.

13 BAREBONE'S PARLIAMENT AND THE PROTECTORATE, 1653–56

1. Marchmont Nedham, *A True State of the Case of the Commonwealth* (London, 1654), TT E.728[5], p. 12; Lomas–Carlyle, ii.289–90; *A Declaration of the Lord Generall and His Councel of Officers* (London, [23 Apr.] 1653), TT E.692[6], p. 8; Massarella, p. 312. The six officer members of the council were Cromwell, Lambert, Harrison, Disbrowe, Robert Bennett and William Sydenham. Of the three later additions two were officers: Colonels Thomlinson and Philip Jones: *CP*, iii.2.

2. Those selected also included three colonels from Ireland: Hewson, Henry Cromwell and John Clarke; the commander of the lifeguard, Charles Howard; the two generals at sea: Blake and Monck; and several garrison commanders: Robert Bennett, William Sydenham, John Bingham, Henry Danvers and Philip Jones: *C to P*, pp. 128–9, 132, appendix B, pp. 410–32; Lomas–Carlyle, ii.295; *CJ*, vii.281; Massarella, p. 323; MS Clar. 46, fo. 8, cited in *C to P* pp. 141–2

3. MS Clar. 45, fos 335, 486^v; D.A. Johnson and D.G. Vaisey, *Staffordshire and the Great Rebellion* (Stafford: Staffordshire County Council, 1965), pp. 73–4, 76–7; *CSPD, 1652–53*, pp. 299–301; *C&P*, ii.284; HMC, *Portland*, iii.200; *Severall Procs in Parliament*, 21–28 Apr. 1653, TT E.211[24], p. 2,952; Massarella, pp. 311–12, 324; Ludlow, *Memoirs*, i.358.

4. *C to P*, p. 141; Johnson and Vaisey, *Staffordshire*, p. 74; MS Clar. 45, fos 381^v, 439.

5. MS Clar. 45, fo. 380ᵛ.
6. Massarella, pp. 324, 328–9; 'Harrison, Thomas', ODNB; CP, v.141.
7. Calendar of the Clarendon State Papers Preserved in the Bodleian Library, ed. O. Ogle and W.H. Bliss and W.D. Macray, 5 vols (Oxford: Clarendon Press, 1872–1970), ii.251 (no. 1,377); C&P, ii.305–6; A True Narrative of the Cause and Manner of the Dissolution of the Late Parliament (London, 19 Dec. 1653), TT E.724[11], pp. 4–5; CP, iii. 9–10; Ludlow, Memoirs, i.366; A Faithfull Searching Home Word (London, 1659), TT E.774[1], pp. 16, 19; An Answer to a Paper Entituled, A True Narrative of the Cause and Manner of the Dissolution of the Late Parliament (London: T.N. for G. Calvert, [4 Jan.] 1654), TT E.725[20]; 'An exact relation of the proceedings and transactions of the late parliament', Collection of Scarce and Valuable Tracts [Somers Tracts], ed. Walter Scott, 2nd edn, 13 vols (London: T. Cadell, W. Davies, 1809), vi.282–3.
8. C to P, pp. 306–11, 343, 346.
9. Ludlow, Memoirs, i.369–70; Farr, John Lambert, p. 124; C to P, pp. 347, 352–3; 'The Instrument of Government', in Const. Docs, pp. 405–17; Blair Worden, 'Oliver Cromwell and the Instrument of Government', in Stephen Taylor and Grant Tapsell (eds), The Nature of the English Revolution Revisited: Essays in Honour of John Morrill (Woodbridge: Boydell, 2013), pp. 123–50, p. 126.
10. Severall Procs in Parliament, 15–22 Dec. 1653, TT E.222[29], p. 3,499; TSP, ii.215. The fifteen who signed the engagement were General Lambert and Colonels Reynolds, Hacker, Constable, Ingoldsby, Worsley, Twisleton, Hewson, Lagoe, Whalley, Barkstead, Goffe, Grosvenor, Haynes and Downing. Allegedly it was opposed by the usual suspects: Harrison and Colonels Rich, Saunders, Alured and Overton: Massarella, pp. 343, 345, 348; A True Catalogue, or, an Account of the Several Places and Most Eminent Persons in the Three Nations and Elsewhere, Where, and by Whom Richard Cromwell was Proclaimed Lord Protector . . . (London: [28 Sept.] 1659), TT E.999[12], pp. 6–9; The Protector (So called,) in Part Vnvailed . . . by a Late Member of the Army ([24 Oct.] 1655), TT E.857[1], pp. 15, 39; Worden, 'Instrument of Government', pp. 142–4, 150; Folger Shakespeare Library, Washington, DC, Robert Bennett Papers, MS Xd 483, fo. 114.
11. TSP, ii.285
12. Ibid., iii.147; Taft, 'The Humble Petition of Several Colonels', pp. 16, 21–2, 33; To His Highness the Lord Protector, TT 669.f.19[21].
13. Some Memento's for the Officers and Souldiers of the Army from Some Sober Christians (London: [19 Oct. 1654]), TT E.813[20], pp. 3, 8.
14. TSP, ii. 733; Ní Chinnéide, 'Political Influence of the Cromwellian Army', pp. 175, 180, 182; Massarella, p. 364; Gentles, 'Agreements of the People', pp. 160–2; Woolrych, Britain in Revolution, p. 610.
15. Taft, 'The Humble Petition of Several Colonels', p. 33.
16. Ludlow, Memoirs, i.434–6; Derek Massarella, 'The politics of the army and the quest for settlement', in Ivan Roots (ed.), 'Into another Mould': Aspects of the Interregnum (Exeter: University of Exeter Press, 1981), p. 120; CSPD, 1656–57, pp. 87–8; Barry Coward, Oliver Cromwell (London: Longman, 1991), p. 104; C&P, iii.5–6; John Milton, A Defence of the English People; in Answer to Salmasius's Defence of the King (?Amsterdam, 1692), p. 116.
17. Woolrych, Britain in Revolution, p. 567; Barry Coward, Cromwellian Protectorate, (Manchester: Manchester University Press, 2002), pp. 30–1; Massarella, p. 351. Each author gives a slightly different total for the number of officers on the first Protectoral Council. See also CSPD, 1653–54, p. 298, which does not list Fleetwood.
18. Diary of Thomas Burton, Esq., ed. Thomas Towill Rutt, 4 vols (London: H. Colburn, 1828), i.lxxxiii, cviii; C&P, iii.45, 49, 211.
19. CP, iii.11; Massarella, p. 383.
20. The Narrative of General Venables, ed. C.H. Firth (London: Royal HS, 1900; repr. 1965), p. 113; CP, iii.203.
21. Ibid., iii.207–8.
22. 'Venables, Robert', ODNB; 'Penn, William (1621–1670)', ODNB.
23. HMC, Seventh Report (London: HMSO, 1879), part 1, p. 571.

24. 'Some account of General Robert Venables', Chetham Soc., vol. 4 (1871), *Chetham Miscellanies*, p. 4; *The Narrative of General Venables*, pp. 9, 14, xxxiii–xxxiv. A pike was normally 18 feet long: *TSP*, iii.506.

25. HMC, *Seventh Report*, part 1, pp. 571–2; *TSP*, iii.505; *Calendar of State Papers, Colonial, America and West Indies: Volume 9, 1675–1676 and Addenda 1574–1674, 1691* (London: HMSO, 1893), pp. 91, 116; *The Narrative of General Venables*, pp. 30, 146. The Caribbean islands were often used as a dumping ground for captured pirates, prisoners of war, criminals and other human 'refuse': see for example *Calendar of State Papers, Colonial Series 1574–1660* (London: Longman, Green, 1860), pp. 419, 427; 'A Brief and Perfect Journal of the Late Proceedings & Success of the English Army in the West Indies . . . by I.S. an Eye-witness' (1655), in *Harleian Miscellany*, 10 vols (London: John White and John Murray, 1808), iii.515; Pestana, *The English Conquest of Jamaica*, p. 54.

26. *The Narrative of General Venables*, pp. 111–12; *TSP*, iii.505.

27. *The Narrative of General Venables*, p. 14; *TSP*, iii.505.

28. Ibid., iv.28; 'Narrative of the expedition to Santo Domingo' by an officer in Colonel Fortescue's regiment, in *CP*, iii.54; Carte, *Coll.*, ii.49; *The Narrative of General Venables*, pp. 21, 155; 'A Brief and Perfect Journal', iii.516.

29. *TSP*, iii.506.

30. HMC, *Seventh Report*, i.572–3; *CP*, iii.56; Granville Penn, *Memorials of the Professional Life and Times of Sir William Penn . . . from 1644 to 1670*, 2 vols (London: J. Duncan, 1833), ii.50; *TSP*, iii.506–7; 'A Brief and Perfect Journal', p. 517; *Narrative of General Venables*, pp. 133, 144.

31. The reported numbers of Santo Domingo's defenders vary widely – from fifty (impossibly low) to 3,000–5,000 (impossibly high). The estimate that they were about a tenth or less of the English force – i.e. a few hundred – seems reasonable. Penn, *Memorials*, ii.89; *CP*, iii.60; 'A Brief and Perfect Journal', p. 516; HMC, *Seventh Report*, part 1, p. 573; *The Narrative of General Venables*, pp. 96, 160–1; Pestana, *The English Conquest of Jamaica*, p. 86.

32. *The Narrative of General Venables*, p. 34; General Penn thought a third attempt, backed up by a naval bombardment, could have worked: *The Narrative of General Venables*, p. xvi; Penn, *Memorials*, ii.51; 'A Brief and Perfect Journal', p. 518; 'Some account of General Robert Venables', p. 5; Pestana, *The English Conquest of Jamaica*, pp. 142–3.

33. *The Narrative of General Venables*, pp. 36–9, 71, 125, 164–5; *TSP*, iii.507; iv.21.

34. 'A Brief and Perfect Journal', p. 521; *The Narrative of General Venables*, p. 142.

35. Penn, *Memorials*, ii.51; *Crom. Navy*, p. 90.

36. *Reg. Hist.*, p. 702.

37. Julius Caesar, *The Civil War*, trans. Jane F. Gardner (London: Penguin, 1967), pp. 150–4.

38. Lomas–Carlyle, iii.454; Christopher Durston, *Cromwell's Major-Generals: Godly Government during the English Revolution* (Manchester: Manchester University Press, 2001), pp. 17, 21. Much of this section draws on Durston's excellent treatment of the topic.

39. *Certain Passages of Everyday Intelligence*, 23–30 Mar. 1655, TT E.481[32]; *Perf. Procs of State Affairs*, 29 Mar.–5 Apr. 1655, TT E.831[6].

40. SP 25/76A, pp. 169–81.

41. SP 18/100/42; *Merc. Politicus*, 20–27 Dec. 1655, TT E.491[9], pp. 5,851–2.

42. *TSP*, iv.149, 207, 411, 216, 225, 334; Anthony Fletcher, 'Religious motivation of Cromwell's major-generals', *Studies in Church History*, vol. 15 (1978): 259–66.

43. Durston, *Cromwell's Major-Generals*, pp. 39–43, 53, 60–70.

44. Ibid., pp. 34, 113; Hutchinson, p. 209.

45. Durston, *Cromwell's Major-Generals*, pp. 142–3, 146–7; Lomas–Carlyle, iii.475; Underdown, *Royalist Conspiracy*, p. 170.

46. Durston, *Cromwell's Major-Generals*, p. 141. The time the major-generals spent on the Decimation tax is reflected in their letters to Thurloe: *TSP*, iv.225, 321, 316, 322, 325, 337, 341, 391, 411, 434, 439, 442, 449, 472, 497, 498, 534, 742; v.9.

47. Ibid., iv.315, 334, 607; v.200.

48. Ibid., iv. 320, 329, 396, 187, 197, 632–3; v.187.
49. Ibid., iv.187, 267, 333, 439, 595–6, 746, 272, 284, 411, 434, 565; Durston, *Cromwell's Major-Generals*, p. 161; idem, 'Policing the Cromwellian church: The activities of the county ejection committees, 1654–1659', in Patrick Little (ed.), *The Cromwellian Protectorate* (Woodbridge: Boydell & Brewer, 2017), pp. 188–206, pp. 201, 205; B.S. Capp, *England's Culture Wars: Puritan Reformation and Its Enemies in the Interregnum, 1649–1660* (Oxford: Oxford University Press, 2012), p. 52.
50. Mortimer, *Reason and Religion in the English Revolution*, pp. 230–1; *TSP*, iv.329–30, 727, v.166, 187–8, 220, 311–12 (Haynes); iv.315, 333, 341 (Worsley); iv,408 (Goffe); iv.434 (Whalley); iv.531(Disbrowe); iv.613 (Berry).
51. Ibid., iv.434, 663, 719; v.211–12, 320.
52. Ibid., iv.187, 523–4; MS Carte 131, fos 183–5; Durston, *Cromwell's Major-Generals*, pp. 157–8.
53. Ibid., pp. 172, 175; *TSP*, iv.411, 434, 663, 686; v.187; *Several Orders Made and Agreed Upon by the Iustices of the Peace for the City and Liberty of Westminster* (20 March 1656), TT E.1065[6], last p. (this tract contains neither page nor signature numbers); *TSP*, iv.273; Capp, *England's Culture Wars*, p. 162.
54. *TSP*, iv.588; Lomas–Carlyle, ii.543, 551.
55. Durston, *Cromwell's Major-Generals*, p. 179. According to Peter Laslett, *Family Life and Illicit Love in Earlier Generations* (Cambridge: Cambridge University Press, 1977), pp. 106, 115, 117, bastardy constituted only 0.5 per cent of births in that decade, compared to the historic rate of around 4 per cent, and today's rate in the double digits. The records go back to the early sixteenth century.
56. *C&P*, iv.255; *TSP*, iv.354. The latter phrase was coined by commissioners in Gloucestershire, in reference to 'the late king's party', but it was applicable to much of the country.
57. Ibid., v.220, 230.
58. Ibid., v.296, 317.
59. Ibid., v.302, 308, 313–14.
60. Ibid., v.234, 299–300.
61. Durston, *Cromwell's Major-Generals*, p. 200; Jonathan Fitzgibbons, *Cromwell's House of Lords: Politics, Parliaments and Constitutional Revolution, 1642–1660* (Woodbridge: Boydell, 2018), p. 220.

14 THE ARMY AND THE END OF THE PARLIAMENTARY RULE, 1656-59

1. *TSP*, iv.228, 642; v.19, 128; 'Worsley, Charles', *ODNB*; J.S. Morrill, *Cheshire, 1630–1660: County Government and Society during the English Revolution* (London: Oxford University Press, 1974), pp. 276–87.
2. Reece, p. 162, n. 122.
3. Lomas–Carlyle, ii.543.
4. On 25 Dec. the Decimation Bill passed by eighty-eight to sixty-three: *CJ*, vii.475. On 29 Jan. it failed by 124 to eighty-eight: ibid., vii.483. Gookin to Thurloe, 27 Jan. 1656: *TSP*, vi.20; Durston, *Cromwell's Major-Generals*, pp. 215–16, 219.
5. Ibid., p. 232
6. 'Remonstrance from the Churches in Gloucestershire', in Nickolls, p. 140.
7. Patrick Little and David L. Smith, *Parliaments and Politics during the Cromwellian Protectorate* (Cambridge: Cambridge University Press, 2007), p. 35.
8. Ibid., p. 15. The text of the Remonstrance is published for the first time as appendix 2 of this book, pp. 306–12; Peter Gaunt, ' "The single person's confidants and dependents"? Oliver Cromwell and his protectoral councillors', *HJ*, vol. 32 (1989), pp. 545–6; Patrick Little, 'John Thurloe and the offer of the crown to Oliver Cromwell', in idem (ed.), *Oliver Cromwell: New Perspectives*, pp. 228–31; Jonathan Fitzgibbons, 'Hereditary succession

and the Cromwellian Protectorate: The offer of the crown reconsidered', *EHR*, vol. 128 (2013): 1,095–1,128, pp. 1,108, 1,114.

9. *Const. Docs*, pp. 447–59; Little and Smith, *Parliaments and Politics*, p. 43.

10. Ivan Roots (ed.), *Speeches of Oliver Cromwell* (London: Dent, 1989), p. 111; *TSP*, vi.93; Charles Harding Firth, *The Last Years of the Protectorate, 1656–1658*, 2 vols (New York: Russell & Russell, 1964), i.138, 191–3; Fitzgibbons, 'Hereditary succession and the Cromwellian Protectorate,' p. 1,117.

11. Nickolls, pp. 142–3; Gerald Aylmer, *The State's Servants: The Civil Service of the English Republic* (London: Routledge & Kegan Paul, 1973), p. 49, n. 28. The officers were four out of fifteen on the council: Generals Fleetwood, Lambert, Disbrowe and Skippon, in addition to two formerly serving officers: Colonels Sydenham and Philip Jones. Those who supported the *Humble Petition* included General Philip Skippon, and Colonels Philip Jones, Richard Ingoldsby, Charles Howard and John Reynolds: Massarella, p. 459; Firth, *Last Years of the Protectorate*, i.190; Woolrych, *Britain in Revolution*, pp. 659–60; Gentles, *Oliver Cromwell*, pp. 175–6; Lomas–Carlyle, iii. 71; Roots (ed.), *Speeches*, pp. 117, 119, 133, 176.

12. Gentles, *Oliver Cromwell*, p. 176.

13. *TSP*, vi.425, 427; Farr, *John Lambert*, pp. 145–53; Firth, *Last Years of the Protectorate*, ii.4; *The Grand Concernments of England Ensured* (London, 1659), TT E.1001[6], p. 61.

14. G.M., 13 Feb. 1658, *CP*, iii.141.

15. Folger Shakespeare Library, Washington, DC, Robert Bennett Papers, MS X.d.483, fo. 114; *C to P*, pp. 389–90; Reece, pp. 68–9.

16. Those who left or were dismissed included Major-Generals Thomas Harrison and John Lambert, Colonels Nathaniel Rich, John Okey, Matthew Alured, Thomas Sanders and Robert Overton, and Major William Packer with his regimental captains: Reece, pp. 70–1; Heath, *Flagellum*, p. 173; *TSP*, vi.412.

17. David Underdown, 'Cromwell and the officers, February 1658', *EHR*, vol. 83 (1968): 101–7, p. 106

18. Lomas–Carlyle, iii.509–10; Firth, *Last Years of the Protectorate*, ii.44–5.

19. Underdown, 'Cromwell and the officers', p. 107; Ralph C.H. Catterall, 'The failure of the *Humble Petition and Advice*', *American Historical Review*, vol. 9 (1909): 36–65, p. 57; Burton, *Diary*, iii.166.

20. *Merc. Politicus*, 18–25 Feb. 1658, TT E.748[16], pp. 339–40; Coward, *Cromwellian Protectorate*, p. 100; Catterall, 'The failure of the *Humble Petition and Advice*', pp. 56–7; *CP*, iii.143–4; *Merc. Politicus*, 25 Mar.–1 Apr. 1658, TT E.750[2], p. 420; Woolrych, *Britain in Revolution*, pp. 689–90. Fleetwood was alluding to Isaiah 40:31; Firth, *Last Years of the Protectorate*, ii.49.

21. Austin Woolrych, 'The Cromwellian Protectorate: A military dictatorship?', *History*, vol. 75 (1990): 207–31 pp. 212, 231; idem, *Britain in Revolution*, pp. 698–9.

22. Ronald Hutton, *The Restoration: A Political and Religious History of England and Wales, 1658–1667* (Oxford: Clarendon Press, 1995), p. 13.

23. *CP*, iii.164; 'The Humble Address of the Officers of Your Highness' Armies', in *Merc. Politicus*, 16–23 Sept., 23–30 Sept. 1658, TT E.756[19, 21], pp. 838, 844–7, 865–6 (corrected pag.); Bodl. Lib., MS Rawlinson A 61, fo.3.

24. Lord Fauconberg to Henry Cromwell, 28 Sept. 1658: *TSP*, vii.414; Massarella, p. 515; *CP*, iii.165.

25. *TSP*, vii.447–9. For example, he promised 'I shall take no comfort in my government until I can see you substantially provided for' (p. 449); *CP*, iii.173; Reece, p. 193; Little, *Lord Broghill*, p. 168.

26. Burton, *Diary*, iv.140–1, 399–401; Reece, p. 194; Aidan Clarke, *Prelude to Restoration in Ireland: The End of the Commonwealth, 1659–1660* (Cambridge: Cambridge University Press, 1999), p. 36.

27. Austin Woolrych, 'Introduction' to vol. 7 of *The Complete Prose Works of John Milton*, ed. Don M. Wolfe, 8 vols (New Haven: Yale University Press, 1953–82), vii.17–18; *CP*, iii.182; *Correspondence of Henry Cromwell*, pp. 457, 461.

28. Massarella, p. 505. Those who backed Richard Cromwell were considered part of the 'Court party', and included Major-Generals Edward Whalley and William Goffe, Lord Fauconberg, Colonels Richard Ingoldsby, Charles Howard, and John Mill, Lieutenant-Colonel Waldive Lagoe and Major Thomas Babington. Their civilian allies included Lord Broghill and John Thurloe.

29. *Correspondence of Henry Cromwell*, p. 475; Woolrych, 'Introduction', vii.61; Farr, *John Lambert*, p. 188.

30. The petition's drafters were Major-General Robert Lilburne, Colonels Richard Ashfield and John Mill, Lieutenant-Colonels John Mason, John Pearson, Haines, William Arnop and John Mayer, and Captain Richard Deane: *CP*, iii.187, 189–90; Massarella, p. 529; *The Humble Representation and Petition of the General Council of Officers*, printed in *Public Intell.*, 11–18 Apr. 1659, TT E.762[4], pp. 355–9; *Correspondence of Henry Cromwell*, p. 500.

31. *CJ*, vii.630–1.

32. *CP*, iii.189–90; Woolrych, 'Introduction', vii.63–4; Reece, p. 196.

33. *CJ*, vii.641; *Correspondence of Henry Cromwell*, p. 502; *CP*, iii.191, 212 (Nehemiah Bourne's account); Woolrych, 'Introduction', vii.63–4; Fitzgibbons, *Cromwell's House of Lords*, pp. 195–6, 214, 217.

34. *CP*, iii.193; Ludlow, *Memoirs*, ii.68–9; Woolrych, 'Introduction', vii.65; Massarella, p. 532; Hutton, *Restoration*, p. 38.

35. Hutton, *Restoration*, p. 39; Massarella, p. 537; *The Humble Remonstrance of the Non-Commission Officers and Private Soldiers of Major General Goffs Regiment . . . to His Excellency the Lord Fleetwood, and the General Council of Officers . . . April 26, 1659*, TT E.979[6]; A. H. Woolrych, 'The Good Old Cause and the fall of the Protectorate', *Cambridge Historical Journal*, vol. 13 (1957): 133–61, pp. 148–51.

36. Massarella, pp. 533–4; Ludlow, *Memoirs*, ii.71.

37. Clarke, *Prelude to Restoration*, pp. 41–2, 51–2, 55, 58, 61, 66, 67; *CP*, iv.19; *CJ*, vii.703.

38. *The Humble Petition and Addresse of the Officers of the Army to the Parliament* ([13 May] 1659), TT E.983[7], pp. 3, 4–5, 6, 9–11; Ludlow, *Memoirs*, ii.75; M. Guizot, *History of Richard Cromwell and the Restoration of Charles II*, trans. Andrew R. Scoble, 2 vols (London: Richard Bentley, 1856), i.383 (Bordeaux); Henry Stubbe, *Letter to an Officer of the Army concerning a Select Senate*, in two parts (London: T.B. [26 Oct.] 1659), TT E.1001[8, 9].

39. *CJ*, vii.670; *CSPD, 1658–59*, pp. 375–6, 378, 379, 384, 394, 395; Massarella, pp. 572, 575–81; *CP*, iv.17, 19, 21. Captain Pride was probably the son of the deceased Major-General Thomas Pride.

40. Ludlow, *Memoirs*, ii.88; *CP*, iv.17, 19, 21, 22; *CSPD, 1658–59*, pp. 375–6, 378, 379, 384, 394, 395; Reece, p. 201; *CJ*, vii.649, 650, 651, 670, 680, 696, 698, 714, 748–9, 781–2; *Reg. Hist.*, pp. 494–5; Massarella, pp. 572, 575–81, 594–5.

41. Reece, pp. 202–3. Cf. Ruth E. Mayers, *1659: The Crisis of the Commonwealth* (Woodbridge: Boydell for the Royal HS, 2004), pp. 55–63, who argues that Parliament and army got along well until after Booth's rebellion. Reece and Massarella show how profoundly alienated the officers were by the purges of the summer of 1659.

42. *Merc Politicus*, 4–11 Aug. 1659, TT E.766[30], p. 650; *CP*, iv.38–9, 42, 46–8; Ludlow, *Memoirs*, ii.112; Hutton, *Restoration*, p. 59.

43. Ibid., p. 64; Farr, *John Lambert*, pp. 192–3.

44. Reece, pp. 175–6; *CSPI, 1647–1660*, pp. 687–8; Clarke, *Prelude to Restoration*, pp. 8–9.

45. *CJ*, vii.766; Godfrey Davies, *The Restoration of Charles II 1658–1660* (Oxford: Oxford University Press, 1955), p. 146.

46. Massarella, p. 606; Richard Baker, *A Chronicle of the Kings of England* (London: George Sawbridge and Thomas Williams, 1670), p. 677.

47. *Public Intell.*, 19–26 Sept. 1659, TT E.771[10], pp. 746–7. The House narrowly defeated a motion that parts of the petition were 'unseasonable and of dangerous consequence', and summoned three officers – Colonels Richard Ashfield, Ralph Cobbett and John Pearson – to come and explain themselves: *CJ*, vii.784–5; Mayers, *1659*, p. 239.

48. The republican officers who opposed the draft petition included Colonels Okey, Hacker and Saunders, as well as Majors Daberon, Barton and Breman: Baker, *Chronicle*, p. 678; Johnston, *Diary*, iii.139; *The Humble Representation and Petition of the Officers of the Army to the Parliament of the Commonwealth of England* (6 Oct. 1659), TT E.1000[5], pp. 3, 4–5, 7, 8–9; Woolrych, 'Introduction', vii.114.

49. Ludlow, *Memoirs*, ii.133; Mayers, *1659*, p. 231.

50. Baker, *Chronicle*, p. 682; Woolrych, 'Introduction', vii.115–16.

51. *CP*, iv. 612; Johnston, *Diary*, iii. 144; Whitelocke, *Diary*, p. 535; *Weekly Intell.*, 11–18 Oct. 1659, TT E.1000[7], p. 191 (corrected pag.); HMC, *Third Report*, pp. 88–9; MS Carte 73, fo. 319; MS Clar. 65, fos 60–1; Ludlow, *Memoirs*, ii.137–40; Hutton, *Restoration*, p. 66.

52. Clarke, *Prelude to Restoration*, pp. 94–5; Ludlow, *Memoirs*, ii.143–51; Mayer, 'Inedited letters', p. 265.

15 THE ARMY BRINGS BACK THE KING, 1659–60

1. The sources refer to fifteen officers, but list only thirteen: Colonels Sir Arthur Hesilrige, Herbert Morley, Thomas Saunders, Matthew Alured, Francis Hacker, John Okey and Henry Markham; Lieutenant-Colonel William Farley; Majors Nathaniel Barton, Arthur Evelyn and George Sedascue; Adjutant-General John Nelthorpe, and Captain Richard Wagstaffe: Ludlow, *Memoirs*, ii.148; *The Declaration of the Officers of the Army Opened* (London: [25 Nov.] 1659), TT E.1010[16], p. 29; *The Armies Vindication of This Last Change* (London, 1659), pp. 3, 4, 20, 22; Baker, *Chronicle*, p. 682; *CP*, v.316–17, 318.

2. Mayer, 'Inedited letters', pp. 265, 271–4; *CP*, iv.95–6n.; Baker, *Chronicle*, pp. 690–1.

3. *The Diary of Samuel Pepys*, ed. Robert Latham and William Matthews, 11 vols (London: G. Bell, 1970–83), i.87, 125; Burnet, *History of His Own Time*, i.89, 125; 'Monck, George', *ODNB*.

4. Baker, *Chronicle*, pp. 685, 686, 688 (Baker says he raised £70,000); Dow, *Scotland*, p. 253; *A&O*, ii.1,284–6; *CP*, iv.69, 70; Reece, p. 207; Hutton, *Restoration*, p. 73; Austin Woolrych, 'Yorkshire and the Restoration', *Yorkshire Archaeological Journal*, vol. 39 (1958): 483–507; HMC, *Leyborne-Popham*, pp. 126–8; Woolrych, *Britain in Revolution*, p. 746.

5. *The Humble and Healing Advice of Collonel Robert Overton . . . to Charles Lord Fleetwood and General Monck* (London, 1659), p. 5; Mayer, 'Inedited letters', p. 280; *CP*, iv.72, 91, 95–6, n. 1, 140, 144, 148; v.319, 322.

6. Ludlow, *Memoirs*, ii.191; *CP*, iv.153, 184–6, 190–1, 192–3, 226, 228, 233, 235, 249, 251, 258–9; *Merc. Politicus*, 28 Jan.–2 Feb. 1660, TT E.195[52], p. 1,054 (Monck's letter to the gentry of Devon, 23 Jan. 1660); Ludlow, *Voyce*, p. 92; Guizot, *History of Richard Cromwell*, ii.384.

7. Stephen K. Roberts, *Recovery and Restoration in an English County: Devon Local Administration 1646–1670* (Exeter: Exeter University Press, 1985), p. 139; Blair Worden, 'The campaign for a free parliament, 1659–60', *Parliamentary History*, vol. 36 (2017): 159–84, pp. 167, 174, 178–9; idem, 'The demand for a free parliament, 1659–60,' in Southcombe and Tapsell (eds), *Revolutionary England, c. 1630–c. 1660*, pp. 179, 184.

8. *CP*, iv.71–2, 77–8, 85; *A Declaration of the General Council of Officers . . . at Wallingford House the 27th of October 1659* (London: Henry Hills, 1659), TT E.1001[12], pp. 17–18.

9. The ten military members of the Committee of Safety were: Generals Fleetwood, Lambert, Disbrowe and Ludlow; Colonels Sydenham, Berry, Hewson, John Clarke, Lilburne and Bennett: Massarella, p. 62; Whitelocke, *Diary*, p. 538; *CP*, iv.92–3; Woolrych, 'Introduction', vii.131–2; Davies, *Restoration*, p. 158; *Weekly Intell.*, 25 Oct.–1 Nov. 1659, TT E.1001[4], p. 202.

10. Whitelocke, *Diary*, p. 543; Massarella, p. 639; Guizot, *History of Richard Cromwell*, ii.284; *Merc. Politicus*, 8–15 Dec. 1659, TT E.195[45], pp. 955–6; Ludlow, *Memoirs*, ii.171–4.

11. Ibid., ii.165–9, 171–4; Johnston, *Diary*, iii.155–6; Mayer, 'Inedited Letters', pp. 281–2; Massarella, pp. 646–7; *A Letter from Sir Arthur Haselrigge in Portsmouth* ([17 Dec.] 1659), p. 5.

12. *CP*, iv.87–8, 93.
13. Ibid., iv.91, 94, 101–3.
14. *An Account of the Affairs in Ireland in Reference to the Late Change in England . . . Dublin, 14 December 1659*, broadside; Clarke, *Prelude to Restoration*, p. 111; *Parl. Intell.*, 9–16 Jan. 1660, TT E.182[18], p. 34; *A Declaration of Sir Charles Coot . . . Feb. 24 1659[-60]* (London: D, Maxwell, 1660), pp. 2–3, 6.
15. HMC, *Portland*, i.690; 'The Declaration of Sir Hardress Waller, Major General of the Parliaments Forces in Ireland, and the Council of Officers There', *Parl. Intell.*, 16–23 Jan. 1660, TT E.182[19], pp. 49–52. See p. 51 for another condemnation of 'fanatic spirits'.
16. Baker, *Chronicle*, pp. 687–8; *CP*, iv.65–6, 87; v.319.
17. *Declaration of the Commander in Chief in Scotland, and the Officers under His Command, in Vindication of the Liberties of the People, and Priviledges of Parliament* (Edinburgh and London: Christopher Higgens, 1659), broadside; *Declaration of the Officers of the Army in Scotland to the Churches of Christ in the Three Nations* (Edinburgh: Christopher Higgins, [20 Oct.] 1659), TT E.1005[7], pp. 2, 3; *CP*, iv.67n.
18. F.M.S. McDonald, 'The timing of General George Monck's march into England, 1 January 1660', *EHR*, vol. 105 (1990): 363–76; *CP*, v.343–6.
19. 'Fleetwood, Charles', *ODNB*; Abbott, iv.728; Johnston, *Diary*, iii.159; *CSPV, 1659–61*, p. 86; Ludlow, *Memoirs*, ii.183.
20. Abbott, iv.728; Whitelocke, *Diary*, pp. 551–3.
21. *CP*, iv.220; Ludlow, *Memoirs*, ii.203; Davies, *Restoration*, p. 188; Massarella, p. 664; *Monthly Intell.*, 1 Dec. 1659–1 Jan. 1660, TT 669.f.22[51], p. 7; *Parl. Intell.*, 19–26 Dec. 1659, TT E.182[15], p. 8; *Publick Intell.*, 19–26 Dec. 1659, TT E.773[33], p. 971; *CJ*, vii.797.
22. *CP*, v.317 (13 Oct. 1659); Baker, *Chronicle*, p. 688; Ludlow, *Memoirs*, ii.191, 213.
23. *CP*, iv.91, 94, 247; Baker, *Chronicle*, p. 700. Monck had 4,000 foot and 1,800 horse.
24. The troops brought by Hesilrige comprised horse from Rich's and Berry's regiments and several companies of foot. Woolrych, 'Introduction', vii,138; Baker, *Chronicle*, pp. 690, 698; Ludlow, *Memoirs*, ii.180; *A Letter from Sir Arthur Haselrigge in Portsmouth*, pp. 4–5.
25. *CP*, iv.164–7; *Merc. Politicus*, 1–8 Dec. 1659, TT E.773[22], p. 939; Woolrych, 'Introduction', vii.145; Hutton, *Restoration*, p. 81.
26. *CP*, v.345, 347, 355; Clarke, *Prelude to Restoration*, pp. 110, 121; HMC, *Portland*, i.690; *Parl. Intell.*, 16–23 Jan. 1660, TT E.182[19], 'The Declaration of Sir Hardress Waller', pp. 49–52; *CP*, iv.216–17, 226, 232.
27. Ibid., iv.233, 237–8; *Fairfax Correspondence*, iv.166–7, 169.
28. *Humble and Healing Advice of Collonel Robert Overton*; *CP*, iv.244–7; *A Letter from the Lord Gen. Monck to Major General Overton: Together with Major Gen. Overtons Answer Thereunto* (London: [Jan.] 1660), TT E.1013[21], pp. 1, 3.
29. Reece, p. 215; *CJ*, vii.697, 704, 807–9, 839; *CSPD, 1659–60*, p. 8; Baker, *Chronicle*, p. 698.
30. *Parl. Intell.*, 23–30 Jan. 1660, TT E.182[20], pp. 65–6; *CP*, iv.240–1; v.356.
31. Davies, *Restoration*, p. 271; *Parl. Intell.*, 16–23 Jan. 1660, TT E.182[19], p. 57; *CP*, iv.238–40; Roberts, *Recovery and Restoration*, pp. 139–40; Ludlow, *Memoirs*, ii.191, 208, 213, 215; *Merc. Politicus*, 28 Jan.–2 Feb. 1660, TT E.195[52], p. 1,054.
32. *CP*, v.361; HMC, *Leyborne-Popham*, p. 145; Whitelocke, *Diary*, pp. 566–7; Hutton, *Restoration*, p. 91; Guizot, *History of Richard Cromwell*, ii.340; *Merc. Politicus*, 2–9 Feb. 1660, TT E.775[1], pp. 1,081–3.
33. David Scott of the History of Parliament informs me that Monck's supporters in Parliament included Cooper, Weaver and Colonel Morley. *CJ*, vii.837–8; *OPH*, xxii.92–3, 98.
34. *A Letter from His Excellencie the Lord General Monck . . . to the Parliament* (London: [11 Feb.] 1660); Pepys, *Diary*, i.50; also printed in *OPH*, xxii.98–103; Baxter, *Reliquiae Baxterianae*, p. 105.
35. Baker, *Chronicle*, p. 709; Ludlow, *Memoirs*, ii.223–4; 'Monck, George', *ODNB*; *CJ*, vii.840–1; Hutton, *Restoration*, pp. 93–4 and n. 47.

36. *CP*, v.361; Guizot, *History of Richard Cromwell*, ii.345–6; Ludlow, *Memoirs*, ii.219–20; Whitelocke, *Diary*, p. 567; *Parl. Intell.*, 6–13 Feb. 1660, TT E.182[22], p. 112; Pepys, *Diary*, i.52. Mark S.R. Jenner, 'The roasting of the Rump: Scatology and the body politic in Restoration England', *P&P*, no. 177 (Nov. 2002): 84–120. Jenner emphasises the themes of cruelty, revenge and obscenity; however, I think the main theme was simple joy at the downfall of the republic, and the near certainty of the king's return. The only recorded nastiness was the breaking of Praise-God Barebone's windows in Fleet Street. No blood was spilt during this ecstatic celebration.
37. Among the great companies (there were twelve) who entertained Monck were the Grocers, Mercers, Clothworkers, Drapers, Skinners, Goldsmiths, Fishmongers and Vintners. Ludlow, *Memoirs*, ii.244; *Parl. Intell.*, 9–16 Apr. 1660, TT E.183[3], pp. 246, 256; Baker, *Chronicle*, pp. 709–10.
38. Ludlow, *Memoirs*, ii.235; Baker, *Chronicle*, p. 713; Massarella, pp. 711–12; Woolrych, 'Introduction', vii.174–5; Ludlow, *Voyce*, p. 92.
39. Pepys, *Diary*, i.86; Guizot, *History of Richard Cromwell*, ii.356, 379; Massarella, pp. 714–15.
40. Baker, *Chronicle*, p. 715.
41. Ludlow, *Memoirs*, ii.251–2.
42. Reece, p. 222; Ludlow, *Voyce*, p. 85.
43. *Parl. Intell.*, 12–19 Mar. 1660, TT E.182[27], pp. 201, 208; Baker, *Chronicle*, p. 214; Ludlow, *Voyce*, p. 96; Massarella, p. 710. My account of this episode differs from that of Reece, p. 221.
44. Hutton, *Restoration*, p. 116; Woolrych, 'Introduction', p. 197; *Merc. Aulicus*, repr. in William Harbutt Dawson, *Cromwell's Understudy: The Life and Times of General Lambert and the Rise and Fall of the Protectorate* (London: W. Hodge, 1938), p. 390.
45. Baker, *Chronicle*, p. 718; *Const. Docs*, pp. 465–7.
46. *Parl. Intell.*, 9–16 Apr. 1660, TT E.183[3], pp. 244–5; Massarella, p. 722.
47. *Eye-Salve for the English Armie* (London, 1660), pp. 6, 7, 8; *An Alarum to the Officers and Souldiers of the Armies of England, Scotland, and Ireland* ([March]1660), pp. 10–11. Note: the Early English Books Online entry for this pamphlet misspells the second word of the title 'Alarm', and this misspelling must be used in order to gain access to the pamphlet.
48. *Parl. Intell.*, 9–16 Apr. 1660, TT E.183[3], p. 256; Ludlow, *Voyce*, p. 90; Baker, *Chronicle*, p. 720; Reece, pp. 220, 224.
49. *To His Excellency the Lord General Monck . . . the Humble Address of the Officers of Your Excellencies Army . . . This 2d Day of May 1660*, broadside.
50. Baxter, *Reliquiae Baxterianae*, p. 105.

EPILOGUE

1. Baxter, *Reliquiae Baxterianae*, p. 105.
2. Austin Woolrych is convinced that the church bells that rang for Monck everywhere after he crossed into England show that most of the country 'guessed [that] he had other business in mind' than restoring the Rump: Woolrych, *Britain in Revolution*, p. 759. Baker, *Chronicle*, p. 673.
3. Ian Gentles, 'The Debentures Market and Military Purchases of Crown Land, 1649–1660' (unpublished PhD thesis, University of London, 1969), appendix 3, pp. 244–356, lists every purchaser. See also idem, 'The sales of crown lands during the English Revolution', pp. 614–35; idem, 'The sales of bishops' lands in the English Revolution', pp. 586, 590–1. *A Friendly Letter of Advice to the Souldiers from a Quondam Member of the Army* (1 Aug. 1659), TT E.993[13], p. 5; *The Sentinels Remonstrance, or, A vindication of the Souldiers to the People of this Common-wealth* (1659), broadside; *The Unhappy Marks-man: or Twenty-Three Queries Offered to the Consideration of the People of These Nations* (London: n. p. [18 June] 1659), TT E.986[5], p. 5; Malcolm Wanklyn, *Reconstructing the New Model Army: Volume 2, Regimental Lists 1649 to 1663* (Solihull: Helion, 2016), pp. 36–40.

4. Josselin, *Diary*, p. 444; Reece, pp. 225, 233. Any estimate of army strength can only be approximate, since the sources mostly provide us with the numbers of regiments, not men. At full strength a horse regiment was 600 men (excluding officers) and a foot regiment 1,000, though sometimes more. Foot regiments in particular were frequently under strength: *Reg. Hist.*, pp. xxix–xxxvi; Wanklyn, *Reconstructing the New Model Army: Volume 2*, pp. 22, 25, 26. A tax strike was reported in Yorkshire in January: *Fairfax Correspondence*, iv.169. Cf. Josselin, *Diary*, p. 460.

5. The army was not completely disbanded at the Restoration. There were still at least 10,000 soldiers and their officers in the summer of 1661, stationed in Scotland, Ireland, Flanders and Tangier: Wanklyn, *Reconstructing the New Model Army: Volume 2*, pp. 19, 27; Woolrych, *Britain in Revolution*, p. 782. For some reason the corpse of Thomas Pride did not suffer the same degradation as the others.

6. Lois G. Schwoerer, *'No Standing Armies!': Antiarmy Ideology in Seventeenth-Century England* (Baltimore, MD: Johns Hopkins University Press, 1974).

SELECT BIBLIOGRAPHY

Primary Sources

The chief manuscript sources for the study of the New Model Army are the Commonwealth Exchequer Papers (SP 28) in the National Archives, the William Clarke Papers in Worcester College, Oxford, and the Tanner Manuscripts in the Bodleian Library, Oxford. The chief printed sources are the tens of thousands of pamphlets and newspapers collected by the bookseller George Thomason between 1640 and 1600, now housed in the British Library and known as the Thomason Tracts.

Secondary Sources

The indispensable beginning for the military, political and religious history of the English Revolution is S.R. Gardiner's *The Great Civil War, 1642–1649* (4 vols, 1893) and his *The Commonwealth and Protectorate, 1649–1656* (4 vols, 1903). The most insightful account of the early years of the Revolution is found in David Scott's *Politics and War in the Three Stuart Kingdoms, 1637–49* (2004). There is also my *The English Revolution and the Wars in the Three Kingdoms, 1638–1652* (2007). The most comprehensive modern general study of the whole period is Austin Woolrych's *Britain in Revolution 1625–1660* (2002), which shows excellent, nuanced judgement on many points. A valuable beginning for the study of the New Model Army is C.H. Firth's *Cromwell's Army* (1902, new edition 1961). Modern work includes Mark Kishlansky's *The Rise of the New Model Army* (1979), my own *The New Model Army in England, Ireland and Scotland, 1645–1653* (1992), Barbara Donagan's *War in England 1642–1649* (2008), and Henry Reece's *The Army in England 1649–1660* (2013). For the important subject of religion in the Revolution, a vitally important study is Sarah Mortimer's *Reason and Religion in the English Revolution: The Challenge of Socinianism* (2010), which is about much more than Socinianism. Some of John Morrill's most important essays are brought together in his *The Nature of the English Revolution* (1993). Also extremely useful is John Adamson's *The English Civil War* (2009). Sadly still unpublished is Derek Massarella's foundational University of York PhD thesis, 'The Politics of the Army, 1647–1660' (1978).

More specialised works include Michael Mendle's *The Putney Debates of 1647: The Army, the Levellers, and the English State* (2001), Philip Baker and Elliot Vernon's *The Agreements of the People, the Levellers and the Constitutional Crisis of the English Revolution* (2012), Stephen Taylor and Grant Tapsell's *The Nature of the English Revolution Revisited: Essays in Honour of John Morrill* (2013) as well as the important essay by Elliot Vernon and Phil Baker, 'What was the first *Agreement of the People*?', *Historical Journal*, vol. 53 (2010). The most recent books on the army and the Levellers are Rachel Foxley, *The Levellers: Radical Political Thought in the English Revolution* (2013), and John Rees, *The Leveller Revolution* (2017).

Among the few studies of the military history of the New Model, the best include Glenn Foard's *Naseby: The Decisive Campaign* (1995) and Malcolm Wanklyn and Frank Jones's *A*

Military History of the English Civil War (2005), as well as Wanklyn's two-volume *Reconstructing the New Model Army* (2015–16). For the regicide we have the matchless, beautifully written *Trial of Charles I* (1968) by C.V. Wedgwood. Valuable modern scholarship is brought together in Jason Peacey (ed.), *The Regicides and the Execution of Charles I* (2001). The standard work for the history of the Rump is Blair Worden's *The Rump Parliament, 1648–1653* (1974). A general account of the Protectorate is Paul Lay's *Providence Lost: The Rise and Fall of Cromwell's Protectorate* (2020). More specialised works include Christopher Durston's *Cromwell's Major-Generals: Godly Government during the English Revolution* (2001), Patrick Little and David L. Smith's *Parliaments and Politics during the Cromwellian Protectorate* (2007), Patrick Little's *Lord Broghill and the Cromwellian Union with Ireland and Scotland* (2004), and Patrick Little (ed.), *The Cromwellian Protectorate* (2007). For the Restoration, Ronald Hutton's *The Restoration: A Political and Religious History of England and Wales, 1658–1667* (1995), and Ruth E. Mayers's *1659: The Crisis of the Commonwealth* (2004).

For the New Model in Ireland, Micheál Ó Siochrú, *God's Executioner: Oliver Cromwell and the Conquest of Ireland* (2008), James Scott Wheeler, *Cromwell in Ireland* (1999), Jane Ohlmeyer, *Civil War and Restoration in the Three Stuart Kingdoms: The Career of Randal MacDonnell, Marquis of Antrim, 1609–1683* (1983), Jane Ohlmeyer (ed.), *Ireland from Independence to Occupation 1641–1660* (1995) and Aidan Clarke, *Prelude to Restoration in Ireland: The End of the Commonwealth, 1659–1660* (1999).

For Scotland, F.D. Dow, *Cromwellian Scotland 1651–1660* (1979), D. Stevenson, *Revolution and Counter-Revolution in Scotland, 1644–1651* (1977) and Allan I. Macinnes, *The British Revolution, 1629–1660* (2005).

Biographies of leading figures in the New Model include my *Oliver Cromwell: God's Warrior in the English Revolution* (2011), Andrew Hopper, *'Black Tom': Sir Thomas Fairfax and the English Revolution* (2007), David Farr, *John Lambert, Parliamentary Soldier and Cromwellian Major-General, 1619–1684* (2003), David Farr, *Henry Ireton and the English Revolution* (2006), and Ismini Pells, *Philip Skippon and the British Civil Wars* (2020).

INDEX